OXFORD STUDIES IN
SOCIAL AND LEGAL HISTORY

OXFORD STUDIES
IN SOCIAL AND LEGAL
HISTORY

EDITED BY

SIR PAUL VINOGRADOFF

M.A., D.C.L., LL.D., DR. HIST., DR. JUR., F.B.A.

CORPUS PROFESSOR OF JURISPRUDENCE IN THE UNIVERSITY OF OXFORD

VOL. VII

XIII. EARLY TREATISES ON THE PRACTICE OF THE
JUSTICES OF THE PEACE IN THE FIFTEENTH
AND SIXTEENTH CENTURIES

By B. H. PUTNAM, PH.D.

LECTURER AT MOUNT HOLYOKE COLLEGE, MASS.

OCTAGON BOOKS

A DIVISION OF FARRAR, STRAUS AND GIROUX

New York   1974

Originally published in 1924 by the Clarendon Press

Reprinted 1974
by special arrangement with Oxford University Press, Inc.

OCTAGON BOOKS
A DIVISION OF FARRAR, STRAUS & GIROUX, INC.
19 Union Square West
New York, N. Y. 10003

Library of Congress Cataloging in Publication Data

Putnam, Bertha Haven, 1872-1960.
    Early treatises on the practice of the justices of the peace in the
fifteenth and sixteenth centuries.

    Reprint of the 1924 ed. published by the Clarendon Press, Ox-
ford, which was issued as v. 7, no. 13 of Oxford studies in social
and legal history.

    1. Justices of the peace—Great Britain. I. Title. II. Series:
Oxford studies in social and legal history, v. 7, no. 13.
KD7309.P88   1974   347′.42′016   73-22305
ISBN 0-374-96166-2

Printed in USA by
Thomson-Shore, Inc.
Dexter, Michigan

PREFACE

THE practice of English 'Self-Government' has attracted the attention of students of Law and Political Science both at home and abroad as one of the most characteristic attempts at solving the problems of local administration. Gneist held it up to Continental statesmen as an example of the proper relation between the power of the Crown and the influence of landed aristocracy for the purpose of social welfare and discipline. J. Redlich, Sidney and Beatrice Webb analysed its elements and described its shortcomings and decay in the face of modern requirements. Miss Putnam's studies have been directed to establishing by patient investigations the true origin and the initial stages of its historical development. The monograph on the Justices of Labourers is universally recognized as the standard authority on fourteenth-century policy in dealing with labour and migration. The present volume takes up the thread of a new phase of the development ranging from the end of the fourteenth to the beginning of the sixteenth century. The institution of the Justices of the Peace, which forms its subject, is undoubtedly one of the most remarkable creations of English administrative history. Its advent marks the end of feudal federations of local potentates endowed with franchises in manors and boroughs. After tentative experiments like the Westminster provisions of 1259, the class rule of the gentry, constituted in county groups, was substituted for feudalism by a definite concentration of judicial and administrative functions in the hands of the Justices

of the Peace. Miss Putnam's monograph traces the
working of this important institution in the fifteenth
century with the help of a detailed examination of the
published and unpublished treatises on the subject.
This piece of literary history is very interesting in itself.
It is shown conclusively that Fitzherbert's treatise
of 1538 was largely based on the *Boke of Justyces of
Peas* of 1506, which itself is a compilation of forms and
precedents for the practical use of clerks of the peace,
while the famous *Eirenarcha* of Lambard was derived
to a great extent from a reading of Marowe, a prominent member of the Inner Temple, *temp.* Henry VII.
A MS. Manual of 1422 has been published by Miss
Putnam as an earlier example of the formulary represented by the *Boke* of 1506. It was compiled under
the supervision of a Worcestershire justice, probably
John Weston, and consists of precedents from Worcestershire practice of the reigns of Henry IV and Henry V.
The cases cited present a curious picture of a set of
country gentlemen alternately keeping the peace and
charged with murder or robbery, sitting on the Bench
and being sent to prison, obtaining pardons from the
king and serving him in his campaigns in France.

The second document published by Miss Putnam is
not less important. Marowe's reading in the Inner
Temple (1503) is no mere collection of precedents and
forms, but the first systematic exposition of the procedure and powers of the justices, based on extensive
knowledge of the law and practice on the subject.
Marowe's personality and career have been described
by Miss Putnam with minute care, and they are certainly
characteristic of the period of Henry VII in its en-
deavours to restore social order. Marowe belonged to
an influential family of the City of London, and was
closely connected in his legal work with two prominent

lawyers of the time—Frowyk, Chief Justice of the
Common Pleas (1502), and Dudley, the hated minister
of Henry VII, executed under Henry VIII in com-
pliance with public resentment. There seems to be
good reason to suppose that the work of this set of
men was by no means prompted by mere cupidity and
arbitrary cruelty. The task of the men who represented
orderly government after the struggles of the Roses
was as necessary as it was invidious.

The publication of the reading is of interest, not
only because the work presents the first complete
manual on the subject, but also as a specimen of a form
of legal teaching which has not received adequate
attention in spite of its intrinsic importance. The
readings constituted the most conspicuous effort of the
Inns of Court of that time to provide systematic teaching for their junior members. By the side of moots
and reports taken in Court, they influenced the forma-
tion of a younger school of students of law, which
attained its culmination in the work of the great
Abridgers—Fitzherbert, Brooke—and of the great
Reporters—Plowden, Dyer. The best readings were
delivered, characteristically enough, in the closing years
of the fifteenth and the early years of the sixteenth
century, that is, at a time when the Year Books were
falling into decay while the Reports had not yet risen
to form a special class of legal literature. We are
indebted to Marowe's protector, Frowyk, for a remarkable reading on the Prerogative, and Marowe himself
achieved distinction in this line by the treatment of the
institution of Justices of the Peace. It is to be wished
that the literature of the readings, of which Miss Putnam
gives us a general survey, should be rendered accessible
by critical editions similar to that which has been prepared for Marowe's *De Pace* by Miss Putnam.

Laws attempt to provide the machinery for solving the most pressing problems of social intercourse. From this point of view no problem is more essential than the problem of social peace, and the growth of self-government in aristocratic England has undoubtedly marked a characteristic stage in the treatment of the subject.

PAUL VINOGRADOFF.

CONTENTS

CONTENTS

ABBREVIATIONS

Ames	Ames, J., Typographical Antiquities, 1749.
Ames, ed. Herbert	The above, ed. W. Herbert, 3 vols., 1785-90.
B.M.	British Museum.
Bodl.	Bodleian.
D.N.B.	Dictionary National Biography.
Dugdale	Dugdale, William.
Chron. Ser.	Chronica Series, bound with the following:
Orig. Jurid.	Origines Juridiciales, 1680.
Monasticon	Monasticon Anglicanum, 6 vols., 1846.
Warwickshire	The Antiquities of Warwickshire, 2 vols., 1730.
E.H.R.	English Historical Review.
Foss, Judges	Foss, Edward. A Biographical Dictionary of the Judges of England, 1870.
Handlists	Handlists of Books printed by London Printers, 1501-56, Biographical Society, 1913.
H.L.S.	Library of Harvard Law School.
Inq. p. m.	Inquisitiones post mortem.
N.E.D.	New English Dictionary, ed. J. A. H. Murray and others.
P.C.C.	Prerogative Court of Canterbury.
P.R.O.	Public Record Office.
Rot. Parl.	Rotuli Parliamentorum, 6 vols., n.d.
S.R.	Statutes of the Realm, 11 vols., 1810-28.
U.L.C.	University Library, Cambridge.
V.C.H.	Victoria County History.

Unless otherwise specified, references to statutes are to the Statutes of the Realm; to Year Book cases, to Les Reports des Cases [Edw. II–27 Hen. VIII], 11 pts. 1678-80; to Lambard's 'Eirenarcha', to the 1602 edition; to Crompton's revision of Loffice, to the 1593 edition.

INTRODUCTION

THE SOURCES FOR OUR KNOWLEDGE OF THE JUSTICES OF THE PEACE PREVIOUS TO THE SIXTEENTH CENTURY

THERE is a strange incongruity between the frequent references to justices of the peace in history and in literature and the serious lack of accurate information on their origin and on their development during the early centuries of their existence.[1] Until the abundant material, most of it in manuscript, has been thoroughly examined, it is useless to attempt a complete account of their powers and their activities for the period before 1500.[2] But even a brief description will show clearly the various classes of sources available for study.

Leaving untouched the problem of origin,[3] my preliminary investigation has covered the latter half of the fourteenth and

[1] The value of similar records for the later period has been admirably described by Sidney and Beatrice Webb, in their work on English Local Government, see especially i. 279, note 1, 295, note 1. Cf. also 'Legal Materials as Sources for the Study of Modern English History', by A. L. Cross, in Am. Hist. Review, xix. 751-71.

[2] The useful monograph by C. A. Beard, The Office of Justice of the Peace in England in its Origin and Development, 1904, is avowedly based on printed sources only. The accounts in the older writers like Blackstone, Gneist, Pike, Reeves, Stephen, &c., suffer from lack of knowledge of MS. material. Holdsworth's brief paragraphs in Hist. Eng. Law, i. 123-35, are excellent as far as they go, but are necessarily meagre. In view of the almost disconcerting amount of material, it is curious that distinguished modern scholars continue to refer to its meagreness for the period before 1600. Cf. the introductions to printed quarter session records ; Mr. J. W. Willis Bund, Worcester County Records, Calendar of Quarter Sessions Papers, 1591-1643 (1900) ; Professor Tait, Lancashire Quarter Sessions Records, 1590-1606 (1917). Professor Firth, in History, April 1920, 50-1, accepts Professor Tait's view. Extracts from MS. proceedings before justices of the peace printed in recent source books are often given in a misleading manner. For example, Miss I. D. Thornley, England under the Yorkists 1460-1485 (1920), refers to Ancient Indictments by ' Bundles ' only, without the number of the membrane (see pp. 160-2, 176), and fails to show that the Cambridge ' Bundle' was a roll of justices of Oyer and Terminer before whom certain quarter session proceedings were being determined.

[3] See Studies in the Hundred Rolls, by H. M. Cam, Oxford Studies in Legal and Social History, vol. vi, pt. xi.

most of the fifteenth centuries. The more obvious printed sources are so well known that it is scarcely necessary to enumerate them : Statutes of the Realm, Rolls of Parliament, Calendars of Close and Patent Rolls, records of gilds and of boroughs,[1] chroniclers, Paston Letters, &c. The following MS. sources, however, need a far more careful examination than has yet been given them.

(1) *Proceedings before justices of the peace.* About sixty rolls are preserved in the Public Record Office, usually classified under Assize Rolls or Ancient Indictments. Nearly all of them have been listed in the ' English Historical Review ',[2] but except for a few extracts,[3] they have not been printed [4] nor have their contents been studied with sufficient thoroughness. Similar records, usually of the borough justices, are listed in the reports of the Historical Manuscript Commission.[5] Quite recently also, additional rolls have been discovered, notably, an ' isolated record ' for Hull *temp.* Henry VI,[6] a meagre fragment for Worcestershire *temp.* Edward IV,[7] and voluminous proceedings for Oxford *temp.* Richard II.[8] The

---

[1] For a recent useful list of accessible town records, see 'The Sources Available for the Study of Mediaeval Economic History', by E. Lipson, Royal Hist. Soc. Transactions, 3rd series, x. 115–58.

[2] 'Early Records of the Justices of the Peace', xxviii. 321–30 ; 'The Ancient Indictments in the Public Record Office', xxix. 479–505 ; 'The Justices of Labourers in the Fourteenth Century', xxi. 532–4 (nos. vi, x, xii, xiv, and note 139). Assize Roll 268 does not properly belong to this list, but Assize Rolls 266 and 523 and Gaol Delivery Roll 221 should be added. The Yorkshire rolls include proceedings for the City of York and the three ridings ; Assize Roll 1143 represents therefore two sets of records and Assize Roll 1145 four.

[3] Putnam, The Enforcement of the Statutes of Labourers, App. 166–9, 192–203, 211–13.

[4] One roll for Wiltshire is in print ; *ibid.* 228–9.

[5] Cf. e.g. iv, for records of the Cinque Ports. As the index is not a safe guide, the actual contents of the reports ought to be thoroughly examined.

[6] 1449 ; Tait, *op. cit.*, iv, note 4.

[7] Among the MSS. of Lord Beauchamp, catalogued by Mr. C. L. Kingsford. The latter kindly called my attention to the roll ; it contains proceedings before Thomas Urswyk, the distinguished recorder of London (p. 120, *infra*), and the great judge Littleton. I am indebted to the courtesy of Lord Beauchamp for the opportunity of examining this document.

[8] Discovered in the archives of the University by the Rev. H. E. Salter.

latter have been printed *in toto* by the Oxford Historical Society.[1]

The indictments for felonies[2] brought before justices of the peace were 'determined' either by themselves acting as justices of Gaol Delivery, or by the regular justices of Gaol Delivery, or by the justices of the King's Bench. In the first two cases, the indictments and the subsequent process appear amongst Gaol Delivery material; in the last case they are found in the custody of the King's Bench, among Ancient Indictments and on the Coram Rege Rolls.[3] It would be possible to reconstruct a large portion of the work of a given session by putting together these scattered records.

(2) *The Exchequer.* On the Memoranda Rolls of the two Remembrancers, among the various rolls of accounts in their respective custody,[4] on the bulky Pipe Rolls, &c., are ound valuable series connected with the justices of the peace: duplicate estreats of penalties imposed in Quarter Sessions, the claims of the Lords of Franchises to their share of such penalties, the amount of salaries paid to the justices, the receipts of the latter for the 'seals' made in accordance with the statute of Cambridge,[5] long drawn out suits in the Exchequer involving the justices, &c.[6] A statistical study of the entries on the Pipe Rolls concerning justices of the peace for a given county would yield interesting results.

(3) *Chancery.* Under Chancery Miscellanea, Writs of Certiorari and Returns,[7] are included many writs summoning into

---

[1] Mediaeval Archives of the University of Oxford, ed. Rev. H. E Salter, ii. ix-xix, 1-125. I am greatly indebted to Mr. Salter and to Mr. R. L. Poole for informing me of the existence of this roll.

[2] Indictments for trespass were more often 'determined' in quarter sessions.

[3] See ch. iii (1), *infra.*

[4] e.g. Exchequer, L.T.R. Foreign Accounts 25 (now included in Lists and Indexes, no. xi). Exchequer, Accounts, K.R.: (1) Lists and Indexes, no. xxxv; Fines and Amercements; Sheriffs' Administrative Accounts. (2) Sheriffs' Accounts (MS. list); Estreats (MS. list no. 137).

[5] pp. 92-93, *infra.*

[6] For similar material on justices of labourers, &c., see Putnam, *op. cit.,* pt. I, ch. i. (6) and ch. iii.

[7] Bundles 47-88; S. R. Scargill Bird, Guide to the Public Record Office, 3rd ed., 59. They were formerly known as County Placita, *ibid.* 85.

Chancery[1] proceedings before justices of the peace. The series needs careful study in connexion with the rolls described under (1).[2] Amongst Chancery Files or Brevia Regia[3] are writs for swearing in justices of the peace, often accompanied by the form of the oath. Moreover, the omission from the printed Calendars of detailed summaries of the commission of the peace renders it imperative to use the MS. Close and Patent Rolls.[4]

In addition to the printed and MS. sources above described, there exists a great mass of legal literature and of legal collections, some of it printed and much of it in MS.: Year Books, abridgements, treatises, manuals, compilations of statutes, and of writs and indictments. A necessary preliminary to a complete understanding of the powers and the practice of the justices of the peace is a knowledge of the treatises and manuals designed primarily for their use; these treatises and manuals have therefore been chosen as the subject of this volume. Further, the easiest method of studying their development in the early centuries is to begin with the familiar printed treatises of the sixteenth century, and to try to discover how far back their origins went. The results of such an investigation are presented in the following pages.

In concluding this brief and necessarily incomplete survey of the sources, it is worth emphasizing that considerable mystery attaches to the long-continued neglect of material so valuable for legal, economic, and social history. The opening announcement of the objects of the Selden Society founded in 1887 does not mention the justices of the peace. The description of the principal classes of records to be dealt with included the records of all the courts of England, past and present, except the courts held before the justices of the peace. Moreover, in connexion with the plan for printing extracts from Eyre Rolls and Assize Rolls, 'with the view of illustrating the state of the criminal law in early times', it is not taken into

---

[1] Or into the court of the King's Bench.
[2] The preservation of a given roll is thus explained; cf. e.g. Chancery Misc. 47, $\frac{8}{125}$, with Assize Roll 32.
[3] Tower Series; Scargill Bird, Guide, 17–18.
[4] See ch. vi (4), *infra*.

account that the justices of the peace played an important part in the administration of such law.[1]

A more recent example dates from July 1921. In a notable discussion on the study of legal records by several of the most eminent living historians of English law, the records of the justices of the peace are conspicuous by their absence.[2] This neglect on the part of those 'learned in the law' has had a dangerous sequence; it has forced a layman to trespass on legal domain. Lambard's words come to my mind: 'Finally, whatsoeuer other thing is done amisse, I protest that it hath escaped of vnskill, and not proceeded of wilfulnesse: and therefore, I desire that I may be allowed the benefit of that *Pardon*, which (as I told you euen now) is in like case grauntable to a *Iustice* of the Peace.'[3]

---

[1] Objects and Work of the Selden Society. I quote from the copy appended to The Court Baron, 1890.

[2] Summarized in History, October 1921, 155–61; Sir Frederick Pollock, Dr. W. S. Holdsworth, Mr. W. C. Bolland. On the other hand, Dr. Hubert Hall, in Repertory of British Archives, pt. i, 111–12, mentions the rolls in official custody (see p. 2, *supra*), but not unnaturally gives no indication of the existence of the innumerable piecemeal records described p. 3, *supra*.

[3] Eirenarcha, Epilogue, 590, quoted by Mr. and Mrs. Webb in their introduction to English Local Government, i. xiii–xiv.

CHAPTER I

PRINTED TREATISES FOR JUSTICES OF THE PEACE, 1506–1599 [1]

FOR an exhaustive study of sixteenth-century printed treatises for justices of the peace, there are two essentials: first, the making of a bibliography that shall be absolutely complete; second, an examination of all editions now known to exist. As far as my present knowledge has made it possible, I have accomplished the latter,[2] but I hardly dare hope that I have achieved the former. Limitations of time and space have confined my search to the more famous libraries of England [3] and of the United States,[4] and have caused the neglect of some valuable smaller collections. All that can be justly claimed therefore for the bibliography in the appendix is that it represents the first attempt—as far as I know—to list *all* sixteenth-century tracts on this one subject,[5] and that it includes more

---

[1] App. I.

[2] Out of the fifty-seven editions, only four have completely eluded discovery; three in Series I, nos. 2, 4, and 21, and one in Series II, no. 5. Further in Series I, of no. 9 only the colophon exists, of no. 10 only the title-page, and of no. 15 only a few folios; in Series II, of no. 4 only the title-page has been found. Fortunately, in all these cases there are excellent reasons for thinking that the variations from known editions are not vital.

[3] London: the British Museum, Guildhall Library, the libraries of the four Inns of Court. Oxford: the Bodleian, the libraries of a few of the colleges. Cambridge: the University Library, and through the generous aid of Miss Fegan of Girton College, the libraries of a few of the colleges. Lancashire: the John Rylands Library, Manchester; the library of Stonyhurst College.

[4] Cambridge, Massachusetts: the library of the Harvard Law School, now the possessor of the legal collection of the late Mr. George Dunn of Woolley Hall, near Maidenhead, Berks. New York: the library of Mr. J. Pierpont Morgan. Philadelphia: the library of Mr. Hampton L. Carson.

[5] In marked contrast, therefore, to the lists printed by bibliographers, who necessarily approach the problem from the point of view of the total output of a given printer. Professor J. H. Beale of the Harvard Law School has made a bibliography of six of the tracts published by Rastell (see App. I, Series I, no. 13), including the 'Justyce of peace'. But he has not added titles known only through earlier bibliographies. It is

titles, and references to the whereabouts of more editions than can at present be found in any one bibliography.[1] Further, it seems certain that the tracts listed afford so wide a basis for investigation that the conclusions about to be presented will not be materially modified by the possible discovery in the future of a few more editions.

As a result of this search, it is possible to say that fifty-seven editions or issues [2] of treatises for justices of the peace were printed between 1506 and 1599.[3] In addition, the Stationers' Registers record the receipt of 6*d.* on 28 June 1585 from ' Master Newbery ' for licence to print ' A booke Intituled, The Office of Justice of peace, by John Goldwell of Graies Inne esquier '.[4] Unfortunately, no copy of the work has come to my attention [5] and except for an entry of his admission to Gray's Inn in 1543,[6] no reference indisputably pertaining to the author.[7]

Account of the four Series.

The fifty-seven editions fall into four series [8] : I. Thirty-two editions of the anonymous ' Boke of Justyces of Peas ', 1506.[9]

hard adequately to express my appreciation of the generous assistance rendered to me by Professor Beale at every stage in my long investigation.

[1] There is at present in preparation a ' Short Title ' bibliography of *all* books printed in England before 1600 which will be more complete than anything hitherto published.

[2] e.g., in Series I, App. I, nos. 13 and 14 are merely separate issues; see *infra*, p. 25.

[3] Omitting the well-known work by Pulton, which is merely a collection of statutes ; see ch. iv, *infra*.

[4] Transcripts, ed. E. Arber, ii. 204. In Ames, ed. Herbert, 918, the date is 1584.

[5] It is possible, but not probable, that the MS. described in ch. iv, *infra*, p. 108, note 6, and p. 113, note 7, is to be attributed to Goldwell.

[6] Register of Admissions to Gray's Inn, 1521–1889, 16. For this reference I am indebted to the librarian, Mr. M. D. Severn, who also writes: ' There used to be the arms of a Goldwell in the Hall at one time, but they have long since vanished, and might have been his or those of Stephen or Thomas Goldwell admitted in 1554 and 1563 respectively ', November 1919.

[7] It is not certain that any of the entries in the Calendars of Letters and Papers, Foreign and Domestic, Henry VIII, or in State Papers, Domestic, Edw. VI and Mary and Elizabeth, refer to this John Goldwell, or that he drew any of the wills now in Somerset House; P.C.C., 20 Cobham ; 42 Kidd ; 54 Windebanck, Sentence, f. 102.   [8] App. I.

[9] The date here given for each series is that of the earliest known edition.

II. Twelve editions of the work by Sir Anthony Fitzherbert, one in the original French form, 'Loffice et auctoryte des Justyces de peas', 1538, and eleven in the English translation, 'The Newe Boke of Justices of the peas', 29 December 1538. III. Nine editions of the 'Eirenarcha' by William Lambard, 1581. IV. Four editions of the revision of Fitzherbert's 'Loffice et auctoryte des Justyces de peas', by Richard Crompton, 1583, virtually a new work.[1]

The fact that Fitzherbert, Lambard, and Crompton were each responsible for one series has of course been long recognized and is proved by even a cursory examination of the titles as printed in Series II, III, and IV. But in the case of Series I, where there are considerable variations in titles,[2] a comparison of content is necessary to prove absolutely that the later editions are all reproductions of the anonymous 'Boke' first printed in 1506, and that there were, therefore, with the exception of Goldwell's missing volume, but four distinct treatises for justices of the peace published in the sixteenth century. Moreover, there have been some curious misconceptions about the French version of Fitzherbert's 'Loffice' of 1538—both in regard to the English translation and to Crompton's revision[3]—and likewise about the authorship of the anonymous 'Boke' of 1506, attributed to Fitzherbert in the only detailed discussion of the question in print.[4] Evidently, therefore, the whole problem of the origin of the sixteenth-century treatises concentrates itself on the 'Boke' and on its relation to Fitzherbert's works, and can best be approached through a consideration of the following subjects:

(1) The general points of difference between the 'Boke' and the treatise universally accepted as Fitzherbert's; namely between Series I and Series II.

(2) The resemblances, within each of the above series, between the later editions and the first edition.

---

[1] As is clearly shown by a study of contents.
[2] From the point of view of title-page, Series I may be divided as follows: (1) nos. 1-7, 9-12; (2) no. 8; (3) nos. 13, 14; (4) nos. 15, 16, 19-23; (5) nos. 17, 18, 24-30; (6) nos. 31, 32.
[3] *Infra*, p. 15.
[4] *Infra*, p. 36, and note 1.

(3) The arguments against Fitzherbert's supposed connexion with the ' Boke '.[1]

The ground will then be cleared for an attempt to trace back the origin of the ' Boke ' to earlier MS. sources,[2] and also for an account of the material drawn upon by Fitzherbert, Lambard, and Crompton.[3]

Evidence will be given later to show that the undated Pynson's ' Boke ' at Stonyhurst was probably printed in 1506 as the first edition in Series I, that on it was based the 1506 Wynkyn de Worde, of which no existing copy is now known,[4] and that the 1510 Wynkyn de Worde, the third, not the first, edition,[5] is almost identical with the Pynson.[6] Since the unique copy of the latter at Stonyhurst is not easily available for comparison,[7] it has seemed necessary for the purposes of this study to use the 1510 Wynkyn de Worde : ' The Justyces of Paes.

[1] In the course of a study of the valuable collection of law books in the library of the Harvard Law School, I became convinced in 1914 of the distinction between Series I and Series II, and of the fact that Sir Anthony Fitzherbert had nothing to do with Series I. In 1918 I learned from an admirable article by the Rev. R. H. C. Fitzherbert, published in 1897 (*infra*, p. 32, note 6), that Sir Ernest Clarke had come to the same conclusion as far back as 1894. In the summer of 1919, in addition to interesting letters from both scholars, I had the good fortune to receive from Sir Ernest a ' Memorandum ' in typewritten form, copies of which had been deposited in various archives, the Bodleian, the British Museum, &c., and apparently completely ignored. In this he made a tentative attempt to show that a number of works had been attributed to Sir Anthony on insufficient grounds, and without giving his evidence and knowing comparatively few of the editions in the two series, he stated emphatically that the Boke was not by Sir Anthony.

In the catalogue of the early printed books in the Harvard Law School made recently by F. A. Ballard, the fact of the two series has been clearly indicated, but it has often been obscured in catalogues of sales of libraries or even in labels of volumes. For example, in the Harvard Law School, no. 31, Series I, App. I, is labelled : Kitchin Aucthoritie of Iustices. A still stranger mistake appears in the catalogue of the British Museum : no. 2, Series II, App. I, The Newe Boke of Justices of peas by A. F. K. . . . is put under ' K ' instead of under Fitzherbert. The notes to my bibliography in App. I show how even the editors of the most important recent bibliographical lists of early printed books in England have fallen into errors by their failure to understand the distinction between Series I and Series II.

[2] In chs. ii and iii.   [3] In ch. iv.
[4] The first edition if my hypothesis as to Pynson is wrong; *infra*, pp. 18–20.
[5] As is so often stated ; see e. g., p. 36, *infra*.   [6] See *infra*, p. 19.
[7] Not only because of the relatively inaccessible situation of Stonyhurst College, but also because there are no other editions within reach for collation.

The boke of the iustyces of peas the charge with all the
processe of the cessyons warrantes supersedias and all that
longeth to ony Justyce to make endytementes of haute treason
petyt treason felonyes appeles trespas vpon statutes trespas
contra Regis pacem.   Nocumentis with dyvers thynges more
as it appereth in the Kalender of the same boke.'[1]

Sometime in 1538—without indicating either the exact date[2]
or the name of the author—Redman published 'Loffice et
auctoryte des Justyces de peas compyle et extrayte hors des
auncient liures si bien del comen ley come dez estatutes oue
moultes auters choses necessaries a scauoir'.   That Sir Anthony
Fitzherbert was the author is proved by the title-page of the
following work also printed by Redman : 'The Newe Boke of
Justices of the peas by A. F. K. lately translated out of Frenche
into Englyshe.   The yere of our Lord God M.D.XXXVIII
The XXIX day of Decembre.'[3]   The changes in the English
version are not numerous ; the most notable are the omission
of the preface, the addition of the tenure of a writ running in
the name of 'Antonius F & socii sui custodes pacis . . . . . . in
Comitatu S. . . . . . .',[4] and several changes in arrangement of
material, some of them made in a peculiarly unintelligent
fashion.[5]   In view of this last fact it seems probable that Sir
Anthony, who died on 27 May 1538,[6] did not himself have
anything to do with the translation.[7]   But since the French
was never reprinted in its original form[8] while the English
went through many editions, and since the differences between
the two versions[9] are so very slight that the analysis of one is

[1] There are copies in the Bodleian and in the British Museum; see
App. I for the references to all the editions discussed.
[2] The year appears only on the title-page: 'Nouelment imprime 1538'.
The preface and some of the later statutes are in English, a few statutes
and the commission in Latin, the rest in French.
[3] Again only a title-page date.   [4] f. 4 b.
[5] There are however some slight improvements ; see *infra*, pp. 11–14,
for the changes.
[6] See D.N.B.; his epitaph at Norbury contains the date of his death.
His will, printed in the Reliquary, vol. xxi, April 1881, 234–6, is dated
12 October 1537, and was proved 26 August 1538.
[7] For the identity of the translator, see *infra*, p. 15.
[8] It has already been said that Crompton's treatise was virtually a new
work.
[9] See *infra*, pp. 11–14.

virtually the analysis of the other, it seems legitimate to use the 'Newe Boke' as a basis of comparison with the 'Boke'. The following brief outlines will make clear their respective contents.

'The Boke', 1510.[1]

[Part I].[2]

What men sholde be Justyces of y^e peas, theyr auctorite & power, y^e fourme of theyr charges and wherof they may enquyre, drawen out of statutes and the comyn lawes.

(1) Summary of statutes.   2 folios.

(2) Two writs of process.   1 folio.

(3) The charge. $7\frac{1}{2}$ folios.

[Part II].

Placita coram A. B. et sociis suis custodibus pacis . . . ac iusticiariis . . . in comitatu M. apud W. . . .

(1) *Circ.* 75 writs of process. $16\frac{1}{2}$ folios.

(2) Table.   3 folios.

(3) 92 indictments of felonies and trespasses, appeals, &c. 24 folios.[3]

'The Newe Boke', 1538.[4]

[Part I].

(1) Table.[5]

(2) The commission of the peace, folios 1–3 b.

(3) The exposition of the commission, folios 4–16 b.

(4) The oath, folios 16–17.

(5) The charge, folios 17–24.

After 'extortion of sheriffs' occurs the unintelligent departure from Fitzherbert's order in 'Loffice' by the insertion into the midst of the Charge of what had been his final section, namely the 'office' of six local officials.[6]

---

[1] App. I, Series I, no. 3.

[2] The fact of two distinct parts is not indicated in the original by any such phrase ; I have adopted it merely for convenience.

[3] To these fifty-four folios must be added two for title-page and colophon, a total of fifty-six.   For signatures and numbering, see *infra*, p. 18 and ch. iii (II).

[4] App. I, Series II, no. 2.

[5] In Loffice a preface had preceded the table ; *infra*, p. 13.

[6] f. 24 : 'Here folowyth incydently the offyce and authoritie of Shyreffes. . . .'   In the translation, the inquiry into the extortion of each of the officials immediately precedes the description of their duties (except

[Part II].

Sheriffs, folios 24–37 b.

Bailiffs, folios 37b–41 b.

Escheators, folios 42–48.

Constables, folios 48–55.

Coroners, folios 55–63.

Ordinaries, folios 63–64.

Then comes the continuation of the interrupted Charge :

[Part I continued].   The charge, folios 64b–78.

[Part III].   Statutes.

(1) Statutes of which justices have power to inquire, hear, and determine by virtue of their commission, folios 78b–89.

(2) Authority of justices by statutes, folios 89–169 b, arranged by regnal years from Edward III through Henry VIII. The order of (1) and (2) exactly reverses that of the French original.[1]

The outlines reveal clearly the fundamental differences between the two works.   Part I of the ' Boke ', as the opening paragraph indicates, contains merely brief summaries of a few statutes that deal with the qualifications of the justices—their number, the date of their sessions, &c.—and the justices' Charge to the jurors, the two writs being evidently out of place.[2]   In Part II, the precedents that make up two-thirds of the volume include writs of process and indictments, but strangely enough, as will be shown later,[3] the indictments have no necessary connexion with the justices of the peace.   Except for a few sentences in the Charge, there is no legal commentary, nor is there a single reference to a ' book case '.   In fact, the ' Boke ' as a whole scarcely deserves the name of a treatise, but is really more like a formula-book, of the same general type as the Registrum Brevium.   On the other hand, Part I of the ' Newe Boke ' begins with the text of the commission (nowhere

in the case of the bailiff), whereas in Loffice it is properly given in the Charge, and is followed by 'Voyes pluis de les offices des Vicountes, Bailiffes des liberties, Escheatours, Constables, Coroners, Extorcion des Ordinaries en le fyne de cest liure a tiel signe . . .' ; ff. 27–28 b.

    [1] i.e. (1) ff. 145 b–58 ; (2) ff. 41 b–144 ; an addition to the Charge appears on ff. 144–5 b ; see *infra*, p. 14.

    [2] *Infra*, pp. 94–95, and notes 1 and 10.

    [3] pp. 99–100.

given in the 'Boke') and continues with an analysis of the powers of the justices, in the form of an exposition of the commission—an able legal commentary. Then come the oath of office and a brief discussion, and finally the Charge, preceded by an interesting explanation of its tripartite division.

Whether Part II is placed at the end of the volume by Fitzherbert[1] or is inserted into the midst of the Charge,[2] presumably by his translator or printer, in either case its significance is the same. It implies that certain local officials are so closely connected with the justices that an account of their duties constitutes an integral part of a treatise on the peace.

Part III, over half the volume[3], contains statutes and chapters of statutes that have to do with justices of the peace. It differs from the first portion of Part I of the 'Boke' in that it purports to be a complete compilation instead of a meagre selection,[4] and that many of the documents are printed *in extenso* instead of being merely summarized. Obviously, in thus emphasizing statutes, Fitzherbert has fulfilled the promise of his English preface to 'Loffice': '. . . And forsomoche as the same lawes and actes be very moch in vre (? use), and dyuers of them made many yeres passed, and so dispersyd in diuers volumes, that the more parte of suche persons as shulde execute and mynister the same lawes and actes haue not the perfyte knoweledge and rememberance of the same as they shulde haue yf they were collecte and compiled together in a lytle boke and volume. For that intent is this lytle treatyze drawen and made in a compendious ordre. . . .' Fitzherbert refers a number of times to Year Book cases, and occasionally to 'Breton', &c.,[5] but, curiously enough, gives no writs of process or indictments,[6] in this last respect differing not only from the compiler of the 'Boke' but also from Lambard and from Crompton.[7]

---

[1] ff. 158 b–207.
[2] *Supra*, pp. 11–12.
[3] In the French, 117 out of 207 folios.
[4] The contrast in the number of folios makes the difference perfectly clear.
[5] See ch. iv, *infra*, for a brief account of his sources.
[6] See *supra*, p. 10, for one writ of process printed in the English version.
[7] *Infra*, ch. vi (5).

The contrast between Series I and Series II is thus well
marked : the ' Newe Boke ', with some legal commentary and
references to Year Books, with its multiplicity of statutes, its
full treatment of a number of local officials, and almost complete absence of writs, is easily distinguishable from the ' Boke ',
with its almost complete lack of legal commentary, its total
ignoring of Year Books, its brief summaries of a few statutes,
its omission of local officials, and its multiplicity of writs.
Still more significant, however, than these general differences
between the two series are certain specific differences, the
discussion of which must be deferred.[1]

On turning to a study, within each series, of the relations
between the various editions, it will be clearer to discuss first
Series II, the shorter and simpler of the two series. It has
already been stated that the English version scarcely differed
at all from ' Loffice ' of 1538 in content, but merely in the
arrangement of material. In addition to the general changes
in order already described,[2] there is a detail worth noting. In
the French edition at the very end of the first group of
statutes—those conferring authority on the justices[3] (the second
group in the English version)[4]—Fitzherbert adds as ' Un article
del charge que lez Justyces de peas deuer doner en lour
Sessions ',[5] an inquiry into two statutes passed in the parliament of June 1536,[6] one on Wines,[7] the other against the
Bishop of Rome,[8] but in the English edition the two statutes

---

[1] *Infra*, pp. 38–9.
[2] *Supra.* I give a few examples of trifling changes in content and
order. In the Newe Boke (f. 83, 83 b) there appears among the chapters
of 12 Rich. II, a statute on Armor of 4 Hen. IV, which in Loffice had
been given after the statute of 20 Edw. III against Maintenance (f. 156).
The Newe Boke omits the repetition of the statute against Washing and
Clipping of money (f. 84; not given on f. 86), which in Loffice appears on
f. 152 and f. 154 b. The latter (f. 12) refers to ' Lancient treatise fait en
le temps le roy E. le primer de forstallours ' (cf. also f. 152); the
translator explains that ' the treatyse of forstallours is in the latter ende
of magna carta ', f. 84 b. Cf. f. 168 b–169 of the translation of the old
statutes by ' Ferrerz ', printed by Redman in 1534, 1540, and again by his
widow, under the title of Magna Carta.
[3] ' Auctorite des gardeins de peas . . .', ff. 41 b–144.
[4] *Supra*, p. 12, and note 1.   [5] ff. 144–145 b.
[6] It sat from 8 June–18 July ; C. H. Parry, Parliaments and Councils, 203.
[7] 28 Hen. VIII, c. 14.
[8] *Ibid.*, c. 10. The statutes themselves appear on ff. 141 b–144.

(the latest quoted) and the articles on them are incorporated into the Charge.[1] The incident suggests that Fitzherbert was perhaps compiling his 'lytle treatyze' not long after the session of 1536, the last parliament that met before his death in May 1538, that he did not revise it for the press,[2] and that after the publication of the French original the translator made the correction in the English version, printed, according to the title-page, on 29 December 1538,[3]—certainly not forty-five years *before* the first French edition, as has been stated on high authority.[4] It is possible that the issue of both volumes was due in part to the attention bestowed during this year on the justices of the peace by the King's Council and by the King's printer,[5] and it would be interesting to know who was responsible for the translation of Fitzherbert's work and for its strange arrangement. Was it, perhaps, the George Ferrers who translated the Great Charter 'out of Latyn and Frenshe into Englyshe', first printed by Redman in 1534?[6] Or was it, perhaps, Redman himself, whose ignorance had aroused Pynson's indignation some years back?[7] In any case, the

---

[1] ff. 74 b–78. The statutes are of course out of place.

[2] It is possible that the book did not actually go through the press till after his death.

[3] Or possibly completed at that date and not printed till a little later.

[4] By the author of the article on Fitzherbert in D.N.B., on the assumption that Crompton's revision of 1583 was the earliest French edition of Loffice. So palpable an error (long ago noted by Miss McArthur, *infra*, p. 36) would hardly deserve attention were it not for recent statements. Cf. introduction to Lancashire Quarter Sessions Records, ed. Tait, i, note 1 : ' First published in an English translation in 1538, republished in the original French and enlarged by Richard Crompton in 1583.' E. Jenks, Short Hist. English Law, gives 1583 as the date, and then adds : ' There is said to be an earlier edition extant ; but the author has not seen a copy of it,' 151–2, note 1.

[5] See *infra*, pp. 26–27, and notes 1, 2.

[6] p. 14, note 2, *supra*. No definite statement can be made until there has been a careful study of the various editions of the Great Charter issued by Pynson, Redman, and Berthelet. George Ferrers was the burgess from Plymouth involved in a *cause célèbre*, Statutes of the Realm, i. xxii ; Adams and Stephens, Select Documents of English Constitutional History, 261–4. R. W. Bridgman, Legal Bibliography, 319, gives several references on George Ferrerz or Ferres, including his admission in 1534 to Lincoln's Inn ; Admissions, i. 48. Another possibility is the Thomas Phayer who was said to have translated the old Natura Brevium ; Bridgman, *op. cit.*, 225.

[7] ' . . . e manibus Rob. Redman, sed uerius Rudeman, quia inter mille

change in arrangement of material is repeated by Redman in another issue with precisely the same title-page, and with merely a few slight changes in phraseology,[1] and perhaps also in his edition of 1540,[2] known only by title-page, and in that of his widow printed in 1541.[3]

The next edition is that of Petyt, also in 1541.[4] In this there is an attempt to modify the inconvenient arrangement already described, but unfortunately instead of a return to Fitzherbert's own logical order, a still different scheme is adopted. After the oath,[5] instead of the Charge, comes the collection of statutes. Thus there is inserted into the body of the treatise what Fitzherbert clearly meant to be an appendix for reference. The statutes are followed by the Charge[6] and then by the section on the six local officials—the latter thus restored to its original place. But there still remains just after the oath Fitzherbert's explanation of the tripartite division of the Charge,[7] now separated from the latter by 103 folios of statutes. Absurd as this arrangement is, it is adhered to rigidly through the remaining editions of the 'Newe Boke': in that of Redman's successor, William Middleton,[8] dated 1543;[9] in those of William Powell, who married Middleton's widow

homines rudiorem haud facile inuenies . . .'; Lytylton tenures, Pynson, 1525, note at end. I am indebted to F. A. Ballard for this reference.

[1] App. I, Series II, no. 3. The most striking change is of the phrase in no. 2, f. 26: 'Shyreffes muste make due eleccion of knyghtes of the parliament' (a literal translation of the French, f. 160 b, from 6 Hen. VI, c. 4) to 'Shireffes must retourne such persons knightes of the parlyament', no. 3, f. 26. As far as I have been able to discover, the change is not perpetuated in any subsequent edition.

[2] App. I, Series II, no. 4. The 'XXIX daye of Decembre' of the title-page is probably a careless survival from the 1538 edition. Redman died between 21 October 1540, the date of his will, and 4 November, when it was proved; E. G. Duff, Century of the English Book Trade, 132.

[3] App. I, Series II, no. 5.

[4] Ibid., no. 6, based on no. 2.   [5] f. 20.

[6] f. 123 b. On f. 130 there is the absurd retention of: 'Loke more of ordinaries in the charge in the XLIII article of Escapes', taken over from the first edition of the Newe Boke, but no longer applicable.

[7] f. 19–20.   [8] Duff, op. cit., 104.

[9] App. I, Series II, no. 7. There are some obvious misprints; e.g. f. 4 b, dicete for direct, repeated by Powell in 1547 and changed by him only in 1551; also f. 19 b (in the oath) regal for egal, repeated in all later editions and first noted by Lambard, Eirenarcha, 1581, 59. In spite of these and similar mistakes, Middleton added to his title-page 'newly corrected', see infra, p. 17.

in 1547,[1] and who printed the 'Newe Boke' twice, in the year of his marriage,[2] and in 1551;[3] and also in the various issues and editions of the indefatigable Tottell,[4] of 1554,[5] 1560 [1561],[6] and 1566,[7] all of them bearing on the title-page the date 1554.[8] Changes of any kind are few in number and slight in character; they are mainly in spelling and only rarely in phraseology. No new statutes are added—even the commission still runs in the name of Henry VIII long after Elizabeth came to the throne. Tottell, however, in 1554 omitted the statute for the 'vtter extynguyshement of the vsurped power of the byshope of Rome',[9] undoubtedly a necessary omission at the time of Mary's accession,[10] but he did not take pains to add any of the important legislation of Elizabeth on ecclesiastical or any other matters. In spite, therefore, of the reiterated 'newly corrected' on each title-page from 1543 on,[11] perhaps designed to tempt an unwary purchaser,[12] the later editions are such exact reproductions of the earlier that the same words nearly always reappear on the corresponding portions of the page. Evidently 'Loffice' in its English form had never been brought up to date. Had Fitzherbert lived longer, it might have had a different fate.

---

[1] Duff, *op. cit.*, 104.   [2] App. I, Series II, no. 8.   [3] *Ibid.*, no. 9.

[4] He became an original member of the new Stationers' Company, incorporated in May 1557, having received a patent for printing law books as early as 1552; Duff, *op. cit.*, xxvii, 157. For later patents see Transcripts Stationers' Registers, ed. E. Arber, i. 32.

[5] App. I, Series II, no. 10. The almost countless variations in the spelling of Tottell's name are well illustrated in the colophons of these and the following volumes.

[6] *Ibid.*, no. 11. Tottell begins his year on 25 March.

[7] App. I, Series II, no. 12.

[8] Cf. Berthelet's similar retention of his '1534' title-page; *infra*, p. 26, note 1.

[9] The phrase used in the table of contents of 'Statutes to be executed by justices of the peace', Berthelet, 1539. The articles of inquiry into the legislation were still kept in the Charge; *supra*, p. 14.

[10] Cf. Duff, *op. cit.*, xxvi. All acts concerned with the break with Rome were repealed in October 1553; Parry, *op. cit.*, 210.

[11] See p. 16, note 9, *supra*.

[12] 'Clearly there was a considerable demand for such manuals, and the publishers of the day seem to have met it by mercilessly borrowing, if that be the right phrase, from each other. The proper thing to do was to reprint your rival's book, adding something to it which would make it yet more attractive to buyers'; The Court Baron, ed. Maitland and Baildon, Selden Society, Introductory Note, 4.

Much more difficult problems are presented by the 'Boke', at least for its first seventeen editions.[1] Unfortunately several of them were printed without a date,[2] while several others, needed for determining chronological sequence, are the very ones of which no copies are at present known.[3]

From the point of view of title,[4] it is obvious that nos. 1–7 and 9–12 are to be grouped together: 'The boke of iustyces of peas the charge with all the processe of the cessyons...' reproduced with minute exactness, sometimes preceded by the briefer title, 'The Justyces of peas', the latter alone being used in nos. 13 and 14, while no. 8 is slightly different from any of them.

The first question concerns the undated Pynson, listed in my bibliography as the earliest edition of the 'Boke' for the following reasons. In the 1510 Wynkyn de Worde,[5] the latest statute quoted is that of 11 Henry VII, 1495, on the Custos Rotulorum,[6] distinctly out of place at the end of the Charge, as if an afterthought.[7] But the writs of process are usually dated ten years later, 20 or 21 Henry VII, the latest being 12 July 1506.[8] This edition is therefore based on a work put into its final shape not earlier than the summer of 1506. Further, the colophon includes the phrase: 'Enprynted at London in Fletestrete *at* the sygne of the sonne', and the signatures run A to I, alternating 8 and 4, making 56 folios in all. What little can be learned about the missing 1506 Wynkyn de Worde reveals two differences, the first slight; the colophon has '*in* the sygne of the sonne' and the signatures run A 6, B 6, C to I, alternating 8 and 4, K 6, making 62 folios in all.[9]

---

[1] App. I, Series I.   [2] *Ibid.*, nos. 1, 8, 10, 11, 12, 16.

[3] *Ibid.*, nos. 2 and 4; no. 15 existing only in a meagre fragment, but see pp. 28–30 *infra*.

[4] See p. 8, note 2, *supra*, and App. I, Series I.   [5] *Ibid.* no. 3.

[6] c. xv, An Acte agaynst Shreiffes and Undershreiffes.

[7] For the significance of this statute and of the dates of Pynson's publication of statutes, see ch. ii, *infra*.

[8] Sig. E i. There are a number of writs dated the same month and year, often returnable at a session to be held on Monday, 27 July; cf. e.g. sig. C viii. The regnal year changed on 22 August.

[9] If the description is accurate: W. C. Hazlitt, Collections and Notes, 1867–1876, 243.

In turning to Pynson it is to be noted that his undated edition,[1] like the 1510 Wynkyn de Worde, includes as the latest statute the act of 1495, and therefore evidently preceded his 1521 edition, in which has been added a later statute.[2] The details of his undated volume are practically identical with those of the 1510 Wynkyn de Worde,[3] and the writs of process have the same dates except that 13 July, 21 Henry VII,[4] 1506, is the latest, not 12 July. But the colophon is worded: 'enprynted at London in Fletestrete *in* the sygne of the George',[5] and the signatures are identical with those of the 1506 Wynkyn de Worde, an unusual form of which no other example has been found.

Apparently, therefore, the undated Pynson and the missing 1506 Wynkyn de Worde duplicate each other so precisely that without further evidence there is no absolute certainty as to which of the two was printed first. But the *a priori* probability is all in favour of Pynson. A Norman by birth and trained at Rouen under Guillaume le Talleur, he succeeded Machlinia as a printer of law books between 1486 and 1490, and became King's printer in 1508.[6] He was responsible for the printing by his old master of Littleton's Tenures[7] and Statham's Abridgement,[8] the two great achievements of the

---

[1] App. I, Series I, no. 1.   [2] *Ibid.*, no. 7.

[3] Even palpable errors in the Pynson edition appear in 1510; e.g. 'hedgemakers' for 'heymakers' in the Charge, sig. B i; 'propter securitatez pacis' for 'preceptum securitatis pacis', sig. C v. The differences are very slight; e.g. 'E. D.' in 1510 for Pynson's 'D. E.' in the first of the two misplaced writs.

[4] The second misplaced writ is thus dated, instead of 10 July, as in the Wynkyn de Worde.

[5] Pynson's address by 1500; Duff, *op. cit.*, 126-7.

[6] *Ibid.* As early as 1504, and possibly in 1499, Henry VII made payments to Pynson; Excerpta Historica, ed. S. Bentley, 122, 131, 132.

[7] About 1490 or a little earlier; Duff, *loc. cit.* It had been printed previously by Lettou and Machlinia about 1482 and by Machlinia between 1483 and 1486; Duff, *loc. cit.* and Fifteenth Century English Books. Cf. *ibid.* for Pynson's 1496 edition. For the whole subject see E. Wambaugh, ed. Littleton's Tenures, lix-lxi, lxvii-lxxxiv.

[8] 1490 (Duff, Fifteenth Century English Books), or a little earlier. Pynson perhaps compiled the index, Duff, *loc. cit.* G. J. Turner, Year Book 4 Edw. II, Selden Society, xxxi, thinks that perhaps Pynson printed it himself. In the introduction to her translation of Statham (2 vols., 1915), Mrs. M. C. Klingelsmith concludes that it may have been printed in Pynson's own shop in England, possibly as early as 1470-1475, and

fifteenth-century lawyers; he was the 'first systematic publisher of Year Books',[1] and among the nearly 400 volumes issuing from his press [2] he included a notable list of other law books,[3] for example, important editions of statutes and abridgements of statutes,[4] the Liber Intrationum,[5] Fitzherbert's Abridgement,[6] by all odds the greatest legal work printed in the first half of the sixteenth century; [7] also, of special significance for the present discussion, a number of editions of eleven of the twelve tracts later collected into one volume by William Rastell,[8] six of them having been already printed by his father John,[9] Pynson's fellow printer.   The contrast with Wynkyn de Worde, Caxton's successor, could hardly be more marked. Out of nearly 800 volumes attributed to his press [10] there is a very small proportion of law books, merely a few editions of statutes of Henry VII and of five of the above-mentioned tracts.[11]   Is it not reasonable to suppose that Pynson led the way with the 'Boke' in 1506 and that Wynkyn de Worde followed in the same year,[12] and later printed two more

probably not later than 1480, xvi.   But, according to Duff, Pynson did not come to England till 1486, Century English Book Trade, 126.

[1] Soule, 'Year-Book Bibliography', 7-8 (reprinted from Harvard Law Review, xiv, no. 8).

[2] Duff, *op. cit.*, 126-7; Handlists, *sub nomine*.

[3] I am not including works on canon law like that of Lyndwood.

[4] They afford strong corroborative evidence of my theory; see ch. ii, *infra*.

[5] 1510; Handlists.   [6] p. 34, *infra*, and note 2.

[7] But cf. J. F. Stephen, History of Criminal Law, ii. 205, 1883 ed. : 'It might have been compiled by any one who with moderate technical knowledge combined time and inclination to go through a great deal of drudgery.'

[8] App. I, Series I, nos. 13 and 14, including the 'Boke'.   Thus far it has not been discovered that Pynson ever printed the Ordinance of the Exchequer.   In an article on 'Verses on the Exchequer in the Fifteenth Century', by Professor Haskins and Mrs. George, the history of the ordinance is given but no references to the printed editions; E.H.R., January 1921, 58-67.

[9] App. I, Series I, no. 8.   [10] Duff, *op. cit.*, 173-4.

[11] The Boke, the Court Baron, the Hundred Court, the Carta Feodi and Returna Brevium; Handlists.   Of these the second and third are bound with the 1510 Boke.   Apparently he did not print the Ordinance of the Exchequer.

[12] It seems quite possible that careful editing of these tracts will prove that Pynson's edition was in every instance the earliest.   It ought perhaps to be mentioned that Wynkyn de Worde was printer to the Countess of Richmond (Duff, *op. cit.*, xix-xx), and that there is an .interesting dis-

editions, namely in 1510 and in 1515?[1] In any case while Robert Copland made new mistakes in 1515,[2] Pynson in 1521[3] was the first to correct obvious errors in the ' Boke ',[4] and was also the first to omit obsolete wage legislation [5] and to add the new and important statute on wages of 1515,[6] which had not been included even in Skot's edition of 3 October 1521.[7]

To this group of early editions of the ' Boke ' Redman contributed four.   The first, known at present only by the colophon,[8] was printed in 1527 ' without Tempull barre . . . . at the signe of the George ', perhaps in the shop once occupied by Pynson and after him by Julian Notary[9]; the second probably a little later in the same shop.[10] The other two, nos. 11 and 12 in my list,[11] were both issued without date from Pynson's old shop within Temple Bar to which Redman had succeeded at Pynson's death early in 1530.[12] Since the dates of the latest statutes mentioned are 1523 in no. 11 [13] and 1532

cussion about her appointment as the first woman justice of the peace ; see ch. vi (4), *infra*.   [1] App. I, Series I, nos. 3 and 4.

[2] *Ibid.*, no. 5, e. g. ' fleonyes ' for ' felonies ' in the Charge, sig. A v. Cf. also ' well dysposed sad men & lawful ' for the usual ' well dysposed men and lawful ' in the opening paragraph. I have found no evidence as to the relative dates of the two 1515 editions.

[3] App. I, Series I, no. 7.

[4] p. 19, note 3, *supra*. ' Henricus ' is substituted for ' D. E.' or ' E. D.', ' Heymakers ' for ' Hedgemakers ', ' preceptum ' for ' propter '. But in the Charge ' within half a yere ' is erroneously put for ' within forty dayes ' (sig. A v) ; see Crompton, Loffice, f. 82 b. There is a slight change in the form of the writ after the ' Placita coram ', i. e. ' preceptum factum ' for ' mandatum quod ' ; and in place of the three entries on the last folio of the writs of process there occurs a shorter entry : ' Relaxatio...'.

[5] e. g. 25 Hen. V (probably an error for 23 Hen. VI, c. 12), sig B i, 1510 ed. ; also the harvest wage clause from 25 Edw. III, st. 2, c. 1, sig. B ii, *ibid.*

[6] 6 Hen. VIII, c. 3 ; printed as 7 Hen. VIII, c. 7 ; sig. A vii-viii.

[7] App. I, Series I, no. 6 ; affording slight though not conclusive proof that Pynson's volume came after 3 October.

[8] *Ibid.*, no 9. The description of the title-page (Ames, ed. Herbert, 387) coincides with title-pages of the preceding editions.

[9] Duff, *op. cit.*, 132. It is natural that Pynson should object to Redman's use of his sign.

[10] App. I, Series I, no. 10. Of the two initials on this title-page, I. M. and I. N., the latter probably stands for Julian Notary.

[11] App. I, Series I.

[12] ' St. Dunstan's parish ' appears in both colophons. Pynson issued no book after 18 June 1528, and Redman's earliest dated book is 23 March 1529 (1530) ; Duff, *op. cit.*, 127, 132.

[13] 14 and 15 Hen. VIII, on Cross-bows, c. 7, and on the Killing of hares, c. 10, are added at the end of the indictments (ff. 68, 68 b) as supplementary articles of the Charge.

in no. 12,[1] and since the important statute on Heresy of 1534[2] appears only in Redman's remaining edition, no. 16, also undated,[3] it seems sound to infer that no. 11 was printed about 1531[4] and no. 12 about 1533. Confirmation of these dates is furnished by the dates of the five tracts bound with no. 11 and no. 12 respectively, constituting two collections similar to that of John Rastell.[5] In each case three of the five tracts are dated; in the first set, two are 1530 and one February 1532,[6] in the second, all three are 1533.[7]

Exclusive of recent statutes, the only important divergence from preceding versions of the ' Boke ' is the addition at the very end of no. 11 of five oaths of office not found in editions issued by any other printer, namely, of the justices of the peace, of the sheriffs, of the undersheriffs, of a ' Bayly errant ', of ' Baylyes of liberties '.[8] Otherwise Redman is evidently following Pynson's careful revision of 1521, and has incorporated almost all his modifications,[9] but with so many inexcusable errors [10] as fully to justify Pynson's scathing abuse.[11]

The changes in the 1533 (?) edition, described as ' nouiter impressa et emendata ',[12] hardly bear out the description. They include the omission of the oath of the sheriff and a stupid running together of the oaths of the justice and of the

---

[1] 23 Hen. VIII, on Clerks convicted of Petty Treason, c. 1, Charge, ff. 13, 13 b ; on Gaols, c. 2, Charge, ff. 13 b–15.

[2] 25 Hen. VIII, c. 14, f. 88 b.

[3] App. I, Series I. Amidst the confusion caused by Redman's undated editions, it is fortunate that the colophon of no. 11 differs from that of no. 12, and that the title-page of no. 16 differs from the title-pages of any of his other issues.

[4] That is, after Pynson's death and before the parliament of 1532.

[5] See *infra*, p. 24.

[6] In the H.L.S. volume ; the U.L.C. edition is bound separately.

[7] Hence in the catalogue of the library of Gray's Inn, the whole volume is given under the date 1533.

[8] ff. 68 b–73 b.   Except for a stupid repetition at the beginning, and for ' and his sayntes ' in place of ' by the contents of this Booke ', Redman's oath of the justices is the same as that printed by Lambard, Eirenarcha, 50–1.   From a comparison of foliation it seems probable that these changes had appeared in the 1527 edition, no. 9 of my list.

[9] See p. 21, note 4, *supra*.

[10] e.g. *Iuramentum feloniarum*, f. 41 b ; *Indictauerunt*, f. 61 b, both for *Indictamentum*.

[11] *Supra*, p. 15, and note 7.

[12] App. I, Series 1, no. 12, colophon.

undersheriff;[1] also a particularly unintelligent reversion in some details to the 1510 Wynkyn de Worde edition.[2]

It is a pleasure to turn from the slovenly productions of Robert 'Rudeman' to the editions of the 'Boke' by the two Rastells, scholarly printers who made their occupation seem a profession rather than a trade.[3] They were educated at Oxford and at the Inns of Court,[4] the father at the Middle Temple,[5] the son at Lincoln's Inn.[6] The latter achieved the distinction of a judgeship by 1558.[7] The family had long been connected with Coventry,[8] John and his brother Thomas holding in turn the post of coroner of the city[9] a few years before Sir Anthony Fitzherbert became recorder.[10] John married the sister of Sir Thomas More, and died in 1536,[11] having done but little publishing after 1530,[12] the year when his eldest son William began his short career as printer.[13]

[1] ff. 6 b–10. The oath now appears in Part I, just before the two misplaced writs.

[2] e. g., 'E. D.' for 'Henricus'; see p. 21, note 4, *supra*. The obsolete wage statute of 23 Hen. VI is given and the current one of 6 Hen. VIII omitted; f. 19 b. Some of the worst misprints are however corrected (cf. p. 22, note 10, *supra*), the articles of inquiry on the two new statutes of 1523 are removed from the end of Part II to the middle of Part I, f. 6 b (they belong in the Charge), and there are slight changes in, and additions to, the qualifications at the beginning of Part I.

[3] John Rastell 'set up the trade of printing, being then esteemed a profession fit for any scholar or ingenious man'; Anthony à Wood, Athen. Oxon., 3rd ed., 1813, i, col. 100.

[4] D.N.B.; A. W. Reed, 'Sir John Rastell, Printer, Lawyer, Venturer, Dramatist, and Controversialist', Trans. Bib. Soc., xv, 1920, 59–82.

[5] Minutes of Parliament, ed. C. Trice Martin, i. 2; 'Rastall' is an Utter Barrister in 1502. Therefore he was not a member of Lincoln's Inn, as stated by Mr. Duff, Century Eng. Book Trade, 129, and art. in D.N.B.

[6] Admitted in 1532; Admissions, i. 46; cf. also Black Books, i, index *sub nomine*.

[7] Foss, Judges. It is often said that like Sir Anthony Fitzherbert they were both ardent Catholics, but Mr. Duff states that John became converted to the reformed religion in 1530; *ut supra*.

[8] Coventry Leet Book, ed. M. D. Harris, index. The earliest reference is to a Thomas Rastell in 1430; *ibid*. 128. Many of the family, including John, belonged to the Gild of St. Anne of Knowle, Warwickshire; see p. 139, note 3, *infra*.

[9] Thomas, 1505–1506; John, 1507–1508; Cov. Leet Bk., 603–5, 619; ch. iii (1), p. 79, note 5, *infra*.

[10] 1509; *ibid.*, p. 78, note 4.

[11] Duff, Century Eng. Book Trade, 129.

[12] Perhaps none; see Handlists.

[13] Duff, *ut supra*, and Handlists.

We know that John Rastell's earliest publications included several legal volumes of the greatest value, the Liber Assisarum,[1] the Abbreviation of Statutes,[2] the Table to Fitzherbert's Abridgement,[3] &c. His prefaces show how much labour as compiler and translator he himself expended,[4] and afford strong confirmation of the hypothesis that it was he who induced Pynson to undertake the actual printing of Fitzherbert's great work.[5] This association with Pynson is important in connexion with Rastell's version of the 'Boke', issued as one of a collection of law tracts, the others being Carta Feodi, Hundred Court, Returna Brevium, Ordinance of the Exchequer, and Court Baron, all six undated, and clearly designed to form one work.[6] In the 'Boke' Rastell followed Pynson very closely, and like him made corrections, most of which were distinct improvements,[7] although neither his additions [8] nor omissions [9] in any way changed the general scheme of the work. The phrase on the title-page is thus justified: 'newly correctyd and amendyd with dyuers new addycyons put to the same'. The date must be between 1523, the year of the latest statutes mentioned [10], and 1530, the year when his printing activities practically cease; [11] perhaps, therefore, earlier than Redman's first edition of 1527, or perhaps just before the issue of the latter's third edition of 1531 (?). In either case, it is probable that Redman's collections of various law tracts under one cover, issued *circ.* 1531 and 1533,[12] were in imitation of the plan of his learned contemporary, and that it is

---

[1] The preface proves that it was earlier than 21 December 1516, the date of the colophon of vol. iii of Fitzherbert's Abridgement, and certainly after 18 November 1510, since Fitzherbert is described as 'seriant at law'; see p. 34, note 2, p. 33, note 2, *infra.*

[2] 25 October 1519; Handlists.

[3] 10 February 1517 (1518); see p. 34, note 3, *infra.*

[4] *Ibid.,* and note 2.   [5] See *infra,* p. 34.

[6] App. I, Series I, no. 8 and note 1 ; and *supra,* p. 22. The qualifications at the beginning of Part I are like those of the 1531 (?) Redman.

[7] See p. 21, notes 4 and 5, *supra.*

[8] e.g., a number of statutes of the reign of Henry VIII.

[9] e.g., he omits 'Markets in Churchyards' in the Charge, and does not give the oaths of office found in Redman.

[10] 14 and 15 Hen. VIII, as in the 1531 (?) Redman (p. 21, note 13, *supra*), but incorporated into the Charge; sig. A viii.

[11] *Supra,* p. 23, and note 12.   [12] *Supra,* p. 22.

to John Rastell that credit must be given for originating and executing the scheme. William Rastell, therefore, in his collection later known as 'Rastell's tracts', two issues of which he printed in 1534,[1] was simply following his father's plan, and amplified it by the inclusion of six more tracts, Natura Brevium, the old Tenures, Littleton's Tenures, the New 'Talys', the Articles upon the new 'Talys', Diversity of Courts.[2] In fact, he reproduced his father's edition of the 'Boke' so closely [3] that he did not bring it up to date.[4]

In spite of the excellence of these Rastell versions of the 'Boke', they seem to have had very little influence on later editions, even on those of Thomas Berthelet, once an assistant to Pynson, and by 1530 his successor as King's printer.[5] There is evidently a close connexion between Berthelet's publications for justices of the peace and his official duties. The latter had begun by the printing of royal proclamations of several statutes to be enforced by the justices,[6] including the proclamation of 9 June 1535 for 'the abolishing of the usurped power of the Pope'.[7] By 1536 he printed his earliest edition of the 'Boke' under a short title: 'The Boke for a Justyce of

[1] App. I, Series I, nos. 13 and 14.

[2] The preface is interesting: 'Wyllyam Rastell to the gentylman studentes of the law . . . Than haue ye the boke of Justice of peas, not onely necessary to those iustices them selfe, to knowe thereby what authoritie they haue and what they ought to do, but as requysite to all theym that any thynge entermedeleyth them with the lawe, includynge the forme of certeyn proces and very many enditementes . . .'

[3] Cf. e.g. the omission of 'Markets in Churchyards'; see p. 24, note 9, *supra*.

[4] e.g., he does not add the important statutes of 1532, printed in Redman's 1533 (?) edition; see p. 22, note 1, *supra*.

[5] Duff, *op. cit.*, 11–12. On the accession of Edw. VI he lost his post and was succeeded by Grafton.

[6] Bibliotheca Lindesiana, v, A Bibliography of Royal Proclamations, 1485–1714, i, 1910: no. 121, For the punishment of vagrants, June 1530; no. 122, Against heretical books, June 1530; no. 132, Against false news, beggars, unlawful games, for archery, against excess in apparel, concerning sewers, 1533; no. 156, For archery, against unlawful games, for reform of apparel and for punishment of beggars, February 1536.

[7] *Ibid.*, no. 153; cf. Act of Supremacy of November 1534, 26 Hen. VIII, c. I. For a brief account of the legislation that brought about the breach with Rome and of the parliament that held various sessions from November 1529 to April 1536, including two in 1534, and also of the parliament of June–July 1536, see H. A. L. Fisher, Political History of England, 1485–1547, chs. xii–xiv, and Parry, *op. cit.*, 202–3.

peace neuer so well & diligently set forth ',[1] incorporating
much of the old title into a note ' To the Reder.'[2]   In this
volume he gives as the latest legislation the two acts of the
June session of parliament, 1536,[3] on Wines and against the
Bishop of Rome.[4] On the whole, apart from his addition
of other recent statutes,[5] he follows very closely the 1510
Wynkyn de Worde,[6] although occasionally using the changes
made in the 1521 Pynson,[7] but not always omitting obsolete
acts.[8]   Then in 1538, a year of great activity on the part of

[1] App. I, Series I, no. 15. This edition known now only by a hitherto
unidentified fragment in University Library, Cambridge, Catalogue of
Early Printed Books, no. 7085, is usually ascribed to the year 1534; see
Handlists, and Ames, ed. Herbert, 425. But among Corrections and
Additions of the latter work, iii. 1787, is a statement that Berthelet's
' Modus tenendi curiam Baronis', colophon 1536 (Ames, 428) was joined
by signatures with the Boke of 1534 (*ibid*. 425). The error in date is
undoubtedly due to the fact that the Boke had a ' 1534' title-page, used
by Berthelet for several years; cf. e.g., the tracts bound up with his
1539 Boke, the Ordinance of the Exchequer, col. August 1537, and the
Statutes, col. 1538, both of which have a 1534 title-page (H.L.S., D. Tr.
26. 2). In the other H.L.S. copy (D. Tr. 26. 3) the Returna has a 1534
title-page but no colophon.

[2] The accuracy of this statement depends on the soundness of my
hypothesis given *infra*, pp. 29–30. But in any case the ' note' appears in
the 1539 edition (App. I, Series I, no. 17): ' This Boke of Justyce of peace is
amended nowe at this imprintyng, as in the allegation of the yeres of
statutes, and the chapyters of the same.   And farthermore many statutes
that in dyuers cases charge the sayd Justyces of peace be added to, that
were neuer before printed in the sayd boke, one cause is for many of them
haue ben enacted, sythe the tyme that the same booke was fyrst compyled;
whiche was a very good acte, for lyghtly, there is nothing belongynge to
a Justice of the peace to do, as concernynge the processe of their sessions,
to make warrantes, supersedias enditementes of haut treason, petye
treason, felonies, appeales, trespasses vpon statutes, and contra Regis
pacem, but it is conteyned in this lytell booke.'

[3] A new parliament; see p. 14, note 6, *supra*.

[4] ' For extinguyshynge of the bysshoppe of Rome '; ff. 27 b–28. Cf.
p. 14 and notes 7 and 8, *supra*.

[5] Acts of 1530, 1531, 1532, &c., in the Charge; very few· of these had
appeared even in the 1534 Rastell or the 1533 (?) Redman.·

[6] e.g. 'within fortye dayes', f. 12 b, instead of 'half a yere', as in
Pynson; *supra*, p. 21, note 4.

[7] The writs of process are almost always as in 1521, not as in 1510,
i.e. after ' Placita coram . . .', f. 33, comes 'preceptum factum' instead of
' mandatum quod'.   Cf. also ' heymaker' for ' hedgemaker', f. 19 b, and
the new wage statute of 1515, ff. 17–19 b.

[8] e.g., the statute of 23 Hen. VI and the harvest clause of 25 Edw. III
are both given; ff. 16 b–19 b, 20. The divergence from Rastell is shown
by the retention of ' Markets in Churchyards', f. 8 b; see *supra*,
p. 24, note 9.

the King's Council in urging the justices of the peace to a zealous performance of their duties, especially in hunting out 'cankered parsons, vicars, and curates',[1] Berthelet printed a volume of 'statutes which to put in execution, the justices of peace, sheriffs, baylyfes, constables, and other ministers of Justice were of late admonished by the Kynges maiestie, on peyne to runne into his grace's moste hyghe indignation and displeasure.'[2]

The very next year Berthelet produced his second edition of the 'Boke',[3] containing no later acts than those of 1536 already mentioned, and bound up with his 'Statutes,'[4] and with the now familiar five tracts.[5] Berthelet printed the tracts separately with their own colophons, but listed them all on his title-page : ' The boke for a Ivstice of peace, the boke that teacheth to kepe a court baron, or a lete . . . etc.' In 1542, the year of legislative changes in the organization of the sessions of the peace,[6] he printed the proclamation of several acts to be enforced by the justices ;[7] in 1543 he re-issued his

[1] A circular letter of December thanked the justices for their previous efforts and bade them make still greater; Letters and Papers, Foreign and Domestic, Hen. VIII, xiii, pt. ii, no. 1171 ; Beard, Office of Justice of the Peace, 125.

[2] p. 26, note 1, *supra*. The statutes are a strange miscellany: (1) Against new-fangled news ; (2) Against unlawful games ; (3) For maintenance of archery; (4) For vagabonds; (5) Concerning commissions of Sewers ; (6) Reformation of excess in apparel ; (7) Against the bishop of Rome. Berthelet had previously printed royal proclamations for all but no. 7 (28 Hen. VIII. c. 10) ; see p. 25, note 6, *supra*. For Redman's publications on justices of the peace in this same year, see *supra*, p. 10.

[3] App. I, Series I, no 17. Cf. Guilielmi Neubrigensis Historia, ed. Th. Hearne, 1819, iii. 784–5 : 'a small scarce Thing, entitled, "The Boke for a Justice of Peace, The Boke that teacheth to kepe a courte baron . . ." in aedibus Thomae Bertheleti . . . Anno MDXXXIX . . . (whereof I have a Copy in my Collection, and it contains only 122 pages).'

[4] With a slightly different title-page from that of the separate edition, *supra*. Cf. also statute 31 Hen. VIII, c. 8, art. ix, 1539, for the duties of the justices in relation to the enactment that royal proclamations are to have the force of law.

[5] *Supra*, p. 24.

[6] 33 Hen. VIII, c. 10, art. 1–19. Dr. Hubert Hall, in Repertory of British Archives, pt. i, England, 111, attaches too great importance, I think, to the changes in 1542 which were abolished by an act of 37 Hen. VIII, c. 7.

[7] e.g. Bib. Royal Proclamations : no. 205, Cross bows, 1542 ; no. 208, Artillery and unlawful games, 1542 ; no. 209, Execution of certain statutes, 33 Hen. VIII, c. 10, 1542. Cf. also another circular letter from the Council to the justices in 1541, urging them to enforce certain statutes

'Statutes';[1] in 1544 he published his third and last edition of
the 'Boke' bound with the same tracts, but omitting the
'Statutes', and preceded by practically the same title-page.[2]
My belief is that Berthelet's 'Boke' of 1539 was a reprint,
without material changes, of his edition of 1536,[3] of which no
copy has been found by recent bibliographers. Certainly the
'Boke' of 1544 is a very exact reproduction of that of 1539,
even to the extent of the repetition of obvious errors;[4] but it
incorporates a number of the new statutes just mentioned,[5]
and from the list of offences constituting petty treason omits
the slaying of his abbot or prior by a monk,[6] no longer
applicable in view of the dissolution of the monasteries.[7]
Before tracing the history of the subsequent editions based on
those of Berthelet, it is necessary to turn once again to Redman. It has been already shown that in 1538—a year of
unusual importance for the literature on justices of the peace—
Redman printed 'Loffice' and two issues of the 'Newe
Boke'.[8] But he also printed an undated 'Boke', containing
the same two statutes of 1536 so often mentioned,[9] and therefore of necessity later than his last previous edition of the
'Boke' of *circ.* 1533.[10] A comparison of this new volume with
the 1539 Berthelet shows that Redman has used the title-
page of the latter's 1536 edition,[11] has omitted the oaths of

(nos. 1, 2, 4, and 7, p. 27, note 2, *supra*); Letters and Papers, Foreign and
Domestic, Hen. VIII, xvi, no. 945.
   [1] The title-page refers to the act of 33 Hen. VIII, cited in note 6,
p. 27, *supra*.
   [2] App. I, Series I, no. 18.　　　　　[3] For proof, see p. 29, note 4, *infra*.
   [4] e.g., f. 10, 'Kings chapiter' for 'charter'.
   [5] Enough nearly to fill up the omitted pages in the 1539 edition between
f. 28 b, the end of Part I, and f. 33, the beginning of Part II. On ff. 31-2 of
the 1544 edition, after the recital of a portion of the act of 1542 (the latest
mentioned), occurs the following note : ' Many other thynges the Justices
of the peace haue auctoritie and are bounde to do, by a special acte for
that cause made & prouided anno 33 H. 8, Cap. 10 '.
   [6] 1539 ed., f. 9 ; 1544 ed., f. 9.　Cf. 25 Edw. III, st. 5, c. 2 : ' or when a
Man secular or Religious slayeth his Prelate '. ' Rex Hybern ' appears in
place of ' dominus Hybern ', e.g. f. 51 b ; but not always ; cf. f. 36.
   [7] By statutes 27 Hen. VIII, c. 28, 1536, and 31 Hen. VIII, c. 13, 1539.
   [8] *Supra*, p. 10.
   [9] App. I, Series I, no. 16. It also includes a number of recent statutes
not found in his earlier editions ; e.g. ff. 8-8 b, on Heresy, 25 Hen. VIII,
c. 14, 1534.
   [10] *Supra*, pp. 21-22, the latest statute being 1532.　　　[11] *Supra*, pp. 25-26.

office, the distinctive feature of his own early editions,[1] and that except for minor differences in spelling, &c.,[2] and for one significant detail to be described below, his volume bears such exact resemblance to that of Berthelet [3] that either one must have copied the other or else they must have been printing from a common source. My guess is that the second alternative is the true one; that the common source is Berthelet's first edition of 1536,[4] and that in the latter's second edition of 1539, he abandoned his new and effective title to his rival,

[1] *Supra*, p. 22.

[2] e.g., in Part II, ' R. S.' in Redman's writs, f. 12, ' W. T.' very often in Berthelet's, f. 44 ; also some stupid errors in Redman, such as the extension of ' coram custod ' to ' coram custodiendis ', f. 1 ; ' Londouici ' for ' Ludouici ', f. 14.

[3] The inclusion of the same statutes, &c. In fact the same words usually appear on the same position on the pages.

[4] My conclusions are based on a study of the fragment, no. 7085, U.L.C., mentioned in note 1, p. 26, *supra*. It contains four folios of Part II of the Boke (bound in wrong order) and on the ground of the type is attributed to Berthelet's press by Mr. Sayle, the maker of the catalogue. The folios have arabic numerals, 19–22, signatures C iii, [C] iiii, C v, [C vi], and a running title *Justice, of peace*. The first folio (f. 19), *of peace*, begins in the midst of a writ of process, ' Norff. ac custodibus pacis '; f. 21 b, *Justice*, has the final entry of the writs, ' Relaxatio securitatis pacis ', followed by ' Indict. de alta proditione '; f. 22 b, *Justice*, ends in the midst of ' Cap. scdo.' of the indictments. Clearly therefore Part II, 'Placita coram . . .', must have begun with f. 1, signature A 1, in order to have the writ ' Norff.' &c. appear on f. 19, signature C iii. But as will be shown later (p. 98) a break in the foliation does *not* occur after the Charge in any of the editions listed in my bibliography earlier than the 1536 Berthelet, and in the 1539 and 1544 Berthelet, as in all the editions based on his (p. 98, *infra*), the arabic foliation and signatures are continuous throughout Parts I and II. In all these, therefore, the above writ comes on f. 51, signature G iii. On the other hand, in the latest Redman edition and in those of all his exact followers (p. 30, *infra*), Part II, 'Placita coram . . .', *does* begin on f. 1, signature A i, and the writ does, therefore, come on f. 19, signature C iii. A careful examination of the unique copy of this Redman (in H.L.S.) and of the editions of his followers (except the missing Smythe) shows slight variations of spelling, &c., between them and the fragment; e.g. in one instance *Justyce* for *Justice* as running title, in other instances roman for arabic foliation ; further, the initial letter on f. 21 b differs from that in the Redman edition, but is identical with that on f. 53 b, the corresponding folio of the 1539 Berthelet. Therefore, by a process of elimination it is sound to infer that this fragment is a part of the missing 1536 Berthelet and a common source of the 1538(?) Redman and of the 1539 Berthelet.

There was a copy in the library of William Bayntun (of Gray's Inn) in 1785, Ames, ed. Herbert, ix, 425 ; probably the same volume that was later referred to by Dibdin as having been in the collection of John Baynes and William Bayntun, T. F. Dibdin, ed. Herbert's Ames, iii. 290, 1816. But, unfortunately, it is not listed in the catalogues of sales ; Bayntun, 1787, Bodleian; Baynes, 1788, B.M.

but otherwise kept very closely to his own model.[1] Further, since the one noteworthy departure from Berthelet in Redman's edition is the occasional appearance of the strange form 'justicer', peculiar to Fitzherbert,[2] it seems reasonable to infer that the 'Boke' was being printed in Redman's shop at about the time of the printing of Fitzherbert's 'Loffice' and the 'Newe Boke', that is, in 1538 or early in 1539,[3] *before* Berthelet's second edition, and that 'justicer' was a not unnatural slip of the typesetters.

Whatever the origin of this Redman edition, it was reprinted in 1544 or 1545[4] by William Middleton, who succeeded to Redman's shop after the remarriage of the latter's widow,[5] and also four times in 1546, by Henry Smythe,[6] Redman's son-in-law,[7] by Nicholas Hyll,[8] Robert Toy,[9] and John Walley.[10] All these five printers use the new title appropriated by Redman, and in almost all details follow him with absolute precision, ignoring, for example, the recent statutes added by Berthelet in 1544.[11]

[1] The very close parallel between the fragment and the 1539 Berthelet suggests that the note to the 'Reder' had appeared in the 1536 volume.
[2] e.g., ff. 3, 5 (Part I) ; contracted from *Justiciar*, according to Lambard, Eirenarcha, 4.
[3] In any case before Redman's death in the autumn of 1540 ; p. 16, note 2, *supra.*
[4] App. I, Series I, no. 19; not dated but bound with the usual five tracts, dated either 1543 or 1544, and with the Office of Sheriffs (abstracted from Fitzherbert), dated 1545. He had printed the Newe Boke in 1543 ; App. I, Series II, no. 7.   [5] Duff, *op. cit.*, 104–5.
[6] App. I, Series I, no. 21 ; not at present known.
[7] Apparently he printed only law books and only in the years 1545 and 1546 ; Duff, *op. cit.*, 150.
[8] App. I, Series I, no. 20. Most of his books were printed for other people ; Duff, *op. cit.*, 72–3.
[9] App. I, Series I, no. 22. Most of his books were printed for him by other people ; Duff, *op. cit.*, 158.
[10] App. I, Series I, no. 23 ; Duff, *op. cit.*, 164.
[11] Excluding the missing Smythe edition, the following similarities are cited as examples: the break in the foliation always appears after the Charge (p. 29, note 4, *supra*), Middleton like Redman using arabic numbers for both parts while the others use roman. Hyll, f. 9 (Part I), departs from Redman in the omission of 'monks slaying their abbot' &c. but otherwise follows him closely, printing *justicer, coram custodiendis*, &c. Toy and Walley reproduce Hyll so exactly as to make one wonder whether they did not all of them bind the identical printed sheets, merely inserting their own names on the title-page and in the colophon. It is to be noted that the familiar tracts bound with the Boke by these various printers usually have their own colophons.

But it was this Berthelet edition of the 'Boke' that eventually triumphed.   Reprinted in 1550 by William Powell[1] with almost absolute exactness, even as to errors,[2] it was selected as his model by Tottell when the series came into his hands in 1556.[3]   His eight issues, the last printed in 1580,[4] include no corrections except the omission in 1556 of the statute against the Bishop of Rome,[5] and a slight change in the title-page of the two final editions.[6]   No new statutes were ever added after 1544 ; the writs late in the reign of Elizabeth still run in the name of Henry VII ; the indictments still include cases of the reigns of Henry VI and Edward IV. The likenesses between the various Tottell editions are in fact so complete that, as in the case of the various editions of the 'Newe Boke', the same words regularly appear on corresponding portions of the pages.[7]

From the study of this one type of legal treatise, one has increased respect for the King's two printers, Pynson[8] and Berthelet, and for the legally-trained Rastells, father and son,

---

[1] App. I, Series I, no. 24. He had married the widow of William Middleton in 1547, two months after the latter's death, and occupied the shop that had been used successively by so many printers ; Duff, *op. cit.*, 104, 125.

[2] e.g., 'King's chapiter', f. 10, still appears for 'Charter'.

[3] See p. 17, note 4, *supra.*

[4] App. I, Series I, no. 25, 1556 ; nos. 26 and 27, 1559; nos. 28 and 29, 1569 ; no. 30, 1574; no. 31, 1579 [1580]; no. 32, 1580. According to Stationers' Registers, ii. 193, Tottell had a licence on 18 February 1582 (1583) to print ' The olde Justice of peace with others &c.' I have not discovered a copy. It is important to note that Tottell adopted the plan of John Rastell, more fully carried out by his son, and made the Boke a part of a collection of the familiar law tracts, his first edition (no. 25 in my list), including also the Diuersitie de Courts and Articuli ad narrationes nouas. The paging is henceforth consecutive, with a table and colophon to the whole volume at the end.

[5] f. 28 b and *supra*, p. 17.

[6] Due to the fact that it became a part of the volume containing Kitchin's new edition of Court Leet, &c.; App. I, Series I, nos. 31, 32.

[7] Tottell's unintelligent, mechanical method is well shown by the following instance. His 1556 volume contained as the next to the last tract the Diuersitie de Courts, and therefore the bottom of f. 195 (the conclusion of the last preceding tract) had the catchword, *Diuer.* In the subsequent issues, this tract is not included, but the catchword is faithfully preserved at f. 195, and by 1574 reduced merely to *Di.* The only differences between the Tottell editions seem to be in spelling or in the omission of marginal headings as in nos. 25 and 26.

[8] See p. 20, note 12, *supra.*

far less for Tottell, and for Redman none at all.[1] It is
characteristic of the age that ecclesiastical matters bulk large
in whatever changes are made, but it is clear that, with few
exceptions, the ' Boke ' and the ' Newe Boke ' both became
stereotyped before the end of the reign of Henry VIII and
therefore fail to include the many important acts of the reigns
of his children that came under the jurisdiction of the justices
of the peace. This failure is particularly serious in the case
of the ecclesiastical, economic, and social legislation of Elizabeth,[2] and shows how great a need there was for the scholarly
work of Lambard.

The preceding analysis leads to a consideration of the
arguments against Fitzherbert's connexion with the ' Boke '.
In the absence of an exhaustive critical study of the career
and writings of Sir Anthony Fitzherbert,[3] there has been a
dangerous tendency to attribute to him far too many works.[4]
Certainly conclusive evidence has been presented to show that
in spite of Skeat's view to the contrary,[5] the ' Book of Surveying ' and the ' Book of Husbandry ' were written, not by
Sir Anthony, but by his elder brother John. There is no
need to rehearse the long controversy.[6] It is impossible to

---

[1] It seems probable that a careful editing of the law books issuing from
Redman's press will prove that they were all based on works already in
print, never on manuscript material ; cf. Duff, *op. cit.*, 132, and p. 17, note
12, *supra*.

[2] e. g., the famous statute of Artificers of 1563, the whole series of Poor
Laws, &c.

[3] The article in D.N.B. is inaccurate and inadequate, p. 15, note 4,
supra. It is strange that the greatest legal scholar of the day should
remain without a suitable biography.

[4] The main purpose of Sir Ernest Clarke in his Memorandum of 1894
(p. 9, note 1, *supra*) was to analyse the insufficient grounds on which
works had been attributed to Sir Anthony. Cf. also his papers of February
1894, read before the Society of Antiquaries, Proceedings, Second Series,
xv. 96–9, and of February 1896, read before the Bibliographical Society,
Transactions, iii. 160–62 ; also an article by J. C. Cox in Journal Derbyshire Arch. Soc., vii, 1885, 221–59.

[5] See his preface to the Book of Husbandry, Eng. Dialect Society, 1882.

[6] The most important contribution to the subject is by the Rev. R. H. C.
Fitzherbert, E.H R., xii, 1897, 225–36, ' The Authorship of the Book of
Husbandry and the Book of Surveying ',cited *supra*, p. 9, note 1. The author
kindly called my attention to an admirably concise summary by Mr. E. F.
Gay in Quarterly Journal Economics, xviii, 1903–1904, 588–93, which
gives specific evidence to show that John had had some legal training.
Distinguished scholars still cling to the old view however ; cf. Select Cases

believe that a man who in dealing with legal matters wrote:
' I remytte that to menne of lawe ',[1] is to be identified as the
author of the great Abridgement and a judge of the Court of
Common Pleas [2] sufficiently distinguished to be chosen to aid
the Privy Council in drawing up the articles against Wolsey.[3]

in the Star Chamber, ed. Leadam, Selden Soc., 2 vols., 1902, 1911, i. 54,
note 3, ii. 165, note 2.

[1] Surveyinge, Berthelet, 1539, ff. 13 b, 14, 15, 17, 17 b.   Cf. f. 47 b,
' and as I sayd in the boke of Husbandrye . . .' Skeat, *loc. cit.*, xii, note 1,
quotes from the prologue to the first edition of the Surveying, that of
Pynson, 15 July, 1523: ' Of late by experience I contriued, compyled, and
made a Treatyse . . . and callyd it the booke of husbandrye '. The latter
was first printed by Pynson in 1523 and then by Berthelet, perhaps in
1534; Fitzherbert, *loc. cit.* The Handlists assign Berthelet's first edition
to 1532. The evidence is certainly conclusive that the same man wrote
both works.

[2] Appointed in Easter 1522 ; Foss, Judges. He was born at Norbury,
Derbyshire, in 1470 (Mr. Gay, however, has some doubt as to this date ;
loc. cit., p. 32, note 6, *supra*), was educated at Oxford and at Gray's Inn
and was made serjeant-at-law on 18 November 1510, king's serjeant on
24 November 1516; D.N.B. Segar's transcripts of the older records
unfortunately lack the folios containing the list of Benchers for this date,
and give Lent 1513-1514 as the earliest specific date for a reading—that
of Spelman—mentioning Fitzherbert as a reader but with no date
assigned; W. R. Douthwaite, Gray's Inn, 1886, 46 ; Pension Book, ed.
R. J. Fletcher, i. xxvi. But that Fitzherbert was admitted a little before
1490 is proved by the instructions in his mother's will drawn that year:
her eldest son John was to pay to Anthony the sum of five marks per
annum ' towards his exhibition at Court (i. e. Gray's Inn) upon condition
that he continue his learning at the same ' ; see p. 234 of art. in E.H.R.,
cited p. 32, note 6, *supra*. At the serjeants' feast held at Ely House in 1510,
' Mr. Fytherbert ' and others gave liberally to a certain church connected
with Gray's Inn ; Pension Book, i. xxvi.
   There is in Gray's Inn library a volume of MS. readings delivered at the
Inn, including one by John Chaloner as early as 1493. Ff. 263-76 are of
different size from the other folios and contain at the end the following
memorandum: ' Iste liber constat Antonio Fyzherberd, Teste Johanne
Ernley '. The latter, a member of the Inn and associated with many
eminent men of law, died in 1520; his will, 3 Maynwarying, P.C.C.,
with a codicil of 7 October 1519, was proved 17 November 1520. It
seems probable that the rest of the collection was transcribed by Robert
Chaloner, Lent reader at the Inn in 1522 (Dugdale, Orig. Jurid., 292),
and that eventually he was the owner of the whole volume; see pamphlet
on The Chaloner MSS. in Gray's Inn Library.
   I am indebted to Mr. Bernard O'Connor not only for a copy of this
pamphlet, but also for a description of the arms of Fitzherbert, formerly in
' Grey's In hall Wyndowe in glasse ' ; MSS. Harl. 2113, f. 107 b ; 2059,
f. 203 ; Dugdale, *op. cit.*, 302. Under date of 1536 the Pension Book
(i. 499) has the entry : ' Called to be Ancients, Fitzherbert . . .' indexed
under Anthony Fitzherbert.

[3] Coke, 3rd Inst., 208, 4th Inst., 89-93, 1644 ed. ; Coram Rege Roll,
Trin. 23 Hen. VIII, rot. 14.

In the present state of our knowledge, it is not safe to attribute to Sir Anthony more than the following works, all of them in French, but even in this short list doubts have been suggested :

(1) 'La Graunde Abridgement'. First printed in 1516 [1] by Pynson for John Rastell. [2] The latter made a valuable table to it which he himself printed a little later. [3]

(2) 'La Novel Natura Brevium'. First printed by Berthelet in 1537, [4] and next by Tottell in 1553, with a table made by

[1] Perhaps his appointment as king's serjeant in this year was a tribute to this monumental undertaking.

[2] The colophon of the third part is: 'Finis tocius istius operi finiti XXI die Dicembris anno domini Millecimo quingentesimo sexto decimo . . .' Until this very difficult problem is solved by further investigation, I am inclined to disagree with Sir Ernest Clarke in his Memorandum, and to accept the theory tentatively suggested by F. A. Ballard, based on a study of type and devices—namely that the edition of 1516 was the earliest and was printed *by* Pynson *for* John Rastell. In Handlists, the first edition is said to be 1514, from the press of Pynson; the second 1516, from that of John Rastell. See also Ames, 120; ed. Herbert, 260; ed. Dibdin, ii. 210, 211, for the traditional references to a 1514 edition. Possibly Mr. W. C. Bolland's hypothesis will prove to be correct (stated in a letter of April 1921), that the three parts were printed in three successive years, 1514, 1515, and 1516. See also Rastell's preface to his edition of Liber Assisarum, printed without date a few years before Fitzherbert was made king's serjeant : 'We pourpose further to put in print another boke which by goddis grace shall be better done & with mich more dylygence than this present boke of assisis that ys now done & fynisshyd in grete hast, which other boke shal be a grete boke of abbregementz of arguyd cases rulyd in many yeres of diuers sondry kyngys conteynyng VI or VII C. leuis of grete paper with diuers grete tables longing therto contriuid orderid & nomberid with figures of algorisme for the grete expedicion & fortherance of the students of this law. And though that I my self smal of lerning and discression haue enterpriside with the eyde and helpe of diuers other gentilmen & taken labor & also entende moo labours to take—as wel for the ordering of the kalenders of the seyde grete boke of abbrigementz as in the nombring of the cotacions & refermentz of the cases therin, yet the only prayse of the making of the seyd grete abbrigement ought to be giuyn to Antony fitzherberd *seriant at the law* (the italics are mine), which by his grete and longe study by many yeres contynuyng hath compylyd and gederyd the same . . . the seide boke of the grete abbregementis which (by goddis grace in as conuenient tyme as can be) shal be imprintid.'

[3] Tabula libri Magni abbreuiamenti, 10 Feb. 1517 (1518). Again Rastell's preface is worthy of note : 'And though the right worchipfull Anthony Fitzherberd *ye kinges Seriant at ye law* (the italics are mine) by his grete and longe study hath gederid & compilid ye seyde grete boke of abbreggement & made & drawyn the kalender to the same . . . yet I haue takyn some payne vppon me in numberyng the seyd casis in the furst parte of this table & markid and notyd the accions namis . . .'

[4] According to Sir Ernest Clarke; but in Ames, ed. Herbert, 423,

John Rastell's son William.[1] It has always been held that Sir Anthony was responsible for the whole work, but it is barely possible that he wrote the preface only.[2]

(3) 'Loffice et auctoryte des Justyces de peas . . .'. First printed by Redman in 1538, just before or just after Sir Anthony's death in May, and again in December in an English translation with which apparently Sir Anthony had had nothing to do.[3]

(4) Readings on the Statute of Beaupleader, delivered at Gray's Inn, probably in 1497 or 1498, and never printed.[4]

there is a reference to a 1534 copy, described in Handlists as in English, probably an error for the 'old' Natura Brevium. It is possible that the mention in the preface to Coke's Tenth Report of a 1534 edition indicates Berthelet's continued use of his '1534' woodcut; p. 26, note 1, *supra*. It is also true that the phraseology of the 1537 title-page perhaps implies an earlier edition, 'La Nouel Natura Brevium nouelment imprime et corrige per laucteur'.

[1] 'La Novvelle Natura Brevium du Iuge tresreuerend Monsieur Anthoine Fitzherbert dernierement reneue (sic) et corrigee par laucteur, auecques vne table parfaicte des choses notables contenues en ycelle nouelment composee par Guilliaulme Rastell et Iammais par cy deuant Imprime.'

[2] Sir Ernest Clarke called attention to the wording in 'La Preface suis cest liure, compose par le reuerend Justice Antonie Fitzherbard' (reprinted in 1553 from the first edition according to the view of Sir Ernest): 'because of the imperfection of the old Natura breuium this treatise has been written . . . en le quel sil y ad ascun chose encounter lopinion des sages, que ount ladministracion des loys del terre, *le request de eux que ount preigne le labour et peyne de faire cel treatise* (the italics are mine) est, que ils voillent amender et corriger . . .'.

[3] *Supra*, p. 15. Loffice de Vicounts mentioned in D.N.B. as a separate work is merely a section of Loffice, sometimes printed by itself; cf. e. g. the B. M. edition, erroneously dated [1535 ?]. In spite of the usual view (see e. g. Handlists under Berthelet, 1535, and D.N.B.), there is no convincing evidence to connect Sir Anthony with the anonymous Diuersitie de Courts, printed first by Pynson in 1526, then by Redman, and included by William Rastell in his twelve tracts. I have found no evidence of the existence of the 1525 edition given in Handlists. For a suggestion as to the origin of the tract, see *infra*, p. 178, note 8.

[4] Described in Cat. Add. MSS. 36079, B. M., as on the statute (36 Edw. III, c. 15) called 'Beaupleader'. It has the following heading: 'Tresdecem Lecturae Domini Antonii Fitzherbert Militis et unius Justiciariorum de Communi Banco lectoris apud Graiis Inne anno regni regis Henrici Octavi decimo tertio. . . .' 'Octavi' is probably a slip for 'Septimi' by a scribe writing after Easter 1522 (p. 33, note 2, *supra*), who has confused the statute for pleading in English with the earlier statute of 1 Edw. III, st. 2, c. 8, that had confirmed the statute of Marlborough. The only reader in 13 Hen. VIII was Robert Chaloner; see p. 33, note 2, *supra*, and Dugdale, Orig. Jurid., 292.

It was, however, suggested by Miss McArthur in 1894 that Sir Anthony was responsible for the 'Boke' of 1510 (she is unaware of any previous edition), and that twenty-eight years later he wrote 'Loffice', basing it on his earlier production.[1] Her main arguments are connected with the following points:

(1) Berthelet's 'Note to the reder' in his 1539 edition of the 'Book of Surveying'.

(2) The similarity in the order of the articles in the Charge, as printed in the 'Boke' and in the 'Newe Boke', the translation of 'Loffice'.

(3) The fact that Sir Anthony was too eminent as a lawyer and as a writer to have 'borrowed wholesale' from another, as he must have done, if he did not himself write the 'Boke'.

(4) The existence of differences between the two treatises is explained by Sir Anthony's intention to make the later a different work from the earlier.

But there is strong evidence against the validity of these arguments as well as definite proof that Sir Anthony had nothing to do with the compilation of the 'Boke'.

(1) Berthelet's much discussed note must once more be quoted: 'Whan I had printed the boke longyng to a Justice of the peace, togither with other small bokes very necessary, I bethought me vpon this boke of Surueyenge, compyled sometyme by Master Fitzherbarde, how good and howe profytable it is for all states, that be lordes and possessioners

---

Another copy, Cat. Cod. MSS. Colleg. Oxon., Exeter, 108, is described as follows: 'Lecturae vndecim Fitzherbert's in Statut de Marlebrige anno 52 H. 3, c. 11, Gallice fol. 42.' There is also a copy in Lincoln's Inn, Maynard MSS., III: 'Lecturae Fitz Herberti super statutum de Marlebridge; cap. 11º. 9 readings.' Cf. the note in the midst of a transcript of a reading by Morgan Kidwelly: 'Vide report de fizherberd de Greys In pur beale pleder'; see *infra*, ch. vi (1). That there are no grounds for attributing to Sir Anthony a reading on the statute Extenta Manerii, in spite of D.N.B., has been clearly shown by Mr. Gay; see p. 32, note 6, *supra*. For the same view arrived at independently, cf. a recent memorandum by Sir Ernest Clark not yet printed.

[1] '" The Boke longyng to a Justice of the Peace" and the Assessment of Wages', E.H.R. ix. 305-14. Miss McArthur's view as to authorship leads her to important conclusions as to wage assessments, and has attracted considerable attention. But the denial by Sir Ernest Clarke in 1894 of Fitzherbert's connexion with the Boke has been almost completely ignored, although mentioned by the Reverend Reginald Fitzherbert on p. 230 of the art. cited in note 6, p. 32, *supra*.

of landes, . . . & also how well it agreeth with the argument
of the other small bokes, as court-baron, court-hundred, and
chartuary, I went in hande and printed it in the same volume
that the other be, to bynde them al togither. And haue
amended it in many places '.[1]

Now, if Skeat's view be accepted that 'Master Fitzherbarde' is Sir Anthony, the note seems to me to show that
Berthelet did *not* consider the latter to be the author of the
'boke longyng to a Justice of the peace'.[2] If, on the other
hand, 'Master Fitzherbarde' is Sir Anthony's brother John,[3]
the note has evidently no bearing on Sir Anthony at all.

(2) By 1538, the 'Boke' was the only manual for justices
of the peace in print, and had gone through at least fifteen
editions. The form of the Charge, the earliest printed version, must have been based on the usage prevailing just before
1506, the date of the first edition, and in fact may have been
employed by Fitzherbert himself when he began his active
service on the commission of the peace in 1509.[4] There had
been, as far as is known, no radical change in usage,[5] so that
one could not expect Fitzherbert to abandon completely the
old form when he came to compile a manual of his own. On
the contrary, it seems reasonable to suppose that he had before
him a copy of the 'Boke', perhaps the latest edition, the 1536
Berthelet.[6]

But the likeness between the Charge in the 'Boke' and in the
'Newe Boke' has been somewhat exaggerated. The similarity
in order is not altogether as great, even in the first ten articles,
as is indicated by the parallel columns printed by Miss
McArthur,[7] while the variations in order in the remaining
eighty or ninety articles are very numerous.[8]

[1] 1539 ed.; see p. 33, note 1.
[2] Miss McArthur has made clear that Skeat's argument on this 'note'
depends on the false premise that Berthelet printed the Newe Boke, but
she herself believes that the 'note' strengthens the case for Sir Anthony;
op. cit., 305–6.
[3] *Supra*, p. 32.   [4] p. 39, note 9, *infra*.   [5] See ch. ii, *infra*.
[6] The first edition, be it noted, to include the two statutes of June 1536,
added in Loffice as if by an afterthought.
[7] e. g. in the 1510 Boke there appears after art. 3, sig. A v, an article
on 'Them that sleeth theyr mayster . . .' (neglected by Miss McArthur)
but it is not found in the Newe Boke.
[8] Two examples will suffice: (1) In the Boke the articles on Purveyors

(3) A glance at the outlines of the two treatises[1] shows clearly that except for the Charge almost no portion of the ' Boke ' was made use of by Fitzherbert ; that he ' borrowed wholesale ' cannot therefore be maintained. But in the composition of legal works there is nothing derogatory in a great lawyer's making use of existing tracts or formula books or compilations. On the contrary, it is an essential part in the production of legal text-books.[2] Thus Sir Anthony himself in his great Abridgement was making a compilation of Year Book cases, perhaps following Statham's Abridgement as his guide, ' the common-place book ' of the time,[3] and he avowedly based his ' Novel Natura Brevium '[4] on the earlier ' Natura Brevium ', an anonymous manual long in use in MS. and already in print.[5]

(4) The general differences between the ' Boke ' and the ' Newe Boke ', radical though they are,[6] do not of course preclude the possibility of a complete revision by Fitzherbert in 1538 of a work first compiled by him in 1506. But there are certain specific differences between the two works ignored by Miss McArthur. In his Abridgement of 1516, Fitzherbert has collected comparatively few cases under the title *Justices de*

---

are grouped together rather late in the Charge, sig. B iii–iv, but in the Newe Boke Fitzherbert's tripartite division necessitates the breaking up of these articles into two groups: felonies, art. 15–19, and trespasses, art. 63 ; see ch. ii, *infra*. (2) In the Boke an art. on Coroners appears in the Charge, sig. A vii, but in the Newe Boke it is in the special section on Coroners, f. 61.

[1] *Supra*, pp. 11–12.

[2] It involves a misconception of the nature of legal formulae to say of the two Charges that ' the similarity would seem too close for them to be the work of two men ' ; E. A. McArthur, *op. cit.*, 308. As Maitland wrote : ' . . . it can seldom have happened that any lawyer set himself to devise an entirely new set of forms, while on the other hand it can seldom have happened that any lawyer set himself or his clerk to copy an ancient collection with rigorous fidelity ' ; *loc. cit.*, p. 17, note 12, *supra*.

[3] ' The Abridgments of the Year Books and Rolle's Abridgments are students' commonplace books in print ' ; Holdsworth, ' The Disappearance of the Educational System of the Inns of Court ', University of Pennsylvania Law Review, March 1921, 219 ; J. Reeves, Hist. Eng. Law, ed. Finlason, iii. 430–1.

[4] If indeed it be his ; see *supra*, p. 35.

[5] Holdsworth, Hist. Eng. Law, ii. 439–40 ; Reeves, *op. cit.*, ii. 439, iii. 431, 438.

[6] See the two outlines, *supra*, pp. 11–12.

peas,[1] in itself a strange fact if he had written a treatise on the subject ten years before; but under *Corone* he declares that justices of the peace cannot inquire of Mort de home,[2] and many years later in ' Loffice ' modifies his statement to the effect that they cannot inquire of murder as murder but only as felony and manslaughter.[3]   In the ' Boke ', on the other hand, it is clearly indicated that the justices are to inquire of murder as such.[4]

In view of Fitzherbert's peculiar interpretation of this important point of criminal law, noted and condemned as an error by the great lawyers of the latter part of the sixteenth century,[5] it is difficult to believe that he could have written the Charge in the ' Boke ' with the vitally different opinion stated in the article on murder; or that if possibly he had done so in his youth, he would have allowed the numerous re-issues of a work containing what he considered bad law.   A less important but exceedingly definite difference between the two treatises is the use by Fitzherbert of ' justicer '[6] in ' Loffice ', instead of the usual ' justice ' which with one exception always appears in the editions of the ' Boke '.[7]   Finally, it is to be remembered that the ' Boke ' is in English and Latin while all Fitzherbert's acknowledged works, including ' Loffice ', are in French.[8]

The above internal evidence is corroborated by external.

(1) Since Sir Anthony was not serving on a commission of the peace until 1509, it is highly improbable that it would have occurred to him to compile a manual in 1506 on a branch of the law in which he had had no experience.[9]

(2) I have not discovered a shred of contemporary evidence in favour of Sir Anthony's connexion with the ' Boke '.   No one of his publishers hints at it, not even the two Rastells, who were so intimately connected with him through their performance of official duties at Coventry, their common devotion to

---

[1] Ten entries. There are, however, many cross-references to *Corone, Laborers*, &c., that involve the action of justices of the peace.
[2] No. 457.   [3] ff. 16, 21, 21 b.
[4] Charge, Sig. A v.   [5] See ch. vi (4), *infra*.
[6] Or justicier.   [7] *Supra*, p. 30.   [8] *Supra*, p. 34.
[9] See Letters and Papers, Foreign and Domestic, Henry VIII, for his service on various commissions from 1509–1536, including those of the peace. He was not recorder of Coventry till 1509; p. 23, note 10, *supra*.

the old faith and their joint work on both the Abridgement and the ' Novel Natura Brevium '.[1] It is inconceivable that they would have been ignorant of the fact had Sir Anthony written the ' Boke ', or that they would have neglected the opportunity of advertising their own editions of the ' Boke ' by heralding them as the early work of the then distinguished judge, ' that greate learned man the Auctour of the saide great abridgement '.[2]

Moreover, toward the end of the century there are definite statements by a distinguished lawyer and writer on law, by the most learned legal antiquarian of his age, and also references by the scholarly reviser of Fitzherbert's ' Loffice ', all implying total ignorance of the identity of the compiler of the ' Boke ' and certainly therefore not attributing it to Sir Anthony.   Recorder Fleetwood in a manuscript treatise on the Justice of the Peace written in 1565 recommends to his readers several sources for further information, including, ' The treatise devised by the late reverend judge Sir Anthony Fytzherbert, Knight ', and also ' The booke called the Justice of peace, the wich booke is inserted & sett forth in a booke called the twelve bookes imprinted by William Rastall in the yeare of our Lord 1534, the wich booke for that purpose is as excellent a piece of work as can be devised.'[3]   Lambard's words in 1581 are decisive : ' And therefore in greedie appetite, I beganne first with M. Fitzherbertes treatise of the Iusticers of Peace ; then went I to another auncient booke, of the same Argument, but of an Author unknowen to me, and thirdly I came to M. Marrowes reading.'[4]   Crompton's preface in 1583, though not equally clear, is also important : ' et que sunt plusors cases de comon ley disperses in les Termes, que poient estre necessaries pur les Iustices de peace, cest assauoire pur le mulx execucion de lour dit office, dount parle le tres reuerend Iudge Monsir Antho. Fitz. jades vn de iudges del common Bank, et auter part vn auter discrete home ore tarde, ont tres bien

[1] *Supra*, p. 23, note 7, pp. 34–5.
[2] An Exposicion of the kinges prerogative, by W. Staunford, preface, 6 Nov., 1548, reprinted in 1567 ed.
[3] B. M., Add. MSS. 26749, ff. 372–3 ; see ch. vi. (5), *infra.*
[4] Eirenarcha, epistle to Chancellor Bromley.

publie en lour lieurs de office de Iustices de peace'.[1] That
the 'other discreet man' is Lambard seems probable; the
description of the work does not fit the 'Boke' but exactly
applies to the 'Eirenarcha' just in print.[2] There is, however,
no shadow of doubt about Crompton's later entry : 'Et vide in
launcient Lieur de Iustice de Peace, inter les Presidents fol.
39',[3] a reference identified in the 1544 edition of the 'Boke'.[4]
In similar fashion, Lambard in the 'Eirenarcha' mentions
'a precedent in the olde Boke of Justices of the peace, folio 41 ',[5]
which can be verified in the very copy of the Tottell edition
once in his own possession.[6] Since both Lambard and
Crompton frequently quote Fitzherbert and his work by
name, it is evident that they are not associating him with the
above references. Finally, in his 1588 edition Lambard prints
in his appendix the following heading: 'The process vpon
enditements and presentments taken out of the old imprinted
Boke of the Justices of the peace',[7] while Crompton in his
appendix has always included almost all the precedents of
Part II of the 'Boke'.[8] Thus it appears that Redman's
adoption of the title 'Newe Boke' for the translation of
Fitzherbert's 'Loffice' marks its contrast to the old 'Boke',
author unknown, and is strictly parallel to the usage that had
already been established in the case of the 'Natura Brevium'
and other early anonymous law tracts.[9]

Origin of the 'Boke'. On the basis of the evidence just
presented, it can be asserted with some confidence that Sir

[1] Address to Chancellor Bromley, Loffice et aucthoritie de Iustices de
peace.

[2] Cf. e. g. the 'cases de comon ley'; see p. 188, *infra.*

[3] f. 129.   [4] Berthelet, f. 39 b.   [5] 1581 ed., 189.

[6] 1569 ed.; the B. M. copy has the autograph, William Lambarde,
1571, and many of his notes on the margin.

[7] A few of the familiar forms from Part II of the 'Boke' are given.
The title-page now contains this note : 'Whereunto there is added an
Appendix of Sundry Precedents touching matters of the Peace.'

[8] The title-page of the 1587 edition contains the phrase: 'et auxy
certeine presidentes dendictments et auters choses'. Since Lambard did
not print these precedents until his 1588 edition, it is possible that he
was influenced by Crompton, but see ch. iv, *infra*, p. 113.

[9] 'Vieux' was applied to the Natura Brevium soon after the publication of Fitzherbert's work; Holdsworth, *op. cit.,* ii. 440; the 'old'
Tenures were distinguished from Littleton's Tenures ; Reeves, *op. cit.,*
ii. 439.

Anthony Fitzherbert had nothing to do with the writing of the 'Boke' of 1506. But is there any possibility of discovering its origin? A solution is suggested by the fact of the composite character of the 'Boke' as revealed in the outline of contents previously given. Part I, including statutes and the Charge, is to be sharply differentiated from Part II, containing only precedents—writs and indictments. Although it is not probable that the identity of the actual writer of the 'copy' for the printer will ever be established, it is possible by a critical examination, first of the statutes and the Charge[1] and second of the writs and indictments,[2] to trace them back to earlier MS. sources. The results of such an investigation are given in the two following chapters.

Sources used by Fitzherbert, Lambard, and Crompton. There remains the problem of the sources used by Fitzherbert, Lambard, and Crompton. In the interval between 1538 and 1581–1583, there was so great an increase of printed law-books— portions of which concerned justices of the peace—that inevitably Lambard and Crompton drew upon a far wider range of printed material than did Fitzherbert.[3] But the surprising fact is that both Lambard and Crompton quote voluminously from a manuscript reading on the peace delivered by Thomas Marowe as far back as 1503—a source which Fitzherbert might have known and which he completely ignored. It is this all-important manuscript treatise that will claim chief attention in the final chapters.[4]

[1] Ch. ii, *infra.*
[2] Ch. iii, *infra.*
[3] Ch. iv, *infra.*
[4] Chs. v and vi, *infra.*

CHAPTER II

FIFTEENTH-CENTURY SUMMARIES OF STA-TUTES ON THE JUSTICES OF THE PEACE AND EARLY FORMS OF THE CHARGE TO JURORS

Summaries of Statutes. It has already been said that Part I of the 'Boke' is to be differentiated from Part II.[1] It must next be pointed out that within Part I there are two distinct portions, the first comprising condensed summaries of the clauses of important statutes on the justices of peace, their qualifications, the number on each commission, the dates of their sessions, &c.,[2] the second consisting of their Charge to jurors.[3] The form of the first portion suggested that it might have been taken bodily from some collection of statutes, and led therefore to an examination of various MS. compilations as well as the earliest printed editions.[4] The subject proved difficult, chiefly because of the lack of any guide to the almost limitless MS. material.[5] But collections of statutes so clearly furnished the clue to the origin of Part I of the 'Boke' that it has seemed worth while to present my conclusions with the warning that they must be regarded as tentative until confirmed by a far wider and more detailed study.

Of the first half dozen printers of the 'Boke' three—

[1] Ch. i, p. 42, *supra.* For Part II, see ch. iii (II), *infra.*

[2] Ch. i, p. 12, *supra.*

[3] *Ibid.*; the two anomalous writs appear between the two; see pp. 94-5, *infra.*

[4] For printed collections, the introduction to Statutes of the Realm, i, is valuable, but needs to be supplemented by a study based on our present increased knowledge. Cf. 'The Early English Statutes' by J. H. Beale, Harvard Law Review, March 1922.

[5] There is great need of a thorough study of the MS. collections and of a careful collation of their entire contents. My investigation has been confined mainly to the archives already described (ch. i, p. 6, notes 3 and 4), and to certain specific points in each collection.

Wynkyn de Worde, Robert Copland, and Skot [1]—published no law books except a few editions of the familiar tracts so often bound with the 'Boke',[2] and in the case of Wynkyn de Worde, in addition, several statutes of Henry VII,[3] notably three issues of the acts of 1495.[4] On the other hand, Pynson, John Rastell, and Redman were all distinguished as law printers. It is natural, therefore, that Pynson should print the same acts of 1495[5] and also the two great collections of full texts of the statutes, known respectively as 'old' and 'new', and that all three of them should print the famous 'Abridgement of the Statutes'.[6] The following list shows the chronological relation between the printing of the Statutes and of the 'Boke'.

Pynson.	Nova Statuta. French and Latin.	Between 1497 and 1504[7] or between July 1501 and December 1502.[8]
	Abbreviamentum Statutorum. French and Latin.	9 October 1499, 2 issues.[9]
	The Boke.	1506 (?).[10]
	Statuta Antiqua. French and Latin.	1508,[11] 1514, 1519.
	Magna Charta. Statuta Antiqua.	1527.[12]

[1] Handlists; and ch. i, pp. 20–5, *supra*.
[2] Copland, the Court Baron; Skot, Carta Feodi, the Court Baron, the Hundred Court; de Worde, the same three and Returna Brevium.
[3] 1 Hen. VII, 7 Hen. VII; Handlists; Duff, Fifteenth Century English Books. Cf. also the statutes of 1, 2, 3, and 4 Hen. VII printed by Caxton in [1489]; Duff, *op. cit.*
[4] 11 Hen. VII [1496]; *ibid.*
[5] [1496]; *ibid.* He also printed the statutes of 38 Edw. III, 1520, and of 19 Hen. VII, n. d.; Handlists.
[6] Handlists. In Statutes of the Realm, i. xxi, Pynson's Abridgement is omitted. Both Rastell and Redman also printed statutes of Hen. VIII; Handlists.
[7] Since the statutes of 12 Hen. VII are included but not those of the 19th year.
[8] On the authority of Mr. Duff, arguing from the state of the devices.
[9] Duff, Fifteenth Century English Books.
[10] Ch. i, pp. 18–21, *supra*.
[11] Statutes of Realm, *loc. cit.* In spite of the copies in B. M., Handlists omit the editions of 1514 and 1519. Holdsworth gives 1588 as the date of the first edition, probably a misprint; *op. cit.*, ii. 175.
[12] Handlists.

Pynson (continued).	Le Breggement de toutes les estatutes . . . French and Latin, ed. Guillaume Owein of the Middle Temple.	8 May 1521,[1] 1528.[2]
	The Boke.	1521.[3]
John Rastell.	Abbreviation of Statutes. English.	25 October 1519.[4]
	Abridgement of the Statutes. English.	22 December 1527.[5]
	Magnum Abbreuiamentum Statutorum. English.	1 December 1528,[6] [1531].[7]
	The Boke.	Between 1527 and 1530.[8]
Redman.	Le bregement de estatutes al xviii H. VIII. French.	3 January 1527.[9]
	The Boke.	1527.[10]
	Whole abridgement of Statutes. English.	1528.[11]
	The Boke.	1531 (?), 1533 (?), 1538 (?).[12]

In relation to the summaries of the statutes in the 'Boke' of 1506 (?), Pynson's 'Statuta Antiqua' of 1508—the first edition of the full text—can safely be ignored.[13] With the first year of Edward III as the dividing line between 'old' and 'new',[14] the 'old' statutes begin usually with Magna Carta as

[1] Handlists give Abbreviamentum Statutorum, 1521.
[2] Handlists. It is merely the 1521 volume with some additions from the parliament of 15 Hen. VIII ; cf. U.L.C. ed.
[3] Ch. i, p. 21, *supra*.
[4] Handlists; Statutes of the Realm, *loc. cit.* Apparently the earliest translation, but unfortunately I have not discovered a copy.
[5] Handlists. Contains an important preface ; see p. 49, *infra*, note 2.
[6] Handlists.
[7] Not in Handlists, but there is a copy in H.L.S.
[8] Ch. i, p. 24, *supra*.
[9] The only copy noted in Handlists is in the Bibliothèque Nationale.
[10] Ch. i, p. 21, *supra*.   [11] Handlists.
[12] Ch. i, pp. 21-3, 28-30, *supra*.
[13] Also the later editions ; ch. i, p. 15, *supra*, note 6.
[14] Statutes of the Realm, i. xxi ; Holdsworth, *op. cit.*, ii. 175. The usage had apparently developed early in the 15th century.

confirmed by Henry III,[1] and continue through the reign of
Edward II only, and therefore all antedate the organization of
the office of justice of the peace.[2]   But Pynson's two other
volumes, the 'Nova Statuta' of 1497–1504, and the 'Abbreuia-
mentum Statutorum' of 1499, need careful consideration.   In
the case of neither of them was Pynson a pioneer.   His predecessor in the printing of law-books, Machlinia, had issued
the first edition of 'Nova Statuta', probably in 1484,[3] and
together with Lettou, during their brief partnership,[4] had
previously printed, probably in 1483,[5] the first edition of the
'Abridgement of the Statutes', commonly known as 'Le Vieux
Abridgement'.

The two 'Abridgements' cover both 'old' and 'new'
statutes, Lettou and Machlinia coming down through 33
Henry VI, 1455,[6] and Pynson through 12 Henry VII, 1497 ;
the two editions of the text of the 'new' statutes begin with
1 Edward III, Machlinia including as his latest statute the
22 Edward IV,[7] and Pynson, as before, the 12 Henry VII.
Now in each 'Abridgement' occurs the title *Justices de peas* and
under it are brief summaries of clauses of statutes—the qualifications of the justices, the number on each commission, &c.—
that immediately suggest the opening paragraphs of the 'Boke.'[8]
Further, in each edition of the 'Nova Statuta' there is an
elaborate analytical index of topics arranged alphabetically
and containing under the same title *Justices de peas*[9] summaries

---

[1] Statutes of the Realm, i. xxix ; various MS. collections ; see pp. 50–51,
infra.
[2] Some of the 'old' statutes, notably Winchester and Northampton,
were, however, included in the commission of the peace and therefore are
important in the Charge ; see *infra*, p. 57.
[3] Duff, *op. cit.*, and Century of English Book Trade, 97.   The
volume has neither printer's name nor date, but since it includes a statute
of 22 Edw. IV enacted early in 1483, the alternative date of 'about 1482'
given in Statutes of the Realm, *loc. cit.*, is scarcely accurate, nor did Lettou
have a part in it.   Holdsworth ignores this volume, and makes Pynson's
the earliest edition ; *op. cit.*, ii. 175.
[4] *Circ.* 1482–1483 ; Duff, Century of English Book Trade, 92, 97.
[5] Rather than 'before 1481' as suggested in Statutes of the Realm,
loc. cit., Ames, ed. Herbert, 112.   [6] Statutes of the Realm, i. xxi.
[7] See note 3, *supra.*   He also printed separately the acts of 1 Rich. III ;
Duff, Fifteenth Century English Books.
[8] The seventeen entries in Lettou and Machlinia are increased to sixty-
three in Pynson ; see *infra*, p. 49.
[9] With cross-references as follows : 'Vide plus des iustices de peas in L
enter Laborers.'

very similar to those in the 'Abridgements'. Although the order of the articles is not identical in the four printed volumes, it is only in the first entries that a marked divergence of phraseology appears :

'Nova Statuta'. Machlinia 1484 (?), Pynson 1497–1504.

Bones & sufficiantes persones soient assigne iustices de peas.

1 Edw. [III], st. ii, c. 17.[1]

'Abridgement'. Lettou and Machlinia 1483 (?).

Grandes homes & auters sages de la ley soient assignez Justices de peas.

2 Edw. III, c. [7].

'Abridgement'. Pynson 1499.

Bons gentz & loialx que ne sount my meyntenours en pais soient assignes a le garde de le peas.

1 Edw. III, st. ii, c. 17.

The actual text shows that the first and second sets of adjectives are due to a misinterpretation of statutes ; that is, to the quotation of certain clauses that in reality did not concern the justices of the peace at all.[2] But in Pynson's 'Abridgement' the adjectives are correct,[3] and the whole entry corresponds very closely to the opening article of his 'Boke'

---

[1] c. 16, in Statutes of the Realm.

[2] In the first case, 4 Edw. III, c. 2 : ' Ensement est acorde qe *bones* gentz & sages, autres qe des places si homme les puisse trover *suffisantz*, soient assignes . . . a prendre les assises . . . & a deliverer les gaoles . . .' Then follows what is apparently the re-enactment of 1 Edw. III, st. 2, c. 16 (the statute is not specified), for the appointment of ' bones gentz & loialx' to keep the peace. (Cf. also ' bones & sufficeantz ' as the qualification for jurors in Lollard cases ; 2 Hen. V, st. 1, c. 7.) In the second case, the statute of Northampton, 2 Edw. III, c. 7 : ' Et quaunt au punissement de felonies, robberies, homicides . . . acorde est qe notre seignur le Roi assigne Justices en divers lieux de sa terre, . . . des *grantz* de la terre qi sont de grant poair, ovesques ascuns des Justices de lun Baunk ou de lautre, ou *autres sages de la lei* . . . denquere . . . et doier & terminer totes maneres des felonies . . .' (the italics are mine). This clause does not apply to justices of the peace at all ; if it did, the statutes of 1344 and of 1361 would have been unnecessary. The mistake is probably due to the fact that c. 3, prohibiting men from riding about armed, and c. 6, providing for the enforcement of the statute of Winchester, were interpreted as coming under the jurisdiction of the keepers of the peace, and that therefore the statute of Northampton was included in the form of their commission. So unintelligent an error renders it very improbable that the great Littleton had a hand in compiling the Abridgement. See Ames, ed. Herbert, i. 112.

[3] From 1 Edw. III, st. 2, c. 16 : ' Item pur la pees meultz garder & meyntener, le Roi veot qen chescun Countee qe bones gentz & loialx, queux ne sont mye meyntenours de malveis baretz in pays, soient assignez a la garde de la pees.'

of 1506 (?)[1]: 'Well dysposed men & lawfull y^t ben not meyntenours of quarrelles sholde be Justyces of ye peas

1 Edward III   c. 18 (sic).'

Evidently it is with Pynson's 'Abridgement' that it will be profitable to compare the 'Boke'. The relation between the two is brought out by the following parallel columns:

The Boke.

(2) Two or iii. men of moost reputacyon & worshyppe sholde be assygned to be Justyces of the peas.

18 Edw. III, c. 11.

(3) Two men of lawe sholde be in euery commyssion of peas to procede to delyueraunce of felons.

17 R. II, c. xi.

(4) In euery commyssion of peas sholde be put vi Justyces with the Justyces of assyses euery Iustyce takynge iiii s. the fyrst day of theyr cessyons & theyr clerke ii s. of fynes.

12 R. II, c. ix.

(5) In euery countye shal be assygned viii Justyces of peas & theyr estreytes shall be dowbled and one parte delyuered to the sheryf to leuye the money ... No Duke, Erle, etc.

14 R. II, c. xi.

The Abridgement.
Justices de peas.

(2) Deux ou troys pluis vaillauntz soient en chescun Counte Iustice de peas & eux oue auters apris en ley terminent felonies & trespas faitz encontre le peas.

18 E. III, st. ii, c. ii.

(3) Deux homes de ley soient en chescun commyssion de peas que deliuerent les felons & procederent a deliueraunce deux a chescun foitz que lour bien semblera.

17 R. ca. vltimo.

(4) Ne soient que vi Justice de peas en vn commyssion ouster le Justice dassize & nul associacion soit fait a iustice de peas apres le primier commission.

12 R., c. ix.

(5) Ne soient que viii iustice de peas en vn commyssyon ouster les seignours ...

14 R., c. xi.

(6) Justice de peas soient faitez de demurrauntez en mesme le counte & de plus sufficient personz forsprise seignours iustice dassise ...

2 H. V, st. ii, c. i.

---

[1] I quote from the practically identical 1510 edition of Wynkyn de Worde; see ch. i, p. 19, *supra*.

(6) No persone shall be assygned to be Justyce of peas
but it soo be he may dispende
xx pounde by yere . . .
    18 H. VI.

(7) Justyces of peas shall be
sworne truly to execute theyr
offyce and to put in execucyon
all statutes and ordynaunces
towchyng theyr offyces.
    14 R. II, c. vii.

(7) Justice de peas eit terres
al value de xx li. par an . . .
    18 H. VI, c. xi.

(8) Seneschall de seignour
ne soit Justice de peas—12 R.,
c. ix. Mes cest repelle Anno
xiii R., c. vii.

(9) Justice de peas serront
iures dexecuter toutz lez esta-
tuts touchaunt leur office.
    13 R., c. vii.

In the remaining ten articles of the first portion of Part I of
the ' Boke ', there are a few slight omissions or additions and
a few changes in order ; for example, a portion of no. 15 of
the 'Boke' appears as no. 53 of the 'Abridgement', but the
resemblance in the arrangement of the summaries and in their
content and phraseology—making due allowance for the
difference in language—warrants the belief that the compiler
of the English 'Boke' had before him a copy of Pynson's
French 'Abridgement'.[1] It is interesting to see that the English
version of the entries under *Justices de peas* had preceded by
a number of years the translation of the 'Abridgement' as a
whole—made and printed by John Rastell in 1519[2]—just
before the publication of Pynson's second French edition.

Pynson's ' Abridgement ', although much more than a reprint
and continuation of the edition of Lettou and Machlinia, was
undeniably based on their work, while his ' Nova Statuta ' and
its index reproduce the Machlinia volume very exactly, the
only significant differences being those caused by the addition
of recent statutes.[3] The next step backwards, therefore, leads

[1] For the far greater number of entries in the Abridgement, see *supra*,
p. 46, note 8.
[2] *Supra*, p. 45. The earliest edition that I have been able to discover is
that of 22 December 1527, with Rastell's explanation of the motives that led
him ' to take this lytell payne to translate out of french into englysshe the
abbreuyacyon of the statutys made before the fyrst yere of the reyn of our
late souereyn lord kyng Hen. the VII '. As far as my limited investigation
shows, Rastell is translating from Pynson's version.
[3] As shown by a somewhat limited collation.

into the realm of MS. collections of statutes. By using the following tests: (1) the dates of the statutes included and (2) the adjectives found in the first entry under the title *Justices de peas*, it has proved possible to put into two groups the collections transcribed in the course of the fifteenth century,[1] in neither of which is there anything that corresponds precisely to Pynson's volumes.[2]

First group. Four Abridgements almost identical with that of Lettou and Machlinia.[3] The form of the summaries is the same, and they cover practically the same period from Magna Carta, Henry III through 33 Henry VI.[4] The adjectives in question are always: 'Grandes homes & auters oue sagez de le ley.'

Second group. Ten collections of the unabridged text of the 'new' statutes, preceded by an alphabetical index,[5] all of them very similar to the Machlinia. They all have as the test phrase: 'Bones & sufficiantes persones . . .' and all begin with the statute of 1 Edward III. The two most closely resembling the Machlinia[6] end with the statute of 1 Richard III,[7] two others with the statute of 3 Henry VII,[8] while the rest stop in

---

[1] In general I have been obliged to accept the statement as to date made in the catalogue description of a given volume, but it is not always to be relied upon. Moreover, as has been already said, my search cannot in any sense claim to be exhaustive. Cf. e.g. the sale by F. Edwards, 83 High Street, Marylebone, in November 1921 of three MS. volumes of statutes from Magna Carta to 8 Edw. IV, once in the possession of Sir James Dyer, the eminent sixteenth-century judge. Undoubtedly there are many MS. collections in private libraries which ought to be examined.

[2] Possibly a proof of the extent to which Pynson was actually an innovator. Cf. however a collection of statutes from 1 Edw. III to 19 Hen. VII, with a different form of index; Lincoln's Inn, MSS. Various Donors, xiv (183).

[3] As far as appears from my somewhat limited comparison.

[4] B.M. Harl. 1317; Harl. 450; U.L.C. Ee. 4. 25 (imperfect); Ff. 4. 14. The last is described as an Abridgment de la ley. At the end later matter is added, *temp.* Edw. IV and Hen. VII.

[5] I omit the countless collections of 'old' or 'new' statutes that have no index.

[6] (1) B.M. Lansdowne 522, incorrectly described in the Catalogue as the source of the Abridgement of Lettou and Machlinia; (2) B.M. Cotton., Nero, c. i.

[7] See *supra*, p. 46, and notes 3 and 7. In no. 1 the writing changes at 7 & 8 Edw. IV.

[8] (3) A volume in the Carson Historical Library; (4) Lincoln's Inn, Hale MSS. lxvi (71).

the midst of the reign of Henry VI, either in the twenty-third [1] or the twenty-ninth year.[2]

It is tempting to urge that the preparation of an index to the unabridged statutes, either 'new' or 'old', or both,[3] suggested the making of an abridgement of both 'old' and 'new' statutes,[4] but all that can at present safely be asserted is this: shortly after the middle of the fifteenth century, great activity developed in the transcribing of collections of the texts of the 'new' statutes,[5] in many cases with an elaborate index, and at just about the same date the earliest Abridgements of both the 'new' and 'old' statutes were compiled.[6] The summaries of statutes on justices of the peace arranged as in the 'Boke' go back therefore into the reign of Henry VI. But transcripts of 'new' statutes had been made earlier,[7] some of the collections coming down only through the first few years of Henry V and some not even so far.[8]

The vital fact for the present discussion is that one volume of the second group contains 'Extracts from divers Statutes of King Edw. III and K. Rich. II for the use, as it seems,

---

[1] (5) Bodleian, Douce MSS. 312 ; (6) Inner Temple, Petyt MSS., 506 ; (7) Cambridge, Trinity College, MS. 928 (R. 15. 1).

[2] (8) Inner Temple, Petyt MSS., 505 ; (9) *ibid.*, 511, no. 8 ; (10) Lincoln's Inn, MSS. Various Donors, xliii (194).

[3] For an example of the last, see *infra*, p. 52. For examples of an index without text, see Bodleian, Douce MSS. 159 ; Tanner MSS. 198, f. 17 *et seq.*

[4] The first entry in the index seems to be always *Accusacions*, whereas in the printed Abridgement it is *Abjuracion*.

[5] Of course the innumerable collections of 'old' statutes go back much earlier.

[6] For the significance of this date, see p. 104, *infra*.

[7] This statement as to date is based on the internal evidence as well as on the catalogue description. It will be observed that in some cases the collections include the 'old' statutes as well.

[8] (1) Lansdowne 469, 1 Edw. III – 3 Hen. V ; (2) Lincoln's Inn, Hale MSS. lxix (74), Magna Carta to 2 Hen. V ; (3) *ibid.*, Various Donors, xxiii (178), 1 Edw. III–3 Hen. V ; (4) *ibid.*, xii (176), 1 Edw. III–3 Hen. V ; (5) Harl. 751, 1 Edw. III–4 Hen. V ; (6) Bodl. Douce MSS. 362, 1 Edw. III–2 Hen. V ; (7) Lansdowne 474, 1 Edw. III–20 Rich. II (only the heading, but a pardon of 21 Rich. II) ; (8) *ibid.* 475, Magna Carta to 6 Rich. II ; (9) Harl. 1311, 1–38 Edw. III. It is possible that in some cases (e.g. in nos. 1 and 8) the early date noted in the Catalogue is wrong, and that the scribe had merely failed to complete a volume that was meant to include the usual statutes of Henry VI.

of some Justice of the Peace, in Law French',[1] and an alphabetical index to the 'old' and 'new' statutes [2] which, instead of giving summaries, merely mentions the regnal year and chapter of the appropriate act. The twenty-three entries under the title *Justices de pees* thus furnish convenient references to the existing law just after the important legislation of Henry V,[3] and make it possible to state that the antecedents of the summaries of statutes in the printed 'Boke', as distinct from their actual source, have been traced back to the first or second decade of the fifteenth century.

But is it possible to discover whether the compiler of the 1506 (?) 'Boke', who, it has been argued, knew Pynson's 1499 'Abridgement', was the earliest to use this series of statutes in a manual for justices?

The answer is found in a MS. volume, Harl. 1777, written throughout in the same hand, perhaps of the early sixteenth century, containing several of the familiar law tracts and also two collections that resemble very closely Parts I and II of the 'Boke', but given separately and in reverse order.[4] Throughout the volume Robert Drury, speaker of the parliament that met in October 1495,[5] constantly appears [6]; Suffolk is usually the county,[7] and the dates are mainly of the time of Henry VII or of his immediate predecessors,[8] 1501 being the latest that I have noted.[9]

---

[1] Harl. 751, ff. 1–18. The description is from the Catalogue.

[2] ff. 20–35. The third section contains the text of all the statutes from 1 Hen. IV–4 Hen. V; ff. 36–99.

[3] Ch. iii (1), p. 92, *infra*.

[4] (1) Court Leet, ff. 7–25; (2) A letter to the king, ff. 26–8; (3) Hundred Court, ff. 29–35 b; (4) La Forme doffice dun Clerk de peas, ff. 36 b–48; (5) Miscellany, including many forms from a Carta feodi, ff. 49–79; (6) What persons shulde be justices of peas, ff. 80–110 b.

[5] D.N.B.; Parry, *op. cit.*, 197. The next parliament met in January 1497 and chose as speaker Thomas Ingelfeld; *ibid.*

[6] Especially as justice of the peace in Suffolk. He was on the commission during most of the reign of Henry VII; that is, from 1488 (except for a few months in 1489); Cal. Pat. 1485–94, 501; 1494–1509, 659.

[7] MS. Harl. 1777, *passim*; occasionally Essex and Norfolk, ff. 38 b, 39.

[8] Cf. e. g. Edward [IV], ff. 32, 33.

[9] f. 45 b; a writ signed by Robert Drury as justice of the peace, 1 May, 16 Henry VII.

The section that corresponds to Part I of the ' Boke '[1] begins in English with the familiar heading : ' What persons shulde bee justices of peas ther auctoryte & power the forme of ther charge and wheroff they maye Inquyre.'[2] Then come the same statutes arranged in precisely the same order as in the ' Boke ', not, however, in the shape of the English summaries of the ' Boke ' nor of the French summaries of the early Abridgements, but in the shape of full quotations in French from the statutes : ' Item pur la peas mellior garder & mayntenir . . . bons gentez & loyals. . . .' The form suggests that the compilation was made before the publication of Pynson's 1499 ' Abridgement' by some one who was familiar with the entries under the title *Justices de peas* either in the 1484 (?) ' Nova Statuta ' of Machlinia or in an earlier MS. collection,[3] but who used the actual text of the statutes.

Charge to Jurors. In turning next to the origin of the Charge, we find confirmation of the early date of this MS. version of the ' Boke '. The ceremony preceding the giving of the Charge is vividly described [4] at the beginning of the collection of writs [5] : ' Et adonque le clerk dirra issint : Criar make an Oiez twiez et apres ceo le clerk ferra le criar adire issint : all maner of menne which haue adoo here before these justicez of the peas of the Shire of Suff', come forth & he shall be horde . . . et donque doit le clerk defair le criour a dire en cel forme, scilicet ; Goode men which haue apperid hear stonde to the barre that ye may be sworn . . . Holde yower hande upon the boke & saye after me ; thus here ye justicez that I shall dewly Inquyr & true presentment make of all such poyntes & articulez wherwith I shall be law-fully charged in the kynges behalff and for no cause lette but the south saye and the kynges councell my felawes & myn owen well & truly

---

[1] ff. 80–110 b.
[2] The next few words differ slightly from the printed version.
[3] The fact that Harl. 1777 must have been written after 1 May 1501 does not of course preclude the possibility of an earlier date for the com-pilation of some of its component parts.
[4] ff. 37–8, preceded by copies of the writs issued by Robert Drury for the summoning of the session ; f. 36 b. For the heading see p. 52, note 4, *supra*.
[5] Corresponding to Part II of the Boke.

holde & kepe as ferre as I can, soo helpe me God, & holydom
& by this booke . . .' After each juror had been duly sworn
and had kissed the 'booke', the clerk continues: 'Godemen
which be sworne stonde forth & here yower charge. Et
donque vn de lez Justices donera a eux lour charge . . .'[1]

An inquiry by sworn jurors into a list of 'poyntes &
articulez' is obviously no innovation on the part of justices of
the peace but rather the inevitable acceptance, with certain
distinct modifications,[2] of a long-established method of legal
procedure. It is scarcely necessary to mention the celebrated
articles of the Eyre,[3] of Trailbaston,[4] of inquiry upon the
statute of Winchester,[5] of the View of Frankpledge in the
Sheriff's Tourn and in the Court Leet.[6] There is need for a
careful comparison of these various lists of articles with the
articles of the Charge of the justices of the peace; by the
sixteenth century the resemblance between these last and
the articles of the Leet has become extraordinarily close.[7]

But my concern here is with the Charge of the justices of
the peace in the 1506 (?) 'Boke', the earliest in print. The list
of articles includes certain offences at common law within the
jurisdiction of the justices as stated in their commission and a

---

[1] f. 38 ; 'quell charge commensa apres fo. 84'. It follows immediately
after the summaries of statutes, without the two anomalous writs ; see
supra, p. 11.

[2] See Lambard, Eirenarcha, 387 *et seq.*, for an interesting discussion of
'the ancient order, of giving the Charge in Eire' and the somewhat
different method used by the justices of the peace.

[3] See Eyre of Kent, 1313–1314, Selden Soc., v. 24, xxxvii–xli, for a
valuable bibliography for the history of the articles ; 1194 is given as the
date of the earliest known.

[4] H. M. Cam, Hundred Rolls, *passim*.

[5] Statutes of the Realm, i. 245–6.

[6] *Ibid.*, 246–7 ; Selden Soc., vols. ii, iv, and v, namely, Select Pleas in
Manorial Courts, xxvii–xxxviii ; The Court Baron, 93–101 ; Leet Jurisdic-
tion in the City of Norwich, xxxiv–xxxvii ; F. J. C. Hearnshaw, Leet
Jurisdiction in England, 43–64 ; W. A. Morris, The Frankpledge System,
passim. Cf. also the many MS. collections containing copies of the
Charge to the Court Leet ; e.g. U.L.C., Dd. 9. 56 ; Bodleian, MS.
Rawlinson, C. 950.

[7] Cf. e.g., B.M. Add. MSS. 25238 ; Articuli curie Baronis, ff. 117–18 ;
Articuli Lete, ff. 119–22 ; Articuli Justiciariorum Pacis, ff. 123–8 ; or
Oxford, MSS. Trin. College, 30, fly-leaf ; the Charge of the Court Baron,
Leet and Sessions. Cf. also Lambard's reference to the 'Articles
delivered to the Enquest of office, in the Kinges Bench, as is to be seene
in the book of Assises, lib. 27. pla. 44' ; *op. cit.*, 390.

great many statutory offences—steadily increasing in number
in successive editions of the 'Boke'—some specified in the
commission and some not.[1]   The essential fact is that the
Charge is mainly a summary of clauses of statutes to be enforced by the justices.   Once again it is necessary, therefore,
to examine collections of statutes, remembering the lawyer's
gibe : ' A Justice of Peace is a Statute Creature & ought to
act no further than the Statutes impower him.' [2]   It proves
possible to identify in Pynson's 1499 'Abridgement' either
under *Justices de peas* or under *Laborers* almost all the articles
of the Charge as far as they are based on statutes.   Further, the
latest acts quoted under either title are those of 11 Henry VII,
1495, including one on the Custos Rotulorum.[3]   This same act
is also the latest in the Charge, where it appears at the very
end as if added as an afterthought.[4]   The resemblance between
Pynson's 'Abridgement' and both portions of Part I of the
'Boke'[5] lends support to the theory previously advanced that
Pynson rather than Wynkyn de Worde was the pioneer in
printing it.[6]

   The order of the articles in the 1506 (?) Charge is important.
They begin with an inquiry into Heretics, continue with
Treason and the more serious felonies, murder, &c.—most of
them (though not all) offences at common law—and end with
a long list of offences, mainly statutory, the majority of which
are trespasses but a few of which are felonies.   This arrangement, though always maintained in later editions of the ' Boke ',
was slightly modified by Fitzherbert in his ' Loffice ' of 1538.
Accepting the old order in relation to heresy,[7] he divided the

---

   [1] For the need of a study of the form of the commission, see *infra*, p. 193.
   [2] B.M. MS. Hargrave 277, f. 86. Cf. also Lambard's quotation from chief
justice ' Hussey ' and his own view that their backs were almost broken
by ' Stacks of Statutes ', *op. cit.*, 33 ; or Maitland, Justice and Police, 84 :
' Long ago lawyers abandoned all hope of describing the duties of a justice
in any methodic fashion, and the alphabet has become the one possible
connecting thread.'
   [3] Under *Justices de Peas*, f. 87.
   [4] See ch. i, p. 18, *supra*.
   [5] See *supra*, pp. 48–9, for the first portion of Part I.
   [6] Only by a few months, however, ch. i, pp. 18–19, *supra*. It must
be remembered that they both printed separate editions of the acts of
11 Henry VII, *supra*, p. 44.
   [7] f. 20 : ' Et pur ceo que heresies & lollardes sount le plus abhominables

articles into three groups: (1) Ecclesiastical matters; (2)
felonies [1]; (3) trespasses—a division which was adopted by
Lambard [2] and which eventually became the usual form.[3] But
leaving these later developments, the problem is to discover
whether the 1506 (?) English form can be traced back to any
source other than Pynson's French 'Abridgement'. A comparison of it with the Charge in MS. Harl. 1777 shows that the
latter, coming immediately after the French statutes,[4] combines
English and French in a curious fashion: ' Le charge d'estre
done par lez justice de peas. Fyrst ye shall inquyre of all
heretykes · & Lollardys '—almost verbally identical with the
first article in the ' Boke '. It is followed, however, not by a
mere reference to the statute as in the ' Boke ' but by the full
French text. Through the remaining articles this method is
pursued,[5] the content, phraseology, and order of the English
summaries being almost the same as in the printed ' Boke '.
But there is a notable difference; the printed Charge includes
two recent statutes, 4 Henry VII [6] and 11 Henry VII,[7] whereas
the MS. Charge has nothing later than 23 Henry VI.[8] It
seems clear, therefore, that the latter represents a form that
was put into shape not long after the middle of the fifteenth
century, undoubtedly based on the collections of statutes then
in existence,[9] and that although this particular copy must have

et execrable al dieu & al roy & as inhabitantes del reame ils commence-
ront oue ceux en tiel fourme.'
    [1] ff. 20 b–27. Divided into felonies by statute (including a few instances
of treason) and felonies at common law. For the effect on the older
order, see ch. i, p. 37, note 8, *supra.*
    [2] Eirenarcha, bk. iv, cap. iv, especially 392, 400, 409.
    [3] Cf. Fleetwood, in MS. Harl. 72, ff. 74 b–75 b; Add. MSS. 25238,
quoted *supra,* p. 54, note 7.   [4] See *supra,* p. 53.
    [5] ff. 84 b–110 b. Oxford, MSS. Trin. College, 30, ascribed to the fifteenth
century (see p. 54, note 7, *supra*), contains a charge slightly more like
the form in Harl. 1777 than like the printed one; but unfortunately it
breaks off in the middle of the article on forestallers and regraters:
' Officium Justiciariorum pacis. Fyrst ye schall enquer off all suche as
we haue power to charge you off Fyrst off all heretykes and lollardez . . .'
It includes almost a dissertation on murder, and also an article on jurors
who reveal the king's counsel, not included in the Boke, but see *infra,* p. 57.
    [6] c. 18; counterfeiting foreign coin current in the realm is declared
treason.   [7] See *supra,* p. 18, and note 6.   [8] f. 96 b.
    [9] *Supra,* pp. 51-2. Perhaps another mark of its relative antiquity is the
fact that the article on ' Vitayllers ' preserves the full text of the old Assize

been made in the latter part of the reign of Henry VII, it did not incorporate the recent legislation. It is tempting to suggest that a Suffolk scribe was stimulated to make such a compilation by the act of 4 Henry VII 'for the due execucion of theire commyssions' by justices of the peace[1] and by the king's mandate issued a few years later to the sheriff of Norfolk and Suffolk for the better administration of the laws by the various local police officers.[2] In any case, the Suffolk Charge[3] or its near relative was very probably the source of the Charge in the 'Boke', brought up to date by the use of Pynson's 'Abridgement'.

But in MS. Harl. 773 there has survived a still earlier form of the Charge, completely in French,[4] with far fewer articles:[5] 'Le Charge et enquerer pur Jurours en Cession du paix deuant Justices de paix &c. En primes vous enquerrez de toutz maniers des felons et de lour felonies, cest assauoir de larons qui gisont en bois, haie, hault chemyns & robbent le people passant....' There is not much evidence of logical arrangement, except that the more serious offences come first, homicide, rape, &c.,[6] also the revealing of the king's counsel by jurors,[7] an offence that has disappeared from the later Charge. Many of the articles are based on the statutes of Northampton[8] and of Winchester,[9] especially on the latter, and a very large number on the legislation of Edward III and Richard II concerned with economic and social matters.[10] One is reminded that

of Bread, ff. 99 b–100 b, not included in the printed Boke. It appears also in a MS. version of Part I of the Boke, closely resembling Harl. 1777, but in a distinctly later hand; Bodleian MSS. 825, ff. 215-27. The Charge ends abruptly with the Assize.   [1] c. 12, 1489.

[2] Cal. Pat. Hen. VII, 1485–1494, 434-7, 1493.

[3] Not necessarily through the medium of MS. Harl. 1777.

[4] ff. 50–51. For the description of the whole volume, distinctly not contemporary with the Charge, see *infra*, p. 102.

[5] Thirty-five certainly, perhaps a few more; it is not always clear what constitutes a separate article. There are but few specific references to statutes, but it has been possible to identify nearly all the statutory sources.   [6] f. 50.

[7] It appears in the 'Articles delivered to the Enquest of office, in the Kinges Bench' quoted by Lambard from 27 Liber Ass., no. 44; *supra*, p. 54, note 7. By the reign of Hen. V it is still important; pp. 90–91, *infra*.

[8] 2 Edw. III, especially c. 3, 1328.   [9] 13 Edw. I, cc. 1-6, 1285.

[10] Especially 23 Edw. III, cc. 1-7; 25 Edw. III, st. 2, cc. 1-7, and various chapters of 12 Rich. II, and of 13 Rich. II, st. 1.

between 1359 and 1361 justices of the peace had taken over the duties of the justices of labourers,[1] and that in the early period offences against economic laws constituted a large proportion of the work of quarter sessions.

Since the important statute against Lollards of 2 Henry V [2] does not appear—a statute that was at once included in the commission of the justices of the peace [3]—and since the latest statute mentioned is one of 4 Henry IV,[4] it is a safe inference that this Charge was in use in the reign of Henry IV, representing the earliest thus far discovered, and that it belongs to nearly the same period as does the earliest known collection of statutes on justices of the peace.[5]   Again therefore it is possible to say that the antecedents of Part I of the ' Boke ' can be traced back to the early decades of the fifteenth century.[6]

The origin of the Statutes and the Charge in the ' Boke ' explains why it was natural for John Rastell and Redman, as well as Pynson, in issuing revised editions of the ' Abridgement ', to issue also revised editions of the ' Boke '.[7] It also serves to reveal certain vital defects even in the first edition of the ' Boke '.   The early collections of statutes, either abridged or unabridged, very rarely indicate the fact of a repeal of a statute,[8] and do not therefore show whether at a given date an Act was in force or not.   The significance of the close connexion between Part I of the ' Boke ' of 1506 (?) and the collections of statutes now becomes apparent.   Two examples out of many will suffice.

(1) Three successive Acts, two of Edward III,[9] and one of

[1] Putnam, Enforcement of the Statutes of Labourers, pt. i, ch. i.
[2] St. 1, c. 7, 1414.
[3] See ch. iii (1), p. 91, note 7, *infra*.
[4] c. 14, on holidays, 1402.
[5] See *supra*, p. 52.
[6] For the significance of the date, see pp. 79, 92, *infra*.
[7] *Supra*, pp. 44-5.   It is to be noted as an example of method that John Rastell, under the title *Justices of peace* in his English translation of the Abridgement, prints the phrase, ' Good men and trew ', &c., while in his edition of the Boke he reproduces the familiar ' Well dysposed men and lawful ...'.
[8] Cf., however, an exceptional case, *supra*, p. 49.
[9] 25 Edw. III, st. 2, c. 7 ; Annunciation, St. Margaret's, St. Michael's, and St. Nicholas ; 36 Edw. III, st. 1, c. 12 ; Epiphany, second week in Lent, between Pentecost and St. John the Baptist, St. Michael's.

Henry V,[1] had established a series of dates for quarter sessions, each differing from the other. Obviously by 1499, or by 1506, only those of Henry V were legal. But Pynson's 'Abridgement' gives all three,[2] and the 'Boke' two, the first and the last.[3]

(2) By 1499 and also by 1506 the statutory maximum rates of wages in force were those of 23 Henry VI, 1445[4]; by 1515, the rates of 6 Henry VIII, 1515.[5] In Pynson's 'Abridgement' under Laborers[6] are given three sets of statutory rates: of 25 Edward III,[7] of 12 Richard II,[8] and of 23 Henry VI.[9] In the Charge in the 1506 (?) 'Boke' the rates of 12 Richard II are correctly omitted, but a portion of those of 25 Edward III[10] appear as well as the rates of 23 Henry VI.[11] To these two sets Berthelet in his 1539 edition adds the rates of 6 Henry VIII.[12] It is clear, therefore, that the presence of a given Act in the 1506 (?) 'Boke' does not prove that the Act was in force at that date, and that even before the form of the 'Boke' had become stereotyped, neither the summaries of statutes nor the articles of the Charge furnished an absolutely accurate account of the existing law.[13]

---

[1] 2 Hen. V, st. 1, c. 4; St. Michael's, Epiphany, Easter, Translation of St. Thomas.

[2] ff. 84–5.   [3] Sig. A iii.

[4] c. 12.   The Act of 11 Henry VII, c. 22, 1495, had been repealed by 12 Hen. VII, c. 3, 1497.   [5] c. 3.   [6] ff. 90–95.

[7] *Ibid.*, f. 91 ; also rates of the ordinance of 1349.

[8] *Ibid.*, ff. 92–3   [9] *Ibid.*, ff. 93–5.

[10] Sig. B i, B ii; wages in harvest time.

[11] Sig. B i. The full text of the statute (not given in the ' Boke') includes rates for harvest wages which must in fact have superseded those of 25 Edw. III.

[12] ff. 16–20.   Cf. Pynson's more accurate edition; ch. 1, p. 21, *supra.*

[13] Although Miss McArthur's main conclusions as to the powers of the justices of the peace under 13 Rich. II (see p. 36 note 1, *supra*) are important and are confirmed by other evidence (see p. 93, note 2, *infra*), the above facts show that it is dangerous to draw inferences from the presence or absence of a given statute in the printed ' Boke'.

CHAPTER III

FIFTEENTH-CENTURY COLLECTIONS OF WRITS AND INDICTMENTS FOR JUSTICES OF THE PEACE

I. A WORCESTERSHIRE MANUAL,[1] *circ.* 1422.

THE next problem to be solved is the origin of the writs and indictments that make up Part II of the ' Boke'.[2] An examination of a great number of manuscript collections of legal formulae has brought to light many compilations of writs[3] quite apart from the famous Register.[4] The earliest having to do with justices of the peace proved to be a manuscript volume preserved in the Public Record Office.[5] It is classified in the official ' Guide' among Records of the Exchequer, Miscellaneous Books, Augmentation Office, no. 169, and is described as : ' Precedents for Writs (" Liber Brevium ") temp. Edward III '.[6] This date is, however, at least half a century too early, and the description by no means sufficiently explicit.[7]

The sixteen folios of the Liber Brevium include two absolutely distinct collections, written by different scribes. Folios one to eleven contain eighty-two separate entries,[8] copies of

---

[1] Folios 1–12 are printed in App. II.

[2] Ch. i, p. 11, *supra.*

[3] See p. 6, notes 3 and 4, and p. 43, note 5, *supra*, for an account of the archives included in my investigation.

[4] F. W. Maitland, ' The History of the Register of Original Writs ', Harvard Law Review, iii ; Holdsworth, *op. cit.*, ii. 431–4, app. 516–51.

[5] It is of course quite possible that future investigation will result in the discovery of still earlier compilations.

[6] S. R. Scargill Bird, 3rd ed., 1908, 182. It is a parchment volume, 10 × 8 inches, bound in boards. For its history, cf. *infra*, pp. 80–82.

[7] On a later page of the Guide, 252, there is a positively misleading account of the same MS. as containing 'Transcripts of writs of various kinds issuing out of the Exchequer.' Throughout this chapter the MSS. mentioned unless otherwise specified are in P.R.O.

[8] For convenience of reference, I have numbered them consecutively in printing the text. I have put the headings immediately below the numbers ; in the original they are usually in the margin.

writs or of indictments or of some legal memoranda, almost all of which, either by specific reference or by clear implication, prove to be precedents for justices of the peace.[1]

Folios twelve[2] to sixteen contain thirty-six separate documents, copies of returns to writs similar to those in the printed ' Returna Brevium ' so often bound with the ' Boke of Justyces of Peas '.[3] The returns are to various writs of process—*capias*, *distringas*, replevin, &c., especially process connected with real actions, but include a few returns to writs of summons to parliament, gaol delivery, &c.[4]

Before analysing the legal content of this collection of precedents or manual for justices of the peace and comparing with it the writs and indictments in similar MS. collections as well as those in the printed ' Boke ', it is necessary to discuss it under the following heads: (1) localization of the writs; (2) their date; (3) the identification of the officials; (4) the identification of the cases and of the parties involved ; (5) the question of the compiler or compilers and of the date of the compilation ; (6) the subsequent history of the MS.

(1) *The localization of the writs.*

The county within which the officials are acting is almost always Worcestershire, either specifically mentioned [5] or else implied by an easily identified place [6] or by the fact that the writ in question is part of a series the localization of which has

---

[1] In twenty-two of the eighty-two forms, justices of the peace are not specifically indicated, but in seven of these twenty-two they are undoubtedly implied (nos. 20, 24, 27, 29, 43, 44, 74), and in three almost certainly (nos. 13, 14, 54). Of the remaining twelve, nos. 53 and 73 deal with the statutes of Labourers, so frequently enforced by the justices of the peace ; no. 3 on Lollardy refers to the recent statute against Lollards, which we know was to be enforced by the justices of the peace (cf. p. 91, note 7, *infra*) ; no. 12 has a heading very common in quarter session records; no. 52 deals with an offence included in the contemporary commissions of the peace; nos. 4 and 6 with offences that are within the jurisdiction of the justices of the peace ; and no. 18 probably (see p. 87, *infra*). There are therefore only four undeniable exceptions, nos. 58 and 76, which have to do with a very special occasion, and nos. 80 and 81, cases of replevin in the county court.

[2] Dorse; for the complete contents of folio 12, see *infra*, p. 81.

[3] See ch. i, *supra*, p. 24.

[4] For an account of this portion, see *infra*, pp. 76-7.

[5] In fifty-three of the eighty-two documents.

[6] In ten instances (nos. 4, 9, 23, 25, 28, 31, 56, 63, 74, and 78).

already been established.[1]   In two instances the justices of
Gloucestershire and Warwickshire respectively demand fugitive
offenders from the sheriff of Worcestershire[2] and in one
instance the justices of Gloucestershire make a similar request
from the sheriff of Oxfordshire.[3]

The place in Worcestershire in which the sessions are held,
if mentioned at all, proves to be the city of Worcester,[4]
evidently at the castle,[5] and the gaol to which prisoners are
sent is the castle gaol.[6]

The towns mentioned, either as the homes of parties to the
actions and bailiwicks of the officials or as the places at which
the offences are said to have been committed, are almost all
in the county of Worcester,[7] in many instances within the
hundreds of Pershore and Oswaldslow.[8]   The few exceptions
are towns in the adjoining counties of Gloucester,[9] Hereford,[10]
Oxford,[11] and Warwick.[12]

(2) *The date of the writs.*

Of the eighty-two documents, fifteen afford positive evidence
as to date by referring to a king or to his deputy or to a regnal

[1] In thirteen instances (nos. 10, 18, 19, 20, 22, 24, 27, 29, 39, 41, 42,
44, 81).   There are three cases in which no county is mentioned (nos. 6,
12, and 73).

[2] No. 61 (county proved by place-name) and no. 67.   [3] No. 55.

[4] The name is written out in twenty-two cases (nos. 7, 8, 9, 11, 17, 21,
23, 25, 28, 30, 31, 32, 45, 48, 49, 50, 51, 60, 65, 71, 75, 78).   In six cases
(nos. 1, 2, 10, 19, 40, 54) merely 'W' is used, and in three cases (nos. 20,
41, 44) 'said place'.

[5] Nos. 68, 69, 77, 82; no. 62 is not so clear.

[6] Nos. 4, 16, 21, 43, 56, 59, 64, 70, 72, 77.   In nos. 55 and 64, the
gaol of Gloucester castle is mentioned.   Worcester is also the place of
the meeting of the county court (no. 26).   For the relation of the 'Shir-
hous' to the castle, see J. H. Round, in '"Shire-house" and Castle Yard',
E.H.R. xxxvi. 210–14; cf. also 13 Rich. II, st. 1, c. 15.

[7] Specifically mentioned in the text: Berrow, Oswaldslow (no. 17);
Broadway, Oswaldslow (no. 58); Droitwich, Halfshire (no. 5); Eckington,
Pershore (no. 51); Evesham, Blakenhurst (nos. 30, 67); Hartlebury,
Halfshire and Oswaldslow (no. 74); Kidderminster, Halfshire (no. 74);
Leigh, Pershore (nos. 48, 75); Mildenham, Pershore (no. 71); town of
Pershore, Pershore (nos. 63, 72, 75, 80); St. Jones, Oswaldslow (no. 69);
Upton on Severn, Oswaldslow (no. 61); Wolashull, Pershore (no. 51);
City of Worcester, *passim.*

[8] The hundred of Pershore is mentioned in nos. 59, 76, 77; of Oswaldslow in nos. 7, 66.

[9] Nos. 44, 55, 61, 64.   [10] No. 65; Munsley, no. 17.

[11] No. 55.   [12] Arrow, no. 36; Coventry, no. 67.

year or by specifying legislation. Of these fifteen, two mention the statute against Lollards passed by the parliament at Leicester in the reign of ' the present king ';[1] one mentions the statute of Labourers of the same parliament,[2] thus in both instances referring to the spring of 1414, the second year of Henry V.[3] One speaks of Edward III as the ' grandfather' of the present king,[4] clearly Henry IV, and belongs to a series of four documents,[5] one of which refers to the 'third ' regnal year ;[6] five speak of Edward III as the 'greatgrandfather' of the present king, clearly Henry V.[7] Without naming the king, one refers to both the ' second' and 'fourth ' regnal years,[8] one to the ' sixth ' regnal year,[9] and one to the ' seventh '.[10] One refers twice to ' Henry ' as king[11] and one is issued by the authority of John, duke of Bedford, ' custos Anglie '.[12] The latter received the title of duke of Bedford in the spring of 1414[13] and was appointed ' custos Anglie ' on 11 August 1415,[14] and again on 25 July 1417,[15] and on 10 June 1421.[16]

In view of the meagreness of the above evidence, it is fortunate that many of the documents prove to be not blank forms for John Doe and Richard Roe but copies of actual writs and indictments, containing therefore abundant details—the names of the sheriff and the justices, and of the parties involved, the nature of the offence, &c.; in fact the only vital omission is usually the actual date of the year. It has therefore been possible to identify nearly all the officials mentioned and to discover many of the actual cases on the Gaol Delivery

---

[1] Nos. 3, 68.   [2] No. 61.

[3] The parliament of Leicester finally met on 30 April ; Parry, Parliaments and Councils, 171.

[4] No. 47.   [5] Nos. 47, 48, 49, 50.   [6] No. 48.

[7] Nos. 53, 55, 71, 75, 76.   [8] No. 32.

[9] No. 13.   [10] No. 5.   [11] No. 17.   [12] No. 58.

[13] 16 May in the parliament at Leicester ; J. H. Wylie, Reign of Henry V, i. 325 ; Cal. Pat. Hen. V, 1413-1416, 187, 230.

[14] *Ibid.* 353. He signed letters from 13 August to 17 November 1415 ; *ibid.* 296.

[15] *Ibid.* 1416-1422, 112. He signed letters from 29 July 1417 to 28 December 1419 ; *ibid.* 88, 149, 214.

[16] *Ibid.* 373. He signed letters from 16 June 1421 to 4 May 1422 ; *ibid.* 335, 426. In the next reign his title was usually ' constable and protector of England', or, simply ' constable of England'; see index to Cal. Pat., Henry VI.

and Coram Rege Rolls and among Ancient Indictments. The
result has been not only the confirmation of the localization
of the writs but also the completion of the chronological
evidence.

For example, the 'seventh' regnal year proves almost
certainly to be Henry IV,[1] the 'second' and 'fourth' regnal
years Henry V.[2] One of the writs describing Edward III as
'great-grandfather of the present king' can be accurately
dated as issued on 22 March 1415,[3] while the writ mentioning
'Henry' as king is proved to be of the reign of Henry V.[4]
Moreover, a number of documents to which there had been no
chronological clue can now be accurately dated. The distribution according to reigns [5] may be summarized as follows:

Henry IV	12	documents	
Henry IV or V	1	"	
Henry V or VI	11	"	
Henry IV or V or VI	4	"	
Henry V	27	"	(certainly)
	2	"	(probably)
No evidence for reign	25	"	
	82	"	

The preponderance is clearly for the reign of Henry V; the
latest date unmistakably referred to is 1419; and it is almost
certain that there are no documents later than the first year
of Henry VI.[6]

(3) The identification of the officials.

Thirty-one men were appointed on the Worcestershire
commission of the peace during the reign of Henry V, including
three Richard Beauchamps—namely, the earl of Warwick, the
earl of Worcester, and the lord of Abergavenny.[7] Of these,
thirteen received salaries,[8] three of them acting only in the

---

[1] No. 5.   [2] No. 32.   [3] No. 76.   [4] No. 17.
[5] For details, see App. II.   [6] Cf. p. 79, *infra.*
[7] Cal. Pat. Henry V, 1413–1416, 21 March 1413; 16 January 1414;
24 June 1415, 425; 1416–1422, 4 December 1417; 8 July 1420; 12 February, 28 May, 3 July 1422, 461–2.
[8] From Monday 2 October 1412, 14 Henry IV to Thursday 18 January
1414, 1 Henry V, Thomas Belne, six days; John Beauchamp, 'chiualer',
four days; Thomas Gower, five days; John Phelippes, 'chiualer', one day;
Richard Oseney, clerk, five days; Pipe Roll 259, 2 Hen. V, Wygorn',

first year of the reign.[1] Therefore leaving out of consideration these three and also the three lords to whom payment would not be made,[2] there were ten who actually sat in session. Six of them appear in the manual, holding sessions and acting individually: John Brace, Thomas Moraunt, John Throgmerton, John Weston, John Wode, and William Wolashull. Of these, Moraunt and Weston were not on the Worcestershire commission in any other reign, but the other four continued to be appointed under Henry VI,[3] John Brace having received his first commission under Henry IV.[4] There are only two other

---

Reddit compotum. From Monday 25 January 1417, 4 Hen. V to Thursday 6 October 1418, 6 Hen. V, John Beauchamp, one day; John Throgmerton, five days; John Brace, ten days; John Weston, four days; John Wode, six days; Thomas Moraunt, four days; William Wolashull, four days; Richard Oseney, clerk, eleven days; *ibid.* 264, 7 Henry V, Wygorn', Reddit compotum. (Under Noua oblata, fines for second to sixth years also are mentioned but not salaries.) From Thursday 12 January 1419, 6 Henry V to Saturday 25 July 1422, 10 Henry V, John Throgmerton, eight days; William Wolashull, fourteen days; Thomas Moraunt, two days; Walter Corbet, three days; John Wode, fourteen days; John Brace, fifteen days; John Vampage, three days; Thomas Heuster, two days; John Forthey, clerk, sixteen days; *ibid.* 268, 1 Hen. VI, Wygorn', Reddit compotum. Under Noua oblata is entered the total sum of fines, &c., before John Throgmerton, &c., justices of the peace for the years 6, 7, 8, 9, 10 Henry V. Cf. Exchequer, K. R. Sheriffs' Accts. $\frac{58}{1}$. The entries for payment of salaries very often refer to Pipe Roll 238, 16 Rich. II, Item Somerset (dorse), the enrolment of the financial clauses of statute 12 Rich. II, c. 10 and 14 Rich. II, c. 11. The justices are to hold sessions at least four times a year, three days at a time if necessary, with salaries of 4s. a day for a justice for the time of the session, and 2s. for the clerk, to be paid out of their fines and amercements. Their estreats, containing the names of the justices, their clerk, and the number of the days of the session, are to be duplicate and one set given to the sheriff that he may collect the money, pay the salaries, and obtain his allowance at the Exchequer, &c. For an account of the earlier procedure, see my Enforcement of the Statutes of Labourers, 44–9, 111–13, 133–5. The Letters Close to the sheriffs seem to have been discontinued after the statutory provisions of Richard II.

[1] Thomas Belne, Thomas Gower, and John Phelippes.

[2] 'Et que null Duc, Count, Baron ou Baneret . . . ne preignent gages pur le dit office'; st. 14 Rich. II, c. 11, quoted in Pipe Roll, *ut supra.* We know that Richard of Abergavenny sat in session at least once, on Friday 6 March 1416, 3 Hen. V; Anc. Indict. K. B. 9, 71, m. 60, wrongly calendared as of the reign of Henry IV.

[3] Cal. Pat. Hen. VI, 1422–1429, 572; 1429–1436, 627; 1436–1441, 593; 1441–1446, 481; 1446–1452, 597; 1452–1461, 681. Brace's last appointment was in 1430; Wode is the only one of the four in the two last references.

[4] *Ibid.* Hen. IV, 1401–1405, 18 November 1403, 521; 1405–1408, 27 January 1406, 499.

Worcestershire justices of the peace mentioned: William Botyller of Yatton[1] who was on the commission under Henry IV,[2] and 'R. H.' acting under the authority possessed by a single justice of the peace out of session,[3] clearly Roger Horton, justice of the King's Bench,[4] on the quorum of every Worcestershire commission of the peace for the reign of Henry V,[5] and sitting in session at least twice, although not recorded as receiving a salary.[6]

There are but two entries in the manual that refer to the clerk of the peace, one to ' Oseny ',[7] the other to ' J. F. '[8] We know that Richard Oseney, a prominent citizen of Worcester,[9] held the office under Henry IV and probably through 1418 under Henry V,[10] and that he was succeeded in January 1419 by John Forthey,[11] also a substantial person,[12] who acted for

[1] No. 79; Yatton, co. Hereford.

[2] Cal. Pat. Hen. IV, 1401–1405, 18 November 1403, 521; 1405–1408, 27 January 1406, 13 February 1407, 499.

[3] No. 57.

[4] Appointed on 16 June 1415; Cal. Pat. Hen. V, 1413–1416, 332; he died 30 April 1423; Foss, Judges, 354.

[5] Proved by an examination of the MS. Patent Rolls ; see p. 75, note 1, *infra*.

[6] With Hugh Huls, &c., on Wednesday 26 July 1413, p. 69, *infra*, and later with Richard of Abergavenny, see p. 65, note 2, *supra*. He was on the commission of the peace in eight other counties ; see App. Cal. Pat. for the reign.

[7] No. 60; cf. no. 51, where he is suing for the king. There are several instances later where the clerk of the peace is the king's attorney ; see *infra*, pp. 102–3.

[8] No 36; possibly the plaintiff in no. 13. Cf. also no. 75.

[9] His name appears frequently in the records of the city. In the reign of Henry VI he served several times as one of the two bailiffs ; Original Charters, Worc. Hist. Soc., ed. J. H. Bloom, 22, 162, 194. Cf. also Collectanea, Worc. Hist. Soc., ed. S. G. Hamilton, *passim*. In 1419 and in 1425 he represented the city in parliament; T. R. Nash, History and Antiquities of Worcestershire, 2 vols., Introduction, 29. Cf. also Th. Habington, Survey of Worcestershire, Worc. Hist. Soc. ii, index *sub nomine*.

[10] Sheriffs' Administrative Accts. (Exchequer, K. R. Accts.) $\frac{592}{20}$, no. 1, at least as early as 11 Henry IV. The latest reference that I have found is Thursday 6 October 1418, 6 Hen. V, Pipe Roll 264, 7 Hen. V, Wygorn', Reddit compotum.

[11] *Ibid*. 268, 1 Hen. VI, Wygorn', Reddit compotum ; the earliest date is Thursday 12 January 1419, 6 Hen. V. Cf. Anc. Indict. K. B. 9, 213, m. 6, 8 Hen. V : ' per manus Johannis Forthey clerici pacis comitatus Wygorn'.

[12] He was escheator under Henry VI, and represented the city of Worcester in parliament twice under Henry V and three times under his son; Nash, *ut supra*, 13 (Fortley), 29. Cf. also Cal. Pat. Hen. V, 1413–1416, 168; 1416–1422, 232.

the remainder of the reign and for at least the first five years of the next reign.[1]

The sheriff, if named at all, is always Richard de Beauchamp,[2] obviously the earl of Warwick, who was hereditary sheriff of Worcester from 1403 until his death in 1439.[3] William Hankford is referred to as delivering the gaol at Worcester Castle[4] together with his companions. We know that his legal career included the position of chief justice of the King's Bench during the whole reign of Henry V[5] and that he delivered Worcester gaol in Michaelmas 1418.[6] The various subordinate officials mentioned, coroners, bailiffs, &c., can in many instances be identified as belonging to the early fifteenth century.[7] There is, therefore, further confirmation of the chronology of the documents, as belonging to the reigns of Henry IV and of Henry V, with the preponderance in favour of the latter.

(4) *The identification of the cases and of the parties involved.*

In turning to a consideration of the cases there are three points to be emphasized. First, occasionally the names of the parties are given in full, so that the date of the action can be established within fairly narrow limits. For example, ' Richard, bishop of Worcester,' against whom an action of replevin was brought by John, prior of Worcester,[8] must be Richard

---

[1] Exchequer, K. R. 137 (Estreats), $\frac{48}{1}$.

[2] Nos. 59, 76, 80; Ricardus B., no. 58.

[3] Lists and Indexes, ix. He returned from France and the Holy Land in 1410, was active in suppressing the Lollards early in the reign of Henry V, was engaged in many important military and diplomatic enterprises, and was entrusted with the education of the king's infant son; D.N.B. He held a great deal of land in the hundreds of Pershore and Oswaldslow. See the Pageant of the Birth, Life and Death of Richard Beauchamp, Earl of Warwick, K.G., ed. Viscount Dillon and W. H. St. John Hope, 1914; also his Household Accounts at Rouen in 1431, recently published, ed. J. H. Bloom. Cf. Holdsworth, *op. cit.*, ii. 438, 528.

[4] No. 59.

[5] He had been justice of the court of Common Pleas under Richard II and Henry IV, and remained chief justice of the King's Bench until his own death soon after the accession of Henry VI ; Foss, Judges, and D.N.B.

[6] On Monday 26 September, together with Thomas Mille and Thomas Harwell ; Gaol Delivery Roll, $\frac{73}{2}$.

[7] See notes to text; App. II.

[8] Nos. 80 and 81.

Clifford, who held the see from 1401–1407.[1] Secondly, in many of the writs, especially in those connected with the process of outlawry or with the taking of recognizances, only the initials of the parties are given and almost no details,[2] so that identification is practically impossible. Thirdly, if actions of trespass, such as on the statutes of Labourers,[3] are begun before justices of the peace, normally[4] the entire process will be completed before them. Unless therefore the session roll itself be discovered, there seems no possibility of finding the actual case. But for Worcestershire no quarter session records for the reigns of Henry IV, V, or VI are thus far known to be preserved.[5] If, however, the cases involve felonies, the chances of identification are far greater. A royal charter of pardon may be enrolled on the Patent Rolls;[6] the case may be summoned into the King's Bench by writ of *certiorari* and therefore will appear amongst Ancient Indictments and on the Coram Rege Rolls;[7] or, since prisoners indicted in quarter session may be delivered either by justices of the peace or by the regular justices of Gaol Delivery,[8] the indictments and the trial will be found amongst Gaol Delivery material.[9]

The most interesting examples of actual cases utilized by the compiler of the manual[10] are those involving accusations against the two Burdets, members of an important county family, both of whom won distinction by serving their sovereign

---

[1] W. Stubbs, Registrum Sacrum Anglicanum, 232. He was then translated to London, *ibid.* 222. The prior must be John Malverne, who held the office from 1395–1420; Priory of Worcester Compotus Rolls, Worc. Hist. Soc., ed. S. G. Hamilton, index *sub nomine*. He was keeper of the spiritualities of the see during its vacancy at the time of Clifford's translation; Worc. Reg. Sede Vacante, ed. J. W. Willis Bund, ii. 387. For the long series of disputes between the bishop and the prior, see V.C.H., Worcestershire, ii. 103.

[2] e.g. nos. 25, 26, 27, 28, or nos. 45 and 46.

[3] See *infra*, pp. 91–92.

[4] Occasionally records of indictments for trespass are summoned into King's Bench; cf. e.g. Coram Rege Roll 610, Rex, rot. 17.

[5] A meagre roll exists, *temp.* Richard II, listed in 'Early Records of Justices of the Peace', E.H.R. xxviii. 328. See also Lord Beauchamp's roll described *supra*, p. 2, note 7.

[6] No. 17 and notes.

[7] Nos. 34–6.

[8] See *infra*, pp. 88–9.

[9] Nos. 16 and 32.

[10] For the other cases identified, see notes to the text, App. II.

in foreign parts.[1] Sir Thomas Burdet[2] of Arrow, Warwickshire [3] (near the Worcestershire border), was sheriff of Warwick
and Leicester under Henry V from 1 December 1415 to 29
November 1416,[4] and during the reign served on several
commissions.[5] His son and heir Nicholas, of Abbot's Lench,
Worcestershire,[6] became great butler of Normandy and was
killed in France in 1440.[7] The legal process connected with
the following indictments brought against father and son in
Worcestershire quarter session lasted throughout the reign.

(1) On Tuesday, 20 June 1413, Nicholas Burdet and six
others were indicted before John Beauchamp de Holt, Knight,
Thomas Belne, and Thomas Gower of an attack at Shipston
on Friday, 28 April, on John Skynnere and Thomas Compton,
constable.[8]

(2) On Wednesday, 26 July of the same year, Nicholas
Burdet and eighty others (eleven named, the rest ' unknown ')
were indicted before Hugh Huls, Roger Horton, Thomas Belne,
and Thomas Gower, of the murder at Shipston on Friday,
30 June, of Thomas Baret and John Clerk.[9]

These two indictments for trespass and for felony were
summoned into the court of King's Bench by a writ of *certiorari*
dated 12 September 1413,[10] but so long was the delay in

---

[1] *Infra*, p. 72.

[2] Son of Sir John ; Dugdale, Warwickshire, 847.

[3] *Ibid.* 845. [4] Lists and Indexes, ix.

[5] Array, 10 May 1418, Cal. Pat. Hen. V, 1416–1422, 198 ; 5 March
1419, 212 ; royal loan, 26 November 1419, 251.

[6] Bruyneslenche, *ibid.* 147 ; Nash, *op. cit.*, App. 71. He was appointed
on the Worcestershire commission of array on 10 May 1418, Cal. Pat.
ut supra, 197. Cf. also *ibid.*, Hen. VI, 1422–1429, 404 ; 1429–1436, 359.

[7] Nash, i. 57 ; V.C.H., Worcestershire, iii. 355 ; Dugdale, Warwickshire, 848. It was the latter's son Thomas who was executed for treason
under Edw. IV as one of the followers of the duke of Clarence, *ibid.*
847-9 ; Nash, i. 58 ; Coventry Leet Book, 378 ; K. H. Vickers, England in
the Later Middle Ages, 479–80 ; Bagae de Secretis as calendared in Rep.
Deputy Keeper, iii, App. II, 213–14 (cf. Vernon Harcourt's art. on ' Bagae
de Secretis ', E.H.R. xxiii. 509).

[8] Anc. Indictments, K.B. 9, 202, ms. 42–44.

[9] Also of an attack on other ' ligeos domini regis ' ; *ibid.* Cf. also the
special commission of 16 July 1413 issued to Hugh Huls and four others
(including Thomas and William Walwayn), to investigate the report of
the attack by Nicholas Burdet and eighty others at Shipston ; Cal. Pat.
Hen. V, 1413–1416, 111.

[10] Anc. Indictments, K.B. 9, 202, m. 42.

securing the presence of the indicted [1] that the quarter session proceedings were not enrolled until Easter 1415.[2] In this term Nicholas Burdet brings into court his charter of pardon,[3] one of the many hundreds granted by the king in accordance with the action of the parliament that had met on 19 November 1414.[4] Since the long list of offences named in the pardon included trespasses and murders committed before 8 December 1414,[5] Nicholas Burdet was *sine die* on both charges. Proceedings connected with the trespass were not completed till Easter 1418,[6] while process against those implicated in the murder and specified by name in the writ of *certiorari*[7] dragged on for several years, until finally by Michaelmas 1417 they had all likewise escaped through similar pardons.[8] Meanwhile the Worcestershire justices of the peace were identifying and indicting some of the eighty 'unknown' (now referred to as 140), who had helped in the murder either as principals or

---

[1] For the writs of *venire facias* and *capias* for the two lists of indicted, cf. Coram Rege Roll 610, Mich. 1 Hen. V, 1413, Rex, rot. 17; for the continuation of the process in the first case, cf. *ibid.* 611, Hill. 1 Hen. V, 1414, Rex, rot. 15 d; 612, Pasch. 2 Hen. V, 1414, Rex, rot. 9; 614, Mich. 2 Hen. V, 1414, Rex, rot. 11; in the second case, *ibid.* 612, Rex, rot. 16; 613, Trin. 2 Hen. V, 1414, Rex, rot. 7 d.

[2] C. R. Roll 616, 3 Hen. V, Rex, rot. 1. There is here no indication that the two lists of offenders had been indicted at separate sessions of the peace, as is proved by Anc. Indictments, *supra*, p. 69, note 8.

[3] Coram Rege Roll, *ut supra*.

[4] 2 Hen. V, Rot. Parl. iv. 34. There is a reference (*ibid.* 40) to a pardon for offences against the statute of Liveries but none to this general pardon. The evidence is however supplied by an extraordinarily voluminous Pardon Roll (Patent Roll, Supplementary), no. 37, 3-5 Hen. V; m. 20 *et seq.* The matter has apparently escaped the attention of the late Mr. Wylie, and is not mentioned in his account of this parliament; Reign of Henry V, i. 431-4.

[5] Excepting any offences committed after 19 November 1414, and also a few especially heinous crimes.

[6] Five of the indicted were then tried and acquitted by chief justice Hankford and William Bishopston holding pleas coram Rege at Evesham; C. R. Roll 617, Trin. 3 Hen. V, 1415, Rex, rot. 17 d; 619, Hill. 3 Hen. V, 1416, Rex, rot. 2; 620, Pasch. 4 Hen. V, 1416, Rex, rot. 5; 622, Mich. 4 Hen. V, 1416, Rex, rot. 10; 624, Pasch. 5 Hen. V, 1417, Rex, rot. 18. The sixth, included also in the second list, had already gone free because of the usual pardon; *ibid.* 619, Hill. 3 Hen. V, Rex, rot. 10 d.

[7] p. 69, note 10, *supra*.

[8] C. R. Roll 619, Hill. 3 Hen. V, 1416, Rex, rot. 10 d; 620, Pasch. 4 Hen. V, 1416, Rex, rot. 5; 623, Hill. 4 Hen. V, 1417, Rex. rot. 13 d; 626, Mich. 5 Hen. V, 1417, Rex, rot. 7 d.

accessories.[1] Of six who were indicted before Weston and Throgmerton, five were acquitted at a Gaol Delivery on 5 March 1416,[2] but the sixth, a certain Robert Monnes of Oxholm, was not tried with his associates. It is therefore interesting to find in the manual that he appeared later before the justices of the peace acting as justices of Gaol Delivery, probably in the spring of 1418—a date for which Gaol Delivery material is missing[3]—and that he escaped punishment by producing a pardon like Burdet's accompanied by a writ *de non molestando*.[4]

There is also a series of charges against not only Nicholas Burdet but also his father, the late sheriff. On Saturday, 8 January 1418, before Throgmerton, Wode, Moraunt, and Brace, the two Burdets, together with William Wodeward, were indicted as accessories [5] to three separate attacks on the property and servants of the abbot of Evesham committed in the late autumn and early winter of 1417 by the servants of Nicholas Burdet and by others, some unknown.[6] On Monday, 23 May 1418,[7] similar indictments were brought before Wode and Brace for two felonious entries into houses.[8] Within a month of the January quarter sessions, 1418, the abbot procured a special commission of oyer and terminer dated 12 February, to inquire into the second of the three attacks.[9] Its preliminary proceedings under chief justice Hankford

---

[1] Cf. e. g. Gaol Delivery Roll 197, m. 6 and m. 6 d ; there is a slight discrepancy in the date of the offence—Friday *in* the feast of St. Peter and St. Paul, instead of *after* as in Anc. Indictments.

[2] G. D. Roll 197, m. 6 d.

[3] See *infra*, p. 89, note 1.

[4] Nos. 32 and 33 ; he is referred to merely as ' R. M.'

[5] ' Per preceptum manutencionem ordinacionem et abettamentum.' See *infra*, note 6.

[6] C. R. Roll 634, Mich. 7 Hen. V, 1419, Rex, rot. 3, 3 d. The details read like schoolboy pranks : ' domos molendinorum ... vocatas Chadbery mulles felonice fregerunt et diuersas billas de ferro et acere factas et lapides vocatos pebeles inter molares ibidem molantes posuerunt ... et les Flodyatys ... cum les hoperys ... fregerunt.'

[7] The Burdets had just been appointed on commissions of array ; see p. 69, notes 5 and 6, *supra*.

[8] C. R. Roll, *ut supra*, note 6. The defendants are William Russell of North Littleton and Simond Pachet of Haggeley. The third accessory in the last case was John Jonettes, not Wodeward.

[9] Cal. Pat. Hen. V, 1416–1422, 147.

lasted till the following summer, when several of the indicted surrendered, including the two Burdets, and when the rest were outlawed.[1]

The next step was the issue early in 1419 of a writ of *certiorari* by the court of King's Bench summoning before it all five indictments made in quarter sessions.[2] When the two Burdets finally appeared in Hilary Term 1420 they were released on bail ' pro eo quod ipsi profecturi sunt in partibus transmarinis in seruicio domini regis in comitiva Johannis Ducis Bedeford '.[3] After their return they were sent to prison and were finally tried by the justices of Nisi Prius in Easter 1422 and were both acquitted.[4] Meanwhile the process against their associates continued to appear on the Coram Rege Rolls —in some instances delayed by their service across the sea— until finally they were all freed,[5] either through acquittal by a jury or by the production of pardons.[6] From the above material the compiler of the manual selected the proceedings connected with the writ of *certiorari* to the justices of the peace demanding the indictments against the Burdets, by far the most conspicuous of the parties.[7]

---

[1] Assize Roll 1038, no. 3. I do not find any record of convictions before this special commission, but cf. Exchequer, K. R. Sheriffs' Accts. $\frac{5}{1}\frac{3}{}$: ' De amerciamentis forisfactis Willelmo Hankeford chiualer et sociis suis justiciariis domini regis ad quasdam transgressiones Rogero abbati de Evesham factas anno VI^{to} regis Henrici quinti ; vicecomes. iii s. xi d.' Note that during the process of exigend and before the writs of *supersedeas*, the two Burdets were appointed on the commission of array ; *supra*, p. 71, note 7.

[2] Noted in Michaelmas term, 1419, 7 Hen. V ; C. R. Roll 634, Rex, rot. 3 d. For the form of the writ and its date, see note 7, *infra*. It seems probable that the proceedings before the commission of oyer and terminer were also summoned into the King's Bench.

[3] C. R. Roll 635, Hill. 7 Hen. V, Rex, rot. 9, rot. 22 ; ' John Brase de Wyche ', one of the acting justices of the peace, was one of the ' manucaptores '.

[4] *Ibid.* 634, Rex, rot. 3 d.

[5] Except John Jonettes.

[6] *Ibid.* 635, Rex, rot. 14 d, 7 d ; 638, Mich. 8 Hen. V, 1420, Rex, rot. 3 ; 639, Hill. 8 Hen. V, 1421, Rex, rot. 17.

[7] Nos. 34-36. The writ in the manual is not dated, but the return was asked for by July 1, and was made by John Forthey, clerk, who began his duties in January 1419. The proceedings were enrolled in Michaelmas term, 1419. It is noteworthy that the justices in their return (no. 36) correct the error as to the county of Thomas Burdet made in the writ of *certiorari* (no. 34). Cf. Year Book, Pasch. 1 Hen. V, no. 8 : contrary

Another case recorded in the manual is the murder of a certain John Milward by an unusually large group of assailants and under especially heinous circumstances—a case that also involved an enormous number of entries on the Coram Rege Rolls and a great many royal pardons.[1] From the above evidence for violence and disorder in the Midlands coupled with the failure to punish the offenders, it seems clear that the king considered that men with the energy and courage to attack their fellow citizens could safely be employed in fighting the French. One is reminded of Pope Urban's plea: 'Let those who for a long time have been robbers now become knights.'[2]

The above investigation has established conclusively certain definite facts as to the material used in the manual, but the two remaining problems are those for which no positive evidence exists. The solution presented is therefore by no means necessarily the right one.

(5) *The question of the identity of the compiler and the date of the compilation.*

It seems plausible to suggest that either a clerk of the peace or else some one of the 'working' justices specifically mentioned in the manual was responsible for its compilation. Of the two clerks, Oseney and Forthey, it is the latter whose term of office fits in with the date of the writs ;[3] but if it be sound to infer that estreats sent up to the Exchequer in his name[4] were written by his own hand, a comparison of the writing in the

to the usage in suits between parties, 'misnaming' of the defendant in an indictment of felony does not render the indictment void.

[1] No. 17 and notes ; App. II.

[2] Speech at Clermont proclaiming the first crusade.

[3] See *supra*, p. 66. It would of course be natural that some of the material belonging to his predecessor should be used.

[4] Exchequer, K.R. 137, $\frac{48}{1}$. The handwriting of indentures made *temp.* Oseney also differs from that of the manual, Exchequer, K.R., Accts. $\frac{592}{20}$, no. 1, as does the handwriting of the estreats of Philip Strethay and John Campion, successive clerks of the peace in Warwickshire while Weston was on the commission there; see p. 77, *infra*. From the general character of the handwriting, I have been assuming that the MS. before us is not much later than the precedents themselves.

two MSS. shows that he did not himself transcribe the documents in the manual. Of the justices named in the latter, there are five who need careful consideration,[1] Brace,[2] Throgmerton,[3] Wode,[4] Wolashull,[5] and Weston,[6] obviously all men of weight in Worcestershire[7] holding important offices, serving on a variety of commissions, and representing either the city or county of Worcester in parliament. Brace was sheriff in the reign of Henry IV and the others were all undersheriffs to the great earl under Henry V or early in the reign of his son, while Throgmerton eventually attained the distinction of being under-treasurer of England.[8]   From their

[1] Thomas Moraunt can be omitted because the only reference to him in the manual gives him a wrong initial, no. 35. William Botyller of Yatton is clearly too early and Roger Horton presumably too busy with more important affairs, *supra*, p. 66.

[2] Sat twenty-five days during the reign, *supra*, p. 64, note 8 ; mentioned seven times in the manual, nos. 5, 72, 74 ; initials only, nos. 32, 45, 46, 54.

[3] Sat thirteen days (p. 64, note 8) ; mentioned eleven times, nos. 21, 62, 63, 65, 66 ; initials only, nos. 7, 32, 38, 45, 51, 56.

[4] Sat twenty days, p. 64, note 8, *supra* ; mentioned five times, nos. 7, 21, 35, 38, 60.   Perhaps no. 45, by initials only.

[5] Sat eighteen days, p. 64, note 8, *supra* ; mentioned three times, nos. 7, 28 ; by initial, no. 42.

[6] Sat for four days (p. 64, note 8) ; mentioned three times [but cf. Anc. Ind. K.B. 9, 71, m. 60, where he sat in a session for which he was apparently not paid] ; certainly nos. 32, 70, 77, and perhaps twice more, nos. 45, 78.

[7] Cf. the qualifications demanded for justices of the peace ; they were to be 'les pluys vaillantz . . . de bone fame et de bone condicion,' ' des pluis suffisantz,' &c., resident in the county ; Rot. Parl., iii, 1 Hen. IV, 444 ; *ibid.* iv, 2 Hen. V, 51 ; Statutes, 13 Rich. II, st. 1, c. 7 ; 2 Hen. V, st. 2, c. 1.

[8] The following references in addition to those for commissions of the peace (given *supra*, pp. 64–5, notes) are perhaps sufficient, though by no means exhaustive. *Brace* of Wych : sheriff and keeper of the Gaol of Worcester Castle, 1401, Lists and Indexes, ix, Cal. Pat. Hen. IV, 1399–1401, 527 ; escheator, 5 Hen. IV, 10 Hen. IV, Nash, Introduction, 13 ; commission of array, Cal. Pat. Hen. IV, 1401–1405, 286 ; Hen. V, 1416–1422, 197, 212 ; against Lollards, *ibid.* Hen. V, 1413–1416, 178 ; royal loan, *ibid.* 1416–1422, 251 ; knight of the shire, 3 Hen. IV, 4 Hen. IV, 9 Hen. V, 2 Hen. VI ; Nash, *ut supra*, 27.

Throgmerton : array, Cal. Pat. Hen. V, 1416–1422, 212 ; against Lollards, *ibid.* 1413–1416, 178 ; royal loan, *ibid.* 1416–1422, 251 ; Hen. VI, 1422–1429, 354, 481 ; 1429–1436, 50, 125, 354 ; 1436–1441, 249, 505 ; 1441–1446, 92 ; referred to as under-treasurer by 1440, *ibid.* 1436–1441, 422 ; under-sheriff 5 Hen. V, 9 Hen. VI, escheator 6 Hen. V, knight of the shire, 8 Hen. V, 1 Hen. VI, 27 Hen. VI, 29 Hen. VI ; Nash, *ut supra*, 16, 17, 13, 27. See pp. 124–5, *infra*, for the marriage of one of his descendants to Thomas Marowe's sister ; cf. also art. in D.N.B.

Wode : array, Cal. Pat. Hen. V, 1416–1422, 212 ; royal loan, *ibid.* 251 ;

repeated association with each other and with the earl of Warwick one gains the impression of a compact little group of intimate friends who were actively engaged in governing the county of Worcester.

Of these five justices of the peace it seems improbable that either Brace or Wolashull had any responsibility for the manual, since neither was ever included in the quorum. Throgmerton, Weston, and Wode on the other hand, if on the commission at all in the reign of Henry V, were always on the quorum; Throgmerton from January 1414, Weston from January 1414 to December 1417 and again from February 1422, and Wode from January 1417.[1] In the eleven Gaol Deliveries at Worcester Castle during the reign, Weston took part four times, once as a regular justice of Gaol Delivery and three times as a justice of the peace, while Wode did not act

similar commissions under Hen. VI, Cal. Pat., *passim*; under-sheriff 1425–1426, Lists and Indexes, ix; escheator, 4 Hen. V, 10 Hen. VI, burgess from city of Worcester, 1 Hen. V, 3 Hen. V, knight of the shire, 8 Hen. VI, 13 Hen. VI; Nash, *ut supra*, 13, 27, 29.

Wolashull: array, Cal. Pat. Hen. V, 1416–1422, 212; royal loan, *ibid.* 251; similar commissions under Hen. VI, Cal. Pat. *passim*; under-sheriff, 1422 (if Wodeshull is the same name as Wolashull), Lists and Indexes, ix; escheator, 2 Hen. VI, knight of the shire, 5 Hen. V, 2 Hen. VI, 8 Hen. VI; Nash, *ut supra*, 13, 27. For his connexion with the distinguished family of Vampage, see *ibid.* ii. 183.

Weston: oyer and terminer with William Boteler of Yatton, Cal. Pat. Hen. IV, 1408–1413, 372; against Lollards, 11 January 1414, *ibid.* Hen. V, 1413–1416, 178; to inquire of treasons, &c., *ibid.* 1416–1422, 269; commission of the peace from 16 January 1414 to 4 December 1417, and from 12 February 1422 to the end of the reign, *ibid.* 1413–1416, 425; 1416–1422, 461; under-sheriff, 20 October 1420-4 February 1421, Lists and Indexes, ix; burgess from city of Worcester (with Wode), 1 Hen. V, knight of the shire (with Throgmerton), 8 Hen. V; Nash, *ut supra*, 27, 29. Perhaps he is the John Weston who was one of the two bailiffs of the city of Worcester in 1409–1410, Original Charters, ed. J. H. Bloom, Worc. Hist. Soc., 77, 193, and who held tenements in the city and acted as witness; Collectanea, ed. S. G. Hamilton, Worc. Hist. Soc., 10, 14, 19. Th. Habington, Survey of Worcestershire, Worc. Hist. Soc., ii. 434, describes the Weston arms in the cloister of Worcester cathedral.

[1] Pat. 1 Hen. V, pt. 1, ms. 34 d, 33 d; 3 Hen. V, p. 1, m. 31 d; 5 Hen. V, m. 26 d; 8 Hen. V, m. 21 d; 9 Hen. V, pt. i, m. 19 d; 10 Hen. V. m. 14 d. It is unfortunate that the editors of the Calendars have adopted a form for printing the commissions of the peace that make it impossible to discover the membership of the quorum, or the identity of the Custos Rotulorum, even when shown in the MS. enrolment. A careful study of both subjects would undoubtedly throw much light on the work of the justices.

at all and Throgmerton only once and then as a justice of the peace.[1]   In the one instance, however, in which the form of the enrolled Letters Patent enables the Custos Rotulorum for Worcestershire to be identified, namely for May 1422, he proves to be Wode.[2]   If therefore it were a question merely of the writs for justices of the peace it would be reasonable to connect the compilation with the justice who had the custody of the records.

But in the same MS. volume with the Worcestershire writs is a collection of thirty-six documents similar to those in the printed 'Returna Brevium', mainly therefore connected with civil pleas.[3]   The bailiwick within which the officials are acting is usually Coventry, and occasionally the county of Warwick.[4]   The dates of the actual cases[5] are early fifteenth century, most of them before 1451, the year in which Coventry was made a county.[6]   The names of the parties are of residents in Coventry or Warwick;[7] the officials include Richard Hastings, sheriff of Warwick and Leicester four times between 1414 and 1432,[8] John Allesley, mayor of

---

[1] See p. 89, note 1, *infra*.

[2] Pat. 10 Hen. V, m. 14 d : ' Et vos prefate . . . .' Lambard, Eirenarcha, 371, implies that the first instance of the appointment of a Custos Rotulorum was in 14 Rich. II ; but cf. Pat. 3 Rich. II, pt. 3, m. 13 d, for an earlier case.

[3] *Supra*, p. 61.

[4] In the cases which require action of the county court as distinct from the court of the city of Coventry.

[5] In many instances it is evident that the names are fictitious, of the Richard Roe and John Doe type ; e.g. William Lot and John Bot.

[6] Dugdale, Warwickshire, 142–3 ; Cov. Leet Bk., 266, 269–70. The last document, however, presents a difficulty. It is the return to the writ of John Weston and his fellows, directed to the sheriff of Warwickshire with instructions for holding a Gaol Delivery at Coventry, and is signed by Johannes Bere vicecomes, never a sheriff of Warwickshire, although a resident of Coventry at this date ; Cov. Leet Bk., index. But the first sheriffs of the city of Coventry after the new charter are John Wylgrys and Reginald Bere, who were formerly the bailiffs ; *ibid.* (1451), 267, 269. Is it possible, therefore, that the document is later than this year and that the scribe who copied it confused both the name and the jurisdiction of the sheriff?

[7] As far as they have been identified. Cf. for example Robert Comaunder and Henry Somerlove, who were bailiffs of Warwick in 1450 ; Warw. Ant. Mag., 179 ; or John Rody, Gaol Delivery Roll $\frac{68}{2}$; Roger Sale, *ibid.* $\frac{68}{1}$.

[8] Lists and Indexes, ix.

Coventry in 1404,[1] and John Weston, referred to three times, as justice of the peace in Warwickshire, as receiving the attorneys by writ, and as justice of Gaol Delivery in Coventry.[2] It appears that John Weston of Warwickshire held lands at Wolston and Weston-sub-'Wethele',[3] and that he was appointed on the quorum of every Warwickshire commission of the peace from 1407 through 1427,[4] and sat frequently in quarter sessions.[5] In 1417, or perhaps a few years earlier, he became recorder of Coventry,[6] probably to be identified with the John Weston who had been common pleader of London from 1402 to about 1415.[7] He was recorder until 1433 or 1434,[8] and therefore *ex officio* justice of the peace in Coventry,[9] serving also on numerous commissions of Gaol Delivery both for Coventry and for Warwick,[10] as well as on other Warwickshire

---

[1] Dugdale, *op. cit.*, 148, spelt Allusley; a Giles Allesley was mayor in 1426, *ibid.* Cf. also Cov. Leet Bk., index.

[2] Folios 13 b, 16, 16 b.

[3] In Knightlow hundred. He is described as John Weston of Weston, serjeant-at-law; Dugdale, *op. cit.*, 34, 296-7; Cov. Leet Bk., 123, note 5, 742.

[4] Cal. Pat. Hen. IV, 1405–1408, 13 February 1407, 498; Hen. V, 1413–1416, 424; 1416–1422, 461; Hen. VI, 1422–1429, 12 July 1427, 571. The next commission, that of 26 October 1433, does not contain his name; *ibid.* 1429–1436, 626, but he evidently sat up to 1433; see note 5. It is necessary to examine the MS. rolls for the quorum. Cf. also the references to receiving the attorneys by writ; Cal. Pat. Hen. V, 1416–1422, 130, 172; Hen. VI, 1422–1429, 202, 461.

[5] 13, 14 Hen. IV, 1, 2 Hen. V, seven days, Pipe Roll no. 259, Warw. Nova oblata; 4, 5 Hen. V, six days, *ibid.* no. 263; 6, 7 Hen. V, nine days, *ibid.* no. 266; 8, 9, 10 Hen. V, 11 days, *ibid.* no. 270; 1–3 Hen. VI, eight days, *ibid.* no. 272 (cf. Exch. K.R. 137, $\frac{46}{4}$); 4, 5 Hen. VI, six days, Pipe Roll no. 273; 7 Hen. VI, six days; 9 Hen. VI, three days; 10, 11 Hen. VI, eleven days (last indenture made in 1434); Exchequer, K.R. Accts. $\frac{590}{33}$. He sat as early as June 1408; Anc. Indict., K.B. 9, 196, ms. 43, 44.

[6] Cal. Pat. Hen. V, 1416–1422, 14 Dec. 1417, 130; Cov. Leet Bk., 44. For evidence that he was appointed shortly after 1415, see note 7, *infra*.

[7] Cal. Lond. Letter Books, ed. R. R. Sharpe, i. 19, 40, 49, 78, 95, 102, 139, 140, 141. The latest reference is to August 1415, perhaps indicating that soon afterwards he accepted the Coventry recordership.

[8] The latest reference in the Leet Book to him as recorder is in January 1433, 144. In January 1434 Donyngton is mentioned as recorder; and on 7 April there is the following entry: 'Also they ordyn that Will. Donyngton be Recordour of the Citie of Couentrie, als long as he is of goode beryng', 150, 157. It is strange that he is apparently also mentioned as recorder as early as 1430, 134.

[9] Cov. Leet Bk., 44, 98, *et passim*.

[10] Gaol Delivery Rolls, 67, 68, 195, *passim*. The earliest reference is

commissions.[1] He is first mentioned in the Year Books in Hilary term 1421, when he was pleading on behalf of the mayor and bailiffs of Coventry.[2] Henceforth through 1432 he appeared frequently in the courts at Westminster,[3] having been made serjeant-at-law in 1425.[4]

If it be sound to infer the identity of John Weston of Worcestershire with John Weston of Warwickshire,[5] we have as the connecting link between the manual and the ' Returna '

to 10 July 1414, no. 195, m. 84; the latest to 13 March, 7 Hen. VI, no. 68, m. 23.

[1] e.g. 26 November 1414, with the mayor of Coventry and others to detect counterfeit money, Cal. Pat. Hen. V, 1413–1416, 266 ; royal loans, *ibid.* Hen. VI, 1429–1436, 6 March 1430, 50 (cf. also Cov. Leet Bk., 123) ; 26 March 1431, 126 ; subsidy, *ibid.*, 12 April 1431, 137 ; grant of monastery at Alcester to the keeping of several, including John Weston, serjeant-at-law, and William Donyngton, *ibid.*, 26 November 1431, 186 ; Dugdale, Warwickshire, 772–3. Cf. also Cal. Pat. Hen. IV, 1408–1413, 26, 295, 380.

[2] Hill. 8 Hen. V, no. 23.

[3] Year Books, Hen. VI, *passim.*

[4] 28 November, Rot. Claus., 3 Hen. VI, m. 12 ; Dugdale, Chron. Ser., 61. It seems clear that the recorder and the serjeant-at-law are the same John Weston, but it is also possible that the experience with this combination of the two sets of duties led the Leet in promising the post to the famous Thomas Littleton (like Weston connected with Worcestershire) to stipulate that he 'remain within the city', Cov. Leet Bk., 234. It appears, however, that Littleton succeeded Donyngton in 1449 (*ibid.* 235), and although called to be serjeant-at-law in 1453 (Dugdale, 65) did not resign as recorder until 1455 (Cov. Leet Bk., 283), when he was made king's serjeant; Dugdale, *loc. cit.*, p. 178, note 4, *infra.* Early in 1486 Thomas Keble, just created serjeant-at-law, when offered the 'next a-voydaunce' of the recordership, explains that 'except that he may be excused of his dwelling and abiding in the Cite, And also licensed to be absent at the ij tymes of the assises and sessions of the peace, he Cannot take hit vppon hym '. He was refused the recordership on these terms in spite of the evidence that he presented for other towns, Cov. Leet Bk., 524–8. But yet Fitzherbert, recorder in 1509 and serjeant-at-law in 1510, did not resign until 1512, and then at his own initiative : 'that he had so grete besynesse by reason that he was seriaunt of the lawe that he cowde not nor myght not occupy the Rome of Recordership ', Cov. Leet Bk. 635 ; see also p. 33, note 2, *supra.*

[5] The multiplicity of John Westons, especially in Surrey (cf. Inq. p. m. iv, 201, 210), makes certainty of identification almost impossible except by an exhaustive study of the abundant material for the purpose of ascertaining the precise dates of the activities of ' John Weston ' in London, Surrey, Warwickshire (including Coventry), and Worcestershire. For example, could one man in the same year act as recorder of Coventry, as undersheriff of Worcestershire, and as knight of the shire for Worcestershire ? The entry on a contemporary Pardon Roll (Patent Roll, Supplementary) is peculiarly disappointing : ' Johannes Weston de London quocumque nomine censeatur ', no. 37, 3–5 Hen. V, m. 27.

the one man of the Worcestershire 'working' justices who was 'learned in the law'. Is it not at least a plausible hypothesis that he was responsible for both compilations, perhaps having the documents transcribed by his own clerks, either private or official; [1] that the manual was put into shape about 1422, before his retirement from the commission of peace in Worcestershire, and the 'Returna' some years later, after his experience as recorder of Coventry had shown the need for such a collection?

As confirmatory evidence it is interesting to note John Weston's connexion with the Coventry Leet Book, the compilation of which was begun during the mayoralty of John Leeder in 1421 : 'Allso that all good ordynaunce of the leetys be sought up and wryton in a regestre, that they may be of record foreuermore, be ouersight of the recorder, for worschip and honesty of this Cite.' [2] If John Weston's 'ouersight'· extended also to the manual for justices of the peace and to the 'Returna Brevium', he is but the earliest of a distinguished group of lawyers connected with Coventry: Thomas Littleton,[3] Thomas Keble,[4] John Rastell,[5] Anthony Fitzher-

---

[1] The difference in handwriting may thus be explained. It seems clear that neither the Worcestershire nor Warwickshire clerks of the peace were the scribes; p. 73, note 4, *supra*. It is of course quite possible that the MS. volume in its present form is later than the precedents it contains. *Ibid.* and p. 76, note 6, *supra*, and Maitland's warning cited *infra*, p. 105.

[2] Cov. Leet Bk. 33. The earliest reference to a town clerk or steward is in 1430, *ibid.* 130, but his name is not given. Is he possibly the Edmund 'Collyshull' who was paid £1 in 1425 for the 'enrollment of presentations of indictments before the justices of the peace in Esterton's mayoralty' [1422]? At the same date, John Weston, recorder, received £20 for his 'labour and advice and the necessary advice of others there'; *ibid.* 98-9.

[3] Born at Frankley Manor House, Worcestershire, between 1407 and 1422; under-sheriff of Worcestershire 1447-1448; recorder of Coventry, 1449-1455; serjeant-at-law, 1453; king's serjeant, 1455; justice of the court of Common Pleas, 1466; died 23 August 1481; E. Wambaugh, ed. Littleton's Tenures, xiii-lvii; Dugdale and Cov. Leet Bk., cited *supra*, p. 78, note 4. For his reading at the Inner Temple see p. 178, and note 5, *infra*. From the date of his recordership, it is evidently not impossible that the author of the Tenures had had a hand in the Coventry Returna Brevium.

[4] For his career and his connexion with Coventry, see p. 78, note 4, *supra*, p. 179, *infra*.

[5] Coroner of Coventry in 1507-1508. For his career and that of his

bert,[1] Edward Coke.[2]   The three greatest of these each held
in turn the recordership, described in 1490 as ' oon of moost
honor and substance ' in the realm.[3]   Coventry's importance
as a legal centre thus almost rivals its importance as an in-
dustrial centre so well illustrated in the Leet Book[4] and in
the ' Discourse of the Common Weal',[5] one of the earliest discussions in English of economic theory.

But granting the truth of the above hypothesis as to the
origin of the manual and the ' Returna ', what was

(6)   *The subsequent history of the MS. volume?*[6]

Obviously the fact of its presence among the Augmentation
records along with chartularies of abbeys and cathedrals,
receivers' accounts of monasteries and inventories of monastic
and church goods, indicates that by the time of the dissolution
it had become the property of some ecclesiastical foundation.[7]

distinguished son, the judge, see p. 23, *supra*.   The compiling and printing of law-books at the end of the fifteenth and in the sixteenth centuries
are thus closely associated with Coventry.   For the marriage of John
Rastell's sister to Sir Thomas More and for the possibility of Thomas
Marowe's connexion with them, see *ibid.* and pp. 135, 140, *infra*.

[1] Recorder of Coventry, 1509–1512, p. 78, note 4, *supra*; for his career
and his relations to John Rastell, see pp. 23, 33–35, *supra*.

[2] Recorder of Coventry from *circa* 1585 (1613, Wambaugh, *op. cit.*,
xxvi) till his death in 1633 ; member of parliament for Coventry, 1623–
1624.   Although holding in succession the posts of attorney-general, and
of chief justice, first of the Common Pleas, and later of the King's Bench,
apparently he kept the Coventry recordership; Foss, *op. cit.*   He was
also recorder of Norwich, and for a time, of London.   It is interesting to
remember that Nicholas Statham came from Derbyshire, not far from
Coventry ; see *infra*, p. 177.

[3] In the king's letter to the mayor, aldermen, &c., asking that he be
informed in advance of the name of the candidate ; the result was the
appointment in 1493 of Richard Empson, Cov. Leet Bk., 537, 547.

[4] Full of details as to craft gilds, &c.

[5] First printed in 1581 ; ed. by Miss Lamond (1891), who has proved
that the scene was laid in Coventry in 1549; introduction, *passim*.

[6] One would expect to find it along with the Leet Book in the ' Comen
Cofur in the Midull Tour chaumbur of sent Mary halle', Coventry, together
with the ' dedes, munimentes, Skrowes, Charters' belonging to the corpora-
tion ; Cov. Leet Bk., 267.   Cf. also index under Council-house, S. Mary
Hall, especially 653.   For the importance of St. Mary Hall in the history
of law, see Wambaugh, *op. cit.*, xxvi–xxvii.

[7] See *supra*, p. 60, and notes 6 and 7.   In 1536, the year of the abolition of the smaller religious houses, a court of Augmentations was established to deal with their property (27 Hen. VIII, c. 27).   After the
surrender of the greater houses, this court was dissolved by Letters

One remembers the connexion of John Weston in 1431 with the monastery at Alcester,[1] near Arrow, the home of Thomas Burdet,[2] and so near the border of Worcestershire, that it was absorbed in 1465 by the monastery of Evesham.[3] But there is another clue perhaps better worth following up. On the folio [4] between the manual and the 'Returna', in a handwriting later than that of either, there is a list of thirteen names, against each of which a small sum is entered, the total recorded at the bottom: Sir John Dygby, Bartholomew and John Brokesby, Thomas Keble, Nicholas Fitzherbert, Robert and Simon Mallory, Thomas Coton, &c. As far as they have been identified they have to do with Leicestershire even more than with Warwickshire and belong to the reign of Henry VII.[5] Dygby was sheriff of the two counties in 1493[6], and Bartholomew Brokesby, a merchant of the Staple in 1505,[7] is perhaps a descendant of the Bartholomew Brokesby who was sheriff in 1419–20.[8] Keble, the serjeant-at-law who was not permitted to hold the coveted recordership,[9] came of a family long connected with Coventry,[10] and held considerable land in Leicestershire, including some at Kirby Bellars.[11] Curiously

Patent of 38 Hen. VIII and a new court of Augmentations created. This in turn was abolished in 1554 (1 Mary, st. 2, c. 10) and its business transferred to the Exchequer; Scargill Bird, Guide, 162–3, 192–3. It seems possible that a careful investigation of all the Annual Reports of the Deputy Keeper and of the reports of early commissions on the Public Records may include a specific reference to the MS. that will determine its provenance.

[1] *Supra*, p. 78, note 1. [2] *Supra*, p. 69.
[3] V.C.H., Warwick, ii. 60; suppressed by Hen. VIII, *ibid*.
[4] Folio 12, App. II. On the fly-leaf just preceding folio 1 is an almost undecipherable entry, apparently an indictment for a felony committed at Sutton Coldfield, Warwickshire, in the fourth regnal year, king not named; App. II.
[5] For references to their careers, see App. II, *infra*. It is worthy of note that several of them are closely connected as friends or relatives.
[6] App. II. [7] *Ibid*. [8] Lists and Indexes, no. ix.
[9] p. 78, note 4, *supra*. It is possible that the reference is to his nephew Thomas Keble; see will of the serjeant, cited *infra*, p. 179, note 3, p. 182, note 3.
[10] There are many references in Cov. Leet Bk. to John, Thomas, and Henry; index *sub nomine*. Henry was mayor in 1484; *ibid.*, 518. Cf. also Pardon Roll (Patent Roll, Supplementary), no. 55, m. 8.
[11] Kirkby upon Wrethek; Cal. Pat. Hen. VII, 1494–1509, 246. Thomas Botheway, another on the list, is a clerk holding land in Leicestershire, including some at 'Kyrkby Malory'; *ibid.* 259.

enough, there is a fourteenth-century MS. in Lincoln's Inn [1] which is said to have been given in 1437 to the priory of Kirby Bellars by the earlier Bartholomew Brokesby and which contains on the fly-leaf a copy of the writ of *dedimus potestatem* to the prior to receive the oath of the sheriff, Sir John Dygby.[2] The coincidence suggests the following theory: that John Weston at the time of his retirement from active work in about 1434 [3] gave to Bartholomew Brokesby (with whom he had been frequently associated [4]) the MS. volume containing the manual and the 'Returna', and that Brokesby within a few years, perhaps at the time of his other gift, gave it to the priory of Kirby Bellars;[5] that while the MS. was in the possession of the priory, the list of Leicestershire names was jotted down, possibly by a monk, and that at the dissolution in 1536,[6] the MS. was transferred to the Court of Augmentations.[7]

[1] Hale MSS. LXVIII (LXXIII).

[2] The oath is given; also a note to the effect that Dygby died in 1533.

[3] *Supra*, pp. 77–8.

[4] The sheriff of Warwick and Leicester and the recorder of Coventry must necessarily have had business relations. Bartholomew Brokesby, after being appointed with the mayor of Coventry and Thomas Burdet on a commission for a royal loan in Warwickshire in 1419, was on a similar commission with John Weston for Coventry in 1430 and 1431; Cal. Pat. Hen. V, 1416–1422, 251; Hen. VI, 1429–1436, 50, 126; Cov. Leet Bk., 122-5. Previously, they each had served on commissions against the Lollards, Weston in Worcestershire, Brokesby in Kent, and a William Brokesby in Leicestershire and Warwickshire; Cal. Pat. Hen. V., 1413–1416, 178. Another link is the fact that Joan, lady of Abergavenny, wife of William de Beauchamp (cf. p. 64, *supra*), sister of the late earl of Arundel and kinswoman of Henry V (Cal. Pat. Hen. V, 1416–1422, 238, 271, 305), was associated with Weston and Bartholomew Brokesby on the two Coventry commissions for royal loans, and made bequests to the latter and to a 'Wauter Kebell' (two of her executors), and also provided for five priests, of whom three were to sing in 'Kirkeby Belers'; Dugdale, Warwickshire, 1031-3. (This reference was brought to my notice by Miss Dormer Harris.) I have been unable to discover the relation of Walter to the Coventry family. In legal material it is sometimes difficult to decide whether 'Keble' refers to him or to Thomas; see p. 179, note 3, *infra*.

[5] For Kirby Bellars, see V.C.H., Leicester, i. 372; J. Nichols, History of Leicestershire, i. xcix, cxxxviii, cxl; A. Savine, English Monasteries on the Eve of the Dissolution, index; Dugdale, Monasticon, vi. 511-14. Dugdale states that a number of its records are in the Augmentation Office.

[6] Savine, *op. cit.*, 16. Since Kirby Bellars is included in the survey of 1535 (Savine, *passim*), Dugdale's statement (*loc. cit.*) that it was dissolved in 1534 must be an error.

[7] This explanation does not solve the mystery of the sums against the

Whatever the origin and the history of this early fifteenth-century Worcestershire manual, its significance in the history of law can be estimated only by an analysis of the writs and indictments and by a comparison with them of the similar forms in the printed ' Boke of Justyces of Peas ' of 1506 [1] and in the various MS. collections covering the intervening period. The analysis and comparison will also serve to establish an hypothesis for the origin of the writs and indictments in the ' Boke '.[2]

Analysis of Legal Content of the Manual.

The absence of orderly arrangement, either logical [3] or chronological,[4] except in a few instances,[5] suggests that the scribe had drawn a number of documents at random from a ' bag ' containing records of the peace [6] and had then chosen for transcription those that seemed important.[7] The presence of the four writs that do not concern the peace is not easily explained.[8] Two are on a case of replevin in the county court, *temp*. Henry IV—the prior of Worcester *v*. the bishop

---

names nor does it show how the other MS. came into the possession of Lincoln's Inn. It is presented merely as a working hypothesis in the hope that it may be either disproved or confirmed by investigations of other scholars. An entirely different explanation is suggested by what seems to me a marked likeness between the handwriting of these names and that of the facsimile reproduced in Cov. Leet Bk., 815, attributed by Miss Dormer Harris to a scribe of the B type, i.e. of the town clerkship of John Boteler, 1480-1507 ; introduction, xv. But Miss Dormer Harris, the final authority on Coventry MSS., does not agree.

[1] See ch. i, p. 11.

[2] *Ut supra*, p. 42. For the origin of the statutes and the Charge as found in the composite Boke, see ch. ii, *supra*.

[3] e.g. the writs on surety of the peace are not all grouped together ; nos. 58 and 76, dealing with the same special emergency, do not follow each other.

[4] e.g. nos. 80 and 81 belong to the reign of Hen. IV, nos. 34-9 to that of Hen. V.

[5] Sometimes a complete series of writs on a given case is given ; see e.g. *infra*, p. 87.

[6] Cf. an entry in Cov. Leet Bk., 132, during the mayoralty of Peynell in 1430 : ' And this said indentur abydithe in Tho. Peynell bag in saynt Mary halle '. The phrase is sometimes found in records of the justices of the peace ; e.g. ' per Bagam Custodum pacis ' ; L. W. Vernon Harcourt, ' The Baga de Secretis ', E.H.R. xxiii. 515 ; Assize Roll 752, m. 3 d.

[7] Under the supervision of the learned recorder, according to my hypothesis ; *supra*, pp. 78-9.

[8] For the possibility of a confusion of records later in the century, see *infra*, pp. 104, 106.

of Worcester [1]—and two are connected with the expedition of Henry V that resulted in the victory of Agincourt in October 1415.[2] From the remaining seventy-eight documents, however, a fairly complete account of legal process for justices of the peace may be obtained, as well as of the form in which their records were kept.

(1) Two headings are given as the 'Style of the Sessions', both of them in common use in Worcestershire and elsewhere: 'Session of the peace', and 'Pleas of the Crown',[3] before justices of the peace and justices for hearing and determining felonies and trespasses.[4] There are also writs to the sheriff to summon twenty-four 'liberos et legales homines magis sufficientes' from every hundred, and likewise all seneschalls, constables, and bailiffs,[5] that they may bring in their presentments and indictments.[6] There are six examples of bills of accusation to be inquired of by the jurors,[7] and three of presentments made in session, one of trespass, two of felonies[8]; also the familiar formula: 'Magna Inquisicio XII juratores . . . dicunt . . . omnia bene',[9] and a brief entry for the recording of fines.[10]

---

[1] Nos. 80 and 81.   [2] Nos. 58 and 76.   [3] Nos. 7 and 51.

[4] Slightly different wording in each instance.

[5] Nos. 78 and 68.   The latter contains also a writ for jurors in Lollard cases; see *infra*, pp. 87, 91.

[6] Lambard makes the following distinction: 'betweene the which two words (howsoeuer they be confounded, or not rightly distinguished, in common speech) me thinketh that there doth easily appeare a true and certaine difference. For I take a Presentment to be, a meere denunciation of the Iurors themselues, or of some other Officer . . . without any other information; and an Enditement to be, the Verdite of the Iurours, grounded vpon the accusation of a third person; so that a Presentment, is but a declaration of the Iurours (or Officers) without any bill offered before; and an Enditement is their finding of a bill of accusation to be true'; Eirenarcha, 458-9.

[7] Nos. 1-6, beginning 'Inquiratur pro rege', so common in the series known as Ancient Indictments (K.B. 9, Public Record Office). Since the first is headed 'Indictamentum', the original was probably 'billa vera', but we cannot tell whether the others were endorsed 'billa vera' or 'ignoramus'.   See Blackstone, Commentaries, 1803 ed., iv. 302-5.

[8] No. 7.   Note that twelve jurors are acting.   According to Blackstone, the number may vary from twelve to twenty-three; *ibid.* 301.   In proceedings before justices of labourers, the number summoned is twelve, eighteen, twenty, or twenty-four; Putnam, Statutes of Labourers, 66-7.

[9] No. 12.   Cf. Assize Roll 1034, ms. 1 and 2, for the phrase 'Magna Inquisicio' in proceedings before Worcestershire justices of the peace, *temp.* Rich. II, summoned into King's Bench.   I am inclined to suspect that the phrase is used when the King's Bench is expected in the county

(2) For securing the presence of those indicted of felonies the usual writs are given : *capias*,[11] *capias alias* (with *seisire facias . . . bona et catalla terras et tenementa*),[12] *exigi facias* [13] ; also *habeas corpus* for fugitives into other counties.[14] This last writ is based on a statute of 5 Edward III [15] enacted before the 'keepers' of the peace had received judicial powers and a little later incorporated into their commission.[16] For those indicted of trespass, there is the writ of *venire facias* [17] and also several references to attachment,[18] but no clear example of the possible stages before the exigend,[19] except in the case of trespass against the labour laws. For this latter, there is an *attachies per corpus* [20] or *pone per vadium et saluos plegios*,[21] with a memorandum that the exigend is to follow the first *capias* if necessary.[22]

(3) Mainprise [23] is illustrated by several documents ; one

or in a neighbouring county and when the justices are therefore trying to do a thorough job. Cf. my art. on 'Ancient Indictments', E.H.R. xxix. 501 ; Anc. Ind., K.B. 9, 213, m. 5 ; Gaol Delivery Rolls $\frac{43}{1}$, m. 16.

[10] No. 44.   [11] No. 8.

[12] No. 9 (cf. also no. 11), equivalent to a *distringas*, I suppose. Marowe refuses to allow the second *capias*; App. III, p. 395, *infra* ; cf. Lambard, *op. cit.*, 497–8.

[13] No. 10. Cf. also no. 21 for the sheriff's returns.   [14] Nos. 55, 64.

[15] c. 11, 1331 ; Lambard, *op. cit.*, 498.   [16] p. 193, *infra*.

[17] No. 8. 'The proper process on an indictment for any petit misdemesnor, or on a penal statute, is a writ of *venire facias*, which is in the nature of a summons to cause the party to appear' ; Blackstone, *op. cit.*, iv. 318.   [18] Nos. 51 and 52.

[19] Lambard states that if the 'offendors may not be found, nor brought in by Attachment or Distresse, (by reason of their insufficiencie) the process of Vtlawrie is to be awarded', and then specifies the sequence as follows : 'And a *Venire facias* first, and then (if thereupon he be returned sufficient) a *distringas*, and so the same Processe infinite till he come in ; but if a *Nihil habet*, etc. bee at the first returned against him, then a *Capias alias* and *pluries*, and after an *Exigent . . .* is the very ordinarie Processe . . .'; *op. cit.*, 493.   [20] Nos. 60, 71, 75, 82.

[21] No. 82. Cf. Blackstone, *op. cit.*, iii. 280, for the writ of attachment or *pone*, as the first step after the summons in a civil suit.

[22] No. 60, quoting 25 Edw. III, [st. 2], c. 7 (5 in Statutes of the Realm). The process is thus shortened to that used in felonies. There is also a writ for a servant fleeing into another county, no. 61, based on 25 Edw. III, st. 2, c. 7, and on 2 Hen. V, st. 1, c. 4.

[23] The term 'ballium' does not appear in the manual. 'But Bailement and Mainprise haue beene taken to differ in the practise of our common law : for he which is properly Bailed by the Justices of any Court, hath bin neuerthelesse reputed to be a prisoner there still, and his suerties to be (as it were) his speciall gardeins ; otherwise it hath beene thought of him that is let to Mainprise, as may bee seene by the Booke cases'; Lambard, *op. cit.*, 332. Cf. also an example of the phrase 'in ballium'; *ibid.* 342

relates to trespass and merely states that sufficient surety has been found,[1] and the others relate to felony. Three of the latter record that four 'manucaptores' bind themselves to produce the indicted on the appointed day.[2] It is noteworthy that in several instances mainprise is recorded before a single justice of the peace,[3] a procedure not permitted toward the end of the century.[4]

(4) Of the eleven writs connected with outlawry,[5] now become merely the final process of compelling appearance in court,[6] the majority are for indictments of felony,[7] but there is one clear case of trespass.[8] The series is fairly complete ; various writs of *exigi facias*, including exaction for the fifth time and proclamation of outlawry in the presence of coroners,[9] also writs of *exigi facias de novo*,[10] *allocatur exigent*[11] and *supersedeas*.[12]

The *locus classicus* for the subject is of course Coke's Treatise of Bail and Mainprize (ed. W. Hawkins, in Three Law Tracts, 1764) ; also 4th Institute, 1644, ed., 179 : ' Every bail is mainprise, ... but every mainprise is not a bail '. Cf. also Blackstone, iii. 127–8 : ' Mainpernors differ from bail, in that a man's bail may imprison or surrender him before the stipulated day of appearance ; mainpernors can do neither, but are barely sureties for his appearance at the day ; bail are only sureties, that the party be answerable for the special matter for which they stipulate ; mainpernors are bound to produce him to answer all charges whatsoever.'

[1] No. 79, perhaps bail.
[2] Nos. 40, 41, 42. Cf. also no. 28, in which mainprise stops the process of outlawry. Lambard holds that from the time justices of the peace became ' complete Iudges ', i.e. by the statute of 34 (35) Edw. III, c. 1, they could bail persons indicted in their sessions, *op. cit.*, 333.
[3] Nos. 28 and 42 ; cf. no. 79.   [4] See Statute, 3 Hen. VII, c. 3, 1487.
[5] Nos. 10, 21–9, 31.
[6] Pollock and Maitland, History of English Law, 2nd ed., i. 476.
[7] Nos. 10, 21, 23, 25–8.
[8] No. 31. In three, nos. 22, 24, 29, the nature of the offence is not stated.
[9] Nos. 21 and 22. Note the possible differences in methods of computation ; Pollock and Maitland, *op. cit.*, ii. 581 ; C. Gross, Coroners' Rolls, Selden Soc., xli.
[10] Nos. 24 and 26. ' If there be the least interruption, the whole is void, and an exigi facias de novo must be awarded and issued ' ; J. Chitty, Criminal Law, 1826 ed., i. 352–3.
[11] Nos. 25 and 27. ' But if there be not five county court days between the delivery of the writ to the sheriff and the return day, and he has called the defendant twice or oftener, without his appearing, then upon this being returned to the exigent, an allocatur exigent is issued, allowing the former exaction, and requiring the sheriff to proceed and complete the requisite number ' ; Chitty, *op. cit.*, i. 353.
[12] Nos. 28 and 29 ; in the first the defendant is mainprised ; no. 31, the defendant ' fecit finem '.

(5) There are also several examples of actions that reach the stage of a jury trial.[1] In one case of felony [2] and also in one case on the statutes of Labourers,[3] the scribe has not only copied the original writs to the sheriff bidding him procure 'XII iuratores liberos et legales homines', *venire facias*,[4] *habeas corpora iuratorum*,[5] and *distringas*,[6] but has also copied the enrolment of the whole process. The fact that the qualification of the jurors is wrongly stated as 100s. a year [7] instead of the statutory 40s.[8] is perhaps a clerical error, due to the confusion caused by the provision of 100s. as the qualification for the juries of presentment in cases on the recent statute against Lollards.[9]

(6) The examples of royal pardons and the accompanying writs *de non molestando* have already been referred to in connexion with two *causes célèbres* of the reign of Henry V.[10] In the Milward murder case,[11] it is to be noted that the defendant is not *sine die* until after proclamation made by the justices of the peace in open session has given an opportunity for further actions against him.

(7) The next document is the release by proclamation of a man arrested on suspicion of felony.[12] If it is correct to infer that the 'justices' mentioned are justices of the peace delivering a gaol, they are exercising an authority which had apparently been allowed them in the reign of Edward III,[13] but which was later denied them.[14]

---

[1] Nos. 14, 15, 16 (with 19 and 20), 30, 47 (with 48, 49, 50), 51, 52, 53.
[2] No. 16.   [3] No. 47.   [4] No. 48.   [5] No. 49.
[6] Nos. 19, 20, and 50. Blackstone, iii. 353, states that in the Common Pleas the writ is called *habeas corpora juratorum* and in the King's Bench a *distringas*, but nos. 49 and 50 imply that the two writs represent successive stages.
[7] Nos. 20 and 48.   [8] 2 Hen. V, st. 2, c. 3 ; Blackstone, iii. 362.
[9] 2 Hen. V, st. 1, c. 7 ; cf. no. 68.
[10] *Supra*, pp. 71, 73.   [11] No. 17.   [12] No. 18.
[13] Cf. e.g. Gaol Delivery Roll 139, m. 5 d ; Gaol Delivery before justices of the peace, 30 Edw. III ; *ibid.* 197, m. 6 ; Gaol Delivery at Worcester before justices of the peace, Huls and Weston, 2 Hen. V : 'capti per suspeccionem latrocinii secundum statutum Wintonie . . . testatum est hic in curia quod sunt bone fame ; ideo deliberantur'. See p. 205, and notes 4, 5, and 6.
[14] In July 1455 (33 Hen. VI) the king refused a request of the commons that justices of the peace should be authorized to deliver by proclamation prisoners arrested by sheriffs on suspicion of felony ; Rot. Parl. v. 332

(8) There is one reference to a regular Gaol Delivery before chief justice Hankford and his colleagues, namely, in the sheriff's writ to a bailiff[1] summoning 'XXIIII probos[2] et legales homines' and all the local officials. There are also cases where the justices of the peace are evidently delivering the gaol of prisoners previously indicted in quarter sessions.[3] The problem of the relation of the justices of the peace to Gaol Delivery during the fourteenth and early fifteenth centuries cannot be solved in the present state of our knowledge. It is complicated by the conflicting evidence presented by statutes, forms of commissions, and actual Gaol Delivery records.[4] But it is at least an undeniable fact that the Wor-

(see p. 197, note 4, for the rest of this petition which has to do with bail). Cf. Lambard, *op cit.*, 518: 'No Justices of the Peace haue authority to deliuer Felons by proclamation, or without sufficient acquitall : nor yet to deliuer such as be in prison for suspition of felony'; Marowe, App. III, p. 404, Coke, 4th Institute, 1644 ed., 168, 177.

[1] No. 59.　　　　　　　　　　　　　　[2] Cf. 'liberos', *supra*, p. 87.

[3] Nos. 16 and 32; proved by the discovery of the actual Gaol Delivery material; see App. II and notes on these cases. Probably also nos. 14, 15, and 17; cf. nos. 55 and 64.

[4] The following brief outline will at least show the problems that need investigation.

By statute 4 Edw. III, c. 2, 1330, keepers of the peace were to deliver their indictments to the justices of Gaol Delivery. With increased powers of hearing and determining felonies under the statutes of 18 Edw. III, st. 2, c. 2, 1344, and of 35 Edw. III, c. 1, 1361, the 'keepers', now become 'justices', were often delivering gaols of prisoners indicted before themselves, as is clearly shown by the Gaol Delivery Rolls from 24–37 Edw. III. Then follows an interesting episode of legislation through changes in the form of the commission. In spite of a petition in parliament (Rot. Parl. ii. 286), the commissions from 38–41 Edw. III (cf. e. g. Pat. 38 Edw. III, pt. 1, m. 43 d) command the justices of the peace to deliver their indictments to the justices of Gaol Delivery. It is interesting to find a reference to an 'ordinance' to this effect 'made with the advice of the council'; Rot. Claus. 40 Edw. III, m. 14 d. In the commission of 42 Edw. III (Pat., pt. 2, m. 29 d), the powers of hearing and determining felonies are again conferred on the justices of the peace; but are somewhat restricted in the reigns of Rich. II and of Hen. V; see ch. vi (4), *infra*. The Gaol Delivery Rolls for this period show both systems in use: justices of the peace were sometimes delivering gaols of their own prisoners and were sometimes sending their indictments to justices of Gaol Delivery. A preliminary study has failed to reveal that they were paying strict heed to the changes in the commissions just described or to the statute of 17 Rich. II, c. 10, that 'where Need shall be, Two Men of Law' resident in each county shall be on every commission of the peace and that they shall deliver gaols,—itself an apparent contradiction of the statute of 8 Rich. II, c. 2, forbidding a man of law to be justice 'of the common Deliverance of Gaols in his own county'.

cestershire justices of the peace delivered the gaol of Worcester castle four times during the reign of Henry V.[1]

(9) The relation of the court of King's Bench to the justices of the peace, a subject on which further investigation will undoubtedly throw new light,[2] is illustrated by two writs of *certiorari* and the returns thereto.[3] One demands the indictments made in quarter sessions against a man who had meanwhile been appealed of the same crime in the court of King's Bench[4]; the other has been already mentioned, as it deals with the case of the Burdets.[5] It is interesting to note that although the writ erroneously describes Thomas Burdet as 'of

---

[1] In the following calendar it is to be noted that Gaol Delivery material is missing for the fifth and eight regnal years.

Gaol Delivery at Worcester Castle.

Wednesday, 26 July 1413, 1 Hen. V. Justices of Gaol Delivery, Huls and Horton. Gaol Delivery Roll 197 m. 5.

Thursday, 1 March 1414, 1 Hen. V. Justices of the peace, Huls &c. *Ibid.*

Thursday, 2 August 1414, 2 Hen. V. Justices of Gaol Delivery, Huls, Horton, Heuster. *Ibid.* m. 5 d.

Monday, 4 March 1415, 2 Hen. V. Justices of Gaol Delivery, Huls and Heuster. G.D.R. 218.

Monday, 4 March 1415, 2 Hen. V. Justices of the peace, Huls and Weston. G.D.R. 197, m. 6.

Thursday, 5 March 1416, 3 Hen. V. Justices of the peace, Horton, Preston, Weston. *Ibid.* m. 6 d.

Thursday, 4 March 1417, 4 Hen. V. Justices of Gaol Delivery, Horton and Preston. *Ibid.* m. 7.

? March 1418, 5 Hen. V. Justices of the peace, Weston, Throgmerton, Brace. No. 32, Worcestershire Manual.

Monday, 26 September 1418, 6 Hen. V. Justices of Gaol Delivery, Hankford, Mille, Harwell. G.D.R. $\frac{73}{2}$. (Cf. no. 59, Worcestershire Manual.)

Thursday, 8 June 1419, 7 Hen. V. Justices of Gaol Delivery, Horton, Preston, and Weston. G.D.R. $\frac{73}{3}$.

Friday, 26 September 1421, 9 Hen. V. Justices of Gaol Delivery, Juyn and Heuster. G.D.R. 197, m. 8.

Wednesday, 9 September 1422, 10 Hen. V. Justices of Gaol Delivery, Cheyne, Juyn, and Heuster. *Ibid.* m. 8 d.

[2] Cf. my art. on 'Ancient Indictments', E.H.R. xxix. 479–505, and Mr. Flower's sharp criticism of my suggestion in his introduction to Public Works, vol. i, xvi–xviii (Selden Society, vol. xxxii). During the serious trouble with Lollards, the court of King's Bench sat at Leicester, Lichfield, and Shrewsbury (Coram Rege Rolls 612 and 613), but never at Worcester during the reign of Henry V. This fact probably explains the comparative paucity of Worcestershire quarter session material amongst Ancient Indictments and on the Coram Rege Rolls.

[3] Nos. 34–6, 37–9. No. 34, though entitled a writ of *certiorari*, is the form which one would like to describe as a writ of *terminari*.

[4] Nos. 37–9.   [5] *Supra*, pp. 68–72.

Worcestershire',[1] the clerk of the peace while denying the existence of any proceedings against such a person, nevertheless returns the indictments against Thomas Burdet of Arrow, Warwickshire,[2] thus himself making the correct ' addition '.[3]

(10) There are numerous illustrations of the procedure used in the binding over of men to keep the peace, in half of the instances before a single justice.[4] Various details are given ; the amount of the recognizances,[5] the number of mainpernors,[6] the part played by the sheriff,[7] bailiffs,[8] and gaoler.[9] The heading is usually: *securitas pacis* [10]—surety of peace—and the context always indicates that the defendant has threatened the plaintiff with bodily harm. The evidence from the manual, therefore, shows the justices of the peace acting under the authority conferred upon them by commission [11] and not taking surety ' of good-abearing ' under the statute of 35 Edward III.[12]

(11) The offences specifically mentioned help to settle several important controversies on the powers of the justices of the peace, the discussion of which will be found below.[13] The felonies include murder,[14] theft,[15] burglary,[16] rape,[17] witchcraft,[18]

[1] No. 34.   [2] No. 36.
[3] It is to be noted that the scribe does not select the writ in which a severe rebuke is administered to the Worcestershire justices of the peace ; Anc. Indictments, K.B. 9, 213, m. 5.
[4] Nos. 5, 46, 54, 57, 62, by a single justice; nos. 13, 45, 63, 70, and 77 by more than one justice.
[5] For the defendant, £100, nos. 13 and 54; £40, no. 46; £20, no. 57; for the mainpernors, £10, no. 57; £20, no. 46; £200, no. 54.
[6] Four; nos. 46, 54, and 57.
[7] Nos. 57, 62, 70.   [8] Nos. 57, 63, 77.   [9] No. 77.
[10] In five instances, nos. 13, 45, 54, 70; by implication, no. 46. In one case the reference in the heading is to ' Securitatem de se bene gerendo ' but in the document to ' securitate pacis ', no. 57 ; in two cases the heading is ' warantum de pees ', no. 62, and by implication, no. 63. One document without a heading mentions a threat to life and limb, no. 77. Cf. also no. 5.
[11] Cf. e.g. Pat. 5 Hen. V, m. 26 d : ' et ad omnes illos qui aliquibus de populo nostro de corporibus suis vel de incendio domorum suarum minas fecerint, ad sufficientem securitatem de pace et bono gestu suo erga nos et populum nostrum inueniendam....'.
[12] c. 1. For a discussion of this whole subject, see ch. vi (4), *infra*
[13] Ch. vi (4).
[14] Nos. 17, 32; ' insidiis ' included in the first, ' conuenticulis ' in the second.   [15] Or to use the later term, grand larceny ; nos. 7, 16.
[16] No. 14.   [17] No. 15.
[18] No. 6. Cf. Anc. Indict., K. B. 9, 72, ms. 2, 3, 6, 19 Hen. VI, for the

'the discovering of the counsel of the king' by jurors,[1] and examples of the law on accessories.[2] The trespasses include rescue,[3] breaking of arrest,[4] breaking of a close and carrying off cattle,[5] and regrating.[6]

(12) There are also actions on the statute against Lollards,[7] on the statute of Northampton,[8] and a surprisingly large number on the statutes of Labourers, sixteen out of the seventy-eight documents, that is, over a fifth. Nine of the sixteen deal with the contract clause of the ordinance of 1349, either departure or retention or both,[9] and six with the compulsory service clause [10] (in one instance combined with the clause of the statute of 1351, commanding the 'usual terms' of service).[11] But there is no mention of either of the famous statutes of Richard II.[12] Except for this one reference to 'usual terms' and for two to the re-enactment under Henry V of the

---

accusation against Roger Bolingbroke and Eleanor Cobham, duchess of Gloucester, of making waxen images of the king. The result is well known; C. Oman, Political History of England, 1377-1485, 332-3. Cf. also History of Witchcraft in England, by Wallace Notestein, especially 1-10.

[1] Nos. 1, 2. There was some doubt as to whether it was felony or treason; 27 Lib. Ass., no. 63; Crompton, Loffice, f. 18. Later it was held to be 'fineable onely'; Lambard, *op. cit.*, 385. Coke, 3rd Institute, 1644 ed., 164, calls the offence perjury. For the history of the oath not to reveal the king's counsel, see 'Antiquities of the King's Council', by J. F. Baldwin, E.H.R. xxi. 1-8. For perjury of jurors see Pollock and Maitland, *op. cit.*, ii. 542; Holdsworth, *op. cit.*, i. 161.

[2] Nos. 14, 15.   [3] Nos. 4, 7.   [4] No. 5.   [5] No. 51.

[6] No. 52. For the inclusion in the commission of jurisdiction over forestalling, regrating, &c., cf. e.g. Pat. 5 Hen. V, m. 26 d.

[7] No. 3 refers to the statute against Lollards passed at the parliament of Leicester, 2 Hen. V, st. 1, c. 7; 30 April 1414. The powers granted to the justices of the peace to enforce this statute appear henceforth in their commissions; cf. e.g. Pat. 2 Hen. V, pt. 2, m. 32; 28 July. No. 68 specifically mentions justices of the peace, but no. 6 may possibly come under the special commissions issued for a number of counties on 11 January 1414 to deal with the Lollard rising in the Midlands; that for Worcester included John Brace, John Throgmerton, and John Weston; Cal. Pat. Hen. V, 1413-1416, 177-8. For proceedings, see Anc. Indict., K.B. 9, 204, 205, 206, 209, and cf. my art. in E.H.R. xxix. 491. For an account of Sir John Oldcastle, see W. T. Waugh, E.H.R. xx. 434-56, 637-58.

[8] No. 65. The statute of Northampton was always included in the commission of the peace.

[9] Nos. 47-50 (one series), 53, 60, 61, 67, 82.

[10] Nos. 56, 69, 71, 72, 74, 75; a larger proportion than was to be expected; cf. Putnam, Statutes of Labourers, 73-4, 175-7.

[11] No. 75. No. 73 refers to both ordinance and statute.

[12] 12 Rich. II, cc. 3-5, statute of Cambridge; 13 Rich. II, st. 1, c. 8.

clause on labourers fleeing into other counties,[1] the documents all relate to those two clauses of the ordinance of 1349, which in the fourteenth century had rarely been enforced by justices of labourers or of the peace.[2] Nor is there a single case covering the receipt of 'excess' wages, the most frequent offence dealt with previously in the local courts[3] in sharp contrast to the overwhelming proportion of actions on the contract clause brought in the two upper courts.[4] The above analysis tends to confirm the view of the importance of the ordinance as compared with the later acts.[5] It also affords ample evidence that in these early decades of the fifteenth century the justices of the peace were giving considerable attention to the enforcement of the labour laws,[6] perhaps as a result of the statute of Leicester in 1414 whereby the sheriffs were to proclaim them in the county courts and to send copies to those justices of the peace who were of the quorum.[7]

Since the manual is obviously intended to serve as a guide for legal procedure, it is not strange that it contains only a few illustrations of the administrative functions of the justices, namely:

(13) The proclamation of the statute of Northampton,[8] the removal of a high constable and the swearing-in of his successor.[9] There are no references to the justices' duties in connexion with the seals for the 'Letters Patent' to be provided[10] under the statute of 1388 for migrating labourers, or to the justices' new powers of assessing wages under the statute of 1390;[11] yet we know from other evidence that earlier Worcestershire justices had received the 'seals' from the

---

[1] Nos. 61, 67.
[2] At least during the decade 1349–59; Putnam, *op. cit.*, 73–7; Mediaeval Archives of the University of Oxford, ii, introduction to 'Courts held under the Statutes of Labourers', xi.
[3] Putnam, *op. cit.*, 77.   [4] *Ibid.* 175–7.   [5] *Ibid.* 179.
[6] For the period after 1359, certainly up to 1485, there is abundant material in the Public Record Office; see Introduction, *supra*. I have already examined it sufficiently to feel sure that the attempts at enforcement continued to be far more energetic than has usually been supposed; cf. e.g. p. 325 of the article by Mr. Tawney quoted *infra*, p. 93, note 2. The huge Oxford roll described *supra*, pp. 2–3, deals exclusively with labour laws.
[7] 2 Hen. V, st. 1, c. 4.   [8] No. 65.   [9] No. 66.
[10] 12 Rich. II, c. 3; like the 'testimonials' of 5 Eliz., c. 4, and the 'certificates' of 8 & 9 Will. III, c. 30.   [11] 13 Rich. II, st. 1, c. 8.

sheriff,[1] and that one of the commission, *temp.* Henry V, John Weston, as an *ex officio* justice of the peace in Coventry, had probably helped to draw up the earliest known assessment under the Act, proclaimed in 1420.[2]

In conclusion, it is clear that although the manual fails to give a satisfactory account of the administrative duties of the justices or an absolutely complete list of the crimes and trespasses within their jurisdiction,[3] yet for judicial procedure it does contain almost everything that justices of the quorum and the clerk of the peace ought to know.[4] Moreover, the exclusion from the compilation of extraneous matter [5] means that the documents form an exceedingly useful precedent or formula book, easily handled, and therefore accessible for practical purposes. But in the absence of any legal analysis or historical discussion of the powers of the justices, it cannot in any sense be called a treatise on the peace.[6]

[1] Many such seals are still preserved in Foreign Accounts, 25, Exchequer, L.T.R.; cf. m. 41 : 'sigilla regis de auricalco facta et et fabricata pro quolibet hundredo [etc.].' In 1391-1392 seventeen seals were made under the instructions of the sheriff, at a cost of 8*d.* each, for the hundreds, cities, and boroughs of Worcestershire and deposited with the justices of the peace; *ibid.* m. 44.

[2] Cov. Leet Bk., 21 : 'Item, at the same lete [1420] was ordenyd by the Justices of peas, with thassent of the same lete, what artyficers and laborers shuld take from Michaelmas vnto Estur aftur the furm of the Statute, ut sequitur.' There follow rates of wages by the day for masons, carpenters, &c. According to the well-known theory of Miss McArthur (E.H.R. ix. 310-14, 554; xiii. 299-302; *supra,* p. 36, note 1), at this date there was no statutory maximum rate, a theory not accepted by Mr. R. H. Tawney in his valuable article on the 'Assessment of Wages'; Vierteljahrschrift für Sozial- und Wirthschaftsgeschichte, Band xi, Heft 3, 318, 324. The evidence of the Leet Book, however, confirms the truth of Miss McArthur's view. Since there are no statutory rates in st. 12 Rich. II except by the year for agricultural labourers, with a vague clause as to 'servants of artificers and victuallers', the latest rates by the day for masons, carpenters, &c., would probably be those of 25 Edw. III, st. 2, cc. 3-4; and they are distinctly lower than those of the Coventry assessment. See pp. xiii-xiv of introduction to the Oxford roll cited *supra,* p. 92, note 6.

[3] Among the felonies, robbery as distinct from theft is not included, and from offences against statutes the most striking omissions are of the statutes of Livery.

[4] Assuming that appeals are not properly within their jurisdiction; see pp. 200-203, *infra.*

[5] It is to be remembered that only four out of the eighty-two precedents do not concern justices of the peace; *supra,* pp. 83-4.

[6] For an account of the 'distinct class of records' known as 'Precedent Books or Registers', cf. Holdsworth, *op. cit.,* ii. 177.

II. A Comparison with the 1422 (?) Manual of the Writs and Indictments in the 1506 (?) 'Boke of Justyces of Peas' and in Manuscript Collections of the Intervening Period.

Part II of the printed 'Boke'[1] contains writs and indictments that constitute a precedent or formula book of the same general type as the Worcestershire manual, but, unlike the latter, divided into two distinct sections: first, seventy-five writs, mainly connected with process; second, ninety-two forms of indictments of felony and trespass, &c.[2] A comparison of the first section with the manual yields interesting results.[3]

(1) The 'Style of the Sessions', instead of coming after the forms of indictments, is the first entry: 'Placita coram A. B. et sociis suis custodibus pacis ... ac justiciariis ... in comitatu M. apud W. ...'. It differs a little from the Worcestershire form, but contains the same clumsy phrase to describe the judicial powers of the justices.[4] Then follows the writ to the sheriff to summon twenty-four jurors and the local officials, so phrased as to suggest that the session was to deal especially with trespasses against the statutes of Labourers;[5] but there are other writs later in the collection that summon jurors to what seems to be a general session.[6]

(2) For securing the presence of parties, the sequence for trespass is more fully given: *venire facias, distringas, capias, capias alias, capias pluries, exigi facias*.[7] But in the case of offences against the statutes of Labourers and in the case of felony, the series are identical with the Worcestershire writs.[8] For some strange reason, however, the writ on felons fleeing into other counties and a memorandum as to a similar writ for fugitive labourers, instead of being included with the other

[1] See ch. i, *supra*, p. 42, and ch. ii, for the origin of Part I, containing the statutes and the Charge.
[2] In the 1510 edition, which has been shown to follow very closely that of 1506; ch. i, pp. 9, 19, *supra*.
[3] I keep to the classification used in the analysis of the manual, *supra*. Since there is no foliation in this edition until the Indictments, I can refer merely to signatures.
[4] Sig. B iiii.   [5] Cf. also sig. E i.   [6] Sig D iiii.
[7] Sig. C i–C ii.   [8] Sig. C ii–C iii.

writs, appear out of place in Part I of the 'Boke' just before the Charge to the jurors.[1]

(3) There are a few examples of mainprise, including writs of *supersedeas*,[2] and, in contrast to the manual, one clear instance of bail.[3]

(4) The process of outlawry, although illustrated by many documents,[4] is less complete because of the omission of the writ of *allocatur exigent*.[5]

(5) Except for one writ to jurors bidding them return their verdict at a given date,[6] there are no illustrations of jury trial, nor (6) of acquittal by royal pardons, nor (7) of the release by proclamation of a man arrested on suspicion of felony.[7] There are, however, several writs issued by a single justice of the peace, ordering constables to produce before him such a 'suspect'[8] or keepers of a gaol to receive him and guard him until the next Gaol Delivery.[9]

(8) Curiously enough, in spite of a number of writs connected with gaols, there is only one having to do with Gaol Delivery, which for some inexplicable reason appears in Part I of the 'Boke' along with the writs on fugitives into other counties.[10]

(9) A *supersedeas* for a writ of *certiorari*[11] is the only illustration of the relation of the court of King's Bench to the justices of the peace, in contrast to the fuller treatment in the manual.

(10) On the other hand, there is a very great increase in the writs on the binding over of men to keep the peace, often under the heading of 'warantum pro pace'[12]—in fact, about a fifth of the documents deal with this subject.[13] The familiar details are given—the amount of the recognizance, the number of mainpernors, &c.—the context almost always showing that

---

[1] Sig. A iii–A iiii. The memorandum follows very closely the form in the manual. [2] Sig. C iii, D iii, E iii.
[3] Sig. C vi; 'Traditur in ballium', but the marginal heading is 'Mainpris'. [4] Sig. C i, C ii, C iii, E iii. [5] *Supra*, p. 86.
[6] Sig. E ii. [7] *Supra*, p. 87. [8] Sig. C viii.
[9] Sig. D ii, E i. See p. 197, *infra*. [11] Sig. E ii.
[10] Sig. A iiii.
[12] Sig. C iii–C iv, C v, C vi, C vii, D i, D ii, D iii, D iiii, E ii, E iii, E iiii.
[13] As compared with ten in the manual, representing about an eighth of the total number, p. 90, note 4.

there had been threats of bodily harm.[1] But there is also one undeniable example of a writ for 'good-abearing' under the statute of 35 Edw. III,[2] not found at all in the manual.

(11) A study of the list of felonies and trespasses referred to in the 'Boke' can be made only by an examination of the second group of documents and will be dealt with below.

(12) Offences against several statutes are specifically included in the writs, notably the statute of Forcible Entries[3] and the statutes of Labourers.[4] The proportion of writs on the latter is just about as great as in the manual; they likewise prove to be almost all on the two familiar clauses of the ordinance of 1349, and not on the later enactments.[5]

(13) The examples of the administrative functions of the justices are the same as in the manual, namely, the proclamation of the statute of Northampton[6] and the removal of a high constable and the swearing-in of his successor.[7]

As in the Worcestershire manual, almost all the writs concern the justices of the peace and are given with a similar disregard of order. Likewise, if one neglects the forms of indictments and list of felonies and trespasses, the resemblance between the contents of the two collections is very close. The historical significance of the Worcestershire collection is thus clear: it affords definite evidence that legal procedure before the justices of the peace had become fixed very early, and that it had undergone little change in the course of a century. In the matter of localization, however, a distinction between the two formula books appears; the printed writs, unlike the manuscript ones, deal with a number of counties, especially with Middlesex, Essex, and Suffolk[8]—the last most frequently—and in contrast with the geographical accuracy of the manual, include the strange error of placing Coventry in Suffolk.[9] The dates when given are 20 or 21 Henry VII,

---

[1] See *supra*, p. 90.
[2] Sig. D iii. The writ is dated 1 March, 21 Hen. VII; cf. ch. vi (4), *infra*.　　　　　　　　　　　[3] Sig. E i-E ii.
[4] Sig. C iiii, C v, C vii, C viii, D i, D iii.
[5] There is, however, one writ on the summer and winter clause of the statute of 1351; sig. C iiii.　　　[6] Sig. E ii.　　　　　[7] Sig. E i.
[8] The other counties specified are: Warwickshire, sig. E ii; Norfolk, *ibid.*; Gloucestershire, sig. D ii; Notts., *ibid.*　　　[9] Sig. E i.

12 July 1506 being the latest mentioned.[1] The writs are
signed by various justices of the peace,[2] most often by
Robertus Sampson [3] of Suffolk and Essex; but thus far it has
proved impossible to identify any of the justices [4] or any of
the actual cases even when specific details are given, such as
a reference to 'auditor generalis Ludowici H. militis domini
DB . . .' [5] The general conclusion, therefore, is that the collection is by no means identical with the Worcestershire manual;
but that it is very similar to it and was undoubtedly planned
for the same practical purpose, and probably compiled by
a clerk of the peace or by a 'working' justice.

An examination of the second group of documents in the
'Boke' shows that they are grouped under seven headings:

(1) Indictamenta de alta proditione	4	f. i–f. iii.
(2) Indictamentum (*sic*) de parua proditione	3	f. iii b.
(3) Indictamentum (*sic*) feloniarum	25	f. iii b–f. viii.
(4) Appella	13	f. viii–f. x b.
Sacramentum probatoris in duello	1	f. x b.
Proclamatio pro rege in duello	1	f. x b–f. xi.
(5) Indictamenta transgressionis contra formam diuersorum statutorum	24	f. xi–f. xix b.
(6) Indictamenta transgressionis contra pacem et ad dampnum partis	15	f. xix b–f. xxiii.
(7) Presentatio nocumentorum, etc.	6	f. xxiii b–f. xxiiii b.
	92	

---

[1] Sig. E i. But the 1506 (?) Pynson edition contains a writ of 13 July;
see p. 19, *supra*.

[2] Indicated merely by initials, sometimes 'T. M.' of Warwickshire, e.g.
sig. E ii.   [3] *Passim*; very often 'R. S.' simply.

[4] The calendars of Patent Rolls have been searched for the fourteenth,
fifteenth, and early sixteenth centuries. A certain Robert 'Saunson',
clerk, is mentioned as promoter of causes in 1494; S. Bentley, Excerpta
Historica, 99. On 17 April 1497 he was appointed a clerk of the Privy
Seal; Cal. Pat. Hen. VII, 1494–1509, 112. He signed warrants for the
Great Seal in November 19 Hen. VII; Series II, File 252 (this file contains Marowe's name as serjeant-at-law). F. Blomefield, Norfolk, refers
to a Robert Sampson in Norfolk and in Suffolk at a little earlier date;
iv. 132, x. 130–2. Cf. also a reference to 'Mr. Robert Sampson', clerk of
the council of requests under Henry VII; 'The Council under the
Tudors', by A. F. Pollard, E.H.R. xxxvii. 345.

[5] Sig. D ii. In most instances the real names appear in cases of surety

H

That this second group of forms in the 'Boke' had a different origin from the first group is proved by the following evidence:

(1) In the early editions of the 'Boke', beginning with the Pynson of 1506 (?) and going through the Rastell of 1530 (?),[1] although the signatures are continuous throughout, there is no paging for statutes, Charge, or writs of process; folio 1 begins either at the *Tabula* just preceding the indictments or at *Indictamenta de alta proditione*.[2] The early Redman editions and that of William Rastell use continuous paging as well as continuous signatures for both parts, while Berthelet in 1536 introduces the fashion of a break immediately after the Charge, and uses new signatures as well as new paging for all of Part II—a fashion adopted by Redman in 1538 (?) and by the small group of his exact followers. Berthelet, however, in 1539 reverts to the earlier Redman method, so that the continuous paging and the continuous signatures of the many later editions of the 'Boke' have obscured the fact of the original break.

(2) There are some striking differences of date and of localization between the writs of Part I and the forms of Part II. The latter are confined to no locality; they usually contain only initials of the officials and parties and no dates; but of those that are dated, many belong to the reigns of Henry VI and Edward IV and concern peculiarly interesting actual cases.[3] A few examples will suffice. Of the indictments for high treason, nos. 1 and 2, *temp.* Edward IV, are for aiding and abetting 'J. lately earl W.', evidently James, earl of Wiltshire, attainted in November 1461.[4] No. 3 is the violation of a safe conduct given by Henry VI to some Genoese merchants who were attacked as they sailed from

of the peace before the justices, only to be discovered therefore in quarter session records.
    [1] pp. 18-31, *supra*; App. I, *infra*.   [2] As in the 1510 ed.
    [3] I refer as before to the 1510 Wynkyn de Worde edition. On f. vi there is a reference to 21 March, 21 Hen. VII, the latest date that I have noted.
    [4] Cal. Pat. Edw. IV, 1461–1467, 186. In no. 1 Southampton is indicated as the place of the rebellion; cf. *ibid.*, Edw. IV, Hen. VI, 1467–1477, 65, under date of 18 February 1468.

Southampton, almost certainly just before February 1451.[1] The indictments for trespass against the peace include an accusation of the adherents of the 'false John Cade, lately dead'.[2]

(3) Most important of all is the following distinction between the two groups. The writs of process of the first section of Part II are writs for justices of the peace, and include only those indubitably connected with their office. But in spite of the title-page of the 1506 (?) 'Boke',[3] there is scarcely a shred of internal evidence[4] to prove that the forms of the second section of Part II have to do with justices of the peace. Not only do they include the trespasses and felonies of the manual,[5] but also a number of offences almost certainly outside the jurisdiction of the justices at the beginning of the sixteenth century.[6] The most striking examples are: high treason,[7] inquisitions of murder before coroners,[8] appeals by approvers,[9] the oath of an approver,[10] inquisitions coram Rege in the

---

[1] Cal. Pat. Hen. VI, 1446–1452, 404, 405, 441, 442. The reference in the Boke to the ship ' vocata a Carik et in Janua vocata Jentilis' suggests a connexion with the Genoese merchant, Balthasar Gentilis, patron of a carrack; ibid., 1452–1461, 438, 443. The fourth indictment for high treason is for the forgery of a Letter Patent of 16 February 27 Hen. VI, issued by ' Kyrkham', clerk of the hanaper, probably to be identified as Robert Kirkham, although the date is puzzling. His earliest appointment is apparently on 7 February 28 Hen. VI, 1450; Cal. Pat. 1446–1452, 307. He was appointed anew on 26 April 1461, and on 23 December of the same year succeeded Thomas Kirkeby as keeper of the 'rolls, books, and records of Chancery'; ibid., Edw. IV, 1461–1467, 52, 82. The next appointment to the office of clerk of the hanaper seems to be that of Thomas Vaughan on 13 January 1469; ibid., Edw. IV, Hen. VI, 1467–1477, 124–5.

[2] Ca. 9. Cade was killed on 12 July 1450; Oman, Political Hist. England, 1377–1485, 349–50. [3] App. I, Series I, no. 1.

[4] In fact the term 'justice of the peace' rarely appears.

[5] Clearly coming within the jurisdiction of the justices of the peace.

[6] It will be shown later that there is some doubt about the precise extent of the powers of the justices, especially in relation to appeals; see infra, p. 101, note 3, and ch. vi (4). But there can be, I think, no doubt that in high treason they had no jurisdiction unless specified by statute; see ibid.

[7] Ca. 1–4; the offences are outside of the statutory list within the jurisdiction of the justices of the peace; see p. 197, infra.

[8] Under indictments for felonies, ca. 14, 20, 21.

[9] Under appeals, ca. 1–13; ca. 2 includes the case of an offender indicted before justices of the peace who became an approver and had a coroner assigned him, apparently by the justices.

[10] Following the appeals.

prison of the marshall,[1] rescue 'in aula Westmonasterii.'[2] Covering as they do the entire range of criminal law, obviously these forms are not to be compared with the indictments of the manual, but represent rather the type of precedents that would be needed by a clerk of the crown for cases coram Rege.[3]

Inasmuch as it has been thus shown that the manual does not constitute the actual basis of either of the groups of precedents in the 'Boke', it is essential in the search for origins to consider again the manuscript collections compiled between *circ.* 1422 and 1506, already discussed in relation to Part I of the 'Boke'.[4] Two classes of collections of writs, although interesting from many points of view, can at once be dismissed as unimportant for the present purpose. First, the class represented by a roll[5] like a Patent Roll, over forty feet long, closely written on both sides, with no numbering of membranes, and containing transcripts of writs of the most divergent character. Most of them deal with actual cases,[6] and their dates range from the very early fifteenth century to 13 Henry VI,[7] covering a great number of counties and a great variety of officials; e. g. commission of sewers, removal of a constable, appointment of a chief justice,[8] a writ of *praemunire*, &c., &c. They include also a very few writs for justices of the peace.[9] It is hard to guess what end such an

---

[1] Under indictments for felonies, ca. 16.

[2] Under indictments against the form of statutes, ca. 21.

[3] For unsound inferences drawn from these forms, see p. 113, note 6, *infra*.

[4] Ch. ii, *supra*. Of course many more manuscript precedent books may be discovered in the future.

[5] B.M., Add. MSS. 35205. For similar rolls, cf. P.R.O., Exchequer, K.R. Miscellanea, $\frac{8}{23}$, perhaps compiled *temp.* Edw. IV; Bodleian, MS. Rawlinson, C. 339, containing material *temp.* Hen. VI and Hen. VII.

[6] The majority include names easily identified. Several of the persons noted in the manual appear; the Earl of Warwick as sheriff, John 'Throkmerton' as justice of Gaol Delivery; also there are some interesting references to John Oldcastle, and to 'Frere Tuk'.

[7] At least that is the latest that I have noted (except for the few documents of 3 Hen. VII at the very end), but the Catalogue gives 1430 as the latest date. An exhaustive study of the names, &c., would make possible a more precise statement. The outer edge includes the names of justices of Gaol Delivery, Frowyk, Kingsmill, &c., friends and contemporaries of Marowe (see ch. v, *infra*), *temp.* Hen. VII, not Hen. VI, as suggested in the catalogue.   [8] The famous Gascoigne.

[9] e.g., a *certiorari* to the Dorset justices, a *supersedeas de exigendo* to the Warwick justices.

inaccessible miscellany was designed to serve; certainly it was not meant for 'office use'.[1]

The second group that may be neglected is composed of miscellaneous legal formulae. The documents on any one subject are too few to constitute precedent books, but often include material connected with justices of the peace: for example, writs issued by John de Veer, earl of Oxford, justice of the peace in Essex *temp.* Edward IV;[2] proceedings before Thomas and Henry Frowyk, justices of the peace in Middlesex 5 Edward IV;[3] or beautifully illuminated Essex writs dated 8 Henry VII, based on the statutes of Labourers.[4]

There are, however, at least three compilations[5] that suggest a possible hypothesis for the origin of the printed precedents.

(1) MS. Harl. 6873[6] contains a copy of the petition in parliament of 1445[7] and of the resulting new statute of Labourers, 23 Henry VI[8]—important because it revived a statutory maximum for wages[9] and because it remained unchanged for half a century.[10] Immediately afterwards comes a copy of the familiar writ found in the printed 'Boke' at the beginning of Part II: 'A. B. & socii sui custodes pacis'. The jurors are summoned to a session in Middlesex at Westminster, apparently to deal especially with trespasses against the labour laws. Writs of process follow, very similar to the printed ones,[11] localized mainly in Middlesex and dated usually in the reign of Henry VI.[12]

---

[1] So described in the Catalogue.

[2] B.M., Harl. 1210; ff. 1-2.   One of the writs is for the arrest of a man suspected of felony; see p. 197, *infra.*

[3] Bodleian, Rawlinson, C. 703, ff. 3-9; the proceedings include an appeal of felony before a coroner, f. 8; see pp. 200-203, *infra.*

[4] B.M., Cotton. Titus, A xxv, ff. 129, 138, 139; there are also some Kent writs on surety of peace. Some of the forms are very like the Essex forms among the writs of process in the Boke.

[5] All in the British Museum.

[6] Probably not put into its present shape until the middle of the sixteenth century, but certainly based on fifteenth-century material.

[7] f. 43; Rot. Parl., V. 112-13.   [8] ff. 43-5.

[9] Cf. pp. 92-3, note 2, *supra,* and especially the article by Miss McArthur there cited.

[10] 11 Hen. VII, c. 22, 1495, is the next wage statute.

[11] ff. 45-53. There are some striking resemblances as well as certain divergences.

[12] There are references to Robert Botiller (Botell or Botyll, &c., in

(2) MS. Harl. 773 includes, in addition to the earliest known example of the justices' Charge to jurors,[1] a number of forms of indictments for justices of the peace and for coroners,[2] and also two distinct sets of writs of process for the former.[3]   The first of these begins precisely as does Part II of the 'Boke',[4] and continues with the familiar writs of process, localized mainly in Lincolnshire, a few in other counties,[5] and usually dated in the reign of Henry VI ;[6] they contain some details absolutely identical with those in the 'Boke'—for example, the mention of 'auditor generalis Ludouici R. militis domini de B . . .'.[7]   But after the opening heading there is a reference to R. Repynghale as the clerk of the justices,[8] evidently the clerk of the signet and king's secretary, who on 1 April 1448 was granted for life 'the office of clerk of the keepers of the peace and of the justices of oyer and terminer' in the parts of Kesteven, Lyndesey, and Holland, co. Lincoln, 'alias the office of clerk of the crown or peace', and also the office of 'king's attorney before the same keepers and justices'.[9]

The early history of the Custos Rotulorum and of his relation to the clerk of the peace and the clerk of the crown has yet to be written,[10] but the phraseology used in Repynghale's appointments suggests several crucial questions.   (1) Is it correct to assume that the clerk of the peace is always the clerk of the

Patent Rolls), prior of St. John of Jerusalem ; e. g. f. 50 b. He was on the Middlesex commission during 1461–1467 ; Cal. Pat. Edw. IV, 567 ; he was prior as early as 1441 (*ibid.*, Hen. VI, 1441–1446, 260) and had died by 21 February 1470; *ibid.*, Edw. IV, Hen. VI, 1467–1477, 189.

[1] p. 57, *supra*.   [2] ff. 47–8.
[3] ff. 51 b–8, ff. 59–69. The second set, Dorsetshire writs mainly, are preceded by a commission of the peace, dated 28 September 26 Hen. VI. On ff. 70–76 b are copies of actual proceedings before Kesteven justices of the peace, *temp*. Edw. III and Hen. V.
[4] That is, pleas at Westminster, 28 Hen. VI, followed by the familiar writ to jurors as in the Boke.
[5] e. g. Middlesex, f. 51 b; Bucks, f. 55; Essex, f. 57.
[6] The volume contains many other legal formulae (see printed Catalogue); the handwriting is for the most part probably late fifteenth century.
[7] f. 57; the initial R. was H. in the Boke; *supra*, p. 97.
[8] f. 51 : 'eorum clerico tunc ibidem existente'.
[9] Cal. Pat. Hen. VI, 1446–1452, 131. Note that Richard Oseney, the Worcestershire clerk of the peace, was king's attorney ; App. II, no. 51.
[10] Cf. Webb, English Local Government, i. 287, note 1 ; Repertory of British Archives, pt. i, ed. H. Hall, 111–13.

crown in the sense that he is the clerk of the justices of the peace who are often described as holding ' Placita Corone' ? [1] (2) Or is it not more usual to confine the use of the term 'clerk of the crown' to the clerk of those justices who are holding ' Placita Corone coram Rege ', or to the clerk of the coroners ? (3) Just what duties are performed by a man appointed as ' clerk of the crown' in a given county with no reference to the peace ? [2] Certainly at about the middle of the fifteenth century it became the custom to make life grants by Letters Patent of the office of clerk of the peace, often described also as clerk of the crown ; in a few instances such grants included definite instructions that the clerk was to have the custody of the records.[3] Then by 1506, after an apparent lapse, the practice seemed to be suddenly revived—the phraseology of the grants implying two distinct offices.[4] Occasionally the clerk

---

[1] Ch. iii (1), p. 84, *supra*.

[2] e.g., on 3 June 1464, George Scalby, one of the clerks of the Exchequer, was granted for life the ' office of clerk of the crown of the county of York ', previously held by Robert Davyson ; Cal. Pat. Edw. IV, 1461–1467, 342.

[3] On 28 December 1446, Wm. Bisshop of Charleton was appointed for life ' as clerk of the peace in Salop and keeper of the records, rolls, and precepts' ; Cal. Pat. Hen. VI, 1446–1452, 28.   On 15 August 1447, Th. Merton was granted offices in Northamptonshire exactly similar to those bestowed upon Repynghale ; *ibid*. 84.   On 7 June 1453, John West (who had been ' attendant in the king's service in the company of the king's clerk, Thomas Greswold,'coroner and attorney in the King's Bench ') was granted for life the ' office of clerk of the sessions of the peace ' and 'of the justices of oyer and terminer' in Warwickshire, *ibid*., 1452–1461, 77. On 13 January 1457, William York the younger was granted the ' office of clerk of the peace in Staffordshire and of the keeping of the rolls pertaining to the office' as John Hegan had had ; *ibid*. 398.   On 27 March 1458, Henry Barbour, an under clerk of the royal kitchen, was granted for life the ' office of clerk of the peace in Staffordshire' in lieu of the above William York ; *ibid*. 420.

[4] On 16 March 1506, the ' offices of clerk of the peace, clerk of the crown, and clerk of sessions ' were granted for life to Henry Everard in Norfolk and Suffolk (*ibid*., Hen. VII, 1494–1509, 446), apparently in place of John Higham as clerk of the peace in Suffolk (at least since 1497); *ibid*. 78.   On 21 September 1506, Higham and Leonard Spencer received a grant of the above offices ' in survivorship', but described a little differently, namely, the ' offices of clerk of the peace and clerk of the crown of all sessions of the peace in the counties of Norfolk and Suffolk'; *ibid*. 495.   A similar grant was made for life on 31 July to Robert Davyson in Essex and Herts., *ibid*. 467 ; life grants of the offices of clerk of the peace and of the crown were made on 29 October to John Lucas in Kent, *ibid*. 501 ; on 21 November to Wm. Conuser in Oxfordshire, *ibid*.

is specifically ordered to 'take over the records pertaining to
these offices from the keeping of the Custos Rotulorum of the
county '.[1] If a clerk of the peace is acting as clerk of the
crown in the second sense, it is natural that he should keep
in one ' baga ' the various records, writs, &c., in his custody,
whether of the sessions of the peace or of inquisitions before
coroners or of proceedings coram Rege. It seems therefore
at least a reasonable hypothesis that shortly after the statute
of Labourers of 1445,[2] several scribes had had access to ' bagae '
containing such a miscellany for Middlesex, Lincolnshire,
and Dorset,[3] respectively, and had made rather unintelligent
transcripts of documents that had once been of practical service
to clerks of the peace and of the crown in the reign of Henry
VI. The presence of indictments for offences outside of the
jurisdiction of the justices of the peace would therefore be
explained by the organization of the office of the clerk.

(3) Finally, MS. Harl. 1777 has been already described as
containing a manual on the peace divided into two sections,
one including the statutes and the Charge almost identical with

504; on 28 November to John Spencer and Thomas Spenser in Bedfordshire and Hunts. 'in survivorship'; to William Hughson and Thomas
Hildersham in the county and town of Cambridge, *ibid.* 519; and on 22
December to John Boteler in Warwickshire, *ibid.* 498.   Many similar
grants are recorded for 1507 and 1508. Cf. also 'Wirall Clerk de Sessions
de Midd.'; Year Book Mich. (Trin.) 16 Edw. IV, p. 5.

[1] e.g. John Boteler, and William Conuser, *supra.*   For Boteler's career
as town clerk of Coventry, see p. 82, note 7, *supra.* The Act of 1545,
37 Hen. VIII, c. 1, is inconveniently vague as to the dates of changes
in the practice, An acte for the office of the Custos Rotulorum and
Clerkes of the peace : previously the Lord Chancellor has appointed the
Custos Rotulorum and ' until nowe of late ' every Custos Rotulorum has
appointed clerks of the peace, but recently people ' beinge not learned nor
yet mete, unable for lack of knowledge & lerning ' to be Custos Rotulorum
or clerks have by labour, friendship, and other means obtained life
appointments from the king by Letters Patent. Therefore many indictments of felony, murder, &c., have been wrong. Henceforth (1) the
Custos Rotulorum is to be appointed only by 'bill signed withe the
King's hande' which shall be a warrant for the great seal. (2) The
Custos Rotulorum is to appoint the clerk ; the latter may appoint a
deputy with permission of the Custos Rotulorum. This enactment does
not cancel existing Letters Patent.

[2] The importance of the new act would thus account for the emphasis
on trespasses against the labour laws.

[3] Undoubtedly many other similar compilations were made, some of
which may later be discovered.

those printed in Part I of the 1506 (?) 'Boke', and the other
a compilation for a clerk of the peace.[1] This compilation
begins with an account of the clerk's duties in opening a session[2]
and continues with a great variety of forms—indictments of
felonies and trespasses—similar to those in the second portion
of Part II of the 'Boke', but with notable differences : there
are constant references to the justices of the peace ; almost all
the precedents are clearly within their jurisdiction ; the few
exceptions are connected with matters about which there is
some legitimate doubt.[3] Then come the familiar writs of
process resembling very closely the writs in the 'Boke'.[4] Since
the county is usually Suffolk, occasionally Essex or Norfolk,
since the justice of the peace is always Robert Drury, justice of
the peace in Suffolk for the reign of Henry VII from 1488 on,[5]
and since the latest and most frequent date is 16 Henry VII,
1501, it is perhaps correct to attribute the compilation to one
of the various men who held the combined offices of clerk of
the peace and clerk of the crown in Norfolk and Suffolk during
the latter part of the reign of Henry VII.[6] But Maitland's
warning must be remembered : 'To fix the date of a manuscript collection of legal precedents is an impossible feat, unless
by the date of the collection we merely mean the date of the
manuscript that happens to lie before us '.[7] It is not safe to dog-
matize about the date of the origin of the collections in MS.
Harl. 1777, either of the writs, or of the tracts on the Hundred
Court, Court Baron, or of the first part of the 'Boke'.[8] It is not
even certain—though highly probable—that the volume was
in existence by the summer of 1506. But it has this peculiar
importance in relation to the printed 'Boke' ; it shows the com-

---

[1] p. 52. [2] p. 53.
[3] Two appeals, one indictment of felony before Robert Drury, justice of
the peace ; two 'informations' to jurors, murder and forcible entry,
respectively; ff. 38-9. Then comes a demand by Robert Drury, justice
of the peace, for a confession before a coroner, followed by a series of
'presentments'; ff. 40-4. For the problem of jurisdiction, see p. 99,
note 6, *supra*.
[4] ff. 44-8. The two groups of forms are given in just the reverse order
from that of the Boke and are far fewer in number.
[5] See p. 52, and note 6, *supra*. [6] p. 103, note 4, *supra*.
[7] The Court Baron, Selden Soc., Introductory Note, 4.
[8] See p. 52, note 4, *supra*.

posite character of the latter and makes clear that the precedents of Part II belong to the clerk of the justices rather than
to the justices themselves,[1] and that Part I is of more direct
concern for the latter.

At the end of this long discussion, one may at least venture
a guess as to the origin of Part II of the 'Boke' and of its
combination with Part I.   In the late summer or autumn or
early winter of 1506, at the time of a marked development of
the life-office of clerks of the peace and of the crown, 'some one
unknown'—as the old indictments run—but almost certainly
from Suffolk, and therefore with full knowledge of the Suffolk
material,[2] and possibly a friend of Robert Sampson, clerk of
the Privy Seal, himself probably of Suffolk origin,[3] had access
to various MS. compilations. They were not necessarily those
that have just been described, but were similar compilations
based like them on records and writs of clerks of the peace and
clerks of the crown of about the middle of the fifteenth century.
Not being 'learned in the law' the unknown scribe failed to
differentiate the two classes of records and unfortunately chose
his indictments from those of the clerk of the crown, transcribing them exactly, even to the original dates, while he or
his printer altered the dates of the writs of process to corres-
pond precisely to the time of the preparation of the volume
for the press.   The second portion of Part II is thus shown to
be exceedingly misleading as a guide for justices of the peace.[4]
In the 'copy' that first went to a printer—Pynson, I believe[5]—
there was prefixed to the collection of precedents the summaries
of statutes and also the Charge, both of them certainly to be
connected with Pynson's 'Abridgement' and perhaps also
with MS. Harl. 1777, but in any case not brought up to a date

---

[1] My theory of the radical difference between the two parts of the Boke
thus finds confirmation ; see ch. i, *supra*, p. 42.

[2] Perhaps even before it was copied into the volume now known as
MS. Harl. 1777. It is noteworthy that this manuscript is the only one
that I have found that contains the combination of the two sections that
together make up the printed Boke.

[3] p. 97, note 4, *supra*.   [4] p. 59, *supra*.

[5] pp. 19–20, 55, *supra*. The two sections in MS. Harl. 1777 would
have made a more accurate manual than the printed Boke, but as Holdsworth has pointed out, it is very much a matter of chance as to what
actually goes to the printer ; *op. cit.*, ii. 527.

later than 1495.[1] To what extent Pynson himself was responsible for the enterprise, it has been impossible to determine.[2]

For the history of law, the significance of the evidence presented in these three chapters is plain. The Worcestershire manual, representing in all likelihood the work of one man actually engaged in the business of the sessions, gives authoritative information on the office of the justices as it was organized in the early fifteenth century, information that is supplemented and confirmed by the MS. French Charge.[3] The ' Boke' of 1506 (?), on the other hand, cannot be accepted as presenting an accurate account of legal theory or practice governing the office of the justices in the early sixteenth century.[4] To find such an account, we must examine the sources of the treatises printed later than the ' Boke '.

[1] pp. 18–19, 53, 55, *supra*.

[2] A number of possibilities readily occur to one's mind. For example, Thomas Keble, who gave a reading on the peace early in the reign of Henry VII (p. 179, *infra*), came from Suffolk, according to Foss, Judges; did he perhaps suggest the need for a practical manual?

[3] In Harl. 773; confirmed also by the early collections of statutes on the justices of the peace; see pp. 52, 58, *supra*.

[4] It is for this reason that the inferences drawn from the contents of the Boke by Professor Jenks (see p. 113, note 6, *infra*) are not sound.

CHAPTER IV

A BRIEF ACCOUNT OF THE SOURCES USED BY FITZHERBERT, LAMBARD, AND CROMPTON, WITH SPECIAL REFERENCE TO MAROWE'S WORK CITED ONLY BY THE LAST TWO

FITZHERBERT'S 'Loffice' of 1538 [1] was based on 'auncient bookes of common law' as well as on 'Statutes' [2] and, as has been already pointed out, the latter made up over half of the treatise. [3] In contrast to the published material available in 1506 for the compiler of the 'Boke', there were in print by 1538 not only the 'old' statutes but also many editions of collections of 'new' statutes as well as separate issues of the more recent acts. [4] Fitzherbert's serious mistake of Canterbury for Cambridge for the statute of 12 Richard II [5] shows that he was relying altogether on printed versions and was not investigating MS. collections. [6] Nevertheless, he performed a real

---

[1] App. I, Series II, no. 1 ; ch. i, pp. 10–13, *supra*.
[2] As stated on the title-page.   [3] p. 13, *supra*.
[4] Ch. ii, pp. 43–5, *supra*.   [5] f. 11.
[6] B.M., MS. Hargrave 429, ff. 4–65, contains a 'Treatise del peace & doffice Justice del peace'. After a series of citations of cases and a copy of Fitzherbert's preface to Loffice (f. 15) comes an exceedingly illegible form of an anonymous tract, mainly in English, but partly in French. It must have been compiled not earlier than 1575–1576 (cf. f. 34), and has many references to 'book cases', and to a large proportion of the sources used by Lambard, including Marowe (f. 11). The writer makes an able refutation (ff. 42–3) of Fitzherbert's mistake as to Canterbury, due, he thinks, to a reliance on printed statutes. In support of Cambridge, he quotes the registers of the bishop of Ely, also 'the booke of the antiquities of the Uniuersities of Cambridge and Oxford' and 'one ould statute booke written by a diligent man' in the reign of Richard II. The whole tract is well worth careful study ; see p. 113, note 7, *infra*, and cf. p. 158, *infra*, for another copy. The Reverend H. E. Salter has kindly supplied me with the precise title of the work on the universities : ' De antiquitate Cantabrigiensis Academiae, Libri duo; in quorum secundo de Oxoniensis quoque gymnasii antiquitate disseritur, etc.', printed anonymously in August 1568, and again in 1574, with the name of the author, Dr. John Caius of Cambridge.

service in giving under one cover the text of the statutes[1] connected with justices of the peace, which had previously been 'dispersyd in diuers volumes'.[2] In view of the difficulty experienced by modern scholars in identifying *all* the sources of 'La Graunde Abridgement',[3] it is peculiarly disappointing to find that Fitzherbert cites so few Year Book cases—only seven in the section on justices of the peace[4] and nineteen in the remainder of the volume.[5] The 'ancient treatise' on forestallers is mentioned, but is merely an 'old' statute or ordinance;[6] Britton is quoted twice, once in the section on Sheriffs and once in that on Coroners.[7] With these exceptions no 'auncient bookes of common law' are specifically mentioned, not even the 'Boke' of 1506 (?)—which he almost certainly knew.[8] Evidently, therefore, positive information on Fitzherbert's sources is lacking. But one negative statement can be made with assurance: he was not making use of the reading on the peace by Marowe.[9] Had he

[1] Is it possible that Berthelet's slim pamphlet of recent statutes to be executed by justices of the peace was printed early enough in 1538 to have suggested to Fitzherbert the need for a more extensive collection? Cf. also Pulton's volume of later date; *infra*, pp. 112–13.   [2] p. 13, *supra*.

[3] 'No one has ever given an account of Fitzherbert's sources and until they are discovered part of the history of the common law must remain a mystery, for no other MS. thus far discovered is parallel with his authorities'; Year Book 12 Rich. II, ed. G. F. Deiser, xxv.

[4] Loffice: f. 12, 3 Edw. II; f. 12 b, Pasch. 7 Hen. IV, 43 Edw. III, Lib. Ass.; f. 15 b, Mich. 7 Hen. IV; f. 17, the opinion of chief justice Fyneux and his colleagues; f. 18, Trin. 9 Edw. IV; f. 29, Mich. 20 Hen. VI.

[5] *Ibid.*, on Sheriffs: f. 173, par Martyn, 4 Hen. VI; f. 173 b, Pasch. 8 Edw. IV, Mich. 28 Edw. III (bis); f. 174, Pasch. 26 Edw. III. On Constables: f. 189, Mich. 5 Hen. VII, Mich. 44 Edw. III; f. 189 b, 3 Edw. III, Iter Northampton; f. 190, 7 Edw. IV. On Coroners: f. 203 b, Mich. 6 Rich. II; ff. 203b–204, Trin. 12 Edw. III; f. 204, 22 Edw. III, Lib. Ass.; f. 204 b, 27 Edw. III, Lib. Ass., 3 Edw. III, Iter Northampton (bis), 8 Edw. II, Iter Canc'.; f. 205, 8 Edw. II, Iter Canc. (bis), Trin. 29 Edw. III.

[6] *Ibid.*, f. 12: 'Donque (de forstallariis) queux persons serront ditz forstallers, il appiert per le ancient treatise fait en le temps le roy E. le primer de forstallours'; also f. 152. See ch. i, *supra*, p. 14, note 2; Holdsworth, *op. cit.*, ii. 175.

[7] f. 174, f. 204. Cf. also a reference to 'Magna Carta Capitulo, 33', f. 171.

[8] See p. 37, *supra*. With the exception of the Charge there was no place in the scheme of Loffice for the material that made up the larger part of the Boke.

[9] In spite of the copy at his own Inn; cf. pp. 151–3, *infra*. Later

done so, he would scarcely have perpetuated in 'Loffice' his strange error on the relation of justices of the peace to murder, an error that dated back to his 'Abridgement'.[1]

The years between 1538, and 1581 and 1583, the dates respectively of the 'Eirenarcha'[2] and of the revision of 'Loffice',[3] witnessed an enormous increase in the number of printed law books.[4] The increase is clearly reflected in the variety of sources referred to by Lambard and by Crompton, possibly also in their habit of precise citations, so much easier to make in the case of printed than of MS. material.[5] The following lists give their sources in alphabetical order,[6] omitting biblical and classical references[7] as not essential to the problem under discussion. The dates are of the first editions,[8] not necessarily those actually used by either Lambard or Crompton. Unless otherwise noted, absence of date indicates that the work is in MS. only :

(1) *Authorities cited by both Lambard and Crompton.*
　　The Boke of Justyces of peas, 1506 (?).[9]
　　Bracton, 1569.[10]
　　Britton, 1540 (?).[11]
　　Brooke, La Graunde Abridgement, 1568.[12]

writers, even Maitland, have failed to distinguish clearly between Fitzherbert's Loffice and Crompton's revision, and therefore have made the mistake of thinking that Fitzherbert quoted Marowe ; see p. 220, notes 3, 4.

[1] pp. 38–9, *supra* ; ch. vi (4), *infra*. Fitzherbert does not himself mention Marowe in his Novel Natura Brevium ; but see *infra*, p. 219.

[2] Published in 1619, according to Jenks, Short Hist. Eng. Law, 151–2, 157 ; written in the reign of James I, according to Holdsworth, *op. cit.*, i. 125. But see ch. i, p. 8, *supra*.　　　　　　　　[3] *Ibid.*

[4] As has already been pointed out ; *ibid.*, p. 42.

[5] Cf. Year Book 4 Edw. II, ed. G. J. Turner, Selden Soc., xv.

[6] I am not attempting to show the relative frequency with which a given authority is cited, nor in doubtful cases to decide whether a MS. or a printed version is being used.

[7] Cf. e.g. Crompton's 'Exhortation to the Iurie', or his quotation from Virgil, f. 65.

[8] The titles are given in the briefest form sufficient for identifying the works in question, *not* precisely as printed by either Lambard or Crompton.

[9] For the term 'old' Book, see p. 41, *supra*. We know that Lambard had in his possession the edition of 1569 (App. I, Series I, no. 28), which is now in the British Museum, and which contains his MS. notes on the margin.

[10] Tottell. Cf. Holdsworth, *op. cit.*, ii. 191.

[11] Redman. Cf. Holdsworth, *ibid.* 268.　　　　[12] p. 210, *infra*.

Dalison.[1]
Dyer, 1581.[2]
Fitzherbert.
    La Graunde Abridgement, 1514–1516.[3]
    Loffice, 1538.[4]
    Novel Natura Brevium, 1537.[5]
Marowe, De Pace.
Plowden, Commentaries, 1571.[6]
Rastell's Abridgment of Statutes, 1533.[7]
Records in the Tower.[8]
Registrum Brevium, 1531.[9]
Staunford, Les Plees del Corone, 1557.[10]
Year Books.[11]
Liber Assisarum, between 1510 and 1516.[12]
Statutes; probably in the main from William Rastell's 'Collection of all the Statutes from Magna Carta to 1551.'[13]

(2) *Authorities cited only by Lambard.*
    Archaionomia, by himself, 1568.
    Glanvill, [1554], 1557.[14]
    New Booke of Entries, 1566.[15]
    Norman Customs.[16]

[1] Not printed till 1689, although a few of his reports appeared in the appendix to Keilwey, printed the year previous. Lambard (who had married Dalison's widow as his second wife ; J. Nichols, Bib. Top. Brit. i, Kent, 503) had become the owner of Dalison's own copy, now MS. Harl. 5141, and cites from it reports not found in the printed edition ; see p. 198, *infra*, note 5. The Harleian MS. has at the end of f. 45 : 'hucusque ex libro manu Willelmi Dallison conscripto Willelmus Lambert exaravit 1569'.

[2] Tottell: 'Cy ensuont ascun nouel cases collectes per le jades tres reuerend Iudge Mounsieur Iacques Dyer'.   [3] See p. 34, *supra*.

[4] Lambard may be using the translation since he refers to it as Fitzherbert's 'Booke' ; Eirenarcha, 50.

[5] Possibly as early as 1534; see p. 34, *supra*, note 4.

[6] p. 158, *infra*.

[7] I am assuming that the reference is to one of the editions issued by William Rastell, 1533, 1534, and without date, under the title 'Great Abridgment', Handlists; a reprint and continuation of his father's earlier volume ; see ch. ii, *supra*, p. 45.

[8] e.g. Eirenarcha, 15, 17, 18 ; Crompton, f. 82 b.

[9] William Rastell, Handlists.   [10] Tottell.

[11] For the early printed editions, see *infra*, pp. 174–5.

[12] p. 34, note 2, *supra*.

[13] Tottell, 1551. Cf. Eirenarcha, 360, 'Statutes at Large'; 390, 'smal volumne of the olde Statutes'.

[14] C. Gross, Sources and Literature of English History, 2nd ed.

[15] Tottell, ed. William Rastell.

[16] 'The booke of the Norman Customes', Eirenarcha, 332. For an

(2) *Authorities cited only by Lambard* (cont.).
        Justinian.[1]
        Law of the Twelve Tables.[2]
        Statham, [1490 (?)].[3]
        Laurence Valla.[4]
        Th. Walsingham, Historia Breuis . . . ab Edwardo
          primo ad Henricum quintum, 1574.[5]
(3) *Authorities cited only by Crompton.*[6]
        Abridgement of Assizes, 1509 or 1510 (?).[7]
        Eyres of Kent,[8] Northampton, and Nottingham.[9]
        Expositiones Terminorum Legum Anglie, 1527.[10]
        Edward Hall's Chronicle, [1542 (?)].[11]
        Hortus Vocabulorum, 1500.[12]
        Liber Intrationum, 1510.[13]
        Littleton, Tenures, [1482 (?)].[14]
        More, Alminacke & Prognostication,. 1567.[15]
        Harvey, Prognostication, 1584.[16]
        Officium Coronatoris.[17]
        St. Germain, Doctor and Student, 1523.[18]
        Stow, Chronicles, 1580.[19]
        Vetus Natura Brevium, before 1500.[20]
        Thomas Wilson, Arte of Rhetorike, 1553.[21]

It is clear that with the exception of Pulton's 'Abstract of penal statutes and authoritie and dutie of Justices &c.' printed in

account of the Norman 'Consuetudines', see Haskins, Norman Institutions, App. D.

[1] Edition not identified.   [2] Cf. note 1.
[3] See p. 19, note 8, *supra.*   [4] Edition not identified.
[5] 'Th. Walsingham in Histo. p. 107,' cited Eirenarcha, 8, identified in the edition of 1574.
[6] See p. 41, *supra*, for the reference to a 'discreete home', probably Lambard. I do not give all Crompton's quotations from his friends and acquaintances, Popham, Fleetwood, &c.
[7] Pynson; see Year Book 4 Edw. II, ed. G. J. Turner, Selden Soc., xxx-xxxi.   [8] See Selden Soc. volumes, ed. W. C. Bolland.
[9] Frequently cited in the printed Abridgements.
[10] Printed by John Rastell, and again without date; Handlists.
[11] Gross, *op. cit.*   [12] [H]Ortus Vocabulorum, Wynkyn de Worde.
[13] Pynson; Handlists.   [14] *Supra*, p. 19, and note 7.
[15] Loffice, f. 88. I have not identified it in the list of Almanacs in W. C. Hazlitt, Bib. Collections, 2nd ser., nor under Ephemerides in the B.M. catalogue.   [16] Loffice; *ut supra*, not identified.
[17] 4 Edw. I, called the Statute de Officio Coronatoris.
[18] John Rastell, Handlists.
[19] See Stow, Survey of London, ed. C. L. Kingsford, i. lxxxii–lxxxvi, for an excellent bibliography of Stow's works.
[20] Pynson, Handlists; Holdsworth, *op. cit.*, ii. 440, note 1, gives 1524 as the date of the earliest edition.   [21] Richard Grafton.

1577,[1] Lambard and Crompton had availed themselves of practically all the legal literature in print important for their subject.[2] Lambard shows his keen historical and legal sense by a careful selection for his appendix of a few pertinent writs of process from Part II of the old 'Boke'.[3] Crompton, on the other hand, uncritically reproduces in entirety both groups of precedents—writs and indictments,[4] sometimes not troubling to bring the indictments up to date[5] and completely ignoring the fact that they have nothing to do with justices of the peace.[6] That Lambard with his antiquarian skill was also investigating a wide range of manuscript material is proved by his numerous references to 'records in the Tower'.[7] But in the matter of sources, the significant point for the history of law has already been indicated, namely that both Lambard and Crompton made extensive use of a manuscript treatise that had been strangely neglected by Fitzherbert. Lambard's own words are the best introduction to the treatise and to its

---

[1] Not mentioned by Lambard even when he entreats 'Master Iohn Tindall of Lincolnes Inne' to make a collection of the statutes 'wherewith all Iustices of the Peace had to meddle'; Eirenarcha, 360. There is no reference by either author to Fleetwood's 'Annalium tam Regum Edwardi quinti, Richardi tertii, & Henrici septimi, quam Henrici octaui', 1579, although under *Peax* it contains excellent summaries of recent reports.

[2] It appears from the dates of the first editions that many of the books were in print at the time that Fitzherbert was writing Loffice.

[3] See p. 41, *supra*.   [4] *Ibid.*

[5] e.g. the indictment of Jack Cade still appears; cf. ch. iii (II), p. 99, *supra*.

[6] *Ibid.* Crompton's uncritical work has misled Jenks in his Short Hist. Eng. Law to believe that justices of the peace (apart from the authority conferred upon them by special statutes) could in 1583 deal with cases of high treason, and also to make unsound inferences about appeals; 152–3, 157.

[7] p. 111, *supra*. In the dedication to the Chancellor printed in his 1581 edition, Lambard writes of making a preliminary sketch for the Eirenarcha: 'I did vpon a seconde reading [of Fitzherbert, Marowe, &c.] plot the matter with my penne and made (as it were) a Module thereof in a small booke ...'. Then after using it he 'enlarged the work'. I had hoped that the Hargrave MS. treatise described p. 108, note 6, *supra*, could be proved to be a copy of Lambard's 'Module'. But unfortunately for this theory the early editions of the Eirenarcha all contain 'Canterbury' for the statute of 12 Rich. II. Not until the 1588 edition is the correction made, with the remark that Fitzherbert 'sucked that errour from the imprinted booke of the Statutes'; 49. Is it possible that the Hargrave MS. called Lambard's attention to the mistake, and that it is a copy of Goldwell's missing work? See ch. i, p. 7, *supra*.

author: ' To write of the Office and Duetie of Iustices of the peace, after M. Marrow (whose learned reading in that behalfe made the 18 yeare of King Henry the 7. is in many hands to bee seene) and after the reuerend Iustice Fitzherbert (who published an excellent treatise thereof, which is yet euerie where to be had) may at the first seeme no lesse vnaduisedly done, then if a man should bring Owles to Athens. . . .'[1] It was this 'Master Marrow' who in 1503 made a scholarly legal analysis of the powers of the justices of the peace, and thus produced a work altogether different in character from the manuals typified by the 1506 (?) 'Boke'. To 'Master Marrow' therefore, and to his 'learned reading', the remainder of this monograph must be devoted.

[1] Proheme to Eirenarcha. I am indebted to Professor C. H. McIlwain for encouraging me to think that a search for copies of Marowe's reading would be worth while.

CHAPTER V

THOMAS MAROWE AND HIS READING ON THE PEACE IN 1503

THE MAROWE FAMILY AND THE CAREER OF THOMAS MAROWE.

THOMAS MAROWE, serjeant-at-law (d. 1505), was the youngest son of William Marowe, grocer, once mayor of London. Previous to the sixteenth century the surname is found frequently in London,[1] and occasionally elsewhere,[2] spelt in a great variety of ways:[3] Marewe,[4] Marogh,[5] Marow,[6] Marowe,[7] Marrogh,[5] Marrow,[8] Marrowe,[9] Marroy,[10] Marue,[11] Marugh,[12] Marw,[13] Marwe,[14] Marwey,[15] Merewe,[16] Mergh (?),[17] Merowe,[18] Merrowe,[19] Meruwe,[20] Merwe.[21] The more common modern

---

[1] Cal. London Letter Books, ed. R. R. Sharpe, Cal. Pat. and Close Rolls, *passim*; H. Harrison, Surnames of the United Kingdom, 2 vols., 1912, 1918, 'Marrow, Eng. companion, mate, lover, ME. Marwe'. Cf. also Murray, N.E.D., for the probable Scandinavian origin of 'marrow' with this meaning and for 1440 as the earliest example of its use in English.

[2] See references below, which are not, however, exhaustive

[3] I give the later spellings also.

[4] Cal. Pat. Edw. I, 1292–1301, 461.

[5] P.R.O., Inq. p. m., Exch. Ser. ii, file 1115, no. 59.

[6] Monk of Coventry, Cal. Close Edw. II, 1323-1327, 556.

[7] 1407, Blomefield, Hist. of Norfolk, iv. 228.

[8] 1641, Hist. MSS. Comm. 5th Report; Ormonde, i, ii, index.

[9] The monk George Marrowe of Nostall Abbey, Yorkshire, author of a treatise on alchemy in 1437 (Bodl. Ashmolean MSS., 1406, iv. 1 ; 1423, 1) is the most distinguished of the name outside of London.

[10] 1539, Cal. Lond. Inq. p. m., ed. R. R. Sharpe, 63.

[11] Bucks., Hundred Rolls, ii. 342.

[12] J. A. Kingdon, Facsimile of MS. Archives of the company of Grocers, 1345-1463, pt. ii, 399.

[13] Cal. Lond. Letter Books, ed. R. R. Sharpe, K, 271.

[14] *Ibid.*, K and L, *passim*; Bristol, Dunstable (Bedfordshire), testament of William Marowe, 1464.　　　　[15] Will cited p. 117, note 7, *infra*.

[16] Sussex, Hundred Rolls, ii. 203 ; Surrey, Cal. Close Edw. I, 1279-1288, 303.

[17] Worcestershire, *ibid.*, Edw. II, 1318–1323, 518.

[18] p. 117, note 2, *infra*.　　　　[19] Kingdon, Grocers, pt. ii, 221.

[20] Cal. Close Edw. I, 1272-1279, 237.

[21] Durham, Cal. Charter Rolls, 1257-1300, 140.

spelling is Marow or Marrow;[1] in the lifetime of the serjeant-at-law, Marowe seems to have been preferred,[2] though Marwe was more usual in the early fifteenth century and Merewe (or Merwe) in the centuries preceding.

We do not know the origin of the London Marowes or whether the numerous individuals in the city bearing the name belonged to one family. But it is tempting to connect them with Merewe in Surrey,[3] modern Merrow,[4] a little parish between Leatherhead and Guildford [5] mentioned as far back as the reign of Henry I.[6] Toward the end of the reign of Henry III a Thomas de Merewe was the seneschall of Lord William de Breus,[7] a large landholder in Surrey;[8] and by the middle of the thirteenth century a John de Merewe is a parson in Surrey.[9] Or perhaps future investigation will show that the London Marowes came from the Midlands. The surname appears constantly in the records of the borough of Leicester from 1271 till 1342.[10] A John le Marwe, member of the 'gild of merchants', was mayor in 1317–1318, 1332–1333, and 1333–1334,[11] and is perhaps the John Marowe who in 1339 was one

---

[1] In the later pedigrees; p. 117, note 5, *infra*, p. 115, note 8, *supra*.

[2] e.g. the signature to his will and testament, and the title of his legal work; App. III.

[3] Spelt in various ways: Plac. de Quo Warranto, 747; Cal. Charter Rolls, 1226-1257, 186, 226; Cal. Close Hen. III, 1227-1231, 321; Cal. Pat., *passim*.

[4] Cf. also Merrow in Connecticut and Galsworthy's Marrow in Worcestershire, The Freelands.

[5] E. W. Brayley, A Topographical History of Surrey, 1850, ii. 101; J. G. Bartholomew, Survey Atlas of England and Wales, 1903, Plate LXIII; General Index to Surrey Archaeological Collections, i to xx.

[6] Brayley, *loc. cit.*, quoting from Testa de Nevill, 225.

[7] Hundred Rolls, ii. 203. For other early Surrey references, see Cal. Close Edw. I, 1279-1288, 303, Geoffrey de Merewe; Abbreviatio Placitorum, Hen. III, 161, Master William de Merewe, probably to be identified with the proctor of the bishop of Durham in 1260, Pat. Hen. III, 1258-1266, 91 (spelt Merewa perhaps in error); cf. *ibid.* 162 and p. 115, note 21, *supra*; John de Merewe witnessed a Sussex charter in 1285, Cal. Pat. Edw. I, 1281-1292, 188.

[8] Cf. William de Braiose, tenant in chief in Surrey, Domesday Book, i. 30.

[9] Cal. Pat. Edw. III, 1354-1358, 117.

[10] Records of the Borough of Leicester, 1103-1603, ed. M. Bateson, 3 vols., 1899-1905, index to vols. i and ii, *passim*; John, Richard, Robert, Thomas, William, often with 'le' before the surname.

[11] *Ibid.* i. 337, 341, 398 (cf. 403); ii. 5, 15.

of the coroners of Leicestershire 'sick and broken with age'.[1]
At any rate, by the middle of the fourteenth century a John
de Merowe, skinner, was a substantial citizen of London.[2] His
will, enrolled in 1352,[3] mentions a son Walter, possibly the
Walter Merwe appointed to the king's mint in the Tower.[4]

Unfortunately, no proof has been found that William
Marowe, grocer, was related to John de Merowe, skinner, or
that his ancestors came from either Leicestershire or Surrey.
In fact, some of the genealogies make him the son of Stephen
Marowe of Stepney, Middlesex,[5] a parish in which the family
was to hold property for many generations.[6] But no other
reference to 'Stephen' has appeared, while there is distinct
evidence pointing to the possibility that William was the son
of the William Marowe, 'citizen and smith of London', who
died in 1430 and who left bequests to St. Botolph's, Bishopsgate[7]—the burial place, it is to be noted, of William the grocer[8]
and of two of his sons.[9] The older William left a widow

[1] Cal. Close Edw. III, 1339-1341, 14, contains an order to cause a
coroner to be elected in his place.

[2] Cal. Close Edw. III, 1349-1354, 277. Probably to be identified with
the John de Merwe assessed to the king's loan in 1346; Cal. Lond.
Letter Books, F, 146, 149.

[3] Ibid., G, 40.

[4] Cal. Pat. Rich. II, 1391-1396, 510, 661. There are many references
to this Walter in succeeding Patent Rolls and in the MS. deeds in the
Guildhall.

[5] The pedigree of 1682-1683, and the one in Dugdale, Warwickshire,
981. Marowe pedigrees are not noted in the heraldic Visitations of either
London or Middlesex (Harl. Soc. Pub. i, xv, lxv), but are found in the
three Warwickshire Visitations: (1) 1563, MS. in the College of Arms;
(2) 1619, Harl. Soc. Pub. xii; (3) 1682-1683, ibid. lxii, and Warwickshire
Antiquarian Mag., pt. ii.

[6] See Marowe wills, Inquisitions post mortem, and deeds, passim. I
am indebted to Miss Drucker for a reference to an entry in the parish
register of St. Dunstan's, Stepney, of the baptism in 1671 of the daughter
of a William Marowe.

[7] Commissary of London, Book More, cclv; will dated 8 June 1430,
proved the following October. Perhaps he is the same as the juror of
1385; Cal. Lond. Letter Books, H, 271.

[8] In his testament (proved 15 May 1465) he requests that he be buried
in the church of 'S. Botulphe withoute Bishoppesgate bytwene the high
auter and auter of the chapel by me late construct'. Stow is not precise as
to the date, and erroneously makes the church St. Botolph's, Aldersgate;
Survey, ed. C. L. Kingsford, i. 309-10. The list of wills preserved in the
Prerogative Court of Canterbury cited in this chapter will be found at
the end, p. 144.

[9] William (will proved 30 October 1499) and Thomas (will proved

Johanna, a daughter Agnes, a son John (with two children, Elene and William), and a son William [1] who, if my theory is correct, is to be identified as the grocer. It seems more than a coincidence that William, 'citizen and grocer and alderman of the citee of London', had a sister Agnes, that his two elder sons were William and John, his eldest daughter Johanna, and that he made a bequest to his 'cosyn' Elene Otesdale and her daughters.[2]

Whatever his parentage, it was William Marowe's success as a member of the great company of grocers and as a city official that first brought the name into prominence. His career was strikingly similar to that of many other prosperous London merchants in the period when native Englishmen were rapidly gaining control of foreign trade.[3] Born probably within the first decade of the fifteenth century, from 1432 on William Marowe is mentioned with increasing frequency in the records of the grocers[4] who had been sharing with the mercers the chief place in the city council.[5] He was master of his company in 1450–1451, 1457–1458, 1463–1464,[6] and represented the city in three parliaments of Henry VI and one of Edward IV.[7] Meanwhile he had gone through the usual routine of city positions, having been auditor,[8] sheriff,[9]

---

10 April 1505) both specify St. Botolph's, Bishopsgate. I quote from the latter: 'within the vaute vnder the tombe there where the body of William Marowe my fader lieth buried'.

[1] Will, *ut supra*, p. 117, note 7. For land held in St. Botolph's by his wife, see MS. deeds, Guildhall.

[2] Testament and will.

[3] The old theory that Englishmen rarely engaged in foreign trade until the very end of the fourteenth century (cf. e. g. A. S. Green, Town Life, i, ch. 3, The Commercial Revolution of the Fifteenth Century) is being modified by new research; E. Lipson, The Economic History of England, ch. x. For contemporary opinion nothing is better than the 'Libelle of English Polyce', *circ.* 1437, printed in Political Poems and Songs, ed. T. Wright, ii, Rolls Series.

[4] Kingdon, Grocers, pt. ii, 221, *et passim*; in January 1436 he made a return on his Billingsgate property; Cal. Lond. Letter Books, K, 197. Cf. also W. Herbert, Livery Companies, i. 247.

[5] A. B. Beaven, 'The Grocers Company and the Aldermen of London,' in Eng. Hist. Review, xxii. 523–5; The Aldermen of the City of London, 2 vols., 1908–1913, i. 329–30.

[6] Kingdon, Grocers, pt. ii; Beaven, Aldermen, ii. 10.

[7] 1447, 1450, 1460, and 1463; *ibid.*

[8] 1444–1446, 1451–1453; *ibid.*   [9] 1448–1449; *ibid.*

alderman,[1] and mayor, the last in 1455–1456.[2] He died in 1465, probably early in May.[3]

His official life was passed in the midst of stirring events. As alderman at the time of the rising of 1450, he had probably gone with the 'meir' and the 'comynes' to the 'kynge bese-kynge him that he wolde tarye in the cite and they wolde lyve and dye with him ',[4] and he must have witnessed Jack Cade's session in the Guildhall in July.[5] He was mayor at the time of the 'hurlynge' between mercers and Lombards in the city streets,[6] and as a result of committing to prison the young mercer who began the 'grete affray', he was attacked in 'Chepe' as he was 'departyng from the [Guylde] hall toward his mancion to dyner'. It was 'with great Jubardy and labour' that the 'mair and shyreffes' succeeded in protecting the foreigners.[7]

He lived through the struggle against Henry VI and saw the triumph of Edward IV early in 1461.[8] Toward the end of Henry's reign, the city and the majority of the aldermen are said to be Yorkist,[9] but Marowe was one of a small group of

---

[1] 1449–1451 for Broadstreet ward; 1451–1464 for Tower ward; *ibid.*

[2] *Ibid.* Despite the evidence of the pedigrees, he was never knighted; *ibid.*, i. 255–6.

[3] His will and testament, dated 8 October 1464, were proved on 15 May following.

[4] Short English Chronicle, ed. J. Gairdner, Camden Soc., 1880, 66–8; R. R. Sharpe, London and the Kingdom, ii. 283. For the relative value of the accounts of the rising in the above Chronicle and in the Chronicles of Gregory, Fabyan, &c., see C. L. Kingsford, Eng. Hist. Literature in the Fifteenth Century, 94–6, 102; R. Flenley, Six Town Chronicles of England, introduction.

[5] Short Eng. Chron., 67.

[6] Cal. Lond. Letter Books, K, 376–7; Stow, Survey, ed. Kingsford, ii. 175.

[7] Chron. Lond., ed. Kingsford, 166–7; Short Eng. Chron., ed. Gairdner, 70; Fabyan's Chronicle, ed. H. Ellis, 630–1. Cf. art. on 'London and Foreign Merchants in the reign of Henry VI' by R. Flenley in E.H.R., xxv. 644–55, for the best recent account of this rising and its effect on foreigners. The entry in Gregory's Chronicle (ed. Gairdner, cited p.121, note 1, *infra*), 199, curiously enough implicates Marowe himself: 'Here was the rysynge and wanton reule of the mayre and the mercers of London agayne the Lombardys'. The result of this riot and of that of the following year was the exodus from London of many of the Italian merchants; Flenley, 654–5.

[8] Edward was crowned at Westminster on 28 June; C. Oman, Polit. Hist. Eng., 409.

[9] For the attitude of the city, see Sharpe, London and the Kingdom, ii,

Londoners who helped to finance Henry just before 1451.
That he was in favour with the Lancastrian government is
perhaps shown by his appointment in 1460 as sole judge for
' Merchants of Almain resident in London ' in pleas of debt
' wherein the mayor and sheriffs do not award speedy justice '.[2]

He was twice married,[3] and by his second wife, Katharine,
daughter of Richard Ryche,[4] a wealthy London mercer,[5] he
had six children, William, John, Thomas, Johanna, Agnes, and
Katharine.[6] Through his second marriage and through his
business and political interests, Marowe came into touch with
a wide London circle, including many members of his wife's
family;[7] her father, her two brothers, John[8] and Thomas,[9]
her brothers-in-law, John Walden, alderman,[10] and Thomas
Urswyk,[11] recorder of London 1454–1471 [12] and later chief
baron of the Exchequer;[13] also William Gregory, skinner, mayor

especially 292–3, 301, 305, 313. Sharpe believes in the Lancastrian
tendencies of the governing body ; Beaven, *op. cit.*, ii. liv, emphasizes
their Yorkist tendencies ; Kingsford, Eng. Hist. Lit. in Fifteenth Century,
109, notes the change in the London Chronicles from Lancastrian to
Yorkist sympathies.

[1] Cal. Pat. Hen. VI, 1446–1452, 472. But toward the end of his life he
was making a loan to Edward IV ; Cal. Pat., 1461–1467, 324.

[2] *Ibid.* 1452–1461, 566 ; Cal. Lond. Letter Books, K, 401.

[3] ' Isabell sometyme my wife and my wife that nowe is ' ; testament.
' Isabell ' is ignored in the pedigrees.

[4] Usually erroneously given as ' John Ryche ' in the pedigrees.

[5] In his testament of 20 April 1463, proved 16 August 1464, a most
picturesque document, he makes his three sons-in-law supervisors of his
will and testament.

[6] The pedigrees are inaccurate as to his children. I take the names
from his will and testament. It is barely possible that Johanna and
Agnes were the children by the first marriage.

[7] For a brief account of the Ryches and of their connexion by marriage
with the Stonors, William Gregory, &c., see Stonor Letters and Papers,
ed. Kingsford, i. xxvi–xxviii. See also their wills listed at the end of this
chapter.

[8] He died in 1458, leaving three sons, Richard, Thomas, and John.
Marowe's eldest son William made his ' cosen Th. Riche ' one of his
executors.

[9] He died in 1475.

[10] In 1454, d. 1464 ; Beaven, *op. cit.*, i. 82 ; Cal. Lond. Letter Books,
K and L, *passim.*

[11] *Ibid.* Urswyk's brass and that of his wife Ann Ryche are at
Dagenham, Essex ; H. W. Machlin, The Brasses of England, 3rd ed.,
1913, 178, 197.

[12] Kingsford, *loc. cit.*

[13] His reward for opening the city gates to the Yorkists in 1471 ; Sharpe,
Lond. and the Kingdom, i. 313.

in 1451, reputed author of the chronicle,[1] William Essex,[2] controller of Petty Customs in London,[3] John Smart, grocer [4] and near neighbour in Billingsgate,[5] Henry Colet of Stepney, mercer,[6] the father of the dean, Sir John Fortescue, the great Lancastrian judge,[7] and—of especial importance for the career of his son Thomas—Henry Frowyk, mercer, alderman and mayor,[8] the grandfather of the chief justice.

Marowe's business enterprises [9] and long list of bequests [10] show that he succeeded in acquiring great wealth. His landed property was mainly in London and in Essex and Middlesex,

[1] Collections of a Citizen of Lond. (including Gregory's Chronicle), ed. Gairdner, Camden Soc., 1876, introduction. His will was proved 23 January 1467; *ibid.* If, however, Gregory accused Marowe of favouring the mercers in their attack on the Lombards, perhaps he ought to be described as his enemy, not his friend; see p. 119, note 7, *supra.*

[2] Cf. phrase in Gregory's will: 'to my cosyn and godson, William Essex, the sone of William Essex'.

[3] Appointed 30 November 1448; Cal. Pat. Hen. VI, 1446–1452, 205; later King's Remembrancer in the Exchequer, 405; *ibid.,* 1452–1461, 326. He and his son Thomas served on various Middlesex commissions; Cal. Pat., *passim.*

[4] Kingdon, Grocers, and Cal. Lond. Letter Books, *passim.* He was overseer of Marowe's will and made Marowe's son Thomas one of his own executors in 1494.

[5] See Smart's will and that of his wife Agnes; also Records of the Parish of St. Mary at Hill, ed. H. Littlehales, Early Eng. Text Society, *passim.*

[6] Of a younger generation, however; sheriff in 1477–1478, mayor in 1486–1487 and 1495–1496; Beaven, *op. cit.,* ii. 15. Cal. Lond. Letter Books, K and L, *passim.* He was in favour at the court of Henry VII, according to F. Seebohm, Oxford Reformers, 14.

[7] Cal. Lond. Letter Books, K, 359–60. Cf. also the entry in a London chronicle under date of 29 March 1450: 'There sittyng Fortescu Chief Justice in Guyldehalle', E.H.R. xxix. 515.

[8] Mayor in 1435 and 1444; Beaven, *op. cit.,* ii. 7. His will was proved 8 March 1460. Marowe's eldest son in his will bequeathes his 'cuppe of jesper' to his 'cosyn Frawyk' (a spelling that occurs occasionally, for example, Cal. Pat. Hen. VI, 1422–1429, 353), but I have been unable to trace any blood relationship between Marowes and Frowyks.

[9] Cf. e. g. his purchase jointly with seven fellow citizens of '2,000 l. worth of roche alum and blak foile'; Cal. Pat. Hen. VI, 1452–1461, 155.

[10] To churches, hospitals, prisons, bridges, the grocers' fellowship, and to innumerable individuals, dependents, friends, priests, and relatives, including Marowes of Bristol and Dunstable. For these latter, cf. Calendar of Deeds, ed. F. Bickley (mainly relating to Bristol), 87–8. To his wife Marowe left £1,000 and plate worth 100 marks; to each son, £400, to each daughter, 500 marks, besides silver; e. g. to each son: '2 siluer cups, a potell pott of siluer, 12 spones, and 2 salt cellars, one covered', &c., &c.

Stepney perhaps serving as his country place.[1]   Only a few of
his holdings in the city are specified in his will,[2] but they
include his city home in the parish of St. Mary at Hill, houses,
shops, and a wharf next to Billingsgate,[3] originally called Le
Culver Key, then Marowe's Key, and finally Smart's Key,[4] the
name under which it appears on a seventeenth century map

[1] Lands in ' Popeler ' and 'Lymostes ', including a wharf on the river.
Poplar was a hamlet of Stepney, and Limehouse was next to Poplar;
D. Lysons, The Environs of London, 1st ed., 1792–1796, iii. 236, 418, 462.
For the country aspect of Stepney, see Wyngaerde's panorama, *circ.* 1543.
In the year of Marowe's shrievalty, 'the water breake in oute of Temmes
be syde Lymeoste'; Short Eng. Chron., 66.

[2] e. g. in St. Giles, without Cripplegate, St. Botolph's, Bishopsgate, &c.
The loss of his London Inq. p. m. and of that of his son Thomas, makes it
difficult to trace the property.

[3] To ' Kateryn my wif... all my tenements with the keye therto lying ...
in which that I dwelle at Billyngesgate in the parish of Saint Mary Hill'.
For the parish, see Littlehales, *op. cit.*, and Stow, *op. cit.*, i. 208–9.   The
latter mentions the 'many fayre houses for marchantes' and the high
rents near the water.

[4] The early history of Le Culver Key needs further investigation,
especially the incident of the deed forged to prove that it had been
conveyed to Henry Julian about 1403 by Richard Pavy and Johanna his
wife; Cal. Lond. Letter Books, K, 20–2.   Cf. also Hustings Roll 180,
no. 38 (in Guildhall), Cal. Pat. Hen. V, 1413–1416, 304–6, and art. on
' Forgery of Fines, 1272–1376,' by H. G. Richardson, in E.H.R. xxxv. 405–
18.   It was from the heir of the above Johanna, Thomas Reynham, that
Marowe on 23 June 1459 obtained seisin: ' de et in tota illa magna
placea cum shopis et domibus ante situatis ac wharfo adiacenti situatis
in parochia beate Marie atte Hill iuxta Billingesgate ... ex antiquo vocato
le Culver...'; Hustings Roll 197, no. 51.   On 4 November 1465 Marowe's
executors use identical terms to describe the premises conveyed to his
widow by his will; *ibid.* 195, no. 40.   Cf. also *ibid.* 197, no. 8.   Marowe's
sons use the family name for the key, and by a specific agreement between
the brothers Thomas receives it on William's death in 1499 (see William's
will), and on condition that it be not alienated, bequeathes ' the grete
place and wharf called Marowes key beside Billyngesgate' to his nephew
and ward Thomas, William's son and heir.   The younger Thomas died
in 1538, seized of ' Marroys Key' (Cal. Lond. Inq. p. m., 63); but possibly
after the elder Thomas's death in 1505, when the younger was still a minor,
the key was occupied by William Smart, son of the old family friend and
neighbour, John Smart, and one of the executors of the elder Thomas's
will, thus accounting for the reference to 'Master Smartes Key' in 1512–
1514 (Littlehales, *op. cit.*, 283, 287).   Perhaps afterwards it was actually
owned by a member of the Smart family, since in 1560 it is referred to by
its later owner, Th. Nicolson, as ' commonly called Smartes Key'; Cal.
Lond. Wills, ed. R. R. Sharpe, ii. 673–4.   By 1582, however, its earlier
name was still remembered: '... quondam cognito deputato et vocato
per nomen de le Marowes key et modo per le nomen de le Smartes key';
Hustings Roll 266, no. 19.   H. A. Harben, Dictionary of London, makes
serious mistakes in regard to this key.

made shortly after the great fire.[1]   He also owned a wharf in Petty Wales, Tower ward,[2] close to the famous Galley Key[3] and near the custom house[4] over which his friend William Essex had presided. Further researches into London customs, national and semi-national,[5] may throw light on the precise methods by which Marowe and other merchants made their profits, but it is obvious that this river frontage was exceptionally advantageous for his overseas trade in spices, drugs, oils, &c.[6]

Such was the heritage into which Thomas Marowe and his brothers and sisters entered—a heritage of friends, wealth, comfortable houses and assured position in the very centre of the economic and political life of fifteenth-century England.[7] John and Agnes did not survive their father many months,[8] and as the eldest son was probably under twelve in 1464[9] it is

[1] Plan of London after the Fire, engraved by Wenceslaus Hollar, 1667. Described in six plates by John Leake. Cf. also Stow's description, *op. cit.*, i. 43, 205, and Agas's spelling 'Smarez' in the facsimile of his map in the library of Guildhall. Agas's map is now supposed to have been made between 1561 and 1576 ; Wheatley, 'Notes on Norden and Map of 1593', Lond. Top. Record, ii. 42.

[2] For the 'grete place in Petiwales' left to his wife with reversion to his sons, see his will and Hustings Roll 169, nos. 20 and 21. It was 'commonly called Marwe's newe key', although in his possession as early as 1440; *ibid.* 195, no. 14.

[3] Acquired by Marowe's eldest son and his wife on 12 May 1488, possibly the date of his agreement with his brother Thomas as to Marowe Key (p. 122, note 4, *supra*); Hist. MSS. Comm., Var. Collect., iv, 1907, 336. Cf. Stow, *op. cit.*, i. 132, 136.   [4] *Ibid.*, *passim.*

[5] N. Gras, in Early English Customs System, 1918, makes an illuminating presentation of the subject. Note especially his account of the tolls in Billingsgate ; 153 *et seq.*, 688. For the exceptional position of this ward, see Stow, *op. cit.*, index. By the reign of Elizabeth, Billingsgate is said to be an open place for the landing of all victuals, grocery wares excepted ; Wheatley, *op. cit.*, 55.

[6] The traditional theory is that the Pepperers and Spicers combined to form the Grocers, great wholesale dealers in products from the East ; E. Lipson, Ec. Hist. Eng., 384.

[7] Sharpe, London and the Kingdom, *passim.*

[8] They died between 8 October 1464—the date of their father's will— and 4 November 1465, when only the other four are mentioned ; Hustings Roll 195, no. 40. Of John I have found no other mention except the erroneous statement in a pedigree ; Harl. Soc. Pub. xii. On 12 May 1466 there is a reference to the death of Agnes ; Cal. Lond. Letter Books, L, 63. The marginal entry is : 'Custodia puerorum Willelmi Marowe orphanorum civitatis'.

[9] For proof, see p. 125, *infra.*

clear that Thomas, the youngest son,[1] did not long come under his father's direct influence. But their father's wealth was an enduring factor in the lives of his children and grandchildren, not only by giving them opportunities for education and for professional and business advancement, but also—in an age when marriages were bought and sold—by enabling them to contract alliances with distinguished county families and by thus eventually removing them from London.

Johanna, the eldest daughter, became the wife of William Clopton of Kentwell Hall, Melford, and of Hawstead, Suffolk,[2] son of John Clopton, sheriff of Suffolk in 1451,[3] a man of great wealth and importance.[4] Johanna and her husband do not seem to have kept in close touch with the Marowes, yet we find that Dorothy, one of the many children, in her will proved in 1508, mentions her 'grete bedes of whyte yvery' and 'xxᵗⁱ nobles' which her 'vnkill Marowe' had given her.[5] It is worth noting that one of Johanna's descendants married Sir Simon Dewes.[6]

Of greater significance for the London Marowes was the marriage, not later than 1479, of Johanna's sister Katharine to Sir Robert Throckmorton,[7] son and heir of Sir Thomas Throckmorton of Coughton, Warwickshire. Coughton,[8] still the country seat of this distinguished family,[9] had been acquired through marriage by Sir Robert's grandfather, Sir John Throckmorton of Fladbury, Worcestershire, under-treasurer of

---

[1] On 8 October 1464, the date of their father's will, and possibly in May 1466 (p. 123, note 8, *supra*), all the children were still minors and unmarried.

[2] The Clopton pedigrees (J. Nichols, Bib. Top. Brit., v. 101), although showing clearly the importance of the family, do not give a complete list of the children of this marriage.

[3] Lists and Indexes, ix.

[4] Cal. Pat., *passim*, and his will, proved 16 November 1497, a document of exceptional interest.

[5] Almost certainly Thomas, the serjeant-at-law.

[6] Nichols, *loc. cit.*

[7] Cal. Lond. Letter Books, L, 63; pedigree, Harl. Soc. Pub. xii. She was his second wife.

[8] Sir Robert is said to have 'erected for himself a fine monument' there; T. R. Nash, Worcestershire, i. 452.

[9] Note the death on 22 December 1919 of a Throckmorton of Coughton.

England in the reign of Henry V.[1] Katharine and Sir Robert
are said to have had five sons and seven daughters.[2] Two of
the boys, Anthony and Michael, took part in the affairs of the
turbulent and brilliant Italy of the Renaissance and were slain
at Pavia,[3] and their father, Sir Robert, died in Rome, almost
the last of the pilgrims.[4] George, the eldest son, succeeded to
Coughton,[5] and it was his grandson Nicholas who became
eminent under Elizabeth as chief butler, chamberlain of the
Exchequer, and ambassador.[6] As will appear below, Thomas
Marowe seems to have remained in close association with his
sister's family and may through them have gained an outlook
on the world outside of England.

William Marowe, the eldest son (d. 1499),[7] spent his life in
and near London without achieving any special distinction.
If he is the William Marowe who signed a deed in 1474,[8] he
must have been at least twenty-one in that year ; he could not
have been much older, since it is not till 1485 that his name
begins to appear on the routine commissions for London and
Middlesex,[9] associated usually with some member of the
Frowyk family—once with the elder Sir Thomas Frowyk [10]
and frequently with his sons Henry [11] and Thomas, the latter

[1] For the Throckmortons, see Nash, *op. cit.*, Dugdale, Warwickshire,
Cal. Pat., *passim*, and article in D.N.B. The pedigrees in Nash, i. 452,
and in Harl. Soc. Pub. xii, omit Sir Robert's third wife (see will) and
contain many errors and discrepancies. For Sir John, see p. 74, *supra*.
The earlier spelling seems to have been ' Throgmerton ', still used in the
late fifteenth century ; cf. p. 139, note 3, *infra*.
[2] Pedigrees, *ut supra*.   [3] Harl. Soc. Pub. xii.
[4] To his will written in England on 2 July 1518 was added a supplement
in Italy on 10 August 1518. It was proved 9 November 1520.
[5] See his father's will. He married Katharine the daughter of Nicholas
Vause of Harwedon (pedigrees, *ut supra*, and Surrey Archaeolog. Collections, i). For his brass and that of his wife and their nineteen children,
see E. W. Badger, Monumental Brasses of Warwickshire, 16.
[6] Stow, *op. cit.*, i. 143. It was from him that Throgmorton Street took
its name.   [7] See his Inq. p. m., p. 126, note 5, *infra*.
[8] Hustings Roll 204, no. 14.
[9] 20 September 1485, commission of the peace and thenceforth until his
death ; Cal. Pat. Hen. VII, i. 493, ii. 650; 21 January 1488, commission
for a subsidy, *ibid.* i. 242 ; 3 March 1497, commission de Walliis et
Fossatis, *ibid.* ii. 171.
[10] The son of the elder Marowe's old associate, Henry Frowyk (*supra*,
p. 121). He died 26 September 1485 ; see will, and Cal. Inq. p. m.
Hen. VII, i. 58.
[11] Died 3 October 1505 ; see will, and Cal. Lond. Inq. p. m., 23–5.

destined to be chief justice[1]—later with his own younger
brother Thomas.[2] William[3] married Joan, daughter of an
alderman, William Chedworth,[4] and at his death in 1499[5] left
his little son, Thomas,[6] to the guardianship of the child's uncle
Thomas. Thomas junior[7] (d. 1538),[8] afterwards to be known
as Thomas senior,[9] married in succession two Warwickshire
heiresses, first, the daughter of Baldwin Douse of Balsall and
second, the daughter of Roger Wigston of Wolston.[10] His son
and heir Thomas (d. 1561),[11] in addition to his estate at
Hoxton, Middlesex,[12] acquired the valuable Warwickshire
manors of Rudfen, Berkswell, and Birmingham,[13] the last two
remaining in the family for many generations. He was trained
at the Middle Temple,[14] had a considerable library,[15] and

[1] See *infra*, p. 132.
[2] For records of proceedings before William as justice of the peace,
see p. 134, *infra*.
[3] The pedigree in Visitation of 1619 (see p. 117, note 5, *supra*) errs in
calling him William of Rudfeld ; cf. Dugdale, Warwickshire, 981.
[4] Dugdale, *loc. cit.* In Visitation of 1619 he is described as John
Chadworth who had been mayor in 1401-1402 ; Stow, *op. cit.*, ii. 170 ;
Beaven, Aldermen, i. 17, spelt ' Shadworth '.
[5] Will ; Inq. p. m. ; (1) Essex, Cal. Inq. p. m. Hen. VII, ii, no. 302 ;
(2) P.R.O. Chancery Ser., ii. 20, no. 32 ; (3) Exch. Ser. ii, file 294, no. 4 ;
London Inq. missing. 20 March 1499 is probably the correct date of his
death (nos. 1 and 2), certainly not 1 May 1500 (no. 3).
[6] In the above Inquisitions the boy's age in 1499 is given variously as
six, three, or five.
[7] His uncle is described as ' Thomas the elder' in 1499 ; P.R.O. Anc.
Deeds, A, 804.
[8] According to Cal. Lond. Inq. p. m., 63, and P.R.O. Ch. Ser., ii. 61,
no. 115, Midd., he died on 2 September, which fell on Monday in 1538 ;
but his unfinished testament shows that he was still alive 'vppon Tuysday
morning' having had a ' pange' the night before. To an urgent request
to make his will, he had replied that ' he had a will or two made whereso-
ever they were'.
[9] Dugdale, *op. cit.*, 981, and Harl. Soc. Pub. lxii ; but he is omitted in
the Visitation of 1619, Harl. Soc. Pub. xii.
[10] *Ibid.* lxii. The Marowe marriage is omitted in the Wigston pedigrees
(*ibid.*), but is proved by the testament.
[11] P.R.O. Inq. p. m., Ch. Ser., ii. 132, no. 38.
[12] He is often called Thomas ' de Hoxtown'; will, and Dugdale, 981.
He married Alice, the daughter of Richard Harry Young ; *ibid.*
[13] For his temporary possession of Rudfen, Rudfeld, or Wrydfen, see
ibid. 254; for Berkswell, *ibid.* 981 ; for Birmingham, W. Bickley and
J. Hill, Survey of Birmingham.
[14] Minutes of Parliament Middle Temple, ed. C. T. Martin, i, index
under Marowe.
[15] See p. 182 and note 7, *infra*.

apparently became a country gentleman of note.[1]   His eldest
son Samuel (d. 1610)[2] married the daughter of John Littleton
of Frankley, Worcestershire.[3]   Henceforth this elder male
branch—the Marowes of Berkswell, and Birmingham—settled
down as a Warwickshire county family, not far from their
cousins the Throckmortons, and while keeping their Middlesex
property, lost their connexion with London.[4]

Of Thomas Marowe's childhood and early youth almost no
specific details have been found, but in his legal career he was
so closely associated with the far more distinguished lawyer,
chief justice Frowyk, that information about the latter is sometimes useful in reconstructing the life of the former.[5]   Since
they seem to have been about the same age and since it is
fairly certain that Frowyk was born in 1460 or 1461,[6] Marowe
was probably born between 1461 and October 1464,[7] in the
parish of St. Mary at Hill.   He perhaps made his first public
appearance at his grandfather Ryche's funeral in the summer
of 1464, carried in his mother's arms, clad in black cloth.[8]   It

[1] Probably the subject of Leland's eulogy : ' Ad Thomam Maronem '
among ' Encomia illustrium virorum ' in Collectanea, ed. Th. Hearne,
1770, v. 143.
[2] For the pedigrees and coats of arms of these later Marowes, see Harl.
Soc. Pub. lxii, and Midland Antiquary, i. 114–16.
[3] Of the family of the great judge, see p. 79, note 3, *supra*, and pedigree
in Harl. Soc. Pub. xxvii.
[4] The will of Samuel does not mention any London property.
[5] There is abundant material for a far fuller and more accurate biography
of Frowyk than at present exists.
[6] Th. Fuller (Worthies of England, 1811 ed., ii. 42) had said that Frowyk
(d. 1506) died ' before full forty years old ', thus interpreting Keilwey's
phrase ' in florida juventute sua ' and making 1466 the earliest possible
date for his birth.   But the will of his grandmother Isabella, widow of
Henry Frowyk (*supra*, p. 121), proves that he was in existence in November 1464, while a phrase in the will of his grandfather Henry makes it
probable that in April 1459 Elizabeth, the first wife of the chief justice's
father, Sir Thomas, was still alive, the mother of two children, Henry and
Isabella, but *not* the mother of the chief justice.   Therefore, to allow time
for her death and for the marriage of her widowed husband to his second
wife Johanna, and for the birth of their son Thomas—the future chief
justice—it seems safe to put this last event not earlier than the end of
1460 or the beginning of 1461.   But a comparison of the chronology of
the legal careers of Frowyk and Marowe makes it unlikely that Marowe
was older than Frowyk, and therefore unlikely that Marowe was born
earlier than 1461.
[7] He is mentioned in his father's will of 8 October.
[8] See Ryche's testament.

is hard to imagine a more fascinating place in which to pass one's childhood than the Billingsgate house, adjoining the great wharf, in contact with ships and people from far-distant lands, within sight of water processions and shows given by the gilds at royal entries,[1] and near enough the heart of the city to see street pageants, night watches,[2] and 'mayings'— these last sometime also celebrated in the Bishop's wood near his Stepney home.[3]   He may have begun his education at the 'scole grammaticalis' of St. Paul's[4] or at the rival school of St. Anthony's in Threadneedle Street[5] and possibly like Frowyk have had a university training,[6] but all that is known is that he pursued his legal studies at the Inner Temple,[7] admitted probably about 1479,[8] just before the death in 1481 of judge Littleton,[9] the most distinguished of the Benchers,[10]

---

[1] Descriptions exist of the river scenes at various royal entries in the late fifteenth century; R. Withington, English Pageantry, especially, i. 150–1, 160–1 ; G. Unwin, The Gilds and Companies of London, 273. Since Thomas's uncle, the recorder, had helped to admit Edward IV in 1471 (supra, p. 120, note 13), the child may well have had a chance to see the barges, &c.   It was shortly before 1460 that the mayor's procession to Westminster took place by water instead of through the city streets ; C. L. Kingsford, Eng. Hist. Lit. in Fifteenth Century, 99–100.

[2] Unwin, op. cit., passim, especially ch. xvi ; Stow, op. cit., i. 91–104, 230–1.

[3] Ibid. 98–9.   [4] P.R.O. Rot. Claus. 8 Hen. VII, m. 4 d, no. 7.

[5] 'The schollers of Paules meeting with them of S. Anthonies would call them Anthonie pigs, and they again would call the other pigeons of Paules' ; Stow, op. cit., i. 75.   Cf. A. F. Leach, Mediaeval Schools of England, for the general subject.   John Colet, the son of Marowe's father's Stepney neighbour (supra, p. 121), and Thomas More, the son of his own fellow serjeant-at-law (infra, p. 134), both studied at St. Anthony's ; D.N.B., art. on Colet and More ; Seebohm, Oxford Reformers, 13, 24.

[6] Frowyk is stated to have been at Cambridge, but on what authority I have been unable to determine ; Athenae Cantabrigienses, ed. C. H. Cooper, i. 10, 522.   That the Countess of Richmond appointed him in 1502, together with Humphrey Coningsby, as arbitrator between the university and the town, proves nothing; cf. Cooper, Annals of Cambridge, i. 258–70.   His mother in her will asked that a 'priest being a scoler of either Oxford or of Cambridge' or of both, should sing masses for her soul, but Frowyk himself left a bequest for a 'good and vertuous priest' to study 'dyuinitie in the university of Oxenford'.

[7] The records of the Inner Temple now in existence begin at 1505, but contain references to earlier ones; Calendar, ed. F. A. Inderwick, i. x. Dugdale's list of readers begins in 1507, Orig. Jurid., 163, but fortunately much additional information as to readers, readings, and moots exists in MS. in various archives; see ch. vi (3), infra, pp. 177–81.

[8] Infra, p. 129, note 8.   [9] p. 79, note 3, supra.

[10] For his reading, see ch. vi (3), p. 178, infra.

and probably a few years later than Frowyk [1] with whom he seemed to have shared a chamber. [2] During these early years he had a chance to hear many readings, [3] in some cases by men whose names are well known : Morgan Kidwelly, Richard Littleton, son of the judge, Frowyk for his first and second readings, and Thomas Keble, whose serjeant's feast in July 1486 he perhaps witnessed. [4]

In this same month, Frowyk, the 'oracle of the law', [5] was made common pleader of London. [6] He had presumably been called to the bar in 1483 or 1484, and was therefore a strangely inexperienced ' utter barrister ' for so important a city position. By Easter term 1489 he first appears in the Year Books [7] and is thoroughly launched on his brilliant career. Marowe must have received his call by 1486 or 1487, [8] for in July 1491 he

[1] *Infra*, note 8.

[2] 'On 3 May 1506 Lawrence Wadham was assigned a chamber where Sir Thomas Frowyk, Kn., chief justice of the Common Pleas, and Thomas Marowe, late serjeant-at-law lay '; Cal. Inner Temple Records, i. 6. Did Marowe perhaps go by water from Billingsgate to the Inner Temple ? Cf. Richard Littleton : ' il poet aler a Grays Inne par barge ou feri bote '; MS. Hh. 3. 6. f. 10 b, U.L.C. Unwin describes the gild of Watermen and the Billingsgate porters; *op. cit.*, 353.

[3] See ch. vi (3), pp. 177-8, *infra*.

[4] p. 179. From just about this date Marowe's name begins to appear in business transactions; Cal. Lond. and Midd. Feet of Fines, 2 Hen. VII, 1486; Cal. Inq. p. m., Hen. VII, i, no. 365, Feb. 1487; Guildhall, Hustings Roll 217, no. 32, 1488; 218, no. 17, 1489; P.R.O. Rot. Claus. 3 Hen. VII, m. 9 d, July 1488.

[5] Fuller, *ut supra*, p. 127, note 6.

[6] 13 July, in place of Richard Higham, later to be serjeant-at-law; Journal 9, f. 114 b, Guildhall. The terms ' common pleader ' and ' common serjeant ' are used interchangeably at this period; Sharpe, Cal. Lond. Letter Books, L, 281.

[7] Pasch. 4 Hen. VII, no. 1. Perhaps the interval of time required in 1574 by the Privy Council and judges was commonly observed at this early date. The ' utter barrister ' was to continue in ' exercises of learning ' for five years after his call before being allowed to practise in the courts at Westminster ; Dugdale, Orig. Jurid., 312 ; Black Books Lincoln's Inn, ed. W. P. Baildon, i, introduct. xi ; Pension Book Gray's Inn, ed. R. J. Fletcher, i, introduct. xii.

[8] Marowe would seem to have spent just about the normal eight years as 'inner barrister' (Cal. Inner Temple Records, i. lxxvii, 346) if he was admitted in 1479 ; he would have been somewhere between fifteen and eighteen years old at his admission. But Frowyk must either have been admitted at fifteen, or must have shortened the normal course ; see p. 127, note 6, *supra*. They may have both spent the first part of their legal course at an Inn of Chancery, Clement's or Lyon's, as did Thomas Roberts of Willesden, later as coroner of London to be frequently associated with

K

succeeded Frowyk as common pleader,[1] both young men doubtless aided in their advancement by their strong family backing.[2] By Michaelmas 1492 Marowe is referred to in the Year Books in terms of respect : ' Marrow del Temple conust le case bien, car il fuit Consel in le dit matter '.[3] On at least one occasion a few years later, in his position as common pleader, he succeeded in influencing the ' comons ' by his ' greate exortacion '.[4]

In view of his staid and industrious career it is natural to

them. Cf. the entry in MS. Harl. 1859, f. 218 b ; on November 10 Hen. VII 'admissus est in societatem hospicii vocati Clementis Inn'. He continued there until 1 August 14 Hen. VII (VIII by an error in the MS.) on which day, 'admissus est in societatem Interioris Templi . . .' The lists of admission, calls to the bar, &c., as given in the records of the four Inns of Court, especially at Lincoln's Inn, where they are contemporary for this period, show that the amount of time spent as an ' inner barrister' varied considerably ; from six to nine years, *temp*. Elizabeth, are mentioned for Gray's Inn; Pension Book, i. xxxiii. Apart from the references in the records of the four Inns, many of them printed by Dugdale in Orig. Jurid., the most famous descriptions of the curriculum are of course contained in ch. 49 of Fortescue, ' De laudibus legum Angliae' written between 1468–1470, referring, I believe, rather to his student days than to the period of his old age (but cf. A. Pulling, Order of the Coif, 160–1, for a very different view); and in the report made to Henry VIII in 1540 by Nicholas Bacon of Gray's Inn and Thomas Denton and Robert Carey of the Middle Temple (printed by E.Waterhouse in Fortescutus Illustratus, 1663, 543–7), distinctly too late to be an infallible source for the end of the fifteenth century. For the same reason Coke's preface to his Third Report is not to be too thoroughly trusted. For the whole subject, see ch. vi (2) and (3), *infra*.

[1] 30 July, 6 Hen. VII, 1491 : ' In isto comuni consilio Thomas Marowe, gentilman, admissus est in communem narratorem ciuitatis predicte [ad] habendum et exercendum officium illud quamdiu se bene gesserit in eodem, capiendum feoda et regarda eidem officio ab antiquo debita et consueta prout Thomas Frowyke habuit et percepit'; Guildhall, Journal 9, f. 275 b; Letter Book L. f. 28 (in the printed Cal. 280–1, erroneously dated 7 Hen. VII, 1492).

[2] According to Fortescue (*loc. cit.*), only gentry who were also men of wealth sent their sons to the Inns of Court; the poor and vulgar could not and burgesses and men of trade would not. Yet these two young men both came of families of ' men of trade', their fathers and grandfathers contemporaries of Fortescue.

[3] 8 Hen. VII, no. 4. The case is a feoffment involving an obligation by statute merchant. It is interesting to note the omission of ' Inner' from Marowe's Inn of Court. For the date of the division into the two Temples, see Cal. Inner Temple Records, i. xiv ; Master Worsley's Book, ed. A. R. Ingpen, 17 ; Bolland, Law Quarterly Review, xxiv. 402 ; Minutes of Parliament of Middle Temple, i. v–xii; Holdsworth, Hist. Eng. Law, ii. 422–3.

[4] 1494, Chronicles of Lond., ed. Kingsford, 201.

find Marowe arguing cases at moots together with Frowyk, Keble, Kidwelly, Littleton,[1] &c., and easy to imagine him reading at the appointed time and keeping his ' Learning ' vacations regularly [2] rather than studying ' music, dancing and other nobleman's pastimes ', in the classic words of his father's contemporary, judge Fortescue.[3] One wonders whether Marowe and Frowyk as inner barristers ever stole quince pies from the kitchen,[4] or whether as utter barristers they were among the ' squyers and gentylmen' who joined ' Therle of Oxford' and other noblemen in witnessing ' ye disgysyng of ye Inner Temple' and of ' Grays Inne ' in January 1490.[5]

Early in 1491 [6] Marowe made a brilliant marriage and in addition to his work as common pleader was acting as counsel for his native parish,[7] with every prospect of as distinguished a legal career as his friend Frowyk. But the latter, after his famous reading on the Prerogative of the King in August 1495,[8] was made serjeant-at-law in the following November, 11 Henry VII,[9] with a notable serjeant's feast at Ely

---

[1] *Infra*, p. 184, in account of Marowe's sources.

[2] See references in note 8, p. 129, *supra*, and Cal. Inner Temple Records, *passim*.

[3] *Loc. cit.*; cf. Holdsworth, *op. cit.*, ii. 415.

[4] On 1 February 1496, a student was amerced 3*s.* 4*d.* 'quia cepit unam picam quynces extra clebanum in coquina . . .'; Black Books Lincoln's Inn, i. 106.

[5] See note on the fly-leaf of a Lincoln's Inn MS., Various Donors, no. xlvi. Mr. W. Paley Baildon was kind enough to transcribe the entry for me. Cf. Pulling, Order of the Coif, 249, for the close alliance between these two Inns and for the Joint Masque of 1612. [6] *Infra*, p 138.

[7] Records of St. Mary at Hill, ed. Littlehales, 178-9, under date of 1491-1492 : ' Coustes spent in the lawe ayenst the priores of Sent Elyns for Iohn Causton chauntrye . . . Item, to Master Wode seriaunt, iii s. iiii d. Item, to Maister Savell and to master marow iii s. iiii d. . . . . Item, [to above three] the xxxiii day of novembere, x s. . . . Item, to mastere morden & to master marow, vi s. viii d. Item, for copyeng out of the testament, to master marows clarke, iii s. iiii d. . . . Item, to master morden and to master marowe, vi s. viii d.' Several other payments to Marowe for the same case were made in 1493-1494; *ibid.* 203.

[8] p. 180, *infra*.

[9] The errors as to the date in almost all the authorities (including Dugdale, Chron. Ser., 75, 1496, and those quoted in note 1, p. 132) are due partly to the almost hopeless chronological chaos of the printed Year Books of this reign and to the confusion between the calendar and regnal years, the latter changing on 22 August. In MS. Hargrave 105, Year Books Hen. VII, the tenth year is not divided into terms ; f. 211 has the following entry : ' Nota qe en fyne de cest terme nouell serieantz fueront

House,[1] and became chief justice of the Common Pleas on 30 September 1502.[2] Marowe, on the other hand, sometime in 1495 accepted the office of under-sheriff of London[3]—a position which has not usually been associated with distinction at the bar [4]— and apparently devoted himself to his duties in the city for seven crucial years of his life.   During most of this time Edmund Dudley of notorious fame and ignominious death [5] was the other under-sheriff.[6] Would Marowe, the eminently respectable

eslieuz Scilicet,'—list follows, assigning Frowyk wrongly to the Middle Temple—' et toutz ceux fueront juriez en le Chauncerye long temps deuaunt qilz fueront faytz etc. anno regni regis Henrici VII X^{mo}, vt supra, quod nota bene'.   Certainly this is a more correct date than Trin. 9 Hen. VII as given in the printed Year Book, Pasch. 9 Hen. VII, no. 6. The warrant for the great seal was signed 9 September, 11 Hen. VII (1495) and was delivered to the chancellor on the next day, with a list that included Mordant, Oxenbrigge, Higham, Frowyk, Constable, Conyngesby, Yaxley Kyngesmyll, and Boteler ; P.R.O., Chancery Warrants for the Great Seal, ii, file 140.   The entry on the Close Roll is dated 10 September 11th year : ' Quia de auisamento consilii nostri . . . ad statum et gradum seruientis ad legem . . . in crastino sancti Martini proximo futuro suscepturi . . .' (Thursday, 12 November) ; m. 7.

    [1] Under date of 1495, among Privy Purse Expenses, there was a payment for ' rowing the King opon Monday to the Sergeants feste ' ; Excerpta Historica, ed. S. Bentley, 106.   For a description of the feast ' at the Bysshops of Elyes place in Holbourn, where dyned the Kyng, the Quene, and all the chyef lordes of England,' 16 November ' anno XI°', see Chronicles of London, ed. Kingsford, 207–9.   The editor in his introduction puts it at the end of 1494, and in a note to his edition of Stow, makes it 21 November ; ii. 362.   R. Holinshed, Chronicles, 1587 ed., 779, makes the date 16 November 1495, 10 Hen. VII.   Bacon gives it correctly ; Life of Henry VII, ed. Montague, 307.

    [2] P.R.O., Chancery Warrants for the Great Seal, ii, file 236.

    [3] On 30 July, 10 Hen. VII (1495) it is ' agreed and granted that Thomas Marowe nowe comen sergeant shall have the next advoydance of the office of oon of the vndersheriffs of London.   Item it is agreed that whan so ever it shall fortune Thomas Marowe comen sergeaunt to come into thoffice of vndersherif or depart oute of the office of the comen sergeaunt that than John Grene, gentilman, shalbe commen sergeaunt of the said citee in place of the said Thomas Marowe' ; Journal 10, f. 50 b, Guildhall. Perhaps it is not a mere coincidence that Marowe entered upon his new duties at just the time that a statute was being enacted containing some new regulations on the office of sheriff and under-sheriff ; see p. 18, supra, note 6.

    On 7 December 13 Hen. VIII (1521) John Greene resigned, ' which by the space of XXVI yeres nowe passed hath contynuelly been in thoffice of comen sergeaunt . . .', Journal 12, f. 154.   I am greatly indebted to the friendly help of Mr. A. H. Thomas, Clerk of the Records, in finding these references.   [4] See note 5, p. 133, infra.

    [5] Executed on 18 August 1510 ; art. in D.N.B.

    [6] From 1497, according to Stow.   See Survey, i. 224, for an account of the ' two faire houses ' of Empson and Dudley, in Walbrooke ward.

city lawyer and friend of judge Frowyk[1] have also lost his head, had he too survived Henry VII? Dudley (and Empson[2]) were not perhaps, as stated in Bacon's memorable phrase, 'turning law and justice into wormwood rapine',[3] but, in a reign important for the development of the administration of the law, were probably aiding the crown in suppressing a too turbulent nobility by legitimate legal processes.[4] It is certainly significant that neither Dudley nor Marowe became unpopular with the London authorities and that on their resignation in the autumn of 1502 they were both rewarded with annual pensions by the grateful city council.[5]

During these years Marowe's duties as under-sheriff kept him, of course, mainly in London,[6] and although he appears occasionally as counsel in the court of King's Bench,[7] his only other activities seem to have consisted in serving on local

---

[1] Commended by Bacon, Life of Henry VII, 413.

[2] For Empson's association with Marowe, see *infra*, p. 139, note 2.

[3] *Op. cit.*, 381–2.

[4] It would be well worth while to investigate anew the evidence for the traditional point of view about Dudley and Empson, as expressed for example in Fisher's recent volume, The Political History of England, 1485–1547, 126–33, or G. Temperley's Henry VII, 278–9. Dudley's own treatise, The Tree of Commonwealth, deserves careful study. Written in 1509–1510 while he was a prisoner in the Tower, it was not published until 1859.

[5] 'XVIImo die Novembris 1502. Ad hanc curiam Thomas Marowe vnus subvicecomitum sponte resignauit officium suum'; Repertories I, f. 116, Guildhall; '13 iour de Decembre (1502). Eodem die consideratum est quod Thomas Marowe et Edmundus Dudley nuper subvicecomites pro eorum fideli concilio antea hec tempora negociis ciuitatis impenso et de cetero impendendo percipient et eorum quilibet annuatim percipiet de camera vnam togam stragulatam et viginti solidos nomine feodi'; *ibid.* f. 118. I am indebted to Mr. Thomas for both these references and also for his emphasis on the fact that the post of under-sheriff in London, as one of the judges in the two sheriffs' courts, was an important one. In view of the evidence presented by Mr. Thomas it is no longer necessary to be surprised that a 'distinguished barrister and a privy councillor' was under-sheriff; see discussion in art. on Dudley in D.N.B. It is also interesting to note that Thomas More accepted the position in September 1510 and apparently received a large income from it ; Foss, Judges.

[6] He is described as 'of London', 12 February 1501, Cal. Pat. Hen. VII, 1494–1509, 232; 7 November 1502, P.R.O., Rot. Claus. 18 Hen. VII, pt. I, m. 13 d.

[7] Year Books, Trin. 12 Hen. VII (1497), no. 1 ; Mich. 14 Hen. VII (1498), no. 19, 'Marowe Apprenti. . .' Unless the chronology is even more faulty than usual (p. 135, note 3, *infra*), the entries prove that an under-sheriff can act as counsel.

commissions, De Walliis et Fossatis in London and Middlesex, and Hertfordshire,[1] Gaol Delivery at Westminster,[2] of the peace in Middlesex,[3] usually associated (as has been already noted) with his brother and with the Frowyks. It is at least a plausible hypothesis that Frowyk, with full opportunity for knowledge of Marowe's ability, had urged him to a more ambitious career and that on his own elevation to the post of chief justice of the court of Common Pleas had persuaded him to resign his post of under-sheriff by promising to secure his election as serjeant-at-law in the near future.[4] Perhaps, too, Frowyk found that the king was favourably inclined toward Dudley's colleague.[5] The learned reading delivered by Marowe in Lent 1503, 'De pace terre et ecclesie et conseruacione eiusdem, Westminster primer, capitulo primo',[6] would be the requisite preliminary.[7] To its preparation he probably devoted his energies during the winter of 1502–1503.[8] The formal appointment of the serjeants, including Dudley as well as Marowe, also Sir Thomas More's father, was made early in

[1] 3 March 1497, Cal. Pat. Hen. VII, 1494–1509, 117 ; 5 April 1502, *ibid*. 285. Henry Colet was included in the latter.
[2] 17 February 1501, *ibid*. 231.
[3] The earliest enrolled commission for Middlesex on which his name appears is 18 October 1501 ; *ibid*. 650, but the following proceedings before Marowe exist : 1499, Friday, 5 July, P.R.O., Anc. Indictments, K.B. 9, no. 444, m. 60 d ; 1500, Monday, 24 February, no. 422, m. 86 ; Thursday, 23 April, no. 445, m. 65 ; Thursday, 30 April, no. 422, m. 58 ; Monday, 6 July, no. 444, m. 56 ; Saturday, 22 August, *ibid*., m. 52 ; 1501, 25 January, *ibid*., ms. 53, 54 ; Thursday, 30 September, *ibid*., m. 55 d.
[4] We know from Fortescue, *op. cit*., ch. 50, that the chief justice of the Common Pleas, with the consent of all the judges, nominated the men to be created serjeants-at-law and sent the names to the chancellor. Cf. Holdsworth, Hist. Eng. Law, ii. 407, and the endorsement of the list of serjeants, cited p. 135. note 1, *infra*.
[5] Dudley was made speaker of the parliament that sat in January 1503 ; Fisher, *op. cit*., 96. Frowyk himself was *persona grata* to the king and to his mother, the Countess of Richmond (art. in D.N.B. ; Bacon, Life of Henry VII) ; and evidently came into close relations with the king ; cf. for example his summons to Richmond in 1501 with all the 'Iudges and servants' ; Plumpton Correspondence, Camden Soc., 161. Various payments to him out of the Privy Purse are recorded : in 1498, 'To Master Conyngesby servaunt and Master Frowick servaunt for writing of sertayn bokes for the King, £3 6s. 8d.' ; Excerpta Historica, 119 ; in 1499, to the same, £14 6s. 8d. and to their clerks in reward, £2 ; *ibid*. 123.
[6] Ch. vi, *infra*, and App. III.   [7] See pp. 167–8, *infra*.
[8] By 1540 (p. 129, note 8, *supra*) it was customary to give the future reader six months notice.

Michaelmas term, 19 Henry VII, 1503,[1] with the statement that the actual creation was to take place on 13 November. The picturesque ceremonies lasted several days and included an unusually brilliant serjeant's feast at the archbishop's palace of Lambeth, in the presence of the king and queen.[2]

The brief remainder of Marowe's life was typical of the career of a serjeant-at-law, destined ultimately for the Bench. He appeared frequently in the courts at Westminster,[3] was

[1] The list includes Fairfax, Brudenell, Elyott, Cutlere, Pollard, Adgore, and Grevill besides the three just mentioned and appears among Ch. Warrants for the Great Seal, ii, file 252, no. 14, under the heading, 'Nomina servientium ad legem de novo faciendorum', but apparently detached from the writ, which I have been unable to find. The list has the following endorsement: ' Memorandum quod XIII die Novembris quod erit anno XIX° Henrici VII procreacione infrascripti seruientes ad legem exfide facti in Curia Cancellarii dicti domini Regis per relacionem dominorum Capitalium Justiciariorum domini Regis de utroque Banco.' The writ appointing Palmes in place of Dudley 'late namyd to be one that shuld take degree to be seriaunt at the law' is dated 1 November; *ibid.* no. 1. As in the case of Frowyk (*supra*, pp. 131–2), Dugdale and Holinshed both give wrong dates, the first, 20 Hen. VII (Chron. Ser., 77), the second, 19 Hen. VII, 1504 (1587 ed., iii. 791). According to Fortescue (*loc. cit.*) sixteen years of study and practice were ordinarily the minimum demanded of those chosen to be serjeants. If my calculations are approximately right (*supra*, p. 129, notes 7, 8, p. 131), Frowyk would have had about nineteen years and Marowe about twenty-four; the longer interval is explained in part by the latter's tenure of the office of under-sheriff.

[2] 'This yere (19 Hen. VII in margin) the XIIIᵗʰ day of November [a Monday in 1503], in the palayes of the Archebisshop of Canterbury at Lambehith was holden the sergeauntes feast'; Chron. Lond., ed. Kingsford, 260; cf. Holinshed *ut supra*, and Bacon, Life of Henry VII, 389. A delightfully vivid and detailed account is recorded in Minutes of Parliament Middle Temple, ed. C. T. Martin, i. 7–9, but presents serious problems as to dates. For example, it is stated that the feast took place on Monday *before* the feast of St. Martin's in winter [11 November], evidently an error for *after*. The actual creation of the serjeants is put on Sunday [12 November], contrary therefore to the entry naming 13 November (*supra*, note 1). Probably the whole episode was written up later, as it is entered under date of 9 November 19 Hen. VII. Dugdale's transcript of this account makes the necessary changes in the dates. For full details of a later serjeant's feast, see Dugdale, Orig. Jurid., ch. 48 ; cf. also chs. 49 and 50, and for Fortescue's famous description, see De Laudibus Legum Angliae, ch. 51. For the farewell to the Inner Temple serjeants in 1521, see Cal. Inner Temple Records, i. 62.

[3] In the present chaos of the Year Books of this reign it is difficult to give dates for his appearance. He almost certainly argued in Trin. 19 Hen. VII, Keilwey, no. 9, f. 53 ; also in Mich. 20 Hen. VII, no. 2, no. 3, 1680 ed. Year Books. But the printed Year Books make him appear long after his death in April 20 Hen. VII. The references are as follows: Hill. 21 Hen. VII ; no. 1, no. 9, no. 11, no. 23, no. 24, no. 25, no. 28

appointed on local commissions with chief justice Frowyk [1]—
the two friends sometimes sitting alone together as justices of
the peace in Middlesex [2]—and on 30 April 1504 he succeeded Frowyk on the western circuit, Cornwall, Devon, Dorset,
Somerset, Southampton, and Wiltshire, acting under commissions of Assize,[3] of Gaol Delivery,[4] and of the peace.[5]
With the beginning of 1505 he was actively employed. He
argued cases at Westminster in Hilary term,[6] and was still in
London by 6 February [7] ; on the eleventh he was in Old Sarum

(identified through Brooke) ; Pasch. 21 Hen. VII, no. 9, identified through
Brooke.   For the references, see p. 210, *infra*, note 6.   The bad gap in
the printed Year Books from 16-20 Hen. VII is partly filled by Keilwey
who gives a few cases for each of the intervening years ; Reports d'Ascun
Cases, 1602. ' Hill. 21 ' is almost certainly ' Hill. 20 '.   The many cases
attributed in the printed editions of the Year Books to Mich. 20 Hen. VII
are divided as follows in MS. Hargrave 105 (B.M.): 20 Hen. VII ;
nos. 1-3, Mich. ; nos. 4-10, Hill. ; nos. 11-15, Trin. ; 21 Hen. VII ;
nos. 16-18, Mich. ; nos. 19-25, Hill.

[1] On the Middlesex commission of peace, 8 September 1503, Cal. Pat.
Hen. VII, 1494-1509, 650. Also on the Middlesex commission of Jan.
1504, for raising the aid for the knighting of Prince Arthur and the
marriage of his sister Margaret ; Rot. Parl. vi. 532-42. The grant is
interesting as having perhaps caused the opposition of Sir Thomas More.
Stubbs, however, is inclined to doubt the story ; Seventeen Lectures on
the Study of Mediaeval and Modern History, 3rd ed. 1900, 418-19.

[2] The following proceedings exist among Ancient Indictments, K.B. 9,
P.R.O. ; Friday, 26 January, 19 Hen. VII, 1504, no. 444, m. 41 ; Thurs-
day, 3 October, 20 Hen. VII, 1504, no. 435, ms. 32-7 ; Wednesday, 18
December, 20 Hen. VII, 1504, no. 436, m. 43 ; Monday, 20 January, 20
Hen. VII, 1505, no. 436, m. 76, no. 444, m. 43.   In the last two instances
Frowyk and Marowe were acting alone ; the latter delivered a record
into the court of King's Bench on 6 February ; no. 436, m. 43.

[3] With John Boteler ; Cal. Pat. Hen. VII, 1494-1509, 360.   Frowyk
after three years on the western circuit was appointed to the home
counties ; *ibid.* 230, 246, 361, 365.   John Caryll was associated with
Boteler and Marowe on 2 July ; *ibid.* 363, and again on 8 February 1505,
ibid. 406.

[4] 20 June 1504. Dorchester, Old Sarum, Winchester, Launceston, Exeter,
'Yevelchester' ; *ibid.* 362 ; 8 February 1505, *ibid.* 436.

[5] 26 June 1504, Devon, *ibid.* 636 ; 12 July, Southampton, *ibid.* 658 ; 25
November and 28 December, Cornwall, *ibid.* 634 ; 28 December, Devon,
ibid. 635 ; 25 March 1505, Dorset, *ibid.* 638.

Various proceedings are preserved before Marowe as justice of the peace,
in one instance, when no commission has been found ; Thursday, 4 July
1504, Wilts. ; P.R.O., Anc. Indict., K.B. 9, no. 435, m. 40 (no commission) ; 29 July, Somerset, *ibid.* no 436, m. 66 ; Chancery Miscellanea,
bundle 77, file 6, no. 223 ; Thursday, 20 February 1505, Exeter, K.B. 9,
no. 439, ms. 44, 45.   For the commissions under which justices of Assize
acted, see art. Circuits and Assizes in Encyclopedia of Laws of England,
2nd ed.   [6] p. 135, note 3, *supra*.   [7] Note 2, *supra*.

hearing a case of Forcible Entry as justice of Nisi Prius[1]; on the seventeenth he delivered the gaol at 'Yeovilchester'[2]; and on the twentieth sat as justice of the peace in Exeter.[3] But his opportunity for the Bench and for fame never came. On 5 April he died in London,[4] having drawn his will and testament a few days before.[5] Within a year and a half Frowyk, too, was dead.[6]

Of Marowe's personal life we have but rare glimpses. He made many bequests of the kind typical of his times—to churches,[7] hospitals, prisons, &c.[8]—and was generous to many friends, servants,[9] and relatives, showing affectionate interest in the family of his brother William[10] and of his sister Lady

---

[1] In W. Rastell's Entries, 1566 ed., f. 403, under 'Nisi Prius, Briefe as executors de iustice d'assise de certifier record de nisi prius in trespas' a form is given with only the initials of the executors, the justice and the parties to the suit. But a comparison with Marowe's will, J. Dyer, Nouel Cases Collectes, 1601 ed., Trin. 4 and 5 Philip and Mary, 163, pl. 54, Coram Rege Roll, 974, Hill. 20 Hen. VII, rot. 18 (die Martis instead of die Mercurie as in Rastell), and with C. R. Roll 977, Mich. 21 Hen. VII, under Fines, Wilts., proves that Marowe as justice of Nisi Prius had quashed the array in a case of Forcible Entry and had died before he had certified the postea, with the result that his executors were sued for the production of the record, instead of his fellow justice, Boteler. For the same case, see H. Rolle, Abridgment, ii. 629 ; Coke, 2nd Inst., 1681 ed., 424 ; J. Chitty, Crim. Law, i. 388–9.

[2] P.R.O., Anc. Indict., K.B. 9, no. 442, m. 32.

[3] *Ibid.*, no. 439, ms. 44–5.

[4] P.R.O., Inq. p. m., Ch. Series, ii. 19, no. 101, Warwickshire (Exch. Series ii, file 1115, no. 59); 2 April may be the correct date ; see Inq. p. m., Ch. Ser. ii. 23, no. 266, Oxfordshire. But the 5 July of the Surrey inquisition is palpably wrong ; Inq. p. m., Ch. Ser., ii. 25, no. 47. His London inquisition is missing. For place of his death, see p. 140, note 2, *infra.*

[5] Dated 31 March, proved 10 April ; his executors were Frowyk, Kingsmill, Sir Edward Ferrers, and William Smart, grocer.

[6] He died on 7 October 1506 ; Cal. Lond. Inq. p. m., no. 23 ; his executors were his wife, Thomas Roberts (*supra*, p. 129, note 8), Kingsmill, and Thomas Jakes.

[7] 'Seynt Botolph witout Bisshoppesgate', 'Seynt Mighell at Quenehithe', 'the parisshe Church of Stebenhithe', 'the parisshe church of our Lady of Baddisley', &c.

[8] For the carrying out of this bequest, cf. will of Sir Edward Ferrers.

[9] One of his servants was named John Marowe.

[10] 'To my nevewe Thomas Marrowe my two best saltes of siluer and gilt with a couer. Item ii pleyn standing cuppes of siluer and gilt with two coueres one of my best wasshyng-basons of siluer and an ewer according to the same, another of my smaller siluer basons and an ewer according to the same, my two pottell pottes of siluer and my two pynt pottes of siluer and my three gilt bolles playne in the botoms with one couer' ; cf. also bequests of money to his nephew's three sisters.

Throckmorton.[1] It seems probable that the latter and her husband had been instrumental in bringing about his marriage early in 1491 [2] to the eldest daughter of Nicholas Brome.[3] Isabella—then not more than seventeen [4]—and her sister Constance, a child of seven, were co-heiresses of their father's manor of Baddesley Clinton,[5] with its beautiful old moated hall, built long before their time.[6] But it was the younger, not the elder, sister who eventually inherited the manor. In 1498 Constance married Sir Edward Ferrers [7] and at the death of Nicholas Brome in 1517 [8] she and her husband became possessed of Baddesley Clinton.[9] Marowe had perforce to be

[1] To 'Sir Robert Throgmerton Knyght a playn standing cupp of siluer and gilt with a couer', to George 'a standing swaged bolle of siluer parcell gilt with a couer', and bequests in money to Richard, Antony, Mighell Throgmerton, and to 'euery daughter of my sister Kateryn Throgmerton'.

[2] The indenture dated 8 January 1491 required the marriage to be celebrated before Easter ; H. Norris, Baddesley Clinton, 28.

[3] For many picturesque details of the career of this distinguished and impetuous gentleman, see Norris, *ut supra*. He usually sat on Warwickshire commissions of the peace (Cal. Pat. Rolls, *passim* under Broun) and was sheriff of Warwick and Leicester in 1504 ; Lists and Indexes, ix.

[4] Her mother, Elizabeth Arundel, did not marry Nicholas Brome till after 20 September 1473 ; Norris, *op. cit.*, 25–6.

[5] P.R.O., Inq. p. m., Ch. Ser. ii. 32, no. 42, Nicholas Brome, Warwickshire, 1517. Constance is thirty-three at this date.

[6] Norris, *op. cit.*, gives an eloquent description of the beauty of the Hall and the church and a good account of the complicated legal history of the manor of Baddesley Clinton. It is not known at what date the Hall was built, but the moat was certainly in existence in 1434 ; Norris, 60–1. See also Rev. William Field, Town and Castle of Warwick, 181–367. Nicholas Brome probably came to live in the Hall in 1483 after his mother's death—but possibly not till later ; Norris, 26–7.

[7] The indenture dated 1 December 1497 required the marriage to take place before 2 February 1498 ; *ibid.* 28. Thomas Marowe was a party to the agreement ; Inq. p. m. of Nicholas Brome, note 5 *supra*. It is hardly necessary to refer to the fame of the various branches of the illustrious family of Ferrers of Groby, and of Chartley, &c. Norris has given excellent short accounts of the Baddesley Clinton branch in the volume cited and of the Tamworth Castle branch in his volume on Tamworth. Cf. also Dugdale, Warwickshire, and the pedigrees in the Visitations of 1619 and 1682–3, cited in note 5, p. 117, *supra*.

[8] On 10 October ; Inq. p. m., note 5, *supra*.

[9] On 10 January 1506, after the death of Marowe, Brome 'sealed his dede of the manour of Baddesley Clinton and certen londs in Warrewyk and in other places to the use of Edward Ferrers, Esquier, and Constance his wyff' ; Norris, *op. cit.*, 27, and by his will quoted in his Inq. p. m. confirmed this deed on condition of a yearly payment of £12 to 'Dorothe Marrow or to hir heires forever'. In January 1531, the agreement was again confirmed in an indenture made between Dorothy and her husband

content with the adjoining Kingswood manor and its far more modest house, which he had received from his father-in-law early in 1497.[1] Shortly afterward Marowe's name appears on the Warwickshire commission of the peace,[2] and the next year, he and his wife, following the example of Bromes and Throckmortons, became members of the Gild of St. Anne at Knowle.[3] Possibly it was at Kingswood manor that Marowe's only child Dorothea was born, sometime between 1497 and 1499.[4]

Francis 'Cokeyn' of the one part and her uncle and aunt of the other part, subject to the perpetual annual payment of £12 13s. 4d. and one buck in season in summer and one doe in winter; Norris, 29. Cf. also Inq. p. m. of Edward Ferrers, grandson of Constance, P.R.O., Ch. Ser., ii. 141, no. 10, Warwickshire. The beautiful hangings, rich plate, &c., in the Hall are vividly described in the wills of Sir Edward Ferrers (1535) and of Dame Constance (1551), abstracts of which are printed by Norris, 133-9.

[1] Norris, 28; on 28 January 1497, Marowe was executing a bond for his father-in-law in connexion with some land at Lapworth, the next parish to Baddesley Clinton; Anc. Deeds, A, 9791, P.R.O. In Marowe's Warwickshire Inq. p. m. (p. 137, note 4, *supra*) it is stated that he died seised of Kingswood manor. The house is famous for a beautiful panelled ceiling and for the fact that Henry Ferrers the antiquarian died in it in 1633; Norris, 120-3 and p. 142, note 12, *infra*.

[2] 5 May 1497, Cal. Pat. Hen. VII, 1494-1509, 663, his very first appointment as justice of the peace. He appears on all succeeding Warwickshire commissions during his lifetime (*ibid.*) associated with his father-in-law, or his brother-in-law, Sir Robert Throckmorton, and with Richard Empson, appointed recorder of Coventry by 1493 through the influence of the king; Cov. Leet Book, ed. M. D. Harris, 537, 547. But the fact that payment of Marowe's salary is noted but once (1 October 1499 and 16 June 1500, P.R.O., Pipe Roll no. 345 under Item Warwick, Reddit compotum) shows that he did not take much part in the sessions. On 18 November 1500 he did, however, deliver into the court of King's Bench, a Warwickshire quarter session record in the name of his brother-in-law, Sir Robert Throckmorton; P.R.O., Bagae de Secretis; pouch 3, bundle 1, ms. 33, 34.

[3] Register, 1451-1535, ed. W. B. Bickley, 122. 'Nicholas Brome (1490), Mr. Robertus Throgmerton & Katerina vxor eius, 1498, Edward Ferrers et Constancia vxor eius, Georgius Frogmerton & Katerina vxor eius, Koghton, 1506, Mr. Thomas Marrow & Margareta vxor eius, 1514, Francis Cokayne Armifer & Dorothea vxor eius, 1526'—to mention relatives of Marowe. The lists include Kebles, Rastells, Shakespeares, &c. (cf. Norris, 122-3). The gild room is still in use in connexion with the church, but the arms of 'Marrow quartering Rich and impaling Brome' are no longer in the window of the church, with the legend: 'et orate pro animabus Thome Marrow seruientis ad legem et Isabellae vxoris eius'; Dugdale, Warwickshire, 961; Norris, 43, 74.

[4] According to her grandfather Brome's Inq. p. m. (p. 138, note 5, *supra*), which makes her twenty in 1517, she was born about 1497; but her father's inquisitions all put the date a little later; the Warwickshire and Oxfordshire inquisitions about 1499 and the Surrey inquisition about 1500 (p. 137, note 4, *supra*).

Perhaps, too, she and her mother spent some time in his city house with ' gardeynes ',[1] in St. Michael's, Queenheath,[2] Isabella's presence serving to excuse him from ' commons ' in the Inner Temple.[3]   One would like to think that Dorothea played with little Frideswyde Frowyk, the only surviving child of her father's friend,[4] either at Frideswyde's home in Finchley [5] or at the famous Ypres Inn,[6] and that the children learned to know Marowe Key which Dorothea's father had inherited from his brother in 1499.[7] Marowe was clearly a man of means with extensive property in a number of counties,[8] but since, apart from his circuit as justice of Assize, his name appears on the commission of the peace only in Warwickshire and in Middlesex, it is evident that he divided his residence between his wife's old home and London and its environs.

Reasoning from chronology, locality, and common interests, it would be easy to construct for Marowe a most interesting group of friends—Sir Thomas More [9] and John Rastell,[10] representing the stimulating legal atmosphere of Coventry,[11] Dean

[1] Will.

[2] ' I bequeath to every poore householder in the parisshe of Seynt Mighell wheryn I dwell xii d. '; Testament.   Similar bequests of ' viii d. ' in the case of ' the parisshe of Seynt Dunstone in the west' and ' vi d.' in the case of ' Stebenhith' may indicate a residence in each.   He is said to have died in the parish of St. Dunstan's; De Banco Roll 975, rot. 409.

[3] Minutes of Parl. Middle Temple, i. 8.

[4] Born about 1498, according to her father's London Inq. p. m. (Calendar, 23), and (in spite of the art. in D.N.B.) the daughter of his second wife Dame Elizabeth, the ' Lady Frowik' to whom Marowe bequeathed ' v li. of money beseching her' to pray for his soul.   She married Thomas Jakes as her second husband; see her will and that of Frowyk, and the Frowyk pedigrees in F. C. Cass, Parish of South Mimms, 70.   [5] See her father's will.

[6] Ibid., and the will of her grandmother, Johanna Frowyk.

[7] p. 122, note 4, supra.

[8] London, Kent, Surrey, Oxford, Warwick, Derby, and elsewhere; see his will and his Inq. p. m., p. 137, note 4, supra.   The London property included tenements in ' Croked Lane ', a ' quytte rent' from the ' Bell and Cheker', and a ' quyte rent' out of a tenement and an ' aley of small tenements . . . in the parish of Alhalowen besides London Wall' which he willed to his executors.   One of them, Sir Edward Ferrers, in turn, willed the two quit rents to the church of Baddesley Clinton; see Norris, op cit., 43–4, for a not altogether accurate account.

[9] He was born in 1478 in St. Giles without Cripplegate, a parish in which Marowe's father had held property; see his will.   For Marowe's own association with Sir Thomas's father, see supra, pp. 134–5.

[10] See p. 23, supra.

[11] Marowe's probable connexion with Coventry suggests various interest-

Colet[1] and Erasmus[2]—to mention the most obvious—and, through his possible connexion with Bristol Marowes,[3] to assume that he had heard of distant voyages across the Atlantic.[4] Apart, however, from his intimacy with his own relatives and those of his wife—Marowes,[5] Throckmortons,[6] Bromes,[7] Sir Edward[8] and Lady Ferrers,[9] and with old family friends like the Smarts[10]—positive evidence tells mainly of his association with people like Dudley[11] or Sir Edward Poynings,[12] and with his colleagues in the city government, Robert Fabian (the chronicler)[13] or Sir John Sha,[14] and especially with men of law, his fellow justices of the peace,[15] his

ing possibilities; see pp. 79–80, *supra*. He was certainly in touch with Empson; see *supra*, p. 139, note 2.

[1] For his father's association with the Dean's father, see *supra*, p. 121. John Colet between 1485 and 1505 was vicar of St. Dunstan and All Saints, Stepney (Seebohm, Oxford Reformers, 529), a church to which Marowe, his father, and his brother, all made bequests. It is, however, believed that Colet probably performed few of his duties in Stepney, and it is known that he was in Italy from 1494 to 1496; Seebohm, *op. cit.*, pp. 1–23.

[2] The meeting of Erasmus with More in London, perhaps at the table of Henry Colet, is supposed to have occurred in 1498 (Seebohm, 113), and therefore at the time that Marowe was under-sheriff. It is interesting to find that Marowe makes a bequest to 'my singler goode lorde Tharchebisshop of Caunterbury for a token & knowlege that I bere hym service and true herte' and to remember that Warham as a patron of letters had received Erasmus and was later to be a protector of Colet; Seebohm, 183–4, 205, 254.

[3] Will of William Marowe, the mayor.

[4] Note the entry of July 1497 : ' To hym that founde the new Isle, £10 ' ; Privy Purse Expenses, Excerpta Historica, ed. Bentley, 113. John Cabot had sailed from Bristol on his first voyage in the spring of 1496, with Letters Patent from the king and had returned in the summer of 1497 ; Fisher, Political Hist. Eng., 1485–1547, 105–9.

[5] *Supra*, pp. 125–6, 137.

[6] *Ibid.*, pp. 137–8.   [7] *Ibid.*, pp. 138–9.

[8] One of his four executors; *supra*, p. 137, note 5. Sir Edward in his own testament left bequests for masses for the souls of Thomas Marowe and his wife Isabella.

[9] ' To my sister Ferys a crymsyn gowne with a deep pursill of shanks which was my wiffes ' ; testament.

[10] William Smart, the son of his father's friend, was one of his executors ; *ut supra*, note 8.

[11] *Supra*, pp. 132–3.

[12] Cal. Lond. and Midd. Feet of Fines ; Trin. 19 Hen. VII, 1504.

[13] Sheriff in 1493 ; Stow, *op. cit.*, ii. 178.

[14] Sheriff in 1496, mayor in 1501 ; *ibid.* ii. 179 ; Cal. Lond. Letter Books and Cal. Pat., *passim*.

[15] The proceedings still in existence show with whom he was actually working ; *supra*, pp. 134, note 3, 136, notes 2 and 5.

fellow serjeants,[1] and the justices at Westminster, notably Kingsmill [2] and Frowyk.[3] Nor is there anything in his learned treatise to suggest that his knowledge or interests extended beyond the range of legal technicalities and history of law.[4]

Marowe's wife may have lived to see her husband made serjeant-at-law in 1503,[5] but must have died soon after, since by December 1504 he is plighting his troth to Anne, daughter of Sir Thomas Grene, once of London.[6] His second marriage did not take place,[7] and at his death his daughter Dorothea, aged seven, was his sole heir.[8] Her parents' position and perhaps the help of her Ferrers and Throckmorton relatives enabled her to make two advantageous marriages, first to Francis Cokain, heir of Sir Thomas Cokain of Pooley, Derbyshire,[9] by whom she had five children;[10] and second to Sir Humphrey Ferrers of Tamworth Castle,[11] a widower with two children. Dorothea seems to have spent much of her married life in Derbyshire and at Kingswood manor, Warwickshire,[12] and is buried in the little church at Baddesley Clinton [13] where

[1] *Supra*, pp. 134–5, and note 1.

[2] One of his executors; p. 137, note 5, *supra*. He was of the Middle Temple, serjeant-at-law in 1497 (should be 1495), justice of the Common Pleas by 1503; Foss, Judges. I am indebted to the Reverend H. E. Salter for interesting details of his connexion with Oxford.

[3] One of his executors; *ut supra*, note 2 ; see also pp. 127–9, 140.

[4] For analysis of its contents, see ch. vi (2), *infra*.

[5] She was alive in Michaelmas term, 1502 ; P.R.O., De Banco Roll 962, rot. 547. I am indebted to Miss Drucker for this reference.

[6] De Banco Roll 975, rot. 409. In his testament he begs Anne to 'be content with suche tokens, summes of money, cheynes of gold and other things' as he had given her.

[7] Hence Marowe's executors recover from Anne's father that portion of the purchase money already paid ; De Banco Roll, *ut supra*.

[8] Testament and Inq. p. m.

[9] See Cokain pedigrees in Harl. Soc. Pub. xii. She was married by 10 May 1515 ; Pat. 7 Hen. VIII, pt. 1, m. 19, Letters and Papers, Foreign and Domestic, 7 Hen. VIII, 434.

[10] Francis Cokayn, P.R.O., Inq. p. m., Ch. Ser., ii. 60, no. 12, Derby ; no. 81, Warwick ; no. 129, Stafford. He died on 5 August 1538. Cf. assignment of dower ; *ibid.* 61, no. 140, and Letters and Papers, Foreign and Domestic, Hen. VIII, 1538, i. 408. Thomas their eldest son was nearly seventeen at his father's death.

[11] By 1540, Norris, *op. cit.*, 28 ; Ferrers' pedigrees in Harl. Soc. Pub. xii.

[12] See Inq. p. m. of her son and heir, Sir Thomas Cokayn ; P.R.O., Ch. Ser., ii. 235, no. 106. His son sold Kingswood manor to an agent of Henry Ferrers on 20 June 1596 ; Norris, 33. For her rights in Baddesley Clinton, see p. 138, note 9, *supra*.

[13] Dugdale, Warwickshire, 974 ; Norris, 49.

probably her mother also lies.[1] Dorothea's eldest son Thomas
Cokain married his step-sister Dorothy Ferrers, and her
daughter Barbara Cokain married her step-brother John
Ferrers, the children of Dorothea's second husband, Sir
Humphrey Ferrers of Tamworth Castle by his first marriage.[2]
Many generations later a descendant of Barbara and of John
married a Ferrers of Baddesley Clinton, thus uniting the two
lines of Ferrers.[3] The present heir[4] to Baddesley Clinton
therefore traces his descent back to Thomas Marowe.

Marowe had requested his executors to ' provide a plate to
be graven with scripture shewing the place of his burying . . .
that plate to be sett vpon the piler at thende of the said
tombe ' ;[5] but he could not foresee that St. Botolph's, Bishopsgate, would survive the great fire[6] only to suffer a worse
disaster in the early eighteenth century.[7] The destruction of
his tomb is typical of the treatment accorded to him by fate.
Notwithstanding his many advantages, his position in the city
through his birth and his wealth, his connexion by marriage
with important county families, his many influential friends;
notwithstanding also his reputation as serjeant-at-law, and his

---

[1] It seems to me probable that the ' small latten effigy of a female figure
kneeling ', now in the chapel of the Hall but formerly in the church, represents Isabella; Norris, 53 ; Badger, Monumental Brasses of Warwickshire, 60.

[2] Harl. Soc. Pub. xii. The last of the descendants in male line of
Barbara Cokain and John Ferrers was the Sir John Ferrers of Tamworth
Castle who died in 1680 leaving Henry Ferrers of Baddesley Clinton as
heir male of both lines ; but Sir John's granddaughter Anne married
Robert Shirley, son of Baron Ferrers de Chartley and continued the
Tamworth Castle line in female descent; Norris, *op. cit.*, pp. 111–18.

[3] Lady Harriet Anne Ferrers Townsend, descendant of Anne (note 2)
married Edward Ferrers of Baddesley Clinton ; Norris, *ut supra*. Their
son was the late Marmion Edward Ferrers, Esq., who died in 1884. His
widow in 1885 married Mr. Edward Dering of Kent and is for her lifetime
the lady of the manor of Baddesley Clinton. To Mrs. Dering I am deeply
indebted for an opportunity to see the beautiful old Hall, and to the rector
and curate of Lapworth cum Baddesley Clinton for their kindness in
showing me the church.

[4] Mr. Edward Ferrers, a grandnephew of the late Marmion Ferrers, Esq.

[5] Testament.

[6] ' London City Churches that escaped the Great Fire ', P. Norman in
Lond. Top. Record, v.

[7] It was rebuilt in 1725–1729 (Baedeker, London), and the old
monuments destroyed, excepting that of Sir Paul Pindar ; C. Knight,
London, 1843, v. 200.

production of a unique legal work, he has been almost ignored through the centuries.[1] The following study of the reading on the peace in 1503 will show how little its author deserved his obscurity.

Wills and testaments preserved in the Prerogative Court of Canterbury and now in Somerset House, cited in the preceding chapter.

Clopton, Dorothy. 5 Bennett, not dated, proved 26 September 1508.
  John. F 17 Horne, dated 4 November 1494, proved 16 November 1497.
Ferrers, Constance. 29 Bucke, dated 26 August 1551, admin. granted 17 October.
  Sir Edward. 29 Hogan, dated 10 July 1535, proved 18 November.
Frowyk, Henry. 20 Stokton, dated 8 April 1459, proved 8 March 1460.
  Henry. 41 Holgrave, dated 2 April 1504, proved 15 November 1505.
  Sir Thomas. 18 Logge, dated 22 September 1485, proved 10 November 1485.
  Sir Thomas. 15 Adeane, dated 13 August 1505, probate act not preserved.
  Isabella. 10 Godyn, dated 26 November 1464, proved 8 August 1465.
  Johanna. 2 Moone, dated 13 April 1500, proved 16 May.
  Elizabeth. 13 Holder, dated 1 December 1515, proved 4 February 1516.
Gregory, William. 16 Godyn, dated 6 November 1465, proved 23 January 1467 (printed in Gairdner's ed., Collections of a Citizen of London).
Marowe, Thomas. 28 Holgrave, dated 31 March 1505, proved 10 April.
  Thomas. 25 Dyngeley, dated 2 September 1538, admin. granted 25 February 1539.
  Thomas. 37 Loftes, dated 6 September 1561, admin. granted 10 December.
  William. 9 and 11 Godyn, dated 8 October 1464, proved 15 May 1465.
  William. 36 Horne (cf. Cal. Wills in Court of Hustings, ii. 606), dated 26 February 1499, proved 30 October.
  Samuel. 91 Wingfield, dated 10 August 1603, proved 22 October 1610.
Ryche, John. 14 Stokton, proved 1458.
  Richard. 4 Godyn, dated 20 April 1463, proved 16 August 1464.
  Thomas. 20 Wattys, dated 2 July 1471, proved 4 October 1475.
Smart, Agnes. 23 Blamyr, dated 30 March 1503, proved 4 July.
  John. 21 Vox, dated 20 June 1494, proved 18 March 1495.
Throckmorton, Sir Robert. 2 Maynwarying, dated 2 July 1518, proved 9 November 1520.

---

[1] *Infra*, ch. vi (5).

CHAPTER VI

A READING ON THE PEACE IN 1503

(1) DESCRIPTION OF THE ELEVEN MSS. THUS FAR DISCOVERED [1]

Of the eleven MSS. here listed, the first ten are in law French, usually with Latin headings, and the eleventh is in English.

University Library, Cambridge.

A.[2] Hh. 3. 6. no. 1646, ff. 74–116.[3]

Prima lectura Magistri Thome Marowe existentis lectoris in quadragesimali vacacione anno Henrici VII^{mi} XVIII°.

De pace terre & ecclesie & conseruacione eiusdem, Westminster primer, capitulo primo.

B. Ee. 5. 20. no. 1074, 47 folios.

Prima lectura Magistri Thome Marowe lector XLme anno XVIII° Henrici VIIⁱ.

De pace terre & ecclesie Westminster primer capitulo primo etc. & conseruacione eiusdem.

C. Ee. 3. 46. no. 1002, ff. 132–161.

Westminster premier. Lectura magistri Thome Marow.

De pace terre [et] ecclesie et conseruacione eiusdem.[4]

D. Ee. 5. 18. no. 1072, ff. 62–95.

Ihesus Maria.

Prima lectura de Magistro Marow. Westminster primer capitulo primo.

De pace terre et ecclesie et conseruacione eiusdem vacacione quadragesimali anno XVIII Henrici Septimi.

E. Gg. 6. 18. no. 1587, 5 folios.

De ingressibus manuforti in terris et tenementis et de remissione partis in possessionem eiusdem.

Lectura nona only.

---

[1] The archives examined are those listed *supra*, p. 6, notes 3 and 4.
[2] The copies will be henceforth referred to by the letters here used.
[3] Printed in full in App. III.   [4] A marginal heading.

British Museum.
>   F.   Hargrave 87, ff. 262–301.
>   De pace terre & ecclesie & conseruacione eiusdem, etc.,
>   Marowe lector anno regni regis Henrici VII XVIII°
>   vacacione quadragesimali.
>   G.   Lansdowne 1133, ff. 55–94.
>   De pace terre & ecclesie et conseruacione eiusdem, etc.,
>   Marrowe lector anno regni Henrici VII XVIII° vaca-
>   cione quadragessimali.

Carson Historical Library, Philadelphia.
>   H.   95 folios.
>   No heading except 'Marrowe' in a hand later than
>   that of the MS.   The last folio ends : 'Finis huius libri
>   per Marrowe.'

Library of Harvard Law School, Cambridge.
>   I.   MS. 14, 39 folios.
>   Lectura Magistri Thome Marowe lectoris in XL^{ma}
>   Henrici VII XVIII, etc.   Westminster primer.
>   De pace terre et ecclesie et conseruacione eiusdem.

Library of Inner Temple.
>   K.   Manuscript Readings.[1]   ff. 98–126.
>   De pace terrae & ecclesiae W. 1. c. 1.

Bodleian, Oxford.
>   L.   Tanner 428.
>   No heading except 'Statut Westminster 1 Anno 3° E. 1'
>   in a hand later than that of the MS.

Lambard had said in 1579 that Marowe's 'learned reading'
was 'in many hands to be seene'.[2]   Two centuries later John
Rayner of the Inner Temple writes : 'We believe this Reading
was never printed, but MSS. copies of it are in Some Hands :
we have seen a very fair one, with the following Title, viz.
Lecture of "Thomas Marrowe, upon the Statute of Westm.
1 Cap. I.   De pace ecclesiae et terrae conservanda." There is
another Copy very different intituled thus " De Pace Terrae, et
ecclesiae, et Conservatione ejusdem, Marrow Lector, Anno regni

---

[1] No number to the volume.   [2] p. 114, *supra.*

regis, Hen. VII. 18º vacatione quadragesimali ".'[1] The 'very
different' copy is evidently F or G or a similar version, but
unless Rayner had partly translated and slightly misquoted
the title of C, the 'very fair' copy cannot at present be identified. Curiously enough, with the exception of an incomplete
copy in Marowe's own Inn,[2] the reading is not now in the
possession of any of the Inns of Court,[3] and unfortunately it
has not been possible to discover the MS. actually written by
Marowe[4] and presumably in his hands when he gave the
lectures.[5] Future research may reveal more copies,[6] but
meanwhile the immediate task is to determine which of the
eleven versions is the most exact reproduction of Marowe's
original work.

The five MSS. now in the University Library, Cambridge—
A, B, C, D, E in my list[7]—were all included in the famous

---

[1] Readings on Statutes, preface 1-2, 1775 ; cf. J. Worrall, Bibliotheca
Legum, 1782 ed., 20, 1788 ed., ii. 191.

[2] Acquired as recently as 1910.

[3] As far as I have been able to discover.

[4] Or by a clerk at his dictation.

[5] Perhaps his own copy was once among the papers of the family of
his brother-in-law and executor, Sir Edward Ferrers (see p. 141, *supra*,
and note 8). It was the latter's great grandson, Henry Ferrers, the
antiquarian, who bought from Marowe's great-grandson Kingswood
manor, Marowe's Warwickshire home (pp. 139, 142, note 12). At
Henry Ferrers' death in 1633, his valuable collection of family papers
became the property of his son Edward of Baddesley Clinton. The
latter lent many of the MSS. to Dugdale ; see Dugdale's letter of 1650,
' For my worthye freinde, Edward Ferrers, Esqʳ., at Badsley ', printed by
Norris, Baddesley Clinton, 31-2. The Ferrers MSS. were frequently
quoted by Dugdale in the Antiquities of Warwickshire, but unfortunately
some of those borrowed were never returned, and became part of the
Staunton Collection in the library at Birmingham. They were therefore
destroyed by the great fire in 1879 ; Norris, *op. cit.*, 32. Norris also
mentions the ' wilful destruction ' at Tamworth Castle of papers belonging
to Henry Ferrers. But there are still valuable MSS. at Baddesley Clinton,
uncatalogued and undescribed (except in Norris's volume). It is greatly
to be desired that the newly organized Dugdale Society be permitted to
examine them.

[6] Perhaps in private collections or perhaps even in the great archives
already investigated. The cataloguing of MS. readings is so inadequate
that without a painstaking examination of literally every collection of
legal material it is impossible to feel sure that all copies have been identified. My own search was as thorough as limitations of time permitted.

[7] In Bernard's Catalogi librorum Manuscriptorum, 1697, they are
nos. 323, 333, 707, 330, 422 respectively ; see key in the Catalogue of
MSS. in the library of the University of Cambridge. The first three

collection of Bishop Moore of Norwich and Ely, given to the University in 1715 by George I.[1] The first four of these merit careful consideration.

A. Hh. 3. 6 is a paper volume, 12 × 8 inches, of 117 folios, containing a number of law readings[2] in a clear handwriting of the early sixteenth century.[3] The first is a short clear reading on Appeals, by Richard Littleton,[4] son of the judge, delivered at the Inner Temple early in the reign of Henry VII.[5] Then after some rather scrappy extracts[6] come two unfinished readings on the Statute of the Prerogative of the King.[7] The second of these consists of three folios[8] of the well-known treatise by Marowe's close associate, under the heading: 'Frowyk lector tempore autumpnali anno X^{mo} H. VII^{mi}.'[9] This fragment is followed by the forty-two folios of the De Pace,[10] representing the latest reading in the collection, and also the fullest and clearest.[11] There is strong evidence to show that the volume is to be associated with the Inner Temple, and that it was put into shape not long after the delivery of the De Pace. The quotations from eminent judges

were mentioned by Th. Tanner, Bibliotheca Britannico-Hibernica, ed. D. Wilkins, 1748, 512: 'Marrow [Thomas] lector, quadragesimalis Interioris Templi London. 18 Henr. VII Adhuc extant ejus Lecturae xv in statut Westmonast. primo. Pr. " En primez voet le Roy ". MS. Norwic. More. 323. 333. 707.'

[1] The 30,000 books and MSS. of John Moore, bishop of Norwich 1691–1707, of Ely 1707–1714, had been sold to the king for 6,000 guineas; see art. in D.N.B., preface to Catalogue of MSS. cited *supra*, and Worrall, Bibliotheca Legum, 1782 ed., 20 (the first edition was in 1731).

[2] Not adequately described in the printed Catalogue.

[3] The hand throughout the collection is the same, I think.

[4] 'Capitulo XII° Westminster secunde Litilton lector in quadragesimali vacacione'; ff. 1–16; then come a few folios on ch. xiii, followed by the signature of a scribe with an undecipherable surname. 'quod . . . Edwarde'. I want to make it 'Cope', referred to in 1506 as a student at the Inner Temple (Cal. Inner Temple Records, i. 5), but experts tell me that it is impossible. For signatures in similar form, see *infra*, pp. 151, 152.

[5] p. 179, *infra*.

[6] Fragments of readings and of discussion on the familiar 'old' statutes, but the precise nature of the legal material in these folios can be determined only after a more careful study than I have been able to give to them.

[7] ff. 55–73.   [8] ff. 71–3.

[9] August 1495; p. 180, *infra*.

[10] ff. 116 b–117 contain a record of a local court and some miscellaneous notes.

[11] Characteristic of all the versions that I have seen.

are from those of the fifteenth century, Fortescue,[1] Littleton,[2] &c. ; and the other lawyers whose opinions are cited, Frowyk,[3] Brown,[4] Brudnell,[5] Sutton,[6] &c., as far as they have been identified at all, are known to have been readers at the Inner Temple before Lent 1503.[7]

Apart from one specific error in arrangement, common to all the complete versions,[8] this copy of the De Pace contains very few mistakes, almost no stupid ones, and only occasionally a careless slip [9]; the meaning therefore is practically always intelligible. It is the longest and most detailed of the eleven MSS., and with the notable exception of a part of Lecture X,[10] omits almost nothing found in the others ; it is the only one besides L to have a table of contents. Finally, the only illustrative dates mentioned in the treatise are here given as 10 November and Easter, 18 Henry VII, and 1503 [11]—an appropriate choice for Marowe if he had prepared the treatise in the late autumn and early winter of 1502-3.[12] The above considerations warrant the conclusion that A is an intelligent and, on the whole, accurate transcript of the De Pace made by some one connected with the Inner Temple at a time so close to the actual reading that it was natural to keep Marowe's allusions to contemporary dates. The version represented by A has been called the A version.

B. Ee. 5. 20 [13] is a paper volume, 12 × 8 inches, containing merely the De Pace in 47 folios in a difficult handwriting of a little after the middle of the sixteenth century.[14] It is at present bound with another paper volume of law readings from Bishop Moore's library, Ee. 5. 19 [15]; the latter includes

---

[1] f. 43. [2] f. 38 b.

[3] f. 1 of Littleton's reading : 'Frowyk a le contrary.'

[4] f. 52 : 'et nota que Broun dist.'

[5] f. 32 b : 'per Brudnell en lecture.'

[6] f. 33 : 'en lecture.' [7] pp. 178–81, infra.

[8] pp. 164-5, 362, 365, infra. [9] Such as leaving out a single word.

[10] p. 365, infra. It contains an additional paragraph at the end of Lect. VI ; see App. III, p. 330, note 2.

[11] App. III, p. 387. [12] See p. 134, supra.

[13] Ascribed to 'Narrow' by a misprint in Bernard's catalogue, no. 333, and therefore not under Marowe's name in the index.

[14] Ascribed to a somewhat later date in the Catalogue of the University Library. [15] Bernard, no. 331.

a reading at the Inner Temple in 1527, delivered by Audeley who died in 1544.[1] The volume bears the signature of William 'Fletewode'.[2]

A careful collation of B with A [3] shows that in spite of certain linguistic and orthographic differences,[4] due to its comparative lateness, B is a very close reproduction of the A version, with identical phraseology, the same illustrative dates, &c. It is, however, often an unintelligent reproduction, omitting whole sentences or half sentences. The important section not found in A is included, but in the wrong place.[5]

C. Ee. 3. 46 [6] is a very badly damaged paper volume, 12 × 9 inches, containing law readings in a hand of the early sixteenth century.[7] It supposedly includes 168 folios, but lacks folios 82–99. The first four readings [8] were delivered at the Inner Temple by Stoughton, Tychborn, Hales, and Malat between the first and fourth years of Henry VIII.[9] The missing folios which turned up unexpectedly as Dd. 3. 41 [10] contain what must be Frowyk's 'single' reading,[11] delivered at least several years earlier than 1495, the date of his reading on the Prerogative of the King.[12] After Malat's reading in Ee. 3. 46 comes an incomplete copy of Frowyk's 'double'

[1] On the statute 4 Hen. VII, on Privileges. For Audeley's career during the critical period of the reign of Hen. VIII, see Foss, Judges, who has no good word for him ; cf. also Dugdale, Orig. Jurid., 164.

[2] f. 217 b. Mr. C. E. Sayle is of the opinion that the joint binding probably goes back only to the seventeenth century.

[3] I am greatly indebted to Mr. Alfred Rogers for the collation of the Cambridge MSS. and also to Mr. Herbert Mills for much valuable assistance.

[4] qi for q, &c.   [5] App. III, p. 362, note 3.

[6] Tanner's reference led to my discovery of this copy. The volume is not listed under 'Marowe' in the index of either Bernard or of the Catalogue of the University Library, and although it is fully analysed in the text of the former, in the latter it is described merely as 'Law readings'.

[7] Ascribed to late sixteenth in the Catalogue of the University Library ; see also p. 151, note 7, infra.

[8] ff. 1–81 ; so illegible that I do not feel sure that its contents are accurately described.

[9] Autumn third year, autumn first year, Lent third year, autumn fourth year, respectively ; Cal. Inner Temple Records, ed. F. A. Inderwick, i. 22, 14, 23 ; Dugdale, op. cit., 163.

[10] Bound with Dd. 3. 40 and Dd. 3. 39.

[11] On all the chapters of Westminster II ; at the beginning, 'Frowyk lector'. For 'single' and 'double', see infra, pp. 167–9.

[12] pp. 179–80, infra.

reading,[1] followed immediately by the De Pace,[2] by far the clearest portion of the MS.

The test dates include Millesimo XIII°—probably a mere slip for MDIII°—and a change from 18 Henry VII to 6 Henry VIII,[3] a regnal year two years later than the date of the latest reading in the volume.[4] If the scribe was the 'Wye, Rychard' whose signature appears so frequently,[5] he was presumably the Richard Wye admitted to the Inner Temple in 1507, and called to the Bench in 1517,[6] and undoubtedly made this collection of Inner Temple material during the year 1514–1515.[7] C is like B in reproducing the A version very closely and in putting the missing section in the same wrong place,[8] but is rather more uneven than B, since the scribe makes some corrections that show intelligence and some that show stupidity.[9]

D. Ee. 5. 18[10] is a paper volume, 12 × 8 inches, of 101

---

[1] ff. 100–130, old numbering. The new nos. 1–30 help to conceal the relation between this MS. and Dd. 3. 41. The extract from the Prerogative is anonymous, but its identity is proved by a collation of it with Hh. 2. 1, ff. 1–26.

[2] ff. 132–61 ; ff. 131 is missing. ff. 161–7 contain almost undecipherable readings.

[3] App. III, p. 387, notes 1, 5.   [4] That of Malat ; *supra*.

[5] e.g. f. 49: 'Explicit per Wye Rychard.' In the present condition of the volume, it is impossible to say whether it was the work of one man.

[6] Cal. Inner Temple Records, i. 7, 39. Probably he is to be identified with the Richard Wye who died early in 1520; cf. his two testaments, 22 March 1518, and 25 March 1520 (proved 9 May), 26 Ayloffe, P.C.C. He left a considerable library: 'books that concerne devynitie humanitie & filocifie', and 'books of law', and gave specific instructions for his burial : ' I will my body to be buryed in the Temple Church in the place where gentilmen of our Company walke as nyghe to the walke as may be and I will that there be a marbull stone . . . leyde upon it and that therebe pictured thereupon the Image of a soule in a shroude.' His epitaph, given in Dugdale, Orig. Jurid., 173, makes the date of his death 19 March 1519 (1520).

[7] But if Mr. Rogers is correct in his judgement that the writing of the copy of De Pace is as late as the middle of the sixteenth century, either the latter part of the collection was transcribed later than the first part, or the whole volume is based on an earlier one dating from about 1514–1515.

[8] App. III, p. 362, note 3.

[9] Perhaps Richard Wye employed a scribe not sufficiently learned in the law.

[10] Not referred to by Tanner ; not ascribed to Marowe by Bernard (no. 330: ' Matters relating to our Laws in the times of Edw. II, III, Rich. II, Hen. IV, V, and VI ') ; and not indexed under Marowe in the Catalogue of the University Library, Cambridge. In the text of the last, Marowe's reading is incorrectly said to be on the statute of Westminster II.

folios, in an early sixteenth-century hand.[1] It contains law readings and some miscellaneous legal material,[2] and has a full table of contents at the end. The most interesting sections are a clear copy of the De Pace [3]—as so often, the most complete part of the collection,—headings from a reading by Morgan Kidwelly at the Inner Temple in 1482 on Magna Carta, ch. XI,[4] and an account of the 'Diversity of Courts', including the sessions of the peace.[5] The scribe has taken great pains to reveal his identity; 'Atwell Walterus' appears frequently,[6] often with pious ejaculations, 'Jhesus Mercy Lady helpe', &c.[7] Except for Kidwelly and Marowe, all of Atwell's authorities prove to be connected with Gray's Inn late in the reign of Henry VII or early in that of Henry VIII: Fitzherbert [8] (including a number of references to what must be the latter's Abridgement),[9] Askett,[10] Dudley,[11] 'Seigneur Fynyux,' [12] Tyngelden,[13] Wynkfeld,[14] 'old' Spylman.[15] Several of

[1] 'About the middle of the sixteenth century', according to the Catalogue. On f. 63 in a later hand than that of the rest of the volume is the entry : 'Emanuel 1576'.

[2] Also copies of receipts, f. 1, and extra folio between f. 52 and f. 53, and a reference to 'Skeltonides', *ibid.*   [3] ff. 62–95.

[4] p. 178, *infra*. On f. 52 there is a record of a Dorsetshire suit involving Morgan Kidwelly and John Atwell, chaplain.

[5] f. 38 b, f. 53, f. 55. See p. 35, note 3, *supra*, and p. 178, note 8, *infra.*

[6] e.g. cf. f. 38, *et passim* for this form and for others; e.g. f. 60, 'quod Walterus Atwell'; also f. 49 b for a reference to his wife Margery. The name is wrongly printed 'Ashwell' in the Catalogue of the University Library.   [7] e.g. ff. 43, 84 b; App. III, p. 413, note 1.

[8] f. 37 b, 'en lyuer A. F.'; f. 32 b: 'Vide report de fitzherberd de Grays In pur beale pleder'. Cf. p. 35, and note 4, *supra.*

[9] App. III, p. 336, note 1, p. 375, note 4, p. 376, note 4, p. 377, note 2, p. 380, note 2, p. 390, note 2, p. 391, note 3. The final volume of the Abridgement was certainly published by 1516; see p. 34, note 2, *supra.* I am assuming that the marginal references are by Walter Atwell.

[10] f. 96 b: 'Vide en lecture de Magistro Askett', Lent 6 Hen. VIII; Dugdale, Orig. Jurid., 292.

[11] f. 68: 'vide en report Dudley de quo warranto folio primo.' See p. 183, *infra.*

[12] ff. 64 b, 66. He was chief justice of King's Bench from 1495 till his death in 1525; Foss, Judges.

[13] f. 99; Lent 7 Hen. VIII, on statute of Gloucester; Dugdale, Orig. Jurid., 292.

[14] f. 100; Lent 8 Hen. VIII, on statute de Coniunctim feoffatis ; Dugdale, *loc. cit.*

[15] f. 20: 'Vide en le Report de old Spylman ... sur lestatut, W. II[d], ca. XXV' (cf. f. 41 b). John Spelman read three times, namely in 5, 10 and 12 Hen. VIII (see Dugdale, *loc. cit.*, and p. 168, note 2, *infra*). He was

the readings are the same as those in the collection made before 1520 by Robert Chaloner,[1] including, it will be remembered, some folios once in the possession of Fitzherbert. The test dates are given in too confused a fashion to count,[2] nor is it possible to say at precisely what time the learned Spelman would have seemed 'old' to the younger generation. But in the absence of Gray's Inn records one may venture the guess that Atwell was a student at the Inn[3] at about the time of Robert Chaloner and that he completed his task not long after Lent 1516, the latest date specified.[4]

The first twelve lectures of the D version of the De Pace reproduce the A version very closely and are so precisely like B that everything that has been said about B applies also to these lectures in D.[5] But the last three lectures depart definitely from A and represent an altogether different type, to be discussed later.

E. Gg. 6. 18 is a paper volume, 8 x 6 inches, of 70 folios,[6] in a late sixteenth-century hand. It contains a variety of rather scrappy anonymous legal material, mainly arguments of cases and readings; one of the latter was delivered in 1552, and another in 1553.[7] The final section turns out to be a condensed version of Marowe's ninth lecture on Forcible Entries,[8] not an exact reproduction of A, but with no significant differences.[9] At the end of a copy of Magna Carta are the initials 'W. F.' in a script closely resembling the signature of 'William Fletewode' in another MS. of Bishop Moore's library already described.[10]

---

serjeant-at-law in 1521, king's serjeant in 1528, and a justice of the court of King's Bench by 1532. He married the daughter of chief justice Frowyk's half-brother Henry and died in 1544; Foss, Judges.

[1] Namely those of Tyngelden and of Spelman; cf. p. 33, note 2, *supra*, and the pamphlet on the Chaloner MSS. there quoted.

[2] App. III, p. 387, notes 1–3, 5.

[3] With some connexion with the Kidwelly family; see p. 152, note 4, *supra*.

[4] *Ibid.*, note 14, *supra*.

[5] Except that the handwriting of D is earlier. Either B was a later copy of D or they were both copies of the same source.

[6] Unnumbered.   [7] 4 August 6 Edw. VI.

[8] No catalogue shows any connexion between this section and Marowe's De Pace.   [9] Probably follows the F version; *infra*, pp. 155, 157.

[10] *Supra*, p. 150. Since Fleetwood died in 1594 (p. 210, *infra*), there is confirmation of the date indicated by the handwriting.

H. The MS. in the Carson Historical Library[1] is a small quarto paper volume of 95 folios, containing merely the De Pace in a late sixteenth-century hand.[2] Although there are some blunders,[3] on the whole H is an intelligent copy of the A version, and follows A itself very closely. It includes the test dates as given in A,[4] several headings found only in A,[5] and, unlike B, C, and D, lacks the portion of Lecture X that was lacking in A.[6]

I. MS. no. 14 in the Library of Harvard Law School is a paper volume, 12 × 8½ inches, of 75 folios, in a handwriting of the end of the sixteenth or perhaps of the beginning of the seventeenth century. The first 36 folios contain Frowyk's reading on the Prerogative of the King,[7] and the succeeding 39 folios a copy of the De Pace.[8] The latter is marred by many omissions of words and sentences that often reduce the text to mere nonsense.[9] It is clearly based on the A version, with the missing section in the same wrong place as in B, C, and D, but is far more like C than like A, B, or D. For example, it gives the test dates as in C, 6 Henry VIII and the same strange year, Millesimo XIII°.[10]

K. In the library of the Inner Temple there is a paper volume,[11] 6 × 8½ inches, of 240 folios, in a seventeenth-century

---

[1] Described in the Catalogue as 'Readings of Mr. Marrow 1504. Containing 14 lectures; referred to by Sir R. Owen in his work, "The Excellency and Antiquitie of the Law of England", who says that they were given in 19 year of Hen. 7. The MS. contains the signature of William Loundes of Lincoln's Inn.'

[2] 'Unusually clear and legible though characteristic Elizabethan hand,' according to the Catalogue.

[3] e.g. f. 15: 'face qui' for 'face gre'; f. 17: 'De Pace terrae et consuetudinibus' for 'conseruatoribus'.   [4] App. III, p. 387.

[5] e.g. f. 31, f. 70. There are differences, however; e.g. H omits a section in A (App. III, p. 330 and note 2), also the Table of Contents, and substitutes 'Leuesque de Rome' for 'Le Pape'.

[6] *Supra*, p. 149, and App. III, p. 365.

[7] Unnumbered. The volume had been for a long time catalogued only under Frowyk, and the existence of Marowe's reading was not suspected. The suggestion of F. A. Ballard led to my examination of the volume and therefore to the discovery of the De Pace.

[8] Numbered 1–39; f. 1 contains a citation from Dugdale on the marriage of Marowe's daughter.   [9] e.g. ff. 11, 14 b, 18.

[10] *Supra*, p. 151, and App. III, p. 387, notes 1, 5. There are many other instances where C and I are like each other and different from the others.

[11] p. 146, note 1, *supra*. Unfortunately, I learned of the existence of this

hand,[1] containing fourteen manuscript readings. The readers, as far as they have been identified, are all members of the Inner Temple who read at the end of the fifteenth or in the early sixteenth centuries.[2] The scribe, late though he is, is clearly familiar with his material; he has supplied a table of contents with the names, and in some cases the dates,[3] of the readers, and has added intelligent comments at the end of several of the readings.[4] The list includes Richard Littleton on Westminster II, cc. 13, 14, and 15,[5] Frowyk on the Prerogative of the King,[6] Keble on Marowe's own subject,[7] followed immediately by the first ten lectures of the De Pace, and a portion of Lecture XI.[8] The copy of the De Pace, as far as it goes, is an accurate rendering of the A version,[9] and has the portion missing from A in the same wrong place as in B, C, and D.[10]

In distinct contrast to the A version represented by seven MSS. is the 'very different' copy noted by Rayner, represented by three MSS., F, G, and L.[11]

F. Hargrave 87 [12] is a paper volume, $9\frac{1}{2} \times 14\frac{1}{2}$ inches, of 457 folios, in writing of about the middle of the sixteenth

collection only as my book was going to the press, too late therefore for a thorough study of its contents.

[1] Attributed to the sixteenth century, in the description of the volume from the catalogue of sales, but on f. 125 (in Marowe's reading) the scribe refers to 'Cooke [Coke] en ses iiii Report'.

[2] 'Manuscript Readings on some of the more Ancient Statutes by Keble, Marrow, Littleton and other Lawyers in the time of King Henry the Seventh', from the above description. A note on the title-page shows that the volume was once in the possession of a member of the Middle Temple.

[3] Only in the case of Keble and Littleton do the names appear in the text.

[4] See notes 7, 8, and p. 161, note 4, *infra*.

[5] ff. 151-70: 'Littilton Lector in Quadragesime', 8 Hen. VII.

[6] ff. 172-86.

[7] ff. 74-96; 'Keble lector, a very good reading' is the scribe's comment at the end. See pp. 184-185, *infra*.

[8] ff. 98-126. The scribe notes at the end that the final portions of the reading are missing.

[9] Easily proved by a comparison of K with passages in A and F that differ from each other. Unfortunately K lacks the lecture containing the test dates. [10] *Supra*, p. 150.

[11] E probably belongs to this second group; see *supra*, p. 153, note 9.

[12] In the index to the printed catalogue there is no reference to this volume under Marowe; but cf. p. 211, note 6, p. 214, note 2.

century.[1] It contains a number of law readings,[2] not always complete, and also many legal arguments, apparently fragmentary extracts from discussions of the reader's points or perhaps of moot cases.[3] The collection resembles, both in content and in form, the manuscript volume that contains A,[4] and includes some of the identical quotations of legal opinion.[5] Except for the puzzling instance of William Wadham[6] the names of the readers are easily identified as belonging to the Inner Temple toward the end of the fifteenth and at the beginning of the sixteenth centuries.[7] Of the readings in the volume the earliest is a fragment by Thomas Keble on Marowe's own subject, delivered not long before July 1486[8]; the latest by Henry Whyte in Lent 1530.[9] There is, however, a reference to the death of Audeley,[10] which did not take place till 1544.[11] Amongst the clearest and fullest readings are Frowyk's on the Prerogative[12] and the De Pace.[13]

The evidence suggests that the collection was the work of some one connected with the Inner Temple, and that it was begun in the reign of Henry VIII not long after 1530, but

---

[1] Early sixteenth, according to the Catalogue; certainly not possible for the entire volume. But it is by no means certain that it is all the work of one scribe.

[2] About thirty, the catalogue states. Cf. the note on f. 2 in a late hand: 'Un profitable livre de divers tres erudites lectures sur severall statutes'.

[3] Cf. also references to the views of readers cited *infra*, p. 172, notes 5 and 6.

[4] Described *supra*, pp. 148-9.

[5] e.g. 'Vide per Brudenell', f. 8; 'per Sutton en lecture', f. 12. The scribe must have had access to the volume or to the sources on which it was based.

[6] ff. 309-25, on Westminster II, chs. 10 and 11, Lent 18 Hen. VII. The date is of course impossible if he was an Inner Temple reader, unless perhaps he was reading at one of the Inns of Chancery. Nor is it correct for William Wadham of Lincoln's Inn; according to Dugdale, Orig. Jurid., 250-1, a reader of that name read in Lent 16 Hen. VII, 20 Hen. VII, and 11 Hen. VIII. The last mentioned reading was on Westminster II, c. 3, and is included in Maynard MSS. lxx, Lincoln's Inn. Is 'William' in the Hargrave collection a slip for 'Lawrence'? See p. 129, note 2, *supra*.

[7] A partial list of the earlier readers is given *infra*, pp. 178-81.

[8] ff. 302-8; see *supra*, 155, and pp. 184-5, *infra*.

[9] ff. 234-61, 'a son 11ᵈ Redynge', Lent 22 Hen. VIII, at the Inner Temple; Dugdale, Orig. Jurid., 164.

[10] f. 427; cf. ff. 427-57 for his reading.

[11] p. 150, note 1, *supra*.   [12] ff. 142-76.   [13] ff. 262-301.

that it was not completed till 1544, or perhaps not till some years later.

A collation of F with A, paragraph by paragraph [1]—the difference between them makes a word to word collation impossible—shows that F is only about half as long as A. Except for the omission of the last part of Lecture XV,[2] its brevity is due to the absence of explanations and amplifications, not to the leaving out of legal points [3]; in other words, it is the result of a condensation performed on the whole with great skill.[4] The greatest single improvement is the insertion in the correct place of the section of Lecture X missing in A[5] and misplaced in B, C, and D.

It has been already noted that the last three lectures in D differ from the A version.[6] It now appears that they are precisely like F, except that they include the whole of Lecture XV.[7] Since the test dates have been changed in F to 10 June, 20 Henry VII and to 1505,[8] it seems probable that the scribe had before him a copy of the De Pace that had itself been transcribed within a few months after Marowe's death,[9] and that this same copy had been used by Walter Atwell as the source for the last three lectures of D. The version represented by F has been called the F version.

G. Lansdowne 1133 is a paper volume, 8 x 12 inches, of 161 folios, containing law readings and other legal material in a handwriting of the latter part of the sixteenth century; the latest date mentioned is 1579.[10] The collection includes readings by Robert Catlin of the Middle Temple, 1547,[11] Thomas Bromley of the Inner Temple, autumn 1566 (?),[12] and

---

[1] I am indebted to Miss Ethel Stokes for the performance of this laborious task and for much valuable assistance throughout this monograph.   [2] App. III, p. 408, note 3.

[3] In fact, it sometimes contains additional information ; cf. e. g. App. III, p. 369, note 6.

[4] There are however a few errors ; see *infra*, p. 158, note 13.

[5] App. III, p. 362, note 3, p. 365, note 1.   [6] *Supra*, p. 153.

[7] Note 2, *supra*.   [8] App. III, p. 387, notes 1, 5.

[9] p. 137, and note 5, *supra*. Certainly a scribe writing just before or after the middle of the sixteenth century would not have been likely to have invented these dates as a substitute for the original ones.

[10] f. 123 b.   [11] ff. 1–29; Dugdale, Orig. Jurid., 217.

[12] ff. 30–54. There were two distinguished Thomas Bromleys of the Inner Temple. The elder read in the autumn of 1532 and became a judge

Marowe's De Pace[1]; also arguments by John Popham,[2] serjeant-at-law in 1578,[3] and by Edmund Plowden,[4] both of the
Middle Temple.[5]   It is to be noted that the famous 'Commentaries' of the latter were printed in 1571,[6] with a Table
by Fleetwood, likewise of the Middle Temple.[7]   There is also
a copy of Fitzherbert's preface to 'Loffice' and a small fragment of the mysterious MS. treatise[8] on the peace which has
been already described, and which has been shown to include
1576 as its latest date.[9]   The names on the whole indicate a
Middle Temple production made by some one or for some one
interested in the subject of the peace.

The De Pace proves to be a copy of the F version, with the
section from Lecture X in its proper place,[10] but shortened by
the omission of all of Lecture XV.[11]   The test dates are given
as 9 June, 20 Henry VIII, 9 July, and 1545,[12] and suggest that
G was based on a copy of the F version made at about the
time of the completion of the volume containing F.[13]

L.   Tanner 428,[14] Bodleian, is a paper volume,[15] $7\frac{1}{2} \times 5\frac{3}{4}$
inches, of 136 folios, in a late sixteenth-century hand.   It con-
tains merely a fairly literal and intelligent translation into
English of the F version of De Pace,[16] and a table of contents[17]

of the King's Bench in 1544; the younger read in 1566, became Lord
Chancellor in 1579 and died in April 1587; Foss, Judges.   For the probability that the Lord Chancellor is the one here referred to, see p. 214,
infra, and note 11.   [1] ff. 55–94.   [2] ff. 123–7.
  [3] Dugdale, Chron. Ser., 95 ; chief justice of the King's Bench in 1592,
ibid. 98.
  [4] ff. 135–6, answered by Dodyngton of the Middle Temple.
  [5] Minutes of Parl. Middle Temple, ed. C. T. Martin, index sub nominibus.
  [6] By Tottell.   [7] See p. 210, *infra*.
  [8] ff. 95–8 ; 'Paget' is written on the margin, perhaps the Sir James Paget
who was justice of the peace in 1570.
  [9] pp. 108, note 6, 113, note 7, *supra*.   [10] p. 157, note 5, *supra*.
  [11] App. III, p. 404, note 2.   [12] App. III, p. 387, notes 1, 2, 5.
  [13] The resemblance between F and G is very close, even in the matter
of errors ; e.g. in both, homicide is discussed under the heading ' de home '
instead of 'Mort de home'.   Cf. also App III, p. 301, note 3.   If F was
transcribed about 1544, it is altogether possible that G was based on it.
  [14] Under 'Jus' in the index of pt. iv of Cat. Cod. MSS. Bib. Bod., 4c8
is given by an error for 428.   But the description is more correct than in
the new catalogue.   In neither is there any reference to Marowe as the
author.
  [15] Once in the possession of John Holland.
  [16] Proved by a comparison of L with passages in A and F that differ
from each other.   [17] ff. 105–6.

(not identical with that in A), and an alphabetical index of subjects.[1] The test date is given as 1 March 25 Henry VII,[2] the missing section of Lecture X is in its proper place,[3] and the reading ends in the middle of Lecture XV,[4] although continuing further than F. There is no contemporary title to the work,[5] no reference to the author, or to the translator, or to the scribe, nothing but the handwriting to indicate the date of this copy, and therefore no clue as to when the translation had first been made. The fact that only one copy of an English version has been discovered [6] and that French copies continued to be produced [7] is evidence, if any is needed, of the persistence of French as the language of law.[8]

Although it is not my purpose to discuss in detail the linguistic peculiarities of the MSS. of the De Pace, a few words ought to be said about the character of the French. The scribe of A—and the statement applies in general to the scribes of the other copies closest in date to A[9]—has an extraordinary disregard for gender and number; for example, 'vne feme' and 'le feme',[10] 'ils serra' or 'ils serront',[11] 'le comen howse del parliement poient'.[12] His inflections are sometimes strange, or are concealed by suspensions capable of several interpretations, but on the whole he writes a fairly consistent and easily understood form of law French.[13] The number of English

---

[1] ff. 110–36.　　[2] See p. 158, note 12, *supra.*　　[3] See p. 157, note 5, *supra.*
[4] App. III, p. 409, note 2.　　　　　　[5] See *supra*, p. 146.
[6] Excluding another English version which was not a mere translation; see p. 212, *infra.*
[7] E and G were perhaps as late as L; and H, I, and K later.
[8] This fact so well known to legal historians is apparently not understood by specialists in other fields; cf. Professor O. F. Emerson's assumption that the statute of 1362 meant the triumph of English in the law courts; History of the English Language, 1907, chs. iv and v, and especially 64–5. But by 1916 he has modified his statement; The Romanic Review, vii, 'English or French in the time of Edward III,' 130. Cf. also the opening paragraphs of ch. viii of The Lollard Bible, by M. Deanesly and her reference to Camb. Hist. Eng. Lit., ii. 80 (not 70 as printed). For the whole subject see Maitland's Introduction to Year Books 1 & 2 Edw. II, Selden Soc., xvii.
[9] Their verbal forms and their vocabulary are however by no means identical with those of A. From the point of view of language the MSS. need more attention than I have given them.
[10] App. III, *passim.*　　　　[11] *Ibid., passim.*　　　　[12] *Ibid.* p. 303.
[13] Cf. instances of substantives ending in -ee (Maitland, *loc. cit.*, xxxix); lessee, for example, is very common.

words is not great, although of course far greater than in the early Year Books.[1] They include the 'common objects of the country and of gentlemanly sport', for which Maitland has shown that the reporters had no French words[2]; barn, bees, dove house, greyhound, 'yonge sperhawkis', &c.,[3] and also such unexpected words as owner, generally, 'meanetemps', 'wesande'.[4] But in spite of the English words there is nothing like : 'Il metta backe oue son dagger vn fenester', or 'Home est let down per le tonel del chimin'.[5] The language is really French—law French, it is true—but not the 'debased jargon' or 'slang' of a later period.[6]

The foregoing account shows that the problem of finding the MS. closest to Marowe's original has been reduced to a simple alternative.[7] As far as we now know, there were in circulation shortly after his death only two versions of the De Pace, the full and detailed A version, and the exceedingly condensed F version. Of these, A[8] and F[9] are the best existing representatives; it is clear, however, from the omissions in Lecture X in the former and in Lecture XV in the latter,[10] that neither can claim to be Marowe's own copy. But did Marowe use the longer or the shorter form in delivering the reading? The following comparison will bring out the nature of the differences between them. After stating that justices of the peace in process on an indictment of a clerk do not

---

[1] The tenacity of French is well illustrated by the fact that statutes of Henry VII enacted in English are cited in French; cf., however, the English quotation at the very end of Lect. XV, App. III.
[2] Maitland, *op. cit.*, xxxvii. [3] App. III.
[4] The material merits careful study by philologists, even though it does not contain the 'rich mine' found in the early Year Books ; cf. W. C. Bolland, The Year Books, 1921, 24-5.
[5] Crompton, Loffice, f. 30.
[6] That is, of the late seventeenth century, according to Maitland, *loc. cit.* xxxiii, but Crompton's jargon was written under Elizabeth. It is difficult to feel sure as to just how closely the language in any one copy represents Marowe's own usage ; see *infra*, p. 190. [7] *Supra*, p. 147.
[8] Very nearly contemporary ; in this group are C and D (first twelve lectures), *circ.* 1514-1516 ; B, *circ.* middle of sixteenth century ; H, I, and K distinctly later.
[9] *Circ.* middle of sixteenth but based on a 1505 MS. ; in this group are D (last three lectures), *circ.* 1516 ; G., *circ.* 1579 ; E (Lect. IX), late sixteenth ; L (English), late sixteenth.
[10] *Supra*, pp. 149, 157.

have the same power as justices of common law, A continues :. 'Et vncore si le vicount fait tile returne al comen leie, lez Justicez al comen leie poient eslier de prendre son proces par Capias al vicount ou agarder vne Venire facias clericum direct al Ordinarie. Mes si home a vne foitz appier sur enditement de transgression & apres fist default, la lenquest serra pris par son default enuers luy; mes si le partie appier sur enditement de Felony & puis fist default, vncore lenquest ne serra pris par son default.' [1]

F summarizes thus : 'Mez si tiel returne soyt al comen ley ilz poyent eslier de prendre son corps par Capias all vicount ou venire facias [clericum] all Ordinarye. Mez in transgression silz appere & puis fist default lenquest serra pris. Autrement est en Felonye.' There are many similar examples in A of redundant phraseology,[2] of carefully phrased explanations and also many instances of illustrative details.[3] The form of A is precisely that which a conscientious teacher might use in presenting difficult material to a group of students who were expected to master the drift of the argument and to take notes on it.[4] In listening to F, on the other hand, one would have no time for note taking. My judgement therefore is unhesitatingly in favour of A as the closest to Marowe's original.[5]

It is tempting to suggest that the F version represents notes taken on the spot by a clever utter barrister.[6] The hypothesis finds support in the fact that the condensation is often so great that the sense is obscured to a modern reader, though doubtless perfectly intelligible to one who had heard

---

[1] App. III, Lect. XIV.

[2] In marked contrast to 'autrement est' so common in F, in place of a restatement of the whole case.

[3] Place-names, &c., are often omitted in F.

[4] Such a form would permit the reader to lecture not 'drawingly' (tractim) but 'rapidly' (raptim), that is to say, 'bringing out the words as rapidly as if nobody was writing before him'; H. Rashdall, Universities of Europe, i. 438. We have the authority of the scribe of the Inner Temple volume (K, *supra*) that Keble's reading was not a perfect copy but only certain notes made by a student; f. 96. But he makes no such comment on Marowe's reading.

[5] It is of course possible (but not probable) that Marowe's own copy was different from either A or F.

[6] Or by one of the reader's assistants; see *infra*, p. 162.

and still remembered the spoken words. If, however, the schedule of hours suggested below is approximately correct, the time allotted,[1] especially without a smoothly flowing 'self-filling' fountain pen, would not have been sufficient for so skilful and so accurate a condensation of intricate arguments.[2] It seems far more probable that the F version was made by some one working at leisure with a fair copy of a manuscript before him. Perhaps Marowe's two assistants, themselves soon to be readers,[3] were responsible for making two copies from the reader's own MS. ; one *in extenso* and the other in the nature of an abstract[4] to serve as a supplement to the rougher notes taken by the students day by day.[5] But this is mere conjecture, and, in our present state of knowledge, not easily susceptible of proof or disproof.

(2) ANALYSIS OF CONTENT

The 'reading' on Westminster first, ch. i, is divided into fifteen [6] 'readings' or 'lectures',[7] as we should call them. The first two—about a tenth of the whole—after a brief paragraph on the enactment of the statute of Westminster, deal with the peace of the church, and the remaining thirteen with the peace of the land.

The former contain a short account of the decrease in the old powers of the keepers of the spiritual peace, bishops and archbishops, and of the present delimitation between their

---

[1] See pp. 172-3, *infra*, and note 1.

[2] Cf. G. J. Turner, Introduction to Year Book 4 Edw. II, Selden Soc. xix : 'Careful note taking is not now, and probably never has been, a popular mode of instruction. It was a difficult pursuit in the Middle Ages, much more difficult than it now is, in an age of cheap writing material, steel pens, and above all of good blotting-paper.' It is sound to assume that for law students in 1503 the language would not have caused a further difficulty ; see p. 159, *supra*.

[3] Cf. Cal. Inner Temple Records, i. xxxii, 33. For assistants in the other Inns, see Pension Book Gray's Inn, ed. R. J. Fletcher, i. 13 ; Minutes of Parliament Middle Temple, i. 21.

[4] It has already been shown that the basis of the F version went back at least to June 1505 ; *supra*, p. 157 ; also that F like A is an Inner Temple production.

[5] As Mr. Turner says of the origin of the Year Books (*ut supra*) : 'The wise student would soon find that he could learn more by reading good notes made by practised reporters than by writing bad notes himself.'

[6] But see *infra*, p. 165.

[7] See *infra*, p. 168, note 7, for the double use of the term 'lectura'.

authority and that of the keepers of the peace of the land. The subject is then discussed under two heads :

(1) Offences against spiritual possessions.

(2) Offences against spiritual persons.[1]

Under the first, Marowe describes the remedies by sanctification, by suit of spoliation and by writ of *De vi laica removenda*. Under the second, he discusses the arrest of spiritual persons by officers of the temporal law, giving a detailed interpretation of two statutes of Edward III and Richard II.[2]

The content of the thirteen lectures on the peace of the land can best be understood by a brief outline which will show Marowe's method of approach to the subject and the logical organization of his material.[3]

A. Historical and descriptive account of the distinction between 'conservator' and 'justice' of the peace and of the sources of their authority.[4]

  I. Methods by which men may be made conservators and not justices.[5]

    a. Office of dignity.

    b. Prescription.

    c. Letters Patent.

    d. Writ.

    e. Tenure.

  II. Methods by which justices of the peace are appointed.[6]

    a. Special Letters Patent.

    b. General commission.

  III. Qualifications of justices of the peace.[7]

B. Analysis of the authority of justices of the peace.[8]

  I. Their authority of keeping the peace exercised out of sessions and without sworn inquest.[9]

---

[1] Lect. II begins with (2).

[2] See App. III, p. 295, notes 2, 4.

[3] The titles of the separate lectures, the various summarizing paragraphs, and the table at the end make his general scheme easy to detect. Unless otherwise specified, I am using MS. A as printed in App. III, but I am not giving literal translations of titles, and I am sometimes adding headings for the sake of clearness. The letters and numerals are mine.

[4] Lect. III–V.   [5] Lect. III.   [6] Lect. IV.

[7] Lect. V.   [8] Lect. VI–XV (in part).

[9] Lect. VI–IX, especially the beginning of Lect. VI.

   a. Surety of peace.[1]

      1. Method of demanding surety.

      2. Method of granting surety.

      3. Process against him from whom surety is demanded.

      4. Method of finding surety.

      5. Method of discharging surety.

   b. Breach of peace and its pacification.[2]

      1. By an individual.[3]

      2. By a multitude of people.[4]

        Riot.

        Assembly.

        Rout.

      3. Forcible Entry and restitution.[5]

II. The authority of justices of the peace exercised in sessions.[6]

   a. Their authority of inquiring.[7]

      1. Method of holding the sessions of the peace.[8]

      2. Offences to be inquired of by virtue of their commission.

        Trespasses.[9]

        Felonies.[10]

      3. Form of presentments.[11]

      4. Process on indictments.[12]

   b. Their authority of hearing and determining offences by virtue of their commission.[13]

      1. Trespass; by any two of the justices.

      2. Felonies; at least one of the quorum must be included.

Marowe's arrangement is so orderly that it is a surprise to find that Lecture XV does not end with its announced subject of 'hearing and determining'. Instead, immediately after a discussion of the arraigning of a felonious clerk, comes a com-

---

[1] Lect. VI.   [2] Lect. VII–IX.   [3] Lect. VII.
[4] Lect. VIII.   [5] Lect. IX.   [6] Lect. X–XV (in part).
[7] Lect. X–XIV.   [8] Lect. X.   [9] Lect. XI.
[10] Lect. XII.   [11] Lect. XIII.
[12] Lect. XIV. Marowe makes no distinction between 'presentment' and 'enditement'; see *supra*, p. 84, note 6.   [13] Lect. XV (in part).

mentary on the words of the commission concerning the Custos Rotulorum and his duties.[1] A glance at the form of the commission[2] makes it appear probable that these two final folios are out of place in Lecture XV,[3] but that they constitute the logical conclusion to Lecture X on methods of holding the sessions.[4] The fact that Lecture X will, with this addition, be longer than any of the other sections may show that it really comprised two 'lectures',[5] making the total sixteen, not fifteen.

The omissions are significant. There are no copies of writs or indictments; no list of statutes; no account of purely statutory trespasses and felonies, but merely a brief note: ' Item sount aultres chosez inquerablez & ceo est par estatutez & purceo ilz ne sount rehercez '.[6] Inevitably, therefore, there is no reference to many important statutory offences, such for example as infringement of the labour legislation, and no copy of the justices' Charge to the jurors which has been shown to be mainly a 'rehersal' of statutes.[7] There is no description of the purely administrative aspect of the duties of the justices, such as their proclamation of the rates of wages,[8] and by no means a complete account of their powers outside of sessions, that is, of their powers as magistrates.[9] Nor are there complete instructions for the making of the endentured estreats nor for the delivery of them into the Exchequer.

Obviously the ' lectures ' would not serve as a manual for the clerk of the peace, like the ' Boke ' printed three years later or like the various fifteenth-century MS. collections of precedents,[10] nor were they suitable for the country gentlemen who made up the majority of the commission. Rather, they constituted a legal treatise that would be of use to the justices of the quorum, who were, supposedly at least, ' learned in the

---

[1] *Ibid.* Followed in the A version by a table of contents.

[2] As printed in Lambard, Eirenarcha, 1581 ed., 39–45.

[3] Although they appear in all the complete copies of Lect. XV that I have read ; but see *infra*, p. 216, note 3.

[4] App. p. 362, note 4, p. 368, note 1.

[5] The confusion in Lect. X is baffling ; see *supra*, pp. 149–50.

[6] App. III, p. 375, note 3 on trespass ; cf. p. 383 for a similar note on felonies.

[7] Ch. ii, p. 55, *supra*.   [8] Cf. ch. iii (1), pp. 92–3, *supra*.

[9] For example, their authority of examining labourers under oath (2 Hen. V, st. 1, c. 4) is not touched on.   [10] *Supra*, chs. i–iii.

law '.[1]   Further, since in the fifteenth century the justices of the
quorum in quarter sessions were exercising a far wider jurisdiction over felonies than at any other time in their history,
it is natural that a trained lawyer like Marowe should feel
compelled to expound the criminal law as he knew it in his
own lifetime.   His discussion of burglary, murder, &c., or of
the intricacies necessary for the correct drawing of indictments,
has therefore a value quite independent of the subject of
justices of the peace.

Marowe's historical sections are exceedingly valuable,[2] his
knowledge of statutes both ' old ' and ' new ' is surprisingly
wide and accurate; but his chief interest, or perhaps better,
his chief pride, lay in subtle legal analysis and in the exercise
of great ingenuity in imagining all possible cases, as in his
discussion of Forcible Entry [3] or of the difference between the
terms ' price ' and ' value '.[4]   To a modern reader the method
often seems both confusing and pedantic,[5] and one can but
regret that Marowe was so ' grave ' and ' sad ' [6] that he allowed
himself little relaxation or lightness of touch.   Picturesque
details are all too rare, such as the reference to the criminal
who keeps a priest's surplice at hand ready to slip on in case
of arrest.[7]   There is none of the discursiveness so delightful in
Crompton's re-writing of Fitzherbert,[8] none of the humour

---

[1] The actual composition of the quorum is one of the many problems
needing investigation.   Mr. W. Paley Baildon has called my attention to
the fact that members of the quorum were not always ' learned in the
law '.
[2] *Infra*, p. 216.   He makes an occasional slip however; cf. e. g.
p. 192, *infra*.
[3] Lect. IX.   Cf. also Lect. VIII on Riots, Routs, and Assemblies.   He
ignores the ' so-called Star Chamber Act of 1487 (3 Henry VII, c. 1) ' ; see
A. F. Pollard, ' Star Chamber under the Tudors ', E.H.R. xxxvii. 520–8.
[4] Lect. XIII ; see ch. vi (4), *infra*.
[5] Cf. the strictures of Bacon and Coke on later readings ; *infra*,
p. 220, note 7.
[6] To use Coke's words of certain reporters, cited by Maitland, Year
Book 1 & 2 Edw. II, Selden Soc., Introduction, 16.   Perhaps Marowe's
spoken words would convey a different impression ; see p. 130 *supra*.
[7] App. III, p. 290.
[8] e. g. under Burglary: ' Come le iour est appoint pur home de trauailer
circa ses besoignes, issint est le nute per dieu pur home de prendre son
rest, car quod caret alterna requie durabile non est, come le poete Ouid
parle . . . & quant home est dormyant, est reason que son corps et biens
soient in peace ' ; 1593 ed., f. 29 b.

that makes the Year Books more 'diverting' than a 'comedy'.[1]
Perhaps the fault lay partly in the immemorial custom that
demanded that a reading should be a strictly legal exposition
of a statute[2] or of a clause of a statute. In Marowe's time
'old' statutes rather than 'new' were the fashionable choice.[3]
Quite naturally, therefore, instead of reading on an act of
Edward III or of Richard II[4] that dealt specifically with
justices of the peace, Marowe selected the opening chapter of
Westminster first, enacted long before their institution: 'En
primez voet le Roy & commaunde que la peas de seint esglis
& de la terre soit bien garde et maintenue en toutz pointez et
que comen droit soit fait as toutz auxi bien as poures come as
riches saunz regard de nully'.[5] The artificiality of the choice
is strikingly shown by the strained interpretation necessary to
make these vague words apply to the authority conferred on
justices of the peace by virtue of their commission. 'Soit le
peas bien garde' signifies the authority of keeping the peace
exercised by the justices out of session and without sworn inquest; 'et maintenue en toutz pointes' denotes their authority
of inquiring exercised in session; and 'que comen droit soit
fait, etc.' implies their authority of hearing and determining.[6]

It is evident that both the form and the matter of Marowe's
treatise were conditioned by the fact that it was a 'reading'—

[1] Roger North's precise words have been chosen as the motto of the
Selden Society.

[2] Report of 1540 (cited on p. 129, note 8, *supra*): he shall 'reade
some one such Act, or Statute as shall please him to ground his whole
reading on for all that Vacation, and that done, doth declare such incon-
veniences and mischiefs as were unprovided for ... and then reciteth
certain doubts and questions which he hath devised, that may grow upon
the said Statute, and declareth his judgement therein'. Cf. Coke on
Littleton, sect. 481: 'Here it is to be observed, of what Authority
ancient Lectures or Readings upon Statutes were, ... First, they declared
what the Common Law was before the Making of the Statute, ...
secondly, they opened the true sense and meaning of the Statute. ...
Fifthly, they read, to suppress subtle Inventions to creep out of the
Statute ...'

[3] For the distinction, see pp. 45-6, *supra*. A superficial examination
shows innumerable readings on Magna Carta, on the statutes of Merton,
Gloucester, Marlebridge, Westminster first, second, and third, &c.

[4] e.g. 35 Edw. III, c. 1, or 12 Rich. II, c. 10.

[5] 3 Edw. I, c. 1, 1275.

[6] Lect. VI; cf. pp. 193-4, *infra*, for the statute of Westminster in the
commission.

a 'double reading'—given with the customary elaborate
ceremony and expense[1] at the Inner Temple, on the eve of
his promotion to be serjeant-at-law[2] and of his consequent
separation from his Inn.[3] A 'double' reading was usually
delivered in Lent vacation [4] (occasionally in the autumn vacation[5]), and normally came nine or ten years after the 'single'
reading.[6]   In the reign of Henry VII it was a more scholarly
and a more elaborate production than a 'single' reading,[7] and

[1] Cal. Inner Temple Records, i. xxxii–xxxiii. The decay of readings
was due in part to the growing expense for the readers ; see the references
cited in note 2, p. 170, *infra*, especially p. 214 of Holdsworth's article.
Marowe's wealth must have been useful ; see pp. 123, 140, *supra*.

[2] The statement in the report of 1540 (*ut supra*), that of 'these
Readers . . . for the most part are appointed those that shall be Serjeants '
(evidently the basis of Holdsworth, *op. cit.*, ii. 423) needs amplification.
It appears that although a man has read twice, on his call to be serjeant
he is forced to read a third time. Cf. the instance of John Baldwin, Cal.
Inner Temple Records, i. 98 ; MS. Harl. 1691, ff. 187–7 b : 'De pri-
sonibus prisonam frangentibus, Baldweyni lectour pro forma seriant '.
Dugdale, Orig. Jurid., 163–4, shows that he read in autumn 8 Hen. VIII,
in Lent 15 Hen. VIII as 'duplex lector', and again in autumn
23 Hen. VIII, 'eo quod ad gradum Servientis ad Legem nunc
electus est '. The following type of entry is common : 'Master Elyot
was chosen Reader for the coming vacation, because he was chosen
Serjeant-at-law' ; Minutes of Parl. Middle Temple, i. 5, 22 May,
18 Hen. VII, 1503.

[3] The double reading has been called a 'swan-song'; Pension Book
Gray's Inn, i. xi.

[4] See the lists in Dugdale and the headings of MS. readings ; cf. also
Dugdale, 315.

[5] e. g. Frowyk read in August 1495, and was made serjeant-at-law in
the following November. Cf. the entry in Minutes of Parl. Middle
Temple, i. 21, 1507 : 'or that a seriant rede for his forme in a Somer
vacacion '.

[6] A study of Dugdale's lists shows that the interval varies from five to
twelve years.

[7] There is evidence to prove that at this date the double reading was
a more specialized treatise and the single reading a mere cursory survey
of all the chapters of an 'old' statute, covering a number of distinct
topics ; the contrast between Frowyk's two readings is a good illustration ; pp. 179–80, *infra*. The preponderance of Lent readings that have
survived would thus be explained. 'Single', 'double', and 'treble', are
clearly synonymous with 'first', 'second', and 'third', applied to the
performance as a whole. Cf. Coke's statement in preface to his Third
Report, which is confirmed by Dugdale's lists. Possibly this terminology
developed in order to avoid the ambiguity arising from the fact that 'first
reading', 'second reading', &c., were also used of the successive instal-
ments of a 'single' or 'first' reading, and of a 'double' or 'second'
reading, &c. Cf. e. g. prima lectura, &c., of De Pace, App. III. Cf. also :
'Such as have Read double, or shall Read double'; Dugdale, Orig.
Jurid., 314. In MS. Hargrave 87, 'lectura 2ᵈᵃ' describes the second day's

had been preceded by a longer period of study at the Inn and of practice in the courts.[1] The reader's audience included not only the students of his Inn, utter and inner barristers,[2] but also distinguished Benchers,[3] most of them already readers, and sometimes serjeants-at-law and judges.[4] Possibly that 'oracle of the law', the chief justice of the Common Pleas, Marowe's close friend, heard some of the lectures on the De Pace.[5] Under such circumstances the reader would naturally try to plan his lectures both to give information to students and also to impress the mature minds of his professional colleagues and

reading by Mounteforde (f. 177 b), and yet 'Son ii^{de} reading' (f. 399) and 'lectour 2da vice' (f. 134) refer to 'double' readings by Coningsby and Rudhale respectively. The double reader has less expense than the single and a larger appropriation; he has two servants instead of one, and is treated as a person of great distinction; Cal. Inner Temple Records, i. xxxii–xxxiii; Pension Book Gray's Inn, i. xii, xiii, 120–1; Dugdale, *op. cit.*, *passim.* For the still more advantageous position of the treble reader, see Black Books Lincoln's Inn, i. xv; but cf. Pension Book Gray's Inn, i. 84, for a change: no double reader shall be asked 'ad lectionem tertiam'.

Professor Roland G. Usher has investigated readings of the end of the sixteenth and of the early part of the seventeenth centuries, and has come to many interesting and important conclusions which it is hoped will soon be published.

[1] Ordinarily, in Michaelmas the readers for Lent were chosen, and in Easter those for the summer; see records of Inns of Court, *passim*; six months' notice therefore were given in both cases; Report, *ut supra.*

[2] *Ibid.*; Black Books Lincoln's Inn, i. xxv. Coke, preface to Third Report, uses 'Mootemen' for 'inner Barristers'.

[3] The governing body of the Inner Temple. 'They selected from the utter bar such as they choose to be readers and such others as they thought fit and proper persons to be made Masters of the Bench. . . . An utter barrister on being elected Reader was in due course called to be Master of the Bench'; Cal. Inner Temple Records, i. xxxi–xxxii. In spite of Coke's statement as to a minimum of twelve years (*ut supra*, note 2), there was no fixed interval between the bar and the bench; cf. Cal. Inner Temple Records, i. lxxxi–lxxxii; Black Books Lincoln's Inn, i. 456–8; Dugdale, Orig. Jurid., 209. But it is, I suppose, probable that regulations such as those of 1466 made by Lincoln's Inn (Bl. Bks. i. viii, 41–2) were in force at the Inner Temple: 'Every Bencher must keep six whole vacations in the three years immediately after his admission, that is, one month in the Lent reading and another month in the Autumn reading, and be personally present for the first week.'

[4] Report of 1540: 'the Judges and Serjeants, if any be present, declare their opinions'; 545. Cf. p. 180, note 4, *infra.*

[5] See p. 134, *supra,* for the probability that Frowyk was responsible for Marowe's call to be serjeant. Frowyk may have been absent on the western circuit during all of Lent 1503; he was certainly in Exeter on Thursday 23 March; P.R.O. Anc. Indictments, K.B. 9, 432, m. 9. Cf. Cal. Pat. Hen. VII, 1494–1509, 305.

superiors with his own legal learning and acumen, and with his mastery of the fine points of the common law. In other words, it seems probable that Marowe was thinking even more of the training of barristers and of his own career as a future serjeant-at-law than of the precise needs of the justices of the quorum in quarter sessions.

Unfortunately, our knowledge of readings, 'the keystone' of the educational system,[1] is more complete for the period of their decline in the late seventeenth century [2] and for what has been called their 'palmy days' under Elizabeth and her immediate successors [3] than for the reign of Henry VII,[4] a period of far greater prosperity for the old system.[5] It is also to be regretted that we know more of the ceremonial aspects of readings, of the food consumed at the reader's feast and of the necessary [6] expenses, than we do of the actual pedagogic methods. It is not easy to discover just how Marowe in Lent 1503 met his responsibilities [7] for teaching his subject to those inner and utter barristers for whom the lectures were compulsory.[8] The following questions need to be answered:

[1] Pension Book Gray's Inn, i. xliii.

[2] Cf. the various introductions to the later volumes of the records of the Inns, and the famous Judges' orders easily accessible in Dugdale, *op. cit.*, ch. lxx. For an admirable recent article, see W. S. Holdsworth, 'The Disappearance of the Educational System of the Inns of Court', University of Pennsylvania Law Review, March 1921.

[3] Pension Book Gray's Inn, i. xxxii.

[4] 'We know next to nothing of the work of readers in the fifteenth century'; G. J. Turner, Year Book 4 Edw. II, Selden Soc., xxv. A good brief account of printed material is given in Holdsworth, Hist. Eng. Law, ii. 414, note 3. The records of the Middle Temple begin with 1501, of the Inner Temple with 1505, of Gray's Inn with 1569 (with extracts from earlier records), of Lincoln's Inn with 1422. The latter give few particulars about early readings. But scholars have thus far failed to utilize many MS. collections of readings, arguments, and moot cases, dating from early Tudor and pre-Tudor times.

[5] Cf. e. g. the greater length of the readings, discussed *infra*.

[6] e. g. Cal. Inner Temple Records, i. 193, 228; Black Books Lincoln's Inn, i. xvi–xvii, 222.

[7] It was probably true of Henry VII's reign that the Reader was the 'member of the bench responsible during his term of office for the teaching of the students'; Holdsworth, *op. cit.*, ii. 417, writing of the middle of the sixteenth century.

[8] We know that in 1507 students were amerced for non-attendance, Cal. Inner Temple Records, i. 7. Cf. also Black Books Lincoln's Inn, i. 183 (1517), 195 (1520).

(1) Who were his assistants and what were their duties?

(2) What kind of notes did the students take?

(3) How many weeks and how many days in the week were covered by his course?

(4) What 'cases' did he put or what 'points' did he submit for discussion? Which of his statements were 'impugned'?[1]

(5) What were his 'sources' or authorities? Did he refer to them as he read?

No further evidence on (1) and (2) has come to my attention beyond what has been said in a previous section,[2] but the answer to (3) is fairly definite. The progressive shortening of the minimum time to be occupied by the reader at the end of the sixteenth and in the beginning of the seventeenth centuries has been frequently described.[3] The three weeks and three days,[4] became three weeks,[5] and included three days a week, usually Monday, Wednesday, and Friday.[6] Next, a differentiation between 'single' and 'double' assigned first nine and then six days to the former, and eventually only three days to the latter.[7] For Marowe's period, however, the normal requirement seemed to have been four weeks, and four days a week.[8] The fifteen or sixteen lectures—so often found in the early MSS.[9]—fit well into such a schedule. It is possible to say with some assurance, therefore, that Marowe began to quote the first chapter of Westminster first in the Hall of the Inner

---

[1] Report of 1540; Dugdale, *op. cit.*, 160, 194.

[2] *Supra*, pp. 161-2.

[3] Definite evidence is afforded by the Judges' orders, cited *supra*, p. 170, note 2.

[4] Cal. Inner Temple Records, i. 142, 1546: 'The readers are to read fully three weeks and three days'; cf. Report of 1540: the two 'learning-vacations' last three weeks and three days.

[5] Dugdale, *op. cit.*, 247.

[6] *Ibid.* 313. But the custom in the various Inns was not uniform as to the days of the week; *ibid.* 319.

[7] *Ibid.* 314, 319.

[8] Black Books Lincoln's Inn, i. xvi; it is uncertain, however, as to just when they began and ended. See *ibid.* 42, 125, for references to four weeks as the 'ancient custom of the Society'; cf. Pension Book Gray's Inn, i. 170: 'at least thrice a week and oftener when it has been the custom'.

[9] e. g. Marowe, fifteen or perhaps sixteen; Frowyk, sixteen in 1495. In the reign of Henry VIII the number is still large; Gilbert, fourteen, B.M. Add. MSS. 36080; Massye, thirteen, B.M. MS. Hargrave 87.

Temple on Monday morning on 6 March 1503,[1] at eight or nine o'clock[2] or as soon after as was permitted by the preliminary ceremonies.[3] He probably read four days a week through the first four weeks of Lent, beginning always on a Monday and finishing the 'course' on either Thursday or Friday, March 30th or 31st.[4]

To answer (4), much MS. material needs to be studied carefully. Several Inner Temple collections of readings contemporary with Marowe[5] and including copies of the De Pace contain notes of the opinions of readers and serjeants that certainly imply a discussion of the reader's 'points'.[6] In at least one instance a clear account of the arguments between the reader and his disputants is recorded.[7] If a discussion of Marowe's 'cases' did take place—the kind of discussion that we know was usual later in the century[8]—then we have convincing proof that his readings occupied fifteen or sixteen days,

[1] See Judges' orders of 1627, for the 'first Monday in Lent'; Dugdale, *op. cit.*, 319.

[2] *Ibid.* 159; cf. Report of 1540: 'Then the first day after Vacation, at about eight of the clock, he that is so chosen read openly in the Hall.'

[3] Dugdale, *loc. cit.*

[4] Since Marowe's lectures vary from six to eleven pages, it is probable that he did not always complete a topic on a given day. It is possible that Lect. I was merely begun on Monday (time being lost by ceremonies) and was finished with Lect. II on the next day, and that the two short Lectures III and IV were delivered in one day. Note also the absence of a break between Lect. II and III in the F version; App. III, p. 301. If Marowe's younger hearers were like modern students, their attention would have been distracted from legal subtleties by the bonfires in the city in honour of the presence of an embassy from Maximilian the emperor; G. Temperly, Henry VII, 235.

[5] MS. Hargrave 87 (see *supra*, p. 155) f. 127 b, in an argument on a voucher to warranty in London: 'et nota que Marow lectour dit expressement que le tenaunt couient iurer son cause de lyen sur le foren voucher in loundr' all commencement & cest aiuge'.

[6] *Ibid.* f. 71 b, after 'Bricknell', 'Kebell seriant, le cas est bon & argumentable Mez semble que . . .'.

[7] B.M. MS. Harl. 1691, ff. 171–86 b, Hall's reading in Lent, 21 Edw. IV: 'Grantam accorde oue le Reder,' etc. (f. 172 b).

[8] Report of 1540: 'one of the younger Utter-barresters tries to prove that the reader's opinion is against the law, etc., and is answered by the reader.' Cf. MS. Harl. 5265, f. 136; Thomas Egerton (*temp.* Elizabeth) the first day of his reading puts a short case, the second day another short case, &c.; MS. Harl. 5103, f. 24: 'Les casez arguez en le lecture que Henley fait sur lestatut de anno 21 H. 8 . . .' Cf. also MS. Harl. 1631, f. 310. Is it possible that the phrase in De Pace, *passim*, 'Semble au lector' is a survival from such an argument?

and that they lasted at least two hours a day.[1] No shorter time would have been possible. Finally, for the solution of (5), the problem of Marowe's sources, there is abundant evidence. To this important subject the next section will be devoted.

(3) ACCOUNT OF SOURCES

An investigation of the sources of the De Pace ought to yield significant results. In the first place, it may help to solve certain problems connected with the later Year Books. A suggestive theory has recently been advanced that fifteenth-century Year Books may have been prepared under the supervision of the Readers, but it has been said that 'actual evidence of the Readers using the Year Books is wanting'.[2] Secondly, unless we know the legal material at Marowe's disposal, it is impossible to determine to what extent his treatise represented constructive pioneer work.

The first task is a mere enumeration of existing authorities. The bibliography of law books in print by the winter of 1502–1503 is not long.[3]

Canon Law.

Lyndwood.

Provinciale, *circ.* 1470–1480,[4] 1496,[5] 1499.[6]

Statutes.[7]

Le Vieux Abridgement, 1483 (?).

Abbreviamentum Statutorum, 9 October 1499.

Nova Statuta, 1484 (?), and between 1497–1504 or between July 1501 and December 1502.

1 Richard III, 1485 (?).

1, 7 Henry VII, n. d.

1, 3, & 4 Henry VII, [1489].

11 Henry VII, [1496].

---

[1] I tried the experiment of having some one read aloud one of Marowe's lectures, and I found that I could barely take sufficient notes in an hour.

[2] Year Book 4 Edw. II, ed. G. J. Turner, Selden Soc., 1911, xxv.

[3] The contemporary custom of printing undated editions makes the list only approximately accurate. There is great need of a thorough study of content by legal historians as a supplement to the work of the expert bibliographer.

[4] At Oxford; Gross, Sources.   [5] Wynkyn de Worde; Handlists.

[6] Wynkyn de Worde, and two editions by Pynson; Handlists.

[7] For printers' names, &c., see p. 44, and notes, *supra.*

Treatises and collections of precedents.

  Littleton's Tenures, 1482 (?), 1483–1486 (?), 1490 (?).[1]
  Natura Brevium (2 editions) ⎱
            ⎰ before 1500.[2]
  Novae Narrationes

Abridgements of Year Books.

  Statham; cases Edward II–39 Henry VI, 1490 (?).[3]
  The Abridgement of Assizes; cases Edward III–
    Henry VI. After 1501.[4]

Year Books printed before 1501.[5]

 Henry VI.

  9, 20, [Pynson, 1500].
  33, 35, 36, [Lettou and Machlinia], n. d.
  34, Machlinia, n. d.
  37, [Machlinia], n. d.

 Edward IV.

  1, 9, Pynson, [1492].
  2–8, [Pynson, 1496].
  11, [Pynson, 1500].

After 1501 the printing of Year Books, especially by Pynson, goes on rapidly, but in the present state of bibliographical lists it is impossible to tell what 'years' were actually through

---

[1] See p. 19, note 7, *supra*. Pynson also printed two undated editions after 1501; Handlists.

[2] Pynson; Handlists; see p. 20, *supra*. Pynson also printed without date but after 1501, Returna Brevium, Articuli ad Novas Narrationes, Carta Feodi (probably 1506), Court Baron, Hundred Court; Handlists. The last three were also printed by Wynkyn de Worde without date but after 1501; Handlists. Some of these may therefore have been in print by 1502–1503, but not the remaining four of Rastell's twelve tracts; see App. I, Series I, no. 13. The colophon of Pynson's 1510 edition of The Boke of Entries, 'noviter impressum correctum emendatum', certainly suggests an earlier edition, perhaps the one owned by Frowyk; p. 182, note 5, *infra*.   [3] See p. 19, *supra*, note 8.

[4] Pynson, without date; erroneously given as Liber Assisarum in Handlists. Mr. Turner assigns it to 1509 or 1510, *op. cit.*, xxxi; Mr. Soule in his 'Year Book Bibliography' (cited *infra*, note 5) to 1490–1501; Coke, with his characteristic ignorance of historical facts, declares that Statham's Abridgement was published in the reign of Henry VI, and the Abridgement of the Book of the Assizes at about the same time; preface to Tenth Report, 28.

[5] My authorities are Mr. Soule's pioneer article, 'Year Book Bibliography', Harvard Law Review, xiv, no. 8, and Mr. Duff's more recent work, Fifteenth Century English Books. Mr. Soule assigns to Pynson's press before 1500 an issue of 3 Henry VI, not included by Mr. Duff.

the press by the winter of 1502–1503, when Marowe was at work on the De Pace.[1] Certainly during his student days between 1480 and 1490 the number must have been almost negligible. An important consideration, however, is that the choice between a beautifully written manuscript on parchment, sometimes illuminated, and very difficult type such as Statham's or Pynson's 'Nova Statuta', is all in favour of manuscripts. What really matters, therefore, is the number and accessibility of legal works in manuscript in these early years of the sixteenth century.

Lyndwood's 'Provinciale' had been completed as early as 1430,[2] and doubtless was in circulation in MS. The MS. volumes of statutes, 'old' and 'new', and of abridgements of statutes have already been described.[3] In addition, there were MS. collections of the dooms and charters of Saxon and Danish kings that included many ecclesiastical laws[4] and that were not in print till half a century after Marowe's death.[5] There were also MS. copies of legal treatises not printed in Marowe's lifetime, such as Bracton, Britton, Fleta, Glanvil, Hengham Magna and Parva, the Mirror of Justice, the Old Tenures, &c.,[6] as well as of the earliest printed treatise, Littleton's new Tenures.[7] MS. precedent books existed in abundance; not only MS. forms of the two that were in print, Natura Brevium and Novae Narrationes,[8] but also of those that were still unprinted, Returna Brevium,[9] Articuli ad Novas

---

[1] The following are listed by Soule, *op. cit.*; 17, 18 Edw. III; 7, 8, 11, 12, 14 Hen. IV; 9 Hen. V; 1, 2, 3 Hen. VI (1510); 10, 20 Hen. VI; 5, 6, 9 Edw. IV; 10 Edw. IV and 49 Hen. VI; 11, 22 Edw. IV; 1 Edw. V and 1 Rich. III; 2 Rich. III; 1–8 Hen. VII. In Handlists, 21 Edw. III is assigned to Pynson.

[2] Gross, Sources.   [3] In ch. ii, *supra.*

[4] See Gross, *op. cit.*, 257–9, 270–1, for a bibliographical account of both MS. and printed versions.

[5] Lambard's Archaionomia of 1568 was the earliest edition.

[6] Holdsworth gives an excellent brief account of works on common law under the head of the 'material used by the legal profession'; *op. cit.*, ii. 431–63: cf. also 267–72, 284, 477–502. Of the five books that 'stand out pre-eminently in the history of English law, Glanvil, Bracton, Littleton, Coke, and Blackstone' (*ibid.* 484), three were available to Marowe.

[7] E. Wambaugh, ed. Littleton's Tenures, lix–lxi.

[8] Professor Beale adds the Old Tenures, Pynson, [1496].

[9] Not mentioned by Holdsworth. For the earliest copy thus far identified, see p. 76, *supra.*

Narrationes, the Court Baron, the Hundred Court, the Carta Feodi.[1] The many MS. collections of writs and indictments for justices of the peace [2] have already been described, including the compilation [3] most closely resembling the 'Boke' of 1506 (?). There were also almost numberless copies of the indispensable Registrum Brevium which had 'reached substantially its final form' by the reign of Henry VI.[4]

Of the difficult subject of MS. Year Books I hesitate to speak at all. But this much may be safely stated. The number of MSS. extant in Marowe's lifetime was very great,[5] and undoubtedly included the reports missing from the old printed editions.[6] Our knowledge of the MSS. for the later reigns is at present exceedingly meagre, especially for the reign of Henry VII.[7] It is, therefore, impossible to try to fill the gaps in the printed Year Books for his reign or to correct the hopelessly faulty chronology, unfortunate though the errors are for a precise understanding of Marowe's career.[8]

In addition to Year Books there are the abridgements. It is important to note that there were at least three MS. abridgements [9] produced in the fifteenth century as full as or even

---

[1] The last two are not discussed by Holdsworth. See pp. 24–5, *supra*.

[2] Ch. iii, *supra*.

[3] *Ibid*. pp. 104–5. It was probably, but not certainly, in existence by 1502–1503.

[4] Holdsworth, *op. cit.*, ii. 431–41, 526, App. V, The Growth of the Register of Original Writs. Perhaps the Boke of Entries had already been put into shape; see p. 182, note 5, *infra*.

[5] As appears from even the most superficial research.

[6] The most obvious are of course those of Richard II; cf. Bellewe's collection reprinted in 1907, and the recent edition of 12 Rich. II, ed. by G. F. Deiser for the Ames Foundation, Law School of Harvard University. See also *infra*, p. 187.

[7] 'Until we get a modern edition of the whole of the Year Books, it is impossible to say much of the MSS. of later years'; Holdsworth, *op. cit.*, ii. 447.

[8] See p. 135, note 3, *supra*, for a statement of the problem. It is greatly to be desired that the MS. Year Books for the reign should be carefully studied.

[9] (1) MS. *temp.* Hen. VI, according to article by G. R. Corner in Archaeologia, xxxix, 1863, 357–72. All that is now extant is the beautiful illuminated illustrations of the four courts at Westminster, judges, serjeants, &c., with a fragment of an alphabetical table of contents at the bottom of the court of Common Pleas. The topics, Accompts-Champartie, are very similar to, but not identical with, Statham's. The MS. was once owned by W. S. Lowndes, a descendant in female line from William Fleetwood of the Middle Temple (see p. 154, note 1, *supra*). It may be older

fuller than the volume attributed to Statham, a member of Lincoln's Inn, who died in 1472.[1] If Mr. Turner's ingenious theory proves sound, namely, that the printed Abridgement was compiled at Lincoln's Inn under the supervision of Statham as part of the official duties connected with his readership in 1471,[2] is it not possible that the three other Inns also compiled Abridgements and that it was a mere accident that sent Statham's to the printer?

Finally, to conclude this account of sources available for Marowe, there were manuscript 'readings',[3] especially those

than Statham's work and may have served him as a model; cf. Introduction, xx, to the recent translation of Statham by Mrs. M. C. Klingelsmith for statement that no model has been found.

(2) B.M. Add. MSS. 16168, 375 folios, latter part of fifteenth century according to printed Catalogue. The alphabetical table of contents is lacking, but the order of the topics is slightly more like no. 1 than like Statham's, but not identical with either. Folio 375 contains the names of ' Sir Wyllyam Huse ', of Gray's Inn, serjeant-at-law in 1478, chief justice of King's Bench, 1481–1495, and of ' Master Thomas Robertson ', crossed through, probably to be identified as the contemporary of Marowe and Frowyk at the Inner Temple; see p. 129, *supra*, note 8.

(3) B.M. Add. MSS. 35936, end of fifteenth century according to printed Catalogue. It is a fragment of eighty-three folios, but in Mr. Turner's judgement it once contained about 650 folios; *op. cit.*, xxxv. It has a few cases, *temp.* Hen. VII and Henry VIII, probably added to the original work.

MS. Kk. 5. 1, U.L.C., 458 folios, is described in the Catalogue as the MS. of Statham, but its index and contents are not identical with the printed edition.

MSS. Ll. 2. 11 and Ll. 3. 1 (with Statham's name on the outer edges of the top), U.L.C., probably both date from the early sixteenth century and are therefore too late for this discussion.

[1] His will was dated 15 July 1472 and was proved on 5 August; 7 Wattys, P.C.C. A portion of it is quoted by Mr. Turner (p. 182, note 1, *infra*), but the whole is delightful reading, especially the reference to his wife, ' the most parfit gentlewoman I have ever known '.

[2] *Op. cit.*, xxxi–xxxvi, especially xxxiv. Mr. Turner quotes as evidence a phrase in the will (proved in 1488) of Sir William Callowe of the Middle Temple and justice of Common Pleas : ' a book of Assises in papir a Dratton (Bracton?) a booke of newe Statutes and ii bookes of Briggementes oon of myne owen labour and the other of Lincolnesin'. It must be remembered, however, that ' Briggementes ' were made not only of reported cases but also of statutes ; see ch. ii, *supra, passim*, and especially p. 50, note 3. There is, therefore, no positive assurance that Justice Callowe meant one type of legal abridgement rather than another.

[3] No reading was printed till 1628, the date of the publication of Francis Ashley's on Magna Carta delivered in 1616; see also Smith's Law Journal, p. 180, note 3, *infra*. In general the few readings that have found their way into print come from just before the middle or latter part of the sixteenth or from the early seventeenth century ; Brooke, Bacon,

of his own Inn.[1]   Since Dugdale's lists for the Inner Temple begin only with Lent 1507,[2] it has seemed worth while to present the following tentative list of readers who read before Lent 1503 or immediately afterward, and to indicate their subjects as far as possible.[3]

Thomas Littleton.   Lent (?) 26 Henry VI, 1448 (?).[4]

Westminster II, c. 1, De Donis Conditionalibus.[5]

In casu quo vir amiserit etc.

Richard Hall.   Lent 21 Edward IV, 1481.

Gloucester, c. 1.[6]

Morgan Kidwelly.   Lent 22 Edward IV, 1482.[7]

Magna Carta, c. 11.

Communia placita non sequantur curiam nostram etc., followed by a list in Latin of the various courts of the realm. It seems probable that the account of the 'Diversity of Courts', including the sessions of the peace, belongs under these headings.[8]

Callis, Calthorpe, &c.   The only exception is the fragment of Frowyk on the Prerogative included in the obscure Law Journal just mentioned. For a useful bibliography of printed readings, see Worrall, Bibliotheca Legum (1731, 1763), ed. E. Brooke, 1782.   What is greatly needed is a bibliography of MS. readings, especially those of the earlier period.

[1] Obviously far more certainly accessible to him than those of other Inns.

[2] In Masters of the Bench ... of the Inner Temple, 1450–1883 (1883), Judge Littleton's is the only name for the period before 1500.

[3] The list makes no claim to completeness, but is merely the bye-product of a search directed primarily to discovering versions of the De Pace.

[4] Certainly before 2 July 1453 when he was made serjeant-at-law, and probably before his 'call' in the preceding February; ch. iii (1), p. 79, note 3, *supra*.   Further, since his recordership was supposed to keep him in Coventry, he ought to have completed his reading by 1449; see *ibid.*, p. 78, note 4.

[5] Not in B.M. MS. Harl. 1691, f. 188, in spite of D.N.B. and of Professor Wambaugh, *op. cit.*, xxix, note 1.   The Harleian reading is by Littleton's son Richard; see *infra*.   Among many readings on De Donis (e.g. B.M. MS. Hargrave 87, ff. 189–94, by 'Malett') I have failed to identify Littleton's.   Cf. Coke on Littleton, sect. 481, 'Jeo aye oye sovent la Lecture de lestatute de Westminster second'; Rayner also is confused as between father and son; Readings on Statutes, preface, 2.

[6] MS. Harl. 1691, ff. 171–86 b; cf. p. 167, *supra*, and note 3.

[7] U.L.C., Ee. 5. 18, f. 26.   'M. K.' almost certainly stands for Morgan Kidwelly; see *supra*, p. 152, especially note 4.   He was appointed attorney general in 1484 and 1485 and died in 1505; Dugdale, Chron. Ser., 73, Cal. Inner Temple Records, i. 1, 2; Testament, 30 Holgrave, P.C.C.

[8] ff. 26–40; cf. f. 53: 'Hic incipit le diuersite enter Court baron,

Thomas Frowyk. Autumn (?) 3 Richard III and 1 Henry VII, 1485 (?).[1]

Westminster II, cc. 1–50.[2]

Thomas Keble. Lent (?) 1 Henry VII, 1486 (?).[3]

Westminster I, c. 1.

Primes le roy voet & commaunde que le peas del terre & seint esglise soit bien garde etc.

Richard Littleton. Lent 8 Henry VII, 1493.[4]

Westminster II, c. 12. Appeals.

Quia multi per maliciam etc.[5]

c. 13.

Quia eciam vicecomes multociens etc.

hundred, Tourne del Viscount, leete, Countie et Cessionz, et le diuersitie del powere et le auctorite de chescun deux etc.' It is tempting to believe that Kidwelly's reading was the basis for the printed tract ; see p. 35, note 3, *supra.*

[1] If the chronology on p. 129, *supra,* and notes 6, 7, is correct, his 'single' reading must have been between his call to the bar in 1483 or 1484 and his appointment as common pleader of London in July 1486. In later times the 'autumn' reading began on Monday after Lammas (August first); Dugdale, Orig. Jurid., 194, 319. Was Frowyk perhaps lecturing on Monday, 22 August, while the battle of Bosworth Field was being fought?

[2] U.L.C., Dd. 3. 41 ; see p. 150, p. 168, and note 7, *supra* ; Lincoln's Inn, Maynard MSS., no. lxx ; perhaps B.M. MS. Lansdowne 1138, ff. 52–104.

[3] MS. Hargrave 87, ff. 302–8, 'Keybell lectour, Westminster primer capitulo primo', fragment only ; for full version, see Inner Temple MS. described *supra,* pp. 154–5, and note 2. The various Kebles are difficult to disentangle, but the contents of both these volumes (*ut supra*) lead us to identify 'Keybell' with the Thomas Keble of the Inner Temple who died in June 1500 (Will, 3 Moone, P.C.C.; Cal. Inq. p. m., Hen. VII, ii, no. 497), and who had been appointed serjeant-at-law in November 1485 (Rot. Claus., 1 Hen. VII, m. 34), the actual creation to take place in July following (1486). Cf. Dugdale, Chron. Ser., 75. The latter by an error includes him also in the list of 1495. But there was a Walter Keble, serjeant-at-law in November 1482, 21 Edw. IV, Dugdale, *op. cit.,* 73, and a Thomas Keble admitted to Lincoln's Inn in June 1503 ; Black Books, i. 130. It becomes possible to understand why the Year Books of Edward IV–Henry VII are literally full of the opinions of 'Keble'.

[4] The date suggested by the scribe of the Inner Temple MS. ; *infra,* note 5. Since Littleton must have been called to the bar some three or four years before his first recorded appearance in the courts at Westminster in 1486 (Year Book, Trin. 1 Hen. VII, no. 3), and since he probably gave his double reading within ten or twelve years after his call, the date is a plausible one. On 2 November 1505 he was elected one of the Governors of his own Inn, in place of Morgan Kidwelly, lately dead ; Cal. Inner Temple Records, i. 1.

[5] MS. Harl. 1691, ff. 188–93 b, fragment only, on ch. xii (p. 178, note 5, *supra*) ; U.L.C., MS. Hh. 3. 6, on ch. xii, and a few folios on ch. xiii (see

Humphrey (?) *Coningsby.*   Lent (?) 10 Henry VII, 1495 (?).[1]
Merton, c. 1.
De viduis que post mortem virorum etc.
Thomas Frowyk.   Autumn 10 & 11 Henry VII, 1495.[2]
Prerogative of the King.[3]
(?) *Green.*   After autumn 1495 and before autumn 1500.[4]
Thomas Pygott.   Autumn 16 [& 17] Henry VII, 1501.[5]
Statute De Quo Warranto.

---

p. 148, and note 4, *supra*); Inner Temple MS., on chs. xii, xiii, and xiv (see p. 155, notes 2 and 3).

For the identification of the Littleton who read on Appeals as the judge's son Richard, to whom the Tenures was dedicated, see Wambaugh, *op. cit.*, xxi, xlix, note; Worrall, *op. cit.*, 1782 ed., 20, and preface to Coke on Littleton. Brooke probably refers to this reading under *Appell*, 62, 125, and *Coroners*, 82.

[1] MS. Hargrave 87, ff. 399-426 ; Humphrey was made serjeant-at-law in November 1495 along with Frowyk; Dugdale, Chron. Ser., 75. The preceding Lent would be therefore a normal time for his 'II^d Redyng'. For their joint services to the king and to the Countess of Richmond, see p. 128, note 6, p. 134, note 5. Unfortunately no initials are given at the first heading, and it is possible that the reading is by Humphrey's son William (see f. 417 for 'W'); the latter read at the Inner Temple in Lent 17 Hen. VIII ; Dugdale, Orig. Jurid., 163.

[2] For his career, see pp. 129-32, *supra*.

[3] One copy in his own Inn in the collection described *supra*, pp. 154-5. Six copies in U.L.C., of which only two are indexed in the Catalogue under his name ; Ee. 3. 46 (*supra*, pp. 150-1); Ee. 5. 22 (probably); Hh. 2. 1, ff. 1-26 ; Mm. 6. 58, 2 copies, ff. 1-8 (incomplete), ff. 9-28 ; Hh. 3. 6, fragment only (*supra*, p. 148). One copy exists in B.M. ; Hargrave 87, ff. 142-76, of which chs. ix and x are printed in Smith's Law Journal, 1804-1807, 238-50. The editors say that it is not extant in Harl. 1691 as stated by Worrall, *op. cit.*, 1788 ed. (ii. 192), but 'only a few loose items from another reading on the prerogative'. The copy in H.L.S., MS. no. 14 (*supra*, p. 154), is not identical with Hargrave's copy. Are there not perhaps two versions as in the case of the De Pace ? Reeves, Hist. Eng. Law, iii. 134, mentions a reading on Villenage by Frowyk, undoubtedly an error. But cf. B.M. MS. Hargrave 318, Law Rules and Maxims, f. 31 ; a statement of the king's prerogative in regard to villeins is followed by a reference to 'Frowick, lectur, fo. 111'.

[4] MS. Hargrave 87, f. 129: 'Grene lector et Frowyk et Kebull presentes, sergeauntez'. My guess as to dates is correct only if 'Kebull' be the serjeant-at-law who died in June 1500; see p. 179, *supra*, note 3.

[5] 'Pygotte lectour . . .'; MS. Hargrave 87, ff. 130-2. Thomas Pygott (died in 1520; testament 26 Ayloffe, P.C.C.) was made serjeant-at-law in 1505 (or 1511) and king's serjeant in 1514; Dugdale, Chron. Ser., 77, 79. B.M. MS. Lansdowne 1138 contains many scrappy notes such as: 'Statutum de mercatoribus secundum Pygot', ff. 111-12 b. Since there was a Richard 'Piggot', serjeant-at-law in 3 Edw. IV, Dugdale, *op. cit.*, 69, there is possibility of confusion.

(?) *Grevell.* Lent 17 Henry VII, 1502.[1]

Gloucester, c. 1.

Thomas Marowe. Lent 18 Henry VII, 1503.

Westminster I, c. 1.

En primez voet le Roy & commaunde que le peas de seint esglis & de la terre soit bien garde etc.

William Rudhale. Lent 19 Henry VII, 1504.[2]

Westminster II, c. 24.

In casibus in quibus etc.

John Fulwode. Autumn 21 & 22 Henry VII, 1506.[3]

To the list of those who almost certainly read before Lent 1503[4] must be added the names of Richard Sutton,[5] Robert Sheffield,[6] Robert Brudnell,[7] later a justice of the King's Bench, and finally chief justice of the Common Pleas,[8] and Gregory Adgore;[9] the two last were made serjeants-at-law along with Marowe.[10] Further, since all who read 'double' must have read 'single', it appears that about a third of the schedule at the Inner Temple for over twenty years has been filled up.[11]

But it is not enough to know that the authorities described

---

[1] MS. Hargrave 87, f. 133; 'Secunda lectura ...'; cf. f. 67 b. He is apparently putting a case; Keble, 'Ruddhall', 'Bric.' (Brudnell) and Frowyk are arguing; f. 69 b, 'per Grevell reder'. He is not Marowe's fellow serjeant, if, as seems probable, the latter was of Gray's Inn.

[2] MS. Hargrave 87, ff. 134–40 b. The heading shows that it is his double reading (p. 168, note 7, *supra*). He was a governor of his Inn by 1505; Cal. Inner Temple Records, i. 1.

[3] According to my interpretation of the entry in Cal. Inner Temple Records, i. 4. Dugdale gives as the earliest on his lists John Skilling, Lent, 22 Hen. VII; *op. cit.*, 163. It is tempting to assign Lawrence Wadham to the period between Rudhale and Fulwode; see p. 156, note 6, *supra*.

[4] Since they do not appear in Dugdale's list, beginning in Lent 1507, they must have read previously.

[5] Hargrave 87, f. 12; U.L.C., Hh. 3. 6, f. 33, *supra*, p. 149, and note 6. He was chief governor of his Inn by 1519; Cal. Inner Temple Records, i. 44; Dugdale, Orig. Jurid., 172.

[6] Hargrave 87, f. 114 b, 'Sheff' dit in lecture'; Dugdale, *loc. cit.*

[7] Hargrave 87, f. 57 b; U.L.C., Hh. 3. 6, f. 32 b; *supra*, p. 149, and note 5; Cal. Inner Temple Records, i. 4.

[8] 1507, 1521, Foss, Judges. The latter does not know his Inn.

[9] Harl. 1691, f. 25 b; he argues with Marowe.

[10] p. 135, *supra*, note 1.

[11] That is, from Lent 1481 to Lent 1503.

were extant in Marowe's day. We want also to know whether they were easily accessible to him. Almost no evidence has been found to show that, like so many fifteenth-century lawyers, Statham,[1] Callowe,[2] Keble,[3] Carell,[4] and Frowyk,[5] Marowe himself was a possessor of legal works.[6] One would like to believe that his own books and MSS. became the foundation of the library known to belong to his grand-nephew, Thomas 'Marow' of the Middle Temple;[7] but the only volume

[1] 'I will that William my clerk haue my lytill olde Statutes couered with ledir, and my natura breuium, and if he go to court to thentente to continue there I wil that he haue my best Registre and my boke of Newe Statutez'; will, quoted by G. J. Turner, *op. cit.*, xxxiii; see p. 177, note 1, *supra*.

[2] See *ibid.*, note 2.

[3] 'I bequeth to my said sonne all my books in scripture, of lawe, of Cronicle or stories and all other my books in Latyn, frensch or Englissh'; will, cited p. 179, note 3, *supra*; cf. 'Inventory of Goods' in Gentleman's Magazine, v. 38, 1768, 257-60.

[4] Marowe's associate on the Assizes; see p. 136, note 3, *supra*. Cf. MS. Harl. 1691, f. 66: 'De anno 4 Henry VII ex libro Magistri Carell'; f. 98: 'Hec habui ex libro Magistri Johannis Caryll'. The reference is possibly to authorship rather than to ownership.

[5] Several MSS. have been identified as having belonged to Frowyk; B.M. Add. MSS. 37659, Year Books Edw. III, Rich. II, Hen. V. Later it was owned in turn by Thomas Jakys, or Jakes, who had married Frowyk's widow, and by four eminent lawyers including Fleetwood (Turner, *op. cit.*, li). At the end of 40 Edw. III, f. 163, is written 'Marow' crossed through. Also Add. MSS. 37657, Year Books, and Veteres Narraciones. It had had two previous owners, and it became later the property of Jakes; cf. f. 2. The latter evidently had a law library; cf. e.g. B.M. MS. Hargrave 210, Year Books, described by Turner, *op. cit.*, li, and note that in his will he begs his wife to give to the Inner Temple his 'fayer boke of the newe Statutes' and his 'greate boke' of entries which were 'my singular good lord Frowyckes', and that he bequeaths a 'boke of lawe' apiece to four friends, including Thomas Roberts, one of Frowyk's executors and an associate of Marowe's; Turner, *op. cit.*, lii, p. 129, note 8, *supra*. It is possible that Jakes's collection had all come to him from Frowyk through his marriage with Lady Frowyk and his position as executor; see *supra*, p. 137, note 6. Was Thomas Roberts's 'boke of lawe' the very beautiful copy of the Registrum Brevium contained in B.M. MS. Harl. 1859 with the following entry on f. 2, 'Thome Robertz pertinet'?

[6] Cf. will of the mayor's eldest son: 'To my brother Thomas a boke that was my fader's'; pp. 126, 144, *supra*. There is no clue as to the identity of the book. Marowe's wealth would certainly have permitted him to accumulate a library.

[7] See ch. v, *supra*, pp. 126-7, and his will of September 1561, 37 Loftes, P.C.C.: 'To my son Samuel my bookes at Hoxton; to my son Thomas my bookes or liberaries at Barkeswell and at Elmedon'. MS. Hh. 2. 12, U.L.C., a collection of Year Books of Edw. III, Hen. IV, V, and VI, contains in several places scribbled across the folios the names

that has been traced containing an owner's signature of 'T. Marowe' proves, curiously enough, to be a MS. on the crusades.[1] It seems reasonable, however, to suppose that the library of Marowe's own Inn included a large portion of the existing legal works,[2] and that he worked on the De Pace in his chamber in the Inner Temple.[3] We know that students at another Inn were bidden 'to leve knockynge on the pottes and makyng of noyse in the Hall, and nott to inquyett Mr Reder in the vacacion of his study'.[4] Undoubtedly also Marowe would have had access to the collection of his friend Frowyk if he needed to supplement the Inner Temple library. Of readings delivered at other Inns he would, perhaps, have known little. But his close association with Edmund Dudley[5] may have made him familiar with the contents of Dudley's two readings at Gray's Inn, on Westminster II, c. 25,[6] and on Quo Warranto.[7]

of Robert Stele, Thomas Denton (one of the writers of the famous report of 1540), and Thomas Marrow : also 'explicit per Thomam Marrowe' at the end of Mich. 21 Edw. III ; f. 148 b. Of course it is possible that this MS. had once been in the possession of the serjeant-at-law.

[1] Formerly owned by the late A. C. Ranyard, Esq. (d. 1894), of Lincoln's Inn, the Inner Temple, and the Royal Astronomical Society; Hist. MSS. Comm. Reports, v, App. 404. In spite of the courteous assistance of Mr. Ranyard's cousins, of the assistant secretary of the Astronomical Society, and of the Earl of Crawford, my attempts to discover the MS. have failed. It is greatly to be regretted, since it would be interesting to compare the autograph with 'Thomas Marow', the signature of the younger Thomas, written soon after 16 May 6 Edw. VI, and preserved in P.R.O., Miscellaneous Books of the Exchequer, Augmentation Office, 513, Inventories of church goods, Warwick, f. 19. It is printed in Warwickshire Ant. Magazine, pt. i, 154.

[2] In Cal. Inner Temple Records, i. xxvii–xxviii, it is stated that the Inner Temple had a library earlier than did any other Inn ; cf. ibid. 6. There is a reference to a library in Lincoln's Inn in 1475 ; Black Books, i. 59 ; cf. ibid. 168. The key of the library is stated to be in the possession of the reader ; ibid. 257.

[3] His home in St. Michael's, Queenheath, was not very far from the Temple ; p. 140, and notes 1, 2.

[4] Black Books Lincoln's Inn, i. 210.   [5] pp. 132–3, supra.

[6] Delivered in Lent 11 Hen. VII, 1496 ; U.L.C., MS. Hh. 3. 10, ff. 59–96. The collection in which it is included was made by William Colyns in a script and style like those of Atwell's Gray's Inn volume ; see pp. 151–3, supra. It was once owned by Fleetwood.

[7] Hh. 3. 10, ff. 1–18. Certainly delivered before November 1503, but perhaps not before the De Pace ; cf. U.L.C., MS. Ee. 5. 18, f. 68 for Atwell's reference : 'Vide en report Dudley de quo warranto'. Material exists for a schedule of early readers at Gray's Inn ; cf. H L.S., Dunn 106, for a

That this great array of law books was easily accessible to Marowe for his perusal does not, however, tell the whole story of the sources of the De Pace. It is also of significance to find that he was arguing in moots[1] with Adgore, Fulwode, Coningsby, &c., often against Frowyk, during the decade 1485–1495,[2] and that some of the cases bore indirectly at least on subjects later to be included in his treatise: the effect on the status of a villein who had been made an abbot,[3] the circumstances under which a petition to the king is permitted to him who is disseised,[4] a question as to the making of a recognizance.[5] Of still greater significance is the fact that Marowe must have had an opportunity of hearing Kidwelly lecture on the sessions of the peace,[6] Richard Littleton outline the criminal law,[7] and Keble expound the statute of Westminster I, c. 1, as the basis for a discourse on the peace.[8] In fact, the degree to which Keble anticipates Marowe is startling. He begins with a brief discussion of the peace of the church, shows the difference between statute and common law, and describes the remedies afforded by the writ *De vi laica removenda*. He then takes as his main subject the question as to who were responsible for enforcing the statutes on the peace, and gives a long list of officials, without special emphasis on conservators or justices. One is forced to believe that Marowe was

reading by Thomas Fitzwilliam in Lent 1465, on the statute of Merton, the earliest extant reading that I have identified. See also p. 33, *supra*, note 2.

[1] 'Argumentes de casez en temps. Ed. 4 et H. 7 in Interiori Templo et en temps H. 8 par Keble, Frowyke, Kedwelley, Welles, Baker, Fullwood, Brudnell, Shelley, Bawldwyn, Vauissor, Pygot, Lyttylton et plusors autres'; B.M. MS. Harl. 1691, ff. 16–55 b. The volume also contains material *temp.* Hen. VIII and Edw. VI, some of it certainly reader's cases; see e. g. ff. 57, 134, 165.

[2] Frowyk is speaking with authority, but is apparently not yet a serjeant-at-law; ff. 16–55 b, *passim*.

[3] ff. 25 b–6   [4] f. 28.

[5] ff. 31–2 b. Sheffeld speaks of 'mon magister Frowyk', and quotes specific book cases, '13 E. 4 and 4 H. 7, fo. 1' (f. 22), despite Coke's statement to the effect that at the bar in ancient times and in moots (in the past and in the Inner Temple of his time) they never 'cited any booke case or authoritie in particular, as is holden in 40 Ed. 3, etc.'; preface to the Tenth Report, cited by J. G. Turner, *op. cit.*, xiv.

[6] That is, if my conclusion is sound; p. 178, notes 7 and 8, *supra*.

[7] *Supra*, pp. 179–80.   [8] *Supra*, p. 179.

thoroughly familiar with Keble's sections on surety of peace, riot, rout and assembly, escapes, and gaoler by inheritance.[1]

Did Marowe perhaps act as one of Keble's two assistants at this reading on the peace,[2] or did he perhaps receive his legal training under the guidance of Keble, with access to the latter's collection of law books?[3] The question cannot in our present state of knowledge be answered.

But it was not only at Marowe's Inn of Court that the subject of the king's peace was deemed important. Marowe must have known of the notable assembly of all the judges at Blackfriars at the very beginning of the new reign that was to be marked throughout by so vigorous an administration of the law. Here the discussion had turned on the best methods of actual enforcement of the statutes of Winchester, Westminster, &c., copies of which had been compiled in the reign of Edward IV and sent to all justices of the peace.[4] Of the two recorded instances[5] before Lent 1503 in which Marowe himself appears in the court of King's Bench, one is in connexion with a long and important case on the power of a justice of the peace to arrest rioters by an oral order to his servants.[6] The Year Books of Henry VII contain many other 'leading'

---

[1] Although the full version was discovered too late for a thorough study, it is clear that Keble has produced a reading altogether different from other early readings on this statute, which ordinarily treat almost exclusively of abuses in houses of religion. Even though he does not, I think, anticipate Marowe completely, it is of great significance that a trained lawyer composed a legal treatise on the peace nearly twenty years earlier than the De Pace.

[2] See p. 162, *supra*. According to my chronology (p. 129, *supra*), Marowe ought to have delivered his 'single' reading shortly after 1486.

[3] Holdsworth, *op. cit.*, ii. 427 : 'We may conjecture that the students had some opportunities for "private reading", perhaps in the chambers of the elder lawyers'; cf. also Cal. Inner Temple Records, i. xxxvi.

[4] Year Books Mich. 1 Hen. VII, no. 3; Rot. Parl. vi. 8; 12 & 13 Edw. IV, 1472 and 1473. Perhaps Keble derived the subject of his reading from this discussion.

[5] Of course, further study of MS. Year Books may show more instances.

[6] Mich. 14 Hen. VII, 1498 (perhaps 13th year, 1497), no. 19. Is the justice of the peace for whom Marowe is arguing the Sir Thomas Green whose daughter Marowe was to have married as his second wife? See p. 142, and note 6. Marowe's other appearance was in Trin. 12 Hen. VII, 1497 (perhaps 11th year, 1496), no. 1; the case involved breach of the peace and also the prerogative of the king.

cases on justices of the peace,[1] and also numerous other cases
concerned with criminal law and involving, therefore, legal
issues discussed in the De Pace.[2]   That Marowe heard many
of the arguments seems certain.   It would be interesting to
know whether he also heard chief justice Fineux give his
historical disquisition on the early history of the conservators
of the peace,[3] or Brian quote a learned doctor of arts to the
effect that priests and clerks can be impleaded at common
law, 'quod Rex est persona mixta, car est persona unita cum
sacerdotibus Saint Esglise'.[4]

In turning next to the A text of the De Pace it appears that
of the authorities just described Marowe cites specifically only
two types, namely, statutes and Year Books.   The former
include (1) the laws of Canute[5] and Edward the Confessor,[6]
of which several MS. versions still exist; (2) a few of the
familiar 'old' statutes, Westminster I, Winchester, De Prisonam frangentibus, to be found in many MS. collections;[7] (3) a
great many 'new' statutes, including those from Edward III
through the 23 Henry VI, one of Richard III and the 11 &
12 Henry VII.[8]   The quotations are usually accurate and full
and are evidently taken from a complete text, not from an
Abridgement.   Since the statutes of Henry VII are cited only

---

[1] They can be easily identified through Fleetwood's Annales (*supra*,
p. 113, note 1), under title *Peax*, and through the index to Year Book
Edw. V–Hen. VII under *Paix*, and also through the references in
Crompton and Lambard; *infra*, pp. 188–9).   A few are cited here as
examples: Mich. 2 Hen. VII, no. 2, recognizances and the Custos Rotulorum; Pasch. 11 Hen. VII, no. 11, distinction between criminal jurisdiction of a Court Leet and of justices of the peace; Trin. 12 Hen. VII,
no. 3, precise title necessary for justices of the peace in heading of criminal
indictments taken before them.

[2] The index of the printed edition is an excellent guide.

[3] Pasch. 12 Hen. VII, no. 1.

[4] Hill. 10 Hen. VII, no. 17; see preface to Fleetwood, cited *infra*,
p. 212.

[5] App. III, p. 289, notes 6, 7, 8; cf. Charter of Canute, *circ.* 1020 in Stubbs,
Select Charters, 8th ed., 75: 'Now I beseech my archbishops and all my
suffragan bishops that they all be attentive about God's right, every one
in his district which is committed to him'; Liebermann, Gesetze der Angelsachsen, i. 273–4.

[6] *Ibid.*, i. 628; 'De clericis et possessionibus eorum.   Omnis clerus et
scolares et omnes eorum possessiones, ubicumque fuerint, pacem Dei et
sancte ecclesie habeant'; cf. also, 273, 274, 631, 637–8.

[7] See ch. ii, *supra*.   [8] *Ibid.*

toward the end, with the rather strange omission of the 3 Henry VII on surety of peace, it is perhaps to be inferred that Marowe was relying mainly on one of the MS. collections that ended with this year,[1] and that just before Lent 1503 he saw Pynson's new edition that had been brought up to date.[2]

The seven citations of Year Book cases are so important that they are given here: xxvii Liber Assisarum,[3] xl E. II (a slip in A for xv E. II),[4] Mich. xxxix E. III,[5] ix H. IIII,[6] vi R. II,[7] anno primo E. III,[8] ii E. III.[9] Five of the seven cases have been identified in the printed Year Books, and few though they are they afford 'actual evidence' hitherto wanting, that a reader, very close to the fifteenth century, was using MS. Year Books; also that he was quoting 'book cases' in particular, contrary to Coke's description of 'general' citing for this period.[10] Further, Marowe was citing Year Books of Edward II, said to be uncommon before the days of Fitzherbert,[11] and was making use of reports not found in Statham.[12]

The remaining task is more difficult; namely, to try to ascertain the Year Book cases and other authorities used by Marowe without specific citations. With one exception, none of the extant versions of the De Pace contain any references beyond those in A. The exception is MS. D, which includes a number of marginal citations of Year Books as well as references to Fitzherbert's Abridgement.[13] For example, opposite Marowe's statement that 'Broker' and 'Chopchurch' are good 'additions' is a reference to 'H. 9 Henry VI'. The case appears as no. 19 in Hilary term, and is evidently the authority for Marowe's opinion.[14] Fortunately, Atwell, the scribe of D,

---

[1] p. 50, *supra*, and note 8.   [2] *Supra*, p. 44.   [3] App. III, p. 332.
[4] Correctly given in B and F; App. III, p. 379, note 4.
[5] *Ibid.*, p. 385.   [6] *Ibid.*, note 8.   [7] *Ibid.*, p. 393.
[8] *Ibid.*, p. 394.   [9] *Ibid.*   [10] *Supra*, p. 184, note 5.
[11] J. G. Turner, *op. cit.*, xxxvi: 'Statham gave comparatively few reports from this reign'. It is interesting to find that the case cited by Marowe is an important one; see Fitzherbert, *Corone*, no. 383; Brooke, *Corone*, 214; Stephen, Hist. Crim. Law, ii. 222; Holdsworth, *op. cit.*, iii. 297.
[12] The reports of Edward II and Richard II; cf. also pp. 207-9, *infra*.
[13] See p. 152, note 9, *supra*. From the form in which the entries are made, it seems clear that they are the work of Atwell and necessarily after 1516.
[14] App. III, p. 386, note 1; the case is thus cited by Fitzherbert in

is not our only guide. As will appear later,[1] Lambard in 1579–1581 and Crompton in 1583, in their respective treatises on the peace, quote voluminously from the De Pace. They differ in their method of quotation. Lambard usually writes merely: 'for Marow saith' or some such phrase, and Crompton is more precise, 'Marrow Lect. 12', &c., but they agree in the frequency with which they add references to earlier authorities. The following examples will prove the significance of these references :

Lambard.

> Surety of peace: 21 E. 4. 40 & Mar[row].[2]
> Determination of the old commission: Mar[row] & 21 H. 6. 29 & 34 lib. Ass. Pl. 28.[3]
> Charters of exemption for jurors: by some other bookes, and namely 42. Ass. pl. 5 and Mar[row].[4]

Crompton.

> Forcible entry: per Marrow Lect. 9.
> Vide 7 H. 6. 14.[5]
> Reasonable chastisement of wife: Marr[ow] Lect. 6. Reg. 89.[6]
> Chastisement of villein: per Marr[ow] L. 6 . . . Litt. 39.[7]

Under trespasses and felonies Crompton very often does not mention Marowe, but gives references to Year Books or to other authorities for his illustrative cases, even when he has taken them from 'Master Staunforde's' 'Plees del Corone'.[8] Many of these cases are easily identified as the basis for the discussion in the De Pace, written half a century before Staunford's work. A few instances are given, with cross-references to Marowe added :

Crompton.

> Stealing goods by wife at command of husband: Bracton, and 27 Lib. Ass. 40.[9]
> Marowe, Lect. XII on Felonies.

Abridgement, *Addicion* 4, but in Statham, *Addicion* 5, it is given as Trin. 27 Hen. VI, either by a slip or else from a report that is not in print ; see ed. Klingelsmith, i. 33.

[1] pp. 214 *ut seq., infra.*   [2] Eirenarcha, 74.
[3] *Ibid.* 65.   The second reference should be Pl. 8.
[4] *Ibid.* 381.   [5] Loffice, f. 58 b.   [6] *Ibid.* f. 118 b.
[7] *Loc. cit.*   [8] p. 215, *infra.*   [9] Loffice, f. 34.

Right of Schoolmaster to chastise scholars : Bracton, cap. 4.[1]

Marowe, Lect. VII on breach of peace.

Forestalling :

43 Lib. ass. 38 ; 27 Lib. ass. 44.[2]

Marowe, Lect. XI on Trespasses.[3]

Taking of vessels, plate, &c., by cook, butler, and 'horse-keeper': 21 H. 7. 15 ; 13 E. 4, 10 & Stamf. 25 . . .[4]

Marowe, Lect. XII on Felonies.[5]

Similar illustrations could be multiplied indefinitely. In fact, Lambard and Crompton together furnish keys to the sources of a large portion of the De Pace. Further, a comparison of the printed Year Books earlier than Henry VII[6] with the De Pace show a number of reports, not cited by Lambard or Crompton, that furnish the basis for Marowe's statements both on questions directly concerning justices of the peace[7] and also on his innumerable 'points' of common law.[8] The most obvious is the historical account of the powers of the justices of the peace delivered in court in the reign of Edward IV.[9] A complete annotation of the De Pace, with references to 'book cases', would prove that Marowe's knowledge of the Year Books was extensive and that he was using it to great advantage.[10] An instance has already been given where Marowe cited reports not found in Statham.[11] It must also

---

[1] Loffice, f. 26. [2] *Ibid.*, ff. 69 b–70.

[3] App. III, p. 369, note 6. Statham, *Corone*, 58, is evidently citing this case, but by an error attributes it to 44 Edw. III.

[4] Loffice, ff. 32–32 b.

[5] The report of Edward IV includes ' cook and butler '. Marowe himself had argued in a case of bailment, assigned to Hill. 21 Hen. VII, no. 23 in the printed edition, an impossible date for him, but certainly belonging to a date after the delivery of his reading. It is also significant that Richard Littleton had used this case in his reading on Appeals, U.L.C. Hh. 3. 6, f. 1 b ; see *supra*, p. 179, and notes 4, 5.

[6] For those of Henry VII, see *supra*, pp. 185–6.

[7] See index to Year Book Edw. IV under *Peax*.

[8] See ch. vi (4), *infra*, for other examples.

[9] Pasch. 22 Edw. IV, no. 33 (cited p. 192, *infra*). Marowe may have heard this case in his early student days.

[10] A large proportion of his ' points ' on criminal law come from Liber Assisarum ; the greater number of cases dealing specifically with justices of the peace are of course found in the later Year Books, especially those of Edward IV and Henry VII. [11] *Supra*, p. 187.

be noted that he gave fuller treatment to certain topics, *Addicion*, for example, that he included new topics,[1] and finally that he failed to follow Statham in an important matter of criminal jurisdiction.[2]   Unless, therefore, Marowe had access to a MS. Abridgement not now known,[3] he was undoubtedly relying largely on the Year Books themselves,[4] perhaps with Statham or a similar work as a guide.

But statutes and Year Books, though the main sources of the De Pace, are not its only sources.   It is not possible to determine to what extent Marowe actually used the early readings, Littleton's, Keble's,[5] &c., but the evidence points to his use of the Register, certainly for ecclesiastical writs,[6] and probably of Bracton ;[7] clearly also his lecture on Forcible Entry shows the influence of the ' most perfect and absolute work that ever was written in any human science '.[8]   Certainly no member of the Inner Temple in Marowe's lifetime would venture to discuss the intricacies of seisin and disseisin without the aid of Littleton's Tenures.

In concluding this account of sources, it would be of great interest to ascertain whether Marowe had on the margins of his own MS. copy full references to ' book cases ', and whether he cited them to his audience, or whether he mentioned only the seven reports incorporated in the text.   It is difficult to believe that so scholarly a reader, whose ' honour ' it was ' to excel others in Authorities, Arguments, and Reasons for Proof of his Opinion ',[9] did not have his references on hand ; far easier to suspect that a careless or lazy scribe did not take the trouble to copy them.[10]

[1] See *infra*, p. 207.   [2] *Ibid.*, p. 200.   [3] *Supra*, p. 176.
[4] Cf. his own citation in court: ' Ceo est adjuge en un Livre ' ; Hill. 21 Hen. VII, no. 33.
[5] One feels that Marowe ought to have referred to Keble ; perhaps he did during the actual delivery of his reading.
[6] *Supra*, p. 163 ; cf. the Register, 1687 ed. for the ecclesiastical writs, *De Vi Laica Removenda*, *De Recto de Advocatione*, and *Quare Impedit* (59, 60, 30), discussed by Marowe in Lect. I and II.
[7] See *infra*, p. 198.
[8] Coke, preface to his Commentary on Littleton ; cf. also his preface to his Tenth Report : ' A book of sound and exquisite learning '.
[9] Coke, cited *supra*, p. 167, note 2.
[10] It is peculiarly unfortunate that we possess no ' author's copy ' of an early reading.

Before trying to estimate the value of Marowe's achievement, his treatment of certain legal and historical problems must be considered.

(4) DISCUSSION OF CERTAIN HISTORICAL AND LEGAL PROBLEMS

Although it is too soon to attempt a complete history and analysis of the powers and practice of justices of the peace,[1] a discussion of Marowe's treatment of certain specific problems may help prepare the way for such an attempt.

Organization of their office.

In the obscure matter of early methods of appointment of the ' keepers ' of the peace, it has recently been suggested that ' election' applied only to the filling of vacancies.[2] But Marowe writes as confidently of the custom of electing keepers of the peace as of electing coroners or knights of parliament.[3] His view was accepted by Lambard, who added confirmatory evidence.[4]

On the debatable question as to when the ' keepers ' of the peace could be described as ' justices', Lambard's opinion expressed very cautiously[5] has been commonly accepted as categorically true.[6] Accordingly, it is usual to say that 'justices' was the correct term only after the statute of 1361[7] had conferred on the old ' keepers' the general power of hearing and determining felonies.[8] Marowe, however, completely ignores this act, so much emphasized by modern scholars, and gives as the three essential statutes, 1 Edward III, c. 17, 2 Edward III,

---

[1] For reason already set forth, see *supra*, pp. 1–4.

[2] Beard, Office of Justice of Peace, 23–44, following the opinion of Stubbs expressed in a letter of 1898. Of course, Marowe's belief in election by no means settles the controversy.

[3] App. III, p. 305.

[4] Eirenarcha, 15–16.

[5] *Op. cit.*, 21 : ' It is not so euident that I dare determine vpon it '.

[6] Cf. Tait, Introduction to Lancashire Quarter Sessions Records : 'As early as 1360 the statute was passed which is regarded as having firmly established the office ', ii–iii. Beard's statement is more guarded : *op. cit.*, 40–1.

[7] Commonly quoted as 34 Edw. III, 1360, but better 35 Edw. III, 1361 ; see Parry, Parliaments and Councils, introduction, 56, and 'Justices of Labourers ', in E.H.R. xxi. 526, note 62.

[8] W. Hawkins, Pleas of the Crown, 1716–1722 ed., 39.

and 18 Edward III.[1] He argues that after the enactment of the last-named statute of 1344 the term 'justice' was applicable, and not before.[2] But he also repeats the error of the early abridgements and quotes from 2 Edward III the clause that gave authority to certain justices to hear and determine.[3] He thus implies that the 'keepers' received judicial powers as early as 1328, an apparent contradiction of his previous statement. There is evidently room for difference of opinion. In Easter 1483 the three peace statutes had been cited accurately in court,[4] with a specific reference to c. 6 of 2 Edward III,[5] but the view had been expressed that the term 'justice' was legitimate even before 1344. The whole matter must be left to future research in the early history of the keepers;[6] it is safe to conclude, however, that powers of hearing and determining were conferred so frequently on the keepers that it became natural to describe them as justices before 1361, and probably even before 1344.[7]

[1] App. III, Lect. III, IV, and V, especially pp. 301, 313. For the references to Statutes of the Realm, see *ibid.*, notes.

[2] *Ibid.*, p. 301.

[3] *Ibid.*, p. 313. His quotation shows that it is c. 7; see p. 47, and note 2, *supra*.

[4] Year Book Pasch. 22 Edw. IV, no. 33 (cited p. 189, note 9, *supra*). It is strange that so long after 1361 the discussion should show that there was uncertainty as to whether 'by commission' ought to appear in the title of justices of the peace when taking criminal indictments; see App. III, p. 313, note 3, and pp. 84-94, *supra*. Cf. also Year Book Mich. 2 Rich. III, no. 20.

[5] The clause empowering the keepers to enforce the statute of Winchester; of course c. 3 ought to have been added.

[6] Miss Cam's study of the commissions of Trailbaston is important in this connexion; see her Hundred Rolls, *passim*, and especially 73-9.

[7] Miss Cam cites a number of rolls that need careful analysis; e.g. Assize Roll 520, 6 Edw. III, 1333, which 'recognizes the judicial powers of the custodes'. Cf. also Rot. Pat. 19 Edw. III, pt. 2, m. 31 d. The following form dating from 33 Edw. III was known to Marowe: Commission al . . . et auters come Gardeins de la peace permy & per touts le counte, d'Oyer & terminer toutz maners de felonie, trespasses, oppressions, etc.; Lib. Ass. 34 Edw. III, pl. 8. See p. 188, note 3, *supra*.

The fact that 'justices' was used in 1351 in the joint commission of the peace and labourers (see my Statutes of Labourers, App. 21-5), and that 'justices de laborers' was very common (see my article on 'Justices of Labourers', E.H.R. xxi. 527-530), perhaps hastened the use of 'justices de la peas'. For early instances *after* 1361, cf. statute of 36 Edw. III, cc. 12, 14, 1362, and Rot. Parl. ii., 36 Edw. III, 271, 46 Edw. III, 312, 50 Edw. III, 333.

These instances seem to have been overlooked by Professor Tait, who

A curious detail in the history of the form of the commission of the peace is the divergence of opinion as to the identity of the statute of Westminster, bracketed with the statutes of Winchester and of Northampton in the opening paragraph.[1] Lambard believes that 'Westminster' refers to the statute of 5 Edward III, c. 14 'against Robertsmen drawlatches, &c.', although he claims that it did not find its way into the commission until 20 Edward III.[2] In reality, 5 Edward III does not concern justices of the peace at all, but since 'Westminster' appears in a commission of 6 Edward III[3]—in spite of Lambard—it is more than possible that the clerks of the Chancery thought that the 'keepers' had this new jurisdiction in the matter of 'Robertsmen'. In any case, 'Westminster' had dropped out by 1351[4] and did not reappear till just after the statute of 1361.[5] Naturally, therefore, modern scholars identify 'Westminster' as this statute of 1361, which they consider the basis of the power of justices of the peace.[6] Equally naturally, Marowe is perfectly clear that it is the 'old' statute of Westminster first.[7] He has powerful support for his theory in the fact that the collection of statutes sent in 1472 to the justices of the peace for enforcement included: 'Westminster primer Wynchestr' Norhampton'.[8] The framers of the reformed commission of 1590 shrewdly avoided the difficulty by their vague phrase: 'omnia Ordinationes & statuta pro bono pacis nostrae,

states that the short form 'justice of the peace' was not used in official documents till after 1378; *op. cit.*, ii–iii.

[1] Another proof, if any were needed, of the crying need of a study of the MS. commissions. Even in the stimulating article cited *infra*, p. 204, note 6, the writers print a commission of 31 Edw. III, with the statement that there 'is no reason to believe that any change was made in the commission before the statute of 34 Edw. III.' But the commission of 33 Edw. III *does* show a change; Rot. Pat. 33, pt. 3, m. 4 d.

[2] Eirenarcha, 38–9, 174. Cf. Professor Tait (*ut supra*) for a recent acceptance of this view.

[3] Cal. Pat. Edw. III, 1330–1334, 292, 296; see proceedings cited p. 192, note 7, *supra*.

[4] See joint commission cited *ibid.*

[5] Commission of 35 Edw. III, printed in article quoted in note 1, *supra*.

[6] *Ibid.*

[7] Lect. IV. Fitzherbert in Loffice arrived at the same conclusion; ff. 10 b-11. Cf. also Crompton, f. 7.

[8] See p. 185, *supra*, and note 4.

ac pro conseruatione eiusdem . . . edita '.[1] Lambard, in expounding this new form, enumerates *four* statutes of Westminster [2] as included in 'all ordinances and statutes', and fails to note his own inconsistency.

Marowe's opinion on the subject of women as justices of the peace is of peculiar interest in connexion with the discussion in the English press in 1919–1920 concerning the Justices of the Peace (Qualification of Women) Bill.[3] After its passage [4] there appeared in a London daily paper under the caption 'First Women J.Ps.' the names of seven distinguished women appointed by the Lord Chancellor.[5] The act provides that ' A woman shall not be disqualified by sex or marriage for being appointed or being or becoming by virtue of office a justice of the peace '.[6] Two arguments are alleged as proving that without such an act women could not be justices of the peace : (1) The old common law disability of women which was re-affirmed by parliament as recently as 1907 [7]; (2) The statute of 1 Edward III, st. 2, c. xvi, ' In every county good *men* (the italics are of the twentieth century) and lawful shall be assigned to keep the peace.'[8] Modern lawyers have failed to remember that this statute of 1327 created 'keepers' not 'justices' of the peace,[9] and that therefore, strictly speaking, it does not apply to the controversy. Marowe in 1503 is unaware of any common law disability, and in considering the various acts dealing with justices of the peace, he evidently interprets the French 'gentz' or 'persones' as human beings.[10]

---

[1] Eirenarcha, 34.

[2] Westm. I, c. 9, 13 Edw. I, and 28 Edw. III, c. 11, 5 Edw. III, c. 14, *ibid.* 43.

[3] The Justice of the Peace, May 31, 1919, 246.

[4] The bill became law late in 1919.

[5] The Daily Mail of 24 December 1919.

[6] See note 3.

[7] *Ibid.* ' The Qualification of Women (County and Borough Councils) Act, 1907, section 1, when granting admission to local offices to women provided that a woman if elected as chairman of a county council or mayor of a borough should not by virtue of holding or having held that office be a justice of the peace.'

[8] The Justice of the Peace, July 5, 1919, 306. For this statute, the opening one in the Boke of 1506, see *supra*, p. 47.

[9] As Marowe knew ; see *supra*, pp. 191–2.

[10] It is possibly significant that the French form of 18 Edw. III has merely 'les plus vaillauntz'.

He implies as a self-evident proposition that a 'feme sole' can be made a justice of the peace by commission; he then shows that a commission to a 'feme covert' is also good, and discusses the legal effects of the marriage of a woman justice of the peace.[1] But Marowe is not the only lawyer of his day to hold such views. His own Inn seems to have been a centre for the teaching of feminist theories.[2] Thus, Humphrey Coningsby, Frowyk's colleague, shows that under certain circumstances widows can appoint justices of the peace,[3] and Brudnell holds that a woman can be a bailiff although a monk cannot.[4] Finally, Marowe's close associate, Edmund Dudley of Gray's Inn, argues that the king can appoint as justices in Eyre any men, whether learned in law or not, two aliens, two villeins, two monks, or even two women, either married or single.[5]

Unfortunately these legal theories were not supported by concrete illustrations.[6] It is significant to find that Marowe's opinion was not even mentioned by Lambard or Crompton. That the subject soon became an obscure and somewhat remote problem is shown by the discussion at Lincoln's Inn in the early seventeenth century as to whether women could be justices of the Forest.[7] In connexion with the celebrated case of the mother of Henry VII, the Countess of Richmond, the king's attorney declared that he had seen 'many arbitraments' made by her, but that he had searched the records in vain for her commission.[8] A certain judge added that he had heard

---

[1] Lect. IV. Apparently women cannot be made justices by special Letters Patent any more than 'persones disablees'; nor does Marowe say that they can be *keepers* of the peace; Lect. III. But a woman can be a gaoleress or a sheriff; Lect. IV. The case of Nichola de Haye has often been cited; cf. p. 196, note 2, *infra*. There is a reference to a woman sheriff in 1657; Fleetwood, Office of a Justice of Peace, 1658, 14.

[2] It was at the Inner Temple in May 1922 that a woman was for the first time called to the English bar; New York Times, 11 May 1922.

[3] p. 180, *supra*, and note 1. But it is possible that I am wrong in identifying him as Humphrey; see *ibid*.

[4] *Supra*, p. 149, and note 5; p. 181, and note 7.

[5] p. 183, and note 7. Walter Atwell in transcribing Marowe's statement on women (Lect. IV) gives a cross reference to Dudley's reading; see *supra*, p. 152, note 11.

[6] At least not in our versions of the readings.

[7] Mr. Atkins was reading on Forests in August 1632; MS. Harl. 980, ff. 81–2. The reading is extant in MS. Hargrave 37, ff. 185–207.

[8] MS. Harl. 980, f. 81. A few earlier instances are given of women as

'from his mother of the Lady Bartlet ... that she was a Justice of Peace' in Gloucestershire.[1]   Some one else quoted the instance of 'Rowse' in Suffolk.[2]   The paucity of evidence certainly proves that there were not many instances of women justices of the peace.   But it is very probable that further research will show that the age of the 'Monstrous Regimen of Women' witnessed a few women on the Bench,[3] and that their 'common law disability' was a doctrine of later years.[4]   A plausible explanation of the tradition as to the Countess of Richmond has recently been suggested.   Her commission was 'probably identical with the Duke of Richmond's for all the Northern Shires.   That it has not been enrolled would only show that, like his, it was an exceptional one.'[5]   It was perhaps not a mere coincidence that the advocates of feminist principles, Marowe,[6] Coningsby, Brudnell, and Dudley, all belonged to a group of lawyers conspicuously favoured by the king and his

justices; Alice Perrers for example.   See App. III, p. 310, note 3, for a reference to St. Alban's History; cf. Daines Barrington, Observations on Ancient Statutes, 243.

[1] 'And did set usually upon the bench with the other Justices ... that she was made so by Q. Mary upon her complaint to her of the injuries she sustained by some of that county and desiring for redress therof that as she herself was chief Justice of all England, so this Lady might be in her own County which accordingly the Queen granted;' MS. Harl. 980, f. 81.

[2] 'Who usually at the assizes and sessions ther held set vpon the Bench among the iustices gladio cincta', *ibid.*   In an article on 'Women as Justices of the Peace' in The Common Cause for May 30, 1919, Mr. Theodore Dodd writes that in Olive *v.* Ingram, 7 Modern Reports, p. 267, it is stated that the Mirror of Justices mentions women justices of the peace.   In addition to the instances given in Harl. 980, he cites that of Nichola de la Haye, but admits that the evidence indicates that she was sheriff.   The reference to the Mirror is strange, since it was probably written *temp.* Edw. I, and therefore before the existence of justices of the peace; ed. F. W. Maitland, Selden Soc.

[3] Only by a thorough examination of the Patent Rolls of the later Tudors can the question be settled.

[4] It may not therefore be strictly accurate to say that the 'exclusion of women from the Bench' was based on 'ancient practice'; see art. quoted *supra*, p. 194, note 3.   But Mr. Theodore Dodd (writing in July 1919) is undoubtedly right in his contention that despite legal theory, 'practically an act of parliament was necessary as the Lord Chancellor would not appoint any women without it.'

[5] R. R. Reid, The King's Council in the North, 88.

[6] Marowe's discussion of the 'reasonable chastisement' of a wife by a husband certainly suggests no thoroughgoing feminism; see App. III, Lect. VII.

mother.[1] Did the appointment of the Countess on the unpopular High Commission in the north perhaps need legal
justification ? [2]

Their criminal jurisdiction.

The authority of justices of the peace in relation to serious
crimes had been greatly increased by recent legislation.
Sheriffs were now compelled to send up their indictments to
justices of the peace ; [3] the latter had been given the power of
bailing men arrested on suspicion of felony ; [4] their hands had
also been strengthened by the attack on benefit of clergy,
notably in cases of Petty Treason.[5]

It has already been shown that Marowe excludes from his
analysis statutory offences, whether felonies or trespasses.[6] It
is therefore natural that he should fail to enumerate the few
forms of High Treason [7] of which the justices of the peace were
empowered to inquire by statute and by commission.[8] Instead,
he devoted his attention to felonies at common law of which
they were not only to inquire but which they could also hear
and determine : Theft, Robbery, Burglary, Homicide, Petty
Treason,[9] Escapes, Accessories to Felonies.[10] The list would

---

[1] The group to which Frowyk belonged ; p. 128, note 6, p. 134, note 5 ;
pp. 180-1, *supra*.

[2] It is probable that Dudley and Empson were associated with her ;
Reid, *loc. cit.*

[3] By 1 Edw. IV, c. 2, 1461.

[4] By 1 Rich. III, c. 3, 1483, modified by 3 Hen. VII, c. 3 (4), 1487.
Petitions of the commons had twice been refused requesting that justices
of the peace should have power to take bail of persons arrested by the
sheriff on suspicion of felony; Rot. Parl. v. 332, 620-1. Cf. also p. 87,
supra, note 14, and p. 101, note 2.

[5] By 4 Hen. VII, c. 13 ; 12 Hen. VII, c. 7. Cf. art. by C. B. Firth on
' Benefit of Clergy in the time of Edward IV ', E.H.R. xxxii. 175-91.

[6] p. 165, *supra*.

[7] (1) Counterfeiting the king's coin, or clipping it, &c., 4 Hen. V
(vel. 3, st. 2), cc. 6 & 7. (2) Threats to burn houses, 8 Hen. VI, c. 6.
(3) Counterfeiting foreign coin, 4 Hen. VII, c. 18. These are all included
in the Charge in the Boke of 1506. A comparison of this list with the
four indictments of High Treason in Part II of the Boke shows that the
latter are distinctly out of place; see pp. 98-9, *supra*, but cf. Jenks, Hist.
Eng. Law, 153, for a very different view.

[8] Rather strangely Marowe holds that there is one form of High
Treason of which the justices can inquire as felony ; App. III, p. 379.

[9] Felony at common law before the statute of 25 Edw. III ; cf. App. III,
p. 379, and note 7.

[10] App. III, pp. 380-1.

call for no special notice were it not for the problem of Homicide.

Marowe gives Bracton's classification of Homicide under four heads[1]: death by misfortune, suicide, manslaughter by chance medley, and murder, and holds that the last two were inquirable by ' the justices of the peace '.[2] Fitzherbert's view as expressed in 'Loffice' has been quoted previously—that justices of the peace cannot inquire of murder as murder but only as felony and manslaughter.[3] The formal rejection of Fitzherbert's opinion in Michaelmas term 1553 by eminent judges assembled in Serjeant's Inn[4] was decisive.[5] Brooke makes the necessary modification of Fitzherbert in his own ' Abridgement' under *Corone* ;[6] Lambard,[7] Crompton,[8] and later Coke,[9] mention the doctrine only to contradict it.

Fitzherbert's prestige as an historian of the law is so enormous that it is of interest to try to discover the basis for

---

[1] He does not mention Bracton, however.

[2] Lect. XII. His definition of murder as including 'malice prepense ' and 'lying in ambush' is perhaps a reminiscence of Bracton's age, when ' murder was restrained to a secrete killing onely '; see Lambard, *op. cit.*, 240.

[3] p. 39, *supra*, and notes 2, 3, pp. 109-10. As has been pointed out, Fitzherbert by 1538 had modified his original categorical statement in his Abridgement under *Corone*, no. 457.

[4] See note 5, *infra*; Hale, justice of the Common Pleas, *temp.* Edw. VI ; Portman, justice of the King's Bench, 1546, chief justice by June 1555; probably Brooke, serjeant-at-law by 1552, and later chief justice of the Common Pleas ; Foss, Judges.

[5] Not in Dalison's printed reports, but in a MS. version in MS. Harl. 5141, f. 10 b (Hill. 6 & 7 Edw. VI) ; ' Loppinion de Fitzherbert en son liver de Justice de Peace non obstante ; et issint est l'experience et opinion des toutes Justices quod nota.' The MS. was once in the possession of Lambard (see p. 111, note 1, *supra*) and is the source quoted in Eirenarcha, 466. Cf. also Lambard's reference to the opinion of the 'justices of the King's Bench, 6 Ed. 6. Collections Dyer, fol. 69.' It is given under Pasch. 5 Edw. VI, ff. 68-9, in the 1601 edition of Dyer.

[6] *Corone*, no. 25. He omits a portion of the report cited by Fitzherbert. Cf. also *Peace*, and *suertie de peace*, no. 3.

[7] See note 5, *supra*.

[8] *Op. cit.*, ff. 19 b-20.

[9] Preface to Tenth Report : ' Wherewith the judges (as I have seen it reported) found fault ; for that he therein affirmed, that Justices of Peace having by their Commission authority to hear and determine Felonies, etc., could not hear and determine murder, which (amongst others) they clearly overruled that Justices of Peace lawfully might do.' The above is inscribed on the fly-leaf of a copy of Berthelet's Boke of 1539, now in the library of Harvard Law School. The writer probably

his discredited theory. The evidence against him is over-whelming. Coram Rege Rolls, Ancient Indictments, Gaol Delivery Rolls,[1] seem literally full of indictments of murder brought before justices of the peace; the cases of the reign of Henry VII that contradicted the theory were fully reported in the Year Books;[2] in fact Fitzherbert cited two such cases without noticing the contradiction;[3] the Charge as printed in the 'Boke' of 1506 (?) represented a widespread practice.[4] The manual of 1422 (?) and the later MS. collections of precedents fully confirm the above evidence.[5] Whatever ambiguity may have existed as to the authority of the justices of the peace in the reign of Edward III ought to have been entirely dispelled by the proceedings in parliament of June 1380. A petition that the justices of the peace should hear and determine murders received the King's assent,[6] and according to the commissions issued immediately afterwards they were em-powered to inquire 'de murdris & aliis feloniis'.[7] The words 'de omnimodis feloniis' were substituted a few years later, and were clearly intended to be an equivalent.[8]

Fitzherbert had relied on two arguments: first, that a statute had provided that in a royal charter of pardon the word 'felonies' cannot be construed to include treason, murder, or rape.[9] Secondly, on a report of 9 Henry IV which he assigns to Hilary term.[10] The precise words as printed by

mistook the volume for the New Boke, the translation of Fitzherbert's Loffice.

[1] See ch. iii (1), *supra*.

[2] e. g. Pasch. 3 Hen. VII, no. 2; Mich. 14 Hen. VII, no. 7; W. Rastell, Entries, 1566 ed., ff. 362, 417; Fleetwood, Annales, under *Peax*.

[3] Abridgement, *Corone*, no. 360, and *Enditement*, no. 22.

[4] p. 39, *supra*.

[5] pp. 90, 105, *supra*.

[6] Rot. Parl., iii. 83–5; note especially the marginal entry, 84: 'Decla-ration faite sur le poair donez as Justices de la Paix, dont il y a une certaine acte enroullez en Roulle de Parlement anno 111º (m. 2).' The 'acte' is described as 'L'Ordinance faite en cest parlement touchant la Poair des Justices de la Paix'. The entire proceedings constitute a most interesting attempt to organize the office of justice of the peace.

[7] Rot. Pat., 3 Rich. II, pt. 3, m. 13 d, 26 May; printed in Rot. Parl., *ut supra*. They were also to hear and determine, but in this case one of the quorum must be present.

[8] Rot. Pat., 6 Rich. II, pt. 2, m. 24 d, 20 December.

[9] 13 Rich. II, st. 2, c. 1; Loffice, f. 21; Crompton, *op. cit.*, ff. 19 b–20

[10] Abridgement, *Corone*, no. 457.

Fitzherbert are significant : ' Vn fuit endite deuant Iustices de peace qe conust le felonie & appel auters & son appel fuit aiudge voide ycy en bank le Roy pur ceo qe les iusticez de paice ne ount power de assigner a luy vn coroner & nota en mesme le plee qe lez iustices de peace ne ount power denquere de mort de home ne treson haut sinon qils aueront especial commission car par lour general commission ils nont power.'

The case appears in practically the same form and under the same date in Statham,[1] but in the printed Year Books it is placed in Michaelmas term, and the last sentence runs thus :[2] ' et Nota, que ils nont pas poyar denquerer de treason, &.' The crucial words ' mort de home' are omitted. Statham may have carelessly expanded ' &' to include ' mort de home' and Fitzherbert may have blindly accepted him.[3] Or the expansion may have been due to an early reporter whose report was used by both Statham and Fitzherbert. There is still another possible hypothesis. In the discussion in court *temp.* Henry IV which evidently took place, some one may have quoted the enactment on charters of pardon and the new phraseology of the commission[4] as proof of a limitation on the authority of justices of the peace. This individual opinion may have been carelessly jotted down by the reporter as the judgement of the court, and thus found its way into the two earliest printed Abridgements. The episode is of peculiar significance for an appreciation of Marowe ; not only because it shows the soundness of his legal knowledge, but also because it affords conclusive proof that he did not depend on Statham for his material.[5]

On vital matters of criminal procedure Marowe is perfectly definite : justices of the peace cannot act on coroners' inquests,[6] they cannot assign a coroner, or take approvements, they cannot hold appeals of any kind whether on indictments before themselves or before coroners.[7] For the first point Marowe's

---

[1] *Corone*, no. 46.   [2] No. 1.

[3] But under *Justices de Peas*, no. 7, he cites the same report in the form in which it appears in the printed Year Book, in Michaelmas term, and with *Mort de home* omitted.

[4] That is, the omission of the specific word, ' murders'.

[5] See pp. 189–90, *supra*.   [6] App. III, p. 363.

[7] *Ibid.*, p. 406. But he holds that ' de rigore iuris' they can take a confes-

authority is undoubtedly the form of the commission;[1] for the others, two Year Book cases of the reign of Henry IV. One has just been discussed; the other is an exceedingly brief report of Easter 1401 ;[2] 'accorde fuit per touts les Justices del common bank que Justices de peace ne poyent my prender nul appeal devant eux de nul provor, ne de auter. Et que lour Commission ne extende my cy largement.'[3] These reports were accepted as decisive not only by Marowe, but also by Fitzherbert,[4] Brooke,[5] and Crompton.[6] Lambard, however, is inclined to follow Staunford, who 'worthilie doubteth of this matter'.[7] Strangely enough, the report of Mich. 44 Edward III[8] which influenced Staunford,[9] and later Hale[10] and Hawkins,[11] mentions 'Justices as gaoles deliver assignes', not justices of the peace, and therefore has no apparent bearing on the controversy.[12]

But there is plenty of room for doubt. Sir Thomas Skelton,

sion themselves. The matter of appeals is important, since they were still usual in Marowe's time. In 1482 the judges held that a person indicted for murder could not be arraigned within the year, so that the suit of the party might be saved; Year Book Hill. 22 Edw. IV, no. 1. The statute of 3 Hen. VII, c. 2, abolished this time limit but provided that acquittal on an indictment was no bar to an appeal; J. Stephen, Hist. Crim. Law, i. 248–9; Holdsworth, *op. cit.*, ii. 307.

[1] Cf. Eirenarcha, 518: 'Their Commission and authoritie extendeth onely to such as stand indicted before themselves, or former Justices of the peace.' They did not act on sheriffs' indictments until specifically authorized by statute; see p. 197, note 3, *supra*.

[2] Pasch. 2 Hen. IV, no. 12.

[3] The commission is again the authority.

[4] Loffice, f. 16 ; Abridgement, *Justices de Peas*, no. 5.

[5] Abridgement, *Appeale*, no. 18.

[6] *Op. cit.*, f. 106 ; he quotes the report of 9 Hen. IV, and refers to Abridgement of Assizes, f. 76. But yet in his appendix he prints from the old Boke forms of appeals as if they were before justices of the peace.

[7] Eirenarcha, 519.

[8] No. 57, in the printed edition ; but in Fitzherbert, *Corone*, no. 95, 'justices de peace' is the phrase, and it was his version that was quoted by Staunford.

[9] Les Plees del Corone, 1568 ed.; ff. 65, 144: 'they can take appeals because their commission is to hear and determine felonies (quere tamen) but they cannot take approvements.'

[10] Pleas of the Crown, 1678 ed., 148 ; he distinguishes between appeals by bill and appeals by writ; only the former can come before justices of the peace.

[11] Pleas of the Crown, 1716–1722 ed., 156.

[12] Unless possibly justices of the peace acting as justices of Gaol Delivery were meant, or unless the printed report is inaccurate.

himself a justice of the peace,[1] had said in court in Easter 1401 that he had taken appeals.[2]   The difficulty of interpreting the statute of 8 Henry VI on appeals[3] was so great that it had caused a long discussion in court three years after its enactment.[4]   The very fact of the petition of 1468 that justices of the peace be empowered to assign a coroner in order to take approvements[5] perhaps showed that they were regularly hearing appeals by others than approvers.

The evidence of formula books is contradictory.   The manual of 1422 (?) contains no appeals.[6]   The precedents of the 'Boke' of 1506 (?)—coroner's inquests, appeals, oath of approver, &c.—have been shown to be of doubtful validity for justices of the peace.[7]   But on the other hand the compilation for a Suffolk clerk of the peace nearly contemporary with Marowe and apparently accurately put together, includes two appeals before Sir Robert Drury as justice of the peace.[8]   There is therefore conclusive proof that the latter was holding appeals at about the date that Marowe was telling his students that justices of the peace had no such authority.   Lambard's suggestion gives the clue for a possible solution of the complicated problem: the commission of 13 Richard II expressly restrained the determination of felonies by justices of the peace 'to the only suite of the King'; but there is no such limitation in the present commission (i. e. *temp.* Elizabeth).[9]   A study of the form of the commission shows that the restraining phrase appeared as early as 5 Richard II,[10] and that it had dropped out by 2 Henry VI;[11] also that from 6 Henry V through

---

[1] For the counties of Cambridge and of Southampton during the reign of Henry IV, Cal. Pat. 1399–1401, 557, 564; 1401–1405, 515, 519; 1405–1408, 490, 497; 1408–1413, 479, 485.

[2] 'Attamen Sir Thomas Skelton la present a cel temps dit, que il avoit fait le contrary'; *supra*, p. 201, and note 2.

[3] c. 10; Lambard, *ut supra*. The wording of the statute is by no means clear.

[4] Year Book Trin. 11 Hen. VI, no. 23.

[5] Rot. Parl. v. 620–1; the petition was refused.

[6] pp. 84–93, *supra*.   [7] pp. 99–100.   [8] *Ibid.*, p. 105, note 3.

[9] Eirenarcha, 1588 ed., 553; omitted from subsequent editions and merely suggested without evidence in 1581 ed., 449–50, and in 1582 ed., *ibid.*

[10] Rot. Pat., 5 Rich. II, pt. 2, m. 22 d.

[11] *Ibid.* 2 Hen. VI, pt. 3, m. 22 d.

1 Henry VI the commission included a proviso that in difficult cases even the quorum should not determine felonies except in the presence of a justice of Assize or of one of the Benches.[1] With such vacillation on the part of Chancery, it is not strange that the justices of the peace and their clerks were frequently genuinely ignorant of the extent of their jurisdiction at a given date, and that legal theory and legal practice often failed to coincide.[2]

Surety of peace and surety of good behaviour.

Marowe's account of surety of peace [3] is fuller than any previous account. Although the main outline closely resembles that presented by Keble many years before,[4] there is much additional material. From an authority on surety of peace one would naturally expect a clear definition of surety of good behaviour; as a matter of fact, Marowe fails even to mention the existence of this form of surety. The history of the latter has so many complexities and Marowe's omission is so baffling that the subject needs investigation.

The writ for taking surety of good behaviour from those *not* of good fame is said to be based on the statute 34 (35) Edward III, c. 1, and is included among the precedents in the 'Boke' of 1506 (?) and in the MS. compilations previously described with the exception of the manual of 1422 (?).[5] A number of judges argued learnedly on the distinction between surety of peace and of good behaviour in Michaelmas 1486,[6] arguments which Marowe might have heard. The writ is cited by

---

[1] *Ibid.* 6 Hen. V, m. 26 d, 7 Hen. V, m. 30 d, 8 Hen. V, m. 21 d, 9 Hen. V, pt. 1, m. 20 d, 10 Hen. V, m. 14 d, 1 Hen. VI, m. 6 d. The proviso is somewhat ambiguously worded.

[2] Until the complete text of the successive commissions are printed or at least typed, it is not easy to compare the changing forms. I do not feel sure that my comparisons are absolutely accurate. Moreover, the actual records of the justices of the peace need to be thoroughly investigated; see Introduction, *supra.* See also App. III, Lect. XV, unfortunately one of the few sections where Marowe is not clear.

[3] Lect. VI.

[4] See pp. 184–5, *supra.*

[5] See p. 96, *supra.*

[6] Year Book Mich. 2 Hen. VII, no. 7, 1486; case of Crofts and Corbet.

Fitzherbert in his 'Abridgement'[1] and likewise by Brooke in his;[2] it is briefly mentioned by Crompton,[3] and elaborately explained by Lambard[4] and by later writers of text-books.[5] But the authors of a recent article[6] have proved conclusively that the phraseology of the writ is wrong and that the wording of the clause as entered on the Statute Roll of 34 Edward III is the only form that makes sense : justices of the peace were empowered to arrest idle returned soldiers 'whom they were able to find by indictment or by suspicion, and to put them in prison, and to take of all those who are of *good fame*' security for their good behaviour . . . and the 'others duly to punish'. They also argue that the clause of the statute framed for a special emergency fell into disuse very speedily and was not revived till the middle or after the middle of the fifteenth century.[7] Finally, they hold that the revival was due to an Exchequer clerk who transcribed a volume of statutes about 1445–1446[8] and inserted the 'ne', 'qui *ne* sont de bone fame' for 'qui sont de bone fame'; that from this volume the early printed editions and translations were made, and that therefore the authority of the justices of the peace to bind over persons not of good fame to be of good behaviour was due to a mere blunder of an ignorant or careless scribe.

The question seems to me more complex, however, than the above explanation suggests. The 'ne' appears in a number of transcripts of statutes made before 1445–1446. The earliest instance that has come to my attention is in a collection presumably completed not later than the beginning of the reign

---

[1] Under *Suerte*, no. 21 (based on the above report). The statute is quoted in Loffice, f. 45, but I do not find the writ in La Novel Natura Brevium, 1553 ed.

[2] *Suretie*, no. 12, based on the same report; cf. Rastell, Entries, 415–16. Fleetwood uses the phrase in his preface (pp. 211–12, *infra*), but gives no instances.

[3] *Op. cit.*, ff. 75, 119, 120–1. He cites the statute of 34 Edw. IV (*sic*), and confines the writ to the arrest of 'barretors'.   [4] *Op. cit.*, 109–16.

[5] The references are given in the article quoted *infra*, note 6.

[6] 'The Powers of Justices of the Peace', by C. G. Crump and C. Johnson, E.H.R. xxvii. 226–38.

[7] The 'earliest victim' that they have discovered was a William Barnard in 1515.

[8] The collection includes statutes up to 23 Hen. VI in one handwriting, and statutes from 23–29 Hen. VI in a later hand.

of Henry IV.[1] On the other hand, it is often omitted.[2] The solution of the problem must be sought, I think, in a study of actual practice during the period before and after 1361. Positive statements cannot be made safely until a vast amount of material has been thoroughly investigated.[3] But the following hypothesis is suggested tentatively. In accordance with the old familiar procedure based on the statute of Winchester,[4] after the arrest of suspicious persons it had been the custom to investigate their general reputation. Although the details of the usage show considerable variation, 'bona fama' naturally assures such prisoners a more favourable treatment than 'mala fama' or 'pessima fama';[5] in fact, in some instances it ensures their immediate release.[6] By analogy, in interpreting the clause of 35 Edward III (which although framed for a special crisis remained on the statute book) many individual justices may have felt that it was unsuitable to proceed against persons of good fame: 'Un common voix & fame est un grand regard in noster Ley' as

---

[1] MS. Lansdowne 474, 'New' Statutes to 20 Rich. II, and a pardon of 21 Rich. II. Other early examples are as follows: B.M. MS. Harl. 751, to 4 Hen. V; MS. Lansdowne 469, to 3 Hen. V; Lincoln's Inn; Hale MSS. LXIX (74), Magna Carta to 2 Hen. V; Various Donors, XII (176), to 3 Hen. V; *ibid.* XXIII (178), to 3 Hen. V (the last reads: 'qe sount de *male* fame'); B.M. MS. Lansdowne 464, to 15 Hen. VI; Bodl. Douce MSS. 362, to 2 Hen. V.

[2] Cf. e.g. MS. Lansdowne 468, to 14 Hen. VI: 'qui sount de bone fame.'

[3] Especially Gaol Delivery Rolls, proceedings before justices of the peace, &c.; see Introduction, *supra.*

[4] e.g. 'Capti pro sinistra suspeccione', Gaol Delivery Roll 139, m. 5 d, 30 Edw. III; 'capti per suspeccionem latrocinii secundum statutum Wynton', *ibid.* 197, m. 6, 2 Hen. V; 'captus pro suspeccione latrocinii et male fame', *ibid.* 137 a, m. 9, 25 Edw. III; 'captus per villatam predictam quia est de mala fama & rettatus de latrocinio', *ibid.*, $\frac{33}{7}$, m. 24, 21 Rich. II.

Cf. also Fitzherbert's interpretation of the statute of 5 Edw. III, c. 14: 'Le Vycountes deuer arestre suspect parsons queux alent par noet ou par iour & sount de male fame'; Loffice, f. 159.

[5] After a proclamation made in court, the entries often run: 'remittuntur Gaole ... eo quod sunt male fame'; G.D.R. 80, m. 12, 7 Hen. V; or 'pessime fame', *ibid.* $\frac{34}{1}$, 9 Hen. V (membrane not numbered).

[6] 'Testatum est hic in curia quod sunt bone fame; ideo ... deliberantur,' &c.; *ibid.* 197, m. 6, 2 Hen. V. But on the other hand, there are instances of the following procedure: 'Sarra ... que capta fuit per suspeccionem dimissa est per manucaptores ... de bono gestu suo eo quod facta inquiscione per vicecomitem de fama ... non male redditur'; *ibid.*

was said much later.[1] Accordingly, they may have taken action
only against those who were *not* of good fame, despite the
phraseology of the Statute Roll.

As a result of this practice, by no means universal at first,[2]
a number of scribes may have thought it sound to insert
the 'ne' in their transcripts; no one clerk can be held
responsible and probably no one justice; nor is it possible in
our present state of knowledge to be precise as to dates. But
whatever the explanation, the strict legality of the writ for
taking surety of good behaviour is very doubtful, based as it is
on a misinterpretation of an enactment meant to deal with
a temporary situation. It is not strange therefore that many
of the keen lawyers of the reign of Henry VII should hesitate
to accept it, even though it had been included in the early
precedent books for the justices of the peace. The court had
not been unanimous in 1486 in the case already mentioned;[3]
and a number of years later there was again considerable
difference of opinion[4] in an action of False Imprisonment.
Keble had justified the arrest of the plaintiff by the defendants
on the ground that they were acting under the oral orders of
a justice of the peace, and he had asserted the right of the
latter to bind over a man suspected 'de male fame . . . de se
bene gerendo'. Marowe, on the other hand, also for the defendants, had based his argument on the authority given a justice
of the peace by the statute of Riots.[5] Thus it is possible
to conclude that Marowe's omission from the De Pace of
surety of good behaviour was due to his critical judgement, and
that it is another proof of the soundness of his legal knowledge.

5, m. 21, 17 Rich. II.   For a similar case before 1361, see *ibid.*, 7 a, m.
24, 12 Edw. III.   Cf. also App. II, no. 18, *infra*, and p. 87, *supra*.
    [1] Year-Book, Mich. 5 Hen. VII, no. 10.   Cf. also Mich. 13 Hen. VII, no. 10.
    [2] It is because my preliminary investigation shows such a variety in
the usage that no dogmatic inferences can be drawn.
    [3] *Supra*, p. 203, note 6: 'Mes uncore les Justices ne furent touts a
avise certeinement coment il serra pris, etc. Quod nota.'
    [4] Mich. 14 Hen. VII, no. 19, 1498, if the Year Book chronology is
correct.   For the case, see p. 185, *supra*, and note 6.
    [5] 'Marowe apprenti. . . .' The statute must be 13 Hen. IV, c. 7. The
main issue had turned on the authority of a justice of the peace to arrest
the plaintiff through oral orders given to servants. Judgement was for
the defendant.   See Lambard, *op. cit.* 170-1, for an account of the case,
with a cross reference to Fitzherbert, Abridgement, *Justice del peace*, 9.

The form of indictments.

It is noteworthy that Marowe gives far fuller and more specific instructions for the framing of indictments than can be found elsewhere at this date. It has already been indicated, for example, that under *Addicion*, he includes a great many more points than does Statham.[1] But his most striking contribution is his elaboration of the 'daintie and nice differences'[2] between *precii* and *ad valenciam* in indictments where valuation is necessary.[3] On the analogy of Writs of Trespass in the Register,[4] Marowe states that for inanimate objects in the plural, *ad valenciam* is necessary, but that for a single inanimate object, and also for live objects whether in the singular or the plural, *precii* must be used.[5]

A modern lawyer has recently examined into the 'arbitrary and fanciful usage', as he terms it,[6] and has concluded that Marowe started the controversy[7] and that the 'difficulty arose largely in his technical mind.'[8] The evidence shows conclusively that the distinction was soon to become a mere historical curiosity.[9] But the Year Books, especially several reports of the reign of Henry VI,[10] show equally conclusively that Marowe was not in any sense the originator of the distinction nor responsible for the controversy, and that he was merely accepting the views of lawyers of the fifteenth century,[11]

---

[1] *Supra*, pp. 189–90.   [2] Lambard's phrase, *op. cit.*, 472 ; see note 11, *infra*.

[3] App. III, pp. 390–3.

[4] 1687 ed., f. 93 b : ' Nota en cas que home porte briefe de transgression de chateux nient moebles: son briefe dirra tants de chateux ad valentiam x s.   Mes si le briefe soit porte de chatelle moeble il dirra precii x s. & non ad valentiam, etc.'

[5] This is his main distinction, but there are many minor points, exceptions, &c., given with the fullest possible details.

[6] 'The Valuation of Property in the Early Common Law', by Nathan Matthews, Harvard Law Review, xxxv, no. 1.   I showed Mr. Matthews Marowe's disquisition on the subject, and I am greatly indebted to him for allowing me to see his conclusions before they were in print.

[7] *Op. cit.*, 23.   [8] *Ibid.* 24.

[9] Cf. *op. cit.*, 25, for the decision in Usher *v.* Bushell, 1651, that swept away the distinction.

[10] (1) Pasch. 21 Hen. VI, no. 5 ; at the end is the following entry : ' Nota que le Registre en ceo accorde.'   The case is cited by Brooke under *Faux Latine & forme*, no. 39.   (2) Mich. 49 Hen. VI, no. 10, cited in the margin of MS. D ; see App. III, p. 391, note 2.   Cf. p. 390, note 2, p. 391, note 3, for other cases.

[11] Many of the early instances listed by Mr. Matthews, *op. cit.*, 26, as

and expounding what was sound law in his day. It is interesting to find once again clear proof that Marowe was making extensive use of ' book cases ', and to note that his exposition of this particular legal subtlety is the fullest that has thus far been discovered.

General estimate.

This study of the content of Marowe's reading, of his sources, and of his method of dealing with legal problems makes it possible to estimate the value of his contribution. A comparison of the De Pace with the MS. precedent books for justices of the peace and with the 'Boke' of 1506 (?) requires no comment.[1] A comparison of it with Fitzherbert's ' Loffice' shows its marked superiority from the point of view of legal history and legal analysis, although of course its omission of the commission, the oath, and of the Charge, &c., prevents the De Pace from serving as a manual of practice.[2] It was not till seventy-five years after Marowe's death that a treatise was produced that combined the merits of the De Pace and of ' Loffice'.[3]

Of the mass of legal literature at Marowe's disposal, we have seen that apart from statutes he had to rely mainly on MS. Year Books. A glance at Statham as typical of the early abridgements reveals the absence of the very topics that would have been of use to Marowe, for example, *Justice de peas*, *Briefe, Enditement, Surety de peas*,[4] and shows also the exceeding brevity of other topics, such as *Addicion*, &c. Evi-

against the validity of the distinction, in reality confirm Marowe's usage of *precii* for a single inanimate object. The evidence from later writers quoted, *op. cit.*, 24, is not convincing. Lambard's scepticism is based partly on a misinterpretation of a Year Book case (Trin. 9 Edw. IV, no. 35). To be sure Fitzherbert in his Novel Natura Brevium, 1553 ed., f. 88 b, is against the validity of the distinction, but Fitzherbert is by no means infallible. W. West in his Symboleography, written *circ.* 1594 (Pt. ii, Indictments, s. 70), and J. Cowell in the Interpreter (1607 ed. under Valewe) accept it, as Mr. Matthews admits. Certainly the opinion of Hale and Hawkins that the 'distinction was never sound' is not borne out by the Year Books.

¹ See chs. i, ii, iii, *supra*.

² Fitzherbert's appendix of statutes must have been of great practical convenience.

³ See pp. 215–18, for the relation of Lambard to Marowe. I do not count Fleetwood for reasons that will be discussed later.

⁴ He was evidently therefore using cases not cited by Statham.

dently, Marowe's task of selection from the Year Books must have been a difficult one and constituted veritable pioneer work.[1]

Finally, his brief outline of criminal law and his account of criminal procedure, even though limited to crimes within the jurisdiction of the justices of the peace, are of the utmost importance. As Maitland wrote long ago: 'The criminal cases in the Year Books are not many and yet they have to fill the long interval between Bracton and Staundford'.[2] One has but to look at the meagre list of references under Statham's *Corone* to realize the significance of Marowe's treatment of the subject.[3] But Marowe's achievement can be most adequately measured by the extent to which the De Pace was utilized as the basis of the standard treatises for justices of the peace. His relation to later legal works must therefore be considered.

(5) RELATION TO LATER LEGAL WORKS

Apart from Year Books and material connected with the Inns of Court, there seems to be no reference to Marowe in legal literature till half a century after his death. Fitzherbert's failure to mention the De Pace in any of his works[4] is the more mysterious inasmuch as a copy was probably produced at his own Inn about 1516 or 1517,[5] and as Marowe was arguing frequently in the courts at Westminster after his call to be serjeant. The oblivion into which the De Pace fell may have been due to the accident of the early death of the author, followed so soon by the death of his two influential professional friends and executors, chief justice Frowyk and justice Kingsmill ;[6] or it may have been in part at least the result of politics. With the accession of Henry VIII and the execution of Dudley and Empson, the group to which Marowe and Frowyk belonged may have come under the ban of public

---

[1] For his possible indebtedness to Keble, see pp. 184–5, *supra*.
[2] The Objects and Work of the Selden Society, 10.
[3] For his possible indebtedness to Richard Littleton, see p. 184, *supra*.
[4] See pp. 42, 109, *supra*.   [5] pp. 151–3.
[6] See p. 137, and note 5, *supra*. Kingsmill died *circ.* 1509 ; Foss, Judges.

opinion.[1] Perhaps, therefore, it was not mere ignorance that led Fitzherbert, a supporter of the policy of the new king, to ignore the work of a close associate of Dudley.

Whatever the reasons, the fact remains that the earliest reference to the De Pace was by the chief justice of the Common Pleas, Sir Robert Brooke,[2] of the Middle Temple, in his 'Abridgement', compiled before 1558 [3] but not printed till 1568.[4] Under the two titles of Commission and Riots, Marowe's reading is cited,[5] and under other titles his arguments in court are quoted.[6] The weight that Brooke attached to 'readings'[7] is presumably the main reason for his familiarity with the De Pace and its author.[8] It is also possible that in his posts as common serjeant of London and later as recorder[9] he had heard of his learned predecessor in the first named office, whose family had once been so important in the city.

The second lawyer to take cognizance of Marowe, William Fleetwood, was also a member of the Middle Temple,[10]

---

[1] Frowyk's Prerogative of the King has had a fate similar to the De Pace; it is not even mentioned by Staunford in his Prerogative Regis. Dudley's Tree of the Commonwealth was not printed till 1859.

[2] From October 1554 till his death in September 1558; Foss, Judges.

[3] The year of his death; pt. i, 1573 ed., f. 187 b, mentions 25 October 1556.

[4] Tottell; reprinted in 1573.   [5] App. III, p. 311, note 2, p. 339, note 3.

[6] (1) Confession et auoydance, no. 26, 21 Hen. VII, 21; on the subject of 'addicion' in a recognizance. Identified in printed Year Book as Pasch. 21 Hen. VII, no. 9; Marowe's name does not appear in the printed version.

(2) Garranties, no. 40, 21 Hen. VII, 9, 10. Identified as Hill. 21 Hen. VII, no. 11.

(3) Prescription, no. 36, 21 Hen. VII, 15. Identified as Hill. 21 Hen. VII, no. 24.

(4) Prescription, no. 37, 21 Hen. VII, 16. Identified as Hill. 21 Hen. VII, no. 28, but Marowe's name is not given in the printed version: 'Et or in Banc fut mouve per plusieurs de Serjants . . .'

(5) Tolle, no. 5, 21 Hen. VII, 16. Identified as Hill. 21 Hen. VII, no. 25. The impossibility of Marowe's appearing in Hilary term 1506 shows the error in chronology in the printed Year Books; p. 135, supra.

[7] See references in the Abridgement, passim, to readings not otherwise known. Note also his frequent citations of Frowyk's Prerogative of the King.

[8] Brooke had himself delivered two readings important enough to be printed; on Statute of Limitations, 32 Hen. VIII, c. 2, 1542, printed in 1647; on Magna Carta, c. 16, 1551, printed in 1641; Foss, Judges.

[9] By 1545; ibid.

[10] Minutes of Parliament Middle Temple, index sub nomine. For his career see D.N.B. and H. W. Woolrych, Eminent Serjeants-at-Law, i. 132–69. He gave his single reading in 1563, his double in Lent 1568, and was made serjeant-at-law in 1580. He died in 1594.

doubtless, therefore, an acquaintance of Brooke, and likewise recorder of London, holding the office from 1572 till 1591.[1] He was 'lerned and riche',[2] the possessor of an extraordinarily extensive law library,[3] and a prolific writer on legal subjects;[4] in fact, altogether a picturesque and eminent figure of the Elizabethan age.

Among his legal productions is a treatise written apparently in 1565,[5] of which at least four MS. copies are now extant.[6] Nearly a century later, long after Fleetwood's death, it found its way into print: 'The Office of a Justice of Peace... Written by W. Fleetwood, Esq., sometime Recorder of London

---

[1] Ousted from his office in that year by Coke, according to Woolrych, i. 158; but cf. Beaven, Aldermen, i. 275-6. It is believed that he lived at 'Shelleyes house now Bacon's house' in Foster Lane; at any rate he dated letters 1576-1578 as from Bacon's house; Stow, Survey, ed. Kingsford, i. 304, ii. 340; Turner, *op. cit.*, xii. Stow's actual words seem to imply that Fleetwood's house was merely near Bacon's house; i. 304.

[2] Cf. 'A viewe of the chyfe Reders, double and single and of the chyfe Baresters'; Cal. Inner Temple Records, i. 470-3.

[3] In the great archives (notably the British Museum and in Bishop Moore's collection in U.L.C.), one comes across a surprisingly large number of MSS.—mostly legal—that are said to have been either composed or transcribed by him, or at least to have been in his possession. The latter often bear his full signature or the initials, W. F.; see *supra*, p. 153. The story of Liber Fletwod, still in Guildhall, is well known; Stow, *op. cit.*, i. xxxii, 271, ii. 333; cf. also the reference to his letters (*supra*, note 1). The will of Fleetwood's widow, Marian, dated 25 April 1613, proved 3 November, Aston Sampford, Bucks., contains the following bequest: 'To Sir William my son the books and plate (except a bason & ewer of siluer guilt) which were sometimes my saide late husbandes his father'; 113 Capell, P.C.C.

[4] The list in D.N.B. is by no means complete.

[5] 'This present seventh year of the Queens heighness raygne', f. 78 b, of the first copy listed in note 6, *infra*.

[6] (1) B.M. MS. Hargrave 15, early seventeenth-century hand, ff. 70-80; A treatyse concerninge the authority of Justice of peace; 'per W. F.' on f. 77 b.

(2) B.M. MS. Harl. 72, late sixteenth-century hand, ff. 50-75; A tretice of the Justice of peace. By M. Fletwood but not imprinted. Some confusion of order and repetition; e.g. Forcible Entry out of place at the end.

(3) B.M. Add. MSS. 26749, seventeenth-century hand, ff. 348-74; Justice of peace by Recorder Fleetwood; 'W. Fleetwoode' on f. 367 and f. 374 b.

(4) MS. 9, Eaton Hall, Chester, seventeenth-century hand (sixteenth according to Hist. MSS. Comm. Report), 20 folios (not numbered), Fletewood Justices of Peace. Cf. Hist. MSS. Comm. Report III, App. 212. I am indebted to the courtesy of his grace the Duke of Westminster for permission to examine this copy. A somewhat hasty comparison of these four versions shows them to be practically identical.

... 1658'. The printed edition has been partly brought up to date, but omits some matter included in the MS. versions.[1]

Fleetwood's own words describe his purpose and method : 'I have presumed, as no Instructor, but as a Rememberer, to clothe these things in English Livery, that have been hidden and obscured in scattered torn Pamphlets written and noted by our elders in the French tongue.'[2] Later, he gives a list of authorities for 'him who desireth further knowledge in these things':[3] Fitzherbert, Staunford's 'Pleas of the Crown', Brooke's reading on Magna Carta, the articles of the Coroner,[4] the Capitula Itineris,[5] and the 'Justice of the Peace', that is, the old 'Boke'.[6]

The omission of Marowe from this list is explained by the discovery that the 'scattered torn Pamphlets' in French evidently contained the De Pace. Fleetwood has translated it, condensed it, omitted certain sections, added a little new matter, or an occasional reference,[7] and has substituted 'Chapters' for 'Lectures', thus obliterating all traces of a reading. He often uses language that implies original research on his part. For example : for Marowe's phrase, 'come fut aiugge XXVIImo libro assisarum etc,'[8] Fleetwood writes, 'As I do gather by the Judgement, 27 Libro Ass.'[9] In his preface he explains that since he has written a treatise on the peace of the church and given it to a 'Reverend Father of this realm',[10] he will begin at once with the peace of the land.[11] The gist of his first six chapters corresponds with

---

[1] In some instances, failure to read the MS. copy correctly results in nonsense in print; cf. e. g. Westmoreland for Westminster in the commission; p. 9. Note also that 'Wiccombe', Bucks. (f. 63 of no. 3), Fleetwood's own county, has become 'Wigorn'; p. 13.

[2] Preface to 1658 ed.

[3] Certain details are omitted in the printed copy; ibid. 89-90, but cf. no. 3, supra (the best MS. copy), f. 373.

[4] 27 Lib. Ass., no. 44; cf. p. 54, note 7, supra.

[5] 'Collected and set forth by Edw. I.'   [6] p. 40, supra.

[7] e. g. Pasch. 7 Rich. II, 1658 ed., 38, but of course it may have been in the copy used by Fleetwood.

[8] App. III, p. 332.   [9] 1658 ed., 43.

[10] Preface. It has not yet been identified, though it is possibly contained in MS. Hargrave 429, f. 106 et seq. or in Add. MSS. 25250, f. 91 et seq.

[11] 'And also for that my leisure serveth not presently to discourse upon the same; and likewise for that this my Treatise may not be over tedious to the Reder . . .'; Preface, ut supra.

absolute precision to Marowe's Lectures III–IX,[1] but Fleetwood cuts ruthlessly. Thus, he omits various interpretations of the qualifications of the justices, and writes: 'And such like Cases as these, a good wit without any great study, as they casually chance, may easily decern of'.[2] Of the elaborate disquisition on Forcible Entries he translates very little, and remarks that ' many cunning Questions may arise ... which may easily be decerned by such as be learned in the laws of this Realm...'.[3]

Fleetwood makes more radical changes in the remainder of the De Pace. For Marowe's lectures on Trespasses and Felonies inquirable by justices of the peace[4] he substitutes 'a Brief of the Charge'.[5] He shortens drastically the final lectures, omitting altogether the lecture on Indictments:[6] 'For because the perfection of Indictments consisteth onely in form, and many things therein contained are rather Ceremonial than Material'.[7]

In view of Fleetwood's great collection of MSS., it is evident that he must have had a copy, or several copies, of the De Pace. In fact, it seems certain that he did possess E—the detached lecture on Forcible Entries[8]—but it has not proved possible to determine which of the full texts he owned and utilized. There is evidence pointing to B[9] or C[10]—or to both— but the evidence is by no means conclusive.[11]

---

[1] Covering therefore the authority of the justices out of session. These chapters end with 'Finis Primi Libri, W. Fleetwood', 1658 ed., 60.

[2] *Ibid.* 24; cf. App. III, p. 315. Under the power of a justice to commit his wife to prison until she gives surety to keep the peace, he adds, 'and this is good to controll a shrew'; *op. cit.,* 33.

[3] *Ibid.* 59–60.   [4] App. III, Lect. XI and XII.

[5] *Ut supra,* 72–90.   [6] App. III, Lect. XIII.

[7] *Ut supra,* 91; see p. 207, *supra.* Fleetwood commits the serious error of referring to the precedents in the old Boke as models; *op. cit.,* 91, but see pp. 99–100, *supra.*   [8] p. 153, *supra.*

[9] pp. 149–51. The section missing from A appears as in B, C, and D; App. III, p. 362, note 3, p. 365, note 1.

[10] If we knew that the present 'torn' condition of C went back to 1565, the phrase in Fleetwood's preface would be explained; *supra.* D, with a portion of the last lecture missing, is not possible, since Fleetwood is using a complete Lect. XV; in fact, he adds a brief paragraph. Identification is difficult because of his omission of Lect. XIII containing the test dates.

[11] It is barely possible that he had access to a copy through Henry Ferrers, the antiquarian. The latter apparently came into possession of the Ferrers MSS. at his father's death in August 1564 (Edward Ferrers of Warwickshire and Bucks.; P.R.O., Inq. p. m. Ch. Ser., ii. 141, no. 10),

Fleetwood's thoroughly discreditable appropriation of Marowe's labours imposed on his contemporaries [1] and on later generations.[2]   But it is at least a satisfaction to know that his unscrupulous attempt to make a successful manual out of a scholarly treatise completely failed. Neither the MS. nor printed version ever achieved popularity ; to-day Fleetwood's ' Justice' is but rarely mentioned.

It is pleasant to turn to Lambard and Crompton, both of whom made extensive use of the De Pace,[3] but with full acknowledgement.   Crompton, although printing his revision of Fitzherbert two years later than the first edition of the ' Eirenarcha ',[4] does not seem to owe his knowledge of Marowe to Lambard,[5] but rather to the continuity of the Middle Temple [6] tradition that went back to Sir Robert Brooke. Crompton also refers to his fellow members of the Inn, Brooke,[7] Popham,[8] Fleetwood, &c. : ' Master Fleetewood Recorder de London dit a moy '.[9]   Since Crompton's quotations from the De Pace are from an F version,[10] it is safe to infer that he was using G, included in the Middle Temple volume previously described.[11]

Crompton was not attempting to write an orderly dissertation on the peace, but rather to collect citations from the chief

just a year before the date at which Fleetwood was writing.   For a connexion between Henry Ferrers and Fleetwood, see P.R.O., Inq. p. m., Ch. Ser., ii. v. 238, no. 69, Bucks.   Cf. also p. 142, note 12, p. 147, note 5.

[1] Cf. MS. Hargrave 318, a collection of law rules and maxims, late sixteenth century, f. 136 b, ' Fletwood en son Justice de peace, fo. 5.'

[2] It is usually included in lists of Fleetwood's works ; see his biographies cited p. 210, note 10, *supra*.   It sometimes appears in legal bibliographies ; B.M. Bagford Collection, Harl. 5928, no. 3, a list of Law Books ; Worrall, Bibliotheca Legum, 1782 ed.   In a recent list of books on justices of the peace, Fleetwood is erroneously described as a 'follower' of Lambard and Dalton ; Webb, English Local Government, i, 1906, 295, note 1. Hargrave is a notable exception.   On the margin of his copy (see p. 211, note 6, *supra*) he wrote : ' This treatise is by Marrow, I apprehend '.

[3] pp. 188–9, *supra*.

[4] Crompton, 1583, Lambard, 1581.   The puzzling MS. treatise, Hargrave 429 (p. 108, note 6, and p. 113, note 7) quotes Marowe several times.

[5] But he was almost certainly referring to the Eirenarcha in his preface ; see pp. 40–1.

[6] pp. 157–8, *supra*.   [7] *Op. cit.*, f. 29.   [8] *Ibid.*, f. 22.   [9] *Ibid.*, f. 39.

[10] Cf. e.g. Crompton, f. 6 b, Banke Le Roy, cited from ' Marrow, Lect. 3 '; App. III, p. 302, note 1.

[11] See pp. 157–8, *supra*.   Was the collection perhaps made at Crompton's suggestion and did it belong to him ?

legal authorities under appropriate headings. Thus after an exposition of the commission and the oath,[1] he states the three divisions of the Charge,[2] and then produces practically a digest of the criminal law.[3] He gives similar digests of a long list of topics: justices of the peace, sessions, surety of peace, breach of peace, riot, &c. For felonies and trespasses, he relies on Staunford as his main source,[4] but for many of the other subjects, including Forcible Entry,[5] he quotes Marowe, often using his exact phraseology for several pages.[6] In other words, a considerable portion of Lecture III, and of Lectures VI–X of the De Pace thus found their way into print.[7] But because of Crompton's chaotic arrangement [8] and impossible language,[9] his volume never had a very wide circulation, certainly not among practising justices, and in spite of its mass of information was speedily neglected.[10] Marowe's reputation therefore was not markedly increased through Crompton.

The history of the ' Eirenarcha ' is altogether different. To begin with, one would expect to find a copy of the De Pace among Lambard's MSS. and books, now widely scattered, but once forming one of the notable libraries of the age.[11]

[1] ff. 1–11 b.

[2] f. 11 b; (1) ecclesiastical causes, ff. 11 b–17 b ; (2) felonies by common law, ff. 18–40; felonies by statute, ff. 40–8 b ; (3) divers other things, ff. 48 b–85 b.

[3] He admits that he has included a number of topics with which it is not necessary to charge the jury. ' Et sont mises ensemble la, pur ceo que serront le pluis readyment troues '; f. 11 b.

[4] e.g. ' Murder, Collect in part per Mast. Staunford '; f. 19 b. He occasionally cites Marowe also ; e.g. f. 34, a reference to Lect. XII.

[5] Put under the Charge, f. 58 b, but ' restitution ' appears later, f. 144 b.

[6] ff. 130, 130 b.

[7] For a reference to Lect. XII, see note 4, *supra* ; for Lect. I see Crompton, 64. The latter omits the topics treated in Lect. II, IV, and V ; Lect. XV was wanting in G, the copy that he presumably used.

[8] A thorough alphabetical digest would have been far better.

[9] Cf. e.g. p. 160, *supra.*

[10] Although it went through a number of editions ; see App. I, Series IV ; also 1606, 1617.

[11] It would be well worth while to try to reconstruct the list of the works belonging to so distinguished a scholar and antiquarian. For a brief account of his writings and of his library, see D.N.B. and J. Nichols, Bib. Top. Brit., i, Kent, 493–529. Some of the MSS. are now at Bradbourne Hall, Sevenoaks, Kent, in the possession of Mr. Gore Lambarde. I am indebted to the latter's cousin, Colonel F. Lambarde, for the information that there is no Marowe MS. there. There are many Lambard MSS. among the Cottonian and Lansdowne MSS., B.M.

Unfortunately, Lambard's copy has not been identified; it is possible that he once owned D,[1] possible that he was also familiar with a copy not now extant,[2] perhaps even the missing original.[3]

Whatever version he used, his preface [4] and his introductory paragraph [5] fully prepare one for the fact of his peculiar indebtedness to Marowe—an indebtedness that is apparent both in form and in matter. Book I of the 1581 edition begins with the history of the office, the distinction between conservator and justice, method of appointment, &c. It continues with an analysis of the authority of justices exercised out of session—what any one justice can do, what any two justices can do, &c.—and includes therefore surety of peace, riot, Forcible Entry, &c.

Book II begins with a description of the sessions and then gives the oath and the Charge. It continues with an account of the form of indictments, and of process, and concludes with the Rewards and Punishments due to justices of the peace.[6]

The resemblance to the outline of the De Pace [7] is clear. But of far greater significance is Lambard's use of its content. Not only does the material from Marowe far exceed that taken from any other one source,[8] but it actually constitutes a very large proportion of the ' Eirenarcha ' as a whole.

The opening pages are taken almost bodily from Lectures

---

[1] The chief evidence is that Lambard, 464, gives the test date, 10 March, as in D; see App. III, p. 387, note 1. Further, the entry on the margin of D in a hand later than the rest of the MS., '1576, Emanuel', suggests that Lambard secured the MS. just before he compiled the Eirenarcha. In his dedication to Chancellor Bromley in the 1581 ed., Lambard states that he began to work on the treatise only after Bromley had appointed him justice of the peace for Kent, i. e. in 1579. The implication is that the preliminary sketch was not begun till then either; see p. 113, note 7.

[2] There is some evidence pointing to the use of an F version, perhaps F itself; cf. Eirenarcha, 79, with App. III, p. 324, note 5.

[3] It is probable, though not certain, that Lambard is citing a copy in which the various portions detached from Lect. X appear in their proper place; see p. 165, *supra*, App. III, p. 368, note 1; Eirenarcha, 367–78. For the problem of the ' Book cases ', quoted along with Marowe by both Crompton and Lambard, see pp. 188–9, *supra*.

[4] p. 40, *supra*.   [5] p. 114, *supra*.

[6] By the 1588 edition, Book I has been broken up into three books, and Book II has thus become Book IV.   [7] See ch. vi (2), *supra*.

[8] Parallel, therefore, to Crompton's use of Staunford.

III and IV; there are voluminous quotations from Lectures VI–X, and XIII, a considerable amount of material from Lectures XIV and XV,[1] and a little from Lectures XI and XII.[2] Of these, Lecture VIII on Riots and Lecture IX on Forcible Entry [3] are often cited word by word for a number of pages, and evidently commanded Lambard's admiration. After printing in full Marowe's elaborate exposition on the issuing of certificates in connexion with Riots, Lambard adds: 'These speculations of M. Marrowes reading are like enough to fall in practise, and therefore I thought it not amisse to acquaint the reader beforehand with some of them'.[4] Likewise, after citing Marowe's opinion on the effect of three years' continuous possession in cases of Forcible Entry, he writes: 'Which opinion I take to be very reasonable, not generally understoode.'[5]

Occasionally, he differs from Marowe; as for example in the matter of special justices.[6] It is interesting to find that shortly after Marowe's death, chief justice Fineux gave a judgement contrary to Marowe's view,[7] but that it was deemed necessary in the reign of Henry VIII to enact legislation in confirmation of the legal opinion expressed in this judgement.[8] The differences between Marowe and Lambard are usually explained either by the interval of time between the De Pace and the 'Eirenarcha', with consequent changes in the law or in legal practice;[9] or by Lambard's failure to understand Marowe, perhaps because of a defective text.[10]

---

[1] Like Crompton, he makes but little use of Lect. I and II (just one reference to the former), and apparently none of Lect. V, but he uses far more of the Lectures XI–XV than does Crompton.

[2] Felonies and trespasses of course appear in the Charge. In discussing them Lambard is apt to cite 'book cases' directly and authorities subsequent to Marowe.

[3] In striking contrast to Fleetwood; *supra*, p. 213.   [4] 322, 1602 ed.

[5] *Ibid.* 151.   [6] *Ibid.* 23–4; cf. App. III, p. 309.

[7] Year Book Mich. 20 Hen. VII, no. 17, but in reality Mich. 21 Hen. VII; see p. 135, note 3, *supra*.   [8] Statute 27 Hen. VIII, c. 24.

[9] e. g. Appeals, *Precii* and *ad Valenciam*, *supra*, pp. 200–3, 207. For the Clerk of the Peace and the Custos Rotulorum, cf. Lambard, 377, with App. III, p. 363, and *supra*, pp. 102–4. Contrary to the custom in Lambard's day, *op. cit.*, 519, Marowe holds that justices cannot try a felon on the same day that the jury is summoned; App. III, p. 409. His opinion is confirmed by a famous Warwickshire case, undoubtedly known to him; Rot. Parl., vi. 173–4, 17 Edw. IV.

[10] Thus Lambard, 519, writes that Marowe 'saith that they can*not*

Only a thorough examination of the two treatises side by side reveals the full extent to which the De Pace was the basis of the 'Eirenarcha'. It is certainly only just to Marowe to remember that quotations from his reading form a very large part of the later treatise. On the other hand, it is due to Lambard to point out that it was his shrewdness that produced a volume which combined sound scholarship with practical common sense and which therefore met the needs of the country gentleman on the commission.

The enormous success of the 'Eirenarcha' was both immediate and permanent. For a number of years it was the popular manual,[1] universally used. When lapse of time necessitated new handbooks, their writers refer in their prefaces to Fitzherbert, Crompton, and others, but actually incorporate the 'Eirenarcha' into their text as far as possible. Lambard, therefore, becomes the basis for the later seventeenth-century treatises of which Michael Dalton's 'Countrey Ivstice' was the most famous.[2]   In the next century, the process is repeated ; Dalton in turn becomes the basis for Burn's 'Justice of the Peace ',[3] to name merely the most conspicuous example.

Lambard has also received adequate notice from historians of the law. Blackstone's paragraph is typical : in his section on justices of the peace he recommends to the student 'the perusal of Mr. Lambard's Eirenarcha, and Dr. Burn's justice of the peace ; where in he will find everything relative to this subject, both in ancient and modern practice, collected with great care and accuracy, and disposed in a most clear and judicious method '.[4]   It is scarcely necessary to cite further illustrations of the fame of the 'Eirenarcha',[5] except to add

award the writ, *Venire facias tot matronas* '; whereas all the texts that I have examined omit the 'not'; App. III, p. 409.   For another instance of inaccurate citation of Marowe, cf. Lambard, 126, and App. III, p. 337, on the authority of a justice of the peace or a constable to break open a house.

[1] Reprinted in 1602, 1607, 1610 (the latest edition that was brought up to date), 1614, 1617.   For earlier editions, cf. App. I, Series III.

[2] 1618.   A full list is given in Webb, *op. cit.*, i. 295, note 1, and a brief bibliography is appended to Seventeenth Century Life in the Country Parish, by E. Trotter, 1919.

[3] The Justice of the Peace, and Parish Officer, 2 vols. 1755, by Richard Burn.   [4] Commentaries, 1803 ed., i. 354.

[5] Under justices of the peace, cf. e. g. Holdsworth, *op. cit.*, i, Reeves, *op. cit., passim.*   The latter also quotes Lambard under criminal law

that the recent monograph on 'The Office of the Justice of the Peace' is based largely on it.[1]

With ·our knowledge of the part played by Marowe's treatise in the composition of the 'Eirenarcha' and of Lambard's generous appreciation so frequently expressed, it seems almost incredible that both Marowe and the De Pace should so soon be lost in obscurity for the second time.[2] The slight recognition that Marowe received at the end of the sixteenth and in the beginning of the seventeenth centuries was mainly through the medium of the 'Eirenarcha'. The earliest references that have come to my attention are in Fraunce, 'The Lawiers Logike',[3] and in Cowell, 'The Interpreter'.[4] Marowe is cited once by Coke [5] and twice in the seventeenth-century editions of Fitzherbert's 'Novel Natura Brevium'.[6] But the later compilers of manuals for justices of the peace previously mentioned, even when they make full use of Lambard and when they also refer in their prefaces to many sixteenth-century legal writers, rarely mention Marowe. The most notable examples are those of Dalton and Burn. Amidst innumerable citations of authorities, Dalton refers to Marowe about half a dozen times,[7] Burn but once.[8] This tradition has

temp. Elizabeth ; e.g. iii. 794. In Stephen, Hist. Crim. Law, ii. 205, the Eirenarcha is called a 'mere book of practice' although 'a particularly good one', and in Webb, *loc. cit.*, it is grouped with 'unscientific (usually alphabetic) statements of the law prepared for the assistance of the Justices and their clerks'. But such derogatory references are rare.

[1] By C. A. Beard.

[2] Not so complete an obscurity as previous to the publication of Brooke's Abridgement.

[3] Abraham Fraunce, 1588, 44. The quotation is through the medium of Lambard.

[4] John Cowell, 1607 ed. : 'Marrow was a lawyer of great accompt, that liued in Henry the seventh his daies, whose learned readings are extant, but not in print, Lamb. Eiren., li. pri. cap. 1'.

[5] On Littleton, s. 153.　　[6] App. III, p. 290, note 8, p. 317, note 2.

[7] Marowe is not mentioned in Dalton's list of authorities; but cf. e.g. Ryots, p. 89, with a marginal reference to 'Marr. Lect. 8. Crompt. 63'.

[8] The only reference that I noted is as follows : 'Mr. Lambard puts a case from Mr. Marrow'; ii. 384. In his preface, xiii, he writes : 'The books of authority concerning the office of a justice of the peace, are those of Fitzherbert, Crompton, Lambard, and Dalton'; when Dalton has adopted these three 'the author hath thought it sufficient to cite Dalton's single authority'.

In the Compleat Justice, 1661, and in the Compleat Guide for Justices of peace, by J. Bond, 2 pts., 1696, there are many references to all the been more than maintained by the author of the twentieth-century monograph.[1] In spite of his reliance on Lambard, he completely ignores Marowe. The latter has, however, received somewhat more attention from historians of law. Many of them give a few sentences to the De Pace ; for example, Sir Roger Owen,[2] Reeves,[3] and more recently Maitland.[4] Marowe is also duly noticed by the specialist on law readings and by the maker of legal bibliographies,[5] and is mentioned, although very briefly, in works on serjeants-at-law.[6]

Undoubtedly other scattered references to Marowe in legal literature will be discovered in the future. But on the whole it remains true that the De Pace had no public recognition till three-quarters of a century after Marowe's death, and that within the next half century it was nearly forgotten. The reasons for the later neglect are not easy to explain. They may have been connected with the disrepute which law readings had acquired by the seventeenth century,[7] and also with the

above and to Brooke, Coke, Staunford, &c., but I have discovered only one mention of Marowe (Bond, pt. 1, 258). Dutton is a notable exception ; see his preface to Justice of the Peace for Ireland, 2nd ed., Dublin, 1727.

[1] See introduction, p. 1, note 2, *supra*, and pp. 218-19.

[2] His treatise cited p. 154, note 1, was apparently never printed. It is referred to by D. Barrington, Observations on Statutes, 116.

[3] *Op. cit.*, Finlason ed., 1869, iii. (1st ed. 1783-7), 198 : 'There are no law treatises of this reign [Hen. VII] in print. But there is a famous book, said to be still in manuscript, written by Marrow, on the office of a justice of the peace ; a work which has been quoted by later writers, such as Fitzherbert and Lambard, with great commendation, and seems to have been followed by them on the same subject.' Reeves makes the usual error as to Fitzherbert's knowledge of Marowe ; see p. 109, note 9, *supra*.

[4] Art. in Pol. Sc. Quarterly for 1889, reprinted in Collected Papers, vol. ii, p. 58 : 'And toward the end of our period, we get some "readings" which should be published such as Marrowe's Reading on Justices of the Peace, a work which Fitzherbert and Lambard treated as of high authority.' It is unfortunate that the error as to Fitzherbert should be perpetuated.

[5] p. 147, note 1, *supra*. Rayner (cited *ibid.*) includes Marowe among 'the first Characters of the Age, in the Profession, for Knowledge and Judgment'.

[6] Dugdale, Foss, &c., Pulling, Order of the Coif, reprinted in 1897 ; but Woolrych, in his Eminent Serjeants, omits him although he includes Fleetwood. For Dugdale's account of Marowe in the Antiquities of Warwickshire, see ch. v, *supra, passim*.

[7] Coke on Littleton, s. 481 : 'But now Readings having lost the said former Qualities, have lost also their former Authorities ; for now the Cases are long, obscure and intricate, full of new Conceits, like rather to Riddles

general indifference on the subject of the early development of justices of the peace.[1]

To this study of the De Pace, the opening portion of Lambard's epilogue is a suitable ending, especially since it is connected with a curious episode in relation to Marowe: 'Thus haue I (by the fauour of God) brought this treatise to an ende: wherein if many things haue escaped me vnseen, I do not greatly maruaile, when I looke backe & behold the variety & multitude of the matter that I haue passed through: and it shall not bee harde for him that meeteth with such estrais to take and lodge them in their right titles here.

Againe, if I shall bee thought to haue heaped vp too many conceites (borrowed out of M. Marrowe's reading) I make answere, that I haue omitted many, and haue made the best choise that I could.'[2]

In the introduction to their standard work on English Local Government, the authors quote these paragraphs *in toto* except that they leave out the words within brackets.[3] This omission of Marowe's name is a typical example of the process that has so effectively concealed his identity and the very fact of the existence of his treatise.[4]

---

than Lectures, which when they are opened, they vanish away like Smoak, and the Readers are like to Lapwings who seem to be nearest their Nests when they are farthest away from them, and all their Study is to find nice Evasions out of the Statute.' For the first part of this quotation, see *supra*, p. 167, note 2. Cf. also F. Bacon, Works, ed. J. Spedding, vii, in introduction to reading on Uses, 395-6; he plans to revive the ancient 'form of reading' (like Mr. 'Frowickes') and 'to open the law upon doubts, and not to open doubts upon the law'.

[1] See Introduction, *supra*.   [2] 1602 ed., 589.

[3] Asterisks are used to indicate the omission; S. and B. Webb, i. xiii–xiv.

[4] See ch. v, *supra*, pp. 143-4.

CONCLUSION

It has long been a commonplace of historians that there are relatively few original sources for the period of Henry VII;[1] 'a dreary life and a dreary reign' is the judgement of his latest biographer.[2] But one of the most significant aspects of the reign is the development of law and of administrative and legislative reforms. Even Bacon, with his deep scorn for Dudley and Empson, asserts that 'justice was well administered . . . save where the King was party'.[3] It is by no means the whole truth to conclude that law was 'mainly an instrument of oppression' and that the king's peace was a 'reign of riot'.[4] That there is a wealth of legal material, much of it in MS. and still unused, is apparent from the preceding study of Marowe and his reading. Similar studies of the group of lawyers to which he belonged may well throw light on a king who has been noted for his partiality to the legal profession[5] and for his interest in the Inns of Court.[6]

Moreover, in spite of constantly increasing work by modern scholars[7] on England in the fifteenth century, it still remains,

[1] Memorials of Reign of Henry VII, ed. J. Gairdner, Rolls Series, preface: 'in no period of English annals are the sources of history so scanty as in the time of Henry VII'; Coke, Third Report, ed. G. Wilson, 1793, xv, note: '. . . the policy of the reign being to leave as few memorials to posterity as possible'. Professor Pollard, in his preface to The Reign of Henry VII from Contemporary Sources, has recently called attention to the danger of exaggerating this paucity.

[2] Temperley, Henry VII, 374.

[3] Life of Henry VII, ed. G. R. Lumby, 213.

[4] Professor Pollard, *ut supra*.

[5] Bacon, *op. cit.*, 217: 'He kept a strait hand on his nobility, and chose rather to advance clergy and lawyers'.

[6] Cal. Inner Temple Records, i. xxxvi.

[7] Cf. e. g. Kingsford, English Historical Literature in the Fifteenth Century, or the work of Professor Pollard, cited *supra*. Important researches on the reign of Edw. IV are being carried on by several scholars, notably Miss Cora Scofield. The recent publication of Miss Thornley's source book is further proof of the growing interest in the period; see Introduction, p. 1, note 2, *supra*.

as a whole, a comparatively unexplored period. Looked upon therefore as a contribution to our knowledge of an important transition age, further information on the justices of the peace ought to have value. Their enforcement of the criminal law at the time when the old local courts were losing their powers, their responsibilities for the labour legislation after the abolition of the justices of labourers, the growth of their jurisdiction in connexion with the Great Revolt—all these special aspects of their office merit investigation in relation to the whole subject of methods of administration.

Finally, there is always the problem of the contrast in the fifteenth century between the ideals of law and justice expounded by lawyers, like Fortescue and Littleton, or Frowyk and Marowe, and the actual anarchy in Quarter Sessions revealed by contemporary documents such as the Paston Letters. It will be the task of some future scholar to determine where the truth lies.

APPENDIX I

A BIBLIOGRAPHY OF PRINTED TREATISES FOR JUSTICES OF THE PEACE, 1506–1599.[1]

NOTE OF EXPLANATION

For Series III and Series IV I have used the complete sets in the library of the Harvard Law School. Since copies of the various editions are so numerous as to be easily accessible in many places, it has not seemed necessary to specify the other libraries that contain them. The situation is, however, very different in regard to the editions of Series I and Series II, many of which are exceedingly rare. The following plan has been adopted. Except in the case of a unique copy, or of a copy unique in England or in America—when it has been essential to name the collection possessing it—only the three most important libraries in England have been indicated, namely, the British Museum (B.M.[2]), the Bodleian (Bodl.), and University Library, Cambridge (U.L.C.), and in America, only the library of the Harvard Law School, Cambridge, (H.L.S.) An * shows that no actual copy nor any part thereof has been discovered and that the edition is at present known only from bibliographical descriptions.

The purpose in printing the list is twofold :

(1) To show .as clearly as possible the relation between the fifty-seven editions and issues of the sixteenth-century printed treatises from the point of view of content, author, publisher, and date of printing.

(2) To facilitate identification of a given copy, in the hope that investigations made by other scholars may lead to the detection of still more editions.

After considerable hesitation I have come to the conclusion that it is sufficient here to reproduce the title-page (whenever it exists) and to give from the colophon (whenever possible) the name of the printer and date of printing. Brackets [ ] around the name or date show that they have been determined from evidence other than title-page and colophon. It remains, therefore, for the bibliographer of expert professional knowledge (to which I can make no claim) to print a list

---

[1] For the extent of my investigation, see p. 6, *supra*, notes 3 and 4.
[2] This abbreviation and the following are used throughout.

which shall include technical details—signatures, foliation, size of the volume, watermarks, character of type, devices and street addresses of the printers. These details have been referred to in the notes to this Bibliography and in Chapter I only when they have seemed essential to the discussion of certain complicated problems, such as the chronological sequence of undated editions, &c.

It is a pleasure to express my appreciation of the invaluable help derived from the 'Handlists of Books printed by London Printers, 1501–1556', published by the Bibliographical Society in 1913. The errors that I have noted in the lists there given are due in part to the changed distribution of copies since the printing of the volume,[1] and in part to imperfect knowledge of the contents of the tracts here discussed, especially important in the differentiation of Series I from Series II.

SERIES I

The boke of Justyces of peas.

Anonymous.

(*Stonyhurst.*)

(1) The boke of[2] Justices of peas the charge with all the processe of the cessions warrantes supersedias & all that longeth, to ony Justyce to make endytementes of haute treason petyt treason felonyes appeles trespas vpon Statutes trespas contra Regis pacem Nocumentis with dyuers thynges more as it appereth in the Kalendar of the same boke.

Col.: Richard Pynson. [1506?]

(*Hazlitt, Collections and Notes*, 1867–76, 243.)

(2) * The boke of Justyces of peas the charge with all the processe of the cessyons warrantes & all that longeth to any Justyce to make endytementes of haute treason petyt treason felonyes appeles . . . Statutes trespas contra Regis pacem Nocumentis with dyuers thynges more as it appereth in the Kalender of the saide boke.

Col.: Wynkyn de Worde. 1506.

(*Bodl., B.M.*)

(3) The Justyces of Paes.

The boke of iustyces of peas the charge with all the processe of the cessyons warrantes supersedias and all that longeth to ony Justyce to make endytementes of haute treason petyt treason felonyes appeles

---

[1] The 'Private Library' referred to in the Handlists proves often to be that of the late Mr. George Dunn, which is now in the possession of the Harvard Law School; see p. 6, *supra*, note 4.   [2] *For* in the Handlists.

Q

trespas vpon statutes trespas contra Regis pacem Nocumentis with dyvers thynges more as it appereth in the Kalender of the same boke.

Col. : Wynkyn de Worde. 1510.

(Ames, ed. Herbert, 152–3.)

(4) * The boke of Justyces of peas, the charge, with all the processe of the cessyons, warrantes, supersedias, and all that longeth to ony iustyce to make endytementis of haute treson, petyte treson, felonies, appelles, trespas vpon Statutes, trespas contra regis pacem Nocumentis, with dyuers thyngs more as it appereth in the Calendar of the same boke.

Col. : Wynkyn de Worde. 1515.

(Bodl., U.L.C. (title-page imperfect).)

(5¹) The Justices of peas.

The boke of iustyces of peas the charge with all the processe of the cessyons warrantes supersedias and all that longeth to ony Justyce to make endytementes of haute treason petyt treason felonyes appeles trespas vpon statutes trespas contra Regis pacem Nocumentis with dyuers thynges more as it appereth in the kalender of the same boke.

Col.: Robert Coplande. 1515.

(John Rylands Library.)

(6) The Justyces of Peas.

The boke of iustyces of peas the charge with all the processe of the cessyons, warrantes supersedias and all that longeth to ony Justyce to make endytementes of haute treason petyt treason felonyes appeles trespas vpon Statutes trespas contra Regis pacem Nocumentis with dyuers thynges more as it apperyth in the Kalender of the same boke.

Col.: John Skot. 3 October 1521.

(U.L.C.)

(7) The boke of Justices of peas the charge with all the proces of the cessions warrantes supersedias and all that longeth to any Justice to make enditementes of haute treason, petit treason felonyes appeles trespas vpon statutes trespas contra Regis pacem Nocumentis with diuers thynges more as it appereth in the kalender of the same boke.

Col.: Rychard Pynson. 1521.

(Bodl., B.M.)

(8) The boke of² the Justyce of peas the charge with all the proces of

¹ Cf. MS. Lansdowne 825 (a miscellaneous collection), f. 70, for description of this volume, its title-page, and colophon.
² *For* in the Handlists.

the cessyons neuly correctyd and amendyd with dyuers new addycyons put to the same.

No col.[1]   [John Rastell, 1527–1530?]

(*Bodl., Douce Add. 142*, p. 207 (*col. only*). *Ames, ed. Herbert*, 387.)

(9) The boke of iustices of peas, the charge with all the proces of the cessions, warrantes, supersedias, and all that longeth to any iustice to make inditementes of haute treason, petit treason, felonyes, appelles, trespas vpon statutes, trespas contra regis pacem, nocumentis, with diuers thynges more, as it appeareth in the kalender of the same boke.

Col.: Robert Redman.   1527.

(*Bodl., Douce Add. 142*, p. 207 (*title-page only*). *Ames, ed. Herbert*, 387.)

(10[2]) The boke of Justices of peas, the charge with all the proces of the cessions warrantes supersedias and all that longeth to any iustice to make enditementes of haute treason petit treason felonyes appelles trespas vpon statutes trespas contra Regis pacem Nocumentis with diuers thingis more as it appereth in the kalender of the same boke.

Col.: Robert Redman.   [1527–1529?]

(*H.L.S., U.L.C.* (*no title-page*).)

(11) The boke of iustices of peace, the charge, with all the processe of the cessions, warrantes, supersedias, and all that longeth to any Justice to make endytementes of haute treason, petit treason, felonyes, appelles, trespas vpon statutes, trespas contra regis pacem Nocumentis, with dyuers thynges more, as it appereth in the Kalender of the same boke.

Col.: Robert Redman.   [1530–1531?][3]

---

[1] The Museum copy was printed separately, but was meant to form one volume with the Carta Feodi, Hundred Court, Returna Brevium, Ordinance of the Exchequer and Court Baron, the last with colophon; Ames, ed. Herbert, 344. There are four of these separate parts in the Museum, including the colophon part; the volume in the Bodleian contains the six parts but lacks the colophon.

[2] This title-page does not belong to nos. 11, 12, or 16. Mr. E. G. Duff is inclined to connect it with the 1527 colophon; see no. 9. But if Ames's transcript of the 1527 title-page is accurate the Douce title-page is not identical with it, and is more probably that of the missing undated edition mentioned by Ames after his account of the 1527 edition: ‘Again without date’. Nos. 9 and 10 are treated as independent by McKerrow in his Printers’ and Publishers’ Devices, no. 81.

[3] The title-page is a perfect hour-glass in form; Ames, ed. Herbert, 399, 1786. ‘1530’ in a fairly late hand is inscribed in the H.L.S. copy.

(Bodl., H.L.S. (col. lacking).)

(12 [1]) The boke of Justices of peas: the charge with all the proces of the cessyons, warrantes, supersedias, and all that longeth to any Justyce to make enditementes of, haute treason, petit treason, felonyes, appelles trespas vpon statutes, trespas contra Regis pacem, Nocumentis, with diuers thynges more as it appereth in the Kalender of the same boke.

    Col.: Robert Redman. [1533?]

(Bodl., B.M., H.L.S.)

(13 [2]) Natura breuium.
    The olde tenures.
    Lyttylton tenures.
    The new talys.
    The articles vppon the new talys.
    Diuersyte of courtes.
    Justyce of peace.
    The chartuary.
    Court baron.
    Court of hundrede.
    Returna breuium.
    The ordynaunce for takynge of fees in the Escheker.
    And fyrste a table to all these XII bokes.
      Col.: W. Rastell. 1534.

(Corpus Christi College, Oxford (imperfect), H.L.S. (imperfect).)

(14 [3]) The same.
      Col.: W. Rastell. 1534.

(U.L.C. (fragment only [4]). Ames, ed. Herbert, 1787.)

(15) The Boke for a Justyce of peace neuer so well & diligently set forth.
      No col. but joined by signatures to
      Modus tenendi curiam Baronis.
      Col.: Thomas Berthelet. 1536.

---

[1] There is a copy in Gray's Inn, omitted from the Handlists. Of Redman's four undated editions, nos. 10, 11, 12, and 16, the Handlists give only two.

[2] The Handlists do not make clear that the *Justyce of Peace* is included in both nos. 13 and 14.

[3] Merely set up differently from no. 13. A few of the titles are, however, given in Latin instead of in English; e.g. Novae Narrationes.

[4] The Handlists refer merely to Ames, ed. Herbert (probably to p. 425 instead of to p. 1787), and give the usually accepted date, 1534.

(H.L.S.)

(16) The Boke for A Justyce of peace neuer so wel and dylygently set forthe.

No col. Title-page : Robert Redman. [1538 ?]

(B.M., H.L.S. (two copies).)

(17 [1]) The Boke for a Ivstice of peace, the Boke that teacheth to kepe a courte baron, or a lete. The boke teaching to kepe a courte hundred. The boke called Returna breuium. The boke called Carta feodi, conteyning the forme of dedes, releasses, indentures, obligations, acquytaunces, letters of atturney, letters of permutation, testamentes, and other thynges. The boke of thordynaunce to be obserued by the officers of the kynges Escheker, for fees takynge. A boke conteynynge those statutes at lengthe, whych Justices of peace, mayres, sheryffes, baylyffes, constables, and other offycers, were of late commaunded by the kynges maiestie, to put in execution.[2]

Col. : Thomas Berthelet. 1539.

(Bodl., B.M., U.L.C., H.L.S.)

(18) The Contentes of this boke. Fyrste the boke for a Justice of peace. The boke that teacheth to kepe a court Baron, or a lete. The boke teaching to kepe a court hundred. The boke called returna breuium. The boke called Carta feodi, conteining the forme of dedes, releasses, indentures, obligations, acquytaunces, letters of atturney, letters of permutation, testamentes, and other thynges. And the boke of the ordinance to be obserued by the officers of the kynges Escheker, for fees takyng.[3]

Col. : Thomas Berthelet. 1544.

(B.M.)

(19) The Boke for A Justyce of Peace neuer so well and dylygently set forthe.

No col. Title-page : William Middilton. [1544 ?]

(H.L.S.)

(20 [4]) The Boke for A Justyce of peace neuer so well and diligently set forthe.

No col. Title-page : Nicholas Hyll. 1546.

---

[1] The Handlists refer merely to Hazlitt, vii. 211.

[2] In spite of the title-page, the tracts are printed separately with their own colophons and are then bound together.

[3] *Ut supra*, note 2.   [4] Omitted in the Handlists.

(*Ames, ed. Herbert,* 706.)

(21 [1]) * The Boke for a iustyce of peace neuer so well and diligently set forth.

>Col.: Henry Smythe. 1546.

(*B.M.*)

(22 [2]) The Boke for A Justyce of peace neuer so well and diligently set forthe.

>No col. Title-page: Robert Toye. 1546.

(*B.M.*)

(23 [3]) The Boke for A Justyce of peace neuer so well and diligently set forthe.

>No col. Title-page: John Waley. 1546.

(*H.L.S.*)

(24 [4]) The Contentes of this Boke. Fyrst the booke for a Justyce of peace. The boke that teacheth to kepe a courte Baron, or a lete. The boke teachynge to kepe a courte hundred. The boke called returna Breuium. The boke called Carta feodi, conteynynge the forme of dedes, releasses, Indentures, obligations, acquitaunces, letters of atturney, letter of permutacion, testamentes, and other thynges. And the boke of the ordynaunce to be obserued by the offycers of the Kynges Escheker for fees takynge.[5]

>Col.: William Powell. 1550.

(*B.M., H.L.S.*)

(25 [6]) The Contentes of this Boke. Fyrst the booke for a Justice of peace. The boke that teacheth to kepe a courte Baron, or a lete. The boke teachynge to kepe a courte hundred. The boke called returna Breuium. The boke called Carta feodi, conteynynge the forme of dedes, releasses, Indentures, obligacions, acquitaunces, letters of atturney, letter of permutacion, testamentes, and other thynges. And the boke of the ordinaunce to be obserued by the offycers of the Kynges Escheker for fees takynge. Wherevnto is added the boke called Articuli ad narrationes nouas, & the diuersitie of courts.

>Col.: Richard Tottle. 13 May 1556.[7]

---

[1] Omitted in the Handlists.

[2] Toye is omitted altogether in the Handlists; but cf. Duff, A Century of the English Book Trade, 158.

[3] Waley is likewise omitted; but cf. *ibid.* 164.

[4] The Handlists refer merely to the ' Merly sale'.

[5] *Ut supra*, p. 229, note 2.   [6] Omitted in the Handlists.

[7] Like no. 8 and even more like nos. 13 and 14, this volume is meant to

(B.M., H.L.S.)

(26) The Contentes of this Boke. Fyrst the booke for a Justice of peace. The boke that teacheth to kepe a courte Baron, or a lete. The boke teachinge to kepe a courte hundred. The boke called returna Breuium. The boke called Carta feodi, conteynynge the forme of dedes, releases, Indentures, obligacions, acquitaunces, letters of atturney, letter of permutacion, testamentes, and other thynges. And the boke of the ordinaunce to be obserued by the offycers of the Kynges Escheker for fees takynge.

Col. : Fletestrete, Richard Tottil.[1]   13 May 1559.

(Bodl., H.L.S.)

(27) The Contentes of this booke. Fyrste the Booke for a Iustice of peace, etc. (as in no. 26 with only slight variations in spelling).

Col. : Fletestreete, Richard Tottil. 13 May 1559.

(B.M.)

(28) The Contentes of this booke. Fyrste the booke for a Iustice of peace, etc. (as in no. 26, with only slight variations in spelling).

Col. : Rycharde Tottel. 1569.

(Inner Temple.)

(29) No title-page—but the same contents as in no. 26.

Col. : Rycharde Tottyl. 1569.

(Bodl., B.M., H.L.S.)

(30) The Contentes of this booke. First the booke for a Justice of peace, etc. (as in no. 26, with only slight variations in spelling).

Col. : Richarde Tottyl. 1574.

(B.M., H.L.S.)

(31) The Avcthoritie of al Iustices of peace, with diuers warrants, presentments, and indictments there unto annexed. Whereunto is added a verie perfect fourme for kepinge of Court leetes, and Court barons, newly set foorth by Iohn Kitchin of Graies Inne an Apprentice of the lawe, with many booke cases concerninge the same. Also the booke called Noue additiones. The booke for keepinge of Court hundredes. And the booke called Returna breuium. With severall Tables for the ready findinge of any thinge contained in the same.

Anno domini 1580.

Col. : Richard Tottell. 16 Feb. 1579 (1580 [2]).

be a whole, and has a table at the end as well as the colophon. The same statement applies to all subsequent editions.

[1] A defective 't' makes the name look like 'Toteil'.

[2] The signatures run A–L, 8, including Kitchin's preface (dated 10 April 1580 like the colophon of no. 32) and table to his Court Leet: the latter then begins with signature B 1 and new Arabic foliation.

(*C.H.L.*)

(32) The aucthoritie of al Iustices of peace, with diuers warrants, presentments, and endictments there-unto annexed.

Where unto is added a verie perfect fourme for kepinge of Court leetes, and Court barons, newly set foorth by Iohn Kitchin of Graies Inne an Apprentice of the lawe, with many booke cases concerninge the same. Also the booke called Noue additiones. The booke for keepinge of Court hundredes. And the booke called Returna breuium. With several tables for the ready findinge of any thinge contained in the same.

Anno domini 1580.

Col.: Richard Tottell. 10 April 1580.

SERIES II

Loffice et auctoryte des Justyces de peas.

By Sir Anthony Fitzherbert.
Translated into English as
The newe Boke of Justices of the Peas.
(*Bodl., B.M., H.L.S.*)

(1) Loffice et auctoryte des Justyces de peas compyle et extrayte hors des auncient liures si bien del comen ley come dez estatutes oue moultes auters choses necessaries a scauoir nouelment imprime. 1538.

Col.: Robert Redman. n. d.

(*Bodl., B.M., U.L.C., H.L.S.*[1] (*no title-page*).)

(2[2]) The newe Boke of Justices of the peas by A. F. K. lately translated out of Frenche into Englyshe.

The yere of our Lord God M.D. XXXVIII, The xxix day of Decembre.

Col.: Robert Redman. n. d.

(*H.L.S., two copies*[3] (*the second lacks title-page and colophon*).)

(3[4]) The newe Boke of Justices of the peas by A. F. K. lately translated out of Frenche into Englyshe.

The yere of our Lord God M.D. XXXVIII, The xxix day of Decembre.

Col.: Robert Redman. n. d.

---

[1] Catalogued as D. Tr. 14. 2.
[2] The Handlists mention only the Bodleian copy, omit the author's name, and give a title used previously for the 1527 edition of the Boke. For the strange entry in the B.M. catalogue see p. 9, *supra*, note I.
[3] Catalogued as D. Tr. 14. 1 ; D. Tr. 26. 1.
[4] The Handlists do not distinguish between nos. 2 and 3. There is a fragment of one of them in U.L.C., no. 6683, but I am unable to say of which.

(B.M. title-page only, Bagford Collection, Harl. 5993, no. 27.)

(4 [1]) The Newe Boke of Justices of peas made by Anthony Fitzherbard Judge lately translated out of Frenche into Englysshe. The yere
of our Lorde God M.D.X.L.

The xxix daye of December.

(Robert Redman's woodcut.)

(Worrall, 1782 ed., 62.)

(5 [2]) * [The Newe Booke of Justyces of Peas.

Made by Anthony Fitzherbard Judge, lately translated out of Frenche
into Englyshe.

The yere of our Lord God MDXLI.

Col.: 31 Jan. 1541.

Elizabeth Pykeringe].[3]

(B.M., Bodl. (two copies, one imperfect), U.L.C., H.L.S.)

(6 [4]) The Newe Booke of Justyces of Peas made by Anthony Fitzherbard Judge, lately translated out of Frenche into Englyshe.

The yere of our Lord God MDXLI.

Col. : Thomas Petyt.   1541.

(B.M., H.L.S.)

(7 [5]) The New Booke of Justices of Peace, made by Anthony Fitzherbard Judge lately translated out of Frenche into Englyshe and
newly corrected.

The yere of our Lorde God M.D.XLIII.

Col.: Wyllyam Myddylton.   n. d.

(Bodl., B.M., H.L.S.)

(8 [6]) The new booke of Justices of peace, made by Anthony Fitz-
herbarde Judge lately translated out of Frenche into Englyshe and
newly corrected.

The yere of oure lorde god. M.D.XLVII.

Col.: Wyllyam Powell.   n. d.

---

[1] Omitted in the Handlists.

[2] Omitted in the Handlists.   According to the catalogue, a copy exists
in C.H.L.; but the volume, from which evidently the colophon has been
torn out, is almost certainly no. 6, Petyt's edition.

[3] I have expanded the description given in Worrall; cf. Bridgman,
Legal Bibliography, 121–2.   Worrall mentions also a 1557 edition,
evidently an error, for Redman's widow did no printing after 1541; see
Duff, *op. cit.*, 104.

[4] The Handlists omit the author's name and use a misleading title; cf.
p. 232, note 2, *supra*.   [5] Omitted in the Handlists.

[6] Bridgman, *loc. cit.*, and Worrall, *op. cit.*, 62, both mention a 1546

(9 [1]) The New BOKF of Ivstices of peace, made by Anthony Fitz-herbarde Judge lately translated out of French into Englyshe, and newly corrected.

The yere of our Lorde God. M.D.L.I.
    Col.: Wyllyam Powell. n. d.

(*H.L.S.*)

(10 [2]) The Nevv Boke of Justices of peace made by Anthonie Fitz Herbard iudge lately translated out of French into Englishe and newlye corrected.

The yere of our Lorde. 1554.
    Col.: Richarde Tottle. 17 Oct. 1554.

(*H.L.S.*)

(11) The Nevve Boke of Ivstices of peace made by Anthonie Fitz Herbard iudge, lately translated out of French into Englishe and newlye corrected.

The yere of our Lorde. 1554.
    Col.: Richarde Tottyll. 7 Feb. 1560 [1561].

(*Bodl.*, *B.M.*,[3] *H.L.S.*)

(12) The Nevve Boke of Ivstices of peace made by Anthonie Fitz Herbert iudge, lately translated out of French into Englishe and newlye corrected.

The yere of our Lorde. 1554.
    Col.: Richard Tottill. 13 July 1566.

SERIES III

Eirenarcha.

By William Lambard.

(1 [4]) Eirenarcha: or of The Office of the Iustices of peace, in two

edition which I have not been able to find. Is the difference in date perhaps due to the confusion between 1 January and 25. March as the beginning of the year?

[1] Omitted from the Handlists.

[2] Not in B.M. as stated in the Handlists.

[3] The fact that the B.M. catalogue by an error gives 1556 as the colophon of this volume probably explains the erroneous entry in the Handlists of a 1556 edition in both B.M. and U.L.C. If there ever was such an edition, I have not been able to discover a copy. The title-page of an Inner Temple volume with colophon missing corresponds precisely with the title-page of no. 12.

[4] A strangely made-up volume in H.L.S. omits the epistle to the Chancellor and the table of contents at the beginning, and has the first sixteen pages from this edition and the remaining pages from that of 1602.

Bookes : Gathered 1579, and now reuised, and firste published, in the 24. yeare of the peaceable reigne of our gratious Queene Elizabeth :
by William Lambard of Lincolnes Inne Gent. . . .
Imprinted by Ra. Newbery, and H. Bynneman,
by the ass. of Ri. Tot. & Chr. Bar.
Anno. Domini.
1581.
No col.

(2) Newbery and Bynneman.   1582.   No col.

(3) Newbery and Binneman.   1582.   No col.

(4) Col. : Nevvberie.   1583.[1]

(5) Eirenarcha : or of The office of the Iustices of peace, in foure Bookes : Gathered 1579 : first published 1581 : and now reuised, corrected, and enlarged, in this 31. yeere of the Peaceable raigne of our most gracious Queene Elizabeth. . . .
Whereunto there is added an Appendix of sundry Precedents, touching matters of the peace.
Anno Domini, 1588.
Col. : Newbery.   1588.

(6 [2]) Eirenarcha : (*almost as in 1588 to* Elizabeth) . . .
Whereunto is added the newly reformed Commission of the Peace, & an Appendix of sundry Precedents touching matters of the peace.
Anno Domini, 1591.
Col. : Newbery.   1588.

(7) Eirenarcha : or of The office of the Iustices of Peace in foure Bookes.   Gathered 1579 : first published 1581 : and now secondly reuised, corrected, and enlarged agreeably to the reformed Commission of the Peace in the 34. yeare of the peaceable raigne of our most gratious Queene Elizabeth. . . .
Anno Domini, 1592.
Col. : Newbery.   1592.

(8) Eirenarcha : Or of The office of the Iustices of peace in foure Bookes.   Gathered 1579 : first published 1581 : and now reuised, corrected, and enlarged agreeably to the reformed Commission of the Peace in the 37. yeare of the peaceable raigne of our most gracious Queene Elizabeth. . . .
Printed by Ralph Newbery
1594.
No col.

[1] The only copy that I have seen is in H.L.S. and lacks a title-page.
[2] For the sake of economy, the reformed commission was inserted into

(9) Eirenarcha: Or of The office of the Iustices of Peace, in foure Bookes. First gathered 1579. published 1581. and now fourthly reuised, corrected, and enlarged in this fortie and one yeare of the peaceable raigne of our most gracious Queene Elizabeth. . . .

Printed by Thomas Wight and Bonham Norton
1599

No col.

SERIES IV

Loffice Et aucthoritie de Iustices de peace.

By Richard Crompton.

(1) Loffice Et aucthoritie de Iustices de peace, in part collect per le iades tresreuerend Iudge, Mounsieur A. Fitzherbert, et ore enlarge per Richard Crompton, vn Apprentice de le common ley: & publie lan du grace, 1583.[1]

A que est annex, loffice de Vicountes, Bailiffes, Escheatours, Constables, Coroners &c. collect per le dit Mounsieur Fitzherbert.

Imprinted . . . by Richarde Tottill.

No col.

(2) Loffice Et aucthoritie de Justices de Peace, in part collect per le tresreuerende, Monsier Antho. Fitzherbert, iades vn de les Iustices del Common Banke, & inlarge per R. Crompton, vn Apprentice de le common ley, & ore per luy reuyse, corrygie, & augment. 1584.

A que etc. (as in no. 1).

Col.: Rychard Tottel. 1584.

(3) Loffice & aucthoritie de Iustices de Peace, in part collect per Sir Anthonie Fitzherbert Chiualer, iades vn de les Iustices del Common Banke: Et ore le tierce foits inlarge per Richard Crompton vn Apprentice de la commen ley: Et imprimye lan du grace. 1587.

A que etc. (as in no. 1 through Fitzherbert).

Et auxy certeine Presidentes dendictments, & auters choses. . . .

By Richard Tottell.

No col.

(4[2]) Loffice & aucthority de Iustices de peace (as in no. 3, through the surplus copies of the unexhausted edition of 1588 ; see Lambard's own preface.

[1] Printed as 1582 in the Stationers' Register, ii. 192 b; the licence is recorded under date of 17 February 1582, really 1583.

[2] Bridgman, *op. cit.*, 122, mentions a 1594 edition by C. Yetsweirt, probably an error for Crompton's ' L'aucthoritie et iurisdiccion des courts . . .' printed by Yetsweirt in that year.

Common Banke): Et ore le quart foits inlarge & corrigee per Richard
Crompton vn Apprentice de la Common ley: Et imprime lan du
grace 1593.

A que est annex Loffice de Viconts, Bailifes, Escheators, Constables,
Coroners &c. collect per le dit Mounsier Fitzherbert in part. Et
auxy certaine Presidents de Indictments & auters choses. . . .

Imprinted . . . by Richard Tottell.

No. col.

APPENDIX II

TEXT OF A WORCESTERSHIRE MANUAL FOR
JUSTICES OF THE PEACE, *circ.* 1422,

from Liber Brevium, folios 1–12, Miscellaneous Books of the Exchequer,
Augmentation Office, no. 169, Public Record Office.

[Fly leaf.[1]]

>   Sutton in Colefeld [2] in comitatu [Warr']
>   . . . . exaltacionis Sancte Crucis [3] anno
>   . . . . quarto Annoque domini . . .
>   . . . . felonice fregit et
>   . . . . vnum par ca[lceorum] coloris
>   . . . . precii iis. viiid. de bonis
>   . . . . . felonice furatus fuit
>   . . . . . in comitatu predicto
>   . . . . . . feloniam predictam
>   . . . . apud [Ba]ldon [4]
> confortauerunt et abettauerunt.

I

[f. 1.][5] Indictamentum versus iuratorem etc. qui publicauit
consilium regis.

Inquiratur pro rege si A. B., qui nuper fuit vnus iurator iuratus
pro domino rege ad veritatem dicendam et consilium regis et sociorum
suorum similiter iuratorum celandum de certis assisis ex parte domini

---

[1] Almost impossible to decipher.
[2] Sutton Coldfield, Warwickshire, a manor belonging to the duchy of
Lancaster; Lists and Indexes, vi. 119.   [3] 14 September.
[4] Baldon, Oxfordshire (?).   [5] No foliation in the original.

regis inquirendis in hundredo de B.,[1] ad sessionem pacis domini regis tentam apud W.[2] die etc. anno etc. coram I. T.[3] et sociis suis iusticiariis pacis in comitatu Wygorn', [cum] per ipsum A. B. et socios suos iuratos presentatum fuit quod quidem L. K. die tali et anno tali domum F. de T. felonice fregit etc., et sic recitandum indictamentum, predictus A. B. veredictam presentacionem illius die tali et anno tali apud tiel lieu plurimis hominibus publice narrauit et discoopperuit, per quod alii iuratores socii sui in inquisicione [illa] multipliciter de vita et mutilacione membrorum sibi imminati fuerunt quod negocia sua palam facere aut pro domino rege in aliis inquisicionibus veritatem dicere ausi non fuerunt, in contemptum domini regis et contra legem antiquitus vsitatem etc.

2

Aliter de eodem.

Inquiratur pro rege cum nuper ante cessionem pacis iam preteritam apud W.[4] tentam tali die tali anno coram iusticiariis ibidem ad pacem in comitatu predicto conseruandam assignatis quoddam breue domini regis vicecomiti Wygorn' directum [est] de venire faciendo coram eisdem iusticiariis ad certos dies et locum in dicto breui contentos de quolibet hundredo et qualibet libertate comitatus predicti xxiiii de liberis et legalibus hominibus maius sufficientibus balliue sue comitatus predicti [? summoniendos], et quod proclamacionem faceret vbique in balliua sua cessionem illam . . . tenendam in forma predicta ; et super hoc proclamacione facta etc. coram prefatis iusticiariis predictus vicecomes retornauit breue predictum cum panellis de quolibet hundredo et de qualibet libertate prout per dictum breue ei precipiebatur, vocatisque panellis videlicet iuratores de quolibet hundredo et de qualibet libertate de tunc ibidem coopertum coram prefatis iusticiariis de pace ad diem supradictum comparuerunt, et quilibet iuratorum predictorum pro se in panellis predictis impanellatorum prestitit sacramentum quod bene ex parte domini regis inquireret et veritatem eisdem iusticiariis de illis que ad tunc ibidem ex parte domini regis [? eis] iniungerentur presentaret et consilium domini regis et sociorum suorum ex parte sua custodiret et quod interim alter alterius domini regis consilium custodiret prout mos est. Postmodum illo eodem die iuratores predicti coram eisdem iusticiariis . . . sua reddiderunt et diuerse bulle de

---

[1] Blakenhurst. [2] Worcester.

[3] John Throgmerton ; ch. iii (1), s. 3. If no reference or explanation is given in the foot-notes for a name in the text, the identification will be found, *ibid.*, or s. 4. [4] Worcester.

felon[um ?] indict[amentis ?] ac alie bulle de aliis . . . post quorum
reddicionem et presentacionem omnia et singula [? indicta]menta . . .
illius cessionis ingrosseruntur ; et sic finita sessione quidam I. B. [unus
iuratorum] crastino eiusdem sessionis videlicet tali die anno etc. apud
S. publice narrauit consilium domini regis et sociorum suorum similiter
ad cessionem predictam inpanellatorum publice dicendo quando E. F.
de etc. fore principalem indictatorem cuiusdam N. B. ad . . . de felonia
qui quidem E. F. ad onus ibidem eidem I. R. . . . cuiusdam bulle de
felonia super eundem N. B. fabricat' . . . ut plenius patet per rotulos, et
hoc coram quam pluribus ibidem demonstrauit contra dignitatem
domini regis et in corone sue preiudicium eo quod per antiquas consuetudines regni . . . defenderuntur ac si talia tollerentur nemine veritas
dicetur.[1]

3

Inquiratur pro rege si W. T. de etc. tali die et anno apud N. in
comitatu Wygorn' inueneruit diuersas opiniones erreticanas contra
fidem catholicam et in scandalum ordinacionis sancte matris ecclesie
pro diversas [leges eciam ?] domini regis [f. 1 b] de hereticanas
opiniones visitando quod ymagines a nullo in ecclesiis deberent . . .
publice nec quod si quis in vigiliis apostolorum Petri et Pauli [2] et Sancti
Iohannis Baptiste [3] cum pane et aqua iennuauerit vlterius confessione
capellanorum non indiget, ac eciam idem tamen W. T. die et anno
predictis apud N. seditiose felonice et proditorie fuit consulens con-
sentiens auxilians et procurans ad [? opiniones] Lollardrie nuper ad
parliamentum Leycestrie prohibitos et prodiciones huiusmodi a predicto die etc. vsque diem fabrice huius mandati scilicet die Iouis etc.
anno etc. diuersis diebus et temporibus continuando contra pro-
hibicionem domini regis nunc ad parliamentum eiusdem domini regis
apud Leycestr' anno regni sui editam etc.[4]

4
De rescussu versus balliuum.

Inquiratur pro rege si I. S. de C. etc. tali die tali anno apud R. in
comitatu predicto in I. Mulle [5] insultum fecit licet quod esset quod

---

[1] The first two precedents are exceedingly illegible.
[2] 28 June.   [3] 23 June.
[4] 2 Hen. V, st. 1, c. 7 ; 30 April 1414.
[5] Cf. no. 7, where he is specifically mentioned as acting in Oswaldslow
hundred, and nos. 80 and 81, where a John Mulle is one of the two bailiffs
of Pershore.

idem Iohannes Mulle deputatus per vicecomitem ad ipsum I. S. virtute cuiusdam ʻwaranti eidem I. Mulle capiendum directi et ad castrum Wygorn' ducendum et saluo et secure ibidem custodiendum, ita quod idem vicecomes corpus eiusdem I. S. ad certum diem iam preteritum coram iusticiariis domini regis apud Westmonasterium habuisse posset ad respondendum Stephano Carpenter[1] de placito debiti, quia I. Mulle virtute waranti predicti prefatum Iohannam S. ibidem ad tunc cepit et arestauit ; et [si] idem I. S. sic ibidem arestatus et captus die et anno supradictis in ipsum Iohannem Mulle rescussum fecit et de vita et mutilacione membrorum suorum ibidem manifeste comminatus fuit, contra pacem domini regis et sic a custodia eiusdem I. Mulle euasit et nunquam in dicta balliua eiusdem vicecomitis postea inueniri potuit etc.

5
De aresto fracto coram iusticiariis pacis.

Inquiratur pro rege cum nuper Iohannes Froxemere de Wyche, armiger,[2] coram Iohanne Braas vno iusticiariorum domini regis ad pacem in comitatu Wygorn' conseruandam assignatorum venerit et securitatem pacis de Iohanne S.[3] etc. et Iohanne Bolton[4] petierit de eo quod ipsi eundem I. Froxmere de vita et mutilacione membrorum suorum minati fuerunt, per quod ipse ad husbandriam seu ad negocia sua facienda propter metum mortis palam incedere non audiebat [sic] quovismodo, sicut idem I. Froxmere coram prefato I. Braas iusticiario per sacramentum suum affidauit ; virtute cuius querele prefatus I. Braas iusticiarius accepto secum Iohanne P. [sic] de etc. et aliis ligeis domini regis pro execucione legis in hac parte fortificanda die Veneris in septimana Pentecostis anno regni domini regis nunc septimo[5] apud N. in prato ibidem ad ipsos I. Salesby et I. Bolton [? parati arestandum] et ipsos I. Salesbury et I. Bolton arestauit ; et iidem I. Salesbury et I. Bolton ex malicia precogitata et nuper inde [sic] vi armata in ipsum

---

[1] Not identified.

[2] Cf. an accusation against John Froxmere, William Boteller of Yatton, John Brace, and many others of an attack in ʻ Wyche ' on a well of salt water called ʻ Shirrevespitt' belonging to Richard, earl of Warwick ; Cal. Pat. Hen. IV, 1401–1405, 423 : Anc. Indictments, 213, m. 5. For Wyche, Halfshire hundred, modern Droitwich, see Th. Habington, Survey of Worcestershire, Worc. Hist. Soc. ii. 295–308 : ʻ the auntient name of Wiche signifyinge fountaynes of salt with the addition of thys Frenche wourd Droyt which Englyshed is Ryght, and so Droytwich, the right salt of thys land '. Cf. also T. R. Nash, Worcestershire, i. 295, *et seq.* The Frogmeres were a family of great antiquity in Oswaldslow hundred ; *ibid.,* i. 209, *et seq.*   [3] Salesby, *ut infra,* but not identified.

[4] Not identified.   [5] Probably 7 Hen. IV, therefore 4 June 1406.

I. Bras iusticiarium etc. vi et armis scilicet gladiis arcubus et sagittis et aliis armaturis adtunc ibidem insurrexerunt et arrestum predicti Iohannis Bras iusticiarii etc. fregerunt, et eidem Iohanni Bras in faciendo ibidem officium suum disturbauerunt et in dictum Iohannem P. vi et armis cum arcubus et sagittis sagittaverunt et fere interfecerunt contra pacem domini regis etc.

6

De nigromancia.

Cum iam tarde infra regnum Anglie per nephandas personas erecta est quadam nova diabolica artis [*sic*] ad perimendum interficiendum et murdrandum quaslibet personas quibus eis placuerit et cum excitacione, confortacione, abettamento et conduccione diuersorum de ligeancia domini regis contra iura et fidem ecclesie catholice sacrosancte quod scelere (?) est, et erit domino regi et ligeis suis et toto Christianitati nisi prius remedium inde subueniatur et succuratur destructio et exanimatio perpetua quod absit; et ideo inquiratur pro domino rege si B. W. etc. die Lune etc. anno [f. 2] tali apud T. in domo W. F.[1] arte diabolica per nigromanciam Lollardiam etc. modo hereticano contra catholicam fidem duas ymagines sereas fecit et eas arte predicta celebrauit cum quadam parte ceree paschalis et aliis inventamentis (?) contra iura ecclesiastica et ad grauem lesionem ecclesie catholice vsque peruenit ad spinam vocatam Thonethorn ibidem arte predicta, videlicet, vnum cereum pro Iacobo B.[2] de etc. et alterum pro I. N. ad eos predicta arte nigromancie Lollardrie et modo hereticano perimendos ac occulte et felonice occidendos. Et si W. F. de etc. predictum B. W. predictas ymagines cereas faciendas celebrandas per dictos I. et I. arte Lollardrie et modo hereticano predictos I. et I. occidendos et murdrandos occulte et felonice dictis die anno et loco conduxit, receptauit, abettauit ac confortauit et [si][3] predicte ymagines arte predicta celebrate in camera dicti Willelmi F. apud W. inuente fuerunt etc.

7

Wygorn'.

Sessio pacis tenta ibidem die Mercurii in festo Sancti Bartholomei[4] anno etc. coram Iohanne T.[5] Iohanne Wode[6] et Willelmo Wolashull[6]

---

[1] Possibly the 'W. F.' of nos. 14 and 65.
[2] Possibly the Iacobus Blount of no. 65 ; see p. 275, note 2, *infra*.
[3] MS. *sic*.   [4] 24 August is the date of the feast.   [5] John Throgmerton.
[6] From the dates of their appointment, the session must be in the reign of Henry V; ch. iii (1), s. 3, *supra*.

iusticiariis domini regis de pace necnon ad diuersas felonias, transgressiones et malefacta in comitatu predicto audienda et terminanda
assignatis etc.

Oswold[eslowe][1] Inquisicio capta coram iusticiariis pacis.

xii iuratores pro rege, scilicet, Ankerus Beauchamp[2] etc., qui
dicunt super sacramentum suum quod Laurentius Andrewes de G. in
comitatu predicto, smyth, die Lune etc. apud P. in comitatu predicto vi
et armis in I. Mulle[3] seruientem domini regis ibidem adtunc venientem
pro execucione cuiusdam waranti domini regis sibi per vicecomitem
directi exequendi et ministrandi insultum fecit, et quod quidem warantum
de quodam breui de Fieri facias predicto vicecomiti comitatus predicti
directo et coram Baronibus Scaccarii eiusdem domini regis nuper
adiudicato versus eundem Laurentium emanauit, eo. quod idem
Laurentius de quadam recepcione denariorum vltime xv^e in predicto
comitatu Wygorn' receptorum coram predictis Baronibus non plene
computasset, et in ipsum Iohannem sic ibidem existentem warantum
predictum exequendum et ministrandum rescussum fecerunt [sic] et
ipsum verberauit et male tractauerit [sic], ita quod de vita sua despera-
batur et vix cum vita sua euasit, et sic per idem tempus execucio
eiusdem waranti ibidem infacta remansit, nec illum permittere vellet
aliquo modo per ipsum Iohannem ministrari. Qui quidem Laurentius
dictam transgressionem iniuste et contra pacem domini regis fecit die
et anno supradictis.

Et dicunt quod faber Hore[4] de etc., H. B. de etc. die etc. anno apud
H. in comitatu predicto quatuor equos nigri coloris precii x librarum
de bonis et catallis Roberti Ingram[5] felonice furati fuerunt et abduxerunt
etc. Et eciam dicunt quod I. N. de etc. die et anno etc. apud R.
predictos H., H. B. et W. B. [sic] in domo sua receptauit sciens ipsos
felonias predictas fecisse etc.

---

[1] Oswaldslow hundred.
[2] He acted as juror in the proceedings against the two Burdets and
others; Assize Roll 1038, Worcestershire, 5 & 6 Hen. V, (1), m. 3, (2),
m. 22. See ch. iii (1), pp. 71-2.
[3] Cf. no. 4 and note 5.
[4] Johannes Hore de Matheme, yeoman, of Worcestershire, is one of the
long list indicted before the justices of the peace for the murder of
Milward ; Anc. Indictments, K. B. 9, 71, ms. 59 and 60 ; Coram Rege Roll
623, Hill. 4 Hen. V, 1417, Rex, rot. 5 d. See no. 17, *infra*, for the indictment of Roger Hore for the same crime. Cf. also the indictment of
a John Hore in 1415 ; Gaol Delivery Roll 218, no. 3, m. 10.
[5] For other thefts from Robert Ingram, see nos. 16 and 19, cases identified on the Gaol Delivery Rolls.

8

Breue de venire facias et capias in eadem.

Rex vicecomiti **Wygorn'** salutem. Precipimus tibi quod non omittas propter aliquam libertatem comitatus tui quin eas ingrediaris et venire facias coram iusticiariis nostris de pace in comitatu tuo conseruanda assignatis apud **Wygorn'** die Iouis etc. proximo futuro Laurentium etc., de etc., ad respondendum nobis de diuersis articulis super ipsum presentatis unde coram prefatis iusticiariis indictatus est.

Precipimus eciam vobis quod non omittas in forma predicta quin capias Henricum B. de etc. si inuentus fuerit in balliua tua, et eum saluo custodias ita quod habeas corpus eius coram prefatis iusticiariis ad diem et locum predictos ad respondendum nobis de diuersis feloniis unde coram prefatis iusticiariis indictatus est; et habeas etc.

Teste etc.

9

Aliter cum clausula de seisiri. Nota quod . . .[1]

Rex vicecomiti salutem. Precipimus tibi sicut alias tibi precepimus quod non omittas etc. quin eam ingrediaris et capias H. B. de etc. si etc. et eos [*sic*] custodiri facias necnon seisiri facias eius bona et catalla terras et tenementa in balliua tua eo quod de exitibus eorundem nobis respondeas; et quod habeas corpus eius coram iusticiariis nostris de pace in comitatu tuo conseruanda etc. [f. 2 b] assignatis apud **Wygorn'** die etc. ad respondendum nobis de diuersis feloniis vnde coram prefatis iusticiariis indictatus est; et habeas etc.

10

Breue de [exigi facias] super . . .[1]

Rex vicecomiti salutem. Precipimus tibi quod exigi facias in comitatu tuo H. B. de etc. de comitatu in comitatum quousque secundum legem et consuetudinem regni nostri Anglie vtlagetur si non comparuerit; et si comparuerit, tunc eum capias et saluo custodiri facias, ita quod habeas corpus eius coram iusticiariis nostris de pace in comitatu tuo conseruanda assignatis apud W.[2] die Lune proximo post festum Epiphanie domini proximo futuro ad respondendum nobis de diuersis feloniis vnde coram prefatis iusticiariis indictatus est; et habeas etc.

[1] Illegible.   [2] Worcester.

I I
Wygorn'.

Preceptum est vicecomiti quod non omittat propter aliquam libertatem
etc. quin capiat H. B. etc., si etc., et saluo etc., ita quod habeat corpus
eius coram iusticiariis domini regis de pace in comitatu predicto conseruanda assignatis apud Wygorn' die Iouis in septimana Pasche
proximo future ad respondendum domino regi de diuersis feloniis vnde
coram prefatis iusticiariis indictatus est; et si, sic [ut] alias capias si
etc., et saluo etc., et quod seisire [sic] facias eorum bona et catalla
terras et tenementa etc. et quod de exitibus etc.   Et quod habeas etc.

I 2
Magna Inquisicio.

xii iuratores pro rege, scilicet, I. B. etc., dicunt super sacramentum
suum omnia bene, etc.

I 3
Quedam securitas pacis.

Memorandum quod die Iouis proximo festum Epiphanie [1] domini
anno regni regis post conquestum sexto [2] coram prefatis iusticiariis [3]
venit I. W., armiger, de etc. in comitatu Wygorn', et recognouit se
custodire pacem erga dominum regem et populum suum et precipue
erga I. F.[4] vsque diem Iouis in septimana Pasche proximo future sub
pena c. librarum quas recognouit se debere domino regi de terris et
catallis suis leuandas si aliquod dampnum corporale eidem I. F. aut
alicui de populo domini regis vsque ad prefatum diem Iouis in septimana Pasche fecerit et si contigerit ipsum I. W. delinquere et modo
inde legitimo conuinci etc.

I 4
Deliberacio vbi indictatus fuit ut accessorius postquam
vtlagati fuerunt.

Ricardus P. de etc. captus pro eo quod indictatus fuit coram prefatis
iusticiariis [5] de eo quod cum Robertus K. de H. in comitatu Stafford'

[1] 6 January is the date of the feast; either ' ante ' or ' post ' is omitted. ·
[2] Almost certainly 6 Hen. V, since no. 13, like nos. 8–12, is apparently
to be connected with no. 7; p. 241, note 6, *supra.*
[3] Almost certainly the justices of the peace of no. 7.
[4] Possibly John Forthey, the clerk of the peace; see no. 36.
[5] Almost certainly justices of the peace.

yoman, et W. H. de etc., die Lune ante festum Petri et Pauli¹ anno etc.
clausum et domos Willelmi F. apud N. in comitatu Wygorn' vi et
armis modo guerrino arrettati [*sic*] noctanter felonice fregerunt etc.², et
si predictus Ricardus P. predictos R. **K.** predictis die et anno receptauit
sciens ipsos feloniam predictam fecisse et quod est communis receptor
felonum. Pro qua quidem felonia predicti R. et W. vtlagati sunt die
Mercurii in vigilia Sancti Michaelis Archangeli³ anno etc. prout patet
per recordum rotulorum coram prefatis iusticiariis residencium. Idemque R. P. per vicecomitem ad barram ductus allocutus qualiter se velit
de felonia predicta acquietare qui dicit quod ipse in nullo est culpabilis
et de hoc ponit se de bene et malo super patriam.

Ideo fiat inde iurata iuratorum de visneto predicto scilicet, T. B. etc.
qui ad veritatem de supracontentis dicendam electi, triati et iurati,
dicunt super sacramentum suum quod predictus R. [in] nullo est inde
culpabilis de felonia predicta nec se retraxit occasione illa. Ideo sit
inde quietus etc.

15

Wygorn'. Deliberacio vbi principalis deliberatur (?) et eius
accessorius eat sine die etc.

Willelmus P.⁴ de B. etc. et Robertus Webbe⁵ etc. captus [*sic*] pro eo
quod indictati fuerunt coram prefatis iusticiariis pacis de eo quod
prefatus Willelmus die etc. anno etc. domum et clausum I. W. de E.⁶
apud S.⁷ noctanter felonice fregit et T. seruientem dicti I. W. ibidem
felonice rapuit et abduxit, et quod R. Wybbe sciens predictum W.
feloniam predictam fecisse et perpetrasse ipsum W. die et anno supradictis in domo sua apud G. receptauit. Prefati W. et R. per vicecomitem ad barram ducti allocuti [sunt] separatim qualiter se velint de
feloniis predictis acquietare et prefatus W. Pedon dicit quod in nullo
est inde culpabilis et de hoc etc. Ideo fiat inde iurata iuratorum de
visneto predicto, scilicet, B. T. et alii etc. qui ad veritatem de supracontentis dicendam scilicet triati et iurati dicunt super sacramentum

---

¹ 29 June is the date of the feast.
² Case not yet identified, but cf. nos. 6 and 65 for other references to a
William F. Both cases are very similar to the attack on the house of
William Russell at North Littleton; see ch. iii (1), p. 71, and note 8.
³ 29 September. ⁴ Poden, *ut infra*; not identified.
⁵ Perhaps Robert Webbe of Evesham, 'barker', one of the defendants
in the suit brought by the abbot of Evesham; see ch. iii (1), p. 71, and
note 9.
⁶ Probably Evesham.
⁷ Probably Shipston-on-Stour, Oswaldslow hundred; Nash, *op. cit.*, ii.
428, and Habington, Survey of Worcestershire, i, index.

suum quod prefatus W. Poden in nullo est inde culpabilis de felonia predicta nec se retraxit occasione illa. Ideo sit ipse inde quietus et quia predictus W. Poden principalis acquietatus est de [f. 3] felonia predicta per iuratam predictam, ideo predictus R. W. qui indictatus est vt accessorius eat inde sine die etc.

16 [1]

Wygorn'.   De equo felonice furato et abducto etc.

I. H., iunior,[2] etc., captus pro eo quod indictatus est coram custodibus pacis comitatus Wygorn' de eo quod ipse die etc. anno etc. apud D.[3] infra manerium de M.[4] vnum equum soreld coloris precii xxs. de bonis et catallis I. G.[5] de D. felonice furatus fuit et etiam quod idem I. H. die etc. anno etc. apud H.[6] in quadam pastura vocata Crippemere vnum equum nigrum precii xxxs. de bonis et catallis R. I.[7] felonice furatus fuit. Idemque Iohannes coram prefatis iusticiariis pacis comitatus Wygorn' per vicecomitem ad barram ductus et allocutus qualiter se velit acquietare qui dicit quod in nullo est inde culpabilis de felonia predicta et de hoc etc. Ideo preceptum est vicecomiti quod non omittat etc. quin venire faciat hic hac instante die Iouis xii etc. de visneto etc. per quos etc. et qui nec etc. ad recognoscendum etc. Ad quem diem vicecomes retornat panellum de nominibus iuratorum etc., et ipsi iuratores vocati quidam veniunt et quidam non, prout in panello annotatur ; et sic iurata illa remanet pro defectu iuratorum etc., et preceptum est vicecomiti quod non omittat etc. quin distringat eos per omnes terras etc. et quod de exitibus etc. et quod habeat corpora eorum hic die Iouis etc. proximo futuro ad recognoscendum in forma predicta etc. ; et vicecomes apponit octo tales etc. et idem dies datus est prefato I. H. etc. et idem I. H. remittitur prisoni castri Wygorn' sub

---

[1] Belongs with nos. 19 and 20.

[2] Johannes Hawkeley, junior. Both these indictments brought before Worcestershire justices of the peace appear on Gaol Delivery Roll 73, no. 3, ms. 3, 3 d. At the Gaol Delivery at Worcester Castle on 8 June 1419 before Preston, Weston, and Horton (p. 89, note 1), Hawkeley was acquitted of both charges. It appears further that at the Gaol Delivery he had also been appealed by one of the two plaintiffs, Robert Ingram, but that the latter had failed to prosecute his appeal.

[3] G. D. Roll 73, no. 3, m. 3 d.

[4] Marteley, mod. Martley, Dodintre hundred ; Habington, *op. cit.*, i. 343.

[5] *Ut supra*, note 3.

[6] For an illustration of the accuracy of the details in the manual, cf. the actual entry on the Gaol Delivery Roll : ' apud Homme in quadam pastura vocata Cripmere vnum equum nigrum precii xxxs.'

[7] Robertus Ingram.

custodia vicecomitis saluo custodiendus quousque secundum legem deliberetur etc.

17 [1]

Wygorn'.

Rogerus Hore de Monesley[2] in comitatu Hereford, gentilman, captus pro eo quod indictatus fuit coram iusticiariis ibidem etc. de eo quod ipse vi et armis modo guerrino noue insurreccionis contra pacem, dignitatem et coronam domini regis iacuit in insidiis apud Bergh[3] in comitatu Wygorn' die Lune[4] etc., et Iohannem Mulleward de M.[5] apud B[ergh] in comitatu predicto ex malicia precogitata circa horam nonam cepit et ipsum ibidem in prisona detinuit vsque noctem eiusdem diei continuando malicia sua predicta et eidem Iohanni Mulleward etc. et tam cito feloniam predictam fecit se retraxit. Idemque Rogerus posteaque bis ad barram ductus et allocutus qualiter se velit de felonia predicta acquietare qui dicit quod dominus rex Henricus nunc pardonauit ei per cartam ipsius domini regis sectam pacis sue que ad ipsum regem pertinet de felonia morte et murdro predictis quam cartam profert hic coram prefatis iusticiariis in hec verba : Henricus dei gratia etc. omnibus balliuis et fidelibus suis ad quos presentes littere peruenerint salutem. Sciatis quod cum Rogerus Hore de M. in comitatu H., gentilman, nuper de diuersis feloniis murdris insurreccionibus transgressionibus et mesprisionibus contra pacem nostram factis et

---

[1] On 6 March, 3 Hen. V, 1416, a large number, including Roger Hore de Monesly, were indicted before the Worcestershire justices of the peace, Beauchamp of Bergevenny, Horton, Weston, Throgmerton, and Brace, for an attack at ' Bergh' on Monday, 17 February, on John Milward and for his murder on the following Thursday ; Anc. Indictments 71, ms. 59, 60. The indictment, summoned by a writ of *certiorari* of 28 March, endorsed by Horton (*ibid.*), was enrolled in Trin. term 1416, Coram Rege Roll 621, Rex, rot. 12, but specified only a few names (omitting Roger Hore), referring to the others as ' unknown '. Process continued through Trin. term 1419, many of the indicted appearing in court with royal charters of pardon, based on the action of the parliament of November 1414 (see p. 70, *supra*); C.R. Roll 622, Rex, rot. 13, 26 d ; 623, Rex, rot. 5 d ; 624, Rex, rot. 1, 3, 14, 17 ; 625, Rex, rot. 2, 10, 16 ; 626, Rex, rot. 13 d, 14, 17 d ; 628, Rex, rot. 23 ; 633, Rex, rot. 16 d. Roger Hore's pardon was produced in Trin. term, 5 Hen. V, 1417 ; (C.R. Roll 625, Rex, rot. 2, and enrolled on the Patent Rolls; Cal. Pat. Hen. V, 1416-1422, 103 ; cf. also 34, 46, 104) and according to the manual was also produced before the justices of the peace. For the necessity of a second production of a pardon, cf. Year Book Mich. 8 Edw. IV, no. 1.

[2] Munsley.

[3] Ancient Berga, modern Berrow, Oswaldslow hundred; Habington, *op. cit.*, i. 130.

[4] 18 February, 3 Hen. V, 1416; Anc. Indict., K.B. 71, m. 60.

[5] Malverne ; *ibid.*, ' Iohannem Milleward de parua Malverne yoman '.

in speciali de murdro et morte Iohannis Mulleward per quandam inquisicionem indictatus existat, super quo quoddam breue vicecomiti comitatus predicti de proclamando in eodem comitatu quod predictus Rogerus super fide et ligeancia nostra fuit et sub pena forisfacture omnium que nobis forisfacere potuit coram nobis in cancellaria nostra die Lune [1] etc. anno etc. ad respondendum super hiis que sibi per nos ibidem obiicerentur compareret extra Cancellariam nostram emanauit; quo die prefatus Rogerus in cancellaria predicta solempniter vocatus minime comparuit proclamacione predicta non obstante; Nos de gracia nostra speciali pardonauimus predicto Rogero sectam pacis nostre que ad nos versus ipsum pertinet pro omnimodis murdris feloniis insurreccionibus transgressionibus et mesprisionibus vnde indictatus rectatus vel appellatus existat. Ac etiam vtlagariam sique in ipsum hiis occasionibus fuerit promulgata et firmam pacem nostram ei inde concedimus, ita tamen quod stet recto in curia nostra si quis versus eum loqui voluerit de morte supradicta, et de uberiori gracia nostra pardonauimus prefato Rogero omnimodas fines et forisfacturas que nobis pertinent seu pertinere possunt occasione non apparencie sue coram nobis in cancellaria nostra predicta ad diem predictum [f. 3 b] aut aliquem alium diem supra aliqua proclamacione in cancellaria predicta vel alibi facta, vel per aliquam causam in breui predicto specificatam siue alia causa inde dependenti eo quod terre, tenementa, bona, catalla ipsius Rogeri ex causa predicta siue earum aliqua manus nostre seisite existunt non obstante. In cuius rei testimonium has literas nostras fieri fecimus patentes.

Teste me ipso apud etc. anno etc.[2]

Prefert etiam quoddam breue domini regis clausum de non molestando predictum Rogerum contra tenorem literarum predictarum in hec verba:

Carta irrotulata coram iusticiariis pacis et irrotulata cum breui de non molestando:

Henricus dei gracia etc. custodibus pacis sue et iusticiariis suis ad diuersas felonias, transgressiones et malefacta in comitatu Wygorn' audienda et terminanda assignatis et eorum cuilibet, salutem. Cum de gracia nostra speciali pardonauimus Rogero Hore de M. in comitatu Hereford, gentilman, sectam pacis nostre que ad nos versus ipsum

---

[1] 6 April 1416: 'die lune proximo ante festum in ramis palmarum anno regni nostri quarto'; Coram Rege Roll 625, Rex, rot. 2.

[2] 'apud castrum nostrum de Wyndesore xxiiii die Aprilis anno regni nostri quinto (1417)'; *ibid.* The enrolled Letter Patent is dated 23 April; p. 247, note 1, *supra.*

pertinuit pro omnimodis murdris, feloniis, insurreccionibus, transgressionibus et mesprisionibus vnde indictatus, rectatus vel appellatus
existit ac etiam vtlagariam si que in ipsum hiis occasionibus fuerint
promulgate, et firmam pacem nostram ei inde concesserimus prout in
literis nostris patentibus inde confectis plenius continetur, et quia idem
Rogerus inuenit coram nobis in cancellaria nostra sufficientem securitatem de se bene gerendo exnunc erga nos et populum nostrum iuxta
formam statuti inde editi et prouisi, vobis mandamus quod ipsum
Rogerum contra tenorem literarum ipsarum predictarum non molestetis
in aliquo seu grauetis.

Teste etc.[1]

Proclamacio.

Et facta est proclamacio quod siquis scit vel loqui voluerit de morte
predicta versus predictum Rogerum quod veniat et audiatur, et nullus
est qui sequitur, quarum pretextu literarum predictarum idem Rogerus
petit se ipsum a prisona domini regis deliberari; et inspectis literis predictis quia dominus rex ad sectam pacis sue de feloniis, morte et
murdro predictis predictum [R. pardonauit], consideratum est quod
prefatus Rogerus eat inde sine die et firma pax ei conceditur etc.

18

Proclamacio.

Thomas P. de F. etc. captus fuit apud F. per vn tiel R. de H. pro
suspeccione robberie catallorum vel per suspeccionem false monete, et
missus ad gaolam et per vicecomitem coram iusticiariis[2] ductus ad
barram quesitus est super causa capcionis etc.   Quiquidem Ricardus
dicit quod causa predicta quesita est a vicecomite et aliis ministris
domini regis comitatus predicti si ipsi ceperint aliquas inquisiciones
qui dicunt quod sic, et quod nullam causam inuenire [sic]; et facta
est proclamacio si aliquis voluerit prosequi pro rege aut pro se
ipso vel iusticiariis informare de aliqua re vel occasione contra ipsum
Thomam super suam deliberacionem quod veniat et audiatur et nullus
venit.   Ideo iuratus est de se bene gerendo et deliberatur etc.

19[3]

Breue ad distringendum octo tales.

Rex vicecomiti salutem.   Precipimus tibi quod non omittas etc. quin
eam ingrediaris et distringas I. W. et alios iuratores summonitos inter

---

[1] Dated 24 April; Coram Rege Roll 625, Rex, rot. 2.
[2] Probably justices of the peace acting as justices of Gaol Delivery.
[3] With no. 16.

eos et I. H., iuniorem de R.[1] in comitatu tuo, yoman, per omnes terras etc., ita quod de exitibus etc., et quod habeas corpora eorum coram iusticiariis de pace in comitatu tuo conseruanda assignatis apud W.[2] tali die proximo futuro ad recognoscendum super sacramentum suum si predictus I. H. sit culpabilis de diuersis feloniis vnde coram prefatis iusticiariis indictatus est necne ; precipimus eciam tibi quod non omittas in forma predicta quin octo tales tam milites quam alios liberos et legales homines in iuratam illam ponas et illos habeas coram prefatis iusticiariis nostris ad diem et locum predictos ad faciendum iuratam predictam ita quod iurata illa ad diem illum pro defectu iuratorum non remaneat capienda, et habeas ibi nomina eorum quos de nouo apposueris et hoc breue.

Teste etc.

20 [3]

Aliter in eodem breue etc.

Vel sic : Precipimus eciam tibi quod non omittas in forma predicta quin octo tales tam milites quam alios liberos et legales homines quorum quilibet habeat c. solidatas terre, tenementorum vel redditus ad minus per annum in iuratam predictam ponas ; et illos habeas coram prefatis iusticiariis nostris[4] ad diem et locum predictos ad recognoscendum simul cum iurata predicta de feloniis predictis, quia predictus I. H.[5] posuit se super iuratam predictam, et habeas ibi nomina iuratorum quos de nouo apposueris et hoc breue.

Teste etc.

21 [6]

Intratio super exigend'.

Preceptum fuit vicecomiti quod non omitteret etc. quin caperet R. W. etc., I. G. et I. T. etc., si etc. et saluo etc., ita quod haberet corpora eorum coram iusticiariis domini regis de pace in comitatu predicto conseruanda assignatis apud Wygorn' die etc. anno etc. ad respondendum domino regi de diuersis feloniis vnde coram prefatis iusticiariis indictati fuerunt etc. Ad quem diem mandat vicecomes quod prefati R. et omnes alii supranominati non sunt inuenti in balliua sua etc. ; per quod adtunc preceptum fuit eidem vicecomiti sicut alias quod non omitteret in forma predicta quin caperet eos etc. si etc. et saluo etc. et

---

[1] John Hawkeley, junior, of Rydmarley ; Gaol Delivery Roll 73, no. 3, m. 3.
[2] Worcester.   [3] With no. 16.
[4] Justices of the peace as in no. 16.   [5] John Hawkeley.
[6] With nos. 22–9 and 31.

quod seisire faceret eorum bona et catalla terras et tenementa [f. 4]
etc. et quod de exitibus etc., et quod haberet corpora eorum coram
prefatis iusticiariis etc. apud Wygorn' die etc. anno etc. ad respondendum domino regi de feloniis predictis. Ad quem diem prefatus vicecomes mandat quod prefatus Robertus et omnes alii defendentes
supranominati non sunt inuenti in balliua sua et quod nulla habeant
bona seu catalla terras neque tenementa vnde etc. Ideo preceptum est
vicecomiti quod exigi faceret eos de comitatu in comitatum quousque
etc. vtlagentur si non etc., et si etc., tunc eos caperet et saluo etc. ita
quod habeat corpora eorum hic die Sabbati proximo post festum
Epiphanie Domini¹ proximo futurum ad respondendum domino regi de
feloniis predictis etc. Ad quem diem coram Iohanne Throkmerton
Iohanne Wode² etc. ad pacem in comitatu Wygorn' conseruandam
assignatis virtute noue commissionis³ eis directe

(*Margin*: Returnum vicecomitis virtute noue commissionis)
mandauit vicecomes quod ad comitatum Wygorn' tentum ibidem die
tali et anno tali prefatus R. W. reddidit se prisoni domini regis castri
Wygorn', cuius corpus coram prefatis iusticiariis hic ad hunc diem
habet etc.; et vlterius mandauit idem vicecomes quod ad comitatum
Wygorn' tentum ibidem die et anno predictis et sic ad quatuor comitatus precedentes predicti I. G. et I. T. exacti fuerunt et non comparuerunt et quia ad nullum eorundem comitatuum comparuerunt vtlagati
fuerunt. Ideo etc. et idem R. W. coram prefatis iusticiariis hic ad
istum eundem diem acquietatus fuit prout patet per recordum rotulorum
de deliberacione inde facta etc.

22

Aliter de vtlagendo coram iusticiariis pacis.

Ad quem diem mandat vicecomes etc., quod ad comitatum etc. tali
die et anno I. B. et omnes alii preter vn tiel quinto exacti fuerunt et
non comparuerunt. Ideo in presencia T. R.⁴ et T. L.⁵ coronatorum
domini regis in comitatu predicto vtlagati sunt.

---

¹ The date of the feast is 6 January.
² The earliest date on which they were simultaneously appointed was
4 December 1417; thenceforth during the reign of Henry V they both
appear on every commission; ch. iii (1), ss. 3, 5.
³ Although there was no statutory provision for the continuance before
new justices of the peace of pleas pending under the former justices, the
phrase in each commission appointing the Custos Rotulorum implies that
normally such pleas were not discontinued; cf. MS. Patent Rolls, *passim*,
and Lambard, Eirenarcha, 491.
⁴ Thomas Rudyng; Gaol Delivery Roll 73, no. 2, m. 2 d. His colleague in 6 Henry V was William Wasseborn. ⁵ Not yet identified.

23

Breue de exigendo coram eisdem custodibus.

Rex vicecomiti salutem. Precipimus tibi quod exigi facias vn tiel de K. de comitatu in comitatum quousque et si etc. ita etc. coram iusticiariis nostris de pace in comitatu tuo conseruanda assignatis apud Wygorn' tali die proximo futuro ad respondendum nobis de diuersis feloniis vnde coram prefatis iusticiariis indictatus est, et habeas etc. Teste etc.

24

Exigi facias de nouo de eadem.

Rex vicecomiti salutem. Precipimus tibi quod de nouo exigi facias vn tiel de comitatu in comitatum quousque secundum legem et consuetudinem etc. si non etc. et si etc. vt supra.

25

Aliter de eadem set non est in usu nisi sit petitum pro rege.

Rex vicecomiti salutem. Precipimus tibi quod allocatis tribus comitatibus tuis ad quos I. T. etc. exactus fuit et non comparuit, prout tuipse iusticiariis nostris de pace in comitatu predicto conseruanda assignatis apud Wygorn' die tali anno tali mandauisti, ipsumque [*sic*] I. T. ad comitatum tuum ex tunc proximo tenendum vlterius exigi facias de comitatu in comitatum quousque secundum legem et consuetudinem regni nostri Anglie vtlagetur si non comparuerit, et si comparuerit tunc eum capias et saluo custodiri facias ita quod habeas corpus eius coram prefatis iusticiariis nostris de pace tali die proximo futuro ad respondendum nobis de diuersis feloniis vnde coram prefatis iusticiariis indictatus est, et habeas etc. Teste etc.

26

Intratio de exigi facias de nouo coram iusticiariis pacis etc.

Ad quem diem mandat vicecomes quod ad comitatum Wygorn' tentum ibidem die tali anno tali predictus [I.] T. tercio exactus fuit et non comparuit et quod non fuerunt plures comitatus etc. Ideo de nouo exigatur in forma predicta etc. ita quod sint [*sic*] hic tali die coram prefatis iusticiariis ad respondendum domino regi de diuersis feloniis vnde etc. indictatus est.

27

Intratio de quodam exigi [facias] et super allocationibus irrotulatis.

Ad quem diem mandauit vicecomes etc. quod etc. tentum tali die et anno tali predictus [I.] T. tercio exactus fuit et non comparuit et quod non fuerunt plures comitatus. Ideo preceptum est vicecomiti quod allocatis predictis tribus comitatibus suis ad quos etc. ipsum [I.] T. ad proximum comitatum suum extunc tenendum vlterius exigi faciat in forma predicta etc. ita quod sit hic tali die etc. ad respondendum domino regi de diuersis feloniis vnde etc. indictatus est.

28

Supersedeas.

Rex vicecomiti salutem. Cum nuper tibi precepimus quod exigi faceres I. T. etc. de comitatu in comitatum quousque etc. si non etc., et si etc. tunc eum caperes et saluo custodiri faceres ita quod haberes corpus eius coram iusticiariis nostris de pace in comitatu tuo con-seruanda assignatis apud Wygorn' tali die proximo futuro ad respon-dendum nobis de diuersis feloniis vnde coram prefatis iusticiariis indictatus est, idem I. T. postea venit coram Willelmo Wollashull vno iusticiario pacis comitatus predicti et inuenit nobis sufficientes manu-captores essendi coram prefatis iusticiariis apud Wygorn' [f. 4 b] ad diem prefatum ad respondendum nobis de feloniis predictis, et ideo tibi precipimus quod de prefato I. T. vlterius exigendo, vtlagendo, capiendo seu in aliquo molestando occasione premissa supersedeas omnino, et qualiter hoc preceptum nostrum fueris executum sciri facias iusticiariis nostris de pace ad diem et locum predictas [sic], et habeas etc.
    Teste etc.

29

Aliter.

Et ideo etc. vlterius exigendo, vtlagendo, capiendo, molestando seu in aliquo grauando occasione premissi supersedeas omnino, et quid inde feceritis iusticiariis nostris predictis ad diem predictum certifecetis indilate, et habeas etc.

30

Venire facias super indictamentum vbi placitauit rien coupible.

Rex vicecomiti salutem. Precipimus tibi quod non omittas etc. quin e am ingrediaris et venire facias coram iusticiariis nostris de pace in

comitatu Wygorn' conseruanda assignatis apud Wygorn' die tali anno
tali de visneto de K. xii liberos et legales homines, et qui nec magistro
Iohanni Weston, clerico,[1] de Euesham in comitatu Wygorn' aliqua
affinitate attingant, ad recognoscendum super sacramentum suum si
prefatus magister Iohannes sit culpabilis de diuersis articulis super ipsum
presentatis vnde coram prefatis iusticiariis nostris indictatus est necne,
quia prefatus magister Iohannes posuit se in iuratam illam, et habeas
ibi nomina iuratorum et hoc breue.

Teste etc.

31

Supersedeas de breue de exigendo in casu vbi quidam indictatus fuit de transgressione et postmodum fecit finem, breue
de supersedendo in comitatu non obstante.

Rex vicecomiti salutem. Cum nuper tibi preceperimus quod exigi
faceres I. T. etc. de comitatu in comitatum quousque etc. vtlagatus si
non etc., et si etc. tunc eum caperes et saluo custodiri faceres ita quod
haberes corpus eius coram iusticiariis nostris de pace in comitatu predicto conseruanda assignatis apud Wygorn' die Lune in festo Sancte
Anne[2] vltimo preterito, venit [I. T.] et coram eisdem coram [*sic*] iusticiariis
nostris finem fieri fecit cum nobis pro dictis articulis super eum
presentatis et inde quietus existit, et ideo tibi precipimus quod de
prefato I. T. vlterius exigendo, vtlagendo, capiendo seu in aliquo
molestando seu grauando occasione premissa supersedeas omnino, et
quid inde feceris prefatis iusticiariis nostris de pace ad prefatum diem
certificetis [*sic*] indilate et hoc breue.

Teste etc.

32

Wygorn'.

Deliberacio facta ibidem die tali anno tali[3] coram Iohanne Weston
I. T.[4] et I. B.[5] iusticiariis domini regis ad pacem necnon ad diuersa
felonias, transgressiones et malefacta in comitatu Wygorn' audienda et
terminanda assignatis.

---

[1] In 1395 there is a letter from the prior of Worcester to John Weston,
bachelor of laws ; Worc. Reg. Sede Vacante, ed. J. W. Willis Bund, ii.
359. In 1389, 1415, and 1425, a John Weston was the incumbent in turn
of each of the following three churches, at Wych, at St. Albans, and at
' Evenload ', Oswaldslow hundred; Nash, *op. cit.*, i. 330, ii, App. 122,
i. 395.　　　　　　　　　　　　　　[2] The date of the feast is 26 July.

[3] Probably at Worcester Castle, in March, 5 Hen. V, 1418 ; ch. iii (1),
p. 89, note 1, *supra*.　　　　　　　　[4] John Throgmerton.

[5] John Brace.

Carta allocata de [regis gracia ?].

R. M.[1] captus pro eo quod indictatus fuit coram iusticiariis domini regis ad pacem in comitatu Wygorn' conseruandam assignatis de eo quod ipse die Veneris etc. anno tali [2] en tiel lieu [3] mane in aurora inter diem et noctem vi et armis contra pacem domini regis in diuersis conuenticulis cum diuersis hominibus modo guerrino arraiatus insurrexit etc., et Thomam B.[4] et I. C.[5] ibidem inuentos felonice interfecerunt et murdrauerunt etc. Idemque R. M. ad barram ductus per vicecomitem allocutus qualiter velit [se] de feloniis predictis acquietare qui dicit quod dominus rex nunc per literas suas patentes pardonauit ei sectam pacis sue que ad ipsum regem pertinet pro omnimodis prodicionibus, murdris, raptibus mulierum, rebellionibus, insurexionibus, feloniis, conspiracionibus, transgressionibus, offensis, et negligenciis, extorsionibus, mesprisionibus, ignoranciis, contemptibus, concellamentis et decepcionibus per ipsum ante octauum diem Decembris anno regni sui secundo factis siue perpetratis,[6] ac eciam vtlagariis sique fuerint versus eum in premissis promulgate ; et profert hic in curia cartam predictam que premissa testatur et breue eisdem iusticiariis directum de non molestando contra tenorem carte etc. cuius data est xvi die Marcii anno regni sui quarto.[7] Pretextu cuius idem R. petit se ipsum a prisona deliberari et inspectis literis predictis consideratum est quod idem R. eat inde sine die etc.

33

[f. 5] Breue de non molestando eiusdem ac . . . de cancellaria.

Rex custodibus pacis sue ac iusticiariis suis ad diuersa felonias, transgressiones et malefacta in comitatu Wygorn' audienda et terminanda assignatis et eorum cuilibet, salutem. Cum de gracia nostra speciali pardonauerimus Roberto etc. quocumque nomine idem censeatur sectam pacis nostre que ad nos versus ipsum pertinet, et sic recitando totum breue ut antea vobis mandamus quod ipsum R. contra tenorem literarum nostrarum predictarum non molestetis in aliquo seu grauetis.

Teste etc.[8]

[1] Robert Monnes of Oxholm ; p. 71, *supra*.　　　[2] 30 June 1413.
[3] Shipston.　　　[4] Baret.　　　[5] Iohannem Clerk.
[6] The exception from the pardon of offences committed after 19 November 1414 and also of a few especially heinous crimes is here omitted ; cf. Coram Rege Roll 616, Pasch. 3 Hen. V, Rex, rot. 1, discussed in ch. iii, (1), p. 70.
[7] The identification of the case proves that the reigning king is Henry V, and the year therefore 1417. For the text of the writ, see no. 33, *infra*.　　　[8] 16 March, 4 Hen. V.

34[1]

Breue de cerciorari iusticiariis pacis etc. ad mittendum coram rege quoddam indictamentum.

Rex custodibus pacis sue comitatus Wygorn' ac iusticiariis suis ad diuersa felonias, transgressiones et alia malefacta in comitatu predicto audienda et terminanda assignatis et eorum cuilibet, salutem. Volentes certis de causis omnia et singula indictamenta de quibuscumque feloniis et transgressionibus vnde T. B.[2] de comitatu predicto,[3] chiualer, et Nicholaus filius eiusdem Thome, ac omnes alii in eodem indictamento contenti coram vobis seu aliquo vestrum indictati existunt coram nobis et non alibi terminari, vobis et cuilibet vestrum precipimus firmiter iniungentes quod indictamenta predicta cum omnibus ea tangentibus adeo plene et integre prout coram vobis capta fuerint et penes vos resident sub sigillis vestris vel vnius vestrum distincte et aperte ac saluo et secure per aliquem pro quo nobis respondere volueritis mittatis, vel vnus vestrum mittat, coram nobis in octabis Sancti Iohannis Baptiste[4] vbicumque tunc fuerimus in Anglia vna cum hoc breui et [sic] vlterius inde fieri faciamus prout de iure et secundum legem et consuetudinem regni nostri Anglie fore viderimus faciendum.

Teste etc.[5]

35

Responsum eiusdem.

Responsum I. Wode[6] et I. Moraunt[7] custodum pacis necnon iusticiariorum domini regis ad diuersa felonias, transgressiones et malefacta in comitatu Wygorn' audienda et terminanda assignatorum patet in quibusdam cedulis huic breui consuetis.

36

Retornum eiusdem.

Omnia et singula indictamenta cum omnibus ea tangentibus de omnimodis feloniis et transgressionibus Thomam Burdet infrascriptum per nomen Thome Burdet de Arwe,[8] in comitatu Warr', chiualer, et Nicholaum filium eiusdem Thome infraspecificatum per nomen Nicholai Burdet de H.[9] in comitatu Wygorn', armigeri, ac omnibus

---

[1] Belongs with nos. 35 and 36.   [2] Thomas Burdet.
[3] An error; his county is Warwick, not Worcester; see no. 36.
[4] 1 July 1419.   [5] Probably early in 1419.   [6] John Wode.
[7] The ' I ' is an error for ' T ', the only mistake that I have noted in the justices' names; see ch. iii (1), s. 3.   [8] Arrow.
[9] Nicholas is of ' Bruyneslench ' or Abbot's Lench (see ch. iii (1), pp. 69–72); I cannot explain the ' H '.

aliis in eisdem indictamentis contentis tangencia adeo plene et integre prout coram nobis custodibus pacis capta fuerint et penes nos resident per I. F.[1] ad diem infrascriptum coram domino rege vbicumque tunc fuerit in Anglia sub sigillis nostris mittimus in quibusdam cedulis huic breui consutis. Et quoad indictamentum Thome Burdet de comitatu Wygorn', chiualer, infraspecificati, nullum indictamentum versus prefatum Thomam Burdet de etc., coram nobis prefatis custodibus pacis de feloniis nec de transgressionibus existit. Ideo nullum indictamentum versus ipsum Thomam Burdet de comitatu Wygorn', chiualer, in breui isto nominatum ad diem infrascriptum coram domino rege mittere possumus ad presens secundum tenorem huius breuis.

37 [2]

Breue de cerciorari custodibus pacis ac iusticiariis suis in comitatu W.[3] etc. ac eorum cuilibet etc. ad mittendum quoddam indictamentum.

Rex custodibus pacis ac iusticiariis suis de diuersis transgressionibus, feloniis et alia malefacta [*sic*] in comitatu Wygorn' audienda et terminanda assignatis et eorum cuilibet, salutem. Cum Agnes que fuit vxor W. B.[4] in curia nostra coram nobis per breue nostrum appellauerit Iohannem Norton [5] et Iohannem Baldok [6] et alios etc. de

---

[1] Iohannem Forthey.

[2] Nos. 37-9 belong together and are connected with the following case. On Thursday 23 September 1417 (5 Hen. V), Alice Norton, and William Norton, son of William Norton, 'et alii' were indicted before Weston, Throgmerton, and Brace, Worcestershire justices of the peace, of the murder of William Bawderipe on Sunday, 4 July. On Saturday, 9 January of the following year, William Norton, son of William Norton, 'et alii' were indicted before the said Throgmerton, Brace, and others, of the same murder on Monday, 5 [*sic*] July; C. R. Roll 631, Hill. 6 Hen. V, 1419, Rex, rot. 15. The indictments were summoned Coram Rege by writ of *certiorari* but not acted on, because meanwhile in the court of King's Bench (probably in the preceding Trin. term), Agnes, the widow of Bawderipe, 'appealed' of the same murder the above-named Alice and William Norton, also others, including John Norton and John Badcok (the latter as accessory). Their 'attachment' is recorded in Mich. term, 6 Hen. V, 1418, C. R. Roll 630, rot. 31 d ; and two of the appellees, Alice and William Norton, were acquitted by a jury on 25 February, 7 Hen. V, 1420, before Babyngton, &c., at Worcester; *ibid.*, and C. R. Roll 631, rot. 15, and Agnes was fined for her false appeal; *ibid.* 637, Trin. 8 Hen. V, 1420, Worcester, Fines and Amercements, rot. 1. Process continued against the rest; *ibid.* 630, rot. 31 d. [3] Worcester.

[4] William Baudryk, alias Bawderipe ; C. R. Roll 631, Rex, rot. 15.

[5] Evidently included in the 'et alii' of the indictment before the justices of the peace.

[6] Clearly an error for Badcok ; see note 2, *supra*.

morte predicti W. etc., quondam viri ipsius Agnetis, ac iam ex parte eiusdem Agnetis in curia nostra coram nobis accepimus quod predictus Iohannes Norton et omnes alii pro morte predicta coram vobis indictati existunt, et nos inde per vos plenius cerciorari volentes, vobis et cuilibet vestrum mandamus quod indictamentum predictum cum omnibus illud tangentibus adeo plene et integre prout in custodia vestra seu alicuius vestrum vt dicitur residet, nobis a die Sancti Michaelis[1] in vnum mensem vbicumque tunc fuerimus in Anglia distincte et aperte sub sigillis vestris mittatis, vel aliquis vestrum sub sigillo suo mittat, cum hoc breui, et [*sic*] vlterius in appello predicto ad tunc consultus [*sic*] procedere valeamus prout de iure et secundum legem et consuetudinem regni nostri Anglie fuerit procedendum.

Teste etc.[2]

38
Responsum iusticiariorum.

Responsum I. T.[3] et I. Wode[4] custodum pacis necnon iusticiariorum domini regis ad diuersa felonias, transgressiones [f. 5 b.] et malefacta in comitatu Wygorn' audienda et terminanda assignatorum prout patet in quadam cedula huic breui consuta.

39
Retornum eiusdem breuis etc.

Indictamentum Iohannis Norton et aliorum in breui isto nominatorum et de quibus in breui isto fit mencio adeo plene et integre prout penes nos dictos custodes pacis cum omnibus illud tangentibus residet coram domino rege ad diem infrascriptum vbicumque tunc fuerit in Anglia sub sigillis nostris mittimus in cedula huic breui consuta; et quoad indictamentum Iohannis Baldok[5] infranominati nullum indictamentum coram nobis prefatis custodibus pro morte W. B.[6] infraspecificati residet eo quod coram prefatis custodibus pacis indictatus non existat [*sic*]. Ideo indictamentum versus ipsum Iohannem coram domino rege ad diem infrascriptum mittere [non] possumus secundum tenorem huius breuis.

---

[1] Evidently 29 September, 6 Hen. V, 1418; see p. 257, note 2, *supra*.

[2] Probably issued in the preceding summer just after the 'appeal' A writ of *Capias* enrolled on Coram Rege Roll 631, Hill. 6 Hen. V, 1418, Rex, rot. 13, specifies John Norton, although he is not referred to by name in the enrolment of the indictments but probably is included in 'et alii'; *ibid.*, rot. 15. If the original indictments could be found they would undoubtedly include the name of John Norton; cf. case no. 32 for the omission on the Coram Rege Roll of some of the names actually given in the files of Ancient Indictments.   [3] John Throgmerton.

[4] John Wode.   [5] See p. 257, note 6, *supra*.   [6] *Ibid.*, note 4, *supra*.

40
Manucapcio.

Memorandum quod ad diem et locum predictos coram prefatis iusticiariis venerunt in propriis personis suis W. R. de B. in comitatu Wygorn', yoman, et I. W. de eadem etc., I. de T. de etc., et I. B. etc., et manuceperunt pro Iohanne B. de B. in comitatu predicto, husband-man, indictato de felonia adtunc coram prefatis, iusticiariis presenti de habendo corpus eius coram eisdem iusticiariis pacis in comitatu Wygorn' necnon ad diuersa felonias, transgressiones et malefacta in comitatu predicto audienda et terminanda assignatis apud W.[1] die tali proximo futuro, et sic de die in diem quousque secundum legem et consuetudinem regni Anglie deliberetur, videlicet, quilibet eorum corpus pro corpore etc.

41
Manucapcio.

Memorandum quod ad diem et locum predictos coram prefatis iusticiariis venerunt in propriis personis suis vn tiel vn tiel vn tiel et vn tiel, omnes de etc., et manuceperunt pro I. B. de etc. indictato de felonia adtunc coram prefatis iusticiariis presenti de habendo corpus eius hic coram prefatis iusticiariis pacis die etc. ad respondendum domino regi de eisdem feloniis, videlicet, quilibet manucaptorum predictorum corpus pro corpore.

42
Aliter.

Memorandum quod die Lune etc. anno etc. coram Willelmo W.[2] vno iusticiario pacis comitatus predicti venit vn tiel, et sic recitando quatuor manucaptores in propriis personis suis et manuceperunt pro I. K. etc. indictament' [sic] de felonia adtunc coram prefatis iusticiariis presenti de habendo etc. die Iouis proximo, ut supra.

43
Remittuntur prisoni.

W. T. de B. in comitatu Wygorn', yoman, I. B. de D. in eodem comitatu, yoman, et I. R. de T. in eodem comitatu, yoman, prisones indictati de felonia remittuntur prisoni domini regis castri Wygorn' sub custodia vicecomitis ibidem moraturi [quo]vsque deliberentur secundum legem et consuetudinem regni Anglie periculo incumbente etc.

[1] Worcester   [2] Wolashull.

44
Fines.

De finibus factis coram prefatis iusticiariis ad diem et locum predictas [*sic*] etc.[1]

De Willelmo F. de M. in comitatu Gloucestr', yoman, de fine pro transgressione per plegium T. R. et I. K. iis.

Et sic de singulis etc.

45
Quedam securitas pacis.
Wygorn'.

Memorandum quod ad sessionem pacis tentam apud W.[2] die etc. anno etc. coram I. T.[3], I. W.[4] et I. B.[5] iusticiariis domini regis de pace in comitatu Wygorn' conseruanda assignatis venit I. G., clericus, in propria persona sua coram prefatis custodibus pacis, et petiit securitatem pacis de T. B. et N. T. presentibus in propriis personis suis, scilicet eo quod ipsi T. et N. ipsum Iohannem minauerunt de vita et mutilacione membrorum suorum per quod ipse ob metum mortis ad negocia sua facienda palam incedere non audebat quouismodo ut dicit et hoc coram prefatis iusticiariis affidauit. Virtute cuius querele dictum fuit per prefatos iusticiarios prefatis T. et N. separatim ad inueniendum securitatem pacis erga dominum regem et cunctum populum suum et precipue erga dominum Iohannem B. [*sic*]. Quiquidem T. et N. ad hoc replicando dixerunt quod ipsi alias in cancellaria in curia domini regis inuenierunt et securitatem fecerunt de pace erga dominum regem et populum suum prout lex expostulat, et petit [*sic*] diem de recordo illo habendo inde de exoneracione eorum ad proximam sessionem pacis; et eis conceditur et dies datus est eis hic die Sabbati proximo etc. proximo futuro apud Wygorn' de recordo illo habendo prefatis iusticiariis deliberando alioquin si prefati T. et N. de recordo illo deficerint quod tunc prefati T. et N. in propriis personis suis compareant coram prefatis iusticiariis [f. 6] ad prefatum diem Sabbati et locum predictum ad inueniendum securitatem predictam sub pena mille marcarum, et ad faciendum et recipiendum ea in hac parte que ex parte domini regis eis adtunc ibidem iniungentur in securitatem predictam faciendam, et medio tempore quod prefati T. et N. vsque ad

---

[1] For the form, cf. e.g. Exchequer, K. R., 137, $\frac{8}{1}$, estreats of Worcestershire justices of the peace, 5 Hen. VI, John Forthey, clerk.
[2] Worcester.   [3] John Throgmerton.
[4] Probably John Weston (cf. no. 32) but perhaps John Wode.
[5] John Brace.

predictum diem Sabbati proximum post festum Epiphanie Domini [1]
proximo futurum sub pena predicta se bene gerent, et vterque eorum
se bene geret pro se et seruientibus suis erga dominum regem et
populum suum et precipue erga dictum Iohannem G., et quod ipsi T.
et N. per se nec per seruientes nec per aliquos alios eorum procuracione
non inferrent aut inferri procurabunt, nec inferret aut inferri procurabit,
per ipsos vel per alios eidem I. G. aut alicui de populo regis in corpore
suo aliquod dampnum corporale vel grauamen per minas insidias in-
sulta seu alio modo quod in lesionem pacis domini regis cedere valeat
quouismodo sub pena mille marcarum predictarum ; quasquidem mille
marcas predictas predicti T. et N. recognoscunt se domino regi debere
et vterque eorum domino regi debere recognoscit de bonis et catallis
terris et tenementis suis separatim leuandas iuxta recognicionem predictam, si contingat dictos T. et N. seu aliquos alios nominibus suis in
premissis seu in aliquo premissorum delinquere et modo legitimo
conuinci etc.

46
Aliter.

Memorandum quod die Lune proximo post festum Purificacionis
Beate Marie [2] anno etc. coram I. B.[3] vno custode pacis domini regis in
comitatu Wygorn' conseruande assignato venerunt I. P., I. T., I. G. et
R. P., omnes de villa de P.[4] in comitatu Wygorn' in propriis personis
suis, et manuceperunt pro I. B., tayllor, in P. in comitatu predicto
adtunc presenti coram prefato iusticiario custode pacis et seruientibus
suis quod ipse I. B. pro se et seruientibus suis amodo se bene geret
erga dominum regem et cunctum populum suum et precipue erga T. H.
de etc., et quod idem Iohannes per se nec per seruientes suos nec per
aliquos eorum nomine [suo] non inferret aut inferri procurabit per se
vel per alios eidem T. in corpore suo aliquod dampnum vel grauamen
per minas insidias insultum seu aliquo alio modo quod in lesionem seu
perturbacionem pacis domini regis cedere valeat quouismodo ; videlicet,
quilibet manucaptorum predictorum sub pena viginti librarum et predictus P. [sic] sub pena xl librarum, et tam predicti manucaptores quam
predictus I. B. recognoscunt se domino regi debere, videlicet, quilibet
manucaptorum predictorum pro se xx libras et predictus I. B. predictas
xl libras ; quasquidem tam viginti libras quam xl libras iidem I.P.,
I. T., I. G. et R. P. concedunt de terris et catallis suis ad opus domini

---

[1] The date of the feast is 6 January.
[2] The date of the feast is 2 February.
[3] John Brace.   [4] Perhaps Pershore.

regis leuari si contingat ipsum I. B. incontrarium facere contra manu-
capcionem supradictam etc.

47 [1]

Placitum coram iusticiariis pacis super breue de statuto laboratorum.

Walterus P.[2] de W.[3] in comitatu Wygorn', laborarius, attachiatus
fuit ad respondendum tam domino regi quam Baldewino Thorn[4] de
Wygorn' de placito transgressionis et contemptus contra formam
statuti de seruientibus nuper editi et prouisi, et vnde idem Baldewinus
qui sequitur etc. in propria persona sua queritur quod cum per dominum E. nuper regem Anglie, auum domini regis nunc,[5] et consilium
suum pro communi vtilitate eiusdem regni ordinatum sit quod si aliquis
seruiens in seruicio alicuius retentus ante finem termini inter eos
concordati ab eo seruicio sine causa racionabili recesserit, penam
imprisonamenti subeat, prefatus Walterus liceat retentus fuisset apud
L.[6] xii die Decembris anno etc. in officio housbrandrie et ad patens[7]
de ligno fabricanda operanda [sic] et alia necessaria sua eiusdem artis
laboranda cum prefato Baldewino a festo Natalis Domini extunc
proximo sequenti anno regni regis predicti predicto vsque in vigilia
eiusdem festi anni sequentis, prefatus Walterus sic retentus primo die
Augusti extunc proximo sequenti absque causa vel licencia extra seruicium dicti Baldewini recessit in regis contemptum et ipsius Baldewini graue dampnum et contra ordinacionem in hoc casu prouisam ad
dampnum ipsius Baldewini centum solidorum, sicut idem B. qui tam
pro domino rege tam pro seipso sequitur dicit et inde producit sectam
etc.[8]

[f. 6 b]. Et prefatus Walterus in propria persona sua venit et defendit
vim et iniuriam quando etc., et dicit quod ipse nunquam fuit retentus
cum ipso B. per tempus predictum in seruicio suo sicut queritur et
declarauit, et de hoc ponit se super patriam et predictus B. similiter.

---

[1] With nos. 48-50.   [2] Not identified.
[3] Worcester; cf. no. 48, *infra*.
[4] In 1433 a Baldwin Thorn was a bailiff of the city of Worcester;
Nash, *op cit.*, ii, App. 111.   [5] Hen. IV.
[6] Lyghe or Leigh, Pershore hundred; Nash, *op. cit.*, ii. 73; Habington,
op. cit., i. 327; cf. no. 48, *infra*.
[7] Patten, wooden shoes; N.E.D. Cf. also *ibid.*, paten, a flat dish.
[8] The form of the count differs slightly from that in use in the upper
courts in the fourteenth century; cf. my Statutes of Labourers, App. 420-2,
where the ordinance is not rehearsed. Cf. Year Book, Hill. 5 Hen. V, no. 26,
for the statement that the rehearsal of the enactment is not necessary in
the count, and cf. no. 53, *infra*.

Ideo preceptum est vicecomiti quod venire faciat hic die Martis in
septimana Pasche proximo future xii etc. de visneto etc. per quos etc.
et qui nec etc. ad recognoscendum etc. quia tam etc.,[1] et idem dies
datus est partibus predictis hic etc. Ad quam diem venerunt tam
predictus B. quam predictus W. in propriis personis suis, et vicecomes
retornauit breue cum panello de nominibus iuratorum, et ipsi vocati
non venerunt. Ideo preceptum est eidem vicecomiti quod habeat
corpora iuratorum predictorum hic die Martis in septimana Pentecostis etc. ad recognoscendum in forma predicta etc.,[2] et idem dies
datus etc. Ad quem diem venerunt tam predictus B. quam predictus
W. in propriis personis suis etc., et vicecomes retornauit breue cum
panello etc., et iuratores vocati non venerunt. Ideo preceptum est
eidem vicecomiti quod distringat eos etc. et quod de exitibus etc.[3] et
quod habeat corpora eorum hac die Iouis proxima post festum Sancti
Michaelis Archangeli[4] proximo futurum ad recognoscendum in forma
predicta etc., et idem dies etc.

48

Venire facias eiusdem placiti.

Rex vicecomiti salutem. Precipimus tibi quod venire facias coram
iusticiariis nostris de pace in comitatu Wygorn' conseruanda assignatis
apud Wygorn' die Martis in septimana Pasche proximo future de
visneto de Lygh[5] xii iuratores liberos et legales homines quorum
quilibet habeat centum solidos etc. terre tenementorum vel redditus ad
minus per annum per quos rei veritas melius sciri poterit, et qui nec
B. T.[6] de Wygorn' nec W. P.[7] de Wygorn', laborer, aliqua affinitate
attingant, ad recognoscendum super sacramentum suum si prefatus W.
retentus fuisset cum prefato B. in officio housbrandrie et ad patens[8]
de ligno fabricanda operanda et alia necessaria sua eiusdem artis
laboranda et exercenda a festo natalis Domini anno regni nostri
tercio[9] vsque in vigilia eiusdem festi anni sequentis secundum formam
statuti de seruientibus nuper editi et prouisi, sicut idem B. qui tam
pro nobis quam pro seipso in hac parte sequitur dicit necne, quia tam
predictus Baldewinus quam predictus Walterus inter quos inde con-
tencio est posuerunt se in iuratam illam; et habeas etc.
        Teste etc.

----

[1] Cf. no. 48.   [2] Cf. no. 49.   [3] Cf. no. 50.
[4] 29 September is the date of the feast.   [5] See *supra*, p. 262, note 6.
[6] Baldewinus Thorne.   [7] Walterus P.   [8] See p. 262, note 7, *supra*.
[9] 3 Hen. IV, 1401 ; cf. no. 47, note 5.

49
Habeas corpora eiusdem placiti.

Rex vicecomiti salutem. Precipimus tibi quod habeas coram iusticiariis nostris de pace in comitatu Wygorn' conseruanda assignatis apud Wygorn' die Martis in septimana Pentecostis proximo future corpora vn tiel vn tiel et vn tiel etc. iuratorum summonitorum coram prefatis iusticiariis inter B.[1] etc., qui tam pro nobis quam pro seipso sequitur querentem, et W. P.[2] defendentem etc., de placito transgressionis et contemptus contra formam statuti de seruientibus inde editi et prouisi ad faciendum iuratam illam; et habeas etc.
Teste etc.

50
Breue de distringas versus eosdem iuratores.

Rex vicecomiti salutem. Precipimus tibi quod distringas vn tiel etc. iuratores summonitos coram iusticiariis nostris de pace in comitatu Wygorn' conseruanda assignatis inter B.[3] etc., qui tam pro nobis quam pro seipso sequitur querentem, et W. N.[4] defendentem etc., de placito transgressionis et contemptus contra formam statuti de seruientibus nuper editi et prouisi per omnes terras et catalla sua in balliua tua, ita etc. ac quod de exitibus etc., et quod habeas corpora eorum iuratorum coram iusticiariis nostris predictis apud Wygorn' die etc. proximo futuro ad faciendum iuratam illam et ad audiendum iudicium suum de pluribus defaltis; et habeas &c.
Teste etc.

51
Wygorn'.

Placita corone tenta ibidem die etc. anno etc. coram I. T.[5] et aliis etc. iusticiariis domini regis ad pacem [conservandam] nec non ad diuersa felonias, transgressiones et malefacta in comitatu predicto audienda et terminanda assignatis etc.

Wygorn'. Placitum super indictamentum transgressionis vbi deficit [iusticiar'?[6]].

Iohannes Palmer[7] et alii attachiati fuerunt ad respondendum domino regi de placito quare ipsi die etc. anno etc. vi et armis agregatis sibi

---

[1] Baldewinum. [2] Walterum P. [3] Baldewinum.
[4] An error for W. P., Walterum P. [5] John Throgmerton.
[6] Illegible.
[7] John Palmer was acting as a juror at Worcester in 6 Hen. V; Gaol Delivery Roll 73, no. 2, m. 6. Cf. also the indictment in 1397 of a John

quam pluribus malefactoribus ignotis clausum et domos Roberti W.[1]
fregerunt, et aueria diuersorum ibidem imparcata ceperunt et abduxerunt contra pacem domini regis, vnde coram prefatis iusticiariis
pacis domini regis comitatus Wygorn' indictati sunt. Idemque I. et
alii venerunt in propriis personis suis et separatim dicunt quod quo
ad veniendum vi et armis seu quicquid quod est contra pacem
domini regis seu ad fraccionem clausi et domorum predictorum
dicunt separatim [sic] quod ipsi in nullo sunt culpabiles et de hoc
ponunt se super patriam, et predictus R. similiter : et quo [f. 7] ad
capcionem et abduxionem aueriorum predictorum dicunt separatim
quod ipsi sunt tenentes domini de Clyfford [2] ut de manerio suo de
Elynton [3] et de predicto domino tenet quilibet eorum vnum mesua-
gium x acrarum terre cum pertinentiis etc. in Elynton vt parcella
manerii de Elynton etc. ; ad que [4] dominus de Clyfford et omnes
homines ac tenentes sui predicti manerii etc., et omnes antecessores sui
et omnes illi quorum statum ipsi habent, in eisdem habere debent communem pasturam in vna pastura ac communa subtus Bredonhull in
villa de Wolashull [5] ad omnimoda aueria sua depascenda annuatim et
per totum annum tamquam pertinentem ad tenementa sua a tempore
quo non existat memoria, per quod ipsi aueria sua predicta in communa sua predicta depascerunt. Et predictus R. Wollashull per
quendam I. W. seruientem suum aueria illa extra communam suam
predictam vi et armis imparcauit, et postea aueria illa eisdem I. P.[6] et
aliis per plegium vn tiel et vn tiel deliberauit, per quod ipsi ea ceperunt
et abduxerunt prout eis bene licuit predictis die et loco quo supponitur transgressionem predictam fieri, absque hoc quod ipsi aueria illa
imparcata vi et armis ceperunt et abduxerunt prout per indictamentum
predictum supponitur, vnde non intendunt aliquam iniuriam in personis suis assignare [sic] posse, et petunt iudicium etc. Et Ricardus
Osemye [7] qui pro domino rege sequitur in hac parte dicit quod ipsi

Palmer of Ekynton before the Worcestershire justices of the peace ; Assize
Roll 1034, m. 2. Elynton, *infra*, is probably a clerical error for Ekynton,
modern Eckington, Pershore hundred ; Nash, *op. cit.*, ii. 180.
   [1] Wolashull ; see *infra*, and cf. William Wolashull, ch. iii (1), pp. 74-5.
The Wolashulls came from Nafford, now part of Eckington ; Nash, *loc. cit.*
   [2] For the connexion of John de Clifford, lord of Westmoreland, with
Worcestershire, see Nash, *op. cit.*, ii. 346 ; cf. also Cal. Pat. Hen. V,
1413-1416, 320, 424 ; 1416-1422, 11, 72, 77, 86.
   [3] See *supra*.   [4] Perhaps a mistake for ' ac quod '.
   [5] The little village of Wolashull is situated on Bredon Hill, Pershore
hundred ; Nash, *op. cit.*, ii. 180 ; Habington, *op. cit.*, ii. 212.
   [6] Iohanni Palmer.
   [7] If the correct reading is Osemye, it is an error for Oseneye ; see
ch. iii (1), pp. 66-7.

sunt culpabiles de omnibus transgressionibus predictis prout per indictamentum predictum supponitur etc. absque causa supra per ipsos preallegata, et de hoc ponit se super patriam ; et predicti etc. similiter. Ideo preceptum est vicecomiti quod non omittat etc. quin venire faciat hic tali die etc. xii etc. de etc.

52
De regraderia et excessu.
Wygorn'.

R. E., R. H. et S. T. attachiati fuerunt ad respondendum domino regi nunc de placito quare ipsi die etc. anno etc. apud A. de I. S. et de aliis diuersis hominibus emerunt xxv torcas [1] pro l. s., et postea eis [*sic*] vendiderunt I. M. coruiser et aliis diuersis sutoribus eodem anno pro octo marcis in regraderia et excessu contra legem etc. Et predicti R. E., R. H. et S. T. per T. B. attornatum suum veniunt et separatim dicunt quod ipsi in nullo sunt inde culpabiles et hoc petunt separatim quod inquiratur per patriam ; et R. C.[2] qui pro domino rege sequitur in hac parte dicit quod ipsi sunt culpabiles prout per indictamentum predictum supponitur, et hoc petit quod inquiratur per patriam. Ideo preceptum est vicecomiti quod non omittat etc. quin venire faciat hic xii etc. de visneto etc. die tali etc. proximo futuro et qui nec etc. et idem dies etc. ; ad quem diem vicecomes non misit breue. Ideo sicut prius preceptum est vicecomiti quod non omittat in forma predicta etc. quin venire faciat hic tali die xii etc. ad recognoscendum in forma predicta etc., et idem dies etc.

53
Breue de statuto de seruientibus.
Wygorn'.

I. G.,[3] B. K.[4] et H. S.[5] etc. attachiati fuerunt ad respondendum tam domino regi quam I. H. de placito quare cum per dominum Edwardum nuper regem Anglie, proauum domini regis nunc,[6] et consilium suum pro communi vtilitate eiusdem regni ordinatum sit quod si aliquis seruiens in seruicio alicuius retentus ante finem termini con-

---

[1] 'Torcha, Torchia, f. Certus coriorum numerus'; Du Cange, Glossarium.
[2] Probably should be O, and therefore refers to Richard Oseneye the king's attorney ; see p. 265, note 7, *supra*.
[3] Becomes I. B. through the rest of the case.
[4] Not mentioned again.
[5] Probably stands for ' seruiens' which is, however, not a good ' addition' ; App. III, p. 386.   [6] Hen. V.

cordati sine causa rationabili vel licencia recessit penam imprisonamenti subeat, et nullus sub eadem pena talem a seruicio suo recipere
vel retinere presumat, predictus I. B. [sic] predictam H. seruientem
ipsius I. H. in seruicio suo apud P. nuper retentam, qui [sic] ab eodem
seruicio ante finem termini inter eos concordati sine causa racionabili
et licencia ipsius I. H. recessit in seruicium ipsius [I.] B., quamquam
ipse de prefata H. eidem I. H. restituenda requisitus fuerit, admisit et
retinuit in regis contemptum et ipsius I. H. graue dampnum ac contra
formam ordinacionis predicte; et de placito quare predicta H. a seruicio predicti I. H. ante finem termini inter eos concordati sine causa
racionabili et licencia ipsius I. H., vt predictum est, recessit in domini
regis contemptum et ipsius [I.] H. graue dampnum ac contra ordinacionem predictam.

[f. 7 b.] Et vnde idem I. H. qui sequitur tam pro domino rege quam
pro seipso per G. P. attornatum suum queritur quod cum predicta I. H.[1]
in festo Sancti Michaelis Apostoli[2] anno etc. apud P. retenta fuisset
cum ipso I. H. ad deseruiendum ei in officio ancille ab eodem festo
per vnum annum integrum extunc proximo sequentem, idem [sic] H.
infra terminum predictum, videlicet tali die, a seruicio ipsius I. H.
sine causa racionabili et licencia ipsius I. H. recessit in regis contemptum et ipsius I. H. graue dampnum et contra formam ordinacionis
predicte. Et predictus I. B. die Veneris predicto ipsam H. seruientem ipsius I. H. in dicto seruicio suo apud [sic] nuper retentam
qui [sic] ab eodem seruicio ante finem termini predicti inter eos concordati sine causa racionabili et licencia ipsius I. H., vt predictum est,
recessit in seruicium ipsius [I.] B., quamquam ipse de prefata H. eidem
I. P.[3] restituenda requisitus fuerit, admisit et retinuit in regis contemptum et ipsius I. H. graue dampnum et contra ordinacionem
predictam. Ideo dicit quod deterioratus est et dampnum habet ad
valenciam x librarum, et inde producit sectam etc.

Et predicti I. B. et H. per T. H. attornatum suum veniunt et defen-
dunt vim et iniuriam quiquid etc. Et predicta H. dicit quod nunquam
retenta fuit cum prefato I. H. ad deseruiendum ei in officio predicto
per tempus predictum prout idem I. H. superius versus eum [sic] queritur, et [de] hoc ponit se super patriam et predictus I. H. similiter.

Et predictus I. B. protestando quod predictus I. H.[4] nunquam
retenta fuit cum prefato I. H. ad deseruiendum ei in officio predicto
per tempus predictum in forma qua idem I. H. superius versus eum

---

[1] Should be H. the servant, not I. H., the plaintiff.
[2] 29 September.   [3] Should be ' I. H.'   [4] Should be ' predicta H.'

queritur, dicit quod predictus I. H. actorum [*sic*] predictum versus eum habere non debet, quia dicit quod predictus [*sic*] H. diu ante predictum festum Sancti Michaelis[1] quo etc. in festo Natalis Sancti Iohannis Baptiste[2] anno etc. apud P.[3] retenta fuit cum ipso I. B. ad deseruiendum ei in officio ancille ab eodem festo Natalis Sancti Iohannis Baptiste per vnum annum integrum proximo sequentem, quiquidem [*sic*] H. infra terminum predictum, videlicet in predicto festo Sancti Michaelis, ab eodem seruicio sine causa racionabili et licencia ipsius [I.] B. recessit, et die Veneris extunc proximo sequente ex mera et spontanea voluntate sua in dictum seruicium ipsius I. B. reuenit, ac idem I. B. ipsum [*sic*] ut seruientem suum amisit[4] et retinuit prout ei bene licuit, et hoc paratus est verificare; vnde petit iudicium si predictus I. H. accionem suam predictam in hoc casu versus eum habere debeat etc.

Et predictus I. H. dicit quod ipse ab accione sua predicta versus prefatum I. B. habenda pro aliqua per ipsum I. B. preallegata excludi non debet, quia dicit quod idem I. B. predictam I. H.[5] seruientem ipsius I. H. in seruicio suo nuper retentam, qui [*sic*] ab eodem seruicio ante finem termini predicti inter eos concordati sine causa racionabili et licencia ipsius I. H. recessit in seruicium ipsius I. B. quamquam etc. requisitus fuerit, admisit et retinuit in forma qua idem I. H. versus eum queritur, absque hoc quod predicta H. retenta fuit cum prefato I. B. ad deseruiendum ei in officio predicto a predicto festo Natalis Sancti Iohannis Baptiste per vnum annum integrum tunc proximo sequentem prout idem I. B. superius allegat, et hoc paratus est verificare; vnde petit iudicium etc. Et predictus I. B. dicit quod predicta H. retenta fuit cum eodem I. B. ad deseruiendum ei in officio predicto a predicto festo etc. per vnum annum integrum tunc proximo sequentem in forma qua ipse superius allegat; et de hoc ponit se super patriam, et predictus I. H. similiter. Ideo preceptum est vicecomiti quod venire faciat hic tali die proximo futuro de visneto etc. xii etc. per quos etc. et qui nec etc. ad recognoscendum etc. quia tam etc.

54

Quedam securitas pacis etc.

Memorandum quod B. H. venit coram I. B.[6] iusticiario domini regis in comitatu Wygorn[7] apud W.[7] die tali anno tali, et recognouit se teneri domino regi in c. libris de terris et catallis suis ad opus domini

---

[1] 29 September. [2] 24 June. [3] Pershore (?) [4] An error for 'admisit'.
[5] Should be H. simply. [6] John Brace. [7] Worcester.

regis leuandis, si contingat eundem B. in posterum per se aut per suos
aut aliquem alium ad eius procuracionem aliquod dampnum corporale
alicui de populo domini regi acere seu fieri [f. 8] procurare soluendis
eidem domino regi cum inde modo legitimo per legem terre fuerit
conuictus. Super hoc A., B., C., D. de comitatu predicto etc. manuceperunt predictum R. [*sic*] de se bene gerendo erga dominum regem
et populum suum, et vlterius recognouerunt se et quemlibet eorum per
se teneri domino regi in cc. libris de terris et catallis suis ad opus
domini regis leuandis si contingat eundem R. [*sic*] aliquod dampnum
corporale alicui de populo domini regis in posterum facere aut fieri
procurare et inde modo legitimo conuinci etc.

55

Breue de venire facias felonem coram iusticiariis pacis in comitatu vbi indictatus existat secundum statutum E. III edito
anno v^{to} capitulo x^o etc.[1]

Iohannes D.[2] et socii sui iusticiarii domini regis ad diuersa felonias,
transgressiones et malefacta in comitatu Gloucestr' audienda et terminanda assignati vicecomiti Oxon' salutem. Cum per statutum domini
E. nuper regis Anglie, proaui domini regis nunc,[3] ordinatum sit quod
si aliqui indictati de felonia coram aliquibus iusticiariis de pace in vno
comitatu, et illi sic indictati fugerunt [*sic*] de comitatu vbi sic indictati
fuerint et commorentur in aliquo alio comitatu, quod iidem iusticiarii
de pace coram quibus iidem felones sic indictati fuerint scribant et
mittant vicecomiti vbi huiusmodi indictati commorantur de habendo
corpora huiusmodi indictatorum coram eis ad standum recto super
eorum deliberacione. Et quia datum est nobis intelligi quod quidam
T.L. etc. qui indictatus est coram nobis de diuersis feloniis in dicto
comitatu Gloucestr' fugit de comitatu Gloucestr' vsque comitatum Oxon'
et ibidem existit, vt dicitur, ideo ex parte domini regis tibi mandamus
quod corpus predicti T. capias et eum Thome G., I. H. et R. S. vel
vni eorum deliberes per indenturas inter te et ipsos debite conficiendas,
ita quod saluo et secure eum vsque ad gaolam castri domini regis
Gloucestr' ducere possint, ita quod ad deliberacionem eius procedere
possumus secundum legem et consuetudinem regni Anglie prout decet;
et hoc nullo modo omittas.

Datum Gloucestr' etc. anno etc.

[1] S. R., i. 267–8 ; should be c. xi.
[2] John Derhurst ; on the Gloucestershire commission of the peace from
13 Rich. II, 1389, through 24 March, 7 Hen. V, 1419 ; Cal. Pat., Rich. II,
Hen. IV, and Hen. V, index *sub nomine*.   [3] Hen. V.

56

Capias versus vacabundum super statutum E. III editum
anno[1] [*sic*].

I. T.[2] vnus iusticiariorum etc. constabulariis de T. E. salutem.
Ex parte domini regis vobis et utrique vestrum mando quod B. R.
de etc. in comitatu predicto, laborer et vacabundum ut dicitur, ad
deseruiendum P. H. in officio housbandrie compellatis vel vnus vestrum
compellat; et si hoc coram vobis facere recusauerit tunc ipsum B. R.
capiatis vel vnus vestrum capiat et ipsum vsque castrum domini regis
Wygorn' duci faciatis vel vnus vestrum duci faciat ibidem saluo custodiendum quousque hoc gratis facere voluerit; et qualiter hoc preceptum
nostrum fuerit executum scire faciatis vel vnus vestrum scire faciat
iusticiariis domini de pace ad proximam sessionem in comitatu predicto
tenendam.

    Datum etc. anno etc.

57

Warrantum pro iusticiariis pacis etc. de non molestando etc. eo
quod inuenit securitatem de se bene gerendo erga populum
domini regis coram dictis iusticiariis in patria.

R. H.[3] vnus iusticiariorum domini regis ad pacem in comitatu
Wygorn' conseruandam assignatorum vicecomiti Wygorn', omnibus
balliuis et ministris suis eiusdem comitatus quibuscumque et eorum
cuilibet, salutem. Quia A., B., C., D. coram me personaliter consti-
tuti manuceperunt pro T. S. quod ipse dampnum corporale P. de C.
seu alicui de populo domini regis contra pacem non faceret nec fieri
procuraret quoquo modo, videlicet, quilibet predictorum A., B., C. et
D. super [*sic*] pena x librarum et predictus T. sub pena xx librarum,
quas concesserint separatim leuari de terris et catallis suis ad opus regis
sique malum vel dampnum corporale contra pacem domini regis
prefato P. aut populum [*sic*] domini regis per predictum T. euenire
contigerit, vobis et cuilibet vestrum ex parte domini regis precipio quod
predictum .T. S. pro aliqua alia securitate pacis alicui inuenienda non
molestetis nec eum in aliquo grauetis, et hoc nullatenus omittatis sub
pena quo incumbit; et qualiter hoc preceptum nostrum fuerit executum
iusticiariis domini regis de pace ad proximam sessionem in comitatu
predicto tenendam scire faciatis.

    Datum etc.

[1] 23 Edw. III, c. 1.   [2] John Throgmerton.   [3] Roger Horton.

58[1]

Warantum factum per vicecomitem constabulario etc.

Ricardus B. vicecomes Wygorn'[2]constabulario de Bradwey[3] salutem. Virtute cuiusdam litere domini Ducis Bedford' custodis Anglie[4] michi directe ex parte domini regis tibi mando quod nocturna custodia vigilacionis sit facta et continuatur in villata tua, vbi solebat fieri secundum ordinacionem statuti inde editi[5] vsque festum Sancti Michaelis proximo futurum sub periculo incumbenti. Item quod venire facias coram me vel meo locum tenente apud Wygorn' die Sabbati proximo post festum Assumpcionis beate Marie Virginis[6] [f. 8 b] proximo futurum ad eorum campane nisi antea aliter premuniaris omnes gentes defensibiles villate tue inter etates sexdecim[7] annorum et sexaginta existentes, bene et competenter armatos, arraiatos et arreratos, quilibet eorum iuxta status sui exigenciam super fidei et ligeancia sua quam debent domino regi et sub pena forisfacture omnium que domino regi forisfacere potuit, ad faciendum et recipiendum ea que ex parte domini regis eis ibidem iniungentur, et quod tunc sis ibidem mane habens totum infrascriptum nomina [sic] omnium hominum defensabilium villate tue et non omittas sub simili pena predicta.

59

Aliud warrantum factum per vicecomitem balliuo hundredi.

Ricardus de Bello Campo vicecomes Wygorn' balliuo de P.[8] salutem. Ex parte domini regis tibi mando quod venire facias coram W. Hankford[9] et sociis suis iusticiariis domini regis ad Gaolam domini

---

[1] With no. 76.   [2] Richard Beauchamp, earl of Warwick.
[3] Modern Broadway, Oswaldslow hundred; Habington, *op. cit.*, i. 107; cf. Priory of Worc. Compotus Rolls, ed. S. G. Hamilton, Worc. Hist. Soc., vi, and full series of Court Rolls, Lists and Indexes, no. vi, 323, 326.
[4] For his appointment, see ch. iii (1), p. 63, and for a full account of the preparation for the expedition to France, see J. H. Wylie, Reign of Henry Fifth, i. 159–63, and chs. 25–7. Instructions for the array of the fencibles were issued on 29 May 1415; Rymer, Foedera, ix. 255–7; Wylie, *op. cit.*, i. 479; but since the sheriff of Worcester refers to the duke of Bedford as Keeper of England, the date of this writ must be between 11 and 17 August; see ch. iii (1), p. 63, and note 14, *supra*.
[5] Statute of Winchester, 13 Edw. I, cc. 4 and 6, 1285.
[6] 17 August 1415.   [7] Fifteen according to the statute of Winchester.
[8] Pershore.
[9] Cf. Gaol Delivery Roll 73, no. 2. The latter contains the commission of 14 April, 1418, to Hankford, Thomas Mille and Thomas Harwell as justices of Gaol Delivery at Worcester, proceedings before them on Monday 26 September, Hankford's writ to the sheriff bidding him have at Worcester on the above date the prisoners, 24 jurors, the reeve and

regis castri Wygorn' deliberandam assignatis apud Wygorn' die etc.
Lune proximo futuro xxiiii probos et legales homines de melioribus et
magis sufficientibus de visneto cuiuslibet ville et loci in quibus felonie
vnde prisones arrettati existunt facte fuerunt balliue tue, per quos rei
veritas melius sciri poterit, et qui prisones predictos nulla affinitate
attingant, vna cum quatuor hominibus et preposito, ad faciendum tunc
ibidem ea que eis ex parte domini regis ibidem iniungentur. Et proclamacione facta [sic] publico in feriis, mercatis et aliis locis publicis
balliue tue dictam deliberacionem dictis die et loco fieri, et quod
omnes illi qui sequi voluerint versus prisones predictos tunc sint ibi
versus eos prout iustum fuerit prosecuturi. Et scire facias eciam
omnibus coronatoribus, iusticiariis domini regis de pace ac balliuis
libertatis ville tue quod tunc sint ibidem cum rotulis et aliis memorandis
suis ad faciendum ea que ad officia sua pertinent ; et habeas ibi nomina
iuratorum corone, iusticiariorum de pace, balliuorum, et eorum per quos
eis scire feceris, et hoc preceptum.

Teste etc.

60

Cest bref est done par lestatut E. III lan xxv etc. c vii [1] et vide
statut etc. Cest est done vers laborers etc. attachiatos per
corpus et lexigent apres le primer capias si mestier soit.

Rex vicecomiti Wygorn' salutem. Quia I. C. fecit iusticiariis nostris
de pace in comitatu tuo conseruanda assignatis securitatem de clameo
suo prosequendo tam pro nobis quam pro seipso versus Iohannam
Fesh [2] de P. in comitatu tuo, spynster, per I. S. et I. M. de placito
transgressionis et contemptus contra formam statuti de seruientibus
nuper editi et prouisi, eo quod ipsa Iohanna in seruicio suo apud P.
nuper retenta ab eodem seruicio sine causa racionabili vel licencia
recessit, tibi precipimus quod attachies per corpus predictam Iohannam
ita quod eam habeas coram prefatis iusticiariis nostris apud Wygorn'
die Iouis etc., ad respondendum tam nobis quam prefato I. B. [sic] de
predicto placito et vlterius faciendum et recipiendum prout lex de [sic]

four men, the coroners, justices of the peace and bailiffs ; and the sheriff's
return, in which he reports that he has informed the coroners William
Wasseborn and Thomas Rudyng, the justices of the peace, John
Throgmerton and John Wode, the bailiffs of Worcester, William Ward
and John Wode, and the bailiff of the liberty of the bishop of Worcester,
William Nasse. His last phrase is as follows: '. . . non sunt plures
coronatores justiciarii de pace siue balliui libertatum comitatus mei quibus
scire facere potui breue domini regis clausum . . .' Yet the manual
apparently contains a copy of the sheriff's writ to another bailiff.

[1] Should be 25 Edw. III, st. 2, c. 5.   [2] Possibly Fisher ; cf. no. 72.

consuetudine regni nostri Anglie inde expostulat. Et habeas ibi etc.
Vel sic, et vlterius ad faciendum et recipiendum quod curia nostra et
de consuetudine in hac parte et habeas etc.

Teste Iohanne Wode etc.

Oseny.[1]

61

Cest bref fut primes done per le statut E. III lan xxv [2] et outre
le Roy H. V comanda le dit estatut estre execute, et touz
les statutz dez laborers furent rehercez par mesme le Roi
H. V etc. en soun estatut fait a Leycestre ou etc.[3]

Rex vicecomiti salutem. Cum in statuto nostro apud Gloucestr' [4]
anno regni nostri secundo edito inter cetera contineatur quod si aliquis
seruiens seu laborator a seruicio alicuius in vno comitatu retentus
deffugerit a seruicio predicto in alium comitatum, quod tunc iusticiarii
nostri de pace comitatus predicti a quo sic defugerit mandent vicecomiti comitatus predicti in quem deffugerit de huiusmodi fugitiuo
capiendo, et ipsum coram prefatis iusticiariis comitatus predicti a
quo sic diffugerit ad certum diem habendo ad respondendum tam
nobis quam parti in huiusmodi causa querelanti; ac ex parte Thome
Hewes de Gloucestr'[5] accepimus quod Alicia N. de Gloucestr' in comitatu
Gloucestr', seruant, in seruicio ipsius T.[6] apud Gloucestr' nuper retenta
ab eodem seruicio de comitatu predicto vsque Vpton super Sabrinam [7]
in comitatu tuo diffugerit, vt accepimus; et quia dictus Thomas Hewes
inuenit nobis plegios de clameo suo prosequendo tibi mandamus
quod predictam Aliciam attachies et corpus suum [sic], ita quod eam
habeas coram iusticiariis nostris de pace comitatus predicti apud
Gloucestr' tali die ad respondendum tam nobis quam prefato Thome de
predicto placito; et habeas ibi hoc breue.

Teste etc.

62

[f. 9] Warantum de pees.

Iohannes Trokmerton, armiger, vnus iusticiariorum domini regis de
pace in comitatu Wygorn' conseruanda assignatorum, vicecomiti
Wygorn' salutem. Quia Willelmus T. de N. michi grauiter conquestus
est quod cum ipse de vita et mutilacione membrorum suorum manifeste per Iohannem Iame [8] de N. et Matildam vxorem eius comminatus

---

[1] See p. 265, note 7, *supra*.   [2] St. 2, c. 7; cf. also 35 Edw. III, c. 10.
[3] 2 Hen. V, st. 1, c. 4.   [4] A clerical error for Leicester.
[5] Probably to be identified with the burgess of Gloucester who was
plaintiff in a writ of debt in 1421; Cal. Pat. Hen. V, 1416–1422, 356.
[6] Thome.   [7] Upton on Severn, Oswaldslow; V. C. H., Worc., iii. 248.
[8] Not yet identified.

est, per quod ipse ad negocia sua facienda propter metum mortis palam incedere non audiebat [*sic*] quouismodo; quare ex parte domini regis tibi mando quod ipsos Iohannem et Matildam corporaliter sine dilacione coram te et coram me vel coram me et sociis suis [*sic*] iusticiariis comitatus Wygorn' venire facias vel vsque castrum Wygorn' duci facias ad inueniendum securitatem pacis de ipsos bene gerendo erga dominum Willelmum et populum domini regis. Et quid inde feceris michi certificas indilate, et hoc preceptum.

Scriptum Wygorn' die etc.

63
Aliter.

Iohannes Throkmerton, vnus iusticiariorum etc., balliuo de Perschore[1] salutem. Quia Willelmus G. mihi grauiter conquestus est quod cum ipse de vita et mutilacione membrorum suorum manifeste per Henricum R. de N. comminatus existat, per quod ad mercandisas suas exercendas propter metum mortis sue palam incedere non audiebat [*sic*] quouismodo; quare ex parte domini regis tibi mando quod ipsum Henricum coram me et sociis suis [*sic*] iusticiariis pacis hoc mandato ostendo [*sic*] corporaliter sine dilacione venire facias ad inueniendum securitatem de se bene gerendo erga dictum Willelmum et populum domini regis; et quid inde feceris michi certificas indilate [? cum] hoc precepto.

Scriptum Wygorn' etc.

64
Breue de habendo corpus ab vno comitatu in alium.

Rex vicecomiti Gloucestr' salutem. Quia T. B. de etc. in comitatu Gloucestr', clerc, coram iusticiariis nostris ad diuersa felonias, transgressiones et malefacta in comitatu Wygorn' audienda et terminanda assignatis ac custodibus pacis nostre[2] de quibusdam feloniis indictatus existat, idem T. a predicto comitatu Wygorn' vsque castrum Gloucestr' diffugiens ibidem per te captus et in castro nostro Gloucestr' sub custodia tua detentus existat, ut accepimus, suas[3] volentes ipsum Thomam in comitatu vbi felonie predicte facte fuerunt super premissis secundum legem et consuetudinem regni nostri Anglie respondere et inde stare iure, tibi precipimus quod corpus predicti T. vicecomiti

---

[1] If this is the hundred, he is probably William Rudyng; cf. nos. 59 and 77; if it is the town, he is probably John Mulle or Simon Castell; cf. no. 80.

[2] An unusual order; 'custodibus pacis' almost always precedes 'iusticiariis'.

[3] A slip for 'nos'.

nostro comitatus Wygorn' vel eius in hac parte attornato per indenturam inde inter vos debito modo conficiendam liberari facias, vsque gaolam castri Wygorn' comitatus predicti ducendum in eadem saluo et secure custodiendum quousque inde secundum legem et consuetudinem regni nostri Anglie predicti deliberetur. Mandauimus enim vicecomiti nostro Wygorn' quod ipse prefatum Thomam a vobis recipiat custodiendum in forma predicta.

Teste etc.

65

Quoddam warrantum de pace super statutum Norhampton'.[1]

Iohannes Throkmerton, vnus iusticiariorum etc. vicecomiti Wygorn' salutem. Quia datum est michi intelligi quod Iacobus Blount, armiger, de comitatu Hereford,[2] ac quidem alii malefactores et pacem domini regis perturbatores armati modo guerrino arraiati clausum et domos Willelmi F. apud C.[3] in comitatu Wygorn' intrare, et bona de possessionibus suis ibidem proueniencia capere et consumere et alia mala que poterunt eidem inferre proponunt pro viribus suis in ipsius Willelmi graue dampnum et contra formam statuti apud Norhampton' de armis factis, tibi ex parte domini regis mando quod ad villam et locum predictas [sic] et allibi in balliua tua vbi expediens fuerit proclamari facias ex parte domini regis, [et] inhibere facias ne quis cuiuscumque status seu condicionis fuerit, ibidem armatus incedat nec armatam potenciam ducat, vel quicquam faciat per quod pax domini regis [f. 9 b] vel statutum predictum ledi, seu eidem Willelmo aut alicui de populo domini regis turbari seu grauari possit, sub pena omissionis armorum suorum et incarceracionis corporum suorum ad voluntatem domini regis. Et omnes illi quos post et contra proclamacionem predictam inueneris contraria facientes vna cum armaturis arestari et capi et saluo custodiri facias quousque secundum legem Anglie deliberentur; et quid inde feceris iusticiariis nostris de pace ad proximam sessionem apud Wygorn' tenendam certificas indilate [? cum] hoc precepto.

Scriptum tali die etc.

66

Breue de exonerando constabularium.

Rex Ricardo Webbe[4] salutem. Quia N. W. coram Iohanne Throkmerton vno iusticiariorum nostrorum ad pacem in comitatu

---

[1] 2 Edw. III, c. 3.
[2] Nash refers to a Herefordshire branch of the Worcestershire family; op. cit., ii. 162ª, 163.
[3] Perhaps the same case as no. 14, with C. instead of N.
[4] Not identified.

nostro Wygorn' conseruandam assignatorum iuratus est in officium
vnius capitalis constabularii hundredi de Oswaldeslow, quoquidem
officio tu hactenus vsus fuisti, volentes te certis de causis ad hoc nos
mouentibus de officio illo penitus exonerari, tibi precipimus quod de
officio illo in nullo te intromittas sub pena que incumbitur.

I. T.[1]

67

Attachies versus seruientem fugientem ab vno comitatu in alium.

Rex vicecomiti salutem. Quia R. C. coram iusticiariis nostris ad
pacem in comitatu Warr' assignatis [*sic*] conseruandam assignatis apud
Warr' inuenit nobis sufficientem securitatem de clameo suo prosequendo
versus Aliciam Kyng de etc. de placito transgressionis et contemptus,
eo quod eadem Alicia in seruicio ipsius Ricardi apud Couentrem
retenta fuisset, eademque Alicia postea a seruicio ipsius Ricardi ante
finem termini inter eos concordati sine causa racionabili et licencia
ipsius Ricardi contra formam statuti nostri recessit a dicto comitatu
Warr' vsque Euesham in balliua tua contra formam statuti de seruientibus ab vno comitatu in alium fugitiuis editi et prouisi fugit;[2] et ideo
tibi precipimus quod attachies per corpus predictam Aliciam et eam
saluo custodias ita quod habeas corpus eius coram prefatis iusticiariis
nostris apud Warr' die tali etc. ad respondendum tam nobis quam
prefato Ricardo de placito transgressionis et contemptus contra statutum predictum et habeas etc.[3]

Teste etc.

68

Venire facias coram iusticiariis pacis pro Lollardez.

Rex vicecomiti Wygorn' salutem. Precipimus tibi quod non omittas
propter aliquam libertatem comitatus tui quin venire facias coram
iusticiariis nostris ad pacem nostram in comitatu Wygorn' conseruandam assignatis, apud castrum Wygorn' die Lune proximo ante
festum Sancti Dionisii [4] proximo futurum de quolibet hundredo infra
comitatum predictum xxiiii liberos et legales homines per quos rei
veritas melius sciri poterit et inquiri, ad faciendum et inquirendum ea

---

[1] John Throgmerton.   [2] Cf. no. 61, and notes.
[3] This case comes before the justices of the peace of the county of
Warwick, although Coventry had had justices of the peace of its own as
early as the reign of Rich. II; Dugdale, Warwickshire, 141. For Coventry
as a separate county, see ch. iii (1), p. 76.
[4] The date of the feast is 9 October.

que eis ex parte nostra ad tunc ibidem iniungentur, necnon omnes senescallos constabularios et balliuos comitatus tui predicti venire facias ad diem et locum predictos coram iusticiariis nostris predictis ad accipiendum et faciendum ea que eis ex parte nostra adtunc ibidem iniungentur. Precepimus eciam tibi sub pena viginti librarum quod venire facias coram iusticiariis nostris predictis ad diem et locum predictos xxiiii liberos et legales homines ac sufficientes necnon suspectos neque procuratos, quorum quilibet habeat terras et tenementa seu redditus ad valenciam centum solidorum per annum ad minus, ad faciendum et inquirendum ea que eis ex parte nostra adtunc iniungentur super quodam statuto contra Lollardes in parliamento nostro apud Leycestr' vltimo tento edito;[1] et publico proclamari facias in locis infra comitatum predictum vbi tibi melius videbitur expedire sessionem iusticiariorum nostrorum predictorum de pace apud castrum Wygorn' ad diem predictum fore tenendam, et omnia breuia et precepta cum omnibus ea tangentibus [f. 10] coram iusticiariis nostris predictis per nuper iusticiarios nostros de pace in comitatu predicto conseruanda assignatos tibi liberata et penes te residentia habeas ad diem et locum predictos; et habeas ibidem tunc nomina senescallorum constabulariorum et balliuorum predictorum et hoc breue.

Teste etc.

69

Istud breue formatum est super statutum E. III anno xxiii capitulo primo[2] et postea inde ordinatum fuit per aliud statutum eiusdem regis editum anno xxv^{mo} capitulo viii[3] etc.

Rex vicecomiti salutem. Si Iohannes atte Nasshe[4] fecerit te securitatem de clameo suo prosequendo, tunc pone per vadium et saluos plegios Galfridum Smyth de Seint Iones[5] in comitatu Wygorn', smyth, quod sit coram iusticiariis nostris ad pacem in comitatu predicto conseruandam assignatis apud castrum Wygorn' die Lune in crastino

---

[1] 2 Hen. V, st. 1, c. 7, 1414.
[2] Made a statute by 2 Rich. II, st. 1, c. 8.
[3] 25 Edw. III, st. 2, c. 1–7; the 'VIII' is therefore an error.
[4] Liber Elemos, ed. J. H. Bloom, Worc. Hist. Soc., 40. For the Nash family of Worcestershire, see Index to Nash, *op. cit.*, ed. J. Amphlett, Worc. Hist. Soc.
[5] Various indictments before the Worcestershire justices of the peace of Galfridus Smyth 'de Sancto Iohanne iuxta Wygorn' are recorded in the Gaol Delivery Rolls; 73, 9 Hen. IV, no. 2, m. 33; 10 Hen. IV, m. 35 (*ibid.* 189, ms. 16 d, 17).

Sancti Iacobi Apostoli[1] proximo futuro ad respondendum tam nobis quam prefato Iohanni de placito transgressionis et contemptus contra statutum ; et attachies per corpus Margeriam Horsman[2] de Seint Iones in comitatu predicto, damysell, ita quod eam habeas coram prefatis iusticiariis nostris ad castrum predictum ad prefatum diem ad respondendum tam nobis quam prefato Iohanni de placito transgressionis et contemptus contra statutum pro seruientibus nuper editum ; et habeas etc.

70

Pro inuenienda securitate pacis coram vicecomite.[3]

Rex vicecomiti Wygorn' salutem. Precipimus tibi quod corporaliter venire facias coram te H. W. de C., Amiciam vxorem eius et R. filium eorum Henrici et Amicie, et eos vsque gaolam castri Wygorn' duci facias ibidem saluo et secure custodiendos, quousque coram iusticiariis nostris de pace in comitatu predicto conseruanda assignatis inuenerint sufficientem securitatem de pace nostra gerenda erga Hugonem Halbert et Aliciam Albert[4] quos de vita sua et mutilacione membrorum suorum comminati sunt ; et habeas ibi hoc breue coram iusticiariis nostris predictis ad castrum predictum die Lune etc.

Teste I. Weston[5] etc.

71

Per statutum E. III factum anno tercio.[6]

Rex vicecomiti salutem. Quia Iohannes Botyler, clericus,[7] inuenit coram nobis sufficientem securitatem de clameo suo prosequendo per Iohannem Curteys[8] et Iohannem Hervy[8] versus Iohannem Berell[8] de Myldenham[9] in comitatu tuo, laborer, tibi precipimus quod attachies per corpus prefatum Iohannem Borell ita quod eum habeas coram iusticiariis nostris de pace in comitatu Wygorn' conseruanda assignatis, apud Wygorn' die Iouis proximo post festum Epiphanie Domini[10] de respondendo tam nobis quam prefato Iohanni de placito quare cum per dominum E. nuper regem Anglie proauum nostrum[11] et consilium

---

[1] The date of the feast is 25 July.   [2] Not identified.
[3] The surety is to be taken before justices of the peace, not before the sheriff.
[4] Not identified.   [5] John Weston.
[6] 'Vicesimo' evidently omitted before 'tercio'. The case is on c. 1 of the ordinance of labourers, 23 Edw. III.
[7] Cf. Index to Nash, *op. cit.*, for John Butler, clerk ; the name occurs frequently in the Coventry Leet Book, index, *passim.*
[8] Not identified.   [9] Mildenham, Pershore hundred.
[10] The date of the feast is 6 January.   [11] Refers therefore to Hen. V.

suum pro communi vtilitate eiusdem regni ordinatum sit, quod quilibet
homo et femina [? dicti] regno [*sic*] cuiuscumque condicionis fuerit
libere vel seruilis, potens in corpore et infra aetatem sexaginta annorum, non vivens de mercatura nec certum exercens artificium nec
habens de suo proprio vnde[1] vel terram propriam circa cuius culturam
se poterit occupare et alteri non seruiens, si de seruiendo in seruicio pro statu suo congruo requisitus vel requisita, seruire teneatur
illi qui ipsum sic duxerit requirendum ; et si talis vir vel mulier de sic
seruiendo requisitus vel requisita hoc facere noluerit,[2] statim capiatur
et mittatur proxime gaole et ibidem sub arta moretur custodia quousque securitatem inuenerit de seruiendo in forma predicta, predictus
Iohannes Borell condicionibus huiusmodi existentibus prefato Iohanni
Botyller in seruicio pro statu ipsius Iohannis Borell congruo quamquam
ipse de seruiendo per prefatum Iohannem Botyller in forma predicta
apud M.[3] sepius fuit requisitus, seruire recusauit penitus in nostri
contemptum et ipsius Iohannis B. graue dampnum ac contra formam
ordinacionis predicte ; et habeas etc.

72

Iohannes Braas vnus iusticiariorum domini regis de pace in comitatu
Wygorn' conseruanda assignatorum constabulario de Pershore salutem.
Quia Iohannes Gaume[4] michi grauiter conquestus est quod cum
Iohannes[5] Fysshere de Pershore qui potens est in corpore ad seruiendum, non vivens de mercatura nec certum exercens artificium, non
habens de suo proprio vnde viuere aut terram circa cuius culturam se
poterit occupare et alteri non seruiens, prefata Iohanna licet sepius
requisita eidem Iohanni seruiendum in officio husbondrie a festo Natalis
Domini vltimo preterito per vnum annum tunc proxime sequentem
iuxta formam [f. 10 b] statuti seruire penitus recusat, in regis contemptum et ipsius H.[6] [*sic*] graue dampnum et contra formam ordinacionis in hoc casu prouise. Quare ex parte domini regis tibi mando
quod si prefata Iohanna sit de condicionibus predictis si alteri non
seruiens, hoc probato per duos fideles homines et seruire recusat,[7] tunc
ipsam Iohannam per corpus suum attachies et eam vsque castrum
Wygorn' duci facias ibidem moraturam quousque gratis seruire

---

[1] 'Vivere' omitted.   [2] 'Hoc probato . . . contigerit' omitted.
[3] Myldenham, *ut supra.*
[4] A John Gam was indicted for murder before the Worcestershire
justices of the peace in 9 Hen. V ; Gaol Delivery Roll 218, no. 3, m. 11.
[5] An error for Johanna. Cf. also no. 60.   [6] Should be 'I'.
[7] The ordinance is not quoted with absolute exactness.

voluerit; et quid inde feceris iusticiariis de pace certifices [? cum] hoc precepto.

Scriptum Wygorn' die etc.

73
Notum.

Nota quod anno xxiii E. III ordinacio de seruientibus facta fuit et anno xxv eiusdem regis statutum de seruientibus factum fuit capitulum xiiii [1] lestatut illeqes done poiar a lez iustices doier et terminer et puis agarder vers lez enditez capias et capias aliter oue lez sumons et apres exigend sils facent defaut.

74

Iohannes Braas vnus iusticiariorum etc. assignatorum constabulariis de Kedermystr [2] et Hertylbury [3] ac balliuis dicti comitatus coniunctim et diuisim salutem. Quia I. H. michi grauiter conquestus est quod cum R. C. de B. etc. qui potens est in corpore etc. vt supra.[4] Quare ex parte domini regis vobis mandamus coniunctim et diuisim quod si idem R. sit de condicione predicta etc. tunc etc.

Teste etc.

Et si talis vir vel mulier sic de seruiendo requisitus vel requisita fuerit et hoc facere noluit hoc probato per duos fideles homines coram vicecomite balliuo domini aut constabulario ville vbi hoc fieri contigerit, statim per eos aut eorum aliquem capiatur et mittatur proxime gaole et ibidem sub arta custodia moretur quousque securitatem inuenerit de seruiendo in forma predicta etc.[5]

75

Rex vicecomiti Wygorn' salutem. Quia abbas de Pershore [6] inuenit coram nobis securitatem de clameo suo prosequendo per Iohannem Fortey [7] et Iohannem Halle [8] versus Iohannem Wheeler [9] de Lee [10] in

---

[1] An error for c. 6.

[2] In ' Halfshyre ', modern Kidderminster; Habington, Worcestershire, ii. 155–68.

[3] Also in ' Halfshyre ', modern Hartlebury; *ibid.* i. 280–4. Cf. V.C.H., Worc., iii. 248, ' mainly in Oswaldslow '.   [4] No. 72.

[5] This addition is a more exact quotation of the ordinance than is no. 72.

[6] Cf. William, abbot of Pershore; Patent Roll (Supplementary) no. 37, m. 33, 2 Hen. V. There is a Pershore chartulary among the Miscellaneous Books of the Exchequer, Augmentation Office, no. 61.

[7] See ch. iii (1), pp. 66–7.

[8] A John Hall represented the city of Worcester in parliament in 11 Hen. VI; Nash, *op. cit.*, introduction, 29. Cf. also Original Charters, ed. J. H. Bloom, Worc. Hist. Soc., index *sub nomine*; and Collectanea, ed. S. G. Hamilton, Worc. Hist. Soc. 13.

[9] Cf. John Wheeler de Shrawley; Gaol Delivery Roll 73, no. 3, m. 3.

[10] See p. 262, note 6, *supra*, for Leigh.

comitatu Wygorn', housbandman, tibi precipimus quod attachies per
corpus prefatum Iohannem Wheler ita quod eum habeas coram iusticiariis nostris de pace in comitatu Wygorn' conseruanda assignatis,
apud Wygorn' die Iouis in septimana Pasche a [*sic*] respondendum
tam nobis quam prefato abbati de placito quare cum per dominum E.
nuper regem Anglie proauum nostrum [1] et consilium suum pro communi vtilitate eiusdem regni ordinatum sit et statutum, quod quilibet
seruiens cuiuscumque status seu condicionis fuerit pro statu nostro [*sic*]
congruo si de seruiendo in seruicio fuerit requisitus seruire teneatur illi
qui ipsum sic duxerit requirendum ad seruiendum per annum integrum
vel per alios terminos vsuales et non per dietas, prefatus Iohannes
seruiens per dietas et non ad terminum dictum prefato abbati in
seruicio congruo, quamquam ipse ad seruiendum per prefatum abbatem
per annum integrum apud Lygh fuerit requisitus, seruire penitus
recusauit, in nostri contemptum et ipsius abbatis graue dampnum et
contra formam ordinacionis et statuti predictorum [2] ; et habeas etc.

Teste etc.

76

Ricardus de Bello Campo vicecomes comitatus Wygorn' balliuo
hundredi de Pershore [3] salutem. Ex parte domini regis tibi mando
quod in balliua tua in locis vbi magis expediens fuerit et necessarie
publico proclamari facias quod omnes et singuli milites, armigeri, et
valetti qui aliqua feoda, vadia siue annuitates de domino rege ex concessione domini Edwardi nuper regis Anglie [4] proaui domini regis
nunc, [5] seu domini Ricardi nuper regis Anglie, [6] aut domini Edwardi
nuper principis Anglie, [7] aut domini Iohannis ducis Lancastr' [8] aui dicti
domini regis nunc, vel domini Henrici patris [9] ipsius domini regis
nunc et de dicti domini regis nunc confirmacione, seu ex concessione
domini regis nunc, annuatim percipiunt, seu de liberata et retinencia
domini regis nunc, sub forisfactura feodorum, vadiarum seu annuitatum
huiusmodi, excusacione quacumque cessante, versus ciuitatem [f. 11]
nostram London' se trahant et festinent, ita quod sint ibidem in crastino
Sancti Georgii [10] proximo futuro ad vltimum de faciendo ea que ex

---

[1] Refers to Henry V.
[2] A combination of the compulsory service clause of the ordinance of
23 Edw. III with the first clause of 25 Edw. III, st. 2.
[3] Probably William Rudyng as in no. 77.   [4] Edward III.
[5] Henry V.   [6] Richard II.   [7] The Black Prince.
[8] John of Gaunt.   [9] Henry IV.   [10] 24 April.

parte nostra in eorum aduentu iniuncta erunt et declarata; et hoc sub
incumbenti periculo nullatenus omittas.

Scriptum Wygorn' die [1] etc.

77

Iohannes Weston et socii sui iusticiarii domini regis ad pacem in
comitatu Wygorn' conseruandam assignati Thome Mulle [2] gaolatori
castri Wygorn' et Willelmo Rudyng [3] balliuo hundredi de Pershore et
eorum cuilibet, salutem. Ex parte domini regis vobis mandamus
firmiter iniungentes quod corporaliter coram vobis venire facias
Radulphum filium Dauid de P.,[4] ita quod eum habeas coram nobis
apud castrum Wygorn' die dominica proxima post festum Trans-
lacacionis Sancti E. regis [5] proximo futurum ad inueniendum sufficientem
securitatem de pace gerenda erga populum domini regis et precipue
erga Willelmum Wanet [6] quem manifeste de corpore et mutilacione
membrorum suorum comminatus est; et hoc sine dilacione faciatis et
non omittatis sub incumbenti periculo; et habeatis ibi tunc hoc preceptum.

Datum Wygorn' xvii die Septembris anno etc.

78

Breue de venire facias xxiiii de quolibet hundredo et de qualibet libertate.

Rex vicecomiti salutem. Precipimus tibi quod non omittas propter
aliquam libertatem comitatus tui quin eam ingrediaris et venire facias
coram iusticiariis de pace in comitatu tuo conseruanda assignatis, apud
Wygorn' die Lune proximo post festum Sancte Trinitatis proximo
futurum de quolibet hundredo et de qualibet libertate comitatus tui
xxiiii liberos et legales homines magis sufficientes balliue tue, necnon
omnes balliuos hundredorum, constabularios, seneschallorum [*sic*] mag-
natum et balliuorum [*sic*] libertatum balliue tue ad faciendum et
recipiendum ea que ex parte nostra tunc eis ibidem iniungentur; et

---

[1] 22 March, 3 Hen. V, 1415; see copy of the writ enrolled in Cal.
London Letter Books, ed. R. R. Sharpe, I, 134. Cf. also *ibid*. xxiv;
Wylie, *op. cit.*, i. 454, and no. 58, *supra*.

[2] Cf. p. 271, note 9, for a Thomas Mille as justice of Gaol Delivery, and
Cal. Pat. Rolls Hen. V, as a Gloucestershire justice of the peace.

[3] Cf. nos. 59 and 76. For the same surname, cf. the coroner in no. 22,
supra, and the jurors in 21 Rich. II before Worcestershire justices of the
peace; Assize Roll 1034, m. 1. Nash, *op. cit.*, i. 439, refers to a William
Ruding in Esch hundred, *temp*. Rich. II.

[4] Pershore.   [5] The date of the feast is 13 October.

[6] Not identified.

proclamari facias vbicumque in balliua tua dictam cessionem fieri predictis die et loco ; et habeas ibi nomina predictorum xxiiii, balliuorum, custodum, senescallorum et hoc breue.

Teste I [1] etc

79
Wygorn'.

Willelmus Botyller de Yatton, vnus iusticiariorum domini regis de pace in comitatu Wygorn' conseruanda necnon ad omnes transgressiones et felonias in comitatu predicto audiendas et terminandas assignatorum, vicecomiti Wygorn' salutem. Sciatis quod I. P. de M. et W. C. de eadem qui indictati sunt coram me et sociis meis de transgressionibus diuersis ad vltimam sessionem inuenerunt coram me sufficientem securitatem de die in diem ad comparendum quousque secundum legem et consuetudinem regni Anglie deliberati fuerint ; ideo ex parte domini regis vobis mando quod ad capiendum vel attachiandum predictos Iohannem et Willelmum omnino supersedeatis ; et si predictos Willelmum et Iohannem causa predicta ceperitis seu attachiaueritis ipsos sine dilacione liberari facias.

Datum

80
Replegiare in comitatu.

Ricardus de Bello Campo vicecomes Wygorn' salutem. Balliuis de Pershore, Iohanni Mulle [2] et Simoni Castell, [3] salutem. Quia Iohannes Prior ecclesie cathedralis Beate Marie Wygorn'[4] inuenit mihi sufficientem securitatem de clameo suo prosequendo ac aciam de aueriis suis returnandis si returnum adiudicatur, quos Ricardus Episcopus Wygorn',[5] Iohannes Pantyk [6] et Ricardus Palmere [7] ceperunt et iniuste detinent vt dicit, ex parte domini regis vobis mando coniunctim et diuisim quod iuste et sine dilacione aueria sua predicta eidem Priori

---

[1] Since Throgmerton, Brace, Weston, Wode, and also the Duke of Bedford, keeper of England, all have John as their Christian name, it is impossible to identify this ' I '.   [2] Cf. nos. 4 and 7.

[3] Not identified, although the surname appears in Coventry ; cf. Leet Book, index.

[4] Cf. ch. iii (1), pp. 67–8.   [5] *Ibid.*

[6] Cf. an indictment before the sheriff (the Earl of Warwick) in 6 Hen. V, of John del Pantyk (?) alias Johannes Ussher de Euesham ; Gaol Delivery Roll 73, no. 2, m. 5.

[7] A Richard Palmer was one of the two bailiffs of Coventry in 2 Hen. V ; Anc. Ind. 207, ms. 29, 30 ; cf. a reference in 1421 to a will of a Richard Palmer of Coventry ; Cal. Pat. Hen. V, 1416–1422, 316.

replegiari et deliberari faciatis vel vnus vestrum deliberari faciat, et ponatis per vadios et saluos plegios predictos Iohannem et Ricardum quod sint ad proximum comitatum etc. ad respondendum prefato Priori de capcioni aueriorum predictorum; et habeatis vel vnus vestrum habeat ibidem hoc preceptum cum execucione eiusdem.

Scriptum etc.

81[1]

[f. 11 b] Replegiare in comitatu tociens quociens.

Monstrauit nobis Prior Wygorn' quod cum Ricardus Episcopus Wygorn', Iohannes Pantyng [*sic*] et Ricardus Palmere aueria ipsius Prioris cepissent et iniuste detinuissent ipseque Prior coram me prosecutus fuisset pro aueriis suis secundum legem et consuetudinem regni nostri Anglie replegiandis; ac licet per Iohannem Mulle balliuum meum quem ad aueria predicta eidem Priori replegiare [? misi] et ipse aueria illa replegiasset et ei dedisset diem ad proximum comitatum etc., predictum Episcopum Iohannem et Ricardum attachiasset ad respondendum prefato Priori de capcione illa[2] idem Episcopus, Iohannes et Ricardus post attachiamentum illud aueria ipsius Prioris interim ceperunt et ea occasione qua prius ceperant et ea sicut prius detinent, et quia hoc iniustum est et manifeste contra pacem domini regis vobis precipimus coniunctim et diuisim quod aueria predicta sine dilacione deliberari faciatis vel vnus vestrum deliberari faciat tociens quociens capta fuerint quousque capitale placitum inde inter eos in comitatu tenetur. Et si inueneritis vel vnus vestrum inuenerit quod predicti Episcopus, Iohannes et Ricardus aueria ipsius Prioris interim ceperunt ea occasione qua prius ea ceperant et ea sicut prius detinent, tunc corpora eorum predictorum Episcopi, Iohannis et Ricardi coram me dicto vicecomite et custodibus placitorum corone domini regis[3] ad proximum comitatum habeatis vel vnus vestrum habeat, ad respondendum prefato Priori de recapcione illa et vlterius faciendum et recipiendum quod curia de eis consideret in hac parte.

Scriptum etc.

82

Breue de statuto.

Rex vicecomiti salutem. Si Willelmus A. de W.[4] fecerit te securitatem de clameo suo prosequendo tunc pone per vadium et saluos plegios W. R. de B. in comitatu predicto, housbandman, ita

---

[1] For the names in no. 81, see no. 80, *supra*.
[2] From 'ac licet' through 'capcioni illa', the syntax is unintelligible.
[3] The coroners.   [4] Worcester.

quod habeas corpus eius coram iusticiariis nostris ad pacem in comitatu predicto assignatis, apud castrum Wygorn' die Martis in septimana Pasche proximo future ad respondendum tam nobis quam predicto W. de placito transgressionis et contemptus contra statutum de seruientibus editum ; et attachies per corpus Aliciam T. de E. in comitatu Wygorn', seruant, ita quod sit coram iusticiariis nostris predictis ad diem et locum predictos ad respondendum tam nobis quam predicto Willelmo de placito quare predictam Aliciam receptauit contra formam statuti predicti ; et habeas ibi nomina plegiorum predicti Willelmi, et hoc breue.

> Teste etc.

[f. 12] [1] Iohannes Dygby, miles [2]	xviis.
De Bartholomeo Brokesby [3]	iiis. viiid.
De Thome Kebyll [4]	vis. viiid.
De Nicholao Fytzherberd [5]	xxd.
De Iohanne Brokesby [6]	xiid.
De Roberto Mallory [7]	iis.
De Simone Mallory [8]	xxxs.
De Thoma Bothewaye [9]	xs.

[1] In a different hand from that of ff. 1–11 b and also from that of ff. 12 b–16 b. For a discussion of the names, see ch. iii (1), pp. 81–2, as well as the notes, *infra*.

[2] In addition to being sheriff of Warwick and Leicester in 1485 (Lists and Indexes, no. ix) Dygby was appointed on all commissions of the peace in Leicestershire during the reign of Henry VII as well as on many other commissions in the latter county and in others ; see Cal. Pat. Hen. VII, index. Note that he was associated with Thomas Coton in 1504 ; *ibid.*, 1494–1509, 359, and also with Thomas Keble, *ibid.* 31.

[3] Merchant of the Staple in 1505, associated with Dygby, Henry Keble, and many others ; *ibid.* 447. The Leicestershire commissions of the peace almost always include a Brokesby ; Cal. Pat., *passim*. For their family, see J. Nichols, Bib. Top. Brit., vii and viii, Leicestershire, index *sub nomine* ; also his History of Leicestershire, i, pt. 2, index volume.

[4] For his career, see pp. 78–82, and p. 179, *supra* ; cf. also Cal. Pat. Hen. VII, 1494–1509, 246, for his connexion with Kirby Bellars (Kirkby on Wrethek).

[5] Referred to frequently in Cal. Pat., mainly in connexion with Derbyshire, on commissions of the peace, &c., during the last years of Hen. VI and Edw. IV ; undoubtedly of the family to which the eminent judge belonged ; p. 33, *supra*.   [6] Not identified, but see note 3, *supra*.

[7] Cal. Pat. Edw. IV, Edw. V, Rich. III, 1476–1485, 183. Like the Brokesbys, the Mallorys were a distinguished Leicestershire family ; see references in note 3, *supra*.

[8] Nichols, History of Leicestershire, i, pt. 2, index volume, *sub nomine*, but the entries in iii. 174, 452, iv. 51 (referred to in the index) give no Christian name to Mallory.

[9] A clerk connected with 'Kyrkby Malory', Leicestershire ; see p. 81, note 11, *supra*.

De Georgii [*sic*] Daives[1] et sociis   iiiis. iiiid.

De Willelmo Harrys[2] pro fine   xs.

De Thome Hody[3] et sociis   iiiis. iiiid.

De Ricardo Pyper[4] et sociis   iiiis. iiiid.

De Thome Coton[5]   xiis.

                              ~~iiii li. xvis.~~ [*sic*]

Summa vere iiii li. xv s. Verius v li. vii s.

APPENDIX III

DE PACE TERRE & ECCLESIE & CONSERUA-CIONE EIUSDEM, WESTMINSTER PRIMER, CAPITULO PRIMO

University Library, Cambridge, MS. Hh. 3. 6. no. 1646, folios 74–116.

NOTE OF EXPLANATION

Of the eleven MSS. now known, A has been shown to be the closest to Marowe's original[6] and has therefore been chosen for printing in full. For reasons already given,[7] it has seemed possible—as far as the text goes—to disregard almost completely the later copies, E, G, H, I, K,[8] and L, but essential to collate A paragraph by paragraph with F, the condensed version, and word by word with B, C, and D, the versions that reproduce A so exactly.[9] Since, however, my main purpose is a study of the legal content of Marowe's own work and not of the paleographic and linguistic peculiarities of the

---

[1] Not identified.   [2] Not identified.

[3] Justice of the peace in Staffordshire in 1487, probably a relative of William Hody, chief baron of the Exchequer; Cal. Pat. Hen. VII, 1485–1494, 500, 139, 216.

[4] The only pertinent reference that I have found is to a 'Richard Pepur' associated in 1420 with the earlier Bartholomew Brokesby and with Joan, lady of Abergavenny; Cal. Pat. Hen. V, 1416–1422, 305, 306.

[5] Usually appointed on commissions in Cambridgeshire; Cal. Pat. Hen. VII, index, *sub nomine*, but occasionally serving in Leicestershire; e.g. in 1504 associated with Dygby; see p. 285, note 2, *supra*. He was one of the executors of Thomas Kebyll's will; p. 179, note 3, *supra*.

[6] Ch. vi (1), *supra*.   [7] *Ibid*.

[8] The statement applies also to this recent discovery.

[9] Ch. vi (1), *supra*.

various scribes, the results of this collation have been used very sparingly. Accordingly, the footnotes contain mainly those differences that serve to clarify or to correct the meaning of A, sometimes merely by supplying a slightly better word or form. The notes also include a small amount of additional matter, usually from F, and, when possible, references to ' Statutes of the Realm ' and to the Year Books in the case of statutes and reports cited by Marowe.[1]

In order to make it easier for the reader to see at a glance the multiplicity of legal points in the reading, I have ruthlessly supplied punctuation and paragraphs,[2] but have kept the scribe's capitalization as far as possible.[3] As for the contractions and suspensions, the problem of how to treat them has not been an easy one, and the solution adopted will undoubtedly meet with criticism. In extensions, my general principle has been to give forms that can be found somewhere in the MS. For example, the scribe is indifferent as to whether he uses a singular or a plural ending for a verb with a plural subject and is exceedingly haphazard as to his genders,[4] but *ils purr'* has been extended to *ils purront*, inasmuch as *purront* very often appears written out in full. On the other hand, *s' vie* has been printed *son vie*, since the latter is often found and never *sa vie*.

For the relative pronoun and for the conjunction one form always appears, Ⓠ, except in one quotation from a statute where it is extended to *que*.[5] Because of this instance, and still more because *que* is very usual in printed law books of the early sixteenth century,[6] it has been adopted here.[7] But the real difficulty comes with the scribe's favourite mark ⊃.[8] It is found after certain final syllables, always after *ion, on, oun, gn, ym, yn, en, ein*, less regularly after *em, in*, and *un*, very frequently after *r* and *x*, occasionally after *t*, and even after a vowel. It is for example so common after *ont* that only two instances of its omission have been noted.[9] That the sign indicates sometimes a con-

---

[1] There are also references to a few other authorities.
[2] For example, I have treated the phrases ' Item ' and ' Mesme le ley ' as introducing new paragraphs.
[3] That is, unless my punctuation necessitates a change.
[4] *Supra*, p. 159.   [5] p. 295, l. 11.
[6] See Pynson's publications, *passim.*
[7] An exceedingly perplexing form has been the abbreviation which I have extended to ' Seignurz ', with no confidence in its appropriateness, as I have never found it written out.
[8] Other scribes use the sign also, cf. e.g. D who writes soñt, but I have not made a careful study of the textual peculiarities of the other MSS.
[9] Puissont, seont ; p. 373, l. 23, p. 364, l. 12.

traction and sometimes a suspension is perfectly clear. Examples
of the former are: atteiƭ for atteint, itm̄ for item, coen̄ for comen,
sinon̄ for sinoun, sonƭ for sount,[1] cheux̄ for chateux,[2] possessin̄
for possession, abiuracon̄ for abiuracion. Examples of the latter
are: eū for eum,[3] faiƭ for faire, recogn̄ for recognicion, com-
maundeƭ for commaunderont, compaign̄ for compaignon, distreyn̄ for
distreyne. But the scribe also very often writes: sinoun̄, comen̄, eux̄,
mielx̄,[4] evidently, it seems to me, from mere force of habit, and with
no possible meaning.[5] The unfortunate result is that there are a
number of words in which there is no way of proving whether the
sign is a contraction, or a suspension, or a mere flourish. For
example, should don̄ be printed doun or done or don? My method
is as follows: I have added or inserted a letter or letters in the case
of all those words ending with the sign in question, if they appear in
their full form somewhere else in the MS.; otherwise I have ignored
the sign. Thus, I have printed sount for sonƭ and fyne for fyn̄,
but in spite of the flourish I have written mon, and son.[6] A far
more logical course has been suggested, namely, to use in the second
group of cases some conventional mark like an apostrophe to indicate
the existence of the flourish. At the risk of incurring the severe dis-
approval of scholars [7] I have rejected the suggestion, for the purely
practical reason that the presence of an apostrophe after every few
words on a page would, in my judgement, seriously increase the difficulty of reading the text. Palaeological accuracy has therefore been
sacrificed in the interests of clearness from the point of view of legal
content.

[1] Cf. also soᵗ; p. 295, l. 27.   [2] p. 400, note 1.
[3] p. 298, l. 17.   [4] p. 399, l. 10.
[5] Cf. English Court Hand, by C. Johnson and C. H. Jenkinson, xxiii:
'In conclusion we may note that in late hands, where English is the
language used, suspension marks over a final consonant (such as d, g, or n)
are very common; and frequently mean little more than that the ending,
had the language been Latin, could only have been that of a suspended,
or incomplete, word, i.e. that the scribe is acting from force of habit, and
that the abbreviation is little more than formal.'
[6] Yet cf. Maitland, Year Books 1 & 2 Edw. II, Selden Society, xxxvii,
note 2, for *moun* and *soun*.
[7] Cf. Maitland's discussion of another sign, *op. cit.*, li: 'Not unfre-
quently an editor will find himself compelled to add a final *e* which he
would rather not write. If he sees in full the words *record, bastard, tort*,
as substantives meaning a record, a bastard, a wrong, but also sees the
little stroke through the final *d* or *t* which should signify an omitted letter,
he has no choice open to him, though he may think that some clerks fell
into a trick of drawing these little strokes without considering whether
they were needful.'

[f. 74] Prima lectura Magistri Thome Marowe existentis lectoris in quadragesimali vacacione anno H[enrici] VII^{mi} xviii°.

De pace terre & ecclesie & conseruacione eiusdem, Westminster primer capitulo primo.[1]

[*Lestatut.*] En primez voet le Roy & commaunde que la peas de seint esglis & de la terre soit bien garde et maintenue en toutz pointez et que comen droit soit fait as toutz auxi bien as poures come as riches saunz regarde de nully.

Le Roy voet que la peas de saint esglis & cetera; cest estatut est en affirmaunce del comen ley & ne fut[2] pas[3] ascun doute que fut al comen ley[4] deuaunt. Mez pur faire le peple timerous purceo que cest estatut fut fait tempore guerre & pur ceo que le peas serra melliour conserue en toutz pointez, cest estatut fut primerment fait en cest parlement.

Et ore est a voier queux fueront conseruatourz de cest esperituell peace purceo que lestatut ne reherse que serront conseruatourz, mez serra entendu ceux que fueront al comen ley deuaunt cest estatut, scilicet, toutz euesch & archeuesques deins son prouynce come fueront en le temps de seint E. le Roy[5] come appiert en lez aunciens leys Knuytt[6] que fut Roie dengliterre deuaunt. Et en temps mesme le Roie[7] lez conseruatourz auauntditz ont poiar de punyssher le trespassours pur loure contumacie fait a dieu & seint esglis par penaunce & huiusmodi & auxi de assesser vne fyne sur eux pur le peas enfreint temporall al vse de le Roie et auxi de agarder damages al partie que fut greue; come si home auoit assaute vne autre en vne esglis & luy batue, doncques lez conseruatourz fueront come est auauntdit. Et lez fynes adoncques fueront cessez en cest fourme: si le peas vst este enfreint en ascun cathedrall esglis le fyne fut assesse certen a vi liuers et si vst este enfreint en ascun autre comen esglis doncques fut le fyne assesse forsque as trois liuers.[8] Et issint il appiert par cez leies que ils ount iurisdiccion a cest iourz de punyssher tout le transgression auxibien pur le spiritualte come pur le temporall acte. Mez

---

[1] For the statute 3 Edw. I, c. 1, 1275, see *supra*, p. 167. Words in the margin of the MS. are either italicized within brackets or preceded by (*margin*).   [2] *Add* fait, C.   [3] pur, B, C, D.

[4] The more condensed form of F appears immediately.

[5] Edward the Confessor.

[6] Canute, Charter of 1020, ed. Liebermann, in Gesetze der Angelsachsen, i. 273; Stubbs, Select Charters, 8th ed., 75.

[7] That is, Canute; see his charter, *ut supra*, ed. Liebermann, 274, also Instituta Cnuti, and Quadripartitus, *ibid.* 279-307, 535.

[8] *Ibid.* 282-3; the sums differ slightly.

apres ceo, en temps de Roy E. le Seint,[1] lez dyuysions dez punyshe-
mentz fuist fait, scilicet, que lez conseruatours del spiritualte punyshe-
rent le contumacye a seint esglise et lez conseruatourz del peas del
terre punyssherent tout ceo que fut fait encountre le coron del Roie
& ses leies,[2] et pur ceo a cest iour ils ne[3] medelerent forsque pur le
contumacie tantum & cetera & lez Justices de Roie punyssherent le
remenaünt & cetera.

Le peas de lesglis poet estre enfreint en ii maners, scilicet, par
violence fait alz spirituelles possessions sanctificate et par violence fait a
lez espirituelles personez sanctificate.   Et en primez par cest letter[4]
est a voier de le peas enfreint a lez spirituelx possessions del esglis,
come si home fait violence par entre on autre maner a vne espirituell
possession come de enfreindre del huys del esglise ou defoundre le
soille le parson ou abbott ; en cest cas pur le temporall tort le parson
auera accion de transgression par le comen ley et pur le spirituell
tort, scilicet, pur le sanctificacion, il auera proces par le spirituell ley.
Mez si vne parson que est loialment en possession de vne benefice
soit ouste par vne autre de son parsonage il est mys a son remedie
par Spoliacion.[5]   Mez sil tient le benefice oue laie power leuesque fra
proces.   Mez si laie power continue,[6] il est mys de suer al euesque de
faire certificat soubz [f. 75 b[7]] son seale al Chaunceler compernaunt tout
le demeaner de lez persons que luy ousterent & tient oue laie power &
cetera,[8] auera vne breue que est appelle De vi laica removenda[9] que
serra direct al vicount de mesme le counte & par auctorite de cest
breue il alera al esglis & la remouera le laie poiar auauntdit.

Et ore est a voier queux personez il remouera la & queux nemi.
Par launcien temps il ne poet remouer clerkis esteaunt en lesglis &
purceo multez de lez misfesourz auauntditz voillount auer vne surplis
sur luy al entent que il serra dit vne clerke & que il ne serra remoue
purceo que lez clerkis adoncques ne fueront remouez purceo que ils
ne fueront entendus laie power.   Mez autre est a cest iour quar ore[10]
coment que eux que tient oue force sount clerkis, ore il serra removez.

Homes que ount pris seintuarie deuaunt pur loure saluacion, scilicet,
pur felonye ou murdre, ne serront remouez ne homez raclusez, scilicet,
autrez ou huiusmodi.

[1] Cf. Leges Edwardi Confessoris, ed. Liebermann, *ibid.* 631, 637–8.
[2] heirz, C.   [3] *Add* poient, B, D.   [4] lecture, B, C.
[5] Cf. Fitzherbert, New Natura Brevium, 9th ed., 1794, i. 36–7.
[6] *Add* possession, D.   [7] f. 74 b, f. 75 are blank.   [8] *Add* et sur ceo, D.
[9] Fitzherbert, *op. cit.*, i. 54, marginal entry : 'Old Na. Br. 33 cont.,
and Marrow in his reading'.   The earliest edition in which this reference
to Marowe appears is that of 1652.   [10] vncore, B, D.

Item quaunt le vicount ad remoue le power, vncore il ne poet mittre lautre, scilicet, le pleintiff en cest breue, en possession de lesglis ; quar doncques lautre auera vne especiall breue al vicount de luy de remouer quar son auctorite nest pluis mez de remouer le laie power.

Le certificat doit estre fait par leuesque ou larcheuesque de mesme le lieu ou le force est et en le temps de vacacion cest certificat doit estre fait par le garden de lez espiritueltez. Mez si le Pape voile faire certificat de ceo force ceo nest bone ; quar il ne poet auer notice de ceo par comen entendement de le ley.

Item cest certificat doit estre southe le sealez lez ordinaries mesme & nemi southe le sealles loure officials ou commissaries. Item cest certificacion nest peremptorie en le title a ascun tile parson ou patron ne pur le fyne. Mez que le partie poet trauerser ceo apres pur sauer son title et fyne. Mes autrement est de Bastardie ou Bigamy certifie par leuesque.

Item si cest certificat soit fait sur vne parson que est exempt de visitacion ou huiusmodi il poet vener en le chauncerie apres le certificat & deuaunt le breue soit pris hors del chauncerie & monstrer cez lettrez de exempcion ou autre mater de luy excuser & estopper le breue. Et si le breue soit pris hors deuaunt son venue il auera Supersedeas direct al vicount de surcesser de lexecucion le primer breue. Mes le vicount ne poet returne sur le breue de vi laica remouenda cest exempcion ne autre mater de excuser le partie le defaute.

Item cest breue de vi laica remouenda est en iii maners de natures dount ii sount originals & le tierce Judiciall. Mes en toutz les iii breues couient de auer Certificat de lordinarie deuaunt que sest breue soit graunt.

Le primer breue est generall & ceo sur espirituall possession que est execute ; come si home fait tile chose oue force en vne esglis mez nemi en le glebe terre ne en le cymytorie.

Item si home tient vne pewe en vne esglis oue force cest breue ne gist. Mez si vne home tient vne tombe en vne esglise oue power le parson auera cest breue purceo que cest chose est annexe al espirituell possession.

Item si lez parysshons soient deforce de vne procession voie par cest force [1] vncore purceo null tile breue purceo que le chose en luy mesme est temporall. [2]

Item si vne disseise moy de vne parcell de terre & puis edifie vne

[1] chemyn par force, D ; apparently something omitted.
[2] *Add* Le breue ne gist pur vn frank chapple [Mez si le] soit unie a ceo vn esglise, donques ill gyst ; quar adonques lordinarie ad jurisdiccion la & issint est deuenues esspirituell, F. The phrase within brackets is supplied from G.

esglis par licence de le Pape & le Roie & puis il que edifia present &
ieo entre & tient luy dehors ouesque force cest breue ne gist. Mez
autre est lou ii personez sont en variaunce pur parcell de vne cymytorie & cetera.

[f. 76] Item si vne parson moy enfeffe en son esglis & puis il tient
possession vers moy oue force cest breue ne gist pur luy[1] quar le feffement est voide ; tantum[2] quere de ceo.

Et auxi si vne parson graunt vne rent oue clause de distreindre a
moy hors de son esglis le rent arerer, si ieo veigne pur distreindre pur
le rent & il tient lesglis oue force,[3] ieo nauera breue de Vi laica
remouenda. Mez autre est si vne parson fait vne lees de son parsonage a moy pur terme de ans & puis tient lesglis vers moy oue force,
quar la ieo auera lauauntdit breue vers luy.

Item si vne Abbathie dissolue par mort ou autrement & le euesque
voille assigner & deputer nouell en mesme le liewe & le foundour
entre & tient vers luy oue laie power, cest briefe ne gist.

Item si le convict parson de ascun Euesque soit tenuz deuers luy oue
laie power cest briefe ne gist pur leuesque quar il nest chose espituell.[4]

Et nota que cest briefe ne gist vncques en ascun cas mez de
chose spirituell & destre fait en vne spirituell lieu come de
faire visitacion, enstallacion dascun abbott ou euesque elect &
huiusmodi & cetera.

Le ii[de] breue est executorie & est founduz auxi sur mater en fait &
est especiall & iugement[5] generall come lautre est. Et cest breue est
ad requisicionem partis[6] & cetera. Et si cest breue soit vne foitz
execute cest breue ne gist apres lexecucion ; come si leuesque inducte
ascun parson par title il nauera cest breue encontre son enduccion
demene. Mez autre est lou lordinarie ad nouell cause come par
recouere apres en vne Quare impedit.

Item il couient que lact lordinarie concerne le spirituall possession,
quar si soit pur dismes[7] ou pur seruyre vne Fieri facias ou huiusmodi
cest breue ne gist, quar ceo est vne temporall acte.

Item il couient que cest acte que leuesque doit affaire ne poet estre
fait aillourz que en cest spirituall lieu & couient que il concerne le
espirituell possession come Induccion, visitacion, eleccion, enstallacion & huiusmodi. Mes autrement est de faire vne admission,
Institucion, ou de prendre de vne Jure Patronatus, quar ceux purrount

---

[1] moy, F.   [2] tamen, B.   [3] *Add* vers moy, C.
[4] espirituell, B, C, D.   [5] nient (?), C.
[6] venerabilis episcopi, etc., F, L.   [7] primes fruytes, F.

estre fait en autrez lieus que en lesglis ou lieu espirituell & cetera & sic nota diuersitatem.

Item si leuesque voille faire Induccion de vne prebende donatiff & est tient hors ouesque laie power, le breue ne gist. Mez si tile prebende donatiff soit annexe a vne parsonage & il voile Inducter le parson en le prebende & cetera, le breue gist, quar transmutatur per annexsiacionem & cetera.

Item si lordinarie voet Inducter vne parson en le glebe terre cest breue ne gist, quar nest en espirituell lieu. Mez autrement est quaunt parcell de le glebe terre est done en augmentacion a vne parson ou a vne viker & cetera.

Item si vne esglis soit suspendue par effusion de sancke & issint esteaunt voide & leuesque voet faire Induccion en lesglis deuaunt que soit resanctificate, le breue gist & cetera.

Item si vne esglis eschuit & puis est reedifie sur le glebe terre de autre seint come lou il fut auaunt de Seint George, ore il est de Seint Margrett & launcient Patron fait presentacion a ceo al nouell esglis reseruaunt a luy launcient esglis & lordinarie voet luy Inducter en launcien esglise, sil soit deforce oue laie power cest breue gist.

Item si vne esglise soit apropure a vne abbe a tener in proprios vsus, et apres vne estraunge present al ordinarie et il voille faire Induccion le breue ne gist, quar par le appropriacion le nature del enduccion est ale. Mes sil ad vne iugement de ceo estre disapropre & doncque lordinarie voillet faire induccion & est tient [1] oue power, cest briefe ne [2] gist & cetera. Mes en cest cas sil voet inducter le parson & outre le vicare cest briefe ne gist.[3]

Item si vne auowson soit aproper a tener en propre vse a vne abbe & puis labbott mesme present son clerke al [f. 76 b] Ordinarie que est institut & induct in mesme lesglis & le parson devie & labbe entre & ent tient en propre vse & puis vi mois passe, lordinarie voile faire collacion et labbott tient oue force, le breue gist. Mes si labbott en le vie lencombent vst purchase nouell licence de apropriacion doncque cest breue ne gist.

Item si vne Maner oue vne auowson soit aprope a tener en propre vse a vne abbe, & apres labbe fait feffement simul cum aduocacione & le feffe present al Ordinarie & il voile enducter son clerke null breue de Vi [4] gist.

---

[1] *Add* de horse, B.   [2] *Omit*, B, D, F.
[3] Mes ... gist wrongly follows Item ... al, but the scribe remedies his mistake by inserting ' b ' and ' a ' before ' Item ' and ' Mes ' respectively.
[4] *Add* laica remouenda, B. C.

Item si ii iointenauntes [1] de vne auowson sount [et] lun de eux done
ceo que a luy affiert a vne abbe a tener en propre vse, et lautre present
al ordinarie, & labbe tient lautre presente hors oue power, lauauntdit
breue gist en cest cas.

Item si lordinarie voille inducter abbe ou prioure que est eligibulle
& nient presentable & il luy resista ouesque power, cest breue ne gist.
Mes autrement est lou il est eligible & presentable. Mes si le Foundour present vne que ne fut eslue,[2] vncore sil soit tenus hors oue
power cest breue gist. Et nota que lou le foundour poet issint auer
present, & apres il reles al abbe et puis lordinarie voile faire enstallacion & il est tient hors oue force, null breue de vi laica remouenda pur
lentres lordinarie est ale par le reles le foundour.

Item lou le foundour present vne que ne fut eligible & il est inducte
par lordinarie, & puis ils eslieront vne autre abbe saunz induccion, si
lordinare voile faire induccion & soit resiste oue laie power, le breue
ne gist. Mes sils eslieront vne que nest abbe & lordinarie luy refusa
& ils eslieront vne nouell, lordinarie voet faire collacion par laps [3] &
sil soit resist, le breue de vi laica remouenda gist.

Le iiicie breue est executorie sur mater de recorde, come si vne
iugement soit done en vne Quare Impedit ou Assise de Darrein Presentment & le breue issist al euesque de admitter son clerke que auoit
recouer & lordinarie luy voile enducter & est tenus hors oue power,
cest breue gist. Mes autre est en vn recouere ewe en breue de Droit
de auowson, quar le vicount luy mittera en possession sur cest recouere. Et en ascun cas tout [4] sur cest recouery, come si recouere en
breue de Droit de auowson & lencombent deuie apres le recouere &
deuaunt ascun execucion sue, doncque il poet auer Scire facias direct al
patron adire pur que il nauera execucion, ou il poet auer breue al vicount
de luy mitter en possession. Mes sil sue execucion par Scire facias & lordinarie luy voet enditer [5] & ne poet pur le graunde power, cest breue gist.

Item mesme le ley que done que cest force serra remoue lou
lordinarie est de Inducter ascun parson al esglis ; mesme le ley est
que cest breue gist lou lordinare voillet remouer ascun parson par
auctorite de ley. Mesme le ley si le breue vient al euesque. Mesme
le ley lou Ne admittas vient a luy & vncore il voet presenter, cest
breue gist. Mez quere si vne Quare non admisit vient al euesque &
tient hors oue power si cest breue gist ou nemi, & cetera.

---

[1] MS. ioint' ; but cf. L for Jointenauntes.
[2] *After* eslue, F *reads* et ou est eligable & presentable, si lordinarie
luy voylle inducter & resistens fayt, le breue gist.
[3] Cf. Fitzherbert, *op. cit.*, i. 32–6.
[4] gist, B, C.   [5] induct, B ; inducter, D.

[Secunda Lectura.] De conseruacione pacis spiritualium personarum ecclesie, scilicet, de lour corps.

Al comen ley si home vst fait violence a vne person spirituall come
a prest ou moigne ou huiusmodi come de batue,[1] assault ou autre
transgression a luy fait, remedie fut done par nostre ley come fut done
a autre temporall person & nient autrement. Mes spirituall penaunce
fut done come est a cest iour. Mes pur arrester de ascun spirituell
person ne fut ascun remedie al comen leie; le quell arrest fut violence
en le spirituell leie auxibien come assault. Sur que le spiritualte soie
complaignount al Roie, sur quell compleint lestatut de anno lmo E. 3,
[f. 77] capitulo vto,[2] fut fait, quell done Que null prest portaunt le
corps de Jhesu Criste oue lour clerkis ou autrez persones de seint
esglis quaunt ils fueront intendaunt a le dyvyne seruyce deins lesglise
& cemytories[3] ne serront arrest sur payn de grevous forfaitur. Mes
par cest estatut null accion fut done pur le forfaitur, quar cest estatut
fut tout en le negatiff & issint en maner forsque prohibicion. Et
purceo apres vient lestatut de anno xvᵒ Ricardi IIᵈⁱ[4] & ceo done
remedie par voie de accion come appiert par le lettre de cest estatut,
Gentz de Seint esglise benefice & autrez : cest parol ‘autrez’ serra
entendu gentz de seint esglis si come prestes de seint esglis deins
lesglis si ceux sount attendauntes as dyvyne seruyce & auxi clerkis,
queresters, sextens & huiusmodi. Mesme le ley est dez gardeins de
vne esglis coment que sount temporall personez sil sount arrestus en
lesglise en fesaunde lour office ils auerount le benefice de cest estatut
auxibien come prestes. Mes autrez temporall persones de le parissh
entendaunt a lour dyvyne seruyce en lesglise ou en alaunt de procession sont hors de remedie de cest estatut. Mes lez Prestes & clerkes
que alent en procession come ceux de le Queere saunz covyn sount
deins le cas de cest estatut. Et cest estatut ne serra entendus sole-
[Nota.] ment lou ils alent[5] Criste tantum. Mez serra entendue sils
alent hors de lesglise ou deins lesglise pur ministrer ascun de
cez sacramentes ou huiusmodi oue son surplis ou revesture accordaunt
a cest act.

---

[1] batrie, B.
[2] 50 Edw. III in all printed copies, but according to S.R. i. 396,
really 51 Edw. III, 1377.
[3] seintwaries, D, a mistake as far as the text of the statute goes.
[4] Primo Ric. 2, cap. xv et ultimo, D ; 1 Rich. II, last chapter, F. Cf.
1 Rich. II, c. 15, 1377, and note that the text of the statute uses
‘ santuaries ’ toward the end ; see note 3, *supra*.
[5] *Add* oue le corps, C, D.

Lestatut est, arreste & cetera ; ceo serra entende [1] lou ils sount arreste par loure corps, scilicet, par Capias & cetera ; quar ils poient estre sommone, garnye ou attache par biens coment que soit fait deins lesglise & est hors de cas de cest estatut.

Si home sue breue de Rauysshement de garde enuers autre & le breue direct al vicount voet que diligenter enquiri facias vbi heres ille est in comitatu tuo, le vicount poet prendre le corps lenfaunt coment que il soit vne querester de cest esglise. Mesme le ley lou vne breue de Habeas corpus vient al vicount pur seruire, il poet seruire en lesglise.

Item cest arrest est auxibien destre entendus de breuez de execucion [2] come dez autrez breuez come en Capias ad satisfaciendum ; si le vicount luy serua vers vne spirituall person deins lesglise, ceo est deins le cas de cest estatut. Mez autrement est en breue de Excommunicato capiendo ; [3] quar si vne prest soit arrest par cest breue en vne esglise null accion gist, quar il ad renounce le benefice de seint esglise deuaunt par cest excommengement. Mes si vne prest soit detect de heresie & de ceo endite deuaunt Justice de peas & puis il est pris par Capias deins lesglise sur cest enditement il auera accion ; quar par cest enditement il nest conuict ne disable par ordinarie, quar poet apres estre troue faux & cetera.

Item toutz maners de seisiers par mater en fait sount hors de cas de cest estatute, come si home ad reteigne vne seruaunt & il ale en lesglise, il poet prendre luy hors par proses ou saunz proses. Et issint est si mon villein entra en lesglise pur estre aide par cest estatut, ieo puisse entrer & seisier mon villen & null accion. Mes si mon villein entre en religion & puis si ieo entra en lesglise & seisier luy, laccion gist vers moy.

Item si ieo present mon villein a vne esglise, [ceo][4] nest enfraunchisement mes ieo puis luy seisier luy [sic] apres deinz mesme leglise. Mes si mon villein soit fait abbe de vne lieu ieo ne puisse luy seisier apres & sil [5] luy seisier il auera accion de Faux imprisonement. Mes si ieo soie vicount & vne precept vient a moy a autre sute pur prendre mon villein & ieo [f. 77 b] luy arrest par vertue de ceo deins lesglise, il auera accion sur cest estatut ; quar par cest acte ieo luy auoie enfraunchise & done luy vne cause de accion & cetera.

Item si ieo prise ascun home a baille, ceo est mon prisoner tancque

---

[1] entendu, C.   [2] excommengement, B, D.
[3] Fitzherbert, *op. cit.*, i. 62 n, 63 a.
[4] MS. s⁰ ; ceo, B.   [5] Clearly an error for ' si ieo '.

a le iour que est done a luy de apperer et sil fue en vne esglise ieo luy prendra hors & null accion;[1] quar il serra toutz foitz aiugge en mon garde. Mes autre est si ieo soie mainpernour pur ascun de garder son iour en le comen place[2] ou pur garder le peas tancque al *[Quere diuersi-* iour; quar la ieo ne puisse luy prendre ne emprisoner *tatem.]* deuaunt le iour; quar en lun cas lez parols sount ceo: home tradatur[3] michi in balliuam et en lautre cas nemi, quod manucaptus.[4]

Item si vne officer arrest vne Preste hors de lesglise & puis il fue en lesglise, vncore il poet luy prendre hors, quar il fut son prisoner deuaunt. Mes autrement est quaunt il viewe lofficer deuaunt il luy ad arrest & fua en lesglise deuaunt larrest; le diuersite appiert.

Item en tout proses lou le Roie est partie enuers vne espirituall person come en surete de le peas ou autre accion lou le Roie est pleintif,[5] ceo nest deins le cas de cest estatut. Et mesme le leie est en accion popular pur lentrest le Roie et sic vide diuersitatem entre le proses le Roie & vne comen person; quar le Roie nest de auer ascun chose forsque vne fyne tantum.

Lestatut est, si soit arrest & trahie hors de lesglise; vncore ne serra pris si generalment, quar si vne preste soit arrestuz deins lesglis & la troua surete al officer il auera accion vncore il ne fut trahie hors. Mez si le vicount areste vne preste deins lesglise & il fait rescous null accion pur luy par cest estatut. Mesme le leie est si ieo delyuer al vicount vne Supersedeas deuaunt le arrest en lesglis; mes si le vicount luy arrest deinz lesglise & puis il eschapa de luy, vncore il auera accion par cest estatut.

Item si le vicount vient en lesglise pur arrester ascun person spirituall & ceo monstra a luy le proses que il ad enuers luy & il done licence a le vicount de luy arrester & le vicount luy arreste, il nauera accion par cest estatut.

Item si vne preste soit arrest deins vne esglise & il eschape en autre esglise & la il est pris, il nauera accion pur lun arrest ne pur lautre; quar pur le primer arreste il ad refuse le benefice par le acceptaunce de lautre esglis & del ii^de prendre il nauera accion, quar il fut son prisoner deuaunt par le primer arrest; quod nota.

Item si vne preste soit arreste deins vne esglise & puis il conust vne Felony par luy fait, si le vicount luy prent hors il auera accion sur cest

---

[1] *Add* eadem opinio Seignur Fynux, D (margin).
[2] banke, B, D.   [3] traditur, B.
[4] manucaptores, B, C, D. For the distinction between bail and main-prise, see p. 85, note 23, *supra*.   [5] partie, B, D.

estatut. Mes sil pria priuelege de seintuarie & ne monstre ascun cause a luy mes pria seintuary generalment, null accion. Mesme le ley est lou vne preste prist esglise pur felony & puis quaunt le coroner vient il ne voet conuster le Felony & est pris hors, il nauera accion sur lestatut.

Item mesme le ley est lou vne preste fait vne affraie ou assault deins vne esglise, il list bien a lez constables, ou a lez autrez officers le Roy, de luy prendre hors & il nauera accion par cest estatut.

Lez parols de lestatut est,[1] Vlle mynester ou autrez; cez parols serrount entende & prise pur ceux que fount larrest & eux que vient oue luy en eidaunt, come vicount, bailly, constable & loure seruauntes & huiusmodi.

Item si vne vient en lesglis et monstra vne warant de le peas vers le parson de lesglis & voet que il vient a son master pur trouer surete & il ale oue luy & troua surete, vncore null accion, quar ceo ne fut ascun arrest. Quar lez parols de [f. 78] le warant sount, quod inueniet securitatem pacis & si nemi, doncque eum [2] Capias & cetera.

Item si le vicount face precept a vne Bailly ou a seruaunt & il fait larreste deins lesglise vne de le spiritualte, laccion [3] gist vers luy que fist larrest & nemi enuers le vicount; mes si le vicount face son precept de luy arrester en lesglise laccion gist vers ambideux.

Item si le vicount arrest vne preste deins vne esglise & apres returne sur le breue non est inuentus ou ne voet returner le breue, le parson [4] poet eslier de auer accion sur lestatut ou auer accion de Faux imprisonement. Mes il ne poet auer ambideux accions; quar sil voile porte accion sur lestatut & pendaunt cest accion il port accion de Faux imprisonement ambideux abateront; quar doncque il serra estoppe par lun accion de porter lautre; quar en maner ils sount contrariaunt par son supposell & cetera.

Item [5] ii vicount sount come en londres & cetera et lun arrest vne preste deins vne esglise laccion gist vers luy tantum.

Item si le partie a que sute [6] vient oue le vicount & monstra luy le person que serra arrest, & le vicount luy arrest deins lesglise null accion enuers celui que monstra. Mes autre est si le partie monstra a luy vne que nest mesme le person que est nome en le breue; quar la le partie auera accion de Faux imprisonement vers ambideux; quod nota.

---

[1] sount si, C.   [2] MS. eū.
[3] *Add* dell spirituall Vi laica emouenda, B.
[4] prest, C.   [5] *Add* si, B, D.
[6] *For* a que sute *read* qui suyst, B; qui sue laccion, D.

Item si le vicount arreste vne preste en lesglise saunz breue ou precept, scilicet, de son tort demene, le partie nauera accion sur cest estatut mes auera accion de Faux imprisonement; quar ne poet estre dit proprement arreste que est saunz auctorite de le ley.

Item mesme le ley lou vne Capias est agarde enuers vne preste & le vicount luy arreste deuaunt que il ad le breue receiue, accion de Faux imprisonement & nemi accion sur cest estatut. Mes si vne Capias soit agarde & delyuer al vicount de arrester vne preste lou null Originall soit ewe deuaunt & le vicount luy arreste par cest Capias deins lesglise, vncore accion gist par cest estatut, quar ceo que le vicount fist fut par garrantie a luy sufficient sil neit luy misuse apres.

Item si le vicount arreste vne preste deins vne esglise & puis vne autre officer que ad autre precept vient & luy prent de luy deins lesglise, le partie greve auera accion sur lestatut enuers celui vicount que luy primez arreste, & enuers lautre, accion de Faux imprisonement.

Item si vne preste soit arreste deins lesglis par seuerall proses al seuerall temps par vne mesme person, il nauera forsque vne accion de toutz arrestes & en cest accion il recouera damages pur toutz. Mes si vne ioint Capias soit vers ii prestes, & le vicount eux ambideux face arrester en vne mesme esglis, ils aueerount seuerall accions sur cest estatut & nemi ioint accion, quar loure tort fut seuerall.

Item si le vicount arreste vne preste en lesglise par iiii^{or} ou xx Capias a vne mesme temps il nauera forsque vne accion & il ne recouera pluis damages que par vne arreste.

Item si le vicount face precept al Bailly & il arreste le preste deins lesglise & puis le vicount ne retourna la breue, le prest auera accion sur cest estatut enuers le Bailly mes nemi accion de Faux imprisonement. Mes si le vicount face precept al Bailly de prendre [*Quere de cest cas.*] vne prest lou le vicount nad ascun breue deuaunt & le Bailly luy arrest deins vne esglise, la gist accion de Faux imprisonement enuers le Bailly & nemi accion sur cest estatut.

Item si le vicount face precept al Bailly & il luy [1] arresta [2] deins vne esglise & ne returne son precept al vicount, le partie poet eslier de auer accion sur estatut ou accion de Faux imprisonement enuers le Bailly. [f. 78 b] Mes si le vicount face precept a son seruaunt que fist larrest come est auauntdit & le vicount ne retourne le breue, il poet eslier de auer accion sur lestatut enuers le seruaunt ou accion de Faux imprisonement vers le vicount & son seruaunt.

[1] *Omit*, B, D.   [2] *Add* prest, B, D.

Item si vne Originall soit vers J.[1] att Stile & le Capias soit vers W.[2] att S., & le vicount luy[3] prist en lesglise W. att S. que est preste et puis le capias est amende J. att S., le partie auera accion de Faux imprisonement.

Item si vne capias soit direct al vicount de arrester vne J. att S. de Dale[4] & sount ii J. att S. de dale & le vicount arrest lun pur lautre deins lesglise, il que est arrest auera accion sur cest estatut. Mes autrement est sil fut areste come est auauntdit sur vne capias ad satisfaciendum, quar la il auera accion de Faux imprisonement ou accion sur cest estatut.

Item si sount ii prestes que ount vne mesme nosme & Capias est agarde enuers vne de eux & le vicount arrest ambideux en lesglise, celui que ne deuoit estre arrest par cest breue poet auer accion sur cest estatut, et sil port accion sur [sic] Faux emprisonement il ne auera autre accion sur lestatut et auxi lautre auera accion sur lestatut mes nemi Faux imprisonement.

Lestatut est, et face gree & cetera; si le prest que est issint arrest auoit vne Master al temps de cest arrest que ad perdue son seruice par tile arreste, le Master nauera accion sur lestatut pur son perdue de son seruice. Mes autre est de feme couert que est seruaunt entre[5] Mynchyns[6] & el est arrest en lesglise, le baron & le feme ioinderount en accion sur lestatut. Mes si ambideux soient seruauntes en lesglise et ambideux arreste en lesglise, le baron auera seuerall accions, scilicet, vne accion pur le tort fait a luy tantum & autre accion en le nome de luy & son feme pur le tort fait a son feme.

Item si vne capias issist vers vne abbe & son commoigne & le commoigne est arrest en lesglise, labbe auera accion sur lestatut, nient nosmant son commoigne. Mes en cest cas si le commoigne soit dereigne deuaunt ascun accion vse par labbe, labbe ne auera ascun accion de ceo apres. Mes si vne commoigne soit arrest & puis il est fait abbe de mesme le lieu, il auera accion pur le tort fait a luy deuaunt quaunt il fut commoigne. Mes si vne abbe soit arrest en lesglise & puis il est depose ou il resigne, son successor nauera laccion. Mes si mesme le abbott apres le resignacion soit reeslue, laccion est reviue a luy & auera accion come deuaunt. Et mesme le ley est sil soit fait abbe de autre meason apres larrest & deuaunt accion sue, vncore il auera accion.

---

[1] John, B.   [2] Wat., B.   [3] *Omit*, D.
[4] J. Stile de dala, B.   [5] all, D.
[6] Minchen, nun, Murray, N.E.D.; cf. mynecenan in charter of

Item si vne moigne purchase licence de prendre vne Benefice & est
present a ceo & il est arrest en mesme lesglis, il nauera accion sur
cest estatut en son nome tantum. Mes son abbe & luy ent auerount
accion. Et ceo appiert maruellous case quar en taunt que il ad licence
de auer Benefice il est[1] personable de vser accion & suer soule pur
toutz chosez a luy concernauntez par[2] son benefice ; quod nota.[3]

[f. 79] [Tercia Lectura.] De pace terre et conseruatoribus
eiusdem.

Lestatute[4] parle de le peas de terre mes lestatut ne parle de
conseruatoribus de peas de terre. Mes chescun Justice de Peas est
conseruatour de peas mez nemi econtra ; quar home poet estre conseruatour & nemi Justice de peas & ceo proue[5] lez parols del commission, scilicet, assignauimus. Et auxi lestatut de anno primo E. 3[6]
prove que fueront conseruytourz deuaunt que fueront ascun Justice de
peas en Englitere. Quar al comen [ley][7] deuaunt lestatut de anno
xviii⁰ E. 3[8] fueront null Justice de peas vt patet per eundem statutum ;
par que Trois chosez sount a voier : Primes, coment home poet estre
conseruatour de peas & nemi Justice de peas ; le ii^de, coment home
poet estre Justice de peas & en quell maner ;[9] le iii^ce, as queux
persones le auctorite de Justice de peas serra commytt.[10]

En primes, home poet estre Conseruytour de peas & nemi Justice
par v maners de voies : primes, ratione officii vel dignitatis ; le ii^de par
prescripcion ; le tierce par letters patentez ; le iiii^te par breue & le v
par Tenure.

[*Ratione officii*.] In primes poet estre ratione officii come nostre
seignur le Roie que est le principall Conseruytour de le peas & poet
commaunder toutz autres & agarder proses vers eux de conseruer le
peas. Mez le Roie mesme ne poet prendre recognysaunce pur le peas,
quar cest recognysaunce serra fait a luy mesme pur que & cetera.
Mes autre est de vne Duke, Erle & Chaunceler par reson de son
office, quar eux purront[11] prendre recognysaunce & [a]garder[12] proses

Canute, p. 289, notes 6 and 7, *supra* ; and mynchen in the translation
printed in Stubbs, Select Charters, 76.   [1] *Add* fait, B.   [2] *Omit*, B, D.
    [3] *Add* Hill. iii H. VI^ti fo. xx, D (margin) ; identified as Hill. 3 Hen. VI,
no. 2. There is no break in F or G between the second and third
lectures, so that the total number of lectures is less than in A, fourteen
in F and thirteen in G.
    [4] That is, Westminster the First, c. 1 ; see p. 289, note 1, *supra.*
    [5] par, C.   [6] 1 Edw. III, st. 2, c. 16 (c. 17 in early citations), 1327.
    [7] ley, B, C, D.   [8] 18 Edw. III, st. 2, c. 2, 1344.   [9] See iiii^ta Lectura, *infra.*
    [10] See Quinta Lectura, *infra.*   [11] poient, B.   [12] agarder, D.

& faire toutz chosez incidentes a ceo office.   Mesme le ley de Master de le Rolles, mez il ne poet faire proses & prendre recognysaunce come incidentes a son office mez par prescripsion que il ad vse de faire tile proses & cetera.

Item le Chieff Justice de le comen Bancke[1] & toutz Justicez de mesme le bancke poient agarder proses & accepter recognysaunce come conseruatourz de le peas come incidentz a lour office.   Mes le chieff Justice de le comen place poet estre Conseruatour par prescripsion, scilicet, de chescun peas enfreint en son presence ou dez chosez faitz deins le precincte de le comen place enciaunt[2] le court.   Et en mesme le maner est de[3] le chieff Baron de lescheker Conseruytour come lautre est en son court & presens & cetera.   Mes lez Justice de assise ne poient agarder proses pur le peas come warant ou huiusmodi; mes si le peas soit enfreint en loure presence ils poient commaunder luy al garde que ad enfreint le peas.   Et si complaynt soit fait a eux que vne tile voille enfreindre le peas ou ils veient occasion en loure presence, ils purront[4] commaunder lez parties sur certein peyn destre en peas mez null surete[5] coment[6] Justice de peas poient.   Mes si lez Jurrourz en assise sount Jurre & mytte en vne meason & lun vient et demanda surete de peas de vne de son compaignon Jurre oue luy en cest assise, les Justicez commaunderont que toutz lour wepens destre[7] pris & assignera vne keper a eux.   Et mesme le ley de Testimoigies[8] que sount jure oue lassise & oue eux.[9]

Item les Justicez de Gaolle delyuere dez prisoners en le Gaile de Seneschall, de court de pipoudres en vne feire, le Coroner & vicount que tient plee par Justicies, le Seneschall de vne lete & de Turne de vicount, null de eux poient graunter proses de surete de peas, quar ils ne sount proprement mes conseruatours de peas.   Mes toutz eux si affraie soit fait en lour [f. 79 b] presence enfesauntz lour officez auaunt-ditz poient committer luy a garde que ad offende en tile maner.   Mes le Seneschall & sutourz en vne court Baron ne maunde le partie al prison pur vne affraie fait deuaunt luy en lour presenee en le court sinoun par title de prescripsion.   Mez toutz lez Justices auaunditz par prescripcion poient prendre surete de peas mes nemi autrement.

Item vne Constable ne poet prendre surete al request dez parties mez il poet garder le peas & sils soient[10] present al temps de laffraie

[1] Bancke le Roy, F, certainly the correct form.
[2] seeant, B ; seant, D.   [3] *Omit*, C, D.   [4] poient, B.
[5] See Sexta Lectura, *infra*.   [6] come, B, C, D.
[7] serront, B, D.   [8] Testimoignes, B.
[9] oue eux en assise, D.   [10] sil soit, B, D.

fait il poet emprisoner luy que fist laffraie mez nemi autrement. Mes lou il est present ne [1] il ne poet cesser son fyne apres il luy ad enprisone. Mes il poet luy prendre & luy compeller de trouer surete par obligacion ou par fideiussores [2] per auncien ley & cetera. Mes autrement est de vicount & dez baillez errauntes quar eux purront lesser a baille par recognysaunce. Mes le Seneschall de le Marshalsie poet prendre ceo [3] deins le vierge del marshalsie surete de peas par recognysaunce par prescripcion. Et en mesme le maner poet le constable marchall del hostell nostre seignur le Roie de affraies faites deins lostell lauauntdit.

Item le comen howse del parliement poient graunter surete de peas al peticion fait a eux par ascun person & ceo saunz lassent dez seignurz de mesme le parlement & auxi ils poient agarder proses de ceo.

Item nota lou home poet tener toutz maners dez plees personel & par graunt le Roie de temps dount memorie ne court oue prescripcion ou ouesque allowaunce de cest liberte en vne Eyre, cestuy poet tener plee de surete de peas & prendre surete de ceo & cetera.

[*Prescripsion.*] Item notandum est coment cest prescripcion serra fait & ceo couient estre en luy ou sez auncestors que heire il est, est bone. Et auxi de alleger le prescripsion en ceux que astate il ad & en tile maner est bone. Et auxi ils poient prescriber pur garder le peas forsque pur certein temps del an, scilicet, pur quarter et de autre nemi & cetera.

Item ils poient prescriber de faire le proses tantum sicome luy distreigner & vender le distreint, & ceo est en maner de surete come si home soit excommenge leuesque luy certifia & le court le Roy fra proses enuers luy de attacher & il serra en prisone tanque il ad fait son caucion [4] par le ley spirituell; quod nota.

[*Lettrez Patentes.*] Le iii[cie] est par lez lettrez patentes; sicome le Roie graunt a vne home destre conseruatour de son peas de tile counte ou hundred, cest bone graunt coment que soit fait a luy & a sez heires. Mes nemi a cez assignes, quar vne Justice ne poet estre par assigne mez il poet auer enheritaunce en son sancke de cest chose.

Item si le Roy fist tile graunt a ii & a loure heires, ceo serra pris come seuerall grauntes a eux & a loure heires. Et si le Roie face tile graunt a vne & a cez heires destre conseruatour de son peas, il poet

---

[1] *Omit*, B, C, D. [2] Cf. Blackstone, iii. 108, 291. [3] *Omit*, C.
[4] Caution or security in both French and English. See Fitzherbert, *op. cit.*, i. 63-4 for writ *de cautione admittenda* after excommunication.

prendre surete par obligacion al request dez parties come chose incident a son office.   Mes il ne poet prendre surete dez parties par
recognysaunce sinoun que ceo soit a luy expressement graunt par le
graunt le Roie.   Mes celui [1] conseruatour ne poet prendre enquerry
par xii homez pur le peas enfreint ou pur riott come Justice de peas
poient.   Mes il poet luy relesser apres que il ad luy pris par mainpernourz ou autrement par obligacion.

[*Quere.*] Mes quere sil poet relesser a luy apres que le prisoner est
en le comen Gaile ; et auxi quere quell [f. 80] proses cest conseruatour
deuoit faire sur surete de peas a luy demande par autre person.

Item si tile conseruytour certifie en bancke le Roy que tile home ad
enfreint le peas en son presence, sur cest certificat le partie serra mytt
a son fyne saunz ascun trauers a ceo.   Mes sil certifie vne rescous fait
a ascun estraunger quere de ceo que serra fait.

Item conseruatour de le peas poet causer chescun home de trouer
surete de peas a luy auxibien deuaunt laffraie come apres [2] & la il
couient destre present come est auauntdit.

[*Diuersite.*]   Item le conseruatour mesme poet arrester vne home luy
mesme & issint ne poet vne Justice de peas come Justice ; quod nota.

Item si cest conseruatour soit requyse de garder le peas entre autrez
persones & il ne voet, il fra fyne si ceo soit certifie en le bancke. [3]

Item si vne conseruatour luy mesme enfreint le peas ouesque autrez
personez il fra fyne al Roie & auxi perdra son office de conseruatour.

Item si tile conseruatour lede ascun home en le garde del peas come
en departyng de ii persones esteaunt enfraiant, celui que est
[*Nota bene.*] lede est saunz remedie enuers luy. [4]   Mes autre est si vne autre
person ad depart eux esteaunt en affraie & lede lun partie, il
auera remedie enuers luy.

Item nota que cest conseruatour ne poet assesser ascun fyne, mes il
poet luy lesse a baille par obligacion & done ioure a luy destre en le
bancke & la son fyne serra cesse par lez Justicez de la Banck.

Item si sount ii conseruatourz de le peas si lun de eux agarde vne
warrant de surete del peas, lautre ne poet graunter Supersedeas de
surcesser de le proses.   Mez autrement est si vne Justice de le peas
agarde vne warant a vne autre Justice de peas deins mesme le counte,
il poet agarder vne Supersedeas sur ceo & cetera.

[1] MS. cè.
[2] *Add* par ceo auctorite.   Mez vn constable ne poet prendre surety
mez apres laffray, C, F ; B and D, omitting the second 'mez'.
[3] Le Roy, etc., B.
[4] *Add* Mez sill mesme soyt lede ill auera accion, F.

Item lez conseruatourz ne poient certifier ascun forcible entre encountre le peas ou reteindre oue force ne ascun autre chose que est
encountre le peas, forsque tantum & solement affraies, assautez ou
baterie, quar ceo est loure office & nient autre par breue.

Le iiii^te est par breue; come si le Roie maunda a vne cest breue de
vener en le chauncerie a certein iour & la de prendre son iurement
destre conseruatour a son peas.   Et en launcient temps si home voet
auer surete de peas, il poet viendre en le chauncerie & la il auera[1]
breue direct al vicount ou autre officer de prendre tile surete & son
surete fut par obligacion & nemi par recognisaunz.

Item home poet estre conseruatour en autre maner par breue;
sicome breue issist al vicount de eslier vne conseruatour de peas en
plein countee come il deuoit faire de vne coroner par le eleccion del
communialte de cest counte, & ils eslieront vne & [par][2] cest eleccion
il est conseruatour sicome Coroner et chiualers de parliament.   Et
issint fut lez vicounts esluz en le counte deuaunt lestatut de anno
xxviii^o [3] E. 3^cii.

Et nota que sil soit eslue par breue il ne poet estre discharge forsque
par breue; quar le Roie poet eux discharger de son office a son plesure
& cetera.   Mes si les gentz del counte esliount vne person destre conseruatour & le vicount returne vne autre sur le breue, celui que fut
eslue est conseruatour & nemi celui que est returne par vicount.   Mez
sils esliount ii & le vicount retourne forsque vne, ambideux sount conseruatourz.

Item si conseruatour de peas soit eslue deins vne counte & le Roie
par cez lettrez patentez graunt a vne [f. 80 b] autre pur terme de vie
destre conseruatour, ceux lettrez patentz ne sount voide en tout.   Mez
il auera Scire facias enuers lautre que fut eslue, en le nature de vne
breue de discharge & cetera.

[*Tenure.*] Item le v maners est par tenure; sicome le Roie graunt
a moy vne acre de terre de tener de luy par le seruice destre conseruatour de peas de tile countie, ceoe st bone tenure & par cest graunt
ieo prendra surete par obligacion & ferra tout come conseruatour ferra
que est fait par lez lettrez patentez.   Mez si ieo soy requyse de garder
le peas & ne face pas, quere si ieo serra distreigne ou nemi.   Mes si

---

[1] *For* & la . . . auera, *read* la estre jure et auer, B; et destre jurie
& la il auera, C; & la estre jurre et auer, D.
[2] *For* & [par], *read* par, B, C, D.
[3] xviii^o, B.   The statute 28 Edw. III, c. 7, 1354, provided that
sheriffs should be removed after one year of office.   As far back as
Edward II their election in the county court was discontinued and

ieo mesme face ieo [1] serra distreigne par fyne mez ieo ne perdra mon terre come Forfait. Quere si ieo puis cesser de cest seruice issint que le Roie poet auer cessauit ; semble que noun.

Mes si vne comen person voillet deuaunt lestatut [2] faire feffement de terre a tener de eux par autile seruice, ceo fut voide & vncore est a cest iour par fait endent. Mes si le Roie ad done a moy vne acre de terre a tener de luy par tile seruice destre son conseruatour de peas deins tile counte, ieo puisse done mesme le acre a vne autre a tener par mesme le seruice assetz bien & ceo est seruice de chiualer,[3] quar est seruice destre fait par le Person de vne home al Roie.

Item si le Roie dona moy terre destre conseruatour de peas, ieo sue conseruatour saunz autrez lettrez patentez. Mes si le Roie done terre a moy a tener de luy destre son Justice de peas il est voide, quar il ne poet estre Justice de peas saunz lettrez patentez de commission come est comement [4] fait.

Item si le Roie en vne fait graunt a moy destre son conseruatour de peas & auxi par mesme le fait vne acura de terre a tener de luy par mesme le seruice de faire loffice, si ieo mesme enfreigne le peas ieo serra distreigne en le terre & auxi perdra mon office & ieo tiendra le terre apres par homage, fealte & escuage & nemi destre conseruatour.

Item si le Roie dona vne acre de terre a ii homez en fee, scilicet, a lun a tener par lez seruice destre conseruatour & a lautre de seruer son preceptes, si le conseruatour deuie, lautre tiendra lacura de terre par seruice de chiualer, et si lautre que seruera le preceptes deuie deuaunt son compaignon, lautre tiendra par le seruice destre conseruatour de peas tantum & cetera.[5]

[f. 81]   iiii[ta] Lectura de Justicez de Peas.[6]

Ore est a voier coment lez Justicez de Peas ount loure auctorite & en quell maner. Lestatut de anno xviii° E. 3 [7] done primez que Justice de peas serrount fait et deuaunt cest estatut ne fueront ascun Justice de peas mez solement conseruatourz come est auauntdit.[8] Mes lez

they were appointed in the Exchequer; Ordinances, 5 Edw. II, c. 17, statute of Lincoln, 9 Edw. II, st. 2, the latter confirmed by 2 Edw. III, c. 4.
 [1] *For* mes . . . ieo, *read* et ieo die qui ieo, D.
 [2] i e. I Edw. III, st. 2, c. 16; see *supra*, p. 301.
 [3] *For* assetz . . . chiualer, *read* et cest assetz seruice de chiualer, D.
 [4] comunement, D.   [5] *Add* Quod nota et quere, C.
 [6] De Justicariis Pacis et eorum autoritate etc. Marowe lector. On margin, in a late hand, vid. Broke Tit. Riots 5, F.
 [7] 18 Edw. III, st. 2, c. 2, 1344.   [8] *Supra*, p. 301.

Justicez de peas sount ceux queux doient veier lexecucion de cest estatut [1] par expresse parols de loure commission, scilicet, Assignauimus vos ad statuta apud Westmonasterium facta & cetera. Et vncore cest estatut fut fait long temps deuaunt que fueront ascun Justicez de peas. Mes nient obstante ceo le Roie poet graunter a autrez persones destre executourz de cest estatut. Sicome lestatut de Wynton' [2] fut fait long-temps deuaunt ascun Justice de peas fueront faitz, scilicet, deuaunt lestatut de anno xviii⁰ E. 3 come est auauntdit fut fait, que provide commission [3] pur oier & terminer. Mes a cell temps lez Justices de peas ne fueront cy requysite come ils sount a ore ; quar a cell temps ils auoient Justice de oiers & terminers & justice en Eyre.

Doncques est a entendre que al primer fesaunce del Justice de peas ils fueront faitz en ii maners & issint sount a ore, scilicet, lun par especiall lettrez patentes le Roy graunt a luy tantum. Et lautre par generall commission fait a luy & as autrez. Et les primerz Justicez par especiall [4] patent sunt appelez Justicez deins eux mesmez, come abbe de seint albons & abbe de Bury sancti Edmundi et autrez auoient par graunt le Roie. Et ceux Justice le Roie ne poet eux discharger apres. Mes lez generall Justice de peas queux sount faitz par generall commission le Roie poet eux discharger a son plesure purceo que refiert [5] a ascun certente.

Et nota le primer que est Justice par especiall patent doit claymer son liberte en Eyre si ascun sount, mes lez autrez Justicez par com-mission, nemi.

Lez justices queux fueront par especiall patentes fueront en cest maner sicome le Roie graunta a moy destre Justice de peas deins vne counte pur terme de vie, ceo est bone graunt. Mes si le Roy graunta a moy & a mez heires cest voide, quar le abilite & discression de mon heire ne poet estre conuz al temps del graunt. Mes si le Roie [6] graunt soit pur terme de vie, coment que ieo ne sue [7] appris ne eridite [*sic*] en le ley, ceo est bone si le patent soit ad audiendum tantum. Mes si soit graunt pur terme de vie a moy ad audiendum & determinandum la il couient que ieo sue erudite en le ley ou autrement le patent est voide.

Item si le Roie graunta a vne home destre Justice de peas pur terme de vie & de tener lez cessions par luy ou son sufficient depute le graunt est bone.

[1] i.e. Westminster the first, 3 Edw. I, c. I.
[2] Winchester, 13 Edw. I, cc. 1-6, 1285.
[3] commysioners, D.   [4] *Add* lettres, B ; graunt et, C.
[5] refert, B ; ne refert, D ; the latter is correct.
[6] *Omit*, D.   [7] soy, C.

Item si le Roie graunta a vne home destre Justice de peas pur terme de vie & ne dit my ad audiendum omnes transgressiones & alia malefacta ; par ceux parols il ad le power de vne conseruatour de peas & auxi le power que est done a eux par statutez mez nemi come ils ount par commission generall.

Item si le Roy graunta a vne home que il serra Justice de peas pur terme de vie sauaunt al Roie que il ne prendra ascun recognisaunce de peas, vncore ceo est bone.   Mes si soit prouiso que il ne tiendra ascun sessions, ore ceo est voide.[1]

Item si le Roy graunt a vne home destre justice de peas rendaunt annuelment xxs. de argent, ceo nest bone graunt.   Mes en cest cas sil graunt a luy destre Justice de peas et auxi de auer toutz les profittez de cessions rendaunt a luy xxs., ceo est bone ; [f. 81 b] quar il reserue riens forsque parcell des profittez le quell sount a luy deuaunt en tout.

Item si le Roy graunta a lez citezyns de London que ii de loure citezyns serrount Justicez de peas, scilicet, lun en Middlesex & lautre en le counte de Surr', ceo nest de autre effect mez pur enfourmer le chaunceler.[2]

Item si le Roie graunta a vne home destre Justice de peas pur terme de son vie & de punyssher offendours de le peas par fyne saunz enquerrer, ce est voide, sinoun que soit de cez chosez que fueront faitz en son presence come luy list.   Mes si soit de tile act issint que le partie perdra son vie ou enheritaunce come felone ou murdour, coment que il soit en son presence fait, il ne poet determiner ceo saunz inquerrer de ceo & cetera.

Item si le Roie graunte a vne home destre Justice de peas en ii countez pur terme de vie, il couient a luy de seer & tener seuerall sessions en ambideux countez & nemi denquerer en lun conte pur ambideux.   Mes si le Roie graunta oustre par le patent que il poet seer en lun counte & prendre lez enquestez dez ambideux countez, cest bone.   Mes si le graunt soit de prendre enquest de lun counte & que cest enquest de mesme le counte presentera lez defautz ambideux. ceo ne vault & cetera, quar eux de vne counte ne poient accepter sur eux notice dez chosez[3] faitz en lautre conte.

---

[1] Clause on recognisaunce . . . voide, repeated but crossed through.

[2] F adds here : Grant to abbot and his successors to oyer only, good ; not to oyer and terminer unless he have a colleague learned in the law, e.g. grant to abbot and his successors and the chief justice for the time being ; the same with mayor and commonalty ; see infra, p. 312, note 6. The same addition is found in L.

[3] For sur . . . chosez, read notice sur eux de chosez, D.

Item si le Roie graunta a vne home destre Justice de peas ad audiendum et determinandum [1] licet ipsemet sit pars,[2] cest graunt est voide. Mes si le graunt soit ad inquirendum tantum, ceo est bone graunt. Et mesme le leie est si son patent soit que il poet faire autrez Justices de peas & que ils aueront power come autrez Justicez aueront de oier & terminer licet sit pars, ceo est bone.

Item si le Roie graunta a vne home de faire Justice de peas de tile hundred come il auoit graunt a dyuers abbeis ou seignurz deins le roialme, cestz generall parolz ne sount pur [3] bone sinoun que il dit & que ils aueront mesme le poiar come Justice de peas ount & doncque par cest graunt il poet faire. Mez nient contristeant, lez generals Justicez de peas deins mesme le conte poient prendre presentement & seer en cessions deinz mesme le hundred de chosez faitz encountre le peas deins mesme le hundrede, sinoun que soit contenue en le patent cest clause, scilicet, quod nullus alius justiciarius pacis se intromittat infra hundredum predictum & cetera.

Item se le Roie graunta a vne home de faire Justice de peas deins vne hundred & que ils ount tile power come est auauntdit, et graunte oustre que si lez generalles Justicez de peas de mesme le counte prent ascun presentement deuaunt eux de ascun chose fait deins le precinct de mesme le hundred, que le graunte auera conysaunce de icell & destre determine deuaunt son Justicez de peas deins [4] le hundred, en cest cas il auera conysaunz al iour de le primer proses retorne enuers les partiez. Et sils ount pris le presentement come est dit & lun de eux liuera le presentement par son propre mayn al Justice de gaole delyuere ou au Justice de Bancke le Roie, vncore le graunte auera conysaunz deuaunt eux sil vient al iour del primer proses retorne ou al primer apparance del partie & deuaunt ascun plede de ceo.

Item si le Roie graunta a vne home que il poet faire toutz Justices de peas deins vne countie & que ils ount autile [f. 82] power que autrez Justices de peas aueront, si le Roie en apres graunt a vne ville deins mesme le counte, le quell vile est corporate, de auer Justice de peas deins eux mesme de eleccion de le Meire et communialte de mesme le counte, cest ii^de graunt est voide. Mes si le Roie graunt al Meire & communialte que ils ferront lez Justicez & que mesme le vile serra counte deins eux mesme come Norwich, Ebor', Exceter & autres sount,

---

[1] terminandum, B.

[2] For an interesting case on the issue, 'although he is a party to the suit', see Year Book, Hill. 8 Hen. VI, pp. 18–21 (not numbered but between nos. 6 and 7).

[3] pas, C.   [4] *Add* mesme, B.

en le cas auauntdit cest bone graunt, quar la le primer graunt est obserue quar a ore nest parcell de mesme le counte & cetera.

Le ii^de est par Commission le quell ad ii chosez en luy le quell lez especiall patentes ne ount my. Et lun est que poet estre fait as personez queux ne poient prendre speciall lettrez patentez, come a moignes professe & autrez de Religion queux sount personez disablez. Et lautre point est que lez Justicez queux ount lour auctorite de commission sount determinablez a le volunte le Roie et lez autrez nemi, come si soit graunt a eux pur terme de vie ou de ans.

Item si Commission soit fait al enfaunt oustre lez ans de xiiii ans, cest bone. Mes sil soit deins age[1] & ioint ouesque autrez de discression, quere & cetera.

Item Commission fait a vne feme couert est bone & el fra warantz par vertue de ceo en son nome sole. Et si commission vient al baron & son feme destre Justice, le baron poet faire warantis en son nome sole ou en ambideux lour nomez. Et en cest darrein cas si le baron soit nosme en le Quorum, le baron & son feme poient lesser home al baille pur suspeccion de felony; quod nota. Et si le baron en cest cas deuie, vncore cest commission demurust bone pur le feme come fut deuaunt en son vie. Mes en mesme le cas si le baron & son feme sount deforse,[2] ceo estoit vers le baron tantum & le feme ad perdue son auctorite. Mes si commission soit fait a vne feme sole & el prist baron, ore le commission est voide, quar il ad luy disable.[3] Mes si soit fait a vne home & vne feme sole & puis ils entremariount, vncore lour ambideux auctoritez demurrount en lour force & cetera.

Item si commission soit fait Maiori Ciuitatis London' & il est corporate par cest nome de meir, par cest auxibien le Meir que est & toutz que serront apres duraunt son commission serront Justice par cell commission & aueront auauntage de ceo. Mes en cest cas si le commission soit fait Johanni Maiori Ciuitatis London',[4] autre est; quar la le commission estoiera a luy apres le Meiralte determine & nemi a lez autrez Meires que serrount apres. Et si le commission soit fait Maiori & comitatu[5] ciuitatis London' ou a tile vile semblable que est

---

[1] Mes sil soit dage de xiii ans ou deins xiiii ans, D.

[2] deuorce, B, D.

[3] quar ell ad perdue son nosme, F. A marginal note (F) states that the Countess of Shrewsbury was justice of the peace, *temp.* Henry VII, 'St. Alban's Historie'.

[4] Perhaps a reference to Marowe's contemporary Sir John Sha, goldsmith, mayor in 1501; Stow, Survey of London, ed. Kingsford, ii. 179; p. 141, note 14, *supra.*

[5] communitati, D.

corporate, ceo est voide auxibien enuers le communialte come enuers le Meire, quar toutz le communialte ne poient seer come Justice [1] & le commission est vne copulative ; ideo & cetera.

Item si vne priour soit en vne commission par le nome de priour & puis mesme le priour est corporate par leuesque destre vne abbe, la le primer commission par la nome priour ad perdue son force. Et en mesme le cas si le corporacion soit defete apres pur cause, vncore il ne poet seer par launcient commission fait a luy quaunt il fut priour.

Item si vne Justice de peas soit fait Chiualer vncore le commission estoiera bone par son auncien nome ; [2] mes si vne Justice de peas soit fait vicount, doncque son office & auctorite de Justice de peas est determine, quar il ne poet estre justice & officer de seruer son preceptes demene. Mes si commission soit fait [f. 82 b] a vne adoncques esteaunt vicount, quere si ceo soit bone.

Item si vne Justice de peas soit fait Coroner de le countie, ceo est discharge de auctorite de Justice de peas. Mes il poet estre soubz vicount, Bailly ou tile semblable & nemi discharge de son primer auctorite, scilicet, de Justice.

Item si vne home soit vicount par enheritaunce & puis est fait Justice de peas deins mesme le conte par commission, ceo est voide vers luy. Mes si vne feme soit vicountesse par enheritaunce & el prist vne Justice de peas al baron ambideux loure auctoritez remayne oue eux ; quod nota.

Item nota que tielx maners de commissions sount determinablez en tout al volunte le Roie ; quar si le Roie graunt nouell commission apres a eux ouesque autrez personez ou a eux tantum & ils aueround notice de ceo come par delyuere a vne de eux ou par proclamacion ou autrement, la launcien commission est determine & expire, & si soit delyuere a ascun Justice de peas de mesme le counte toutz lez autrez Justices deins mesme le counte ount [3] tenus de prendre notice de ceo ; quere tamen ; [4] quar semble que noun tancque ils ount notice en Fait. Mes si le commission soit vne foitz lie en les Cessions & Cessions a vne foitz tenus par force de ceo, toutz ceux sount tenus de prendre conisaunce sur eux de ceo.

---

[1] *For* come Justice, *read* come Justices de peas, B ; all cessionz, D.
[2] Vide in lectura marrow que ou Justice de peace est fait chiualer *ou prist autre dignitie,* vncor son auctority remainera, & *sic Justice del comen bank est fait chiualer son commission remainera in force* & 1 E. 6, ca. 7 ; Brooke, La Graunde Abridgement, 1573 ed., Commissions, no. 4. The words in italics do not occur in any text of Marowe that I have seen.
[3] sont, D.   [4] tantum, B, C.

Item si vne nouell Commission vient a eux pro hac vice tantum pur determiner, vncore ils ne poient seer & tener Cessions apres par force de lez auncient commission.   Mez ils couient de suer pur nouell commission.

Mes si le Roie face commission as autrez Justicez de oier & determiner toutz maners de Felonyes & robories, vncore ceo nest detraccion de launcient commission.   Mez que lez Justices de peas poient seer par force de cest auncien commission en apres.   Item mesme le ley si le Roie [face]¹ justice en Eyre ou lez Justices de Bancke² de seer & enquerrer deins mesme le countie si proclamacion ne soit fait.

Item si le Roy graunt nouell commission as nouellis Justices de peas ad inquirendum tantum, vncore ceo est determinacion de launcien commission.   Et issint est si le ii^de Commission soit ad audiendum et determinandum, ceo est en determinacion de launcien commission. Et mesme le ley est si nouell commission soit fait a lez Justices de peas ad determinandum tantum ; quere.   Mes si le nouell commission que vient a lez Justices soit ad audiendum et determinandum omnia felonias, ceo va solement al felony & cetera.

Item si le Roie graunt³ commission par cez lettres patentz a vne home pur terme de vie, il ne seera ouesque eux & vncore launcien commission est determine.   Et si le Roie voet graunter en mesme le case que il seera ouesque eux par expresse parols cest graunt est voide ; quar lestatut fait anno xii^mo Ricardi II^di voet que null associacion serra fait a eux ;⁴ quod nota.

Item si le Roie graunt a vne home destre Justice de peas pur terme de son vie sur condicion que il deuoit seer sur chescun riott deins vne moys, & sil ne fait que le Roie reseisera loffice tancque il ad fait fyne oue luy ; & puis le Roie reseisist par cause auauntdit & puis graunt nouell patent a vne pur terme de son vie destre Justice de peas generally ; & puis le primer patente le Roie paia son fyne al Roie, ore ambideux patentes serront bone & effectuelx & estoieront bone en [apres & cetera].⁵

[f. 83] Item nota que vne commission fait a vne abbe solement pur enquerer tantum est bone, mes nemi de enquerer & determiner sinoun que vne autre apris en le ley soit ioynt oue luy en le commission & doncques cest commission fait a eux de enquerer & determiner est bone & cetera.⁶

---

¹ face, B, D.   ² Clearly King's Bench.   ³ *Add* novelle, D.
⁴ c. 10 ; statute of Cambridge, 1388.   Brooke, *ut supra*, Commissions, nos. 5–10, summarizes much of this lecture and concludes : ' & omnia hec in lectura, Marwod [*sic*] seriant.'   ⁵ apres & cetera, B.
⁶ See p. 308, note 2, *supra*, for the same clause in F.

[Quinta Lectura.] Ore est a voier queux persons serront myse
en commissions de peas et queux nemy.

Nota lestatut anno xviii⁰ H. VI^{ti 1} inde factum.

In primes anno primo E. 3 ² Gardeins de peas fueront auctorise par
mesme lestatut come appiert. Et anno ii^{do} mesme le Roie done poiar ³
de oier & determiner omnimodas felonias.⁴ Et apres anno xviii⁰ mesme
le Roie est done par estatut⁵ que deux ou trois dez vailiauntes de
chescun counte soient assignes Justices de peas deins mesme le counte
& que eux mesmez oue autrez sagez de la ley doient oier & terminer
toutz maners de felonyes; et nient obstante ceo ils voillent, scilicet, le
chaunceler que fait commission voet mitter plusourz autrez que fueront
compris par lestatut en lez commissions.   Pur que apres, scilicet, anno
xii⁰ Ricardi II^{di}, capitulo xi^{mo},⁶ vne estatut fut fait que done que ne serra
en vne counte forsque vi Justices de peas al pluis oustre lez Justices de
assise & done oustre que null patent de associacion sera fait a lez
Justices de peas en null counte.

Et puis apres, mesme lestatut fut afferme par vne estatut fait apres,
scilicet, anno xiiii⁰ mesme le Roie, capitulo,⁷ que voet que ne serrount
plusourz Justices de peas en vne counte que viii oustre lez seignurz.

Mes ceo nient obstante, lez auauntditz vi Justices de peas que fueront
oustre lez Justices ⁸ a cest iour ne fueront erudites en le ley. Pur que
fut vne autre estatut fait, scilicet, anno xvii⁰ mesme le Roie Ricardi II^{di},⁹
par que fut ordeigne que en chescun commission de le peas soient
deux homez apris en le ley de mesme le countie & que ils procederount
tauntz foitz come busoigne soit a gaole deliuere deins mesme le counte;
& nient obstante toutz lez auauntditz faitz, vncore ils voillount mitter
persones insufficientes en commissions par labour ou fauour de loure
amyes & auxi voillent mitter en lez commissions diuers persones demurrauntes en forein countez. Pur qe fut vne estatut fait anno ii^{do} H.
V^{ti}, capitulo primo,¹⁰ par que est estably que lez pluis sufficientes
persones deins mesme le countie serrount assignes destre Justices de
peas & nemi de foroin [sic] countez except lez Justices de assise & le
Stuarde de le Duchie.¹¹

---

¹ c. 11, 1439.   ² *Add* capitulo 16, D.   See Tercia Lectura, *supra*.
³ *Add* par commission, B, D.
⁴ Statute of Northampton, 2 Edw. III, c. 7, 1328.
⁵ See p. 306, note 7, *supra*.
⁶ Should be c. 10; see p. 312, note 4, *supra*.
⁷ Should be c. 11, 1390.   ⁸ de Assize omitted by error.
⁹ c. 10, 1394.   ¹⁰ 2 Hen. V, st. 2, c. 1, 1414.
¹¹ Cf. the statute : '& forspris auxi les Chiefs Seneschalx du Roy des

Mes de quell sufficiente en certen ils serront, ceo ne fut mys en certen par cest estatut. Mes apres par vne estatut fait anno xviii° H. VI^ti, capitulo [1] le sufficiente fut mys en certen en tile fourme, scilicet, que chescun que serra fait Justice de peas en ascun counte auera terres ou tenementz al value de xx li. par an al meins vt patet statutum & litera inde.

Lestatut parle de terres & tenementz al value de xx li. par an, mes ceo serra pris pluis largement que lez parols sount ; quar terres, tenementz, rentes & autrez enheritaunces que sount annuell al value de xx li. de claro & poet auer continuance par comen entendement a toutz iours serra pris par lequite. Mes vncore si vne home ad vne comen en grose ou vne auowson ou annuite ou tielx semblablez al value de xx li. par an, vncore il ne serra dit sufficient pur ceux chosez, quar ne sount de certen value.

Item si homme ad tenementes que sount fynable [f. 83 b] al temps del mort de loure tenauntez come en Deuenshire & aillourz en Englitere soloncque le maner, ne serra accounpt pluis en value pur le fyne come [2] que le terre fuera pluis en value par [3] xx li. sil fut en lez mains le seignur. [4]

Item terre tenus par Copie de court Rolle coment que vault xx li. par an ne serra aiuge destre en value destre Justice de peas accordaunt a lestatut.

Item si home eit terres en auncien demene al value de xx li. par an, vncore il est hors del cas de cel estatut. Mes vncore si homme ad terres en auncien demene al value de x li. & terre al comen ley as value dez autrez x li. & il fait vne ioint les de eux a vne home pur terme de ans ou de vie, reseruaunt a luy xx li. de annuell rent pur tout, il serra dit destre en value destre Justice de peas. [5] Mes autre est lou il ad vne rent de xx li. issuant hors de terre forsque al value de x li. par an, il ne serra mys en le commission pur cell rent.

Item si home ad terres ou tenementes al value de xx li. par an en Galis, Irelonde ou Cales [6] ou tielx lieus semblablez, il ne serra Justice de peas pur cell terre coment que soit en value. [7] Mes sil ad terres de tile value en le v portez, Counte palantyn ou Loundourz [*sic*], il poet estre Justice de peas. [8]

terres & seignuries del Duchee de Lancastre en le North & le South pur le temps esteantz.'   [1] Should be 11; see p. 313, note 1, *supra.*
   [2] coment, B, C, D.   [3] qui, B ; que, C.   [4] In F the locality is omitted.
   [5] *Add* quia majus dignum trahit ad se minus dignum, F.
   [6] France, F.   [7] *Add* quar nest Tryall de ceo ycy, F.
   [8] *Add* quar ceo puit estre Trye etc., F.

Item il couient que il ad astate en mesmez lez **terres** & tenementes
que sount al value auauntdit, scilicet, pur terme de son vie ou de autre
vie en son droit demene ou en droit son feme, issint que il auoit
Fraunck tenement en ceo al meins, ou autrement il ne poet estre
Justice de peas; quar coment que il ad astate en terres al value de
xx li. pur terme de ans ou a tener a volunte le lessour, il ne serra
Justice de peas pur ceo.

Item sil ad terres al value de xx li. & fait lees de ceo pur terme de
ans reseruaunt [1] null rent ou petit, le lesse ne le lessour ne purront
estre [2] Justice de peas pur cest terre duraunt le lees. Mes si le lessour
reserue rent al value de xx li. duraunt son terme, doncque pur cest
reseruacion de cel rent il poet estre Justice de peas.

Item si homme [soit] [3] seisi de taunt de terre que vault xx li. par an &
fait feffement as dyuers persones a son vse, vncore pur cell terre il
poet estre Justice de peas coment que il nad ascun possession en ceo.
Mes son feffes ne couient coment que il nad forsque vne feffe en mesme
le terre, il ne serra vncques Justice de peas pur tielx terrez. [4]

Lez parols sount : al value de xx li. & cetera; vncore si home ad
terre que saunz le comen que est appendaunt a mesme le terre ne
vault xx li. mes oue le comen vault xx li., vncore purceo il serra dit de
bone value & il poet estre Justice de peas pur ceo coment que il nad
ascun autre terre. Mes si le terre ne vault xx li. oustre lez villeins
regardant a cest terre & oue cez villeins ceo est de value de xx li.,
vncore il ne serra Justice purceo. [5]

Item si homme ad vne garrein sur cest terre que vault xx li. par an,
cest sufficient pur estre Justice de peas.

Item si home ad vne bois de quell il fait chescun an xx li., il poet
estre Justice de peas sil ad vse issint de vendre luy par custom de an
en an deuaunt cest temps, mes autrement il nest sufficient & cetera.

Item si homme ad vne pomeraye, scilicet, orcharde de frute de quell
il fait chescun an xx li. il nest sufficient; mes sil luy lessa a vne autre
[f. 84] person rendaunt xx li. de rent, doncques il est sufficient destre
Justice de peas.

Item si homme ad pischerie en vne ryver quell il lesse pur xx li. par
an, il poet estre Justice de peas purceo. Mes autre est sil fait xx li. par

---

[1] *Add* a luy, C.
[2] *For* reseruaunt . . . estre, *read* ou a tener a vote le lessour, il ne
serra, B ; ou a tener al volunte le lessor il ne serront, D.
[3] soit, D.
[4] *Add* & vncore ill serra mys en jure, quere le cause, F.
[5] Que nest casualte, D ; Quar ceo nest forsque casuelty, F.

an de vne stangue deins son meason ou manse [1] annuatim, quar ceo
nest en value.

Item si [ad] vne mynde de cole ou de plombe, ceux chosez ne serront
entendus de auer continuance & purceo ne serra Justice de peas pur
eux coment que soient de value de xx li. par an & cetera.

Item si vne homme ad vne maner a que appent vne court Baron &
le maner ouesque lez issues & profitz de cest court sount al value de
xx li. par an, il poet estre Justice de peas ; mes sil ad vne maner oue
vne viewe de frauncplege & le maner oue lez Issues de le lete sount le
value de xx li. & nemi le maner sole, il nest sufficient destre Justice de
peas.

Item mesme le ley si home ad lez profittes par graunt le Roie dauer
tolle en merket ou feire ou stallage ou wharfage, ceo ne serra dit sufficiente destre Justice de peas coment que il auoit astate en eux pur
terme de vie ou en Fee.

Item si le Roie graunt a vne home vne hundred & deprendre lez
profittez de ceo ensemble [2] issint que lez profittes de ceo vault a luy
par an xx li., vncore ceo nest sufficient destre fait iustice de peas.

Item si home ad corrodie al value de xx li. en vne abbe, vncore
purceo il ne serra dit Justice de peas.

Mes si home ad terres hors de quell rent est issuant oue penaltes,
scilicet, que a quell iour que le rent soit arere al graunte, le tenaunt
forfetra xl d. nomine pene et distreint [3] purceo done tociens quociens
ceux penalties serront [4] forfaitez, si le terre vault oustre le rent clere
xx li. par an mez nemi ouesque [5] les penaltes si ascun sount, vncore
ceo est [6] sufficient value destre Justice de peas. Mes si home ad terre
al value de C li. par an hors de quell rent est issuant par son graunt
demene a vne autre, & graunt oustre que le rent serra chescun an
double al graunte oue clause de distreint, vncore cest terre ne serra dit
le value destre Justice de peas coment que a cest temps que le commission vient a luy il vault C li. par an.

Item si home soit emplede en Precipe quod reddat & il vouche vne
autre a garranty,[7] le quell entra & perdra, issint que. iugement est done
que le tenaunt recouera en value enuers le vouche, & puis le vicount
extende le terre perdue al value de xx li. & deliuera a luy terres queux
ne sount de mesme le value en nome de xx li. par an, vncore coment
que soit par mater de recorde vncore il ne serra dit sufficient & cetera.

Item mesme le ley est si ieo auoie cause de prier en aide de Roie

---

[1] MS. mans̄.   [2] en fee, C.   [3] MS. dist͠r.   [4] sount, C.
[5] ouster, F.   [6] nest, F, probably wrong.   [7] MS. gar͠r.

sur especiall parols de recompense, & ieo sue emplede & perde, issint
que recompens est delyuer a moy pur Roie, scilicet, terre pur le value
de xx li. par an par extent de vicount, vncore sil ne soit issint en value
en fait, le Roie ne serra estoppe a dire apres cest delyuere a luy sur
vne commission fait a luy que le terre nest de mesme le value, scilicet,
de xx li. par an.

Et les parols de lestatute[1] sount outre : Et si ascun soit ordeigne que
nad terre al value de xx li. & cetera, que il notifia ceo al Chaunceler
deins vne mois apres que il mesme ad notice de cest commission.
Nota que le temps de cell mois serra entendue en tile maner, scilicet,
destre accounpt par xxviii iourz & nemi accordaunt al mois contenue
en le kalendre, quar ceo est en auauntage de le Roy. Mes en [f. 84 b]
vne breue de Quare Impedit le ley est autre, quar pur le lapse & le
recouere de auowson le mois en tile breue serra accounpt accordaunt
al kalendre & nemi autrement.[2] Et sic vide diuersitatem istorum
casuum.

Item a ore est a voier coment cest notice poet estre fait & en quell
maner ; & ceo serra entendue fait par parolle del partie a le chaunceler,
ou par vne escript south le seale le partie myse all Chaunceler, ou par
vne Certificat fait en le chauncerie par autre person par son commaundement come[3] par son seruaunt ou autre par son commaundement. Mes si vne estraunger voillet faire notice al chaunceler en le
nome celui a que le commission fut fait, & apres le mois le partie voet
agreer a cest notice destre fait par son commaundement, vncore cest
notice ne excusera le partie de son forfett, scilicet, de xx li. & cetera.

Item notandum est en cest cas de notice destre fait le distaunce de
le chaunceler ; sil soit deins lez iiiior miers en ascun lieu de Englitere il
ne excusera le partie en cest cas sil ne fait notice ; quar par comen
entendement il poet estre oue luy deins vne mois sil soit deins lez iiiior
miers come est auauntdit.

Item si le partie sur cest accion port vers luy voille luy excuser par
emprisonement de luy, ou que il ne poet vener pur ieopardie dez ewes
par le voie,[4] ou tielx excusez semblablez, ceux ne excuseront le partie
de cest forfaitt.

---

[1] Still the statute of 18 Hen. VI, c. 11, *ut supra*, p. 313, note 1, p. 314.

[2] Fitzherbert, *op. cit.*, i. 37, under Ne admittas, marginal entry :
'33 Ed. 3. Quare impedit 194. Note: In Marrow's Reading it is holden,
that the six months shall not be accounted by 28 days, but according to
the calendar months.' The earliest edition in which this reference to
Marowe appears is that of 1666.

[3] ou, D.

[4] *For* pur . . . voie, *read* pur creduer dez ewes et cetera, B ; pur

Item si vne commission vient a vne & deuaunt il fait notice vne autre
commission vient a luy deins mesme le mois destre Justice de peas, la
sil ne fait notice deins le moise apres le primer commission, il poet faire
notice de ceo deins vne mois apres le ii^de commission a luy direct, &
cest notice excusera luy pur ambideux commissions; quar par le ii^de
commission agarde le primer fuist determine.   Mes autrement est si
vne commission soit agarde, & apres vne Supersedeas vient a luy hors
del chauncerie pur luy[1] discharge de commission; quar la nient contristeant tile Supersedeas, vncore il couient al partie de faire notice de
son substaunce, quar en cest cas poet estre graunt a luy vne procedendo apres que proue que le commission ne fut determine a ascun
temps deuaunt, mes en suspens pur le temps.

Item si vne enfaunt deins age soit mys en vne commission, il couient
de faire notice de son substaunce deins le mois apres il ad notice de
cest commission auxibien come il[2] fut de plein age, & ne demurrer le
notice tancque a son plein age.

Item si vne feme couert soit fait Justice de peas par commission[3] el
couient de faire notice deins le mois en mesme le maner; mes en cest
cas le baron poet faire notice pur luy ou el mesme en propre person.
Mes si vne moigne soit mys en vne commission par le nome de moigne
de tile lieu, il ne couient de faire notice, quar il appiert quaunt il est
moigne professe que il ne poet auer terre a son vse demene & ideo &
cetera.

Item si home que nad ascun terre soit mys en Commission, & apres
le commission il purchase terre, ou terre a luy discendist deins le mois
apres le commission par ascun de sez auncestors, ou vient al terre par
autre maner apres le commission, & il ne auoit terre al value deuaunt,
scilicet, al temps del commission a luy direct, il couient a luy de faire
notice; quar son purchase ou discent ne serra pris sufficiauncy accordaunt a lestatut.

Item si homme ad terre al value de xx li. al temps de le commission
de[4] luy direct, pur terme de autre vie ou en droit son feme, &
[*Nota* puis apres, celui que vie deuie ou son feme deuie issint que son
cest astate est determine, en cest cas il couient a luy de faire notice
cas.] al chaunceler que il nest de tile value accordaunt al estatut,
deins vne mois apres le determinacion [f. 85] de son astate & nemi
autrement.

credeuer dez ewez par le voye pur ieopardie deux, C; pur certen credeu
de ewe par le voie, D.   [1] *Add* destre, C.   [2] sil, B.
  [3] Margin, late hand: Feme couvert ne poit estre justice de peas, F.
    [4] *For* de, *read* a, B, C, D.

Item de ¹ terre que est del value de xx li. par an discende a ascun home deuaunt le commission, & il ne entra en ceo issint que il ad vne possession en ley al temps del commission a luy direct, il ne couient de faire notice de nome le value; ² quar quaunt il auoit entre en fait, son possession serra aiugge de temps de mort de son auncestor & cetera.

Item si deux persones sount iointement enfeffez en terre esteaunt al value de xx li. par an, & liuere de seisin est forsque a lun & il est fait Justice de peas a que liuere de seisin fut fait, & lautre a que le liuere ne fut fait disagrea a cest feffement deins le mois apres le commission, vncore celui que fut fait Justice de peas couient de faire notice deins le mois apres le commission & nemi deins le mois apres le disagrement ; quod nota.

Item si vne home soit seisi de vne seignurie de xx li. par an [&] graunta son seignurie a vne autre par fait, & deuaunt ascun attorne-ment del tenaunt le grauntour est fait Justice de peas & puis le tenaunt attourna al graunte del seignurie deins le mois apres le commission, vncore si le grauntour fait notice de ceo deins vne mois apres lattourne-ment fait par le tenaunt, ceo est sufficient, quar il fut en parfitt possession de le seignurie toutz foitz deuaunt lattournement ewe.

Item si homme fait a moy vne les pur terme de ans de terre esteaunt al value de xx li. par an sur condicion que si ieo paia a luy x li. a tile iour que adoncques ieo auera fee, & puis deuaunt le iour de paiement le lesse est fait Justice de peas par Commission & al iour assigne entre eux que est deins le mois le lesse paia al lessour lez x li., en ceo cas le lessour ³ ne doit faire ascun notice ; quar ore son astate serra aiugge destre bone de le temps de le primer liuere de seisin ent fait.

Item si vne les soit fait a vne home pur terme de ans de terre al value auauntdit sur condicion que si le lessour graunta le reuersion a ascun autre person duraunt son terme que le lesse auera Fee, et puis le lesse est fait Justice de peas & deins le mois apres le lesse ⁴ graunta le reuersion de mesme le terre a vne autre, la le lesse couient de faire notice deins le mois apres le commission ; quar le condicion fut voide & cetera. Mesme le ley si le condicion soit sil soit ouste deins le terme & cetera.

Item si Justice de peas soit que ad xx li. de terre par an en son mayn al temps de le commission & apres il venda mesme le terre a vne autre & puis fait astate de ceo accordaunt a le vendicion, le Justice en

---

¹ si, B, D ; si le, C.   ² *For* nome le value, *read* noun value, D.
³ lesse, D, correctly.   ⁴ Mistake for ' lessour '.

cest cas deuoit faire notice deins le mois apres le vendicion par luy
fait & nemi deins le mois apres lastate ent fait & cetera.   Mes nota
que si vne que est Justice de peas soit seisi de deux maners & chescun
maner esteaunt de value de x li. par an, & puis il vende vne dez ii
maners a vne autre & ne assigna a luy le quell de eux le vende auera ;
mes apres il assigna a luy lequell de eux il auera & liuera a luy seisin de
ceo, la il couient al vendour de faire notice al chaunceler deins vne mois
apres lastate fait & nemi deins vne mois apres le vendicion, ne assigne-
ment, & cetera.

Item si vne que est Justice de peas eit terre al value de xx li.
eschaungea ceo pur taunt de terre en mesme le countie, & lautre
ouesque luy fist eschaunge & entra en son terre mes le Justice ne entra
pas en lautre terre [f. 85 b] par le temps de vne mois ou pluis apres,
vncore il ne couient de ceo faire ascun notice apres. .

Item si vne Justice de peas soit emplede de le terre que il ad al value
de xx li. par an par Precipe quod reddat, & ils apparier & vouche et
puis iugement est done vers le tenaunt & que il recouera taunt en
value, par force de quell iugement le demandaunt entra en le terre
saunz ascun suer dexecucion, la le Justice de peas couient de faire
notice ou autrement il forfetra son payn del estatut.   Mes autrement
est si le demandant sua execucion par vne Habere facias seisinam oue
vne Extendi facias ad valenciam ; quar en cest cas il ne couient de faire
notice, quar ambideux dez executorz, scilicet, ambideux de le tenaunt
come le demandant serra aiuge a vne mesme foitz saunz ascun distaunce.[1]

Lestatute est : sil [face][2] precept ou waraunt ; cest clause serra pris
generalment auxibien apres le mois come deuaunt, & ne auera relacion
al mois mez solement que sil face ascun tile precept a ascun temps
apres ceo que il ad notice del commission & cetera.   Et nota que cez
parols, preceptes ou warantes, ne serront prisez solement come de
faire warant de peas, mes auxi sil fait Supersedeas ou lesse vne home
arrest pur le peas a baille par recognisaunz ou ascun tielx semblez [sic].
Et coment que lez preceptez de lez Justices de peas que nest de le
value del terre auauntdit, scilicet, de xx li. par an, soit fait par luy en le
nosme le Roie, vncore ceo ne luy excusera de son forfaiture pur cest
cas & cetera.

Item si ascun Justice que ne poet expendre xx li. par an apres le
commission sea en lez cessions ouesque autrez Justices de peas & ne
fait autre chose, vncore sil fait notice deins le mois apres, cest notice
luy excusera de son penaltie done par lestatute.   Mes en cest cas sil

---

[1] *Add* & cetera ; quod nota & vide etc., C.   [2] face, B ; fait, D.

face ascun precept deins le mois coment que il face notice apres deins le mois accordaunt a lestatut, vncore il encourgera le peyn de lestatut pur cest precept fait.

Item si vne soit myse en le commission destre Justice de peas, & deuaunt que il auoit ascun conisaunce de ceo il fait precept come Justice de peas & ceo apres le date de le commission, coment que il fait notice deins le mois, vncore il ad forfait son peyn. Mes si home face precept come Justice de peas deuaunt le date del commission, & puis vne commission est direct a luy destre Justice de peas & puis le precept que il ad fait est seruye apres le commission, en ceo cas coment que il ad fait precept deuaunt, vncore sil fait notice al chaunceler deins le mois apres le commission accordaunt a lestatut que il nest de taunt value, ceo luy excusera ascun forfeture.[1]

[Sexta Lectura] De securitate pacis & quomodo il serra fait.

Lez parols de lestatute de Westminster primer sount[2]: Soit le peas bien garde. Et notandum est que ceux parols oue lez parols subsequentes deins mesme lestatut compris lentiere auctorite dez Justices de peas; le quell auctorite de eux estoier en iii chosez. Le primer est en ceux actuell chosez le quell ils poient faire saunz cessions ou enquerre; come de chose fait [f. 86] en loure presence encountre le peas, ils poient ceo committer al garde saunz ascun inquerre de ceo & auxi ils poient ceo certifiera[3] en le bancke saunz autre enquere de ceo; & ceo est par mater par[4] fait & le power de cest actez est done par le primer clause del commissions lou est dit: Assignauimus vos ad pacem & ne dit Justice & cetera.

Le ii^{de} chose est dez queux chosez ils poient faire pár enquerre & cetera. Et le power de lenquere est done par le ii^{de} clause del commission lou est dit: Assignauimus vos Justiciarios nostros ad inquirendum; quar par cez parols del commission ils sount faites Justices de peas & nemi par lez parols prochun deuaunt en le commission; quar ceo done null power a eux en maner forsque come conseruatourz de peas & cetera.

Le iii^{cie} chose est de ceux chosez de queux lez Justices de peas

---

[1] *Add* Chacun home scient & erudite en le ley puit estre in le commyssion & le science & nesciens ne viendront in debate. Quere si home nient sufficient soyt mys in le commyssion & deinz le moys vn nouell commyssion issist as autrez il ne couient defayre notice, pur ceo que le primer commission est determine; mez autrement est lou supersedias vient; car ceo nest forsque sequestracion de lour power pur le temps & apres illz poient auer procedendo, etc., F.

[2] *Ut supra*, p. 289. [3] certifier, B. [4] en, B, C.

doient non solement enquerer mez auxi a determiner, et cest power est
done a eux par autre clause en le commission lou est dit : Assignauimus
vos xx[ti] & cetera Quorum duo vestrum sount & cetera ad omnia &
singula felonias et transgressiones & cetera audienda et terminanda.
Et nota que ceux trois auctorites sount compris deins lauauntdit estatut
de Westminster primer, capitulo primo ; quar en ceux parols de
lestatut :· Soit le peas bien garde, est implie toutz lez actes que lez
Justices de peas doient faire saunz enquerre. Et par ceux parols : Et
maintenue en toutz pointes, est implie toutz ceux actez queux il purra [1]
faire par enquerre. Et par ceux parols : que comen droit soit fait
auxibien as poures come as Riches, sount implie toutz actez queux ils
purrount deuaunt eux en lour cessions enquerer & determiner eux [2] par
loure commission.

Et issint sur le primers parols de lestatut de Westminster primer &
sur le primer clause de le commission sount iiii[or] choses a voier : le
primer, coment lez parties serront mys southe surete de peas pur
ieopardie denfreindre le peas en fesaunt cest act.[3]

Le ii[de] est, Qux chosez serront dit enfreindre de le peas & queux
nemi & coment que serra pacifie apres lenfreindre de ceo.[4]

Le iii[ce] est si tile enfreindre soit oue multitude dez gentz quell pluis
punysshment [5] lez Justice de peas poient faire de cest enfreindre que
dez autrez.[6]

Et le iiii[te] est, scilicet, si ascun home soit par reson de tile enfreindre
de peas oue multitude dez gentz soit [sic] devict hors de son possession
dez terres ou tenementes, coment & en quell maner lez Justices de
peas doient auoider cest force & de restorer le partie greue a son
possession.[7]

Et notandum est que ceux iiii[or] chosez sount lez principall chosez
que appartient al garde del peas saunz enquere & cetera.

Et quaunt al primer point de eux, scilicet, coment home serra mys
south surete saunz ieopardie de enfreindre de peas, v chosez sount a
voier de ceo : le primer coment cest surete serra demande & en quell
maner.

Le ii[de] est coment cest surete serra graunt.

Le tiercie coment le proses de tile surete de peas serra fait enuers
celui vers que il est demande par le partie.

Le iiii[te] coment le surete serra troue.

---

[1] doient, D.   [2] *Omit*, B, D.   [3] Treated in this present lecture.
[4] See Septima Lectura, *infra*.   [5] MS. punysshe[t].
[6] See Octaua Lectura, *infra*.   [7] See Nona Lectura, *infra*.

Et le v^{te} est coment que cest surete de peas que est a vne foitz pris poet estre en apres discharge & cetera.

[*Coment cest surete serra demande.*] Sciendum est que les Justice de peas poient causer le partie de trouer surete al peas [f. 86 b] a toutz iours ou tancque a certen iour par eux destre lymytt, & ceo ils poient faire de loure auctorite saunz ascun demande de ascun partie sil veient rationable cause & cetera. Mes sils fount issint, le partie ne poet ceo reles vncques cest surete [1] ne lez Justices mesme ne poient ceo reles apres ceo si le recognisaunce soit de garder le peas a toutz iours. Mes autrement est si soit de garder le peas tancque [2] vne iour certen ; quar la lez Justices poient ceo reles deuaunt le iour.[3] Mes si surete de peas soit graunt al demande de vne partie iesque a certen iour, le partie ceo poet relesser deuaunt le iour, mes nemi lou le surete est pris a toutz iours coment que il soit al demande del partie, il ne vncques relessera apres.

Item si surete de peas soit demande enuers vne enfaunt esteaunt de age de xii ans ou oustre, il serra compelle de trouer surete & issint il poet demander surete de peas enuers autrez a tile age ; mes en le cas auauntdit il ne serra lie mes sufficient surete serra lie pur luy en vne recognisaunce ou autrement. Et issint serra fait al prier de Feme couert de baron ou de vne moigne professe. Et auxi surete serra demande, vers eux & ils trouerount surete al peas, mez ils ne serront liez ne pluis que lenfaunt serra en cas auauntdit & cetera.

Item si vne feme demande surete de peas vers son baron, el auera, & en semblable maner auera le baron enuers son feme & vncore le baron poet luy chastiser par resonable chastisment.

Item vne villeyn auera surete de peas enuers son seignur sil voet ceo demander, & le seignur poet trouer surete saunz faire ascun protestacion [4] & vncore ceo nest enfraunchisement al villeyn. Et issint poet le seignur demande surete de peas enuers son villeyn, & ceo couient trouer surete de peas & vncore null enfraunchisement & cetera.

Item si homme que atteint est de Felony voet demander surete de peas il auera, et auxi surete de peas poet estre demandé vers luy esteaunt atteint.

Item home conuict de heresie auera surete de peas sil ceo demande & auxi serra agarde vers luy. Mes si home ad iugement done enuers

---

[1] *For* ne . . . surete *read* ne poet unques relesser son surete, B.
[2] *Add* a, C.
[3] *Add* xxi E iiii^{ti}, fo. 38, D (margin) ; identified as Mich. 21 Edw. IV, pp. 38–44, not numbered but between nos. 4 and 5.
[4] proses, C.

luy en vne breue de Premunire & puis voille demander surete de peas
dez autrez il ne auera, mes il serra mys a surete de peas sil soit demande
enuers luy.

Item si homme ad abiure le Roialme & puis il demande surete de
peas de autrez persones il auera, & vncore il remaindra en garde tout
temps apres le abiuracion[1] tancque il vient a son port le quell le
Coroner ad luy assigne, scilicet, en le garde dez constables de chescun
vile tancque al prochun vile & cetera.

Item si vne alien que fut nee hors del liegeaunce nostre seignur le
Roie & nient fait denizyn voet demander surete de peas de ascun autre
il ne auera ceo, mes surete de peas serra demande enuers luy assetz
bien.[2]

Item si vne home que est de noun sane memorie voet demande
surete de peas enuers ascun, il ne auera ne autrez naueront suretes
vers luy par recognisaunce ne obligacion.[3]

Item si home que est mute voet demander surète de peas enuers
ascun par signes, il serra graunt sur cest demande, et auxi il couient
trouer surete as autrez sil soit demande vers luy & ceo par signes poet
demander.

[*Item nota.*] Item lez Justices de peas nient obstante le demande le
partie de auer surete de peas enuers vne tile ils ne sount tenus par le
leie de luy graunter, coment que il voet iurre sur vne [f. 87] liuere,
sinon que loure discression dez Justices de peas soit que il [ne][4] ceo
demandera pur malice, mes pur fere de son vie ou de baterie destre fait
a son person ou de arcer de son measons & similia. Et pur ceux ils
ne voillount graunter deuaunt que le partie auoit jurre a eux sur vne
liuere de ceo & cetera.[5]

Item si vne home demande surete de peas enuers vne Justice de peas
deuaunt autre Justice de peas deins mesme le countie, il poet ceo
graunter enuers son compaignon, et issint lou surete de peas est
demande de vne Justice de peas en plein cessions il mesme doncques
seeaunt sur le bancke il poet graunter son surete & vncore loure seaunt
la est ioint.

Item si surete de peas soit demande enuers vne home que est
empanell en le Jure de le Cessions, lez Justices ne voillent par lour

---

[1] pur temps de abiuracion, C.
[2] *Add* & mesme le ley est de enymy le Roy, F.
[3] For the distinction between obligation and recognizance, see Blackstone, *op. cit.*, ii. 340–1.   [4] ne, D.
[5] *Add* & Pur ceo si le partye soyt impotent de que cest suerty est
demande il poyent denier, F.

discression luy compeller de trouer surete adonques, mes quaunt le Cessions soit fynye ils voillent graunter proses, scilicet, vne warraunt enuers luy ; quar sils compeller[1] lez iurrourz de trouer surete en plein cessions ils ne voillent faire apparaunce apres al cessions autrefoitz & cetera.

Item si surete de peas soit demande enuers vne Officer come vers vicount ou bailly erraunt ou seriaunt de London,[2] lez Justices voillent luy compeller de trouer surete enuers le partie et nemi vers cunctum populum domini Regis.

Item si homme demande surete de peas enuers vne feme de vne de lez Justice de peas, vncore il mesme poet ceo graunter, scilicet, son baron & poet prendre surete de ceo. Et issint poet labbe que est Justice de peas prendre suretez pur son commoigne si ascun ceo demande.

Item le baron poet demander surete de peas enuers son feme & auera, & econtra, scilicet, le feme auera surete de peas de son baron et issint poet le moigne de son soueraigne auer & auxi le soueraigne de son commoigne & cetera.

[*Coment le proses de ceo serra fait.*] Si cesty person de que surete de peas est demande soit present al temps del demande deuaunt lez Justicez de peas deuaunt que & cetera, le Justice de peas poet commaunder le vicount ou bailly adoncque esteaunt[3] la present ou autre officer iurre que est en son presence que il prendra celui enuers que le surete est demande saunz ascun proses. Mes il ne poet commaunder[4] vne de cez seruauntes de luy prendre la saunz proses, scilicet, warraunt. Mes en cas que celui de que le surete est demande soit absent al temps que cest surete est demande vers luy, coment que le vicount ou autre officer que est Jurre & conus deins mesme le counte soit la present, lez Justices de peas en cest cas ne poient eux ne ascun de eux commaunder par parols saunz autre precept de luy prendre ; quar sil fait, le partie auera accion de Faux imprisonement enuers le Officer & cetera.

Mes si vne warraunt soit direct al vicount de prendre vne home pur surete de peas ou autrement, la le vicount poet commaunder Bailly ou autre officer iurre come est auauntdit & conuz, de prendre mesme le home saunz autre precept de luy & ceo est bone. Mes en cest cas si le

---

[1] compellerunt, C.
[2] Marowe had been common serjeant (or common pleader) of London from 1491 to 1495 ; see ch. v, *supra*, pp. 129–32.
[3] *Add* auxi, B.
[4] *Add* en ceo case, B, C ; en ceo cause, D.

vicount voilleit commaunder vne estraunge ou son seruaunt de ceo seruer, ceo nest bone sinoun que il fait a luy vne precept.

Item si vne warraunt ou autre precept vient al Bailly pur seruer, il mesme doit ceo seruer en propre person & ne poet faire precept ou commaundement a ascun autre de ceo seruer ; et issint est si soit direct [f. 87b] a vne dez seruauntes dez Justicez de peas ou a vne autre estraunge pur seruer come il bien poet, eux ne poient faire ascun precept ne commaundement as autrez.

Item si vne precept soit direct a ii iointement si lun ceo serua saunz lautre, ceo est bien fait.

Item si vne precept soit fait al vicount & a vne autre estraunge iointement & ils ii fount vne precept outre a vne autre person, cest bone & ceo pur lentres que le vicount ad en son office deuaunt.

Item si le vicount ou autre bailly ou officer iurres & conuz arrest ascun person par force de ascun precept a eux fait, & le partie que est arrest demande de luy quell garrantie il ad de luy arrester, il nest tenus en ceo cas de monstrer a luy son garrantie.

Mes autrement est si le precept soit direct a ascun estraunge que nest officer conus deuaunt ; quar la si le partie demande de [*de le ley cest cas.*] luy de voier son garrantie & il ne voet monstrer, il poet faire rescous ou auer accion de Faux imprisonement. Mes en cest cas si le partie ne ceo demande de luy, il ne couient demonstrer de necessite ; quod nota.

Item si vne Justice de peas agarde vne precept, si le partie voet vener deuaunt ascun Justice de peas & troue surete, le Baille que ad le precept ne poet luy arrester & mitter en prison. Mes sil refuse de trouer surete il poet luy mitter en prison.[1]

Item si vne Supplicauit soit direct al vicount de causer home de trouer surete & le vicount face precept a vne Bailly de luy faire vener deuaunt luy de trouer surete, en cest cas le Bailly ne poet luy carier al prison. Mes il couient returne cest mater & sur cest returne il auera Capias ; quere.

Item si vne Justice de peas soit demurrant hors de counte, vncore il poet graunter precept destre serue deins le countie. Mes le bailly couient luy arrester deins le countie ou il demurre. Mes apres que il ad luy arrest deins le countie il poet luy carier hors del countie al dit Justice de peas que fist le precept de trouer suretez. Mez quere sil soit arrest apres par autre officer en le mesme countie semble que cest ii^{de} arrest est voide ; quar il fut en garde deuaunt a lautre.

[1] *Add* & ceo par expresse parolx in le precept, F.

Item si vne Justice de peas procure vne home de demander surete
de peas dun autre & il mesme graunta a luy vne precept sur cest procurement, par force de quell le partie est arrest, le partie que est arrest
ne vncques auera accion de Faux imprisonement vers le Justice de
peas. Mes autrement est si le seneschall en vne court Baron procure
home de affermer pleint [1] & puis il luy arrest sur colour de prescripsion
come conseruatour ; quar la le partie auera son accion de Faux
imprisonement & cetera.

[*Coment le surete serra troue.*] Item notandum est que le sufficiente
de ceux queux serront suretes, le nombre de eux & le some en quell ils
serront lies est toutzfoitz en le discression dez Justice de peas, et sils
ount pris surete que nest sufficient ils poient causer le partie de trouer
melliour surete a lour plesure. Et auxi si le partie ad enfreint le peas
a vne foitz apres le reconisaunce fait, launcient suretes sount come
voide pur que ils poient luy compeller de trouer nouell suretes a la
peas.

Auxi ils poient prendre surete par plegge ou gage auxi bien come
par recognysaunce, et auxi les Justicez de peas poient prendre surete
par obligacion oue condicion fait a eux mesmez par le nome de Justice
de peas ; ou sil soit oblige a lez Justicez oue condicion par son nome
[f. 88] demene, ceo est bone & nemi voide par lestatut de anno xxii°
H. VI^ti [2] fait enuers vicount de prendre obligacion & cetera.[3]

Item si les Justices de peas cawse celui que duist trouer surete destre
oblige al partie que ceo demande de luy ad vsum domini Regis, ceo
est bone par obligacion. Mes sil fait recognisaunce al partie ad vsum
domini Regis, ceo est voide. Mes sil fait recognisaunce al Roie & al
partie iointement, cest recognisaunce est bone al Roie & voide enuers
le partie.

Item si les Justicez auauntditz preignount vne comen [4] recognisaunce [5]
& nemi resitaunt [6] le peas destre obserue en ceo, cest recognisaunce
nest bone. Mes si lez Justice prent recognisaunce de peas & omytt en
cest recognisaunce le iour a le quell le partie [7] deuoit apparer, vncore
ceo est bone recognisaunce. Mes si le iour soit inz & ne dit de
apperer deuaunt luy come Justice de peas, en cest cas il poet apperer

---

[1] *Add* de dette ou transgression, C.

[2] Should be 33 Hen. VI, c. 3, 1455, the famous ordinance of the
Exchequer so often printed ; see p. 20, note 8, p. 24, *supra.*

[3] *Add* Mez semble que un gage ne serra forfeyt. Mez il myttera gage
que il gardera le peace sur certeyne payne quell payne ill forfetra, F.

[4] *Omit*, D.   [5] *Add* generalment, D.
[6] recitaunt, D.   [7] counsour, D.

deuaunt luy en ascun lieu hors de le cessions. Mes si lez parols sount
en le recognisaunce que il deuoit apperer deuaunt luy vne dez Justices
del peas & sociis suis ad tile vile, la son apparaunce couient estre fait
solement en plein cessions.

Item si vne Justice de peas voet doner vne Iniuncion a vne home
de garder le peas vers cunctum populum domini Regis sub pena xx li.
tancque a cest iour, ceo est voide.

Item si le Justice prist vne recognisaunce de xx li. de le partie de
paier chescun an xxs., ceo est bone recognisaunce. Mes si le condicion
soit que il paiera de xx ans xx s., ceo nest bone.

Item si le Roie soit endett al partie & il est lie en vne recognisaunce
de garder le peas, ou autrement que le Roie auera cest dett, cest voide
recognisaunce.

Item si le recognisaunce soit fait par vne home de xx li. destre leue
de vne acre de terre, ceo nest bone.

Item si le recognisaunce soit fait de xx li. destre leue de son bienz
tantum ou de son terre tantum, ou de son corps tantum, semble que
ceo nest bone.

Item si vne home fait recognisaunce de garder le peas enuers vne
home tantum, ceo est bone. Mez si le condicion de le recognisaunce
soit que il ne doit maihemer le partie ou bater le partie tantum, ceo
nest bone.[1]

Item si le recognisaunce soit de garder le peas vers le partie &
heredes suos, ceo est bone recognisaunce & son heires auerount
auauntage par cest recognisaunce. Mez nemi le pusne fitz que est
heire par le custom ne serra construe[2] deins le recognisaunce forsque
tantum leir al comen ley.[3]

Item si le recognisaunce soit fait de garder le peas enuers le partie
& omnes homines suos, ceo va forsque as homagers & villeins & nemi
enuers son seruauntes manuelles.

Item si le recognicion soit fait de garder le peas enuers le partie &
seruientes suos, ceo serra entendue auxibien enuers son seruauntes
demurrauntes deins son meason come autrez loialment retenuz oue le
partie. Mes si le partie reteigne nouell seruauntes apres le reconysaunce
fait & il enfreint le peas enuers ascun de eux, il[4] forfett le some del

---

[1] *Add* Quar il serra lie de garder le peace & le peace puit in autre
maner estre infreynt, come sill luy tua ou arca son meason ou tielx etc., F.

[2] *For* ne . . . construe *read* nest compris, D.

[3] *For* Mez nemi . . . ley *read* Mez nient pur especiall heyr come par
custom, sicome puisne filz in Borough inglyse, F.

[4] *Add* ne, D.

recognisaunce. Et si ascun de eux queux fueront primerment retenus ale hors de son seruice apres le recognisaunce, il est auxi discharge enuers eux & cetera.

Item si le recognisaunce soit de garder le peas enuers luy & tenentes suos, ceo ne serra entendu mez enuers tilx tenauntes que il auoit saunz mene[1] [f. 88 b.] de que astate que ceo soit, except frauncke almoign. Mez tenauntes en fraunck mariage serront compris destre deins mesme le recognisaunce.

Item [si][2] le recognisaunce soit de garder le peas enuers luy, scilicet, le partie & omnes aherentes[3] suos, ceo serra pris pur eux queux ount[4] mult pluis estre conuersauntz oue luy & son company & cetera.

[*Coment cest surete serra discharge.*] Et ceo poet estre dyuers voies.[5] Par vne voie si le partie que ad demande le surete deuaunt enuers luy voet relesser deuaunt ascun iustice de peas deuaunt le iour de son apparaunce, ceo est bone. Mes sil voet relesser par son fait, ceo est voide. Et si le partie ad reles a luy deuaunt vne iustice deuaunt le iour de cessions, il ne couient de apperer al cessions. Mes nient obstante cest reles, lez Justices que ount pris le recognisaunz couient certifier cest recognisaunce al cessions pur sauer son penalte que est done enuers eux par lestatut.

Item si le Roie pardon le partie deuaunt que il ad enfreint le peas, le pardon est voide. Mes si vne generall recognisaunce soit fait al Roy pur paier vne certen somme a ascun iour, la si le Roie graunta pardon al partie ou reles deuaunt le iour de ceo est bone, et auxi sil ad enfreint le peas deuaunt le pardon, ceo est bone.

Item si ii sount iointment liez al Roie, [si][6] le Roie pardon lun ceo est voide enuers ambideux. Mes sils sount lies iointment & seueralment & puis le Roie pardon lun, ceo est bone enuers luy a que & cetera & nient vers son compaignion.

Item cest surete que il trouer deuaunt vne Justice poet estre apres discharge par vne Supersedeas de autre Justice de peas de mesme le countie, ou par Supersedeas de Justice de Banck ou del chauncerie, mez nemi econtra, scilicet, de Supersedeas de le base court al haute court.

Item si surete soit troue deuaunt vne Justice de peas par vne Supplicauit direct al Justice, vne Supersedeas de autre justice de peas de mesme le countie ne poet ceo discharger.

[1] MS. mᵉ, also B, C, D ; cf. Fleetwood, Office of a Justice of Peace, 39, for his rendering of it as 'menalties'.
[2] si, B, C.   [3] adherentes, B.   [4] Probably an error for sount.
[5] Et . . . voies repeated ; the error is corrected in D.
[6] si, B, D.

Item si le Supersedeas port date deuaunt le precept, vncore ceo est assetz bone.

Item si le Supersedeas vient deuaunt le iour de apparaunce, il nest lie de garder cest iour si soit Supersedeas del chauncerie. Mes si soit par Cerciorare retournable a vne iour apres le iour de cessions, il couient de garder son iour en le cessions & cetera.

Item si le partie que ad troue suretes del peas ad enfreint le peas apres deuaunt le iour, ou sil nad enfreint le peas mez fist defaute al iour que fut done a luy destre deuaunt lez Justicez en plein cessions, lez Justices de peas ne ount ascun poiar de agarde ascun proses enuers luy pur le forfeture.

Mes sil soit lie en Banck le Roie al peas & puis fist defaute a son iour, ils voillent agarder Fieri facias maintenaunt enuers le partie. Mes sil ad enfreint le peas, la ils agarderont vne Scire facias enuers luy primez. Mes si home soit lie en autre comen recognisaunz deuaunt eux de garder son iour, coment que il ne fist defaute ils ne voillent agarder Fieri facias mes Scire facias. Mes sils sount assertenu [1] que il ad enfreint le peas par mater en fait, ils voillent agarder Fieri facias. Quere quo iure & cetera.

[*Nota & bene nota.*] Lez justicez de peas poient directer le waraunt a quecomcque que ils plerrount, & est si bone sicome fut direct al vicount ou autre officer conuz ou jurrez & cetera.

[f. 89.] Si le partie soit lie en vne reconisaunce pur garder le peas & pur apparer a certen iour & ad enfreint le peas en le meane temps, ore lez Justices de peas ore certifieront ceo en bancke le Roie, & ils voillount agarder Scire facias vers le partie que forfett sil sciett ascun chose dire pur que le Roie ne auera le forfett, ore le partie auera trauers a ceo; quar ceo nest mes vne nude surmys & nude mater en fait. Mes sil ne garda son iour deuaunt eux done a le cessions, ore ceo est mater de recorde, & de cest chose ils sount Justices de recorde, & ils ceo certifieront en lescheker & le partie la nauera trauers purceo que est mater de recorde & ore lez barons del escheker voillent agarder Fieri facias ; quod nota. [2]

[Septima Lectura] De fraccione pacis et pacificacionis [3] eiusdem.

Et ore par cest lecture est a voier queux choses serrount ditz enfreindre le peas & queux nemi & cetera.

---

[1] acertein, B, C.
[2] From Lez justicez . . . quod nota omitted in B, C, D.
[3] pacificacione, D.

Et sciendum est que ascunz chosez sount que sount encontre le peas
& vncore eux ne serrount ditz enfreindre de peas de que cest estatut[1]
parle. Sicome [vne] entre encountre le peas en ascun terre & luy disseisist, ou si ascun prist lez bienz de ascun autre, ceux chosez ne sount
enfreindre de le peas quaunt a ceo que ascun recognisaunce de le peas
fait serra forfait. Et vncore eux sount suppose par vser de accion sur
ceo destre encountre le peas. Mes si ascun recognisaunce serra forfett
par ascun enfreindre de le peas, il couient que lact que est fait soit
encountre le peas et auxi fait al person de ascun home & ceo est cause
de forfaiture & cetera.

Item si vne manasse vne autre par parols ou sil gisoit en agayt par
voie de luy bater, ceux ne sount enfreindre de le peas. Mes si home
face assault ou affraie sur vne autre, ceo serra dit enfreindre de le peas ;
et vncore en ceo cas lun poet estre troue coulpable de lassault & lautre
coulpable de laffraie ; quere coment & cetera.

Item si homme soit oblige en vne recognisaunce de le peas tancque
a certen iour & deuaunt le iour il batist ou mayme vne home, ceo serra
dit enfreindre de le peas & il forfetra son recognisaunz. Mes si home
rase lez crynes ou herere[2] de vne autre, ceo nest enfreindre le peas
coment que soit encountre son volunte fait. Mes si home enprison
vne autre encountre son volunte, ou luy giser en vne ryuer issint que il
est en ieopardie destre drowne, ceo serra dit vne enfreindre de le peas.

Item si home rauyssh vne feme encountre son volunte, ceo est vne
enfreindre de le peas. Mes autre est si vne home rauyssh vne garde
hors de possession de vne autre, il ne serra dit enfreindre & cetera.

Item si homme fait riotous assemble oue multitude dez gentz, ceo
est enfreindre de le peas. Mes si home face forcible entre fait par luy
mesme & nemi autrement ne serra dit vne enfreindre de le peas.

Item si home emble vne chiuall ou autre chose que est Felonye,
vncore il nest enfreindre de le peas. Mes autrement est si vne home
face Burglarie, roborie al person, murdre ou manslaughter ; quar en
toutz cez cases le peas est enfreint al person mesme, & sic nota diuersitatem entre Theft & ceux cases & cetera.

Item si home commytt ascun treson al person le Roie, serra dit vne
enfreindre de le peas & vncore [f. 89 b] le recognisaunce est : quod
ipse geret pacem versus cunctum populum domini Regis & precipue

---

[1] i. e. Westminster First, c. 1.
[2] *For* crynes ou herere *read* crynes hedre, B ; crynes, C ; crynes sur le
chieff dun home, D. The interpretation in F differs : sill rase parsell de
son auriell . . . est infreindre dell peace.

versus J. de T.[1] & ne parle de le Roie. Mes purceo que lact que est fait encountre luy que est le principall Test[2] de le Roialme, est adiuge en preiudice a toutz cez subgettes & issint encountre le peas.

Et nota que en diuerses casez le baterie tantum ne fait lenfreindre de le peas mes le maner de Baterie ceo fait; sicome home bate son seruaunt, son feme ou son villeyn, quar ceux persons il poet loialment chastiser saunz enfreindre de le peas. Mes sil eux batue excessiue come de Maymer eux ou autre excessiue batue, ceo serra dit vne enfreindre de le peas. Et sil Mayheme son seruaunt il poet loialment departer de luy & auxi auera accion de transgression ou appelle.[3] Mes son feme si soit issint batuz ne poet departer de son baron ne el nauera accion & cetera. Mes si vne home chastisa son villeyn excessyuely il serra dit enfreindre de le peas et auxi vne enfraunchisement al villeyn, come de luy mayhemer & cetera.

Item en ascun cas coment que le Chastisement soit fait nient excessiue, vncore il serra dit enfreindre de le peas; come sil chastisa son villeyn ou seruaunt en le presence de le peas[4] ou en son palais, come fut aiuge xxvii^mo libro assisarum[5] & cetera.

Item si mon seruaunt departe hors de mon seruice deinz son terme saunz licence, ieo puisse luy reprendre mez nemi luy chastiser pur son departir. Mez pur son male seruice ieo puisse luy batue. Mes si mon feme depart de moie ieo puisse luy reprendre & auxi luy chastiser pur son departure; mes le seruaunt ne serra sinoun pur son male seruice.

Item vne Scole master de Gramer poet chastiser cez scolers, & vne Gailer son prisoners, & issint poet le vssher de le scole ou le south-gailour saunz ascun especiall commaundement de loure maisters, & null enfreindre de le peas en cest cas. Mes le seruaunt de le gailour ou scole master ne poient ceo faire sinoun par especiall commaundement de loure master; quar le southgailour & vssher ount vne general commaundement quaunt ils entrent en lour officez que suffist saunz autre.

Item en diuerses casez homme poet faire baterie a vne persone & vncore null de eux ad enfreint le peas; sicome home percucute[6] a

[1] J de C, in MSS. B, C, D.
[2] Capteygn, B; Cap[teyn], C; Capteign, D.
[3] *Add* de mayhem, B.   [4] roy, B, C, D.
[5] Identified as 27 Edw. III, no. 49; in a case of trespass 'fait ... deins le Pallays de Westminster en la presence de Roy', it was held that a man 'ne puit prendre son villein en le presence de Roy,' &c.
[6] percute, B, C; percust, D.

mure, ou autre soy defendendo percucte [1] vne autre a son dorse nient
veiaunt luy, ceo nest enfreindre de le peas ; quar ceo fut fait encountre
son volunte.

Et en diuers cases coment que le baterie soit fait oue son volunte,
vncore il ne serra dit enfreindre de le peas si le cause auoit vne loiall
commensement deuaunt ; sicome le Roie commaunde Justice [2] Roiall
destre deins son roialme pur son plesure et si ascun person soit lede
en Justis roiall, ceo nest enfreindre & cetera & vncore il fut fait oue
son volunte.

Item si home gage bataille en vne breue de droit lou le originall est
bone, ceo est null enfreindre & cetera.   Mes si lez parties ioynerount
bataille lou null originall est deuaunt ou apres que le pleintif est noun
sute en cest breue, cest ioindre de bataille serra dit lenfreindre de peas
si lun lede lautre.   Mez autrement est lou lez Justicez voillent agarder
bataille destre fait, en cest cas lou [f. 90] null tile bataille gist, come en
cas lou vne enfaunt voille porter appelle de roborie ou murdour, & le
defendaunt gage bataille oue lenfaunt coment que lun de eux soit lede,
ceo nest enfreindre de le peas & semble purceo que ne fut ascun
defaute en eux mesmez mez en lez Justices & cetera.

Item si vne homme voile commaunder autre home de sagitter a luy
& sur ceo lautre issint fait & luy lede, ceo est vne enfreindre de le
peas ; quar le commaundement ne fut loiall al commensement.   Mes
si vne home tient vne cotell en son mayn, & vne autre luy percute sur
son brache al entent de faire luy que tient le cotell de leder vne autre
stante [3] prochun a luy, par force de quell il luy lede, ceo est enfreindre
de le peas en celui que cause cest acte destre fait & nemi en celui que
fist lact & cetera.

Et auxi nota que en diuerses casez home poet faire baterie a autre
person, & vncore cest baterie serra dit enfreindre de le peas en celui que
est batuz & nemi en celui que fist le baterie ; sicome vne home moy
assault & ieo fue en taunt que ieo puisse pur ieopardie,[4] & doncque ieo
face defence & en mon defens lede lautre, ceo serra dit enfreindre de
peas en luy & nemi en moy.

Item en cest cas il nest solement loiall a moy mesme de faire defens
pur moy defendaunt,[5] mez auxi list bien a mon seruaunt moy defendre
en cest cas & null enfreindre de peas serra aiugge en mon seruaunt
nient pluis que en moy mesme.   Et en mesme le maner poet le master
defendre son seruaunt oue baterie pur le perdue de son seruice.   Et

---

[1] percute, B, D ; soi defend[endo] percute, C ; si come home percute
un home a son dorce soy defendendo, F.   [2] Justis (?), B.
[3] esteant, D.   [4] doute de mort, D.   [5] defendre, D.

vncore semble que le master ne poet mayntener son seruaunt en ascun sute de le ley; quere de ceo.

Item si vne home ad vne bailly de son maner il poet defendre son master oue baterie; mes si home ad vne fermour que paia rent a luy, le fermour ne poet defendre son lessour oue baterie; quar il nad ascun lyvyng par luy.

Item vne commoigne[1] poet defendre son abbott & econtra oue baterie, mes labbe ne poet defendre son Ordinarie que est son visitour oue baterie. Mes vne abbe poet defendre son foundour oue baterie.

Item chescun de vne Communialte de vne cite Corporate ne poet iustifier en defens de le meire de mesme le cite. Mes chescun home poet iustifier en defens de le Roie mesme oue baterie; quar il est le principall par que & cetera.

Item si ii reteignent vne seruaunt & lun dez masters voet lede lautre, le seruaunt poet faire defence enuers lun pur lautre defendre. Mes si home ad vne seruaunt & il ad autre seruaunt, le seruaunt de le seruaunt ne poet defendre le primer master oue baterie saunz enfreindre de le peas. Mes si home soit reteigne oue vne graunde home en seruice come oue vne seignur & cetera et il done gages a luy pur luy[2] & son seruaunt de seruer luy, ore le seruaunt del seruaunt poet faire defence pur le primer master oue baterie saunz enfreindre de le peas & cetera.

Item si home ad vne garde il poet luy defendre oue baterie, et issint si le garde soit graunt a moy al vse de vne autre, le graunte de son garde & ieo auxi puissomus faire baterie en defence de mesme le garde. Et issint poet gardein en socage et garden per cawse de Norture faire defence de lour gardes.

Item le villeyn poet defendre son seignur oue baterie et auxi le seignur poet defendre son villeyn. Mez si le seignur ad vne Nieff que est marie el ne poet faire defence de son seignur duraunt le couerture; [f. 90 b] quar duraunt le couerture el est enffraunchise.

Item le fitz poet faire baterie pur son pier en son defens et auxi en defence de son mier; & issint poet chescun[3] de[4] consanguinite de quell. pluis long degre que il soit continue sil sciet faire son pedegre, il poet[5] faire defence pur luy oue baterie & ceo justifia & cetera. Et auxi poet vne Frer ou soer de dimi sancke defendre autre de eux oue baterie saunz enfreindre de le peas, & vncore lun de eux ne poet enheriter a lautre par null possibilite & cetera.

Item en ascun cas de aliaunce lun de eux poet defendre autre oue

---

[1] moigne, C.   [2] *Add* seruer, B.   [3] *Add* en defens, D.
[4] *Add* son, D.   [5] *Omit* il poet, D.

baterie, mes le alliaunce couient estre tile que ils ne poient par le ley de
seint esglise entremarier. Sicome en cas que non Frer ad marie vostre
[*Nota*]   soer & deuie, ieo puisse en cest cas defendre vostre soer oue
        baterie mez ieo ne puisse defendre vous que estez nostre [1] frer
saunz enfreindre de le peas.[2]

Item si home ad issue Bastarde, le Bastarde poet defendre son mier
oue baterie mez nemi son pier; quar il nest certen que est son pier.
Mes si le pier apres prist mesme le feme a feme par espouselx & ad
issue autre fitz, cest ii^de fitz defendra le bastarde & le bastarde poet
defendre luy oue baterie & cetera.

Item notandum est que homme poet auxibien faire defens oue
baterie pur cez [*sic*] bienz come de son corps. Mes si home ad pris
mez bienz hors de mon possession, ieo ne puisse eux prendre de luy
oue baterie esteaunt en son possession; quar la il poet claimer
proprete. Mes si ieo baille mez bienz a vne a mon vse & vne
estraunger voille eux prendre hors de son possession, quar en cest cas
ambideux de nous, scilicet, mon baille & moy poiomus defendre cez
bienz oue baterie. Mes si ieo deliuera bienz a vne G.[3] a delyuer
a vne S.[4] par certen iour, si ascun estraunge voillet prendre lez bienz
deuaunt le iour hors de le possession mon bailly, G.[5] & S.[6] poient
defendre lez bienz oue baterie. Mez ieo ne puisse my defendre; quar
le propurte est ale hors de moy.

Item si vne homme ad vne Garrein ou parke ou autre liberte & vne
autre voet entrer en ceo, il poet luy defendre oue baterie. Mes autrement est de terre saunz liberte sinoun que il ad continue possession
en mesme le terre par le space de iii ans deuaunt lentre, come appiert
par lestatut de anno viii^o H. VI^ti.[7] Mes al comen ley deuaunt cest
estatut ils [8] puissount luy defendre en cest cas & cetera.

Item si home voet faire comen nusaunce, chescun home poet luy defendre en fesauns de cest act oue baterie saunz enfreindre de le peas.[9]

(*Margin*) Coment cest enfreindre de le peas serra pacifie.

Item le constabull ou bailly sils semblerount que ascunz persons

[1] son, B, D, F.
[2] *Add* quar si un de nous fuissomus femme nous puissomus entre
mary, F.   [3] C. A. in MS. B; C. in MS. D; B. in MS. F.
[4] C. in MS. F.   [5] C. in MS. B.   [6] G. in MS. C.
[7] *Add* ca^o ix, F; see 8 Hen. VI, c. 9, 1429, the very last clause of the
statute on Forcible Entry.   [8] *Add* ne, F.
[9] On margin of D is a reference to 'statute of Marlebridge c. xxv' and
to opinion of 'Seignur Fyneux at the end of this book'; probably the
entry on f. 96 b, a reference to Statute de Malefactoribus in Parcis, to
Fyneux, &c.

voillount affraier deins mesme le vile, ils commaunderont ambideux
parties de avoidre sur peyn de imprisonement; & sil semble destre
graunt affraie ils poient eux commaunder al prison pur petit temps pur
saver le affraie.   Mes le constable eux couient en cest cas delyuerer
saunz fyne.

Item si ii hommes sount en affraiauntes chescun home poet eux
departer par le ley.[1]   Mes sil soit lede en le departyng il nauera[2]
accion de transgression enuers celui que ad luy lede.   Et en mesme le
maner aueround lez autrez accion enuers luy sil lede ascun de eux en
le departer.   Mez autre est[3] [f. 91] en cest cas si vne constable,
gardein de peas ou autre officer vient & eux depart & le Constable ou
autre officer est lede, il auera accion.   Mes si lofficer lede ascun de
eux, celui que est lede nauera ascun accion enuers le officer & cetera.

Item si vne affraie soit en le haute[4] strete & home vient oue wepons
defensible trahie en son mayn ou en harnes, issint que est de entend
que il voille prendre ascun partie en le affraie, chescun home que luy
suspect en tile maner poet luy tarrier tancque laffraie soit fynye.

Item si ii homes sount a cedicious language le quell par comen pre-
tense voet enducer eux a vne affraie, null poet eux departer loialment
tancque lour wepens soient trahie en loure mains ou autre semblable
chose fait par eux.

Item si vne affraie soit fait en le presence de le constable & il ne
luy endeuera de ceo pacifier, il ferra fyne si ceo soit troue par
enquestes deuaunt lez Justicez de peas al prochun cessions & cetera
par loure discression.   Mes si laffraie soit fait en autre lieu del vile, &
autre vient al constable & monstra ceo a luy & sur ceo monstraunce
il ne voet ceo pacifier, en ceo cas il ne fra fyne & cetera.

Item si affraie soit fait chescun home sur ceo poet luy prendre que
est en defaute & luy amesner al constable, mes il ne poet en cest cas
luy amesner al prison.   Mes si ascun home soit en ieopardie de son
vie par mesme laffraie, la chescun home poet luy arrester & amesner
al prison, scilicet al gaile maintenaunt ou il poet luy delyuer al constable.   Mes en cest cas le constable nest tenus de luy receiuer &
doncque couient a eux de luy amesner al prochun gaile.   Mes lou il
fist affraie solement & il luy prist sur ceo & il luy amesna al prison, ou
il[5] poet luy lesser aler a large & cetera.

<hr>

[1] At the top of the corresponding folio in D are the following references:
Trespas 246, Baile 245, Barre 119 (should be 110), Barre 291.   All but the
second have been identified in Fitzherbert's Abridgement, 1516 ed.
      [2] auera, B, C, D, F, but A is correct.   [3] Mez . . . est, *bis.*
      [4] *Add* chemyn ou, C.   [5] *For* ou il *read* null, B ; il null, D.

Item si vne affraie soit fait & le constable veigne & voile arrester celui que fist laffraie & il fua en vne meason & closa le huys, en cest cas le Constable ne poet debruser le huys per luy prendre nient obstante que soit sur fressh sute. Mes si ascun home soit tue [1] en cest affraie issint que il est en ieopardie de son vie, il poet enfreindre le meason & luy prendre dehors. Et issint il poet si ii homes sount affraiauntes en vne meason & le huys en quell ils sount inz est clause, coment que null home soit lede deuaunt lentre, vncore il poet entre en le meason & ceo debruse de voier le peas garde, & issint poet chescun autre person affaire.

Item si affraie soit fait en vne countie & est continue en autre counte, le Constable de lun countie ne poet luy pursuer en lautre countie & deprendre luy la come constable de lautre conte. Mes chescun home poet luy pursuer en autre countie mez nemi de luy prendre dehors. Mes si laffraie soit fait en vne vile et continue [2] tancque a autre ville que est fraunchese deins mesme le countie, le Constable de le primer vile poet luy pursuer & luy prendre hors del fraunchese pur son fressh sute & cetera.

Item si affraie soit contenue de vne counte en autre counte, & sur ceo [f. 91 b] fresh sute est fait par lez Constablez & la il est pris en le darrein conte, ils couient de amesner le prisoner al prison en le conte ou il fut pris. Mes sil que est pris auoit occis vne home ou le home que il ad lede est en ieopardie de son vie, en cest cas il que fist le pursute poet eslier de luy amesner al prison en lun countie ou en autre a son plesure.

[*Margin*] Coment le Constable doit enprisoner vne home en son meason.

Item si le Constable arrest vne home sur affraie il ne poet luy emprisoner en son meason ouster resonable temps, issint que il poet luy auer al gaile en conuenyent temps et saunz ieopardie de rescous. Mes autre est de vicount ou Gailor que ad le charge de gaile; quar ils poient eux emprisoner en loure meason a lour plesure & faire Gaile de son meason quaunt il voet pur son charge. Mes si vne Justice de peas arrest vne home par son seruaunt, il ne poet luy enprisoner en son meason par ascun longure [3] temps que il poet luy conuenyentment mitter al comen gaile, come appiert par lestatut fait pur cest mater anno v^{to} H. IIII^{ti}, capitulo x^{mo} [4]; quod nota.

---

[1] troue, D.   [2] MS. contiə.
[3] long, B.   [4] 5 Hen. IV, c. 10, 1404.

[Octaua Lectura] [1] De fraccione pacis cum multitudine
gencium.

(*Margin*) Vide statutum de anno xiii° H. quarti [2] pur cest mater.

Ore est a entendre que al comen ley deuaunt le fesaunz de ascun
estatutes faites encountre cest Riotours, Riott ne fut mez come comen
transgression est a ore.   Mes si ascun home ent fut troue coulpable de
ascun riott al comen ley, lez Justicez voillent cesser pluis graunde
fyne en cest cas que ils voillent en autrez transgressions; quar lez
Justicez de peas adoncques auoient poier denquerer de ceo come de
autrez transgressions & ceo fut considre adoncques pluis haute transgression que autrez & cetera.

Et auxi deuaunt lestatut ent fait si ascun home fut lede en cest riott,
lez constablez & autrez officerzs puissent eux arester & amener al
prison.   Mes si vne Riotous assemble ad este fait encountre le peas
& null acte execute sur ceo come baterie, murdre, arcer dez measons
ou huiusmodi, vncore en cest cas deuaunt le fesaunz de lestatut
auauntdit ils ne auoient ascun poier de eux arrester et imprisoner.
Mes ils poient seuere lez compaignes ne ils ne medeler & issint poet
chescun home que fut comen person faire.   Et si lez parties sur cest
seueraunce ne voillent aler en loure meason, ils puissent eux imprisoner
pur le temps & nemi autrement & cetera.

Et auxi par le comen ley fut vne autre mischieff; quar si vne tile
riotous assemble ad este fait, le vicount ne puisseroit compeller homez
de le countie de aler oue luy de garder le peas; quar par le comen ley
null puit commaunder lez homez de conte de aler oue luy en cest cas
forsque le Roie tantum; quar cest commaundement fut entendue vne
sequestracion de loure liberte.   Et pur le graund partie lou il est done
par estatut que le vicount poet prendre oue luy le power de le counte,
ceo est sur le ii^{de} contempt fait par le partie & nemi sur le primer contempt; come en cas lou en breue de Replegias lez auerz sount
conveiez a vne Forcelett & proclamacion est fait accordaunt al estatut
de W ii^{de}, [3] la il poet prendre oue luy le power de la conte & debruse
le castell ou forcelett.   Et mesme le ley lou le breue de Replegias est
agarde & le bailly retorne que il ne poet replevyn faire pur ceo que est
resistence fait enuers luy & cetera.   Par [4] quell remedie vient lestatut
de anno xvii° Ricardi secundi, [5] & done power al vicount & as autrez
officerz le Roie que si ascun tile riott soit fait deins ascun conte, [f. 92]

---

[1] viii^{ta} lectura, B.   [2] 13 Hen. IV, c. 7, 1411.
[3] Westminster primer ca° xvii°, D, F, the correct reference.
[4] Pur, B.   [5] *Add* ca° viii, F ; see 17 Rich. II, c. 8, 1394.

que adoncques le vicount & autrez officerz poient prendre le power del counte oue luy & aler al lieu ou le Riottourz sount & la arester lez misfesourz,[1] coment que null baterie soit execute entre eux deuaunt. Mes vncore cest estatut ne done ascun power en le cas auauntdit a lez Justices de peas de prendre tile power de le countie; pur que lestatut de anno xiii° H. IIII[ti], capitulo [2] fut fait que done que ils poient prendre le power del countie en cas auauntdit auxi bien come le vicount, come appiert par le lettre de mesme lestatute & cetera.

Les parols de lestatut sount: que si ascun Riott, assemble ou Rowte soit fait & cetera. Ore est auoier le dyuersite parentre Riott, assemble & Rowt.[3] Riott serra dit proprement lou nombre dez gentes sount assemblez al entent defaire chose que est encountre le ley, & execute mesme lact appres que ils sount assembles come est dit; come sils batue ou mayme ou murdre vne home ou plusourz homez par cest riott.

Assemble est lou ils sount assemblez en fourme auauntdit al entent defaire chose que est encountre le ley & ils ne executent lact de loure entent mez apres le assemble departount.

Rowte est dit proprement lou vne graunde assemble dez gentz est faire [4] & ceo defaire vne chose encountre le ley, & en lour quarellis demene & en le quarell de chescun de eux & nemi en le quarell de vie [5] priuate person esteaunt entre eux; sicome lou home ad fait vne enclosure en vne ville & tout lez communiers de mesme le ville assembleront eux [6] de bruser mesme le close, ou autrement de bater vne person que ad fait a eux comen displesure come de seruer vne warant, breue ou huiusmodi en mesme le vile, ceo serra dit proprement vne Rowte dez comens.

Item deux chosez sount requisites a chescun de ceux trois, scilicet, Riott, assemble ou Rowte. Et lun est que ils sount ii [7] persons al meins que sount assemble; le ii[de] chose que ils couient de faire chose que est encountre le ley, sicome exhort ascun estraungers de aler oue luy de bater vne home a tile lieu & ils aleront [8] de ceo faire, ceo est vne

---

[1] *For* lez misfesourz *read* et lez myse en prison, D.

[2] *Add* vltimo, D; see p. 338, note 2, *supra*.

[3] Brooke, Abridgement, 1573 ed., Riots & routs & assemblies, no. 5 (margin, Difference inter ryott rowte & assemble): 'nota par Marrow seriant in son definition de riots routs & assemblees, in son lecture in inferiori (*sic*) templo, sur lestatut de pease, que riot est ou tres vel plures font illoyal act in fait, . . .'

[4] fait, B, C, D.

[5] vn, B, D.   [6] *Omit*, C.

[7] See note 3, *supra*, 'tres vel plures'.   [8] *Add* oue eux, D.

riotous assemble. Mez si diuers personez sount assemblez en vne
compaigne a loiall entent come de faire vne chirch[1] a[2] le Gilde ou
similia, ou de manger ou boier, et ascun de eux fait affraie sur
estraunger, ceo ne serra dit Riott. Mez si ascun de mesme le compaigne preignount lun partie & ascunz de eux lautre parte, ore il
serra dit Riott & vncore loure assemble fut loiall al commencement &
cetera.

Item si homme ala ouesque son meniall seruauntes oue queux il ad
vse de aler auaunt, coment que il soit oustre son degre de aler ouesque
tauntz dez seruauntes, & fait affraie par le voie et lez seruauntes
esteauntes oue luy present, ceo ne serra dit Riott. Mes si le master
fesoit cez seruauntes priue a son entent deuaunt le affraie fait & puis
ceo execute en fait, la il est Riott coment que ne sount la forsque son
meniall seruauntes & cetera.

Par queux persones assemble poet estre fait et par queux nemy.

Si plusours femmez ou enfauntz south lans de discression assemble
par eux mesme pur loure propre cause, ceo nest riott. . Mes si ascun
autre person cause de assembler tile persones de faire tile Riott, en
cest cas serra dit vne Riott.

Item si vne meire & communialte de vne vile fount ascun riott en
le quarellis de tout le communialte, ceo serra adiuge vne Riott en
loure particuler persons que fesoient le Riott & nemi en tout le politik
[f. 92 b] corps del cite & cetera.

Item si xii iurrourz queux sount iurre en ascun enquest & mys en
vne meason, & vi dez iurrourz voillount pugner et batue oue lez autrez
vi iurrourz, ceo nest ascun riott & cetera.[3]

Item si plusourz homez sount assembles & null de eux sciet a quell
entent ils sount assemblez, ceo nest riott deuaunt que lentent soit conuz
a eux.

Item le maner de le fesaunce de le assemble poet faire vne Riott
lou lassemble fut loiall deuaunt ; sicome home que entende de aler al
cessions ou merkett & vient en harnes & ceux seruauntes auxi oue luy
en harnes, & vncore parauentur son entent ne fut de faire ascun Riott,
mes le maner de luy face le Riott pur le pretens[4] del people.

Item home poet faire assemble al entent defaire vne chose que est
encountre le ley & vncore ceo ne serra dit Riott, sicome dyuers homez

[1] Church-Ale, Fleetwood, Office of a Justice of Peace, 51.
[2] ou, D.   Probably a le in A is an error for ale.
[3] *Add* purceo que ilz furont loyalment assemblez & auxi ut par compul-
syon fueront mys einz &c., F.
[4] presens, C.

assemblerount de iewer al classhe,[1] dise ou cardis ou autrez tilx iews que ne sount pas loiall, vncore il ne serra dit Riott; quar il nest a preiudice de ascun home mez a eux mesmez & cetera. Et mesme le leie lou home fait tort, scilicet, deprendre vne chose come vne pece de mereme[2] ou huiusmodi que ne poet estre fait mes oue plusourz gentz, ceo ne serra dit Riott. Mes si le nombre que vient oue luy soit excesse pur tile cause, ceo serra dit Riott.

Lestatute est[3]: que lez Justices de le peas, trois ou deux de eux, oue le vicount ou southvicount. Par cez parols de lestatut ils purront prendre oue eux le power de countie, & cest power poet estre prende soloncque loure discression que serra conuenientment par le mater & cetera, scilicet, plusourz ou meinz a loure plesure & cetera.

Item femez & enfauntz deins lage de xv ans & pluis[4] sount exemptes en cest cas de le commaundement de lez Justices. Mes [quaunt][5] vne enfaunt vient al age de xv ans & pluis, doncques il serra compelle de aler ouesque lez Justicez de peas en cest cas; quar doncque a cest age il couient de auer harnes de luy mesme & cetera.[6]

Item toutz Religious persons come abbes, ancres, heremites, Reclusez & toutz ceux qe serrount infra sacros ne serrount compellable de aler oue les Justicez & cetera.[7] Mes toutz les seignurz deins mesme le countie serront compellable de aler oue eux come Dukes, Erles, Barons & huiusmodi.

Item toutz seruauntes, apprenticez, villeins & Gardes sount compellable de aler oue eux. Mes si home soit en prison ou est lesse a baille a autrez pur dett ou transgression ou huiusmodi, il nest compellable de aler.

Item lez Justices & vicount poient eux prendre oue compulsion magre eux, mez si cest compulsion serra par fyne & emprisonement fait, quere & semble que cy, scilicet, que ils poient eux emprisoner & mitter fyne.

---

[1] cloyssh, B, cleshis, C, chesse, F. Cf. 17 Edw. IV, c. 3, 1478, 'disloialx Juez come dise . . . diuersez nouelx ymaginez Jeuez appellez Cloishe Kayles'. Apprentices are forbidden to play 'at the Tenys, Closshe, Dise, Cardes, Bowles', except at Christmas; 11 Hen. VII, c. 2, s. v, 1495. N.E.D. states that closh was a game with a ball or bowl, obsolete before the time of Cowell, 1554–1613.

[2] Godefroy gives 'Mairien' and a long list of alternatives with 'mereme' as the last, 'bois à bâtir'; cf. the Latin form, p. 392, *infra*.

[3] i. e. 13 Hen. IV, c. 7, see p. 338, note 2, *supra*.   [4] *Omit* & pluis, B.

[5] quaunt, B, D.   [6] See statute of Winchester, 13 Edw. I, c. 6.

[7] *Add* & issint homez que ount continuell infirmyties, F.

Item si hue et crie soit fait a lun fyne de vne vile de prendre vne lareyn que auoit robbe, & le vicount vient de autre fyne del vile & commaunda a eux de aler oue luy de pacifier vne Riott accordaunt al estatut, en cest cas ils couient de aler oue le vicount & nemi deprendre le lareyn; quere tamen.

Lestatute est auxi: pur eux arrester & eux arrestent. Ceo serra entende si lez parties sount presentz quaunt lez Justicez de peas vient en le lieu ou le Force & Riott fut fait, doncque il poet eux arrester & mitter en prison. Mez si lez·Justices & le vicount obuia eux par le voie en alaunt a cest lieu, sils sount en harnes ou en auter maner nient loiall, ils purront eux arrester & apres que ils ount eux arrest, le power de counte couient de aler oue le vicount de carier lez prisonerz al Gaile. Mes sils ount pris vne felone [f. 93] en le compaigne de le vicount par hue & crie ils ne couient de aler ouesque le vicount al gaile [1]; quere diuersitatem.

Et eient mesme lez Justices, vicount ou southvicount, power de Recorder tile Riott & cetera.[2] Et nota que cest recorde couient estre en escript & remayne oue vne dez Justices de peas, & les Justices de peas sur cest recorde fait poient eux emprisoner, & auxi mesme lez Justices que ount tile recorde ferront & cesseront loure fyne en ceo cas & null autrez Justicez de peas de mesme le countie ceo ferra.

Item si lez Justices voient le riott & deuaunt que il purra prendre lez misfesourz ils eschaperount, ils doient recorder cest mater. Mez lez Justicez de peas ne poient eux prendre a autre temps apres pur cell Riott ne ils ferrount ascun proses vers eux en cest cas. Mes ils poient mitter cest recorde en bancke le Roie & la lez Justices de Bancke ferront proses sur cest certificat. Mez lez parties ne aueront trauers a cest certificat, mez ferrount lour fyne meintenaunt. Mez lez Justicez de peas ne poient mitter cest certificat en le bancke entre autrez recordes de le cessions mez par luy mesme.

Item si lez Justicez veignount de voier vne riott & puis vne autre Riott est fait en loure presence, ils poient recorder cest ii[de] Riott coment que ils ne vient la pur mesme le cause.

Item si lez Justices de peas & le vicount sount en company pur autre cause que de voier Riott paise, il poient Recorder vne Riott fait en loure presence coment que ils ne veignount pur tile cause. Mes si les Justices & le vicount vient deprendre lez Riottourz & ils fuant en autre conte & lez Justicez pursue eux en autre conte, lez Justices en

---

[1] *Add* quar la quaunt ilz ont luy delyuer ilz serront dischargez, F.
[2] Quoted from the statute, *ut supra*, p. 341, note 3.

cest cas ne poient recorder le Riott que ils fount en autre conte. Mes si lez Riottourz fuount a vne Forcelett ou chastell deins mesme le countie, la lez Justices sils eux pursuount purront enfreindre le force-lett & prendre dehors & cetera.

Item si les Justices & le vicount vient de cesser vne Riott & quaunt ils veignount la lez Riottourz fount riott sur mesme lez Justices et le vicount, en cest cas ils poient recorder cest riott fait sur eux mesmez. Mes si lez Justices de peas & le vicount sount assemblez en vne lieu pur autre cause & doncque vne [affray¹] est fait sur eux ensemble, en cest cas lez Justices & le vicount ne poient ceo recorder ; quar ils ne poient estre iugez en lour cause demene lou ils ne veignount a lentent de peaser le Riott. Mes si home soit occise en le Riott, lez Justices & vicount poient recorder sur cest mater que lez Riotourz ount occise vne home riotose & nemi felonice. Et issint ils poient recorder en tile fourme que un tile, tile iour & an riotose mayhamauit. Et issint poient lez Justices de peas de vne rescous fait a vne officer en loure presence que voet arrester lez Riottourz, mes ils ne poient recorder ascun Rescous fait a ascun autre officer hors de loure presence.²

Item si les Justices de peas fount vne recorde de le Riott & sur ceo ils teignount lez offendourz en prison tancque ils ount fait loure fyne, coment que sur le viewe de le recorde [f. 93 b] il appiert destre null Riott, vncore ils sount saunz remedie en cest cas. Et vncore lez Justicez ne ount ascun power pur eux enprisoner forsque pur riott tantum & cetera.

Et par lez Recordes de mesmes lez justices soient tielx trespassourz & mysfesourz conuyct & cetera.³ Cest conuiccion serra entendue destre sur son recorde mys al prison la a demurrer tancque ils ount fait fyne. Mes si lez Justices certifiount que il ad tue ou mayheme vne homme riotose, lez parties ne serront conuictez de vie & de vie et de membre par cest recorde dez Justices de le mort ou mayme, tanc-que ils sount endite & arreigne sur cest mater nient obstante le Recorde. Et puis si mesme le home soit endite al sute le Roi de Maiheme ou de felony, il poet pleder rien coulpable a ceo nient obstante le recorde auauntdit de le Justice de peas. Mes sil soit endite en ⁴ apres al sute le Roie en transgression apres le riott recorde

¹ affray, B ; affrai, D ; riot, C.
² *Add* Et en icell cas le party ne serra estoppe de pleder nient culpable all felony ou all rescous, nient obstaunt le record dez Justice de peace, mez nient all riott, mez serra de ceo quiete, come appiert par le breue dell estatut, F.
³ Quoted, *ut supra*, p. 341, note 3.   *Omit*, C.

come est dit, il ne pledera rien coulpable en cest cas, mes ferra fyne pur cest recorde. Mes si le partie port vne accion de transgression enuers luy apres le recorde fait par lez Justicez de peas, vncore en cest cas il pledera rien coulpable & cetera.[1]

Item si vne homme soit lie al peas par recognysaunce al Roie & puis lez Justices de peas fount tile Certificat de Riott vers le reconisour en le bancke le Roie, & ils ne iustifieront leynfreindre de peas ne plederont[2] rien coulpable en cest cas sur le Scire facias agarde enuers luy sur le reconisaunz & cetera.

Et sil aveigne que tielx trespassours sount departus & cetera Inquireront mesme lez Justicez.[3] Ceo ne serra entende en null cas forsque lou lez Justicez de peas aleront de viewer le Riott, mes coment que ils ne vncques alerount de voier ceo, vncore ils poient enquerer de cest Riott apres. Et auxi si lez prochun Justices alent pur voier le Riott & ils sount departez deuaunt lour venue, vncore si[4] ii autrez Justices de peas & le vicount de mesme le conte poient enquerer de cest riott & ceo est bone enquerry nient obstante que lestatut dit que mesmez lez justices enquirerount.

Item si ii justices de peas & vicount alent de voier le Riott & ii autrez Justices de peas fount lenquerre, ceux Justices queux fount lequerre [*sic*] ou lez autrez Justices poient faire le certificat.

Item nota que si lenquerre ne soit fait deins le mois apres le Riott fait, le Certificat nest bone. Et auxi si lez Justices de peas queux ount pris lenquerre ne fount certificat deins le mois apres lenquerre de ceo ewe, le certificat nest bone & cetera.

Item si lez Jurrourz par lenquerre troue lun partie en le Riott, vncore lez Justices poient certifier lautre partie en le Riott; quar la verite nest troue deuaunt & cetera.

(*Margin*) Nota cest cas.

Item si lez Jurrourz troueront ascunz hommez en le Riott & ils omittent certen persones que fueront partiez al Riott, lez Justices de peas poient certifier que ceux queux sount endites & autrez que fueront omys fieront le Riott, & en cest cas ne serra en le liberte de le Roie de arreigner eux [f. 94] que fueront endites sur lun ou sur lautre. Mes ceux que sount endites par enquest serra arreigne sur lenditement & le Certificat vers eux come voide. Mes lez autrez

---

[1] *For* Mes sil soit endite . . . & cetera *read* Mez nient sur Indytement de transgression, mez in accion de transgression ill ferra, F.

[2] *For* & ils ne iustifieront . . . plederont *read* il ne iustifiera . . . pledera, B.

[3] Quoted, *ut supra*.   [4] Should be omitted.

queux fueront omys surront [*sic*] arreigne sur le Certificat sinoun que lenditement expresse le nombre dez persons que fieront le Riott en generalte.

Item si lez Jurrourz troue que le riott fut fait oue xii personez lou en verite il fut fait oue C. personez, lez Justices poient faire Certificat accordaunt al verite & le Certificat serra pris & nemi lenditement. Mes si lenditement & le certificat dez Justices variount forsque solement en le iour de le fesaunce de le Riott, la lenditment serra pris & nemi le Certificat. Mes si lenditement soit de xii & le Certificat rehers le Riott destre fait oue xii hommez en hernes, la le certificat serra pris & nemi lenditement; quod nota.[1]

Et nota si les Justices de peas arreignont vne de le Riottourz deuaunt eux en le counte ils ne poient faire certificat apres cest arreignement.

Et les parols de lestatut sount oustre: Et si la verite ne poet estre troue doncque & cetera. Si deux Justices de la peas, vicount et southvicount alent de voier vne Riott, & vne dez Justices & le vicount fount vne certificat & lautre Justice de peas & le southvicount fount autre certificat, ambideux certificat sount voide. Mes si iiiior Justices de peas & le vicount & southvicount alent a cell entent, et puis ii de lez Justices de peas & le vicount mesme fount vne Certificat & lez autrez ii Justices & le southvicount fount autre Certificat, cest certificat a que le vicount mesme fut partie serra pris & nemi lautre ne serra en eleccion de le Roy en cest cas.[2] Mes si iiiior Justices de peas sount & le vicount & alent pur voier le Riott, & le vicount et ii de lez Justice fount certificatt & auxi le vicount & autrez ii Justices fount vne autre Certificat, ore cest certificat serra pris que est mielx beneficiall pur le Roie. Mes si iiiior Justices de peas sount & le vicount alent & cetera, et ii de lez Justices & le vicount fount vne Certificat en tile maner, scilicet, que vne A. riotose tua vne J. atte S.,[3] et lez ii autrez & le vicount certifia que un C. mesme le iour & an & lieu tua mesme le J. atte S. riotously, ore en cest cas le premer Certificat serra pris, pur ceo que ambideux de lez Certificattes ne poient estoier ensemble & cetera.

Item si ii Justices de peas & le vicount face vne enquerre del Riott et sur ceo il fount vne certificat & apres ils mesmez fount autre certi-

---

[1] *Add* si lenditement soyt que ilz riotous assauta J atte S, ilz poient certyfier que ils riotuus bate mayheme ou occist a mesme le iour & ill serra mys a responder sur ambideux, F.

[2] *Add* quar le south vicount nad null auctorite in le presens dell vicount, F.

[3] Stile, B, D.

ficat, en cest cas le primer certificat serra pris. Mes si le primer Certificat abate pur faute de mater ou fourme come il poet, doncque quell remedie et [1] serra fait de lautre ; quere de ceo.

Item si le vicount deuie apres lenquerre fait & ad executourz si lez executourz & lez Justices de peas voillent faire Certificat, ceo nest bone.

Item si lez Justicez & vicount veient le Riott & enquerre est fait, & puis vne dez Justices de peas queux veiount cest riott est mys hors de le commission, vne certificat apres fait par luy & par lautrez [2] nest bone. Mes autrement est sil ad recorde vne Riott sur le viewe & ils eschapent, il poet certifier cest recorde en Bancke le Roie apres que il est mys hors de le commission & cest certificat est bone & cetera.

Et que le certificat soit de tile force come le presentment de xii hommez [3] ; ceo serra entende de mitter le partie al reponz [f. 94 b] mes si le partie soit acquite sur cest certificat, vncore il ne vncques auera breue de conspiracion en cest cas. Mes sur le presentment de xii homez, sil soit acquyte il auera cest breue. Et nota auxi que cest certificat ne oustera le partie de son bataille gager si vne appelle soit port vers luy apres le Certificat fait ne que il enquerera dez abettourz. Mes si lappell fut commence sur vne enditement ewe deuaunt, le partie serra ouste de son bataille gager & ne enquerera dez abettourz & cetera.

Item cest Certificat doit estre certein & auer fourme, scilicet, conteignaunt le an, iour & lieu auxibien come vne enditement. Mes addicion ne serra requisite en cest Certificat ; quar null proses de vtlagaria git sur ceo, mes proses sur lestatut tantum & cetera.

Et [4] tielx trespassourz & cetera ; semble que cest clause de lestatut fait chescun home de le counsell le Roie destre Justice de recorde, scilicet, a delyuerer cest certificat en Bancke le Roie, & il couient en cest cas de auer vne Venire facias deuaunt le Capias soit agarde vers le partie sur cest certificat, nient obstante que lestatut ne parle forsque de Capias ; quar il dit sil ne veigne, doncques Capias issera.

Et nota que cest proses poet estre returne deuaunt le Counsell ou en Bancke le Roie. Mes si le councell agarde vne Sub pena ou Priue seale sur cest certificat, cest proses est hors de cas de cest estatut & le partie nest lie de apperer sur ceo pur cest cause & cetera.

---

[1] Perhaps for 'et cetera'; si, in B and D, is clearly wrong.
[2] *Omit* & par lautrez, B.　　　　　　　[3] Quoted, *ut supra*.
[4] *Add* si, B, C, D. The statute reads: 'Et si tielx trespassours & meffaisours traversent la matire ensy certifie . . . '.

Et lestatute dit oustre : que lez Justicez pluis prochuns ceo ferront.
Mes vncore nient obstante tilx parols, si ascun autrez dez iustices de
mesme le countie sount come lestatut rehers auaunt, ceo serra sufficient de excuser sount[1] que sount pluis procheins Justices demurrauntz
deins mesme le conte ou dehors de le conte a le lieu ou le Riott ceo
fut fist. Et auxi lez Justices de peas demurrauntz, prochun coment
que ils demurrent en autre conte, vncore il est deins le cas de lestatute.

Item si ii Justices prochun demurrauntes a le lieu veignount pur
veier le Riott & le vicount ne vient pas, en cest cas lez Justices serront
excusez de lour penaltes. Et issint serra le vicount sil vient & lez
autrez sount defaute, il serra excuse et le Justicez nemy & cetera.

Item si les Justices de peas enquirerount deins le mois & done iour
al jurre outre le mois de doner lour verdit, vncore ceo est sufficient
enquerre deins le mois.

Item sils chargeront vne Jurre & dona a eux iour de doner lour
verdit par vi semaignes apres, & le iour apres que ils sount Jurres vne
graunde Riott est fait & ils donent loure verdit a iour a eux done
apres & dit riens en loure verdit de cest Riott, vncore lez Justicez de
peas sount excuses ; semble le cause fut pur ceo que loure charge fur[2]
generall al commencement & cetera.

[Nona Lectura]   De ingressibus mainfortis[3] in terras & tene-
menta & de remiscione partis grauate in possessione[4]
eiusdem.[5]

(*Margin*) Vide lestatut anno viii⁰ H. VI^ti [6] & auxi lestatut fait
anno v⁰ Ricardi Ricardi[7] & anno xv⁰ meme le Roie Ricardi II^di.[8]

Al comen ley deuaunt le fesaunz dez ascunz dez ditz estatutes de
Forcible entre come appiert & cetera, chescun home puissoit entre
en terres ou tenementes & eux deteigne oue force sil auoit bone [f. 95]
title dentrer en ceux, auxibien come home poet prendre ou deteigner
son bienz & chateux a cest iour ; & lissue serra en accion de transgression port sur ceo si le defendaunt auoit title ou nient title, & si le title
fut troue pur le defendaunt le force fut excuse, & ceo proue le comen
accion de transgression a cest iour ; pur que vne estatut fut fait
anno v^to Ricardi II^di, capitulo,[9] & cest estatut en maner prohibite que

---

[1] ceux, B, C.   [2] fuit, C.   [3] manufortis, B.   [4] possessionem, B.
[5] *For* De . . . eiusdem *read* De ingressubus manufortis et de partibus
grauatis in possessionem remissis eiusdem, C.
[6] 8 Hen. VI, c. 9, 1429.
[7] Perhaps for secundi: see 5 Rich. II, st. 1, c. 7, 1381.
[8] 15 Rich. II, c. 2, 1391.
[9] *Add* v^to, D ; but should be c. 7, see note 7, *supra*.

ne list a ascun person dentre en ascunz terrez ou tenementz oue force
coment que son entre fut loiall, & cest estatut fait le force destre
materiall en accion foundue sur cell entre.

Mez vncore par cest estatut ne fut done ascun power al Justice de
peas de entromitter ouesque ascun tile sinoun par vne generall enquerre de ceo en loure cessions de peas & nient autrement; par que
vient lestatut de anno xv^{mo} Ricardi II^{di},[1] & ceo done que si ascunz
homez entreront en ascunz terrez ou tenementes & ceo oue force &
deteigne oue force apres son entre, que lez Justices ou vne de eux
deins mesme le conte veignount oue le power del conte & voisent le
lieu ou le forcible entre fut fait; & si mesmez lez Justices de peas
trouount ascun home teignaunt mesme le lieu oue Force, que adoncque
ils prenderont eux & eux de[2] committer al gaile come persons conuictez de lour Forcible entre par loure recorde, la a demurrer tancque
ils ount fait fyne par le discression de mesme lez Justices.

Mes cest estatut ne done ascun remedie enuers ceux que entreront
pesiblement & apres cest entre teignount oue force, ne done ascun
remedie si lez persons que fount lentre oue force sount remoues
deuaunt le venue dez Justices de peas, ne null payn par cest estatut
fut done al vicount sil ne voet entendur[3] sur lez Justices de peas
quaunt ils ou ascun de eux voillent enquerer de cest matter par lour
commaundement; par que cest estatut de anno viii^o H. VI^{ti}, capitulo ix^o,[4] fut fait que done autile remediez come appiert par le lettre
de mesme lestatut.

Lestatute est: Et voet desore en auaunt.[5] Cest braunche de mesme
le statut affirma lestatut de xv^o Ricardi II^{di}, & oustre ceo done remedie
de remouer del Force auxi bien lou celui que entre pesiblement &
apres deteigne oue force terres ou tenementes come lou lentre primerment fut fait oue force. Et auxi done que cest remouement de le
force serra toutz foitz a lez costes de le partie greue par son entre;
par que couient al Justices de peas de auer ceo ou[6] lour costez tenduz
a eux ou luy[7] deuaunt, ou autrement il nest tenus de aler oue luy de
remouer ceo force & cetera.

Item vne Justice de peas saunz vicount ou southvicount esteaunt oue
luy poet aler a tile lieu lou la force est fait & poet recorder cell entre
ou deteigne oue force sil voia ceo par cest estatut, et issint ne poet

---

[1] See p. 347, note 8, *supra*.   [2] *Omit*, B, D.
[3] entendaunt, B, C: attendre, D.   [4] See p. 347, note 6, *supra*.
[5] Cf. text of 8 Hen. VI, c. 9: Ajoustant a icelle que si desorenavaunt.
[6] en, B; perhaps the word should be s. for 'scilicet'.
[7] *For* ou luy *read* a, D.

vne Justice de peas Faire sur vne Riott fait ; quar la couient destre
ii Justice de peas, vicount ou southvicount al meins, de recorder ou
certifier tile riott. Et auxi par cest estatut le power de le countie serra
fait[1] al commaundement de lez Justices de peas & nemi del vicount,
mes en le cas de Riott le power serra fait[2] al commaundement de le
vicount & sic nota diuersitatem.

Item si les Justices de peas veignount al lieu lou le force est fait &
troua le huys clausez, & coment que soit forsque vne person en cest
meason si mesme le person ne voet suffre le Justice dentre, ceo est
vne deteigne oue force & le Justices poet committer ceux que sount
deins le huys a garde & cetera.

Item si les Justices troueront en le meason graund nombre de gentz
ou ascuns persones en harnes ou sils sount hors de harnes & loure
harnes gisount par eux deins le [f. 95 b] huys come bowes, arowes,
billes, espees, gonnes, ou stonys, ceo serra dit auxi vne deteigner oue
force.

Item si hommes en harnes soit en autre mansion place par petit
distaunce a lentent de bater celui que voet entre en autre lieu, ceo
serra dit auxibien deteiner oue force sibien come sils fueront en
mesme le meason en quell il voet entrer. Mes si cell meason que est
tenuz oue force soit in confinio comitatus & ils que voent defendre
lentre en cest meason sount en harnes en autre meason & en autre
conte adioynaunt, en cest cas lez Justicez de peas ne poient riens
faire a ceo deteigner oue force. Et issint est si le meason que est
tenuz oue force soit en ii contees, & ils remouent le force en cest partie
de le meason que est en lautre countie quaunt lez Justices vient, en
ceo cas lez Justice ne poient oue force.[3]

Item si homme clayme vne rent ou comen en ascun terre, & le terre
est deteigne oue force quaunt il voet vser son comen ou quaunt il voet
distrainer pur le rent, en cest cas lez Justicez de peas poient aler a le
terre hors de que & cetera & remouer le force que est la, et vncore le
partie ne vncques auera breue de Restitucion al possession come il
serra en cas de terres ou tenementz.

Item si vne mitte autre hors de son meason & mitta inz vne de son
seruauntes en pesible maner & tient le partie que il a mys hors de son
possession en prison, nient obstante tile emprisonement ceo ne serra
dit deteiner oue force, coment que il emprison lez parties que il ad mys

---

[1] prise, D.   [2] prise, D.
[3] *For* ne . . . force *read* & ne poiet auoide cest force, B ; ne poient
auoides cest force, D.

hors de possession en prison en mesme le lieu, ceo ne serra dit
deteigner oue force & cetera.

Et outre ceo coment que tilx persones & cetera : coment que tielx
parols de lestatut sount coment que tilx personez sount presentes ou
auoides deuaunt loure venue, ceo nest materiall a lenquerre coment
que lez Justices ne aleront de veier le terre & cetera.

Et auxi lez parols sount : Et mayntenaunt doient enquerer. Vncore
lez Justicez poient enquerer a ascun temps apres cel entre oue force
fait a lour plesure & cest enquerre est assetz bone.   Et auxi lestatut
done power a vne justice de le peas de mesme le conte solement denquerer de tile Forcible entres & deteigners oue Force.   Et cest
Braunche de lestatut done auxi power a mesmez lez Justices de luy
remitter en son possession. Mes il ne poet sur cest conuiccion
deuaunt luy del viewe del force mitter le partie en possession.   Mes il
deuoit faire enquerre de ceo deuaunt, et doncque sur cest enquerry le
Justice mesme poet eslier de mitter le partie en possession luy mesme
ou de faire vne precept al vicount de mitter le partie en possession de
le terre & cetera.

(*Margin*) Nota que vne Justice de peas apres lenquerre fait poet
mitter le partie en possession ou autrement nemi.

Et coment que lestatut parle solement de lez Justices de peas,
vncore si le presentement de tile Forcible entre ewe deuaunt lez
Justicez de peas soit remoue deuaunt lez Justices de Bancke le Roi,
en cest cas lez Justices de Bancke poient graunter breue de restitucion
par lequyte de mesme lestatut, mes eux mesmez ne poient mitter le
partie en possession.

Et issint est si celui Justice de peas que auoit enquerre de cest
Forcible entre est mort deuaunt que le partie est mys en possession,
lez autrez Justices de peas de mesme le conte poient graunter breue
de Restitucion, mez lez autrez Justices de peas ne poient mitter le
partie en possession eux mesmez sicome il puissoit que est mort sil
viueroit & cetera.

Item [1] si lenquest troue que ieo fue seisi tancque vne J. C.[2] entre
sur moy oue force, sur ceo [f. 96] verdit ieo ne auera vncque breue
de Restitucion ; quar il poet entrer en mon terre & nemi [3] outre moie
a cest temps.   Mes couient estre troue que un J. atte S.[4] entra & moy
ousta oue force & armis.   Quar si mon pier deuie seisi de terre & vne

---

[1] The scribe has written what may be initials just below Item.
[2] S. in MSS. B, D ; a S. in MS. C ; A. in MS. F.
[3] & nemi, *bis.*   [4] *Omit* J. atte, B.

estraunge entre en cest terre deuaunt que ieo entra, en cest cas si
lenquest troue le mater issint ieo ne auera vne breue de restitucion a
mon possession ; quar ieo nay ascun [1] possession en fait deuaunt mez
possession en ley & serra aiugge mon folie que ieo ne entra en fait
issint que ieo puisse estre ouste de cell possession. Mes si troue soit
par enquest que ieo fue seisi tancque par vne J. atte S. ouste & disseisi oue force, ou autrement que ieo fue seisi tancque par J. atte S.
pesiblement ouste, lequell J. atte S. ceo tient oue force, en cez ii cases
ieo auera breue de restitucion.

Item si lenquest troue que ieo fue seisi tancque par J. atte S. disseisi
& que ieo luy re-ousta oue force, le disseisour auera breue de restitucion & vncore il appiert que son possession est defete par mon entre
& outrement determine.

Item si lenquest troue que ieo fue seisi tancque par vne J. atte G.[2]
oue force disseisi & ouste, & auxi que mesme le J. atte G.[3] issint fut
seisi tancque par vne J. atte N.[4] oue force disseisi, en cest cas si J.
atte G.,[5] scilicet, le primer disseisour a moy sua oue [6] breue de restitucion destre restore al terre, ieo puisse apres cest prier mon breue de
restitucion par mesme le verdit vers luy. Mes si ieo sua mon breue
de restitucion primes, en cest cas mon disseisour ne vncque apres
auera breue de restitucion ; quar il ad perdue son auauntage & cetera.

Item si soit troue par enquest que ieo fue seisi tancque par force
ouste & disseisi par vne J. atte S., et auxi est troue par autre enquest
en mesme le cessions deuaunt mesmez lez Justices que ieo fue seisi de
mesme le terre tancque par vne J. atte Nok [7] ouste & disseisi oue force,
en cest cas ieo puisse eslier sur que de ceux verditz ieo voille suer
restitucion, & si ieo pria restitucion sur lun & ceo est returne que ieo
auoy possession, ieo nauera apres restitucion sur lautre verdit. Mes
si ieo soy mys en possession par le primer breue & le breue nient [8]
returne, coment que lautre [9] entra, ieo auera [10] autre breue de restitucion
enuers luy & luy oustera & cetera.[11]

Et si troue soit par enquest que ieo fue seisi tancque par J. atte S.[12]
oue force ouste & disseisi, et par autre enquest deuaunt mesmez lez
Justices est troue que J. atte S. fut seisi de mesme le terre tancque par

[1] vnques, C.   [2] S in MSS. B, C, D ; Stile, MS. F.
[3] S. in MSS. B, C, D, F.   [4] Watt N, F.   [5] *Ut supra*, note 3.
[6] *Omit*, C.   [7] J. atte N., B, C ; John at N, D.   [8] *Omit*, C.
[9] *Add* estraunge, D.   [10] nauera, D ; incorrectly, I think.
[11] *For* & si ieo pris restitucion . . . luy oustera & cetera *read* Et si jeo
pria sur lun & ceo retourne coment qe lestraunge entre, jeo auera breue de
restitucion & luy outer, F.
[12] J. A. usually in MS. F.

moy disseisi & ouste oue force, en [ceo] cas chescun de nous poiomus
prier breue de restitucion enuers autre & celui que est primes remyse
par cest breue est en le maius perille ; quar lautre poet auer breue de
restitucion apres & doncque est le primer que auoit sue restitucion
deuaunt saunz remedie mez de auer assise.

Item si soit troue que J. att S. fut seisi de terre pur terme de vie de
vne A. & que vne C. luy ousta & disseisit oue force, coment que A.
deuie deuaunt que J. att S. auoit sue restitucion, vncore il poet apres
auer son breue de restitucion sur son verdit a son perelle.   Et sil prist
restitucion en cest cas ou ascun autre cas fait lou son title nest bone
deuaunt, le partie que [f. 96 b] est ousta [sic] auera assise de nouell
disseisin nient obstante que il soit mys inz par lez Justices.

Item si troue soit par enquest que deux iointenaunt fueront seisiez
tancque oue force ouste & disseisiez par J. att S., en cest cas lun dez
iointenaunt poet auer breue de restitucion saunz lautre & saunz ascun
seueraunce.

Mes nota que si troue soit par enquest que mon pier fut seisi tancque
par vne autre oue force ouste & disseisi & mon pier deuie deuaunt
restitucion, en cest cas ieo que sue heir a luy ne auera breue de
Restitucion sur cest mater, ne auxi son [1] executourz lou il fut ouste de
vne chatell rialle en son vie oue force naueront restitucion.   Mes si le
lesse pur terme de ans soit ouste & soit troue, il auera breue de
Restitucion.

Et nota que si vne breue de Restitucion soit agarde al vicount de
mitter le partie en possession, & le vicount returne sur cest breue que
tile resistens est fait vers luy issint quil ne poet le breue seruer, en cest
cas le vicount serra amercie [2] pur cest returne ; quar il poet auer prendre
posse comitatus & aler icy & cetera.   Mes vncore en cest cas nouell
[breue] serra direct a lez Dukes, Erles & Barons de mesme le countie
de ceo faire & cetera.

Lestatute dit : Et si ascunz apres tile entres fait feffement ou discontinuance.   Cest discontinuance ne serra entende vne discontinuance
de autre droit mez solement le discontinuance de son torcious
possession que il ad come per feffement.   Mesme le ley est de done
en le taille ou les pur terme de vie ou Fyne ou recouery, come par
feffement lou le vse est expresse en le fait, en toutz ceux casez le
pleintiff auera auerement a dire que cest feffement, done ou fyne fut
fait as persones pur maintenaunce et issint maintener son breue coment
que lez feffez ne donees ne sount pas nosmes en le breue.

---

[1] *For* ne ... son *read* ne cez, C.   [2] MS. amercerie.

Et nota bene que est diuersite entre le pleder & auerer vne destre pernour del profittez & cest cas pleder de maintenaunce.   Come si ieo sue disseisi & le disseisour fait feffement as dyuers persones a moy disconuz en Fee.   Et puis ieo port assise enuers luy & il plede noun tenure par reson que il ad fait tile feffement deuaunt, en cest cas ieo que sue pleintiff puisse eslier de auerer luy generalment destre tenaunt & monstra le mater en evidence al Jurre, ou monstrer le speciall mater & de auerer luy destre pernour de lez profittez.

Et nota lou le pleintiff monstra le especiall mater, scilicet, que il ad enfeffe certen persons pur maintenaunce, en cest cas le defendant couient de respondre al feffement ou al maintenaunce.   Mes lou le pleintiff en assise ou en breue dentre sur disseisin en son Replicacion auerra le tenaunt destre pernour de lez profittez, en cest cas le tenaunt poet trauerser que il nest pernour de lez profittez.[1]   Mes en ambideux cases le tenaunt poet trauerser le disseisin.

[f. 97] Item si cestuy que entre en ascun terre oue force fait feffement as autrez graundes personez pur maintenaunce & apres il reprist astate a luy & a vne autre, en ceo cas si assise soit port enuers le disseisour tantum, [et] il voet plede iointenauncie, le pleintiff de necessite serra mys de monstrer tout le especiall mater & sur ceo il serra aide nient obstante le re-feffement.[2]

Item si assise soit port vers celui que ad entre oue force & son feffe que fut enfeffe pur maintenaunce, et chescun de eux pledount vne barre enuers le pleintiff, en ceo cas le pleintiff ne poet eslier celui que entra sur luy oue force pur son tenaunt saunz monstrer de lespeciall mater, scilicet, le feffement fait pur maintenaunce & issint il poet eslier destre son tenaunt.

Mez si deux homez entrent oue force en ascun terres & cetera & apres fount feffement as autrez pur maintenaunce, & le feffe enfeffe vne de eux areremayn que entre oue force & vne estraunge oue luy, si assise soit port enuers eux deux, & ils pledont iointenauncie que fut disseisi deuaunt & lautre plede vne barre,[3] ore en cest cas le pleintiff poet demurrer sur ambideux lour plees, mes il couient de monstrer le speciall mater en ceo cas.

Item si assise soit port vers le feffe que est fait pur maintenaunce & enuers celui que entra oue force & disseisi le pleintiff, & le feffe vouche

<hr>

[1] *Add* & ne puit trauerser le feffement, F.
[2] *Add* pur mayntenauncye, C.
[3] *For* & ils pledont ... barre *read* & lun plede joyntenauncye & lautre plede un barre, F.

celui que entre oue force par vertue de mesme le feffement que est prist
en le court & entra en le garrantie & plede vne barre, en ceo cas le
pleintiff nauera trauers a cest feffement pur auoider luy de le voucher,
come a dire que cest feffement fut fait pur maintenaunce & cetera.

Item si home entra oue force en terre & cetera al vse de vne
estraunge, & lestraunge fait feffement oustre pur maintenaunce, ceo est
auxi bien deins le cas de lestatut come si le disseisour auoit entre oue
force a son vse demene & ent fait feffement pur maintenaunce as autrez.
Mes si ii homes entre oue force et puis lun reles tout son droit en le
terre a son compaignon pur maintenaunce, ceo est hors de cas de
lestatut.

Lez parols de lestatut sount : Cest feffement serra voide auxi bien si
soit plede en barre come autrement. Doncque ieo pose que si vne
moy disseisi & puis enfeffe mon pier[1] de cest terre a que ieo sue heir
apparaunt & mon pier luy refeffe oue garrantie & deuiast, si ieo port
assise [vers][2] le disseisour & il plede le feffement mon pier oue garrantie
enuers moy en barre, ieo ne vncque auoidera cest garrantie par maintenaunce ; quar ceo est vne covenaunt reall que est hors de cas de
feffement & cetera.

Item si celui que est pier a ma feme est tenaunt en taille & il fait
vne discontinuaunce en son vie, & ieo entra sur le discontinue en le vie
le pier a ma feme oue force & ent enfeffa le pier ma feme, & il deuie
& le discontinue port assise vers moy, et ieo plede en barre que ieo nay
riens en le terre forsque en le droit de ma feme, en cest cas le pleintiff
poet monstrer le feffement que fut fait par luy[3] al pier apres le disseisin
oue force pur maintenaunce, & auoider ceo plee par cest especiall mater.[4]

Et auxi quaunt tilx Justice ou Justices facent tile enquerre & cetera ;
par cest clause de lestatut est done que chescun Jurrour que serra
iurre en ascun tile maner de inquire auera xl s. de terre, & serra retourne
en issues al primer iour sil fist defaute xx s̨., et a le ii[de] iour xl s., & al
tierce iour sil fist defaute C s., & done oustre quell punysshement le
vicount auera pur son misdemener en cell partie.

Item si lez presentourz ne auoient xl s. de terre par an, vncore le
presentement est bone, mez sur cell [f. 97 b] presentement le partie ne
auera restitucion par cest enquerrer et le partie auera auauntage de
monstrer ceo al temps de le restitucion praie[5] & cetera ; quar il ne

---

¹ *Add* pur mayntenaunce, D, F.   ² vers, B.   ³ Should be 'moy'.
⁴ *For* en cest cas . . . mater *read* le pleintiff ne auoydera ceo pur
monstrer le feffement pur mayntenaunce a son pere, F.
⁵ prie, B, D.

poet auer auauntage de ceo deuaunt le prier de restitucion.   Mes si le vicount retorne ascunz dez auauntditz Jurrourz issint en panell en pluis petit isseiez[1] que est compris deins lestatut, vncore le partie nauera auauntage de ceo.   Mes le vicount en cest cas serra punysshe accordant a lestatut.

Et oustre ceo si ascun person[2] ouste ou disseisi oue force ; cell braunche de lestatut done le partie accion par assise de nouell disseisin ou par breue de transgression sil soit ouste oue force ou sil soit ouste pesiblement & apres ceo tenus oue force, & ceo est troue pur le pleintiff en mesme laccions que le pleintiff recouera en cest cas son damages a treble & cetera.

Mes si tile force soit troue par vne enquest en vne generall accion de transgression le pleintiff ne auera treble damages, mes sil voet[3] auauntage de lestatut il couient de porter son accion de transgression sur lestatute & cetera.   Mes si le partie greue port assise & recouera & le disseisin est troue oue force, en cest cas il recouera treble damages. Mes autrement est en vne breue dentre sur disseisin en nature de assise,[4] coment que le disseisin soit troue oue force, le pleintiff ne recouera iii[ble] damages en ceo cas.   Mes si accion de transgression soit porte enuers vne sur lestatut & lez xii homez troueront pur le defendaunt, vncore sil port[5] breue de atteint & reuerse le primer iugement, en cest cas il recouera iii[ble] damages en cest breue de atteint ; quod nota.

Cest braunche de lestatut est tout en le disiunctiff, scilicet, sil soit ouste oue force ou ouste pesiblement & apres tenuz oue force. Vncore nient obstante cez parols si home soit ouste oue force & apres mesme le terre est tenuz oue force, vncore le partie greue auera vne ioint accion sur ambideux sur cest estatut & auera auauntage dez ambideux forcez, scilicet, lentre oue force & le teignaunce oue force.

Mes autre est sil voet vser accion sur lestatut de Ricardo[6] anno v[to][7] que done que home ne doit entre en ascun terres ou tenementz mez lou son entre fut loiall, & in illo casu non manuforti nec multitudine gentium ; quar en cest cas lun serra contrarie a lautre.   Et en cest accion sur lun couient le breue destre Quare vi & armis & lautre nemi.

Item si home soit disseisi de ascun rente par le tenaunt de le terre come par rescous oue force fait par le tenaunt & ceo est troue en

---

assise, vncore le tenaunt en cest cas ne rendra iii^{ble} damages al pleintiff. Mes en cest cas si assise soit port de tile rent vers vne come pernour de le rent & troue est par le assise que il disseisit le pleintiff oue force & cetera, en cest cas le partie[1] rendra treble damages; quere diuersitatem.

Prurveie[2] toutz foitz que ceux que gardent loure possession oue force & cetera; cest braunche de lestatut va en abriggement del comen leie & ne voet seruer enuers le Roie sinoun que soit troue par le primer Jurre & couient estre done a eux en evidens. Mes si home soit endite sur cest Forcible entre, en cest cas lendite ne[3] apres lenditement par voie de Justificacion.

Mes si le partie sue breue de transgression [f. 98] sur cest estatut
[*Nota.*] il auera auauntage de ceo & pledera ceo assetz bien pur le force & monstra ceo en euidence, sil ad continue possession en mesme le terre par iii ans. Mes si vne entre fut fait sur luy ou son auncestor ou sur ceux que astate il auoit deins cez trois ans, coment que ils re-entrent deins vne iour coment que il & sez auncestors ount continue par mesme le title, vncore ceo nest bone cause de iustifier le deteigner oue force.[4] Et issint si le feffour eit pesible possession par vne an & apres le feffe continue son possession par ii ans prochein apres, ceo est bone cause de iustificacion & cetera.

Item issint est si home recouere vers autre par covyn en Precipe quod reddat & celui enuers que il recouera auoit possession pur iii ans, en ceo cas celui que recouere poet iustifier le deteigner oue force & vncore il ne auoit continue possession par le title de cest recouere par iii ans.

Item il couient que cest auerment de continuaunce de possession soit entendue de continuaunce de possession en mesme le terre par iii ans apres le title accrue al pleintiff que voet entrer. Come si home lessa terre pur terme de autre vie & le lesse auoit possession de le terre en le vie celui que vie pur xx ans, vncore si celui que vie morust & le lessour voet entre come en son reuersion deins iii ans apres le mort de celui que vie, en cest cas si le lesse voet deteigner oue force il serra punye accordaunt al estatut, & vncore le tenaunt auoit possession deuaunt par xx ans mes nemi par le temps de iii ans apres le title le

---

[1] pernour, C.

[2] purveu, text of statute and B; purvue, C; purueu, D.

[3] *For* ne *read* nauera, F.

[4] *Add* mez vncore si le possession eit este contine en son pere par ii anz en son vie et puis contine en luy par le temps dun an, cest bone cause de Justifier le deteyner oue force, B, C, and D (slight differences in spelling).

lessour a luy accrue apres le mort de celui que vie, & ceo est le cause que il serra punye.

Mes si le possession soit continue en le tenaunt[1] par iii ans apres title accrue a vne home dentre en mesme le terre & il deuie que auoit title dentre, vncore en ceo cas le tenaunt poet deteigner oue force mesme le terre encontre toutz que claymount inz apres[2] luy par mesme le title; come en cas si home disseisist mon pier de vne acre de terre & est en possession pur iii ans en le vie de mon pier & mon pier deuie, en cest cas si ieo que sue heire a mon pier voillet entre sur le dissisour, il poet deteigner enuers moy oue force & vncore le title en cest terre ne accrue a moy mez apres le mort mon pier. Mes pur ceo que ieo afferme mesme le title de mon pier & null autre title entaunt que il puissoit deteigner encountre mon pier par force, par mesme le reson poet il deteigner enuers moy par force; quod nota.

Item si vne[3] moy disseisist & apres continua son possession enuers moy pur iii ans, coment en ceo cas que ieo face continuell claym sur mesme le terre duraunt ceux trois ans, vncore nient obstante cest claym fait par moy si ieo voille entre apres lez iii ans, il poet deteigner vers moy oue force.

Item si vne disseisour ad continue son possession en ascun terre que il auoit par disseisin pur iii ans, & puis le disseisi port assise ou breue dentre sur disseisin vers luy de mesme le terre & recouere vers le dis-seisour, si le disseisi voile entre en mesme le terre par force de celle recouere saunz proses, vncore le disseisour poet deteigner oue force. Mes sil que recouera sua vne Habere facias seisinam, doncques il ne poet deteigner oue force; ou si vne breue de Restitucion vient al vicount & le vicount voet mitter le partie en possession par force de ceo, il ne poet deteigner oue force.

Item si vne disseisist moy & vne autre luy disseisist, & le primer disseisour tient par vne an & le ii[de] disseisour continua possession apres pur ii ans, en ceo cas si ieo voille entre [f. 98 b] sur le ii[de] disseisour, il poet deteigner oue force. Et mesme le ley est si mon disseisour fait vne les de le terre que il moy disseisist a vne pur terme de vie le remeindre oustre en fee, si le tenaunt pur terme de vie tient le terre par ii ans & deuie & puis celui en le remeindre tient par vne an, en ceo cas si ieo voille entrer sur celui en le remeindre, il poet deteigner le terre enuers moy oue force, & vncore il ne auoit possession en mesme le terre forsque par vne an. Mes le possession de le primer disseisour serra dit son possession enuers moy & cetera.

---

[1] terre, B, D.   [2] enuers, B.   [3] *Add* home, B, C, D.

Item si vne que est tenaunt pur terme de autre vie en vne Quid Juris clamat port enuers luy clayma Fee simple & puis continua son possession vne an apres, et puis celui que vie deuie & il continua son possession apres le mort de celui que vie pur ii ans, en cest cas si celui que fut pleintiff en [Quid][1] Juris clamat voet entrer sur le tenaunt, vncore il poet deteigner oue force & vncore il nauoit le possession par iii ans apres le title a luy accrue; quar son title a luy accrue par ii ans deuaunt, scilicet, de le temps de mort de tenaunt pur terme de autre vie. Et en mesme le maner est si le tenaunt disclayme en vne Precipe quod reddat lou il ad bone astate, & puis apres cest disclaymer il continua son possession par iii ans, en cest cas si le pleintiff voet entre sur le tenaunt par reson de le disclaymer ewe deuaunt, vncore le tenaunt poet luy deteigner oue force & cetera; quod nota bene.

[Decima Lectura]   De modo tenendi Cessiones pacis.

Lestatut de Westminster primer est : Et mayntenue en toutz pointes.[2] En cestz parols de lestatut est compris lauctorite que Justices de peas ount de enquerer & dez queux pointes ils poient enquerer; & ceux pointz apperount par le ii[de] clause de le Commission de lez Justices de peas lou est dit : Assignauimus vos Justiciarios nostros etc. ad inquirendum & cetera.[3] Par que primes est a voier coment lez Sessions serront tenuz;[4] le ii[de] de queux chosez sount destre enquirez par force de le commission;[5] le iii[cie] coment lez presentementz serront faitz;[6] le iiii[te] point quell proses ils ferront sur ceux presentementz.[7] Et toutz cez pointz apperount par expresse parols en le ii[de] clause de le commission auauntdit & cetera.

Et quaunt al primer poynt, lestatut de anno xxxvi⁰ E. 3, capitulo xii⁰ [8] done que en chescun commission de le peas serra mencion fait que lez Cessions serront tenuz iiii foitz par an, scilicet, vne foitz deins le vtas de Epiphany; le ii[de] foitz deins le ii[de] semaigne quaresme; le tierce entre le festes de Petencoste [9] & Seint John Baptiste; le iiii[te] deins le vtas de Seint Michell.

Et puis apres par vne estatut fait anno xii⁰ Ricardi II[di] [10] est done que lez Justices de peas teignerount loure cessions chescun quarter del an sur peyn destre punyssh par avise de le councell le Roie; en quell estatut sount exceptez lez Justice & lez seriauntez de la ley.

---

[1] *Quid*, B, D.   [2] *Supra*, p. 289.   [3] p. 321, *supra*.
[4] In the present lecture.   [5] Vndecima et duodecima Lecturae, *infra*.
[6] Terciadecima Lectura, *infra*.   [7] Quartadecima Lectura, *infra*.
[8] 36 Edw. III, st. 1, c. 12, 1362.   [9] Pentecost, B, C, D.
[10] 12 Rich. II, c. 10, 1388.

Et puis apres par vne autre estatut fait anno ii^do H. V^ti, capitulo iiii^to,[1] [est][2] done que ils tiendrount lour Cessions iiii foitz par an, scilicet, le primer semaigne apres Seint Michell, le primer semaigne apres'le Translacion de Seint Thomas, le primer semaigne apres le Epiphany,[3] le primer semaigne apres le clause de Pake;[4] except lez Justices de lun bancke & de lautre, le chieff Baron, lez seriauntes & lattourney [f. 99] le Roie entendaunt lez courtes le Roie, & accordaunt a cest estatute sount toutz cessions tenuz a cest iour. Mez par lestatut fait apres anno xiiii° H. VI^ti, capitulo[5] est done que en le counte de Midd', lez Justicez ne tiendront Cessions forsque ii foitz par an & pluis cy mystre[6] soit pur riottes ou forcible entres.[7]

Et nota que par lestatut de anno xii° Ricardi secundi auauntdit[8] est done que chescun Justice de peas prendra pur luy mesme pur son costes iiii s. pur chescun iour del cessions & ii s. pur loure clerkes, destre levies dez Fynes & amerciementes de mesme le Cessions par le main del vicount, et que lez seignurs dez fraunchise serrount contributories a lez gages de les Justices auauntditz soloncque le affermaunce & quantite de loure parte de lez fynez.

Et puis apres par lestatute de anno xiiii° le Roie Ricardi le II^de, capitulo,[9] est done que lez estretes dez Cessions serra double, & que lun parte remayne oue le vicount & lautre parte oue lez Justices de peas, & lez nomez de lez Justices de peas oue lez iourz en queux ils ount tenus lour Cessions serront escries en endenture al entent que le vicount conustra as queux Justicez il deuoit paier que scieront[10] a mesme lez cessions & as queux nemi.

Et puis par mesme lestatut est ordeigne oustre que Dukes, Countees, Barons, ne Banerettes ne prendront ascun gages pur le temps de le Cessions & cetera.

Item lez primers estatutes faitz de Justice de peas voet que ne serra forsque viii Justices de peas en vne conte outre lez seignurs & cetera.[11] Et si a cest iour le Chaunceler voet mittre plusourz Justices en lez

---

[1] 2 Hen. V, st. 1, c. 4, 1414.   [2] est, B.
[3] The second and third dates are given in wrong order in A and B, but are corrected in A.
[4] Page, B, C, D.   [5] 14 Hen. VI, c. 4, 1435.
[6] moister, B; mittre, C; meister, D.
[7] *Add* & ceo pur lour eace pur ceo que ilz inquirent deuaunt Justice de Bank & sont faytz vener la pur inquirer etc., F.
[8] By c. 10.   [9] 14 Rich. II, c. 11, 1390.
[10] MS. scieꝑ; seeront, C; seer, D.
[11] According to 14 Rich. II, c. 11, but 12 Rich. II, c. 10 had said six, not eight.

·commissions que viii, & ils sceerount[1] en lez cessions &[2] force de cell commission, vncore toutz lez Justice de peas en cest cas nauerount gagez pur le temps de le Cessions mez solement viii de eux, & ceux serront lymytt par le discression de lez barons del escheker quaunt le vicount face son accounpt queux viii serront allowe & cetera. Mes quere si le vicount voilleit de son propre test[3] assigne lez viii Justices que prendront gagez & paiera eux, si serra allowe de ceo ou noun & semble que noun.

Ceux gages couient destre leuiez dez Fynes & amerciementes de le cessions & cetera ;[4] mes si vne home forfeit al Roie vne recognisaunce de peas purceo que ils ne teignount son iour quell est done par lez Justicez de peas destre al prochun cessions, ou pur ceo que le recognisour ad enfreint le peas, cest forfeit ne serra liable a lez gages de lez Justicez de peas. Et issint est si le vicount retourne issues sur vne distres enuers lez Jurrourz destre deuaunt mesme lez Justices apres venire facias, scilicet,[5] issues ne serra liable a lez gages de lez Justices. Mes si le enquest de le primer enquerre ne veignount al cessions issint que lez cessions remanent en loure defaute & null enquire pris, ils serront amercies & mesmez lez amerciementes alerount al gages dez Justices nient obstante que null enquerre fut fait deins mesme le cessions & cetera.

Item ceux gages couient auxi destre leuies dez Fynes & amercie- mentes de mesme le cessions & nemi de autre cessions deuaunt ne apres ; quar le vicount ne poet prendre lez gages dez Justices de Fynes & amerciementes de vne autre cessions & paier pur le seer dez autrez Justices apres. Mes si le cessions sount adiournes, scilicet, de lun iour tancque a vne autre iour, doncque le vicount poet paier lez Justices de peas que sceerount[6] en ambideux lez cessions de lez fynes & amerciementes que fueront forfaitz en mesme le cessions; quar ambideux iourz fount forsque vne cessions.

[f. 99 b] Item si homme soit endite a vne cessions & al prochun cessions il fait son fyne, cest fyne serra liable a lez gages de mesme lez Justices queux cesserount le fyne & nemi a lez gages de mesme lez Justices deuaunt queux lenditement fut pris & cetera.

Item si home que est endite mitte inz plegges pur son fyne a vne cessions & lez fyne est assetz par lez Justices & il ne paia pas le fyne,

[1] seeront, C.   [2] par, B, C, D.   [3] tete, C.
[4] Cf. 12 Rich. II, c. 10, and 14 Rich. II, c. 11 ; I do not find the exact phraseology, but Marowe is quoting from the first, see p. 361, note 4, *infra*.
[5] MS. s., perhaps better ' sez '.   [6] seeront, B, C ; seer, D.

par que a autre cessions apres le proses est fait enuers lez plegges &
ils paiount cest fyne, en ceo cas cest fyne serra loiable[1] a lez gages de
ceux Justices queux cesserount le fyne & nemi a ceux Justices deuaunt
queux le fyne fut paie.

Et mesme le ley est si lez Justices de peas en vne cessions amercie
vne officer pur son noun apparaunce & il paia le amerciement a autre
cessions, vncore lez Justices que luy amercient aueround son gages de
son levie[2] & nemi ceux deuaunt queux il paia son amerciement. Mes
autre est lou les Justices de le primer cessions recordount le defaute de
ascun officer & rien fount oustre de le amerciement tancque al prochun
cessions, et doncque lez Justices queux seeround al prochun cessions
luy amersient pur son defaute, cest amerciement alera a lez gages de
ceux Justices que assesserount le amerciement & nemi a ceux queux
recordount le defaute & cetera.[3]

Item si les Cessions sount tenus par ii iourz & par diuers Justice de
peas, scilicet, par ii vne iour & par autre ii le ii^de ioure, en ceo cas si
lez fynes & amerciementes de tout mesme le cessions ne voillount ex-
tender de paier ambideux lez Justices forsque pur vne iour, vncore ceo
serra deuyde entre eux & sils ne extend a taunt, scilicet, pur une iour,
doncque le vicount eux paiera soloncque le quantite & porcions dez
auauntdites amerciementes & fynes, et issint coment que lez fynes ne
amountount a iiii s. par iour. Et vncore lestatut est que lez Justices
aueround iiii s. par iour dez fynes & amerciementes,[4] par que sils ne
amount a taunt come lestatut parle doncque ils nauerount riens. Mes
en ceo cas le mielx ne[5] serra pris pur le Roie ; quar ils sount en son
seruice & cetera.

Et nota que lez Justices de peas aueround accion de dett enuers le
vicount pur loure gages de cessions nient paiez a eux, coment que lez
fynes soient insufficiauntes[6] & cetera ; ou sils soient nient sufficiauntz a
iiii s. par iour, doncque accion de dette pur le porcion dez fynes & amerciementes coment que ils soient allowe al vicount en lescheker ou nient
allowe.[7]

Item si apres le cessions & deuaunt le alowance[8] en lescheker, le

---

[1] liable, B, C ; liablez, D.   [2] cest leue, B.
[3] *Add* si lez justicez veignount de tener Cessions & null dell County
apparust par que ilz eux amercient, ceo alera a lour gagez & in ceo case
null Cessions furent tenuz, F.
[4] Clearly 12 Rich. II, c. 10.   [5] *Omit*, C.   [6] sufficiauntes, B, C, D.
[7] *Add* sinoun que soyt in le case auauntdit lou sont plusors Justices que
viii, quar la le vicount se sauera etc., F.
[8] all viscount, B ; all vicount, D.

Roie graunta a vne que il auera cell dett le quell le Roie est endett
a luy destre leuye de mesme lez fynes & amerciementes de vne tile
cessions, et vne deliberat[1] est delyuer al vicount deuaunt lez estretes de
mesme le cessions a luy delyuer par endenture par lez Justices de
peas, en ceo cas nient obstante le deliberat delyuer al vicount pur
paier, vncore lez gages de lez Justices de peas serrount paies & nemi
le dett le Roie par le Deliberat & cetera.

Et lestatute voet oustre : que lez seignurz de fraunchisez serront
contributories & cetera.   Et ceo serra entendue que si ascun seignur
de fraunchise ad lez fynes & amerciementes de toutz son tenauntz &
enhabitauntes deins tile vile, en cest cas le rate del seignur serra ratifie
soloncque le porcion dez fynes, & le vicount reteignera taunt de lez
fynes & amerciementes quaunt le seignur demanda lez fynes sur le
allowaunce de le vicount en lescheker.   Mes si le seignur ad lez fynes
de graunt le Roie destre leuies par son officerz demene, doncque lez
Justice aueront lor gages vers le seignur par accion de dette.   Et si
[f. 100] le graunte le Roie soit destre[2] fait a ascun seignur destre
leuyes par le vicount a son vse, doncque gist laccion de dett vers le
vicount en cest cas coment que il soit allowe ou nemi.[3]

De custodicione sessionis pacis & de Gaole deliberacione in quolibet comitatu & quociens per annum & quomodo fiant.[4]

In primis est avoier coment lez Justices de peas doient garner lez
cessions & en quell fourme.   Et serra fait en tile fourme, scilicet, al
primes deuaunt lez cessions serront prisez, lez Justices de peas ou ii de
eux al meins couient de faire vne precept al vicount de mesme le
counte de sommoner le paiis, videlicet, xxiiii^{or} probos & legales
homines de chescun hundred ou wapentage deins mesme le counte ; &
par mesme le precept de commander toutz Constables, Bailles et autrez
officerz le Roie come de coroner ou autrez, de faire lour attendaunce
sur mesmez lez Justices a tile lieu & iour al cessions & la de presenter
toutz tielx choses queux chescun officer ad fait puis le darrein Cessions
par reson de lour offices.

Mes vncore si tilx Justice de peas teignount ascun cessions saunz
faire ascun tile precept, toutz presentmentes ewe deuaunt eux en

---

[1] deliberate, D.   [2] *Omit*, B, C.
[3] The section within brackets (pp. 365–6, *infra*) follows here in B, C, D, I,
and K, but is distinctly out of place ; cf. F, G, and L, p. 365, note 1, *infra*.
[4] Perhaps this should be a separate lecture, in spite of the numbering.
If the last portion of Lect. XV is added to it, it would be about the right
length ; see p. 368, note 1, and p. 411, note 1, *infra*.

mesme le cessions par verdit de xii hommez, officers ou huiusmodi, sount assetz sufficiant.   Mes ils ne poient en ceo cas amercier en ceo cas[1] lez Inquisitourz ne lez autrez officers queux ne apparent deuaunt eux la, sinoun que tile precept vst este fait deuaunt & cetera.

Et nota que tile precept que serra direct al vicount de sommoner lez cessions en fourme auauntdit come[2] de auer Teste south lez nomez de ii Justices de peas al meins & nemi south lez nomez de Custos Rotulorum tantum & cetera.

Item si les officers sur tile precept fait fount defaute come Bailly, vicount ou Coroner & huiusmodi, ils serront amerciez par mesme lez Justices.[3]   Et vncore le coroner ne poet retorner cest Inquisicion deuaunt eux[4] en lour cessions, mes il couient al coroner destre la pur ceo que il est partie a lour exigentz al iour del exigent retorne & cetera. Mes si ascun autre person voille demander le Coroner pur le Roie, vncore lez Justices ne poient prendre sur ceo approwment pur le Roie coment que il fist defaute sur tile demande & cetera.

Item si le Clerke de peas fist defaute al cessions, vncore il ne serra [*Nota.*] pur ceo amercie, quar il nest officer de le court, mez solement il est le clerke de le Custos Rotulorum,[5] & pur ceo il poet assigner vne autre de ce faire a cest temps que excusera lautre & cetera.

Item si ascun dez Justices de peas de mesme le conte fist defaute a tile cessions, lez autrez Justices ne poient luy amercier.   Mes si vne dez Justices de peas fist defaute al Gaole delyuerer, en cest cas lez Justices de Gaole delyuerer luy poient amercier.

Item si lordinarie ou son depute face defaute al cessions, il ne serra amercie ne son temporaltes seisi pur cest cause, quar il nest tenus defaire attendaunce la coment que soit generall cessions ou speciall & cetera.

Item si[6] ii Justices de peas poient tener cessions & faire enquires, prendre baillez & recorder apparaunce coment que null de eux soit de le Quorum, mes ils ne poient arreigner vne home de Felony ne de transgression ne lesser home all baille que est enprison pur suspeccion de felonye ne tielx semblez, sinoun que vne de eux soit de le Quorum.

Item si vne Justice de peas tient lez cessions [f. 100 b] par luy mesme tantum, mez il fist le stile de le cessions en le nome de deux & prist presentmentz deuaunt luy, en cest cas celui que est issint endite deuaunt luy poet dire que ne fueront a mesme le cessions forsque vne

---

[1] *Omit* en ceo cas, C.   [2] couient, B, C.
[3] Queried in F for sheriff and coroner.
[4] *Add* mez deuaunt Justice dassize, F.
[5] *For* de le Custos Rotulorum *read* dez Justice de peace que est Custos rotulorum, F.   [6] *Omit*, B, C. D.

Justice de peas & issint voide lenditement. Mes si le stile de le cessions soit fait en le nome de iii Justicez il ne dirra que vne de eux ne fut la; quar sil fut fait deuaunt deux, ceo est sufficiant.

Item si lez cessions par le precept sount appoyntes destre en vne ·vile & puis apres lez Justices tient lez cessions en autre ville, toutz lez presentementz deuaunt eux en lautre vile sount assetz bone, mes en ceo cas lez Justicez ne amercierent ascun person que fist defaute la pur son noun attendaunce.

Item si deux Justicez de peas fount vne precept al vicount pur sommoner le paiis & que ils voillent tener lez cessions en vne vile, & autrez ii Justices fount autre precept de tener cessions en autre vile mesme le iour, et ambideux iusticez seont en lez ambideux villes & prenent presentmentz, ambideux presentmentz ewe deuaunt eux sount bonz.

Et mesme le leie si lez cessions sount garny destre tenuz en vne vile a certen iour, & ii de lez Justicez voilount seer en lun part de le vile & autrez ii en autre part del vile, en cest cas lez presentmentz ewe deuaunt chescun de eux sount bonz pur lauauntage le Roie. Mes en le cas auauntdit si entre chescun de lez ii Justices lun de eux eit[1] Justice de le Quorum, & vne felon est arreigne en primez deuaunt ii dez Justices & puis mesme le iour il est arreigne deuaunt lez autrez ii Justicez que seer en lautre part de le vile, & le felon est acquyte deuaunt lun dez Justicez & deuaunt lautre ii Justicez il est troue coulpable, en cest cas le primer verdit ne prendra effect. Mes cest verdit doit prendre effect que est deuaunt eux Justicez que primez luy arreignent; quod nota.

Item si deux Justicez de peas sount, & vne home que ad mesme le nome que lun dez Justicez auoit sea par force de le commission, en cest cas toutz presentmentes ewe deuaunt luy sount voidez, et vncore lautre que est Justice en fait poet seer par force de mesme le commission apres saunz nouell commission & cetera.

Et doncques sur cest precept le vicount doit retorner son panell et auxi vne panell de corpore comitatus mes il ne couient de returner vne panell en chescun hundred, mez lez Jurrourz de diuers hundredes serra iurrez ensemblez lun ouecque autre; et lez Justicez de peas en ceo cas par lestatut de anno ximo H. VIImi in fine de attein:[2] done poiar as Justicez de peas[3] de chescun conte de adder & mynyssher lez

---

[1] est, B ; sont, C.　　　　[2] 11 Hen. VII, c. 24, s. vi, 1495.
[3] Clearly the first Justicez de peas should be omitted and 'est' inserted before 'done'.

nomez dez Jurrourz retorne deuaunt eux en lour cessions, et que ils poient causer le vicount ou son depute demitter autrez en le panell en le lieu de eux queux lez Justices ount retrete & mynyssh hors de mesme le panell. Mes en cest cas lez Justicez de peas ne poient ceo faire eux mesmez. Et si lez Justices en cest cas commaunde le vicount de chaunger lentier panell que il auoit returne deuaunt eux, le vicount couient de ceo faire par loure commaundement, & sil ne voet, lez Justicez poient assesser vne fyne sur luy. Mez cest addicion ou mynyssheng dez iurrourz ne poet estre fait par vne ou ii Justicez de peas saunz lassent de toutz loure compaignons esteant Justices de peas & seant en mesme le cessions, & issint ils couient toutz en cest cas accorder ou autrement est voide.

Item si lez Jurrourz que sount returne par le vicount ne voillount apparer al cessions, vncore lez Justices de peas poient faire enquerrer par circumstaunces & cest enquire est bone.

MS. Ee. 5. 20, f. 28.[1] [Item il couient ceux persons qui doient enquirer en tielx cessionz soient jurries ou autrement linquire est voide ; mez en ceo case si le record face mencion qui lez jurriourz fuerent jurriez, coment que ilz ne fuerent issint en fait, vncore cest enditement est assetz bone & cetera.

Item le nomber dez jurriourz qui doiet faire presentmentes en ascun case couient estre xii jurriourz all meynz. Mez lez justices de peas poient charger xv ou xviii personz en vn enquest pour enquirer & discharger ascun deux a lour pleasure apres. Mez lez justices de peas ne poient eux garder apres que ilz sount charges saunz manger & voier,[2] tanque ilz ont done lour verdit come lez justices de Banke poient quaunt lez jurriourz sount chargez entre partie & partie ; ne lez justices de peas ne poient eux carie hors dell vill de doner louer verdit, mez lez justices de le peas poient doner iour all enquest de doner lour verdit apres le cessionz, et cest verdit couient estre prise par ii justices de peas all meynz. Mez nemi requisite en ceo case qui lun dez justices ne soit de le quorum.

Item cest enquire doit estre per probos & legales homines ; et nota qui probi homines serra entenduz ceux qui ne sount disablez par le ley ; sicome home atteinpt de faux surett[3] en atteinpt ou decies tantum, ou soit ambidexter &c., le partie qui est greue par tiell verdit poiet monstre ceo & voidera le presentement. Mez si en ceo case sount xii

---

[1] The section within brackets, Item il couient . . . est assetz bone & cetera is taken from B ; see p. 362, note 3, *supra*. It appears here in F, G, and L. It is the only serious omission from A.

[2] boyer, F.   [3] serement, F.

Jurriourz oustre luy qui est issint atteinpt & cetera, vncore il presentement est assetz bone & cetera.]

Item 'legales homines' sount ceux queux sount[1] ne sount vtlagez
ou hommes abiurez, home enuers que iugement est done en Premunire
facias, home atteint de felony ou treason, et le presentment [f. 101] pris
par eux est voide. Mes si vne clerke que fut conuict deuaunt ou
homez queux sount conuictez[2] [*quere quia credo quod caret*] et
homez que ne sount de sane memorie sount Jurrez en ascun tielx
enquestez come deuaunt est dit & ils fount presentement, cest bone.
Et si vne villein soit iurre en ceo enquest [est bone],[3] quar le precept
que va al vicount nest 'liberos', mez le precept est probos et legales
homines & cetera.

Item nota que moigne professe, femez, infauntz & ceux que sount
infra sacros ne enfaunts south lage de xiiii[4] ans ne aliens neez hors de
roialme de le Roie, coment que il soit iurre al Roie deuaunt destre
son true liege home en son lete ou aillourz, le presentement fait par
ascun dez personez auauntditz sount voidablez[5] par le iuraunce[6] del
mater.[7]

Item si persons queux sount de consanguinyte fait presentement
vers son amy, ou si le partie mesme que est vne dez Jurrourz fount
presentement enuers luy mesme, vncore en ceux deux casez le presentment est bone; mez en le cas auauntdit si lez Justicez suffrent luy
mesme destre iurre sil auoit conusaunce deuaunt de son misdemenour,
ceo nest bone discression en eux. Mez si vne dez Jurrourz que est
iurre en le panell present luy mesme en transgression, baterie ou
felony, cest presentment est bone et il mesme ne auoidra ceo en apres
ne auera trauers a ceo.[8] Mes il couient de[9] felony que soient xii homez
iurres oustre luy que presenteront, ou autrement il poet trauerser
lenditement & cetera; quere de felony.

Item il couient en cest cas que lez enquisitourz[10] soient de mesme le
counte, scilicet, que ils soient demurauntez deins mesme le conte ou
ount terre deins mesme le conte; mez coment que ils ount chatelx en
mesme le counte, vncore pur ceux il ne serra my iurre.

Item si ascuns dez inquisitourz queux sount returnez par le vicount
destre deuaunt Justice de peas ount perpetuall infirmyte ou est de age

---

[1] *Omit*, B; in C, the second 'sount' is omitted.
[2] mutes, B. [3] est bone, B, D. [4] xiii, F. [5] void, D.
[6] iurans, C. [7] partie, C.
[8] *Add* en transgression ou baterie coment que ne sont forsque xii oue
luy, B, D.
[9] en, C. [10] jurrourz, B, D.

de lxx ans ou est decrepute ou huiusmodi, ils ne poient eux chalenge mez ils sount mys a lour accions sur lestatut de Westminster ii^{de} enuers le vicount.[1] Mez si ascun dez iurrourz que sount returnez ad ascun chartre de excepcion, ils poient pleder lour chartre, mez en ceo cas le chartre ne voet seruer pur luy sinoun que il ad ceux parols en le chartre : licet tangat nos. Et vncore si lez parols sount compris deins le chartre, si ne soient plousourz sufficientz homez destre iurrez il mesme serra iurre nient obstante son chartre.

Lez parols del commission sount : tam infra libertates quam extra ; ceo sera entendue de tielx libertez & fraunchise queux ount Retorna breuium, mes ne serra entendue en tilx libertez & fraunchisez queux sount countez deins eux mesmez come Loundon, Norwich, Ebor'[2] & huiusmodi. Et mesme le ley est sil ne soit counte en luy mesme, mez ad vne iurisdiccion graunt a eux par le Roie de auer Justice de peas deins eux mesmez & que null autre Justice de peas seera deins mesme le vile, en cest cas lez autrez justice ne doient enquirer deins mesme le vile.

Mes autre est del lete en[3] autre court que auoit poiar de tener toutz plees personelx ; quar lez Justicez[4] ount poiar denquerer de chosez faitz encountre le peas deins le precinct de tile lete ou court. Mes si lez Justices de peas enquireront de vne chose troue deuaunt mesme le Senescall en mesme le lete, & auxi est troue deuaunt eux en lour cessions si le partie ad fait fyne a moy a vne foitz, ceo excusera luy enuers le Roie. Et sil nad paie son fyne a moy deuaunt, [f. 101 b] quere a que il doit faire son fyne ou al Roie ou al moy.

Et nota que lez Justicez de peas ount poiar de proceder sur vne presentment fait en vne lete, mez nemi de faire proses vers le partie sur ceo & cetera.

Et lez parols de le precept sount oustre : per quos rei veritas melius sciri poterit ; & la il couient de voier si ascun chose soit fait que soy extende en ii countez coment il serra trie ; come en cas si assault soit fait en vne conte[5] lez Justices de peas de ambideux counteez poient enquerer de cest assault, & issint si vne robbe vne autre & fue en autre conte, ils purrount enquerer de ceo en ambideux contez. Mes si vne moy batera en vne conte & puis ieo deuie sur ceo baterie en autre conte, en cest cas lez Justicez de le conte lou ieo fue batuz enqueront de ceo mater[6] & nemi ceux Justices de peas lou ieo murust, & le reson

---

[1] 13 Edw. I, Westminster Second, c. 38, 1285.
[2] Loundrez, Couentre, etc., F. [3] ou, B, C, D. [4] *Add* de peas, B, C.
[5] *Add* et est contine en autre countie, D. [6] mort, B, D.

en cest cas est ceo, quar le principall occasion de le mort fut le bate-
ment en le primer conte & cetera.[1]

Vndecima Lectura.

(*Margin*) De rebus inquirendis coram Justiciariis pacis per commissionem.

Lez parols de le commission de Peas done poiar as Justice de peas
denquerer de transgressionibus, & ceo serra entendue auxi bien de tilx
transgressions queux sount faitz en terre ou en bienz sicome en transgressions de Baterie ou huiusmodi. Mes transgression que est sur le
cas ne serra enquire par force de le commission.[2] Mes si home soit
mayme, ceo serra enquire deuaunt mesme lez Justicez de peas & vncore
lez parols sont felonice & cetera.

Item engettement de garde & rauysshement de garde sount compris
deins le transgression de [3] enquire deuaunt lez Justices. Mes entru-
sion de garde de maritagio non satisfacto nest compris deins lez
parols del transgression auauntdit.

Item si homme fait rescous al seignur lou il distreigne pur rent, ceo
serra enquise et auxi serra de parco fracto lou le pounde est enfreint
contra pacem. Et si home entre en mon parke ou en mon waren ou
ascun autre liberte que ieo ay saunz mon volunte & la fait tort a moy,
ceo serra enquise deuaunt lez Justices de peas come de transgression
& cetera.

Item si vne Officer fait vne voluntarie eschape de vne prisoner que
il ad en prison lou leschape nest forsque fynabull al Roie, ceo est
enquirabull par ceux parols de transgressions. Mez si leschape soit
necligent [4] fait, ceo ne sera enquise & cetera.

Item si vne purpresture ou autre noisaunce soit leue par ascun
person en le haute estrete, ceo est enquerable par lez parols de transgressions. Mes si vne home leue le noisaunce en son terre demene
que est al noisaunce a vne comen voie, ou si home voet distreigner
ascun person par cez bienz en Regia via, ceux ne sount enquerable
par lez parols auauntditz, scilicet, transgressions, mez en ceo darrein
cas le partie poet auer accion sur lestatute de Marlebrigge [5] encountre
celui que luy issint distreigne & cetera.

---

[1] It almost seems as if the last part of Lect. XV belongs here : ' Et lez
parols de commission . . . & nota ceo bene & cetera.' This clause on the
Custos Rotulorum comes immediately after ' per quos rei veritas, etc.' in
the actual commission.

[2] *Add* purceo que nest suppose encountre le peace, D.

[3] destre, B, C, D.   [4] negligenter, B, D.

[5] 52 Hen. III, c. 15, 1267.

Forstallariis; cest parolle forstaller serra auxi bien entendue de
marchandise come de vitaille, si soient en veignaunt a ascun [1] merkett
ou Feir destre la venduz ou si lez merchandise ou vitaille sount en
veignaunt al hostell le Roie destre venduz; quar cest hostell est vne
merkett en chescun lieu lou le Roie est & a chescun iour & cetera.

[*Nota bene.*] Item nota que cest forstallerie doit estre fait hors de
le merkett, faire ou port, par empcion fait par le Forstallour de mesmez
lez chosez al entent de faire le chose issint par luy empt destre pluis
care quaunt il vient al merkett [et aussi poet estre forstallour en ascun
casez coment qui ne fait empcion de les chosez],[2] come en cas si vne
home par le voie obvia diuers persons veignaunt al merkett & il dit a
eux que cest vitaille queux ils ount la come greynys ou autrez mer-
chandises prist pluis pris en le market [f. 102] que il prist en fait,
al entent de causer eux de teigner lour vitaille all haute pris [issint] [3]
que il poet [vender] [4] son vitaille ou merchandise le pluis haute &
care.

Et mesme le leie est sil obuia eux & dit a eux que sont [5] veignaunt
al markett oue vitaille & cetera que cest vitaille ne prist ascun bone
pris al markett, al entent de causer eux de transire oue lour ware ou
autre vitaille a autre markett ou vile & nemi a ceo markett, issint que
il vendra son vitaille que il ad en le markett pluis care, en ceux
deux casez ce est forstallarie auxi bien sicome il ad fait empcion dez
chosez.[6]

Item al comen ley cest forstallerie fut solement fynable si le partie
vst este conuyct de ceo & cetera. Mez a ore par lestatut de assisa
panis & seruicie [7] est done & ordeigne que chescun que est troue
forstaller come auauntdit, que al primer foitz que il soit troue coulpable, il serra amercie & paiera fyne; al ii^de foitz que il est troue
coulpable il auera iugement de pillorie; al tierce foitz destre enprison
& de faire redempcion al volunte le Roie, & le iiii^te foitz que il doit

---

[1] *Add* port, B, C, D.   [2] [et .. chosez] added from B.
[3] issint, B, C, D.   [4] vender, B; vendre, C, D.
[5] MS. s'; son, B, C, D.
[6] *Add* et ad este aiuge que lou vn vient in Cotteswold & dit a lez mer-
chauntes que in cell an null leyn duist passer outre le mier, par force de
quell il venda ceo pur le meyndre somme, que ceo fuit vn forstallerie, F.
[7] Not in Assisa Panis et Ceruisie, S.R. i. 199-200, but see Statutum
de Pistoribus: primo convictus grauiter amercietur & *amittat res sic
emptas* et hoc secundum consuetudinem & constitucionem ville; secundo
convictus paciatur judicium pillorie: tercio incarceretur & redimatur;
quarto abjuret villam; *ibid.* 202-4. It is headed: Incipit composicio ad
puniendum infringentes assisam panis & ceruisie forstallarios, cocos etc.
Note that Marowe has omitted the clause that I have put in italics.

abiurer le vile. Et puis vient lestatut de anno xxv^{to} E. 3 de Pannis,[1] et cest estatut ordeigne que le forstaller en ceo cas perdra lez chosez que il auoit empt par forstallyng, et sil nad paie my pur eux le pris ne eit[2] sufficient de eux paier, doncquez le forstallour auera lemprisonement de deux ans, et celui que voet suer pur le Roie auera lun moite de le forfaitur & le Roie lautre moite.

Item si home forstalle en vne countie chosez veignaunt al markett que est en autre conte, ceo poet estre enquyse en ambideux contez.

Item si home Forstalle sur le ryuer de Tamys lou Essex [est][3] de vne part & lautre partie en le counte de Kent, en ceo cas ils ne deuoient enquirer en ambideux contez, mez par le File de le water il serra mesure & accordaunt a ceo file que proue le fait en ascun conte de eux, la il serra enquyse. Mez home poet forstaller merchaundise esteaunt sur le miere & ne serra puny pur le forstallyng; quar en cest cas lez merchaundisez ne fut a ascun temps passe'[4] laduenture de le mier & cetera.

Item si vne forstalle merchaundisez en vne countie & ceux conveia par vne mesne conte al markett esteaunt en le iii^{cie} conte, lez iusticez de peas de le meane conte ne doient enquirer de ceo forstaller & cetera.

Item si home vse de vener oue cez merchaundisez iesque a vne markett & de cest markett tancque a autre markett, & issint oustre a diuers markettes tancque toutz son merchaundisez sount venduz, si en ceo cas vne home luy forstalla deuaunt il vient al primer markett, ceo ne serra dit forstaller a ii^{de} markett.[5]

Item si home ala a son meason que auoit vitaille ou autre marchaundise a vendre & la il ema son vitaille ou merchaundise de eux, ceo ne serra dit forstallyng & cetera.

Item si vne home vsurpe de auer vne markett lou il auoit[6] tile liberte en fait de auer son markett, ceo nest forstallery. Mes si home ad vne purpris & vne forstalla vitaille ou autre merchaundise al iour de le purpris, ceo est forstallerie & serra puny.[7]

---

[1] 25 Edw. III, st. 3, c. 3, 1351, in S.R. i. 314-15; statute the *Fourth* in all former printed copies, and entitled 'Statutum de Pannis'; *ibid.* 314, note.

[2] soit, B, C, D.   [3] est, B, D.   [4] *Add* le ieopardie ne, C.

[5] *Add* ne a null autre markett forsque solement all primer markett ne enquirable en le Court de ii^d markett, B.

[6] Probably a mistake for 'nauoit'.

[7] *For* Mes ... puny *read* Mez autrement est si home purpris vn iour come sill eyt markett le lundey & il purpris le marteday, si home forstall a ceo ior purpris cest forstallerie quar la ill ad colour etc., F.

Item si mon seruaunt saunz mon commaundement & oue mon money forstalla a mon vse & apres que il ceo fait ieo agrea a ceo, vncore null forstallerie serra dit en moy mez tantum en mon seruaunt & cetera.

[*Regratourz.*] Regraters; ceux serront entendue proprement ceux queux ement merchaundise ou vitaille al entent pur reuendre eux en vne mesme markett, & que autrez emerount de luy pur le pluis care en mesme le markett, et ceo act de Regraterie couient estre fait deinz le markett, & nemi hors & cetera.

Item si vne homme ema vitaille & ceo en vne markett al entent de eux vendre en autre markett, cest empcion ne serra dit regraterie. Mesme le leie [f. 102 b] sil ema vitaille a vne markett, iour & cetera, al entent que il voile eux vendre en autre markett autre iour, ceo nest regraterie. Mes si le Feir ou markett continua par iii iourz & il ema al primer iour al entent de vender ceo a le ii^de ou le iii^cie iour en mesme le markett ou feir, ceo serra dit regraterie. Et mesme le leie est si ii markettes sount tenuz en vne vile & a vne iour, et home vient & ema merchaundises a lun markett al entent de ceo vender en autre markett, ceo est regraterie.

Item si homme ema merchaundise a vne certen pris & venda mesme le merchaundise a vne autre a mesme le price, coment que soit en vne mesme markett, ceo nest regraterie, sinoun que son entent fut al commencement de vendre pur pluis que il ema & cetera. Mes sil bartera en mesme le markett son vitaille que il auoit ema deuaunt pur autre merchaundise, en ceo cas lentent fait le mater; quar son entent poet faire regraterie & nient regraterie & cetera.

Item si home vient a vne markett & ema tout le vitaille que est deinz mesme le markett pur luy mesme, coment que il ne revende ceo apres en mesme le markett, ceo est vne regraterie si soit[1] a reuendre. Mes si home ne ema forsque parcell de mesme le vitaille & lessa parcell, quere.[2]

Item si home que ad blees en son barne vt[3] son necessarie expence & ala al markett & ema autrez bleez, la ceo est Regraterie de taunt que il ema & serra forfett.[4]

[1] *For* si soit *read* si come fuit, B.
[2] *For* Mes ... quere, *read* Mes si home achate forsque parcell, autrement est, F.
[3] oustre, B, D ; pur, C.
[4] *For* & serra forfett *read* & est finable pur ceo & neit forfeyt come forstaller, F. *Add* si home attacha toutz lez Greynes in le markett all intent que si le markett sourde a graund prise que ill voet vendre pur meyndre [*sic*] price, ceo nest regraterie come semble, F.

[*Extorcion.*] Extorcion ; ceo serra entendue lou home par colour de son office ou auctorite prist pluis argent de comen pepull que ils deuoient par le leie auer de droit pur dowte de lour office ou auctorite ; le partie fait ceo ou [1] pur feer de luy pur son office, sicome de vicount, southvicount, Bailles ou huiusmodi, que preignount pluis de le pepull pur fair lour office que ils doient de droit auer par le ley & cetera. Mes si home priste vne chose de moy saunz faire ascun title de ceo chose a luy ou par coloure de ascun office que il auoit, ceo prendre ne serra dit extorcion mez solement transgression.

Item si vne Justice de peas ou autre Justice de Roie prist ascun chose ou bienz de ascun home lou il nest entitle dauer ascun Fee de mesme le person, ceo ne serra dit extorcion mez transgression.   Mes si vne Fee soit incident a mesme le Justice de mesme le home coment que il prist pluis pur son fyne que il deuoit auer de comen droit, ceo est extorcion ; sicome lez Justicez de Nisi Prius lou ils doient auer de le pleintiff pur vne Nisi Prius vi s. viii d. pur lour seer sur ceo, sils preignount x s. ceo est extorcion, et issint est si vne ordinarie prist pluis pur vne iugement done en le spirituell leie [2] & auxi pur probatez dez Testamentes & similia, ceo est extorcion ; [3] quar il est colore officii sui, et en cest cas de extorcion de probate de testament sil soit endite de ceo il couient destre specialment declare en lenditement par lestatut de anno xxv^{to} E. 3.[4]   Et nota que si ascun tile officer come vicount, senescall, bailly ou huiusmodi, prist pluis que ils deuoient prendre de le peple, coment que cest prendre ne soit a lour vse demene mez al vse de le Roie ou al vse de autre seignur, vncore ceo est extorcion & cetera.

[*Conventiculis.*] Conuenticulis ; ceo serra entendue vne entreparlaunce entre diuers personez al entent de faire vne chose que est encontre le ley, coment que ils ne vncques apres tile enparlaunce assemble ne fait mesme le chose que ils ount entendue deuaunt destre fait ; come si ieo ala a vne home & dia a luy mon oppinion que ieo entendue defaire vne chose encontre le ley come de occider vne homme, & il parla oue vne autre person destre de mesme le purpos & le ii^{de} parle oue le iii^{cie} al mesme lentent & ils toutz agreount a mesme lacte destre fait distincte, en ceo cas coment que il ne vncques assemblerount apres a mesme le purpos, vncore ceo est vne conventicull &

---

[1] *Omit*, C, D (crossed out).   [2] court, B, D.

[3] Cf. F ; the ordinary 'ne puit fayre extorcion come juge', but only in proving wills.

[4] *Add* capitulo vltimo, D, F ; see 25 Edw. III, st. 6, c. 9 (the last).

ils serront toutz punys pur ceo si soit present deuaunt Justicez de peas [f. 103] par fyne & cetera.

Item si vne homme voillet faire covenaunt oue autre de prendre son partie et son opinion en toutz chosez ou enuers vne tile home nosmant son nome, cest covenaunt serra aiugge vne conuenticle. Et nota que cest conuenticle est & fut al comen loie fynable saunz autre faire de ascun act sur ceo & cetera.

Et auxi par ceux parols 'conuenticles' en le commission lez Justicez de peas poient enquerrer de Riotous assemblez sils fueront faitz al entent pur faire ascun chose encountre le leie, et auxi ils puissount enquirer de donourz del liuerez a autrez persons que a son menialz seruauntes,[1] mez par ceux parolx nest forsque fynable.

Item lez Justicez de peas poient enquirer de conspiracies & confiderasies; sicome home voet moue vne autre de prendre vne faux accion, come de mouer vne enfaunt de prendre appelle de felony[2] ou huiusmodi & cetera, ceux sount enquirablez par ceux parols 'conuenticles'.

Item si deux hommez conspirount de forger vne faux fait ou sount agree entre eux que lun ceo forgera & lautre ceo proclaymera mesme le fait, en cest cas ceo est vne conuenticulle. Mes si vne home forge vne faux fait & vne autre ceo proclayma apres & nient par covenaunt fait entre eux deuaunt, ceo nest conventicle & cetera.

Et auxi par ceux parols lez Justicez puissont enquirer de champartie;[3] come si home enfeffe vne autre en ascun parcell de terre que il ad par tort pur eider luy enuers celui que droit ad, et auxi dez[4] maintenaunce dez accions queux sount torcious & nemi conuse[5] de son counsell ou aliaunce que port laccion & cetera.

& lez parols de le commission sount oustre: Vi armata ierunt et equitauerunt. Et ceux parols serra entenduz en tile fourme si home ala ou chiuaucha en harnes mez sil ne face ceo a male entent, ceo nest offence; come sil ala en harnes pur son defence, ceo nest prohibite par le leie. Mes si home ala en harnes al entent de faire male come de faire vne assaute, affraie, baterie, murdre ou huiusmodi, coment que cest harnes que il auoit sur luy soit couert,[6] vncore ceo est enquirable.

---

[1] *Add* & ceo deuaunt lestatut dez liueres, F; there is also a query as to the taker of liveries. Cf. 1 Hen. IV, c. 7. 1399, and the numerous other statutes on liveries.

[2] *Add* all intent que le deffendaunt serroyt ouste de son battell Gager, F.

[3] *Add* et mayntenaunce, D.

[4] pur, C.

[5] *Omit*, B, D; come, C.

[6] *Add* ou previe, D.

Mes si home ceo face deuaunt ascun iustice de le Roie ou autre mynester le Roie sil mesme si ne soit officer, il forfetra son harnes [1] par lestatut de anno ii^{do} E. III.[2]

Et cest estatut done poier as gardens de peas de faire execucion de mesme lestatut, & ceo serra entendue si home ala en harnes en lour presence que ils purrount saisier saunz enquire de ceo & sils ne voillount saisier, vncore ils purrount enquirer de ceo & cetera.

Item si lez Justicez de peas alount de voier vne riott & ils trouent eux en harnes, vncore ils ne forfatrent lour harnes en ceo cas ; quar ils ne presumeront par eux mesmez de vener en loure presence vi & armis & cetera.

Item si vne justice de peas vient army a lez cessions, en cest cas vne autre iustice de peas poet prendre son armer de luy si bien come de vne estraunge ou autre home.[3]

Item si home vient arme en le presence de Justice de peas & lez iustices ne prendrent cest harnes de luy, si apres a autre temps mesmez les Justicez trouerount mesme le armour en autre lieu, ils ne poient ceo prendre adoncque, mes deuaunt quaunt il fut en loure presence ils puissount bien ceo prendre.

Item si lez Justicez de peas veiount vne homme en harnes en loure presence & ils pristerount le harnes de luy, en cest cas le Justice nauera [f. 103 b] le harnes ne armure a son vse demene mes il couient ceo delyuerer al vicount pur accounpter de icell & cetera.[4]

[*Insidiis.*] Insidiis ; cest parolle serra entendue de bater de prison [5] ou de murdre ascun homme & issint serra le presentment fait, ou autrement ceo nest bone. Mes en cas lou home gist en agaite de bater ascun home & vncore il ne ceo fait en fait, en ceo cas le partie nauera accion enuers luy de tile agayte. Mes si home fist assault sur vne homme coment que il ne leda luy, vncore le partie auera accion de transgression sur cell assaute. Mes si home gist en agaite par le voie en [6] autre lieu al entent de faire felony ou roberie ou rape a ascun feme ou huiusmodi, ceo nest inquirable par ceux parols, Insidiis.

Item si homme fait mynez a autre person de leder ou bater luy,

---

[1] *Add* En mesme le maner, si home ala in harness in le merkett, ill serra forfeyt, F.

[2] Statute of Northampton, 2 Edw. III, c. 3, 1328.

[3] *Add* Et si toutz veignent in armur le vicount prendra, quar in ceo cas le vicount auera [*sic*] come conseruatour, F.

[4] *Add* harnez serra pris chescun chose que est defensible de quacumque mettall ou matter ceo soyt, come de mayles, briggondirez ou huiusmodi, F.

[5] *For* de prison *read* le person, B.   [6] ou, C.

ceo nest inquirable coment que il ne poet faire ne neit faire[1] son
bosoignez, mes en cest cas le partie auera accion de transgression sur
cest mater, quia tales & tantas minas[2] vt non potest circa negocia sua
ibidem facienda & cetera.[3]

Duodecima Lectura.

(*Margin.*)   De feloniis inquirendis coram Justiciariis pacis.

Par cest parolle en le commission ' Feloniis ' diuers chosez sount enquerablez deuaunt lez Justicez de peas.

' Theft ' est enquerable par ceux parols, sicome homme prist & emble
ascun biens al value de xii d. ou oustre, ceo est felony.   Et issint est
si home prist ascunz bienz felonysshement coment que ils ne sount
forsque al value de vi d., cest inquirable deuaunt mesme lez Justices de
peas, vncore le vie del partie en ceo cas ne serra mys en ieopardie &
cetera.   Et nota que le torcious pris dez bienz ne fait le felonye
tantum, mes le felonyous entent fait le felony ; quar home poet prendre
mez bienz torciousment come trespassour & nemi come Felon.   Et
vncore coment que homme ad pris mez bienz come felon, vncore ieo
puissoie faire cest felonye destre forsque transgression a mon plesure et
issint poet le Roie faire a son plesure ; quar vne tort ne voet estre
excuse par autre tort & cetera.

Item si vne home delyuer cez bienz a autre pur carier ou autrement
pur sauement garder & il eux prist come felon oue felonous entent,
vncore cest entent en ceo cas ne poet ceo faire Felony pur lenteress
que il auoit en mesme lez bienz deuaunt par le liuere de eux a luy fait
& cetera.   Mes si ieo delyuer a mon horskeper vne chiuall ou a mon
Butteler mez pecez de plate pur moie seruer oue eux & de sauement
eux garder, en ceux casez sils prent le chiuall ou le plate & depart de
moy saunz licence oue ceux, cest prendre serra aiugge felony ; quar
nient obstante le delyuere fait a eux le possession serra aiugge en moy
toutz foitz & cetera.[4]

---

[1] *For* ne poet . . . neit faire *read* ne poet seer ne sciet faire, C.
[2] *Add* de vita sua, B, C, D.
[3] *Add* Item fueront in auncien temps Insidiatores viarum & ceo fuit
enquirable & pluis especialment pur clerkes que aleront oustre le pays
mendiauntz & fuit annull all request dez seignurz espirituellez.   Item il
auer depopulatores agrorum & est auxi annull etc.   Item sount autre's
chosez inquerablez & ceo est par estatutez & pur ceo ilz ne sount rehercez
etc., D, F.
[4] *Add* Vide in prima parte fo. cclx title de Corone & specialment 40
Corone, D (margin).   The first citation is to Fitzherbert's Abridgement,
Corone, no. 52, and the second is to the same work.

Item si bienz soient delyuerez a vne [1] pur sauement garder al vse de B, & A delyuer mesmez lez bienz a vne C a mesme lentent & puis A oue felons entent prist mesmez lez bienz de le possession de C, en cest cas ceo nest felony en A, et vncore il ne auoit ascun proprete ne possession de eux al temps de le prendre de eux mes vne sole enterest par le baillement. Mes si bienz soient delyuerez al A pur delyuer a vne B & [A] [2] delyuer eux a mesme le B, & puis apres A prist lez bienz hors de le possession de B oue felonous entent, ceo est felonye & cetera. [3]

Item si home delyuer bienz a vne autre pur sauement garder & le baille chaunge le fassion de mesme lez bienz, come il poet de plate [f. 104] et similia, en ceo cas si le baillour apres eux prist oue felonous entent ceo est felony, & vncore fueront cez bienz proprez en fait mez le proprete fut chaunge par le chaunge de le facion & cetera.

Item si home moy robba dez biens & puis apres vne autre luy robba de mesmez lez bienz, ceo ii[de] robberie est Theft fait a moie & Felony & ieo auera lappelle de le ii[de] robberie. [4] Mes si homme prist mez bienz come trespassour & puis vne autre luy robba de mesmez lez bienz, ceo nest theft fait al moie mez al trespassour; quar trespassour afferme proprete & cetera.

Item si vne feme feloynssement [5] prist lez bienz son baron, & ala de son baron ouesque eux, ceo nest felony en le feme pur ceo que el ad entresse en lez biens son baron.

Item si home bailla cez bienz al baron pur sauement garder & le feme prist mesmez lez bienz felonyoussement, vncore ceo prendre par le feme nest Felonye. Mes en cas lou biens sount baillez al baron & le baron eux bailla oustre a vne autre, & doncques le feme le primer baille prist mesmez lez bienz hors de le possession de le ii[de] baille feloniousment, ceo serra dit felony en le feme. Mes en mesme le cas si le baron mesme ad pris mesmez lez bienz felonyously hors de le possession de le ii[de] bailly, ceo nest felony & cetera.

Item nota que lou hom̃e ad biens & murust en tile lieu que le custom est que le feme auera le iii[cie] parte de mesmez les biens queux fueront a son baron al temps de son mort, en ceo cas si le feme apres le mort son baron voet prendre parcell de cez biens son baron al felonous entent, cest prendre est felony nient obstante lentrest que el ad en eux

---

[1] *Add* A ; MSS. C, D.   [2] A ; MS. B.

[3] *Add* quar il nauera null entrest in eux apres que ill auer delyuer etc., F.

[4] *Add* 62 Corone, D (margin) ; identified in Fitzherbert, *ut supra.*

[5] solement, D.

deuaunt pur [1] le certente queux biens el auera pur son part ne fut assigne deuaunt & cetera.

Item si le baron commaunde son feme deprendre lez bienz de vne estraunge & el fait ceo par son commaundement,[2] ceo est auxi bien felony en le baron come en le feme.   Mes si le baron coherta son feme de ceo faire & el ceo fait par son cohercion, en cest cas ceo est felonye en le baron & nemi en le feme.   Mes si le master cohert son seruaunt de faire vne felonye & il ceo fait, cest felony auxi bien en le master come en le seruaunt.   Et issint est si le baron cohert son feme de murdrer vne home, cest felonye en ambideux, scilicet, en le baron & le feme auxi ; quar lact fait le felony & cetera.

Item si vne garden de vne esglise prist lez bienz de mesme lesglise oue felonous entent, vncore ceo nest felonye.   Et si vne commoigne prist lez bienz de son meason oue felons entent, ceo nest felony pur lentrest.   Mes si vne moigne prist lez bienz de labbe mesme felonysse- ment, ceo serra dit felony.

Item si vne home de vne communialte que est corporate come London & autrez prist lez bienz de mesme le communialte, ceo est felony en luy.

[*Robberie.*]   Robery est auxi enquerable deuaunt Justices de peas & est felony coment que le chose que est prist ne soit de value de xii d. Et cest Robberie couient destre entendue proprement quaunt vne prist ascun chose de le person mesme, issint que par le prisell de icell il est en fee [3] & ieopardie de son person.   Mes sil assaulte le person & luy mitte en graund feer mez prist null chose de le person, en ceo cas ceo nest felony.

Item si vne home scia vne purse & ceo prist, ceo nest Roberie, quar le person ne fut en ascune feer ou ieapardie par cest scier.   Mes en mesme le cas si le somme que est conteigne en le burse soit oustre xii d.

[*Nota cest diuersite & quere.*] il serra pendue come laron, & si le some ne amount al value de xii d. doncque il ne serra pendue pur ceo.   Mes si apres que le laron ad scie le burse, le burse gisoit al terre issint que il ne fut vncques en possession, ceo nest felony mez fynable par discression dez Justices.

Item si home vient a moy [f. 104 b], & dist que si ieo ne voile luy mutier [4] xx s. que il voile moy murdrer, sur que ieo delyuer a luy xx s.,

[1] quar, B D.

[2] *For* & el . . . commaundement *read* et ell ceo fayt oue felons entent, F, D (margin).   The latter *adds* : 199 Corone (identified in Fitzherbert, *ut supra*) ; also case 40 Lib. Ass. (proves to be 27 Edw. III) on the other margin.

[3] fere, B, D ; feer, C.   [4] metua, B ; myttyer, C ; metuer, D.

cest Roberie. Mes si home cause moy de iurer que ieo portera xx s.
de argent a certen lieu a certen iour ou autrement il voillet moy murdrer, ceo nest [1] felony.

[*Burglary.*] Burglary ; ceo est auxi enquirable par lez Justices de
peas par force de ceux parols en le commission ' Feloniis ', et est proprement lou home enfreint ascun meason al entent de murdrer ascun
home esteaunt deins mesme le meason [2] & par noet ceo est felonye,
mes si tile enfreindre soit fait par iour, doncques ceo nest felony.

Item si home vient a vne esglis en le noet & enfreindre ceo & enter
al entent [3] de robber mesme lesglise, ceo est felony & vncore en cest
cas il pose null person en ieopardie ne en Feer ne autre choce mez
solement son enfreint.

Item si home ad enfreint vne meason en le noett al entent de
rauyssher vne feme esteaunt deins mesme le meason ou de bater ascun
person que est deins, cest enfreindre de le meason ne serra dit Burglarie.

Item si home [4] enfreint ascun closure al entent de prendre hors de
ceo ascun chateux felonyousment, ceo nest felony sil ne prist riens hors
& cetera.

[*Mort de home.*] Mort de home est auxi enquerable par lez iustices
de peas & ceo poet estre fait en iiii maners, scilicet, par mysfortune ;
sicome home est occise par chaunce de vne mure gismaunt sur luy ou
par thonder ou autre maner dez chauncz, en toutz ceux casez ceo nest
enquirable deuaunt Justices de peas, ou si home soit felo de se lou
home tua luy mesme, ceo nest enquirable deuaunt Justicez de peas.
Mes de manslawghter ils poient enquerer & ceo serra entendue lou
home tua vne autre par chaunce medle il est enquirable deuaunt eux.
Le iiii[te] est murdre & ceo est lou home par malice prepense gitta en agaite
& tua ascun home, cest auxi enquirable deuaunt lez Justices & cetera.

Et nota que en mort de home lentent de celui que fait le mort ne
fait le felony come il fait de Theft come est auauntdit & cetera ; quar
si home entende de bater ascun person & en cell baterie il tua vne
autre, ceo est felony nient obstante son entent ne fut de luy occider.
Mes en ascun cas de mort de homme lentent ferra le felony ; sicome
vne home dona a vne autre corrupt vitaille al entent de luy oue cest
vitaille de poysoner & murderer & il deuia de maunger ou boire de ceo
vitaille, ceo est felony. Mes sil ne sauoit le corrupcion ne entend de
luy poysoner al temps quaunt il luy dona, ceo nest felony & issint
lentent en ceo cas fait le felony & cetera.

[1] *Add* robrie ne, D.   [2] *Add* ou de fayre autre felony, F.
[3] al entent, *bis*.   [4] *Add* in le noet, F.

Item en auncien temps lentent en murdre oue vne notorious act fait
de perfourmer mesme le murdre fut felonye coment que il ne fist le
murdre en fait, sicome [1] en cas vne garcoun voile auer tue son master
quaunt il fut endormant & come il voillet auer [2] scie son gutter, il
gisoit sur luy cy dure que il mesme vigiloit & eschape ceo, & ceo fut
aiugge felony en le garcoun et vncore le master fut en vie.

Et issint est si feme que est auowtres & le feme & son auowterour
scierount le guttour de le baron, et le wesande [3] de luy ne fut tout scie
issint que il recouer ceo, vncore ceo fut aiugge felony en lauowterour
& en le Feme & vncore le baron fut en vie, anno xl [4] E. II^di.

Item si vne enfaunt soit tue en le ventre son mere, ceo nest felony.
Mes si home tue vne autre home que nest conuz en Engliterre, vncore
est felony et vncore en ceo cas poet estre que il fut vne alien & enemy,[5]
mez aiugge fut pluis stricte [f. 105] enuers luy que ceo fist & cetera.

Item si vne enfaunt tua vne home, lez Justicez agarder ceo destre
felony soloncque le discression de lenfant. Mes si home que est
lunatik en son rage tua home, ceo nest felony.[6]

Item si home tua le chieff Justice seant en son place, ceo est treason
& lez Justicez de peas ne poient enquirer de ceo come treason. Mez
ils poient enquerer de ceo come felony. Mes de treason fait al person
de Roie mesme ils ne poient enquirer come treason ne come felony.

[*Petit treason.*] Petit treason est enquirable deuaunt lez Justicez de
peas par ceux parols ' feloniis ' & ceo fut felony par le comen leie, mez
par lestatut a ore est done que ceux que fount petit treason & de ceo
soit atteint, que il serra trahez & penduz,[7] et auxi par autre nouell
estatut il est ouste en ceo cas de son clergie.[8] Et auxi si le seruaunt
tua son master ou le feme tua son baron ou le moigne son souereigne,
ceo est petit treason par estatut fait anno vii^mo [9] H. VII^mi.[10]

<hr />

[1] *Bis.*   [2] *Omit*, C.

[3] pipe, B ; pier, C ; pype, D. See Century Dictionary for *weasand*,
wind-pipe.

[4] xv, B, F. The reference is to Pasch. 15 Edw. II, Appell., p. 463.

[5] *Add* Et ne serra issint intende, F.

[6] *Add* Mez si home tua vn autre quant il est dronkyn, ceo est feloni &
serra pendue quaunt il est sober etc., B, C, D ; mez autrement est dun
que est dronke, F.

[7] 12 Hen. VII, c. 7, 1497. In 25 Edw. III, st. 5, c. 2, 1352, petty
treason is defined as follows : ' When a servant slayeth his Master or a
Wife her Husband, or when a man Secular or Religious slayeth his
prelate.' But no penalty is stated.

[8] In reality by the same statute of 12 Hen. VII, but Marowe may be
thinking of 4 Hen. VII, c. 13.

[9] *Omit* vii^mo, B, D.

[10] *Omit* par . . . VII^mi, F, the correct reading.

Item si le seruaunt tua son master apres que il est hors de son seruice pur malice que il auoit a luy quaunt il fut en son seruice, vncore[1] ceo est petit treason.[2] Mes si vne seruaunt commaunda ou abetta vne autre de tuer son master & il ceo fait, ceo nest petit treason, mes en cest cas lact est felony & le seruaunt est vne accessorie a cest felony & cetera.

[*Accessories.*] Item accessories; lez Justicez de peas ne ount solement poiar denquerer de Felonys mez auxi de accessories de mesme le felonies. Et nota que accessories sount en iii maners, scilicet, lun deuaunt le felony fait, le ii[de] al temps de le felony, & le iii[cie] apres le felony fait. Le primer que est deuaunt le felony fait, sicome vne home commaunda vne autre de tuer vne home ou luy robber, ou sil procure ou wage ou labour[3] vne home de tuer autre home. Mes en cest cas si homme commaunda vne enfant de tuer vne home ou commaunda vne home de noun sane memorie & ils ceo fount, en cest cas le commaundour est principall, & lez enfauntz ou celui que nest de sane memorie sount excusez.

Item si A commaunda B de commaunder C de tuer vne home & il ceo fist, ambideux, scilicet, A & B, sount accessoriez. Mes si A commaunda B de tuer vne home & B commaunda C de ceo faire, B est accessorie & A est excuse de cest felony. Et mesme le leie si A commaunda B de tuer vne home en le cas auauntdit, & puis A reuoke son commaundement & nient obstante cest reuocacion B ceo fait, en cest cas il nest accessorie a le felony ou murdre.

Mes si home tua vne autre par lez commaundementes de la leie il est excuse, sicome le vicount auoit precept a luy fait par lez Justicez de Gaolle delyuerer de faire execucion de vne home, scilicet, de luy prendre ou decoller ou huiusmodi. Mes si le vicount decolle vne home lou son precept est de pendre luy, ceo est felony en le vicount.[4] Mes si vne iuge voille doner iugement saunz auctorite que home serra pendue & commaunder le vicount de luy pender, en cest cas le vicount est principall & le iugge est accessorie a ceo murdre. Mes si le iuge auoit auctorite & voiet doner iugement que il serra decolle lou il serroit penduz et commaunde le vicount de luy decoller que issint fait, en cest cas le Justice & le vicount ambideux sount excusez de ceo. Mes si

---

[1] *Bis.*

[2] *Add* 210 Corone, D (margin); identified in Fitzherbert, *ut supra*.

[3] *For* ou sil . . . labour vne home *read* Mesme le ley de procurer, coger ou labourer luy etc., D.

[4] *From* Et mesme le leie . . . vicount, the phraseology differs markedly in D.

ascun iuge voille prendre sur luy de arreigner ascun homme saunz ascun inditement ewe deuaunt de ceo felony, & sur ceo done iugement sur luy destre pendue & le vicount face execucion de ceo, en cest cas le vicount est excuse & le iuge est vne felon & principall.[1]

[*Le ii^{de} accessorie.*] Item le ii^{de} accessorie sount ceux queux fueront la al temps de le felonie fait, sicome vne vient en company oue vne autre al entent de murdrer vne autre home & il est present mez ne fait ascun chose al temps de le murdour [f. 105 b] committe, en ceo cas il est accessorie a lautre come de felony.   Et nota que en Robberie toutz que veignount a mesme lentent en company pur ceo faire, coment que vne de eux luy robba tantum, vncore toutz sount accessoriez,[2] & le cause est pur le feer que est fait par toutz eux al person & cetera. Mes si vne tient vne home come vne autre luy tua, en ceo cas ambideux sount principall.   Et issint est si ii hommez percussent vne autre a vne temps & il morust de ceo, ambideux sount principalles.   Mes autrement est en Rape; quar si vne home tient vne Feme iesque que al soit rauyssh maugre luy, celui que tient nest forsque accessorie.

Item si vne home done a vne autre vne plage dount il voille murere[3] & puis apres a autre temps vne autre luy occist, en cest cas celui que dona le primer plage nest principall ne accessorie al murdre.[4]

[*Accessorie apres le felony fait.*] Accessories apres le felony fait sount ceux que comfortount ou resceitount autre scient que il ad fait le felony ou murdre, en cest cas il est accessorie.   Mes sil luy rescetta & ne comforta ou rescue lez bienz & ne scient que ils furent emblees, ou ema de luy mesmez lez bienz coment que il sciet lez bienz destre felonousment pris, ceo nest felony en lez casez auauntditz.

Item home poet estre accessorie par resceit de cez biens proprez, sicome home bailla a vne home biens pur sauement[5] garder a son vse, & puis vne robbe le baille de mesmez lez biens & eux port a le baillour, & il eux receiua & comforta le felon al entent que il voillet auer amendes de le baille pur mesmez lez biens, en cest cas il est accessorie al felon & cetera.

[*Eschapes.*] Eschapes auxi sount enquerablez deuaunt Justice de peas, sicome voluntarie eschape de vne felon, sicome le Gailour ou vicount suffre vne que est en lour garde pur felony de eschaper volun-

---

[1] *Add* quere de ceo etc., B ; quere de ceo quod notandum quia ?, C ; quere, D.

[2] principalles, D, F.   [3] morer, B.

[4] *Add* nient obstante que il dona a luy vn plage mortall etc., C.

[5] MS. sauenent.   In this paragraph and the last the phraseology in MSS. B, C, D, differs slightly.

tarie, ceo est felony & enquirable par lez parols de le commission
'Feloniis' & cetera.

Item si vne Officer come vicount, Bailly ou Gailour, suffre vne felon
que est en lour garde de eschaper voluntarie & deins son viewe il luy
reprist, nient contristeent que ceo fut voluntarie, vncore ceo nest eschape.
Mes en cest cas si le felon prist vne esglis deins le viewe de le Officer
coment que il ceo prist en apres, vncore cest eschape est Felony en le
officer.

Item si le officer commaunde le felon de aler al prochun vile[1] &
revener a luy & le felon face issint, ce nest eschape. Mes en mesme
[*Nota.*] le cas si le felon alast a vne autre vile oustre son licence &
commaundement, ceo est eschape & Felony.

Item si le vicount lessa vne home a mainpris que nest maynpernable,
ceo nest voluntarie eschape mez est finable. Et issint est si lordinarie
suffre vne Convict de faire son purgacion lou il ne doit & cetera, ceo
est finable & nemi eschape voluntarie.

Item si vne home ferust vne autre issint que il est en ieopardie de
son vie & il est en garde pur ceo, si le gailour suffre luy deschaper
voluntarie & puis celui que est ferue murust, ceo nest felony en le
gailour & cetera.

Item si vne Constable que ad pris vne felon amena mesme le felon
al Gaile & le gailour ne voet ceo resceiuer, si le constable suffre le
felon de aler a large, vncore ceo nest felony en le constable. Et mesme
le leie est si home abiure est amene par vne Constable de vne vile
iesque a vne autre vile & null constable est la pur luy resceiuer, si lautre
constable suffre le felon[2] de aler a large, vncore null felony en luy pur
ceo & cetera.

Item si vne felon prist esglis & le vile suffre luy deschaper voluntier-
ment, ceo nest felony mez ils ferrount fyne pur cest eschape. Et en
cas que sount diuers esglis en vne mesme vile & le felon prist vne dez
esglise et apres eschape dehors de ceo, en cest cas tout le vile respondra le fyne & nemi le parysshe tantum. Mes si iii villes [f. 106]
nount forsque vne esglis & cest eschape est fait hors del esglis, en ceo
cas celui vile en que lesglis est respondra al Roie le fyne & nemy lez
autrez ii villez.

Item si ii Gailours sount par graunt le Roie et lun de eux fait voluntarie eschape de vne felon esteaunt en loure garde, ceo est felony en
luy que suffre leschape & forsque fynable en son compaignion.

---

[1] *Add* Sur lez besoignez, D ; sur son Besoynez, F.
[2] prisoner, C.

Item si vne feme soit gailoures par enheritaunce & prist baron & le baron fait voluntarie eschape, ceo nest felony en le baron ne en le Feme.

Item si feme esteaunt Gaioleres come est dit prist[1] vne dez felons esteaunt deins mesme le prison al baron & ceo eschape, ceo nest felony en ascun de eux & cetera.

Item si le gailer deuie & lez Felons en le gaile eschape, ceo nest felony en le heir coment que il ad loffice par enheritaunce; ne en lez executourz ne ils ne ferront fyne pur ceo.

Item sount diuers autrez felonies queux serront enquirablez deuaunt lez Justicez de peas, sicome homme que est abiure revient en le Roialme, ils purront de ceo enquerer, mes ils ne enquereront dez homez queux sount vtlagez ne de tielx hommes queux fugam fecerunt pur felonie sinoun pur arreignement de mesme le felon. Et auxi ils purront enquirer de ceux queux sount en prison pur felony & enfreynt le prison; quar ceo est felony par lestatut de Frangentibus prisonam.[2]

Et nota bene que toutz ceux chosez queux sount faitz felonies par estatut, come vers Purveours[3] ou vers hunters oue visourz oustre dez oielx[4] & similia, toutz ceux sount enquirable deuaunt lez Justicez de peas par ceux parols 'Feloniis', coment lestatut ne expresse que lez Justicez de peas doient enquerer de ceo que fait felony & cetera; nota bene & cetera.[5]

xiii^ma Lectura.

(*Margin.*) De presentacionibus contra pacem capiendis in cessiones pacis & circumstanciis eiusdem.

Ore est a voier coment lez Justicez de peas doient voier lez present-mentes fait deuaunt eux. Et son poiar est done a eux par expresse clause en le commission que ils purrount veier lez presentementes. Mes a ore lez Justicez de peas ount mielx vse que ceo fut; quar a ceo iour ils vsount de voier le sufficiente de tielx billez de presentementes deuaunt que ils sount deliuerez al enquest, & pur cell cause lez Justice

---

[1] *Bis.*

[2] 23 Edw. I, 1295. Note states that in old printed copies it is I Edw. II.

[3] For unlawful purveyance as felony, see Articuli super cartas, 28 Edw. I, c. 2, 1300, and a number of statutes of Edward III listed in index of S.R., I, under purveyance.

[4] Cf. I Hen. VII, c. 7, 1485.

[5] Throughout this last paragraph, as throughout the remaining three lectures, D now varies so greatly in phraseology that word to word colla-tion is often impossible. On the whole it is henceforth more condensed than A and is like the F version.

de peas de chescun counte vsount de commaunder lenquest apres que
ils sount iuriez que ils ne pristerount ascunz billes de ascun person
sinoun par le court ou par lez mains de vne Justice de peas ; mes
vncore en cest cas sils pristerount ascun bille de autre person & ceo
troue, ceo est bone presentment & liera le partie si fort sicome il fuist
delyuere par lez Justices de peas si soit sufficient en le leie, scilicet, de
Fourme & mater.

Et si le presentment en cest cas ne soit sufficient en Fourme come
sil ne conteigne lan, ioure ne lieu ou huiusmodi, la lez Justices de peas
poient mander pur lez presentourz queux fount tile presentment destre
deuaunt eux a certen iour, & doncques la ils purrount refourmer cest
omission en le presentment. Mes en cest cas si le presentment soit
remoue en le Bancke le Roie deuaunt ascun reformacion de ceo fait,
lez Justices de le Bancke ne poient faire proses vers lez presentourz
pur refourmer lour presentment de lez casez auauntditz.

Mes si tile presentment soit fait en le conte de Midd' & tile omission
soit en fourme de icell presentement, & puis remoue en bancke le Roie
deuaunt ascun reformacion ewe de ceo, la lez Justices de Bancke
poient faire proses enuers lez Jurrourz queux fount [f. 106 b] le presentement de reformer luy & cetera.

Et nota que a chescun tile presentment deuaunt lez Justicez de peas
destre trouez v chosez sount requisitez & necessarie a ceo destre bone &
loiall en leie : lun est de auer laddicion de le partie endite ; le ii^de est
de conteyner le an, le iour & le lieu lou lact ou loffence fut fait ; le
iii^cie est a quell person loffence fut fait ; le iiii^te est de nosmer le
chose en lequell loffence fut fait ; le v^te le nature de mesme loffence,
scilicet, sil soit transgression, felony, murdre ou huiusmodi & cetera.

Et quaunt al primer poynt de laddicions ; lestatut de anno primo
H. v^ti [1] done que addicion serra done a celui que est endite en tile presentmentes ou proses de vtlagarie gist enuers luy, si bien come en toutz
accions personelx en queux proces de vtlagarie gist vers le defendant.
Et vncore al comen leie home couient de auer done addicions al partie
en presentementes, mez ceo fut lou lendite auoit vne nome de dignite
come de Duke, Erle, vicount, counte, euesque, chiualer ou seriaunt de
le leie ; quar toutz ceux nomez sount nomez de dignite & fait par
creacion. Mez autrement fut de Barons, Banerettes, esquyers ; quar
tielx hommez [2] de dignite ne fueront faitz par creacion & issint al
comen leie home ne fut tenuz doner a eux addicion pur cause de loure
dignite.

[1] 1 Hen. V, c. 5, 1413.   [2] nosmes, B.

Mes si home soit vne countie[1] en Irelonde, il ne couient de auer tile addicion par cest nome & vncore bone, quar il nest tenuz de vener a notre parlement. Mes si tile presentment soit fait de vne countie en Scotlonde, la il couient.de doner a luy tile addicion ou autrement est voide, come de le vicount[2] de Angwis[3]; vide tile mater Mich. xxxix[o][4] E. 3.[5]

Mes si vne home ad vne nome de dignite par reson de son office come Chaunceler, Tresorer, & chamberleyn & huiusmodi, en ceo cas il ne couient deux nosmer en tilez comen presentementes accordaunt a mesme le nome. Mes si tile presentment fait enuers ascun tile officer soit de charger luy par reson de son office, doncque couient que il soit nome en le presentment accordaunt a son office sil soit office de dignite ou nemi, come vicount, Eschetour, Baillez & similia & cetera.

Item al comen leie si le pier & le Fitz fueront de vne mesme nome, si vne presentment deuoit estre fait sur le fitz, il couient en cest cas de doner a luy addicion en le bille de enditement, scilicet, Junior. Mes si le presentment serra fait enuers le pier, la ne couient null addicion destre fait en le bill; quar il ne chaungera son nome par le nome de son fitz.

Mes si soient ii estraungers ou ii officers[6] queux ount mesme le nome & de vne mesme vile, le presentement fait enuers ascun de eux saunz ascun addicion fut bone al comen leie. Et en cest cas si lez Justices agarderont proces enuers luy sur tile presentment iesque al exigent & il vient & demande vne addicion a luy destre done, il nauera tile addicion; quar lez Justicez de poiar[7] chaunger le verdit saunz lenquest, & issint diuersite lou vne accion est sue enuers vne tile lou deux sount de mesme le nome & vile & lou est fait par presentement, & de ceo mater vide anno ix[o] H. IIII[ti][8] & cetera.

Et doncque vient lestatut auauntdit, scilicet, anno[9] H. V[ti], capitulo v, que done que en tile presentment en accion personell & en appelle que le partie defendaunt serra nome par son astate, degree ou mister,[10] & auxi de le vile, hamlett ou lieu conuz & de quell conte il est conuersaunt & cetera.

---

[1] *For* vne countie *read* vn home qui demurre, B.
[2] county, F.   [3] Angus.
[4] xxxviii, B. *Add* fo. a fine, D; 4[o] fol., F.
[5] The reference is Mich. 39 Edw. III, p. 35, Briefe.
[6] frerz, D, F.
[7] *For* de poiar *read* ne poient, B; nont power de, C.
[8] Mich. 9 Hen. IV, no. 11. Idemptitate nominis.
[9] *Add* V[to], B; primo, C; and see p. 384, note 1, *supra*.
[10] mistree, C; mistre, D.

Estate ou degree serra pris come home soit esquyer, gentilman, chiualer, Baron ou huiusmodi & par cest nome poient estre conuz par autre de mesme le nome. Et issint est de yoman, quar il couient de auer tile addicion. Mes si sur tile presentment lez Jurrourz done vne addicion al [f. 107] Indite come seruaunt de vne tile, cest addicion nest bone, quar il est generall auxi bien a gentilman come a yoman & cetera. ·

[*Mistre.*] Mistre est vne nosme de occupacion come mercer, Grocer, Draper ou huiusmodi. Et issint est de husbondman, laborer & huius-modi. Mes cest Mistre couient de estre de tile occupacion que nest prohibite par le leie, come Diser, vsurer, Symoner & huiusmodi, quar cez addicions sount de mistres queux sount encontre le leie & issint voide addicions. Mes Broker & Chopchirch[1] sount bone addicions, quar ils poient estre bene vsez & sount sufferablez en viles & citees pur loiall mistres. Mes cest chose que nest mistre ne degree nest addicion, come si homme soit present & endite par cest addicion Citezyn de London ou enheritaunt de tile borowgh ou vile & huiusmodi, ceo nest bone, mes alderman est bone addicion, quar ceo est degree.

Item en cest addicion il couient de monstrer de quell vile. hamlett ou lieu conus, lendite est conuersaunt ou fut conuersaunt, & pur ceo laddi-cion est nuper de tile vile, ceo est bone addicion. Mes si le addicion soit vne tile nuper mercer, ceo nest bone addicion. Mes si ne soit ascun vile ne hamelett la lou il est ou fut conuersaunt, en ceo cas il couient destre nome de lieu conuz hors de ascun vile ; quar sil soit lieu conuz deins vne vile, ceo nest bone sinoun que addicion soit de tile vile & nemi de lieu conuz deins mesme le vile.

Item si le lieu ou il est ou fut conuersaunt ceo extende en ii villes, il ne couient estre nomez dez ascunz dez villes mez de parochia, & cest bone addicion, coment que ceo extende en ii ou iii villes & cetera.

Item ils vsount en diuers presentementes de auer vne alias dictus & ceo nest mult apurpos en tielx presentementes, quar si lendite ne soit bien nome en son nome de Baptism, surnosme, addicion de son maistur,[2] degre & vile ou il est ou fut conuersaunt, doncques le alias dictus ne voet faire ceo destre bone que fut voide deuaunt ceo & cetera. Mes tile alias dictus seruera bien en toutz accions queux sount fonduz sur vne escript, come sur obligacion ou endenture & tielx semblablez

---

[1] Chopchurch, a dealer or trafficker in ecclesiastical benefices, N.E.D. On margin of D is H. IX H. VI[ti] fo. The reference is Hill. 9 Hen. VI, no. 19. Addition. The case mentions ' Chopchurch' and ' Brogger'; cf. Statham, Addicion, no. 5.

[2] misterie, B.

queux sount faitz par ascun homme, si come il fut esquyer ou gentilman & puis il est fait chiualer ou Banerett & similia deuaunt que le
partie sua son obligacion, en tile case il couient de auer alias dictus de
faire le brieff accordaunt oue lescripte que fut fait par autre nome &
cetera, & en cest cas le alias dictus serra fait accordaunt al obligacion
pur que il est bone nosme deuaunt & cetera.

[*Le ii*de *lan & le ioure.*] Le ii^de est que en laddicion soit specifie lan
& le iour en quell loffence fut fait, si come le x iour de Nouembre
anno regni regis H. VII^mi xviii°,[1] ceo est bone & en certente. Mes si le
bill soit generalment le x iour de Nouembre [2] & ne specifie pluis, ceo
nest bone. Mes si le bille soit le x iour de Nouembre darrein passe
coment que il ne specifie lan de reign le Roie, vncore ceo est bone
presentment.[3] Et si le bille soit de loffence fait le xx iour de Pasch,
anno xviii°,[4] ceo est bone & le xx iour de Pasch serra accounpt inclusiue
en ceo cas & exclusiue. Mes si le bille soit que loffence fut fait en le
Vtas de Pasch, ceo nest bone presentment. Mes si le bille soit que il
fut fait en Octobis [*sic*] Pasche, ceo est bone, & en cest cas il serra pris
destre fait en le iour de Vtas & nemi le iiii^te iour apres & cetera ; quod
nota.

Item si le bill soit que loffence fut fait anno domini [f. 107 b] M°
DIII°[5] & cetera, ceo est bone & cetera, & ceo serra accounpt soloncque
le computacion de Anglia[6] & nemi de Roma.

Item si loffence soit fait en le Nute si soit deuaunt mydnoet ceo
serra pris pur le iour deuaunt, & si soit fait apres mydnoet pur le iour
consequent & nemi de meredie in merediem.

Item si le bille compris que loffence fut fait en tile fest come en feste
Sancti Johannis Baptiste ou huiusmodi, ceo est bone & serra pris pur le
iour de mesme le fest & nemi de primer vespris en darrein vesperis de
mesme le Fest.

---

[1] 10 November, 6 Hen. VIII, C ; 10 March, 8 Hen. VII, D ; 10 June,
20 Henry VII, F ; 9 June, 20 Hen. VIII, G ; 1 March, 25 Hen. VII, L.

[2] 10 March, D ; 9 July, G ; 1 March, L.

[3] *For* Mes si . . . presentment, *read* Mez sil dit darrein passe, lenditement est sufficient, quar le stile de cessions monstra lan, etc., D.

[4] Sexto, C.

[5] Millesimo, etc., B, L ; Millesimo xiii°, C ; anno domini, etc., D ;
1505, F ; 1545, G.

[6] *Add* si commensa all fest de natiuite, D ; videlicet, to begin at the
feast of the natyuitie, L. But 25 December was not the date of the new
year in England at this time, and 'secundum consuetudinem ecclesie
Anglicane' means that the year began on 25 March, instead of on
1 January according to the Roman usage ; R. L. Poole, Medieval
Reckonings of Time, 43–45.

Item si tile presentement deuaunt lez Justicez de peas soit fait en le negatiff, en cest cas lan & le iour nest materiall, sicome home soit present al Sessions que il nauoit scowre vne sewer, gutter ou Diche & cetera; quar lez Justicez de peas poient enquerer de ceo come con-seruatourz de le ryuer par estatutez.[1]

Item si tile presentment soit fait en le negatiue oue affirmatiff pregnans surdaunt sur mesme le negatiff, sicome homme est endite pur ceo que il nad bien scowre vne sewer par reson de quell noisaunce tiel prees sount surroundes, ou pur nounfesaunce de tilx murez tile eirable grounde est surounde, eñ ceux casez lan & le iour ne sount materiall, quar il est destre entendue que il fut nusaunce par continuaunce.

[*A que tile offence fut fait.*] Le tierce est a que tile offence fut fait; mez vncore ceo ne serra pris si generalment en chescun cas; quar en ascun casez lenditement est bone coment que le person a que loffence fut fait ne soit conuz, come en cas que le bill soit que vne tile, scilicet, J. atte S.[2] & cetera bona cuiusdam ignoti felonice cepit & abduxit, ceo est bone en Theft. Et issint est si le bille soit tile : quod ipse quem-dam ignotum felonice murdrauit, ceo est bone. Mes si le presentement soit tile : quod ipse bona cuiusdam ignoti cepit vi & armis, ou quod ipse quemdam ignotum depredauit, si ne soit felonice, ceo nest bone; ou si le presentment soit que un tile maund quemdam ignotum de tuer ascun home & ceo il fist par son[3] commaundement, ceo nest bone. Mes si soit de tile transgression ou treason lou toutz sount principalles, ceo est bone presentment adire que un tile procurauit personas ignotas de imagener[4] ou faire treason, ceo est bone, quar en mayme & treason toutz sount principalls & null accessorie & cetera.

Item si lez Jurrourz voillount enditer ascun person de prendre dez biens de vne abbe, le bill de lenditement couient estre tile, scilicet, que un tile felonice prist lez biens domus & ecclesie et nemi lez biens de J. att S., abbott de mesme le lieu. Et issint couient estre fait si labbe deuie apres lez biens sount feloneusment prisez & deuaunt lenditement, vncore le bille serra fait dez bienz domus & ecclesie & cetera. Et mesme le leie est si lenditement serra fait dez biens felonysment pris que fueront de vne communialte, le bill serra bona comitatus cepit & cetera & nemi bona maioris cepit & cetera. Mes si lez propres bienz de vne parson de vne esglis sount issint prisez, le bill couient estre fait

---

[1] Cf. Westminster II, c. 47, 1285; 13 Rich. II, st. I, c. 19, 1390; 17 Rich. II, c. 9, 1394.

[2] Stile, B. [3] cell, B; cest, C.

[4] mayhemer, B; machener, C; but cf. Statute of Treasons (p. 379, note 7, *supra*) for the use of imaginer.

de bonis Rectoris de tile esglise felonysment prisez et nemi bona
ecclesie.   Mes si lez biens de lesglise sount felonysment prisez le bill
couient estre tile, scilicet, bona parochianorum & nemi ecclesie.   Mes
[si] lez bienz de vne propositor ou garden de vne[1] chapelle que appartient a le chapell sount prisez, le bille couient estre bona capelle de C
& cetera.   Et vncore en cest cas nest ascun successour[2] en ceo chapelle
ou propositour, quar[3] il fut saunz remedie & cetera.

Item si vne soit endite deuaunt lez Justicez de peas, scilicet, quod
ipse verberauit Johannem a S.[4] & vnum equum precii xxs. cepit &
abduxit, & ne dit equum ipsius Johannis att S. cepit & vncore cest
enditement est bone.   Et si lenditement soit tile, scilicet, quod vne tile
vnum [f. 108] equum predicti Thome[5] cepit & cetera, cest enditement
est voide pur ceo que Thomas ne fut nome deuaunt en lenditement &
cetera.

Item si lez biens de vne home sount prisez de luy en son vie & il
fait cez executourz et deuie, en ceo cas lenditement couient estre quod
bona testatoris in vita sua cepit & nemi bona executorum.   Mes si
biens sount prisez hors de le possession dez executourz apres le mort
del Testatour, en cest cas lenditement couient estre bona Testatoris in
custodia executoris existentia, ceo est bone.

Item si vne cote armure desuis vne Tombe en lesglise soit pris hors
de lesglise, en cest cas lenditement couient estre bona executorum de
celui que fut le owner de & cetera.   Mes si vne Grauestone que est en
lesglis soit issint pris, lenditement couient estre bona ecclesie & nemi
rectoris & cetera.[6]

Item si vne home prist mez biens de moie & puis vne autre prist
mesmez lez biens de luy, en ceo cas si celui que eux prisoit pluis
darrein soit endite de cest prisell, lenditement couient estre bona celui
que fut darrein en possession & nemi bona de moy de que ils fueront
primerment prisez.   Mez en mesme le cas si ieo baille mez biens a
vne autre pur savement garder & vne autre eux prist hors de son
possession, la lenditement serra dit bona de moy que eux baille &
nemi bona de le baille cepit & cetera.   Et issint si vne home moy
robbe & vne autre luy robba apres de mesmez lez biens,
[*Nota diuersite.*]   en ceo cas lenditement couient estre bona de moy que fut
primerment robbe & nemi bona celui que moie robbe,

---

[1] *Add* free, B, C.   [2] succession, F.
[3] *Add* autrement, B, D, F.   [4] Style, B, C.
[5] J. att S. throughout F.
[6] *Add* Trin. ix E. 4[ti] fo. xiiii, D (margin) ; identified as Trin. 9 Edw.
IV, no. 8.

quar robberie ne chaunge ascun proprete, mez biens pris par transgression chaunge le propurte en toutz casez par supposell.

[*Le quart.*] Le iiii^te chose est le chose en quell loffence fut fait ou
le pris de icell. Et ore nota si le pris de le chose soit suppose par
lenditement de vne chose en le singuler nombre, sil soit de chose viue
ou de chose mort, lenditement dirra tile chose come vne chiuall ou
vne robe precii xxs.[1] & nemi ad valenciam & cetera. Mes si lenditement soit de chosez en le plurell nombre, sil soit de chose viue come
chiuall, vachez ou huiusmodi, la lenditement couient destre precii &
nemi ad valenciam. Et si lenditment soit dez chosez mortez en le
plurell nombre, la lenditment doit estre fait que il prist tielx chosez
come pottez, pannes, ou huiusmodi, ad valenciam & nemi precii &
cetera.[2]

Et nota que si lenditement soit de chatell viue il ne dirra bona &
catalla de vne tile, mez si lenditement soit dez chateux queux sount
mortez, ils serront nomez en lenditement bona & catalla vne tile &
cetera.

Item si vne home soit endite pur ceo que il auoit pris tilx bestez
queux sount Feer de natur come hertes, fesaundes, dere & huiusmodi,
ceo nest bone sinoun que ils sount prisez hors de ascun parke, Forest,
warrein queux sount libertees par graunt le Roie, & doncques est bone.
Mes en cest cas de warrein ou parke, si vne soit endite que il prist
sauagez ou Fesauntes, il ne dirra en lenditement precii ne ad valenciam
en ceo cas.

Mes si lenditement soit tile, scilicet, quod clausum fregit & tot
cuniculos, scilicet, x couple, ibidem cepit, la il dirra precii. Mesme le
ley est si lenditment soit de pris de vne Dame que est Domesticall, ou
si soit de vne Foule que est feer de nature & il scia vne pate[3] ou vne
whyng, en ceux deux casez lenditement serra precii & nemi ad
valenciam, & cetera; quod nota.

[f. 108 b.] Item si lenditement soit quod vne tile in viuariis de A.
piscatus fuit & pisces ibidem cepit, il ne dirra precii nemi ad valenciam
& ceo est vne chose viue. Mes si home soit endite quod piscem de
stagno cepit, en cest cas il couient que le nombre dez pissez sount
expressez en lenditement come xx & cetera; et auxi en ceo cas il
dirra precii & nemi ad valenciam. Mes si home soit endite pur ceo

---

[1] Quinque solidorum, B; xs., C.
[2] *Add* Trin. p. 10 H v^ti f. 3, 842 Brefe, D (margin). The first reference
has not been identified; the second is to Fitzherbert, *ut supra.* The
latter cites a report of Mich. 19 Edw. II, pp. 624–5.
[3] pee, B, D, F; pece, C.

quod ipse pissem in stagno enudauit [1] & nemi cepit, en ceo cas il dirra
ad valenciam & nemi precii & vncore est chose viue & cetera.

Item si lenditement soit quod intrauit boscum de vne tile & pullos
esperuorum, scilicet, yonge sperhawkis, cepit, en cest cas il couient de
monstrer en lenditement le nombre de eux & precii.[2] Et issint est si
home soit endite quod ipse intrauit in vnum columbarium & columbas
ibidem inuentas cepit, la il couient de monstrer le nombre & price de
eux.

Et nota bene que en toutz casez lou home ne dirra en lenditement
le pris ne ad valenciam, la il ne monstra le nombre de eux chosez
issint prisez. Et en toutz casez lou il couient de monstrer le nombre,
en ceux casez il couient dire precii vel ad valenciam come le cas gist
& cetera.

Item si home ad delyuere a moy bestez par lez pur certen terme pur
compescer mon terre, & il eux reprist de moie deins le terme & puis ieo
luy endita de ceo, lenditement serra bone vers luy sur le especiall mater
quare vi et armis il eux prist & vncore le proprete de eux fut en luy
mesme al temps de le transgression. Mes en cest cas, ieo ne dirra en
lenditement precii ne ad valenciam, & vncore le enditement est de
chatell viue & cetera.

Item si home soit endite pur ceo quod ipse equos vel vaccas ad
talem locum fugauit, ceo est bone enditement de transgression & en
cest cas il ne dirra precii ne ad valenciam.[3] Mes en mesme le cas si
lenditement soit oustre, scilicet, quod equos vel vaccas fugauit vnde
mortui sunt, doncque il dirra precii de eux en lenditement.

Et nota si lenditement soit de prisell de vne chatell mort, come dez
harbres, herbes, blada en grangia ou cressauntes [4] & huiusmodi, la il
dirra toutz foitz en lenditement ad valenciam & nemi precii quia
mortui sunt. Mes si home soit endite de le prisell dez chartres ou
evidences concernaunt ascun terre ou Fraunk tenement, la ne serra
precii de eux ne ad valenciam, quar le value [5] de eux ne poet propre-

---

[1] enuditur, B; emundauit, D, F.

[2] *Add* et vncore est chose uiue, etc., C.; Mich. x E. iiii[ti] fo. xv,
Maxim en ley pur precii & valenciam, D (margin). The report is Mich.
49 Hen. VI, no. 10.

[3] *Add* 13 Mich. x E 4[ti], D (margin); identified as Mich. 49 Hen. VI,
no. 9. The reference applies, I think, to the passage a few lines further
down about 'chartres'. On the opposite margin D has 629 Brefe, identified in Fitzherbert, *ut supra*.

[4] *For* blada . . . cressauntes *read* blada ou grane cressauntes, B ; blada
ou grenez, C.

[5] valumentt, D.

ment estre exsteme. Et issint en cas lou home est endite de ceo que
il ad pris le corps de vne enfaunt esteaunt en garde hors de possession
de vne tile, la il ne dirra precii ne ad valenciam, quar ceo est vne
chatell realle.

Et nota en toutz casez de chatell reall il ne dirra precii ne ad valenciam en lenditement. Et mesme le leie est de vne precious stone &
de relickez, quar de eux il ne dirra precii ne ad valenciam, quar il¹ ne
poient estre value bien & cetera.

Item si lenditement soit quod ipse domum fregit & meremium inde
cepit et asportauit, en cest cas il couient dire en lenditement ad valenciam de² & cetera, & vncore ceo fut annexe al soyle & cetera.

Item si home defalke lez herbez de vne autre en son close & puis
apres depasture part de mesmez lez herbez oue son auerz, en cest cas
sil soit endite de tout cest mater, il couient de auer en lenditement ii
foitz ad valenciam, quar le value de eux que fueront defalke ne fut le
value dez autrez que fueront depastus.³ Mes en mesme le cas si
lenditement fut quod ipse tantas herbas defalcauit & easdem herbas
depastus [f. 109] fuit cum aueriis suis, la il ne dirra forsque vne foitz
ad valenciam pur tout le mater & cetera.

Et nota que si home soit endite pur ceo que il ad mispris ascun
chose mort que va par weight ou mesure, coment que soit chose mort,
vncore il dirra en lenditement precii & nemi ad valenciam ; sicome
home soit endite de prisell de ii lagyns de vyne ou de ii quarters de
Frument ou deux libres de peper ou de huiusmodi, la il dirra precii
& nemi ad valenciam. Mes si home soit endite en tile fourme, scilicet,
quod ipse duas lagenas vini de vno doleo vini extraxit & eundem
doleum cum·aqua repleuit sic quod residuum eiusdem vini putridum
remansit, en cest cas lenditement couient destre en le premissez duas
lagenas vini precii & cetera. Et lou il apres en mesme len-
[*Nota bene*] ditement [dit] quod residuum putridum remansit, il dirra la
ad valenciam. Et issint en cest cas il dirra precii⁴ ad valenciam en vne mesme lenditement & en maner pur vne⁵ chose.

Item si homme soit endite de le prisell de moneẏ il ne dirra
en lenditement precii ne ad valenciam, quar il purport vne pris en luy
mesme. Mes en mesme le cas si lenditement soit de prisell de vne
coyne que est curraunt en autre roialme & nemi en cest roialme, come
de Dukettes, Rennyssh gildourns & huiusmodi, la il couient a dire en
lenditement precii de eux & nemi ad valenciam. Mes si lenditement

---

¹ eux, B.   ² *Add* celui, B.   ³ MS. depasẟ ; depastuz, B.
⁴ *Add* et, B.   ⁵ *Add* mesme, B.

soit de money que est curraunt en autrez roialmes & auxi curraunt en mesme le roialme, come de plackez & huiusmodi, la il dirra viginti libras en plackes & ne dirra precii ne ad valenciam & cetera.

Mes si home soit endite pur ceo quod ipse proditorie fecit grossos ou denarios, en cest cas lenditement ne serra precii ne ad valenciam ne xx libras en grossis ne xx libras in pecuniis domini Regis, mes lenditement serra quod ipse proditorie fecit tantos grossos ad instar pecuniam domini Regis; quod nota bene.

[*Le v est le natur de loffence.*] Et hic nota que si ascun enditement soit fait de transgression il couient de auer ceux parols en mesme lenditement, vi et armis, ou parols que amount a taunt; sicome lendite ad entre en ascun terre oue force, coment en cest cas que il ne dirra vi & armis, vncore ceo est bone quar il amount a taunt.

Item si le mater de lenditement soit foundue sur ascun estatut, la il couient dire en lenditement quod ipse fecit & cetera contra formam statuti ou contra forman statutorum, come en cas del franger dez parkes [1] ou huiusmodi. Mes en cest enditement il ne couient reherse lestatut mez solement loffence fait encontre tile estatute.

Item si homme soit endite de mayhem, il couient dire en lenditement quod ipse felonice maymeauit, ou autrement lenditement nest bone & vncore ceo nest felony.

Item si home soit endite de Burglarie il couient que lenditement soit Burglariter; quar coment que il monstra en lenditement que lendite en le nute entra son meason al entent de luy murdrer & ne dit Burglariter, lenditement nest bone. Mes si home soit endite quod ipse vi et armis rapuit vne tile, vncore ceo est bone enditement de felony saunz dire felonice en lenditement; quar Rape est fait felony par estatut,[2] & pur ceo quaunt il dit rapuit ne poet estre entendue forsque felony. Mez si home prist mez biens, ceo poet estre felonice ou come trespassour, & pur ceo en cest cas il couient dire felonice en lenditement; mes en le cas auauntdit si lenditement soit que un J. att S. felonice cepit vxorem vne tile & eam carnaliter cognouit, vncore ceo nest felony sinoun que il dit en lenditement rapuit & cetera.

Item si lenditement soit tile, scilicet, quod vne tile vnum ciphum furatus fuit & ne dit felonice en cest [f. 109 b] enditement, et vncore ceo fut aiugge bone enditement de felony anno vi[to][3] R. II[di][4] saunz dire felonice & cetera.

---

[1] Cf. 3 Edw. I, Westminster I, c. 20, 1275, and 21 Edw. I, 1293, Statutum de Malefactoribus in Parcis.
[2] Cf. 13 Edw. I, Westminster II, c. 34, 1285.
[3] v[to], B.   [4] Not identified.

Item si lenditement soit que un tile auoit occise vne home, ceo nest bone saunz dire felonice, & vncore contrarium est aiugge anno primo E. III^{cii},[1] quar home poet occider vne autre loialment par diuerses voies, come en son defence ou en batell gager ou huiusmodi & cetera.

Item si home soit endite quod ipse quendam A amesna hors de le meason en le champe par le nute dount il pur frigour murust felonice, cest enditement nest bone, mes couient estre quod ipse felonice ipsum A murdrauit & ceo est aiugge anno ii^{do} E. III.[2]

Item si home soit endite quod ipse felonice abduxit vnum equum & ne dit cepit, ceo nest bone enditement de Felony mez il couient dire en lenditement cepit. Et si lenditement soit que ipse felonice cepit vnum equum, vncore ceo nest bone mes il couient dire [3] cepit & abduxit. Et si lenditement soit quod ipse vnum equum cepit & abduxit felonice, ceo nest bone mes couient dire felonice cepit & abduxit.[4]

Et nota que si home soit endite pur ceo quod ipse felonice succidit arbores & il asportauit, ceo nest bone. Et sil dit quod ipse vi & armis succidit arbores & felonice asportauit, vncore semble a moy que nest bone ; mes si lenditement soit quod ipse vi & armis succidit arbores & quod ipse postea al autre iour eux cepit & asportauit, ceo est bone & cetera ; quod nota.

Quartadecima Lectura.

(*Margin.*) De processu super indictamentis contra pacem.

Auxi est compris deins mesme le clause en le commission que dona le auctorite denquerer a lez Justicez de peas que mesmez lez Justices ne doient solement inspexer le sufficiente de lez enditementes mez auxi que ils doient faire proses sur mesme lenditement ; & ceo auxi sur enditementes deuaunt autrez Justicez [5] en mesme le counte auxi come sur lenditementes ewe deuaunt eux, & auxi sur enditementes ewe en temps dez autrez Roies ; & ceo eux ne puissent auer fait sinoun que ceo vst este graunt a eux par expresse parols en le commission, quar lez auncientz Justices fueront de cy haute de [6] recorde come lez nouelles, & pur ceo ils ne auoient poiar de faire breue a eux ne ils ne puissount mitter inz lez enditementes en le Bancke le Roie par lour

---

[1] Not identified.

[2] The reference is to Hill. 2 Edw. III, no. 1, p. 18, under the heading : 'Note that these cases of the 11 year of Edward the third were taken out of another Report, and by advice placed here, as followeth.'

[3] *Add* felonice, C.

[4] *Add* quar si le felonice soit apres, ceo auera relacion forsque all abduxit, etc., D.

[5] *Add* de peas, C.   [6] *Omit*, B.

mains come de recorde. Mes deuaunt lez Justicez de Gaole delyuerer ils puissent mitter inz loure enditementes par loure mains,
quar ils fueront pluis haute.

Mes nient obstante que ils poient proceder sur enditementes deuaunt autrez Justicez de peas, vncore en cest cas si le partie ad
trauers lenditement issint que il ad este a vne issue ou autrement en
proses, ceo vst este discontinue par le determinacion de launcient
commission & cetera ; par que lestatut de anno xi^{mo} H.VI^{ti} capitulo vi^o [1]
voet que par ascun nouell commission fait que toutz sutez, plees &
proses queux fueront pendaunt deuaunt lez auncientes Justices ne serront my discontinuz, mes que lez nouelles Justicez eiant poiar de proceder sur mesme les plees, Inditementes & procez que fueront deuaunt
rendauntes [2] lez auncientes Justices & cetera.

Doncque le proses de le commission que lez Justicez poient faire
sur lez enditementes est le veraie procez dutlagerie que est al comen
leie ; & ceo est sur enditement de transgression vne Venire facias,
iii Capias & Exigent, et sur toutz enditementes de felony forsque vne
Capias et Exigent & cetera.[3] Mes lez Justices de peas ne ount poiar
de faire ascun collaterall procez sur les enditementes sicome lez
Justicez al comen leie poient faire ; quar si lez Justicez agarder vne
[f. 110] Venire facias enuers vne home sur vne enditement de transgression, & le vicount retorne sur le breue quod ipse clericus est &
beneficiatus non habens laicum feodum, en cest cas ils ne poient
agarder vne Venire facias clericum al euesque de faire son clerke de
apparer deuaunt eux, mez ils purrount agarder solement Capias. Et
vncore si le vicount fait tile returne al comen leie, lez Justicez al
comen leie poient eslier de prendre son proces par Capias al vicount
ou agarder vne Venire facias clericum direct al Ordinarie. Mes si
home a vne foitz appier sur enditement de transgression & apres fist
default, la lenquest serra pris par son default enuers luy ; mes si le
partie appier sur enditement de Felony & puis fist default, vncore lenquest ne serra pris par son default.

Item si vne seignur come Duke, Erle, Baron ou huiusmodi, que
sount seignurz de parliament, soient enditez de transgression, Riott ou
huiusmodi, null proses de vtlagarie gist enuers eux, ne lez Justicez de
peas ne poient agarde vne Testatum en autre conte enuers mesme le

---

[1] 11 Hen. VI, c. 6, 1433.
[2] *For* deuaunt rendauntz *read* dependaunt deuaunt, B.
[3] *Add* 81 22 anno lib. Ass., D (margin) ; identified as 22 Edw. III,
no. 81.

seignurz ; mes ils poient faire proses dutlarie enuers vne seignur de
Irelonde ou vne Testatum en autre conte enuers luy, quar le seignur
de Irelonde ne vient a notre parlement.   Mes lez Justicez de peas ne
poient agarder proses de vtlagarie enuers vne seignur de Chesshire,
Lancashire & huiusmodi, coment que le breue le Roie ne courge la,
vncore ils veignount al parliament tenuz en engliterre & pur ceo null
proses dutlagarie [gist] enuers eux.   Mes si ascun tile seignur de parliament fait ascun rescous ou autre contempt en le pretence[1] de lez
Justicez come sil fesaunt[2] ascun Riott, Rowte ou huiusmodi, en cest cas
sils sount enditez sur cest, proses de vtlagarie gist enuers eux & cetera.

Et doncques vient vne autre estatute que fut fait anno v E. 3, capitulo xi^{mo},[3] que done lou hommez sount enditez, appellez ou vtlagez
de felony en vne conte, sils sount demurrauntez & conuersauntz en
vne autre conte, que lez Justicez ount poair de oier et terminer tielx
felonies & facent breue en chescun conte de prendre tilx enditees.
Et par lequyte de mesme lestatut est pris que si ascun tile endite
remayne en prison en autre conte que lez Justices de peas deuaunt
que il fut endite voillount agarder Habeas corpus de luy remouer
deuaunt eux.   Mes si home fut endite en vne conte & en lenditement
il est appelle de vne autre conte, en ceo cas lez Justicez voillount
agarder proses de vtlagarie enuers luy & luy utlager saunz faire
ascun proses en cest forrein conte lou il fut appelle destre demurant ;
par que est vne autre estatut fait anno viii^o H. VI, capitulo x^{mo},[4] que
done que si ascun home soit endite en vne conte & par mesme lenditement il est nome de autre conte que lez Justices facient le ii^{de} Capias
destre direct al vicount de le conte dount il est appelle en mesme
lenditement, conteignaunt le space entre le Teste & le retourne de
trois moys, lou le conte est tenuz chescun mois, et le space de iiii mois,
lou le counte est tenuz forsque chescun vi semaignes.   Et en cest cas
si le vicount de le forein conte ne poet trouer lendite, que il face proclamacion en plein conte de tile enditement & cetera.   Et si ascun
home soit vtlage en tile cas saunz fesaunz de tile proses, que cest
vtlagarie serra voide et que null home sur tile vtlagarie perdera son
vie ne sez bienz mes serra outrement come voide & cetera.

Item si homme soit nosme de vne vile par lenditement deins mesme
le conte lou il est endite & auxi soit nosme en mesme lenditement

[1] presence, B.   [2] fesoit, B.
[3] 5 Edw. III, c. 11, 1331 ; the statute reads ' que les Justices, assignez
doier & terminer tieles felonies facent lour brefs . . .'
[4] 8 Hen. VI, c. 10, 1429.

nuper de autre vile en vne Forein conte, null proses en cest cas serra
fait en le Forein conte. Mes si homme soit endite par le nome
[f. 110 b] de J. att S.[1] nuper de B., que est deins mesme le conte lou il
est endite, oue vne alias dictus de vne autre vile deins vne Forrein
conte, en cest cas proses serra fait en le forrein conte pur ceo que il
est nome destre tile vile en forein conte. Mes si home soit endite par
nome de A. de B. que est en forein conte, & nuper de C.[2] que est en
autre forein conte, en cest cas le breue serra direct solement al vicount
de le primer conte de que il fut primerment nome, & nemi en lautre
forein conte de que le nuper se extende. Mes si lenditement soit que
vne A. nuper de B., que est en forein conte, nuper de C. en autre
forein conte, en cest cas le brieff serra direct en ambideux forein
contez.

Et mesme le ley est sil soit nome de A. que est en forein conte,
alias dictus de B. que est en vne autre forein conte, le proces serra direct
en ambideux forein contez. Mes sil soit nome en lenditement de A.
deins mesme le conte lou lenditement est, alias dictus de C. que est en
vne forein conte, la null proses issera en le forein conte; quar il fut
appelle de A. que fut en mesme le conte que serra entende[3] lou est
demuraunt a cest temps & nemi aillourz.

Item si vne abbott soit endite deins vne conte par le nome de J. B.,
abbott de C., le quell monasterie est en autre conte, coment que il soit
en lenditement de vne vile que est en mesme le conte lou il est endite,
vncore en ceo cas proses serra direct al vicount de mesme le vicount[4]
lou le abbathie est, par lequite de cest estatut ou autrement le vtlagerie
est voide & cetera.

Et doncques apres en[5] vne autre estatut fait in anno xxv° E. 3,
capitulo xiiii°,[6] & ceo done que si home soit endite de felony al cessions
deuaunt Justicez assignez de oier & terminer felonies, & si le vicount
sur le primer Capias returne quod non est inuentus & cetera, que sur
cest returne serra vne autre Capias fait par mesme lez Justices direct
a mesme le vicount, en quell breue serra compris que le vicount
seisiera toutz ceux chateux & eux sauement gardera al vse le Roie sil
tarie[7] lexigent, ou autrement al vse del partie. Et si le vicount returne
sur cest breue que il nest inuentus ne apparust deuaunt lez Justices,
soit lexigent agarde & son bienz forfaitz. Mes si le vicount ad luy

---

[1] J. a. E., MS. B ; no initials in MSS. D, F.
[2] E, MS. B.
[3] MS. adds que serra entendue, evidently a slip.
[4] contie, B, C.   [5] est, B.
[6] 25 Edw. III, st. 5, c. 14, 1352.   [7] terge, B.

pris par vertue de cest ii^de Capias ou autrement le partie apparust deuaunt lez Justicez, en ceux ii casez sez bienz serront saue a luy et si le vicount en cest cas prist son corps, il ne poet seisier son biens auxi par statut Ricardi tercii, capitulo.[1]

Doncques est a voier quellez chosez il poet seisier & quell nemi & cetera; quar sil ad frument en garbez, si le vicount poet eux garbez seisier, & en ceo cas il ne poet seisier eux quar il ne poet eux sauer quaunt il deuoit eux delyuerer & cetera. Mes si Frument ou autrez graynes sount en le barne en lez garbez il poet eux seisier, quar en ceo cas il poet eux a taunt sauer quaunt il eux prist.

Item si homme ad greihoundes, hawkes ou autrez chosez de plesure, le vicount ne poet eux seisier par cause de tile ii^de Capias sur enditement, ne auxi le vicount ne poet seisier pissons esteauntz en estange ne poions[2] esteaunt en vne dowue howse ne rabettes ne conyes en vne garrein ne tielx semblablez; quar en toutz tilx casez le vicount ne poet eux sauement garder sil couient eux redelyuer al partie sil apparust deuaunt lexigent. Mez le vicount poet seisier bees que sount encloses en vne hyffe mes nemi lez bees queux sount en swarme en vne arbe par tile proses.

Item le vicount sur cest ii^de Capias sur enditement ne poet seisier son apparell que est pur son corps, mes si lendite ad vne eire lome, scilicet, vne chatell come chalis, cuppe de argent ou autre chose que ad use de aler oue son enheritaunce par le volunte son auncestres, le vicount [f. 111] poet ceo seisier sur cel proses.

Item le vicount ne poet seisier ascun evidence concernaunt ascun terre ne obligacion que fut fait a luy tantum, mez a luy & vne autre sur cest proses de ii^de Capias; quar ceux chosez ne sount forsque chosez en accion. Mes le vicount seisiera vne lez pur terme de ans & ceo manmera (?).[3]

Item si tile endite ad vne garde de terre & de corps, le vicount poet luy seisier le terre & le corps ambideux, mes en cas seisiera[4] le corps de vne garde & luy maria deuaunt le iour de retourne de mesme le Capias par force de quell il luy seisit, & puis le partie apparust a cest iour de retourne, en cest cas le partie auera accion sur son cas enuers le vicount & recouera en[5] son damagez pur le mariage al value. Mes si lendite auoit a vne foitz tende convenable mariage al garde deuaunt le seisier de le vicount et puis le vicount luy maria, en cest cas le

---

[1] 1 Rich. III, c. 3, 1484.   [2] pigeons, B.   [3] maynura (?), B.
[4] *For* mes ... seisiera *read* mez en ceo cas si le viscount seisier, C.
[5] *Omit*, B.

partie ne recouera le ii^de value de le mariage enuers le vicount, sicome il deuoit enuers leir sil ad luy maria & cetera.

Item si vne dona vne villein a vne autre & puis le done est endite & cest ii^de Capias agarde enuers luy pur seisier cez bienz, en ceo cas le vicount poet seisier le villein. Mes si lendite soit seisi de vne villein appendaunt a son maner, le vicount ne poet luy seisier; nota diuersitatem de ceux casez & cetera.

Item si home ad ii chiualx & dona celui que est endite vne de mesmez lez chiualx & ne monstra le quell de eux en certen, en cest cas sur cest proses le vicount ne seisiera le mielx de eux come le partie poet, ne il seisiera ascun de eux.

Et mesme le leie si lendite soit entitle de auer hariett par custom et chuett[1] a luy ne lou il deuoit auer waiffe ou straie, en ceo cas le vicount ne poet eux seisier deuaunt que le partie est en possession de eux. Mesme le ley lou lendite est entitle de auer wreke de mier, mes si le partie seisiera le wreke & deuaunt prove, & deinz le an le vicount seisist & apres lan passe si le partie a que le propurte fut ne apparust, doncque sount forfaitz & le vicount eux retiendra pur le Roie & cetera.

Item si homme ad retourne irrepleuysable de bestez queux il ad en pounde, le vicount ne eux seisiera sur tile proses. Mes si vne autre home ad lez bestez le Indite in pownde irrepleuysable, le vicount poet seisier eux mez vncore mesmez lez bestez ne serrount deliuerez, mes le partie que ad eux en pounde en cest cas serra compell de eux sauement garder oue manger & boier necessarie & le Roie luy allowa de ceo apres.

Item si ii ount bienz iointement & lun de eux est endite & le vicount ad Capias enuers luy de seisier cez bienz, en cest cas le vicount seisiera toutz mesmez lez biens, mes quaunt lexigent est agarde ils serrount preisez par le pays & le Roie[2] eit forsque le moite. Mez si lautre que est son compaignion deuie deuaunt lexigent agarde, doncque le Roie auera lentier bienz & cetera.

Item si vne vile soit corporat par le nome de Maire & successour, & le maire de mesme le vile est endite par le nome de maire, & proses entre eux fait tancque al exigent, en cest cas le maire forfetra solement cez bienz demene & nemi lez bienz de le communialte, et vncore il ne apparust que il fut endite pur vne cause de le communialte ou pur luy mesme.

---

[1] enchuett, B; escheit, C; eschuyt, D; eschuit, F.
[2] Viscount, B.

Mes si vne abbe de vne lieu soit endite & tile ii^de Capias agarde
enuers luy de seisier cez bienz, en cest cas le vicount seisiera lez biens
de son esglise & domus, mes nemi lez oblacions & dismes que il deuoit
auer [f. 111 b] come oblacions ou dymes.   Mes vncore si vne parson
soit al exigent sur tile enditement, il forfetra toutz cez bienz, oblacions
& dymes, mez nemi lez bienz que sount de son esglise & cetera. [*Quere.*]

Item si feme couert soit endite, le vicount ne seisiera sur tile Capias
lez biens queux el ad come executrice ne si el auoit vne garde de corps
de vne enfaunt, vncore ceo ne serra seisi pur le entresse que le baron
ad en son garde & cetera.

Item si celui que est endite apres cest ii^de Capias agarde enuers luy
aliene ascunz de sez biens, le vicount seisiera eux nient obstant tile
alienacion.   Mes sil aliene cez bienz apres le primer Capias & deuaunt
le ii^de Capias agarde, en cest cas le vicount ne seisiera eux apres.

Item si vne villein soit endite, si le vicount sur le ii^de Capias seisist
lez bienz de le villein, & deuaunt le iour de lexigent agarde, le seignur
de le villein seisist & puis lexigent est agarde, en cest cas le seignur de
le villein auera lez bienz & nemi le Roie ; quere.

Et lez parols de le commission sount oustre : & lez sauement
garderount tancque al iour de le brieff.   Et ceo serra entendue en tile
maner, scilicet, que vicount apres que ad seisi lez bienz par vertue de
ascun tile proses que il deuoit mittre eux en suretie par Inuentorie ou
de eux mittre en vne meason ou de garder eux luy mesme.   Et si le
vicount delyuer mesmez lez biens issint seisiez al constable de mesme
le vile, nient obstante que il est lofficer le Roie, vncore si lez biens
sount empairez ou wastes en le custodie de le constable, ceo serra al
perell de le vicount, quar il respondra al Roie pur mesmez lez bienz
& de chescun parcell.   Mes si le vicount deliuera lez bienz apres tile
seisier a vne autre home pur sauement garder eux, al request de celui
partie que est endite, en cest cas coment que lez bienz sount wastez,
si le partie apparust al iour deuaunt lexigent agarde enuers luy, la le
vicount est discharge enuers le partie.   Mes en mesme le cas si le
partie ne apparust my deuaunt lexigent, le vicount nest discharge par
ceo vers le Roie & cetera.

Si le vicount retorne sur cest ii^de Capias, non est inuentus & le
partie ne apparust, soit lexigent agarde & son chateux[1] forfaitz soloncque ceo que le leie de le crowne demande.   Et par ceux parols deins
mesme le commission, coment que le vicount retorne non est inuentus
sur cest ii^de Capias, vncore si le partie apparust deuaunt lexigent

---

[1] MS. cheux ; chateux, B.

agarde, il ne forfetra cez bienz nient obstante le premier seisin[1]; quod nota. Et nota que si lexigent soit agarde enuers ascun tile endite, il forfetra toutz cez bienz & chateux mez nemi cez dettes ne accions que va al person, come accion de Baterie & huiusmodi. Mes en cest cas accions de Detenue sount ale, quar la propurte de la chose que est deteigne est chaunge par cest agarde de lexigent & mys en le Roie. Mes si lendite soit entitle de auer ascun accion de Transgression dez bienz emportez enuers autre, vncore il auera cest accion, nient obstante tile exigent agarde; mes en cest cas si le speciall mater soit monstre par le defendaunt, le pleintiff ne recouera damages solement pur lenparture[2] & nemi pur le value de lez bienz. Et nota auxi que cestuy enuers que tile exigend est agarde ne forfetra par cest exigent solement lez bienz queux fueront seisiez deuaunt lexigend par le vicount, mes auxi toutz autrez biens queux il ad en possession iour de lexigend agarde.

Mes si le primer enditement soit de Felony & puis il est vtlage sur cest enditement, doncque il perdra son terre par cest vtlagarie, mez il ne forfetra son terre par le agarde le exigent enuers luy [*Diuersite et nota*] sicome il forfetra cez bienz, et sic nota diuersitatem entre terre & biens en cest cas. Et auxi sur le vtlarie de felony le partie que est vtlage ne forfetra [f.112] solement le terre que il ad al temps del vtlagarie enuers luy pronounce, mez auxi tout le terre que il auoit al temps de le felony fait. Et auxi sur cest vtlagarie de felony il forfetra toutz sez dettes. Et issint il ne ferra sur le exigend agarde sil apparust sur le exigent & plede pardon deuaunt lexigent agarde, lez bienz serront sauez a luy; quere & semble a le lectour que cy & cetera si ceo[3] mainpernourz sount returnez inz en le court accordaunt a lestatut ent fait anno x^mo E. III^cii[4] & cetera.

Item si lexigend issist erronious & le vtlagarie reuers apres pur cell cause, nient obstante le primer seisier de le vicount dez bienz lendite, vncore il recouera cez bienz. Mes si home soit vtlage de felonie & puis le partie reuers ceo pur tile cause, scilicet, pur ceo que il fut en prison al temps de le vtlage pronounce enuers luy, en ceo cas il ne auera cez bienz que fueront seisiez deuaunt ou nient seisiez, quar en cest cas apparust que lexigend bene issist. Mes sil soit vtlage sur

---

[1] Probably for seisier.
[2] *For* ne . . . lenparture *read* ne recouera damages sinon pur porter, B; ad recouera damages solement pur lemporte, C; ne recouera damages forsque solement pur lemporte, D.
[3] *Omit*, B; cez, D; son, F.
[4] 10 Edw. III, st. 1, c. 3, 1336.

enditement de transgression, si le partie apres reuers cest vtlagarie pur
ceo que il fut en prison al temps & cetera, en cest cas il reauera cez
bienz, quar la lez bienz fueront solement forfaitz par le vtlagarie
& nemi par le isser de lexigende & cetera.

Item si exigent soit agarde enuers vne & apres deuaunt il est vtlage
il apparust & est acquyte, il perdra cez bienz pur ceo que il tarie [1] lexigend ; mes si le ii^de Capias soit agarde enuers ii iointement & lun de
eux tarie lexigend & lautre apparust, & celui que apparust deuaunt
lexigent auoide le enditement sur que tote le proses issist pur noun
sufficiente de icell, vncore en cest cas lez bienz de lautre que ad tarie [2]
lexigent sount sauez, nient obstante que ils fueront primerment seisiez
par le vicount sur le ii^de Capias.

Auxi lez parols de le commission sount oustre : scilicet, sil veigne
ou soit pris deuaunt le retorne del ii^de Capias par le vicount, doncques soient son biens & chateux sauez. Ceux parols serrount entenduz si le vicount ne voet delyuer lez bienz que il ad issint seisi sur tile
ii^de Capias apres que le partie ad apparue & ceo plede, que doncques
les Justicez de peas ferrount vne especiall breue al vicount de eux
deliuerer.

Et si le vicount sur tile breue retorne que lez chateux sount mortz
en son custodie ou autre tile excuse, en cest cas le partie ne prendra
issue sur cest retourne, mez est mys a son accion sur le cas enuers le
vicount ou accion de Detenue. Mez il ne poet auer accion de transgression vers le vicount pur eux coment que il ad mysdemeane
mesmez lez bienz, sicome il errie [3] son terre ou chiuauche dithiauyst (?) [4]
oue lez bestez issint prisez. Mes si le vicount seisist lez bienz de
vne autre sur tile ii^de Capias, et puis apres le vicount retorne sur
mesme le breue non est inuentus & ne retorne que il ad seisi cez bienz,
en cest cas le partie auera son remedie enuers le vicount par accion
de transgression quare vi & armis,[5] & recouera cez damages al value
dez bienz.

Item si vne especiall breue soit direct al vicount par lez Justicez de
peas a delyuerer lez bienz arer al partie, & il retorne sur mesme le
breue que il ad delyuere eux al partie par vertue de tile breue, en cest
cas le partie nauera auerrement al contrarie de ceo, mes est mys a son
accion & cetera. Mes si le vicount retorne sur cest breue que le partie
mesme ad pris mesmez lez bienz deuaunt le venue de ceo breue hors

---

[1] ad terge, B ; terge, C.   [2] terge, B, C.   [3] drie, B.
[4] *For* ou . . . dithiauyst *read* ou eschemchest, C. Dithiauyst is omitted
in B and crossed through, I think, in A.
[5] *For* quare . . . armis *read* de biens emportes.

de son possession, en cest cas le partie poet auer auerment al contrarie; mez lez Justicez de peas ne poient trier cest auerment deuaunt
eux & cetera; quod nota.

Item si lez bienz que le vicount ad issint seisi sur cest proses sount
arcez par reson de soden tempest esteaunt en le possession de le
vicount, ou autrement sount prisez hors de le possession de le vicount
par enemys le Roie, le vicount est excuse en ceux ii casez. Mes
autrement est si lez bienz sount prisez hors de le possession de le
vicount par vne autre estraunge, quar la le vicount auera son remedie
enuers lestraunge [1] & ideo il auera son accion vers le vicount & cetera.

Item si le vicount seisist tilx bienz & eux amesna en son propre
meason, et celui a que le propertie [f. 112 b] dez biens sount ad vne
autre meason adioynaunt a mesme le meason de le vicount [2] lou lez
bienz sount deinz,[3] & le meason celui a que lez bienz sount est arce
par le necligence de son seruauntes, par cause de quell le meason de le
vicount lou lez bienz fueront sount arcez, cest arcer est bone excuse
pur le vicount sur le speciall breue de deliueraunce a luy fait. Mes
en mesme le cas si le meason celui a que lez bienz sount fut arce par
vne estraunge & nemi par le necligens de luy ne de son seruauntes,
ceo nest excuse al vicount sur tile breue & cetera.

Item si vne hostiller soit endite & cez biens sount seisiez sur le ii[de]
Capias & deliuerez al vicount, et en mesme le meason deuaunt le aler
de le vicount lez bienz sount enbesilz & pris hors de le hostrie, en cest
cas ceo est bone excuse pur le vicount, quar le hostiller est chargeable
oue toutz biens que sount deins son meason par estatut & cetera.

Item si lez bienz sount empairez par le custodie de le vicount, & le
vicount dit sur tile breue de deliueraunce que il est [prist][4] a deliuerer
lez biens al partie oue tielx amendez que lez Justices voillent pur ceo
assesser, en cest cas lez Justices de peas ne ount poiar de assesser les
amendes. Mes si le mendis soit assesse & le partie ceo rescue,[5] le
vicount est discharge enuers le partie toutz iourz.

Item si le vicount ad seisi lez bestez de vne home par vertue de tile
ii[de] Capias ou autre chose viue, et lez Justicez de peas agarde vne
especiall breue al vicount de faire redelyueraunce, & le vicount dist
que il est prist a delyuerer eux al partie, sil voet paier luy pur loure
viander en le meane temps, ceo nest bone excuse, quar en cest cas le
partie paiera rien pur le viandre de eux en le meane temps; quere.

<hr>

[1] *Add* par accion. Mez issint ne poet celui a qui le propertie fuit auer
enuers lestraunge, B, and more briefly in D, F.
[2] *Bis.*   [3] *Omit*, B.   [4] prist, B; prest, C, D.
[5] resceue, B; resceit, D.

Et vncore le vicount est tenuz de doner a eux viandre apres tile seisier et si le partie tarie[1] lexigent, le Roie alowera le vicount pur cest viandre de eux; quere diuersitatem.

Quintadecima Lectura.[2]

(*Margin.*)   Coment lez Justices de peas poient oier & terminer.

Lez parols de lestatute[3] sount: et que comen droit soit fait auxi bien as pouris come as richis. En cest clause de lestatute est compris le iii^cie auctorite dez Justicez de peas, scilicet, que ils poient oier et terminer, & auxi est compris deins cest clause de le commission lou est dit: Assignauimus vos Justiciarios nostros quorum. Et par cest clause de le commission est done que dez extorcions et Regrateriez lez Justicez ount poier de proceder al sute de le partie pur luy & le Roie, ou le Roie tantum. Mes mesmez lez Justices de oier & terminer ount poiar de proceder sur presentementes deuaunt eux de transgression, forstallerie, felony & de toutz autrez articulez conteigne en le commission al sute del Roie tantum. Mes vncore dyuers estatutez sount que done poiar a mesmez lez Justices de oier & terminer le offence al sute le partie, come especiall estatut de riott queux nest expresse en le commission. Et auxi vne estatut fait anno xi^mo H. VII^mi [4] que done poiar a lez Justices de peas de oier & terminer toutz accions conteynuz[5] sur estatut lou le mater nest felony, murdre ne treason, ne cest accion concerne ascun terre destre perdue al partie compleignaunt. Par que ore ieo voile monstrer solement a vous coment lez Justices de peas doient oier et terminer Felonies, & autrez chosez queux sount pluis conuenient vse destre determine en lez cessions, & le diuersite de loure poiar entre eux et autrez Justicez en cest cas.

[f. 113.] Justicez de peas ne ount ascun poiar si home soit imprison pur suspecions de felony de delyuerer ceo pur ceo; mes en cest cas couient que le prisoner soit remoue en bancke le Roie & la lez Justices de le Banke ferrount vne breue de gestue & fama en le conte ou le pris de felon fut suppose, & ils ne ount poiar de luy deliuerer saunz tile breue. Mes si home soit pris en Midd' pur suspecions de vne felony fait deins mesme le conte & puis apres remoue en le Bancke le Roie, en cest cas lez Justices de Bancke poient delyuerer le prisoner

---

[1] terge, B, C.   [2] The whole lecture is omitted in G.

[3] Westminster First, c. 1, *ut supra.*

[4] 11 Hen. VII, c. 3, ss. i, ii, and iii, 1495; but 'uppon informacion for the King tofore them to be made', the crucial words in the text of the statute, are omitted by Marowe.

[5] concevez, D.

saunz ascun tile breue. Mes si home soit pris en Midd' pur suspecions de vne Felonye fait en le conte de Essex & puis il est remoue par breue en le Bancke le Roie, vncore en ceo cas lez Justices de Bancke ne poient luy deliuerer saunz agarder vne breue de gestu & fama en Midd', pur ceo que le felon fut pris en cest conte.

Item Justicez de peas ount poiar de delyuerer vacabundes queux sount imprisonez en le gaile & ceo par lour discression par estatutez ent faitz & cetera. Et auxi lez Justicez de peas ount poiar de deliuerer tielx vacabundez auxibien hors de le cessions come en le temps de le cessions. Et nota que vne Justice de peas poet ceo faire auxibien come ii ou iii, mez en cest cas lez Justices de peas vsount de iurrer le vacabunde deuaunt que il soit deliuere coment que il soit deinz age ; quar cest serement serra fait al Roie & cetera.[1]

Item si homme soit endite que il ad procure vne home en le countie de Midd' de murdrer autre home en le conte de Essex, & que celui que il issint procura fist mesme le murdre en le countie de Essex par cest procurement & est endite de ceo en le conte de Midd', en cest cas lez Justicez de peas de le countie de Midd' ne poient escrier al lez Justicez de peas en le conte de Essex de eux certifier si le principall fut endite ou nemi, sicome lez Justicez de Bancke le Roie puissent. Mez en cest cas lez Justicez de peas de le conte de Midd' dischargera le accessorie.

Mes si tile accessorie fut endite en bancke le Roie, lez Justicez la voillent mitter breue a lez Justices de peas de le conte de Essex de certifier a eux si le principalle fut endite deuaunt eux ou nemi, & nemi dischargera laccessorie saunz tile breue. Et si le principall ne fut endite deuaunt lez Justicez de peas de E., doncques ils voillount mitter le accessorie south surete de apparer deuaunt eux quaunt le principall est pris. Mez lez Justicez de peas ne ount tile power en ceo cas deprendre tile surete & cetera.

Et si le principall en le cas auauntdit vst este mys en execucion en autre conte, lez Justicez de peas de cest conte lou laccessorie est endite ne ount poiar de mitter a lez autrez Justicez de peas pur lour recorde & de arreigner celui que est endite come accessorie. Mes en cest cas ils couient de remouer lenditement deuaunt eux en le bancke le Roie, & lez Justicez de le bancke le Roie escrieront pur lautre recorde deuaunt lez autrez Justicez deuaunt queux le principall fut mys en execucion, & sur ceo arreigne le accessorie & cetera.

Item si homme soit endite de ceo que il auoit robba vne B. & auxi est troue par mesme lenditement que le dit B. fist fressh sute enuers

---

[1] *Add* Le vicount ne poet eux deliuerer, vncore est vse al contrary, D, F.

luy, cest verdit graunt al fressh sute nest riens al purpos pur le partie
greue, et issint est si lez enquestez que endite ascun home de Felony
dicount par mesme lenditement que le partie fugam fecit pur cest felony,
ceo nest bone verdit sur le [f. 113 b] primer enditement. Mes si tile
fugam fecit soit troue par le ii^de enquest sur le triall lou le partie est
acquyte de ceo, doncque lez Justicez de peas poient apres cest verdit
done agarder vne brieff direct al eschetour de seisier lez biens de lendite saunz maundre le verdit en bancke le Roie, & vncore le felony fut
determine deuaunt.

Item si vne Capias issist sur vne enditement de felony & le vicount
retorne que le partie fist vne rescous sur luy en le prendre de lendite,
en cest cas mezmez lez Justicez de peas poient agarder vne autre
Capias enuers luy, & mitter lendite a respondre sur cest rescuse auxi
bien come de lenditement. Mes si le vicount retorne que il ad luy
prist & puis apres mesme lendite ouesque autrez a luy fist rescous, en
ceo cas le partie ne serra arreigne sur ceo rescous par le retorne de le
vicount, mez ceo couient¹ troue par enditement deuaunt eux & cetera.

Item si homme voille entre appelle de Felonie ou murdre deuaunt
lez Justicez de peas sur vne enditement de felony ou murdre que est
deuaunt eux ou deuaunt le coroner, lez Justicez de peas ne ount ascun
poiar de tener plee sur cest appelle & cetera.

Item si vne homme que est endite deuaunt eux & arreigne de felony
voet conustre le felony & pria vne coroner al entent devener approuour
pur le Roie, en cest cas lez Justicez de peas ne ount poiar deprendre
tile approvement & cetera. Mes de Rigore iuris lez Justicez de peas
doient en ceo cas prendre son confession & luy discharger de ascun
coroner.

Item si home abiure que returne saunz pardon le Roie soit pris &
port deuaunt lez Justices de peas, vncore lez justicez de peas ne ount
poiar de luy arreigner sur son abiuracion, nient obstante que le
abiuracion fut done a luy deins mesme le conte.

Item si homme soit endite de murdre super visum corporis deuaunt le
Coroner, & puis le partie que est endite est pris & port deuaunt lez
Justicez de peas, en cest cas lez Justicez de peas ne poient luy
arreigner sur cest enditement coment que lenditement fut ewe deins
mesme le conte & cetera.

Mes si home soit endite deuaunt le vicount en son turne de transgression, baterie ou huiusmodi, & le vicount mitta mesme lenditement
deuaunt lez Justices de peas, en cest cas lez Justices de peas poient

¹ *Add* destre, B.

mitter lendite a son fyne sur cest enditement, mes ils ne poient faire
proses ne discharger lendite de ceo par voie de plee.   Et en mesme le
cas si le vicount mitta inz lenditement par son mains saunz proces ceo
est sufficient, sicome lez Justicez de peas doient faire de enditement par
loure mains en le bancke le Roie & cetera.

  . Mes si home soit arreigne deuaunt lez Justicez de peas de felony &
est acquyte de ceo, & puis apres il est arreigne sur mesme le felony en
le Bancke le Roie, en cest cas lez Justices de peas ne poient mitter le
recorde en le bancke saunz vne brieff direct a eux de certifier tile
recorde & cetera.[1]

Item si homme soit vtlage de felony sur procez deuaunt lez Justicez
de peas & puis il est pris, en cest cas lez Justicez de peas poient luy
arreigner sur tile vtlagarie.   Mes si home soit vtlage de felonie par due
proses en vne counte & puis il est pris en vne autre conte, lez Justices
de peas de ceo conte lou le partie est pris ne poient luy arreigner sur
tile vtlagarie.   Et issint est si home soit vtlage de felony par proces
fait hors de Banck le Roie & en mesme le conte lou il est pris, vncore
lez Justices de peas ne poient luy arreigner sur tile vtlagarie & cetera.

Item si home que est endite deuaunt eux mesme est vtlage par
proses fait par mesmez lez Justicez, & puis il est arreigne sur mesme le
vtlarie & il voet [f. 114] pleder vne pardon de le Roie, en cest cas lez
Justicez de peas poient ceo allower, et vncore lour commission est que
ils ount poiar [de oier][2] et terminer toutz felonies deuaunt eux quousque
vtlagetur.

Item si le vtlage en mesme le cas voet pleder que sount ii de mesme
le nome[3] que il est vtlage & en vne mesme vile & que il nest celui que
est outlage, & lattourney le Roie ioigne vne issue oue luy sur ceo, en
cest cas lez justice de peas ount poiar denquerer de ceo par verdit &
cetera.   Mes si celui que est vtlage voet dire que il fut en prison en
vne forein countie al temps del vtlagarie enuers luy pronounce, la lez
Justicez de peas ne ount ascun poiar denquerer de ceo, quar ils ne
poient enquerer de tile chose en autre counte.

Mesme le leie si le vtlage voet dire que il fut enprison deins mesme
le conte al temps del vtlagarie & cetera, ils ne poient enquerer de ceo,
mes ils poient agarder vne Scire facias enuers lez seignurz enuers que
son terre fut forfaite par cest vtlarie, a dire pur que il ne auera restitucion de son terre.

---

[1] *Add* En mesme le maner dun acquitell en le Turne, le Vicount ne
mittera ceo einz par ses maynes, D, F.
  [2] de oier, B ; de oyer, C.   [3] *Add* par, B, C.

Item si tile vtlage voet pleder que il ne fut deinz lez iiii miers al temps
& cetera, & vne replie pur le Roie que il fut a tile lieu deinz mesme le
conte, en cest [cas][1] lez Justices de peas nount poiar de trier ceo deuaunt eux. Mesme le leie est si le Replicacion soit que il fut en tile lieu
en vne forein conte, lez Justicez ne ount poiar de trier ceo & cetera.

Item sil voet dire que il fut al temps del vtlagarie hors de roialme
en le seruice le Roie south le retenue de vne tile Capteyn, nosmant son
nome, en cest cas lez Justicez de peas ne ount poiar de escrier al capteyn de ceo certifier a eux & cetera.

[*Nota bene.*] Item si vne enfaunt deins lage de xii[2] ans soit arreigne
deuaunt lez Justicez de peas, ils poient luy chastisier par loure discression auxibien come autrez Justicez de Bancke poient faire.

Item si homme que serra arreigne deuaunt eux a cest temps que il
serra arreigne est en vne rage ou de noun sane memorie, en cest cas
lez Justicez de peas poient luy reprier tancque a autre temps a lour
plesure & cetera.

Item si home soit arreigne deuaunt lez Justices de peas sur vne enditement de Mayheme, & lendite pria que le mayheme poet estre viewe
deuaunt mesme lez Justicez sil soit mayhem ou nemi, cest viewe ne
serra fait sur cest enditement. Mes si le defendaunt en appelle de
mayme pria que le mayme soit viewe, la lez Justicez aueround le viewe ;
nota diuersitatem.

Item si homme que est mute serra arreigne deuaunt eux & il stea
mute & ne sauoit dire riens, en ceo cas lez Justicez de peas poient
enquerer sil soit mute par lacte de Dieu, ou sil mesme cause luy
destre mute pur malice, auxi bien come autrez Justicez poient faire.[3]

Item si le lange, scilicet, son tonge, de lendite de felony soit scie
issint que il ne sauoit parler, en cest cas lez Justice de peas doient
enquerer si cest scier de son lange fut fait deuaunt le felony sur que il
serra arreigne ou apres & en quell maner ceo fut fait & cetera.

Item si cestuy que est arreigne deuaunt lez Justice de peas dit que
vne de son enditourz fut vtlage al temps de lenditement, en ceo cas il
auera iour de porter inz son recorde prouaunt lutlage deuaunt mesme
lez Justices si ceo fut trauers pur le Roie & cetera.

Item si cestuy que est arreigne deuaunt eux sur transgression plede
vne mater de Justificacion par mater de recorde que est deuaunt autrez
Justicez come recouery ou huiusmodi, la le partie auera iour de porter

---

[1] cas, B.
[2] xiii, B, C ; deins age, D.
[3] MS. F (folio 301) ends thus : ‘ Si home mute soyt prist deuaunt eux
ilz poyent inquirer. Finis lecture Magistri Marowe.’

inz [f. 114 b] mesme le recorde deuaunt lez Justicez de peas sil soit trauers deuaunt & cetera.

Item si cestuy que est arreigne deuaunt eux de felony plede que il fut pris hors de Seintuarie a tile lieu,[1] en cest cas lez Justicez de peas ount poiar de trier ceo si le seintwarie soit en mesme le conte lou il est endite.   Mes si lez Justicez ne sciount parfettment si cest lieu soit seintuarie ou nemi, ils ne ount poiar descrier al abbe, Priour ou huius-modi de tile lieu de monstrer son chartre de le seintuarie.   Mes sil soit troue deuaunt lez Justicez de peas que lendite fut pris hors de seintuarie, vncore mesmez lez Justicez ne ount poiar de luy restorer al seintuarie & cetera.

Item si lendite plede al felony de rien coupable deuaunt Justicez de peas, en cest cas ils poient agarder vne Venire facias[2] retornable deuaunt eux a vne autre iour, mez nemi returne[3] mesme le iour de le Teste & cetera.   Mes lez Justicez de Gaole deliuerer purront faire en cest cas Venire facias retornable mesme le iour deuaunt eux & ceo est bone & cetera.

Item si vne Feme que est arreigne de felony deuaunt eux plede que el est enseint, en cest cas ils poient agarder vne Venire facias tot matronas ad ventrem inspiciendum de terminer si el soit enseint ou nemi, auxibien come autrez Justicez de Gaole Deliuerer poient faire.

Item si vne seignur que est Baron soit endite deuaunt eux de felony & il trauers lenditement, en cest cas lez Justicez de peas purrount agarder Venire facias tot Barones ad triandum cest mater & cest par son peris de roialme.

Item si cestuy que est arreigne deuaunt les Justicez de peas challenge lenditement pur ascun cause ou prist a ceo ascun excepcion queux lez Justicez ne voillount allowe, en cest cas lez Justicez de peas deuaunt queux il est arreigne poient sealer a luy vne bille de excepcion come autrez Justices de lun Banck ou lautre poient faire & cetera.

Item si cestuy que est arreigne voillet demurer en leie sur le evidence que est done enuers luy deuaunt lez Justicez de peas, ils poient recorder son demurer en leie.   Mez si vne autre voille praie[4] de voier dire sur cest felony, vncore lez Justicez de peas ne poient luy examiner sur cest praier,[5] pur ceo que le Roie est partie & cetera.

Item si home soit endite de ceo que il auoit felonyssement prist le chiuall de vne A., & troue est apres par especiall verdit que vne B.

---

[1] MS. adds (clearly an error): en cest cas lez justicez de peas ount poair de trier ceo si le seintwarie soit a tiele lieu.

[2] MS. L ends at this point.   [3] returnable, B.

[4] prier, C.   [5] prier, C.

felonyssement prist mesme le chiuall hors de possession de mesme ce
A., & que apres le primer endite [felonsement prist mesme le chiuall
hors del possession de lauauntdit B, en ceo cas le primer endite][1] serra
discharge par tile verdit, & null proses fait enuers luy sur le nouell
presentment de felony troue par le verdit encontre luy.   Mes si deuaunt
lez Justicez de Gaole Deliuerer vne home est arreigne sur vne enditement super visu corporis deuaunt eux & il plede de rien coulpable, &
lenquest troua que vne autre luy tua & nemi lendite sur especiall verdit
come oportet & cetera, en cest cas sur cest especiall verdit troue
deuaunt eux lez Justicez de Gaole Deliuerer facent proses vers celui
que est troue coulpable de nouell par ceo verdit, auxibien come ils
deuoient faire sur vne autre enditement & il serra mys a respons[2] sur
icell, come il serra sur vne enditement & cetera.

Item si xii hommez iurrez de acquitell de ascun home continus[3]
ensemble en vne [f. 115] meason, & lun dez Jurrourz done money a
vne autre de mesme lez Jurrourz pur doner le verdit accordaunt a son
volunte, & celui que issint dona apres monstra a lez iustice de peas
tout cest mater & lautre ceo denye, en cest cas lez Justice poient
assesser vne fyne maintenant sur luy que conust son fait par son
conusaunz demene, & pur lautre que dona,[4] ceo serra vne Venire facias
par mesmez lez justice, pur ceo que enuers luy le recorde doit estre
maunde en bancke le Roie.

Item si ascun que est arreigne de felony deuaunt lez Justicez de peas
demanda son liuer, ils ount poiar de luy deliuerer al ordinarie si'
lordinarie ou son depute soit la present, & sil soit absent, lez Justice de
peas poient faire notice de ceo al Ordinarie ou a son depute & reprier
le prisoner en mesne temps.   Mes en cest cas lez Justice de peas ne
ount poiar pur amercier lordinarie pur son absence & cetera, & coment
que il ne vient deuaunt eux sur le notice a luy fait, vncore il ne serra
amercie.   Mes en cest cas lez Justice de peas maunderount le prisoner
en Bancke le Roie & cetera.   Mes si lordinarie ne voet vener deuaunt
lez Justice en le counte palentyn, come Chester, Lancastre & similia,
quaunt lendite pria son clergie, la lez Justice couient defaire le prisoner
destre reprie a toutz iourz, ou causer lordinarie de luy prendre, quar le
breue de Bancke le Roie ne vient a eux.

Item si lendite demanda son lyuer deuaunt lez Justicez de peas &
vne autre allege Bigamy enuers luy, en ceo cas lez Justice de peas ne
ount poiar descrier al Ordinarie de certifier a eux sil soit Bygamy ou

---

[1] Added from B ; similar phrase in D.   [2] responder, B.
[3] sont myse, B.   [4] denia, B ; denya, D.

nemi & cetera. Et mesme le leie est si lendite dit que il est moigne professe, & le attourney le Roie ou vne autre dit que il nest professe ; mes en cest cas lenditement & le plee couient destre remoue en Bancke le Roie, & lez Justicez de Bancke deuoient escrier al euesque de certifier a eux tile Bigamy ou profession & cetera.

Item si lordinarie soit present quaunt le prisoner est arreigne & le prisoner pria vne liuere, & lordinarie voet accepter luy come clerke, lou il ne lie come clericus, vncore en ceo cas lez Justice de peas ne ount poiar de assesser ascun fyne pur son acceptaunce sur lordinarie de seisier son temporaltez & cetera.[1]

Et lez parols de commission sount ouster : Et quod vos prefatus R. ad dies & loca predicta omnia breuia, precepta, processus & indictamenta predicta coram vobis et sociis vestris venire faciatis & cetera. Ore est entendue par ceux parols de le commission que cest clause done poiar al Custos Rotulorum de garder lez Recordez de le cessions come Justice & nemi come officer, quar le Commission ne dit: Assignauimus vos custodem Rotulorum. Et pur ceo si le Justice que eit le custodie dez Recordez nad lez recordez la present en le cessions, vncore il ne serra pur ceo amercie come vne officer doit estre. Mes en cas que le Recordes fueront prisez hors de le cessions par vne estraunge nient Justice, en cest cas toutz lez Justicez de peas ne doient ioyndre en accion sur ceo enuers celui que prist lez recordez, mes le Custos Rotulorum auera accion de ceo en son nome tantum, quar son possession nest le possession dez autrez Justicez de peas, quar par ceux parolx de le commission il ad power de deteigner lez recordez de lez autrez Justicez de le peas, & null dez Justicez poet escrier en ascun de cest recordez forsque le custos Rotulorum ou son clerke; quod nota.

Item le commission de peas ne apparteigne al custodie de le custos Rotulorum, quar lez autrez Justicez de peas poient auxi bien tener lez cessions par force de tile commission come il mesme poet.[2] Et issint de tilx especialles recordez queux sount de Riottes ou preceptes de le peas & similia, [f. 115 b] le custos Rotulorum ne auera le custodie de ceux recordez pluis que un autre Justice de peas auera, quar le auctorite que est done a le custos Rotulorum est doner[3] le custodie de tielx

---

[1] It seems probable that the remainder belongs at the end of Lect. X ; see p. 368, note 1.   I suspect that the correct conclusion of Lect. XV is missing.
[2] This paragraph in D begins thus: Cest custodie sera entende solement dez recordez del cessions come presentementez billes & huiusmodi. Mes le commission . . .
[3] dauer, B, C.

recordez le Roie queux sount de le generall cessions et nient autrement, et cestes cessions sount forsque iiii foitz par an.

Item si lez Justicez de peas queux ount recordez en lour mains ne voillount deliuerer eux al custos Rotulorum quaunt il eux demanda, come breuez de Cerciorare que vient a eux de pluis haute court ou similia, doncques poet le custos Rotulorum sur cest clause de commission que done poiar a luy de auer le custodie de tilx recordez oue vne surmyse fait en le chauncerie de cest deteigner de tilx recordez auer vne breue hors de le chauncerie de delyuerer mesmez lez recordez, & sil ne voet delyuerer sur cest breue doncque issera vne autre breue hors de le chauncerie oue vne contempt pur delyuere mesmez lez recordez a le custos Rotulorum.

Mes le custos Rotulorum en le cas auauntdit ne poet auer accion de Detenue vers vne dez Justicez de peas que ad tile recorde de luy, pur ceo que il ad entresse en mesme le recorde par reson que il est vne dez Justicez & cetera. Mes si vne estraunger ad le possession de tile recorde & ne voet ceo deliuerer al custos Rotulorum quaunt il ceo demanda, en cest cas le custos Rotulorum auera accion de transgression en son nome sole enuers tile estraunger & cetera.

Item nota que null dez Justicez de peas ne doient escrier en lez Rolles de le cessions forsque solement le custos Rotulorum & cez clerkes, & toutz son clerkes poient escrier en lez rollez a son paroll si soit male entre ou huiusmodi & cetera.

Item si ascun fauxine ou deceit soit fait sur lez auauntditz rolles de le cessions par ascun estraunge & nient par luy ne par son clerkes, vncore le custos Rotulorum ferra fyne pur son negligent custodie de tilx recordez & cetera.

Item le custos Rotulorum auoit poiar de assigner ii Justicez off the peas att the generall cession to haue the examinacion & ouersight of the shireffes & off his clerkes for mysentrying of the plaintes hadde before hym yn the shireffes Tourne and also yn makyng of their streites, vt patet per statutum factum anno xi^{mo} H. VII^{mi}, capitulo.[1]

Et nota que toutz lez proses queux serrount faitz par lez Justicez de peas hors de lez enditementes, come Capias, Exigent & huiusmodi, serrount faitz en le nosme le Roie & le Teste de tile proses en le nosme de Custos Rotulorum. Mes si ascun precept serra fait al vicount de garner lez cessions de peas ou huiusmodi, cest precept couient estre fait en le nome de le custos Rotulorum & vne autre Justice de peas, ou en lez nomez de deux Justicez de peas dount lun soit de le Quorum

---

[1] *Add* xv, D. Cf. 11 Hen. VII, c. 15, ss. i–iii, 1495.

saunz le custos Rotulorum. Et issint vide diuersitatem lou le proses
serra fait en le nome de Roie & lou nemi & nota ceo bene & cetera.[1]

Explicit Lectura Magistri Thome Marowe Lectoris Interioris Templi
in quadragesimali vacacione anno regni regis H[enrici] VII^{mi} xviii.^o

[f. 116.]   Tabula libri precedentis inferius patet.

De pace terre et ecclesie & conseruacione eiusdem.

De conseruacione pacis spiritualium personarum ecclesie, scilicet de
lour corps.

De pace terre & conseruatoribus eiusdem.

De Justiciariis pacis.

Queux persons serront misez en commission de peas & queux nemi.

De securitate pacis & quomodo il serra fait.

Coment ceo surete serra demande.

Coment le surete serra graunt.

Coment le proses de ceo soit fait.

Coment le surete serra troue.

Coment le surete serra discharge.

De fraccionis [sic] pacis & pacificacionis [sic] eiusdem.

Coment cest enfreindre de peas serra pacifie.

Coment le Constable doit enprisoner vne home en son meason.

De fraccione pacis cum multitudine gentium.

Par queux persons assemble poet estre fait et par queux nemi.

De ingressibus manufortis & de partibus grauatis in possessionem
remissis.

Coment cest breue de Restitucion serra fait.

De modo tenendi cessiones pacis.

De rebus inquirendis coram Justiciariis pacis per commissionem.

De Regraters & Forstallers de le markett.

De Extorcion.

De conventiculis.

De insidiis.

De feloniis inquirendis coram Justiciariis pacis. Vide lou home poet
estre Felon pur prendre de cez proprez biens.

De Roberie.

De Burglarie.

De mort de home.

De petit treason.

---

[1] *Add* finis, B, C; finis laudetur deus quod Walterus Atwell cuius anime
propicietur deus amen Ihesus Ihesus Ihesus esto mihi Ihesus amen, D.

De accessoribus.

Le primer accessor.

Le ii^{de} accessor.

De accessoribus apres felony fait.

Eschapes.

De presentacionibus contra pacem capiendis in cessiones pacis & circumstanciis eiusdem.

Mistre et postea de petit treason coment inditement de ceo soit fait.

De processu super indictamentis contra pacem.

Coment lez Justicez de peas poient oier & determiner.[1]

Difference parentre vne assemble, vne Riott & vne Rowte.

[1] After each of the first seven entries of the *Tabula*, ' fo ' is added.

INDEX

to pp. 1–223

The index contains references to the more important manuscripts, persons, places, and subjects, but is designed not to duplicate the Table of Contents, or the Bibliography in Appendix I.[1]

[1] I am indebted to Miss M. P. Roesel for the arduous task of compiling the index, but she is not responsible for its imperfections.